Professional XML Development with Apache Tools

Xerces, Xalan, FOP, Cocoon, Axis, Xindice

Professional XML Development with Apache Tools

Xerces, Xalan, FOP, Cocoon, Axis, Xindice

Theodore W. Leung

Wiley Publishing, Inc.

Professional XML Development with Apache Tools: Xerces, Xalan, FOP, Cocoon, Axis, Xindice

Published by
Wiley Publishing, Inc.
10475 Crosspoint Boulevard
Indianapolis, IN 46256
www.wiley.com

Published by Wiley Publishing, Inc., Indianapolis, Indiana

Published simultaneously in Canada

For general information on our other products and services or to obtain technical support, please contact our Customer Care Department within the U.S. at (800) 762-2974, outside the U.S. at (317) 572-3993 or fax (317) 572-4002.

Wiley also publishes its books in a variety of electronic formats. Some content that appears in print may not be available in electronic books.

Library of Congress Control Number: 2003115130

ISBN: 0-7645-4355-5

Manufactured in the United States of America

10 9 8 7 6 5 4 3 2 1

Credits

Author
Theodore W. Leung

Executive Editor
Robert Elliott

Production Editor
Vincent Kunkemueller

Copy Editor
Tiffany Taylor

Compositor
Gina Rexrode

Book Producer
Ryan Publishing Group, Inc.

Vice President & Executive Group Publisher
Richard Swadley

Vice President & Executive Publisher
Robert Ipsen

Vice President and Publisher
Joseph B. Wikert

Executive Editorial Director
Mary Bednarek

Editorial Manager
Kathryn A. Malm

About the Author

Theodore W. Leung

Ted Leung is a Member of the Apache Software Foundation. He is a founding member of the Apache XML Project and served as the chairman of the XML Project Management Committee from March, 2001 to June, 2003.

He is also the principal of Sauria Associates, LLC, a Pacific Northwest consultancy focused on high-impact software development. He has served companies such as F5 Networks, IBM, Enkubator, Apple Computer, and Taligent in roles spanning technical lead through chief technology officer. Ted holds a S.B in Mathematics from the Massachusetts Institute of Technology and a Sc.M. in Computer Science from Brown University.

Ted has given a number of technical presentations at industry conferences, including Software Development West and ApacheCon. A full list of his speaking engagements is available at http://www.sauria.com/presentations.html.

Acknowledgments

Writing a book is a journey, and the journey begins well before the keys on the keyboard start clicking. In my case, the journey to this book has led through a number of organizations, and I want to thank those that have helped me along the way.

Without the Apache Software Foundation, this book—and more importantly, the software described in this book—would not exist. It has been my privilege to work with the contributors, committers and members of the ASF. I'd like to give special thanks to Dirk-Willem van Gulik, Stefano Mazzochi, Pierpaolo Fumagalli, Davanum Srinivas, and James Duncan Davidson.

My involvement with the ASF would not have happened were it not for the hard work of the developers and management of the IBM Cupertino XML4J team: Mike Pogue, Andy Clark, Glenn Marcy, Ralf Pfieffer, Andy Heninger, Tom Watson, Eric Ye, Mike Weiner, Rajiv Jain, and Paul Buck. I'd also like to thank Rachel Reinitz, from IBM's Software Services for Websphere, for starting me down the road of interacting with real people who were trying to get their jobs done using XML technologies.

The actual act of writing a book cannot happen in a vacuum. Various people have provided much needed help or advice. My neighbor Kate deVeaux dropped everything to help me beat an eleventh hour deadline by taking the photograph that graces the cover of this book. My other neighbors Alex Torres and David Shenk provided valuable advice about how to handle various aspects of the book writing process.

Apache is about community software development, performed across great distances via the wonder that is the Internet. But people also need a local, physical community, so I'd like to thank the members of our spiritual community, for their support, understanding, and prayers during this project, especially the Campbells, Woleslagles, Ziakins, Bests, and Larsens. Extra thanks to Larry Gonwick for physically standing in for me this summer.

To Mom and Dad: Thank you for your love and all the years of prayers and hard labor.

To Abigail, Michaela, and Elisabeth: Daddy is finally done with the book. We can go play now.

To Julie, the love of my life, thank you for standing over me and guarding my time, hearing my frustrations, and enduring my absences.

One of the many characterizations of the open source culture has been as a gift culture. Jesus Christ gave himself as a gift for the world. I want to thank him for the inspiration to be a gift giver. I hope that I will be able to follow his example.

Contents

Acknowledgments **ix**
Introduction **xvii**

Chapter 1: Xerces **1**

Prerequisites **2**
Well-Formedness 3
Validity 4
Entities 6
XML Parser APIs **6**
SAX 8
DOM 13
Installing Xerces **15**
Development Techniques **16**
Xerces Configuration 16
Deferred DOM 20
Schema Handling 20
Grammar Caching 23
Entity Handling 29
Entity References 31
Serialization 34
XNI 38
Using the Samples 43
CyberNeko Tools for XNI **44**
NekoHTML 44
ManekiNeko 44
NekoPull 45
Practical Usage **48**
Common Problems 49
Applications **50**

Chapter 2: Xalan **53**

Prerequisites **53**
XPath 53
XSLT 62
Installing and Configuring Xalan **69**

Development Techniques **70**
TrAX 70
Xalan Specific Features 81
XSLTC 91
Xalan Extensions 97
Practical Usage **104**
Applications **104**

Chapter 3: FOP **113**

Prerequisites **114**
Basic XSL 115
Flows 115
List Blocks 116
Generating XSL with XSLT 117
Tables 119
Installing and Configuring FOP **123**
Hyphenation 124
Development Techniques **125**
Embedding 125
Using the Configuration Files and Options 127
SAX 129
DOM 131
XSLT 133
Validating XSL 135
Command-Line Usage 135
Ant Task 137
Fonts 138
Output 140
Graphics 143
FOP Extensions 145
Practical Usage **146**
Applications **146**

Chapter 4: Batik **155**

Prerequisites **156**
Static SVG 156
Dynamic SVG 164
Installing and Configuring Batik **169**
Development Techniques **170**
SVGGraphics2D 171
JSVGCanvas 183

ImageTranscoding 187
SVG Scripting 191
Security 197
SVG Rasterizer **202**
Command Line 202
SVG Browser **205**
SVG Pretty-Printer **206**
SVG Font Converter **207**
Practical Usage **208**
Applications **209**
Rich Client User Interfaces 212

Chapter 5: Cocoon Concepts **213**

Prerequisites **213**
Concepts **214**
Sitemap 214
Generators 223
Transformers 225
Serializers 229
Matchers 231
Selectors 233
Actions 234
Action Sets 236
Readers 236
Views 238
Resources 239
<pipeline> elements 239
Cocoon URIs 241
XSP 242
Sessions 253

Chapter 6: Cocoon Development **255**

Installing and Configuring Cocoon **255**
Configuring Cocoon 257
Development Techniques **258**
Database Access 258
Simple Application 269
Practical Usage **283**
Performance 283
Applications **284**

Chapter 7: Xindice **285**

Prerequisites **286**
XML:DB 287
XUpdate 293
Installing and Configuring Xindice **299**
Command-Line Tools **300**
Runtime Environment 300
Adding to the Database 300
Retrieval 302
Deleting 303
Indexing 304
Other 306
Development Techniques **307**
XML:DB API 307
Practical Usage **329**
Applications **329**
XMLServlet: Accessing Xindice 330
XSLTServletFilter 334
Deployment Descriptors 337
XSLT Stylesheets 338
A SAX-based Version 341
XPathResultHandler 346

Chapter 8: XML-RPC **349**

Prerequisites **350**
Concepts **350**
XML Encoding RPCs 351
Using HTTP as an RPC Transport 354
Installing and Configuring XML-RPC **356**
Development Techniques **356**
A Simple Client 357
Mapping to Java Types 358
A Simple Server 359
Asynchronous Clients 361
Getting More Control Over Server Processing 363
Handling BASIC Authentication on the Server 365
XML-RPC in Existing Servers 366
Using SSL 368
Practical Usage **373**
Applications **373**
Simplifying XML-RPC 373

Chapter 9: Axis **379**

Prerequisites **380**
Concepts **380**
SOAP 380
WSDL 384
JAX-RPC 392
Installing and Configuring Axis **399**
Deployment Environment Setup 400
Development Environment Setup 401
Development Techniques **402**
Axis Conceptual Model 402
Axis and WSDL 407
Accessing the ServletContext 434
Message Service 436
Handlers 442
.jws Web Services 448
Tools 449
Practical Usage **453**
Applications **454**

Chapter 10: XML Security **455**

Prerequisites **456**
One-Way Hashing 456
Symmetric Key Encryption 457
Public Key Encryption 457
Digital Signatures 457
Concepts **458**
Canonicalization 459
Installing and Configuring XML Security **470**
Development Techniques **471**
Canonicalizing and Computing the Digest 471
Signing 474
Verification 485
More Signatures 490
Resolvers 493
Encryption 495
Practical Usage **501**
Applications **502**

Index **503**

Introduction

XML is growing in popularity for use in all kinds of applications. Some have called it the new ASCII, believing that XML will be used as widely as the ASCII character set is today. XML's simple rules for markup, utilization of Unicode, and endorsement by the World Wide Web Consortium (W3C) have made it a good choice for representing various kinds of data in a human-readable manner. In addition, many new technologies have been built on top of XML—from technologies that convert XML from one vocabulary to another, to those that render formatted XML as PDF or Postscript, all the way to technologies that digitally sign and encrypt XML documents or pieces of XML documents.

To use XML or one of its related technologies, you need to have a toolset, and one such toolset is the topic of this book. The Apache Software Foundation hosts a number of projects related to XML. The aim of this book is to give you an overview of the XML technology the projects implement and then show you how to use the projects in your own applications.

How to Use This Book

This book is intended for Java developers who are already familiar with XML and who want to use one of the Apache XML projects in an application setting. The focus of the book is the unique features of the Apache tools we'll cover. This isn't intended to be a tutorial book for any of the XML technologies standardized by the W3C. In particular, you shouldn't use this book as a tutorial on XML, XML Namespaces, SAX, DOM, XSLT, XSL, SVG, SOAP, WSDL, XML Signature, or XML Encryption. Although each chapter contains some material to make sure that you can understand the functionality provided by the Apache projects, each one of these technologies could be the subject of an entire book (and many of them are). Our goal is to help you see how to use the Apache libraries to perform the kinds of tasks needed to build real-world applications.

This book also doesn't cover every Apache XML-related project—a book must have a finite scope, just like a software project. We'll examine the most useful tools provided by Apache, as well as real-world techniques for using them.

Unless noted, all the examples have been written for and tested under the Java SDK version 1.4.2. Many of the examples will run fine on earlier versions of the JDK, but a few will not, and these are noted for you.

The tools presented are mostly independent of one another, with the exception of Xerces. XML parsing is a fundamental aspect of all the Apache XML tools, so knowledge of Xerces can be helpful in many circumstances. It would be a good idea for you to at least browse the contents Chapter 1, "Xerces," to make sure you're familiar with all the concepts. After that, you can jump to the chapter that discusses the particular tool you're interested in.

All the code and sample applications in this book can be downloaded from www.wrox.com.

Organization

This book is divided up into three parts. Part I contains an overview of all the tools in this book, and it explains the details of Xerces, a tool which is used in conjunction with almost all the other tools discussed in this book. Part II focuses on tools that are particularly useful for developing Web applications—these tools have other purposes as well, but the focus is on Web applications. Part III covers tools that are primarily used to build back-end applications.

Part I: Getting Started with the Apache XML Tools

Part I includes a chapter on Xerces, which is foundational for all the other tools described in the book.

Chapter 1: Xerces

Xerces-J is an XML parsing library that has been used in many large Java applications. It provides support for XML 1.0 with Namespaces and has preliminary support for XML 1.1. Xerces-J supports the W3C DOM Level 2 tree-based API, the SAX 2.0.1 event-driven API, and the Java API for XML Parsing (JAXP) 1.2, which is based on the DOM and SAX APIs. In addition, Xerces-J provides full support for the W3C XML Schema 1.0 recommendation, allowing you the choice of using DTDs or XML Schema when validating XML documents. XML parsing is the foundational layer for any XML processing application, and Xerces provides a stable and flexible foundation. Xerces has been incorporated into so many applications that you may be using it today and not know it.

We'll look at how to use JAXP with Xerces-J to obtain a parser that you can use from within your application. Then we'll discuss how you can use either the SAX or DOM APIs to process an XML document. Xerces-J provides additional functionality that isn't described by any of the standards, so we'll look at how to use the Xerces configuration mechanism and the Xerces Native Interface to perform tasks that are outside of what the standards describe. Xerces includes a library for serializing XML, taking either SAX event callbacks or a DOM tree and turning them back into an XML document. One of the newest features of Xerces is the ability to cache XML Schemas to avoid reprocessing them when you're processing a number of documents that use the same schema.

Part II: Web Application Development

Part II is devoted to tools that are useful when you're developing Web applications. That's not to say that these tools don't have other applications; it's recognition that they can be particularly useful in developing Web applications.

Chapter 2: Xalan

Xalan is the ASF library for working with XSLT, the eXtensible Stylesheet Language (XSL) Transformations language. XSLT is an XML grammar that allows you to specify how an XML document using one vocabulary can be converted into an XML document that uses a different vocabulary. These transforms let you add or subtract information from the document, as well as rearrange the structure of the document. Xalan implements the XSLT 1.0, XPath 1.0, and JAXP 1.2 APIs. You can use XSLT to convert XML of various sorts into HTML, WML, or other display languages based on XML. You can also use it to convert data files from one vocabulary to another.

The JAXP API is the primary method for interacting with Xalan, so we'll look at how to use it to perform XSLT transformations. Xalan can operate in two modes, interpretive and compiled. In interpretive mode, Xalan interprets the XSLT stylesheet as it transforms the document. In compiled mode, Xalan uses an XSLT-to-Java compiler called XSLTC to compile the stylesheet into a Java class that can then be executed directly. If you're passing a large number of documents through the same stylesheet, using XSLTC can improve the performance of your application substantially. We'll also examine the Xalan mechanism for implementing extensions to XSLT using libraries of functions and via custom Java code. The chapter ends by showing you how to implement a Java servlet filter that can be used to add XSLT capabilities to many servlet applications.

Chapter 3: FOP

The XSL recommendation comes in two parts: XSLT and XSL, which is sometimes referred to as XSL-FO (XSL formatting objects). Whereas XSLT is concerned with transforming one flavor of XML into another, XSL-FO takes XML in the form of XSL formatting objects and formats it for output to non-XML formats such as PDF, PCL, and Postscript. The Apache FOP project is an implementation of an XSL processor. It's capable of rendering XSL formatting objects to PDF, PCL, Postscript, SVG, text, and other file formats.

We'll look at the FOP SAX- and DOM-based APIs to see how to embed FOP in a Java program. FOP provides some command-line tools that are useful for debugging and testing, as well as some Ant tasks. At the end of the chapter, we'll discuss how to implement a Java servlet filter that uses FOP as an output stage. We'll also see how to chain that filter together with the Xalan XSLT filter to obtain a complete system for rendering XML to non-XML formats.

Chapter 4: Batik

People are finding applications for XML in a wide and varied number of problem domains. The Scalable Vector Graphics (SVG) recommendation specifies an XML vocabulary for describing vector graphics operations. SVG allows you to describe dynamic as well as static images, so you can use it to perform animation and build user interfaces. There are two methods for describing SVG animation: a scripting-based method based on an SVG-enabled version of the DOM, and a more declarative method based on elements taken from the Synchronized Multimedia Integration Language (SMIL). SVG provides a way to integrate visual content into XML data. The Batik project is Apache's library for working with SVG.

The Batik toolkit contains both end-user and developer components. We'll look at the Batik tools for generating images from SVG files, an SVG browser based on Batik components, and tools that Batik supplies for generating fonts and pretty-printing SVG files. Batik provides a library of classes you can integrate into your application so you can generate SVG documents by using the Java2D drawing API. There is also a Swing-based component for displaying SVG documents; you can add it to your Swing applications to obtain SVG display capabilities. We'll also examine how Batik integrates with scripting languages such as ECMAScript/JavaScript and JPython.

Chapter 5: Cocoon Concepts

Cocoon is a sophisticated Web publishing framework based on XML. It's different from most of the other tools we'll discuss because no standard defines how it works. It's purely the invention of the Cocoon committers, and it makes heavy use of the rest of the Apache XML libraries.

Cocoon is based on the notion of XML processing pipelines. These pipelines are used to process request URIs and generate results of varying types, including HTML, XHTML, WML, PDF, and others. Cocoon defines eXtensible Server Pages, an XML-compliant equivalent to JavaServer Pages, which you can use to generate XML data for Cocoon pipelines. A new feature in Cocoon is FlowScript, which provides a compact mechanism for capturing complex Web page interactions such as multipage forms.

Cocoon is a big topic, so it's covered in two chapters—this chapter focuses on Cocoon concepts and terminology, and we look at how to build pipelines.

Chapter 6: Cocoon Development

This chapter focuses on practical applications. We'll discuss installing and setting up Cocoon. We'll approach database access from a number of different angles because Cocoon provides a diversity of database access methods. And we'll show you how to tie all these components together in a simple database-backed Web application.

Chapter 7: Xindice

Once you start marking up data as XML, you'll discover that you quickly accumulate a lot of information. The question then becomes how to manage all this information. The Xindice project is an attempt to answer that question. Instead of trying to store your XML data in files or as columns or rows in a relational database, Xindice gives you the option of storing your data in a database that has been designed from the beginning to deal with XML. Xindice lets you create collections of documents, index them, and query them using XPath. There are no widely adopted standards in this space, although Xindice does support an API called XML:DB that has been developed by a few native XML database vendors.

We'll look at setting up a Xindice database and how you go about creating, retrieving, updating, and deleting XML from it. To do this, we'll discuss the Xindice command-line tools, as well as Xindice's implementation of the XML:DB APIs. We'll demonstrate how to integrate Xindice into an XML application by using Xindice as the source of XML data to be processed by the servlet filters developed in earlier chapters.

Part III: Back-End Application Development

Part III discusses three tools that are involved at the back-end plumbing level. You can use them in Web applications and many other back-end application situations.

Chapter 8: XML-RPC

The XML-RPC protocol uses XML to mark up the arguments of a remote procedure call. The resulting XML document is transported to the server using HTTP. This protocol is fairly easy to implement and use, which makes it a popular choice for integrating applications. The main details you need to be aware of are how the XML-RPC library maps types in the host programming language (Java, in our case) onto the set of types defined by XML-RPC. The Apache XML-RPC library is part of the Web services projects at http://ws.apache.org; it's called Apache XML-RPC.

This chapter shows how to build XML-RPC clients and servers using the Apache XML-RPC library. We'll also talk about how to perform basic security tasks such authentication and encryption using SSL. The chapter concludes with an example of how to make XML-RPC calls a bit more type safe.

Chapter 9: Axis

Some of the creators of XML-RPC went on to create a more sophisticated version of an XML over HTTP protocol called the Simple Object Access Protocol (SOAP). The SOAP protocol is one the cornerstones of the Web services technology stack. Web services is an attempt to construct systems using an architecture based on loose coupling. Using XML as a marshalling format and HTTP as a transfer protocol is one way to obtain loose coupling. Another cornerstone of the Web services technology stack is the Web Services Description Language (WSDL). This XML vocabulary is used to describe a Web service. A WSDL description can then be used to generate the code that implements a Web service. Apache Axis is a part of the Apache Web services project and is the ASF implementation of both SOAP and WSDL. Axis provides an implementation of the Java API for XML-based RPC (JAX-RPC).

We'll look at how you write both service providers and service requestors using the Axis / JAX-RPC APIs, and we'll discuss the Axis deployment descriptor format and how it controls the deployment of Web services when you use Axis. Axis includes powerful command-line tools for taking a WSDL file and generating Java code that implements the service being described in the WSDL file. It also includes tools for processing an existing Java class and creating a WSDL file based on it. In addition, Axis provides a mechanism for creating a message-based service where the Axis runtime does not interpret the contents of the SOAP message, allowing your application to have total control over how the XML message is processed.

Chapter 10: XML-Security

XML is increasingly being used to mark up data that has various kinds of security requirements. Either the data needs to have a guarantee of authenticity, or the data needs to be private or secret. The W3C has developed two recommendations to deal with these issues. The XML Signature Syntax and Processing recommendation details how to represent digital signature information as XML and how to use digital signatures to sign portions of XML documents. The XML Encryption Syntax and Processing recommendation contains a parallel technology for using encryption.

The Apache XML project hosts the XML-Security project, which provides a Java API for working with digital signatures and encryption. The digital signature functionality is stable and has been available for some time. The encryption functionality is in the alpha stage but is usable. This chapter explains the APIs provided by the library and walks you through signing, verifying, encrypting, and decrypting documents and portions of documents.

The Apache Software Foundation

You may wonder where all this software comes from. How was it developed? Who developed it? Who paid for it? What can you use it for and under what terms? What if you have a problem? In this section, we'll talk about the Apache Software Foundation and, along the way, answer all these questions.

History

The Apache Software Foundation started out in 1995 as a group of eight Webmasters called the Apache Group. Their purpose was to continue the development of the public domain HTTP server daemon that was developed by Rob McCool at the National Center for Supercomputing Applications (NCSA) at the University of Illinois at Urbana-Champaign (UIUC). McCool had left NCSA in 1994, and no one was developing the NCSA code base. The problem was, the NCSA HTTP server was the most popular Web server in 1995, and many people wanted to keep using it. The group of Webmasters used e-mail to coordinate the changes each of them made to the NCSA HTTP code. The changes were distributed as patches, generated by the UNIX diff command and integrated using the UNIX patch command. All these patches led to the Apache name: "a patchy server." Since 1996, the Apache HTTP server has been the number-one Web server on the Internet.

In 1999, the members of the Apache Group formed the Apache Software Foundation (ASF) in order to provide organizational, legal, and financial support for the Apache HTTP Server. The ASF is a membership-based, not-for-profit corporation formed for the following reasons:

- Provide a foundation for open, collaborative software development projects by supplying hardware, communication, and business infrastructure.
- Create an independent legal entity to which companies and individuals can donate resources and be assured that those resources will be used for the public benefit.
- Provide a means for individual volunteers to be sheltered from legal suits directed at the foundation's projects.
- Protect the Apache brand as applied to its software products from being abused by other organizations.

New Projects

The ASF initiated the Apache XML project in the fall of 1999 with code donations from a variety of sources including IBM, Sun Microsystems, Datachannel, and several individuals. These projects formed the core of the new project. Since that time, the Apache XML project has added several new projects as the XML area has continued to grow. Early in the spring of 2003, some of the projects in the XML project were spun off into a Web Services project, and the Cocoon project became a top-level project as well. This was done to facilitate the foundation's ability to oversee these projects, and so that the projects could build more cohesive communities around their areas of interest.

The projects are frequently referred to by the URLs of their Websites. The XML project is at http://xml.apache.org, the Web Services project is at http://ws.apache.org, and Cocoon is at http://cocoon.apache.org. The ASF has a number of other projects, including Ant, APR, Avalon, Commons, DB, Incubator, Jakarta, James, Maven, Perl, PHP, and TCL.

What does this mean to you? The software you download from the ASF is owned by the ASF and is licensed to you, as is all software. As you'll see in the next section, the terms of the license aren't restrictive. Development of the software is the responsibility of the ASF through individual contributors.

Licensing

The ASF differs from some of the other large open source efforts in a number of ways. One of them is the area of licensing. You may have heard that open source software is *viral*, meaning that if you use it in your application, you must distribute your application as open source. Whether this is true depends on the license you're using. The GNU General Public License (GPL) is the primary license that has this property. The GNU Lesser General Public License (LGPL) may also have this property when applied to Java code. This issue is still being resolved at the time of this writing.

The Apache Software Foundation has its own license called the Apache Software License. For your convenience, the entire content of the license follows.

```
/* ====================================================================
 * The Apache Software License, Version 1.1
 *
 * Copyright (c) 2003 The Apache Software Foundation. All rights
 * reserved.
 *
 * Redistribution and use in source and binary forms, with or without
 * modification, are permitted provided that the following conditions
 * are met:
 *
 * 1. Redistributions of source code must retain the above copyright
 *    notice, this list of conditions and the following disclaimer.
 *
 * 2. Redistributions in binary form must reproduce the above
 *    copyright notice, this list of conditions and the following
 *    disclaimer in the documentation and/or other materials provided
 *    with the distribution.
 *
 * 3. The end-user documentation included with the redistribution,
 *    if any, must include the following acknowledgment:
 *       "This product includes software developed by the
 *        Apache Software Foundation (http://www.apache.org/)."
 *    Alternately, this acknowledgment may appear in the software
 *    itself, if and wherever such third-party acknowledgments
 *    normally appear.
 *
 * 4. The names "Apache" and "Apache Software Foundation" must
 *    not be used to endorse or promote products derived from this
 *    software without prior written permission. For written
 *    permission, please contact apache@apache.org.
 *
 * 5. Products derived from this software may not be called "Apache",
 *    nor may "Apache" appear in their name, without prior written
 *    permission of the Apache Software Foundation.
 *
 * THIS SOFTWARE IS PROVIDED "AS IS" AND ANY EXPRESSED OR IMPLIED
 * WARRANTIES, INCLUDING, BUT NOT LIMITED TO, THE IMPLIED WARRANTIES
 * OF MERCHANTABILITY AND FITNESS FOR A PARTICULAR PURPOSE ARE
 * DISCLAIMED. IN NO EVENT SHALL THE APACHE SOFTWARE FOUNDATION OR
 * ITS CONTRIBUTORS BE LIABLE FOR ANY DIRECT, INDIRECT, INCIDENTAL,
 * SPECIAL, EXEMPLARY, OR CONSEQUENTIAL DAMAGES (INCLUDING, BUT NOT
```

```
 * LIMITED TO, PROCUREMENT OF SUBSTITUTE GOODS OR SERVICES; LOSS OF
 * USE, DATA, OR PROFITS; OR BUSINESS INTERRUPTION) HOWEVER CAUSED AND
 * ON ANY THEORY OF LIABILITY, WHETHER IN CONTRACT, STRICT LIABILITY,
 * OR TORT (INCLUDING NEGLIGENCE OR OTHERWISE) ARISING IN ANY WAY OUT
 * OF THE USE OF THIS SOFTWARE, EVEN IF ADVISED OF THE POSSIBILITY OF
 * SUCH DAMAGE.
 * ====================================================================
 *
 * This software consists of voluntary contributions made by many
 * individuals on behalf of the Apache Software Foundation. For more
 * information on the Apache Software Foundation, please see
 * <http://www.apache.org/>.
 *
 */
```

There are seven items you need to be aware of:

- You're free to redistribute the source code and/or binaries of an Apache-licensed piece of software. This is true even if you make modifications to the source code. You aren't required to make your product open source. You also aren't required to give out the source code, but you're allowed to do so if you choose. There are some conditions, and they basically come down to this: You must credit the fact that you used Apache-licensed code. So, if you redistribute the source code to an Apache project, you must include the license file (which appears at the top of every source-code file).
- If you redistribute binaries (including binaries you write that include the Apache code), then you need to distribute a copy of the license file somewhere in your distribution.
- If you make a distribution (including building software that uses the Apache code), then you need to include the clause "This product includes software developed by the Apache Software Foundation (www.apache.org/)" somewhere in the end-user documentation, in the software, or wherever you acknowledge the use of third-party software.
- You can't use the name *Apache* or *Apache Software Foundation* to endorse or promote your product unless you get written permission from the ASF.
- You can't use *Apache* in the name of your software product unless you get written permission from the ASF.
- There is no warranty for the software.

Under the terms of the Apache License, it's fine for you to build a product that uses one or more pieces of Apache software and sell the product in binary form. You don't have to distribute the source code for your product, and you don't have to make it open source. You don't have to pay the ASF, although they would never turn down your donation. As long as you give the ASF a little credit and don't try to misuse the Apache name, you should have no problems. A number of commercial Java products do this on a regular basis (IBM's WebSphere application server comes to mind as an example).

Community

Another way the ASF is different from other open source projects is in its focus on community-developed software. For an ASF project, the health and diversity of the development community is as important as the technical quality of the project code. The knowledge and expertise about the code resides in the community of developers.

A good way to keep abreast of developments in the broader ASF community is via the Apache Newsletter at www.apache.org/newsletter/index.html.

The ASF is a virtual organization; it has no central meeting place, so everything happens via the Internet. An Apache project uses several tools to create a virtual meeting place:

- **Mailing lists**—The most important tool is mailing lists. Usually a project has two or three mailing lists. One mailing list is for users to ask questions, get help, and help each other. Another list is used by the people who are developing the software for the project. This mailing list is public and open to anyone who is interested. There may also be a third mailing list that records all the changes made via the source-code control system, CVS. Sometimes the developer list and the CVS list are the same. The XML and Web Services projects each have a project-wide mailing list called *general*. This cross-project list facilitates interaction between the various subprojects and the public working area for the project management committee (PMC).
- **CVS source-code control system**—CVS is an open-source version-control system that allows developers to work in parallel without locking files. If two developers change the same file, then a conflict occurs, and they have to merge their changes. The importance of CVS is obvious. It's where the code lives, and because people are there for the code, CVS is essential.
- **IRC channel**—Sometimes a project has an IRC channel where people can gather and discuss issues interactively. This tool can be useful but can also be a barrier to community development unless the IRC session is logged and the logs are posted to the mailing lists.
- **Wiki**—The ASF also hosts a *wiki* (a collaboratively edited Website) at http://nagoya.apache.org/wiki/apachewiki.cgi. It's useful for working on documents in a collaborative manner. Mailing the final document or snapshots of the document to the appropriate mailing list is encouraged.

Roles

There are different categories of involvement with an Apache project, all of them voluntary. The first and most important category includes people who are using the software. Without the users, there is no reason for the project to exist. They use the software, make requests for new features, report bugs, and let the developers know where the software is hard to use or understand. These users are also doing the marketing and sales for ASF projects. If someone has a good experience using a piece of Apache software, they are likely to let their friends and colleagues know about it. So, although most users don't contribute code, they supply lots of information that shapes the way the code is written.

Some users do a bit more: They send changes to the documentation or to the software itself. Typically these changes are sent to one of the mailing lists as patches (generated using the diff command) to the existing documentation or software, although occasionally someone sends an entire file. One of the committers (explained next) examines the patches and decides whether the changes should be incorporated. If the changes should be incorporated (or modified and then incorporated), the committer makes the changes and commits them to the CVS repository. A contributor can contribute in other ways as well, such as by helping resolve disputes or making significant suggestions for features.

Contributors who consistently make valuable contributions may become committers. The term *committer* comes from the CVS commit command used to make changes to the CVS repository. The committers form the core development team for the project. Because they have been recognized as doing significant amounts of work, they decide on the direction of the project. In order to become a committer, a person must be nominated by an existing committer. A contributor can ask to be nominated, but a committer must be willing to propose that the contributor be given commit rights. All the committers for the project vote on whether the person should be granted commit rights. If the person receives three +1 votes and no -1 votes, then they are given commit privileges.

Voting

Let's change topics for a moment and talk about voting. All major decisions for an Apache project are made by voting. Voting is typically used in three areas: major code modifications, project releases, and procedural matters. However, voting is so much a part of the way Apache projects work that it often happens spontaneously as a way of expressing agreement or disagreement on an issue. Depending on the project, a good rule of thumb is that a vote lasts for 72 hours in order to allow people to participate—this is especially important because the committers may be distributed around the world.

Votes are stated using numbers. Voting +1 means you're in favor, voting -1 means you aren't in favor, and voting 0 means you're neutral. In addition, +0 and -0 votes indicate that you're leaning, but your inclination isn't strong enough to be in favor or against.

Code modification votes work like this. Someone makes a proposal for a code change they would like to make and requests a vote (people may also vote spontaneously to show that they believe a vote is necessary). At that point, the proposal needs three +1 votes and no -1 votes. In this setting, a -1 vote is a veto. Vetoes should be exercised reasonably, and the person exercising the veto must give a valid technical reason for it. It's possible to get someone to retract their veto after addressing their concerns.

Code release votes are typically called by the person acting as the release manager for that release. Typically, the project develops a release plan and votes on it using procedural style voting. A twist in the voting on release plans is that +1 is assumed to mean the voter will help make the release happen, whereas +0 and -0 indicate that the voter will not help or hinder the release process. Once all the items in the release plan have been completed, the release manager calls for a vote to make a release. Release votes can't be vetoed, but they do require a minimum of three +1 votes to be approved.

Procedural votes on issues such as developing release plans are done via a simple majority. There must be more +1s than -1s, and there are no vetoes.

Another voting style can be used: *lazy consensus*. In such a vote, someone says something like "I'm going to modify the code to do this instead of that unless someone objects within three days." If no one objects, then the change is made. This process can be used effectively for smaller code changes that may not be important enough to vote on. If another committer believes the change is important enough for a vote, then a vote can be taken. Lazy consensus is mostly used for code modification votes, although it can be used for minor procedural matters. Another name for lazy consensus is *silence implies consent*.

PMCs

All the top-level ASF projects have a project management committee (PMC). The top-level projects are those that have their own Websites. Of the projects we'll discuss in this book, the XML project (http://xml.apache.org), the Web Services project (http://ws.apache.org) and Cocoon (http://cocoon.apache.org) are all top-level projects. Xerces, Xalan, FOP, Batik, Xindice, and XML-Security are all subprojects of the XML project, and XML-RPC and Axis are subprojects of the Web Services project. You may hear the term *umbrella PMC* used to describe the XML and Web Services PMCs (as well as Jakarta) because they form an umbrella over a number of (sub) projects. The subprojects operate as projects in their own right, but many of them don't want to deal with having their own PMC.

The role of the PMCs is to ensure that the ASF guidelines on voting and culture are followed, to ensure that projects continue to be developed in a reasonable fashion, to help resolve conflicts, and to help take care of administrative or legal issues that might arise. The PMCs don't determine the direction in which the software is developed. The members of the PMCs are drawn from the committers of the project or subprojects and are voted on by the existing members of the particular PMC.

The PMC for a particular project does most of its business in the project's general mailing list (general@xml.apache.org, general@ws.apache.org, dev@cocoon.apache.org). The PMC also has a private mailing list, pmc@, which is used only for sensitive matters.

New Projects

The last issue we'll address is the question of how new ASF projects (or subprojects) are created. It's fairly common for groups of developers or a corporation to approach the ASF with the desire to start a project around some piece of code that has been developed.

Remember that the most important criterion the ASF uses in evaluating the proposed project is the health of its development community. After much experience, the ASF has learned that this is the key factor for success. If the project is a closed-source project that wants to become open source, as is often the case with a code base that has come from a company, then it's very important to have a diversity of committers to the project. If the code base has been developed by a single person, there is a similar concern over the size of the community around the project. Neither of these issues is insurmountable, but if you want your project to be accepted by the ASF, you should be aware that these are among the most important issues.

New project proposals are sent to general@incubator.apache.org. The Apache Incubator project is designed to help new projects learn to function within the ASF framework. This includes following the voting guidelines, learning to work in an open community development style, and finding necessary resources and infrastructure within the ASF. The ultimate decision of whether a project is accepted for incubation is up to the ASF board or, if the new project would fall under the domain of one of the umbrella PMCs, the PMC for the appropriate project. If the board or the PMC decides to accept the project, then an ASF member is asked to help shepherd the new project through the incubation process. The project spends some time in incubation, learning to work in the Apache style, before leaving the incubator. The decision on whether a project is ready to leave incubation is a joint one, involving the members of the project, the ASF board or relevant PMC, and the Incubator PMC.

W3C Process

All the projects described in this book are under active development. A number of them implement specifications developed by the W3C. In order to understand the development status of a project that is implementing a W3C specification, it's useful to understand the W3C process for developing specifications.

The documents that many people refer to as standards are actually called *Recommendations* by the W3C. Recommendation is the highest status a specification can reach within the W3C process. In practice, this distinction doesn't mean much, because most people treat a W3C Recommendation as a standard. The following figure illustrates the steps a specification goes through on its way to becoming a Recommendation.

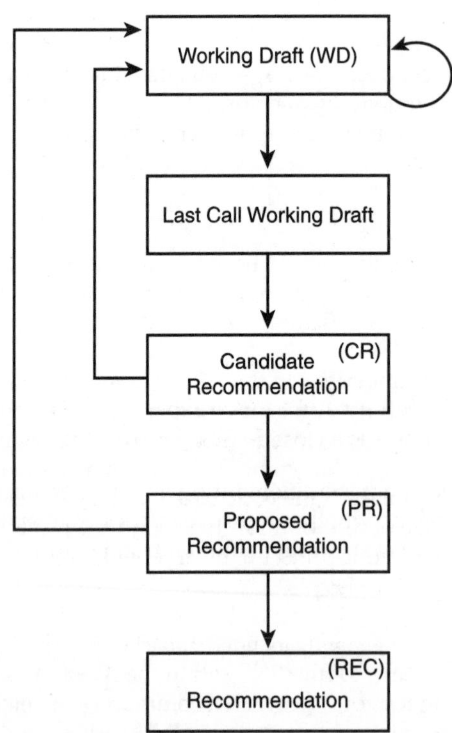

The W3C creates specifications in a *Working Group*—a group of experts from W3C member companies who gather for the purpose of creating a specification. The specification begins its life as a Working Draft (WD), which is a public document meant for public review by the W3C, the public, and any interested organizations. A specification typically goes through a number of WDs (three to four seems to be the rule for many of the XML-related specifications). A three-month rule dictates that a Working Group must update the WDs every three months.

Once the Working Group is satisfied that it has met its requirements and taken into account dependencies with other related specifications, it can announce a *Last Call Working Draft*. The Last Call announcement indicates to the rest of the W3C and the public that the WD is ready to advance to the next stage in the specification process. After the Last Call announcement is a review period during which other W3C groups and the public may comment on the draft. This review period must last at least three weeks but may last longer. If the comments warrant it, the specification may be returned to the WD stage in order to address the comments; otherwise it advances to the next stage.

The next stage in the process results in the specification being labeled a *Candidate Recommendation* (CR). The director of the W3C issues a call for implementations. The Working Group specifies a minimum duration for the implementation period as well as an estimate of the amount of time it will take to gain the relevant implementation experience. The Working Group may identify some features in the specification as being *at risk*; depending on the experience gained with implementations, these features may be removed from the specification without sending it back to the WD stage. This stage may be skipped if no implementation needs to be done, as in the case with the XML Infoset.

If the implementation phase doesn't uncover any problems with the specification, then the specification can advance to the penultimate stage: *Proposed Recommendation* (PR). If the specification was implemented, the Working Group must show two independent and interoperable implementations of each feature of the specification. During the PR stage, the specification must be reviewed by the W3C Advisory Committee. When a specification enters PR status, the review period must last at least four weeks. During this stage, representatives on the Advisory Committee may appeal the decision to advance the specification to Recommendation status (the next and final step).

Once the PR review period has been completed and the Advisory Committee has provided its feedback, the decision is made whether to issue the specification as a Recommendation. If the specification isn't published, it may be returned to the Working Group or possibly canceled. If the specification is published as a Recommendation, the W3C is saying that it believes the specification is ready for wide-scale deployment and implementation.

If you're working with a project that is implementing a W3C specification, understanding how the process works can help you decide whether to use features of that specification in your application. A number of Apache projects serve as implementation testing grounds for some of these specifications, so it's important to know how mature the specification is before you use a feature. The more mature the specification is, the better. Specifications in the Working Draft stage can be very volatile—they may change a great deal from on draft to the next, and may even be cancelled. It's better to wait until a specification is in the Candidate or Proposed Recommendation stage before seriously using related functionality in your application.

1

Xerces

XML parsing is the foundational building block for every other tool we'll be looking at in this book. You can't use Xalan, the XSLT engine, without an XML parser because the XSLT stylesheets are XML documents. The same is true for FOP and its input XSL:FO, Batik and SVG, and all the other Apache XML tools. Even if you as a developer aren't interacting with the XML parser directly, you can be sure that each of the tools you describe makes use of an XML parser.

XML parsing technology is so important that the ASF has two XML parsing projects: Xerces and Crimson. The reason for this is historical. When the ASF decided to create http://xml.apache.org, both IBM and Sun had Java-based XML parsers that they wanted to donate to the project. The IBM parser was called XML for Java (XML4J) and was available in source code from IBM's AlphaWorks Website. The Sun parser was originally called Project X. The code base for IBM's XML4J parser became the basis for Xerces, and the code base for Project X became the basis for Crimson. The goal of the parsing project was to build a best-of-breed parser based on the ideas and experience of XML4J and Project X. This did not happen right away; it wasn't until late in 2000 that a second-generation Xerces effort was begun.

Throughout this chapter and the rest of this book, we'll use Xerces for Java 2 (hereafter Xerces) as our parser. Xerces for Java 2 is replacing both Xerces for Java 1 and Crimson. At the time of this writing, the plan is for a version of Xerces to be the reference implementation for XML parsing in the Sun Java Developer's Kit (JDK). Xerces is a fully featured XML parser that supports the important XML standards:

- XML 1.0, Second Edition
- XML Namespaces
- SAX 2.0
- DOM Level 1
- DOM Level 2 (Core, Events, Range, and Traversal)

- Java APIs for XML Parsing 1.2
- XML Schema 1.0 (Schema and Structures)

The current release of Xerces (2.4.0) also has experimental support for:

- XML 1.1 Candidate Recommendation
- XML Namespaces 1.1 Candidate Recommendation
- DOM Level 3 (Core, Load/Save)

A word about experimental functionality: one of the goals of the Xerces project is to provide feedback to the various standards bodies regarding specifications that are under development. This means the Xerces developers are implementing support for those standards before the standards are complete. Work in these areas is always experimental until the specification being implemented has been approved. If you need functionality that is documented as experimental, you may have to change your code when the final version of the specification is complete. If the functionality you need is implemented only in an experimental package, be aware that the functionality may change or be removed entirely as the standards process continues. A good example is abstract support for grammars (both DTDs and XML Schema), which was supposed to be part of DOM Level 3. However, the DOM Working Group decided to cease work on this functionality, so it had to be removed from Xerces. This is a rare and extreme occurrence, but you should be aware that it has happened. Most situations are less severe, such as changes in the names and signatures of APIs.

Prerequisites

You must understand a few basics about XML and related standards in order to make good use of the material in this chapter. Following is a quick review. If you need more information, *XML in a Nutshell, Second Edition* by Eliotte Rusty Harold and W. Scott Means is a good source for the relevant background. Let's begin with the following simple XML file:

```
 1: <?xml version="1.0" encoding="UTF-8"?>
 2: <book xmlns="http://sauria.com/schemas/apache-xml-book/book"
 3:   xmlns:xsi="http://www.w3.org/2001/XMLSchema-instance"
 4:   xsi:schemaLocation=
 5:    "http://sauria.com/schemas/apache-xml-book/book
 6:     http://www.sauria.com/schemas/apache-xml-book/book.xsd"
 7:   version="1.0">
 8:   <title>Professional XML Development with Apache Tools</title>
 9:   <author>Theodore W. Leung</author>
10:   <isbn>0-7645-4355-5</isbn>
11:   <month>December</month>
12:   <year>2003</year>
13:   <publisher>Wrox</publisher>
14:   <address>Indianapolis, Indiana</address>
15: </book>
```

Like all XML files, this file begins with an XML declaration (line 1). The XML declaration says that this is an XML file, the version of XML being used is 1.0, and the character encoding being used for this file is UTF-8. Until recently, the version number was always 1.0, but the W3C XML Working Group is in the process of defining XML 1.1. When they have finished their work, you will be able to supply 1.1 in addition to 1.0 for the version number. If there is no encoding declaration, then the document must be encoded using UTF-8. If you forget to specify an encoding declaration or specify an incorrect encoding declaration, your XML parser will report a fatal error. We'll have more to say about fatal errors later in the chapter.

Well-Formedness

The rest of the file consists of data that has been marked up with tags (such as <title> and <author>). The first rule or prerequisite for an XML document is that it must be *well-formed.* (An XML parser is required by the XML specification to report a fatal error if a document isn't well-formed.) This means every start tag (like <book>) must have an end tag (</book>). The start and end tag, along with the data in between them, is called an *element*. Elements may not overlap; they must be nested within each other. In other words, the start and end tag of an element must be inside the start and end tag of any element that encloses it. The data between the start and end tag is also known as the *content* of the element; it may contain elements, characters, or a mix of elements and characters. Note that the start tag of an element may contain attributes. In our example, the book element contains an xsi:schemaLocation attribute in lines 4-5. The value of an attribute must be enclosed in either single quotes (') or double quotes ("). The type of the end quote must match the type of the beginning quote.

Namespaces

In lines 2-4 you see a number of namespace declarations. The first declaration in line 2 sets the default namespace for this document to http://sauria.com/schemas/apache-xml-book/book. *Namespaces* are used to prevent name clashes between elements from two different grammars. You can easily imagine the element name title or author being used in another XML grammar, say one for music CDs. If you want to combine elements from those two grammars, you will run into problems trying to determine whether a title element is from the book grammar or the CD grammar.

Namespaces solve that problem by allowing you to associate each element in a grammar with a namespace. The namespace is specified by a URI, which is used to provide a unique name for the namespace. You can't expect to be able to retrieve anything from the namespace URI. When you're using namespaces, it's as if each element or attribute name is prefixed by the namespace URI. This is very cumbersome, so the XML Namespaces specification provides two kinds of shorthand. The first shorthand is the ability to specify the default namespace for a document, as in line 2. The other shorthand is the ability to declare an abbreviation that can be used in the document instead of the namespace URI. This abbreviation is called the *namespace prefix*. In line 3, the document declares a namespace prefix xsi for the namespace associated with http://www.w3.org/2001/XMLSchema-instance. You just place a colon and the desired prefix after xmlns.

Line 4 shows how namespace prefixes are used. The attribute schemaLocation is prefixed by xsi, and the two are separated by a colon. The combined name xsi:schemaLocation is called a *qualified name* (QName). The prefix is xsi, and the schemaLocation portion is also referred to as the *local part* of the QName. (It's important to know what all these parts are called because the XML parser APIs let you access each piece from your program.)

Default namespaces have a lot of gotchas. One tricky thing to remember is that if you use a default namespace, it only works for elements—you must prefix any attributes that are supposed to be in the default namespace. Another tricky thing about default namespaces is that you have to explicitly define a default namespace. There is no way to get one "automatically". If you don't define a default namespace, and then you write an unprefixed element or attribute, that element or attribute is in no namespace at all.

Namespace prefixes can be declared on any element in a document, not just the root element. This includes changing the default namespace. If you declare a prefix that has been declared on an ancestor element, then the new prefix declaration works for the element where it's declared and all its child elements.

You may declare multiple prefixes for the same namespace URI. Doing so is perfectly allowable; however, remember that namespace equality is based on the namespace URI, not the namespace prefix. Thus elements that look like they should be in the same namespace can actually be in different namespaces. It all depends on which URI the namespace prefixes have been bound to. Also note that certain namespaces have commonly accepted uses, such as the xsi prefix used in this example. Here are some of the more common prefixes:

Namespace Prefix	Namespace URI	Usage
xsi	http://www.w3.org/2001/XMLSchema-instance	XML Schema Instance
xsd	http://www.w3.org/2001/XMLSchema	XML Schema
xsl	http://www.w3.org/1999/XSL/Transform	XSLT
fo	http://www.w3.org/1999/XSL/Format	XSL Formatting Objects
xlink	http://www.w3.org/1999/xlink	XLink
svg	http://www.w3.org/2000/svg	Scalable Vector Graphics
ds	http://www.w3.org/2000/09/xmldsig#	XML Signature
xenc	http://www.w3.org/2001/04/xmlenc#	XML Encryption

Validity

The second rule for XML documents is *validity*. It's a little odd to say "rule" because XML documents don't have to be valid, but there are well defined rules that say what it means for a document to be valid. Validity is the next step up from well-formedness. Validity lets you say things like this: Every book element must have a title element followed by an author element, followed by an isbn element, and so on. Validity says that the document is valid according to the rules of some grammar. (Remember diagramming sentences in high-school English? It's the same kind of thing we're talking about here for valid XML documents.)

Because a document can only be valid according to the rules of a grammar, you need a way to describe the grammar the XML document must follow. At the moment, there are three major possibilities: DTDs, the W3C's XML Schema, and OASIS's Relax-NG.

DTDs

The XML 1.0 specification describes a grammar using a document type declaration (DTD). The language for writing a DTD is taken from SGML and doesn't look anything like XML. DTDs can't deal with namespaces and don't allow you to say anything about the data between a start and end tag. Suppose you have an element that looks like this:

```
<quantity>5</quantity>
```

Perhaps you'd like to be able to say that the content of a <quantity> element is a non-negative integer. Unfortunately, you can't say this using DTDs.

XML Schema

Shortly after XML was released, the W3C started a Working Group to define a new language for describing XML grammars. Among the goals for this new schema language were the following:

- Describe the grammar/schema in XML.
- Support the use of XML Namespaces.
- Allow rich datatypes to constrain element and attribute content.

The result of the working group's effort is known as *XML Schema*. The XML Schema specification is broken into two parts:

- *XML Schema Part 1: Structures* describes XML Schema's facilities for specifying the rules of a grammar for an XML document. It also describes the rules for using XML Schema in conjunction with namespaces.
- *XML Schema Part 2: Datatypes* covers XML Schema's rich set of datatypes that enable you to specify the types of data contained in elements and attributes. There are a lot of details to be taken care of, which has made the specification very large.

If you're unfamiliar with XML Schema, *XML Schema Part 0: Primer* is a good introduction.

Relax-NG

The third option for specifying the grammar for an XML document is Relax-NG. It was designed to fulfill essentially the same three goals that were used for XML Schema. The difference is that the resulting specification is much simpler. Relax-NG is the result of a merger between James Clark's TREX and MURATA Makoto's Relax. Unfortunately, there hasn't been much industry support for Relax-NG, due to the W3C's endorsement of XML Schema. Andy Clark's Neko XML tools provide basic support for Relax-NG that can be used with Xerces. We'll cover the Neko tools a bit later in the chapter.

Validity Example

Let's go back to the example XML file. We've chosen to specify the grammar for the book.xml document using XML Schema. The xsi:schemaLocation attribute in lines 4-5 works together with the default namespace declaration in line 2 to tell the XML parser that the schema document for the namespace http://sauria.com/schemas/apache-xml-book/book is located at http://www.sauria.com/schemas/apache-xml-book/book.xsd. The schema is attached to the namespace, not the document.

There's a separate mechanism for associating a schema with a document that has no namespace (xsi:noNamespaceSchemaLocation). For completeness, here's the XML Schema document that describes book.xml.

```
<?xml version="1.0" encoding="UTF-8"?>
<xs:schema
  targetNamespace="http://sauria.com/schemas/apache-xml-book/book"
  xmlns:book="http://sauria.com/schemas/apache-xml-book/book"
  xmlns:xs="http://www.w3.org/2001/XMLSchema"
  elementFormDefault="qualified">
  <xs:element name="address" type="xs:string"/>
  <xs:element name="author" type="xs:string"/>
  <xs:element name="book">
    <xs:complexType>
      <xs:sequence>
        <xs:element ref="book:title"/>
        <xs:element ref="book:author"/>
        <xs:element ref="book:isbn"/>
        <xs:element ref="book:month"/>
        <xs:element ref="book:year"/>
        <xs:element ref="book:publisher"/>
        <xs:element ref="book:address"/>
      </xs:sequence>
      <xs:attribute name="version" type="xs:string" use="required"/>

    </xs:complexType>
  </xs:element>
  <xs:element name="isbn" type="xs:string"/>
  <xs:element name="month" type="xs:string"/>
  <xs:element name="publisher" type="xs:string"/>
  <xs:element name="title" type="xs:string"/>
  <xs:element name="year" type="xs:short"/>
</xs:schema>
```

Entities

The example document is a single file; in XML terminology, it's a single *entity*. Entities correspond to units of storage for XML documents or portions of XML documents, like the DTD. Not only is an XML document a tree of elements, it can be a tree of entities as well. It's important to keep this in mind because entity expansion and retrieval of remote entities can be the source of unexpected performance problems. Network fetches of DTDs or a common library of entity definitions can cause intermittent performance problems. Using entities to represent large blocks of data can lead to documents that look reasonable in size but that blow up when the entities are expanded. Keep these issues in mind if you're going to use entities in your documents.

XML Parser APIs

Now that we've finished the XML refresher, let's take a quick trip through the two major parser APIs: SAX and DOM. A third parser API, the STreaming API for XML (STAX), is currently making its way through the Java Community Process (JCP).

A parser API makes the various parts of an XML document available to your application. You'll be seeing the SAX and DOM APIs in most of the other Apache XML tools, so it's worth a brief review to make sure you'll be comfortable during the rest of the book.

Let's look at a simple application to illustrate the use of the parser APIs. The application uses a parser API to parse the XML book description and turn it into a JavaBean that represents a book. This book object is a domain object in an application you're building. The file Book.java contains the Java code for the Book JavaBean. This is a straightforward JavaBean that contains the fields needed for a book, along with getter and setter methods and a toString method:

```
/*
 *
 * Book.java
 *
 * Example from "Professional XML Development with Apache Tools"
 *
 */
package com.sauria.apachexml.ch1;

public class Book {
    String title;
    String author;
    String isbn;
    String month;
    int year;
    String publisher;
    String address;

    public String getAddress() {
        return address;
    }

    public String getAuthor() {
        return author;
    }

    public String getIsbn() {
        return isbn;
    }

    public String getMonth() {
        return month;
    }

    public String getPublisher() {
        return publisher;
    }

    public String getTitle() {
        return title;
    }

    public int getYear() {
```

```
        return year;
    }

    public void setAddress(String string) {
        address = string;
    }

    public void setAuthor(String string) {
        author = string;
    }

    public void setIsbn(String string) {
        isbn = string;
    }

    public void setMonth(String string) {
        month = string;
    }

    public void setPublisher(String string) {
        publisher = string;
    }

    public void setTitle(String string) {
        title = string;
    }

    public void setYear(int i) {
        year = i;
    }

    public String toString() {
        return title + " by " + author;
    }
}
```

SAX

Now that you have a JavaBean for Books, you can turn to the task of parsing XML that uses the book vocabulary. The SAX API is event driven. As Xerces parses an XML document, it calls methods on one or more event-handler classes that you provide. The following listing, SAXMain.java, shows a typical method of using SAX to parse a document. After importing all the necessary classes in lines 8-14, you create a new XMLReader instance in line 19 by instantiating Xerces' SAXParser class. You then instantiate a BookHandler (line 20) and use it as the XMLReader's ContentHandler and ErrorHandler event callbacks. You can do this because BookHandler implements both the ContentHandler and ErrorHandler interfaces. Once you've set up the callbacks, you're ready to call the parser, which you do in line 24. The BookHandler's callback methods build an instance of Book that contains the information from the XML document. You obtain this Book instance by calling the getBook method on the bookHandler instance, and then you print a human-readable representation of the Book using toString.

```
/*
 *
 * SAXMain.java
 *
 * Example from "Professional XML Development with Apache Tools"
 *
 */
package com.sauria.apachexml.ch1;

import java.io.IOException;

import org.apache.xerces.parsers.SAXParser;
import org.xml.sax.SAXException;
import org.xml.sax.XMLReader;

public class SAXMain {

    public static void main(String[] args) {
        XMLReader r = new SAXParser();
        BookHandler bookHandler = new BookHandler();
        r.setContentHandler(bookHandler);
        r.setErrorHandler(bookHandler);
        try {
            r.parse(args[0]);
            System.out.println(bookHandler.getBook().toString());
        } catch (SAXException se) {
            System.out.println("SAX Error during parsing " +
                se.getMessage());
            se.printStackTrace();
        } catch (IOException ioe) {
            System.out.println("I/O Error during parsing " +
                ioe.getMessage());
            ioe.printStackTrace();
        } catch (Exception e) {
            System.out.println("Error during parsing " +
                e.getMessage());
            e.printStackTrace();
        }
    }
}
```

The real work in a SAX-based application is done by the event handlers, so let's turn our attention to the BookHandler class and see what's going on. The following BookHandler class extends SAX's DefaultHandler class. There are two reasons. First, DefaultHandler implements all the SAX callback handler interfaces, so you're saving the effort of writing all the implements clauses. Second, because DefaultHandler is a class, your code doesn't have to implement every method in every callback interface. Instead, you just supply an implementation for the methods you're interested in, shortening the class overall.

```
/*
 *
 * BookHandler.java
 *
```

```
 5:  * Example from "Professional XML Development with Apache Tools"
 6:  *
 7:  */
 8: package com.sauria.apachexml.ch1;
 9:
10: import java.util.Stack;
11:
12: import org.xml.sax.Attributes;
13: import org.xml.sax.SAXException;
14: import org.xml.sax.SAXParseException;
15: import org.xml.sax.helpers.DefaultHandler;
16:
17: public class BookHandler extends DefaultHandler {
18:     private Stack elementStack = new Stack();
19:     private Stack textStack = new Stack();
20:     private StringBuffer currentText = null;
21:     private Book book = null;
22:
23:     public Book getBook() {
24:         return book;
25:     }
26:
```

We'll start by looking at the methods you need from the ContentHandler interface. Almost all ContentHandlers need to manage a stack of elements and a stack of text. The reason is simple. You need to keep track of the level of nesting you're in. This means you need a stack of elements to keep track of where you are. You also need to keep track of any character data you've seen, and you need to do this by the level where you saw the text; so, you need a second stack to keep track of the text. These stacks as well as a StringBuffer for accumulating text and an instance of Book are declared in lines 18-21. The accessor to the book instance appears in lines 23-25.

The ContentHandler callback methods use the two stacks to create a Book instance and call the appropriate setter methods on the Book. The methods you're using from ContentHandler are startElement, endElement, and characters. Each callback method is passed arguments containing the data associated with the event. For example, the startElement method is passed the localPart namespace URI, and the QName of the element being processed. It's also passed the attributes for that element:

```
27:     public void startElement(
28:         String uri,
29:         String localPart,
30:         String qName,
31:         Attributes attributes)
32:         throws SAXException {
33:         currentText = new StringBuffer();
34:         textStack.push(currentText);
35:         elementStack.push(localPart);
36:         if (localPart.equals("book")) {
37:             String version = attributes.getValue("", "version");
38:             if (version != null && !version.equals("1.0"))
39:                 throw new SAXException("Incorrect book version");
40:             book = new Book();
41:         }
42:     }
```

The startElement callback basically sets things up for new data to be collected each time it sees a new element. It creates a new currentText StringBuffer for collecting this element's text content and pushes it onto the textStack. It also pushes the element's name on the elementStack for placekeeping. This method must also do some processing of the attributes attached to the element, because the attributes aren't available to the endElement callback. In this case, startElement verifies that you're processing a version of the book schema that you understand (1.0).

You can't do most of the work until you've encountered the end tag for an element. At this point, you will have seen any child elements and you've seen all the text content associated with the element. The following endElement callback does the real heavy lifting. First, it pops the top off the textStack, which contains the text content for the element it's processing. Depending on the name of the element being processed, endElement calls the appropriate setter on the Book instance to fill in the correct field. In the case of the year, it converts the String into an integer before calling the setter method. After all this, endElement pops the elementStack to make sure you keep your place.

```

    public void endElement(String uri, String localPart,
      String qName)
      throws SAXException {
      String text = textStack.pop().toString();
      if (localPart.equals("book")) {
      } else if (localPart.equals("title")) {
          book.setTitle(text);
      } else if (localPart.equals("author")) {
          book.setAuthor(text);
      } else if (localPart.equals("isbn")) {
          book.setIsbn(text);
      } else if (localPart.equals("month")) {
          book.setMonth(text);
      } else if (localPart.equals("year")) {
          int year;
          try {
              year = Integer.parseInt(text);
          } catch (NumberFormatException e) {
              throw new SAXException("year must be a number");
          }
          book.setYear(year);
      } else if (localPart.equals("publisher")) {
          book.setPublisher(text);
      } else if (localPart.equals("address")) {
          book.setAddress(text);
      } else {
          throw new SAXException("Unknown element for book");
      }
      elementStack.pop();
  }

```

The characters callback is called every time the parser encounters a piece of text content. SAX says that characters may be called more than once inside a startElement/endElement pair, so the implementation of characters appends the next text to the currentText StringBuffer. This ensures that you collect all the text for an element:

```
    public void characters(char[] ch, int start, int length)
        throws SAXException {
        currentText.append(ch, start, length);
    }

```

The remainder of BookHandler implements the three public methods of the ErrorHandler callback interface, which controls how errors are reported by the application. In this case, you're just printing an extended error message to System.out. The warning, error, and fatalError methods use a shared private method getLocationString to process the contents of a SAXParseException, which is where they obtain position information about the location of the error:

```
    public void warning(SAXParseException ex) throws SAXException {
        System.err.println(
            "[Warning] " + getLocationString(ex) + ": " +
            ex.getMessage());
    }

    public void error(SAXParseException ex) throws SAXException {
        System.err.println(
            "[Error] " + getLocationString(ex) + ": " +
            ex.getMessage());
    }

    public void fatalError(SAXParseException ex)
        throws SAXException {
        System.err.println(
            "[Fatal Error] " + getLocationString(ex) + ": " +
            ex.getMessage());
        throw ex;
    }

    /** Returns a string of the location. */
    private String getLocationString(SAXParseException ex) {
        StringBuffer str = new StringBuffer();

        String systemId = ex.getSystemId();
        if (systemId != null) {
            int index = systemId.lastIndexOf('/');
            if (index != -1)
                systemId = systemId.substring(index + 1);
            str.append(systemId);
        }
        str.append(':');
        str.append(ex.getLineNumber());
        str.append(':');
        str.append(ex.getColumnNumber());

        return str.toString();

    }

}
```

DOM

Let's look at how you can accomplish the same task using the DOM API. The DOM API is a tree-based API. The parser provides the application with a tree-structured object graph, which the application can then traverse to extract the data from the parsed XML document. This process is more convenient than using SAX, but you pay a price in performance because the parser creates a DOM tree whether you're going to use it or not. If you're using XML to represent data in an application, the DOM tends to be inefficient because you have to get the data you need out of the DOM tree; after that you have no use for the DOM tree, even though the parser spent time and memory to construct it. We're going to reuse the class Book (in Book.java) for this example.

After importing all the necessary classes in lines 10-17, you declare a String constant whose value is the namespace URI for the book schema (lines 19-21):

```
 1: /*
 2:  *
 3:  * DOMMain.java
 4:  *
 5:  * Example from "Professional XML Development with Apache Tools"
 6:  *
 7:  */
 8: package com.sauria.apachexml.ch1;
 9:
10: import java.io.IOException;
11:
12: import org.apache.xerces.parsers.DOMParser;
13: import org.w3c.dom.Document;
14: import org.w3c.dom.Element;
15: import org.w3c.dom.Node;
16: import org.w3c.dom.NodeList;
17: import org.xml.sax.SAXException;
18:
19: public class DOMMain {
20:     static final String bookNS =
21:         "http://sauria.com/schemas/apache-xml-book/book";
22:
```

In line 24 you create a new DOMParser. Next you ask it to parse the document (line 27). At this point the parser has produced the DOM tree, and you need to obtain it and traverse it to extract the data you need to create a Book object (lines 27-29):

```
23:     public static void main(String args[]) {
24:         DOMParser p = new DOMParser();
25:
26:         try {
27:             p.parse(args[0]);
28:             Document d = p.getDocument();
29:             System.out.println(dom2Book(d).toString());
30:
31:         } catch (SAXException se) {
32:             System.out.println("Error during parsing " +
33:             se.getMessage());
34:             se.printStackTrace();
```

```
35:         } catch (IOException ioe) {
36:             System.out.println("I/O Error during parsing " +
37:             ioe.getMessage());
38:             ioe.printStackTrace();
39:         }
40:     }
41:
```

The dom2Book function creates the Book object:

```
42:     private static Book dom2Book(Document d) throws SAXException {
43:         NodeList nl = d.getElementsByTagNameNS(bookNS, "book");
44:         Element bookElt = null;
45:         Book book = null;
46:         try {
47:             if (nl.getLength() > 0) {
48:                 bookElt = (Element) nl.item(0);
49:                 book = new Book();
50:             } else
51:                 throw new SAXException("No book element found");
52:         } catch (ClassCastException cce) {
53:             throw new SAXException("No book element found");
54:         }
55:
```

In lines 43-54, you use the namespace-aware method getElementsByTagNameNS (as opposed to the non-namespace-aware getElementsByTagName) to find the root book element in the XML file. You check the resulting NodeList to make sure a book element was found before constructing a new Book instance.

Once you have the book element, you iterate through all the children of the book. These nodes in the DOM tree correspond to the child elements of the book element in the XML document. As you encounter each child element node, you need to get the text content for that element and call the appropriate Book setter. In the DOM, getting the text content for an element node is a little laborious. If an element node has text content, the element node has one or more children that are text nodes. The DOM provides a method called normalize that collapses multiple text nodes into a single text node where possible (normalize also removes empty text nodes where possible). Each time you process one of the children of the book element, you call normalize to collect all the text nodes and store the text content in the String text. Then you compare the tag name of the element you're processing and call the appropriate setter method. As with SAX, you have to convert the text to an integer for the Book's year field:

```
56:         for (Node child = bookElt.getFirstChild();
57:             child != null;
58:             child = child.getNextSibling()) {
59:             if (child.getNodeType() != Node.ELEMENT_NODE)
60:                 continue;
61:             Element e = (Element) child;
62:             e.normalize();
63:             String text = e.getFirstChild().getNodeValue();
64:
65:             if (e.getTagName().equals("title")) {
66:                 book.setTitle(text);
67:             } else if (e.getTagName().equals("author")) {
```

```
                book.setAuthor(text);
            } else if (e.getTagName().equals("isbn")) {
                book.setIsbn(text);
            } else if (e.getTagName().equals("month")) {
                book.setMonth(text);
            } else if (e.getTagName().equals("year")) {
                int y = 0;
                try {
                    y = Integer.parseInt(text);
                } catch (NumberFormatException nfe) {
                    throw new SAXException("Year must be a number");
                }
                book.setYear(y);
            } else if (e.getTagName().equals("publisher")) {
                book.setPublisher(text);
            } else if (e.getTagName().equals("address")) {
                book.setAddress(text);
            }
        }
        return book;
    }
}
```

This concludes our review of the SAX and DOM APIs. Now we're ready to go into the depths of Xerces.

Installing Xerces

Installing Xerces is relatively simple. The first thing you need to do is obtain a Xerces build. You can do this by going to http://xml.apache.org/dist/xerces-j, where you'll see a list of the current official Xerces builds. (You can ignore the Xerces 1.X builds.)

The Xerces build for a particular version of Xerces is divided into three distributions. Let's use Xerces 2.4.0 as an example. The binary distribution of Xerces 2.4.0 is in a file named Xerces-J-bin.2.4.0.*xxx*, where *xxx* is either .zip or .tar.gz, depending on the kind of compressed archive format you need. Typically, people on Windows use a .zip file, whereas people on MacOS X, Linux, and UNIX of various sorts use a .tar.gz file. There are also .*xxx*.sig files, which are detached PGP signatures of the corresponding .*xxx* file. So, Xerces-J-bin.2.4.zip.sig contains the signature file for the Xerces-J-bin2.4.zip distribution file. You can use PGP and the signature file to verify that the contents of the distribution have not been tampered with.

In addition to the binary distribution, you can download a source distribution, Xerces-J-src.2.4.zip, and a tools distribution, Xerces-J-tools-2.4.0.zip. You'll need the tools distribution in order to build the Xerces documentation.

We'll focus on installing the binary distribution. Once you've downloaded it, unpack it using a zip-file utility or tar and gzip for the .tar.gz files. Doing so creates a directory called xerces-2.4.0 in either the current directory or the directory you specified to your archiving utility. The key files in this directory are

- **data**—A directory containing sample XML files.
- **docs**—A directory containing all the documentation.
- **Readme.html**—The jump-off point for the Xerces documentation; open it with your Web browser.
- **samples**—A directory containing the source code for the samples.
- **xercesImpl.jar**—A jar file containing the parser implementation.
- **xercesSamples.jar**—A jar file containing the sample applications.
- **xml-apis.jar**—A jar file containing the parsing APIs (SAX, DOM, and so on).

You must include xml-apis.jar and xercesImpl.jar in your Java classpath in order to use Xerces in your application. There are a variety of ways to accomplish this, including setting the CLASSPATH environment variable in your DOS Command window or UNIX shell window. You can also set the CLASSPATH variable for the application server you're using.

Another installation option is to make Xerces the default XML parser for your JDK installation. This option only works for JDK 1.3 and above.

JDK 1.3 introduced an Extension Mechanism for the JDK. It works like this. The JDK installation includes a special extensions directory where you can place jar files that contain extensions to Java. If JAVA_HOME is the directory where your JDK has been installed, then the extensions directory is <JAVA_HOME>\jre\lib\ext using Windows file delimiters and <JAVA_HOME>/jre/lib/ext using UNIX file delimiters.

If you're using JDK 1.4 or above, you should use the Endorsed Standards Override Mechanism, not the Extension Mechanism. The JDK 1.4 Endorsed Standards Override Mechanism works like the Extension Mechanism, but it's specifically designed to allow incremental updates of packages specified by the JCP. The major operational difference between the Extension Mechanism and the Endorsed Standards Override Mechanism is that the directory name is different. The Windows directory is named <JAVA_HOME>\jre\lib\endorsed, and the UNIX directory is named <JAVA_HOME>/jre/lib/endorsed.

Development Techniques

Now that you have Xerces installed, let's look at some techniques for getting the most out of Xerces and XML. We're going to start by looking at how to set the Xerces configuration through the use of features and properties. We'll look at the Deferred DOM, which uses lazy evaluation to improve the memory usage of DOM trees in certain usage scenarios. There are two sections, each on how to deal with Schemas/Grammars and Entities. These are followed by a section on serialization, which is the job of producing XML as opposed to consuming it. We'll finish up by examining how the Xerces Native Interface (XNI) gives us access to capabilities that are not available through SAX or DOM.

Xerces Configuration

The first place we'll stop is the Xerces configuration mechanism. There are a variety of configuration settings for Xerces, so you'll need to be able to turn these settings on and off.

Xerces uses the SAX features and properties mechanism to control all configuration settings. This is true whether you're using Xerces as a SAX parser or as a DOM parser. The class org.apache.xerces .parsers.DOMParser provides the methods setFeature, getFeature, setProperty, and getProperty, which are available on the class org.xml.sax.XMLReader. These methods all accept a String as the name of the feature or property. The convention for this API is that the name is a URI that determines the feature or property of interest. Features are boolean valued, and properties are object valued. The SAX specification defines a standard set of feature and property names, and Xerces goes on to define its own. All the Xerces feature/property URIs are in the http://apache.org/xml URI space under either features or properties. These URI's function in the same ways as Namespace URI's. They don't refer to anything—they are simply used to provide an extensible mechanism for defining unique names for features.

The configuration story is complicated when the JAXP (Java API for XML Parsing) APIs come into the picture. The purpose of JAXP is to abstract the specifics of parser instantiation and configuration from your application. In general, this is a desirable thing because it means your application doesn't depend on a particular XML parser. Unfortunately, in practice, this can mean you no longer have access to useful functionality that hasn't been standardized via the JCP. This is especially true in the case of parser configuration. If you're using the SAX API, you don't have much to worry about, because you can pass the Xerces features to the SAX setFeature and setProperty methods, and everything will be fine. The problem arises when you want to use the DOM APIs. Up until DOM Level 3, the DOM API didn't provide a mechanism for configuring options to a DOM parser, and even the mechanism described in DOM Level 3 isn't sufficient for describing all the options Xerces allows. The JAXP API for DOM uses a factory class called DOMBuilder to give you a parser that can parse an XML document and produce a DOM. However, it doesn't have the setFeature and set Property methods that you need to control Xerces-specific features. For the foreseeable future, if you want to use some of the features we'll be talking about, you'll have to use the Xerces DOMParser object to create a DOM API parser.

Validation-Related Features

A group of features relate to validation. The first of these is http://apache.org/xml/features /validation/dynamic. When this feature is on, Xerces adopts a laissez faire method of processing XML documents. If the document provides a DTD or schema, Xerces uses it to validate the document. If no grammar is provided, Xerces doesn't validate the document. Ordinarily, if Xerces is in validation mode, the document must provide a grammar of some kind; in non-validating mode, Xerces doesn't perform validation even if a grammar is present.

Most people think there are two modes for XML parsers—validating and non-validating—on the assumption that non-validating mode just means not doing validation. The reality is more complicated. According to the XML 1.0 specification (Section 5 has all the gory details), there is a range of things an XML parser may or may not do when it's operating in non-validating mode. The list of optional tasks includes attribute value normalization, replacement of internal text entities, and attribute defaulting. Xerces has a pair of features designed to make its behavior in non-validating mode slightly more predictable. You can prevent Xerces from reading an external DTD if it's in non-validating mode, using the http://apache.org/xml/features/nonvalidating/load-external-dtd* feature. This means the parsed document will be affected only by definitions from an internal DTD subset (a DTD in the document). It's also possible to tell Xerces not to use the DTD to default attribute values or to compute their types. The feature you use to do this is http://apache.org/xml/features/nonvalidating/load-dtd-grammar.

Error-Reporting Features

The next set of features controls the kinds of errors that Xerces reports. The feature http://apache.org/xml/features/warn-on-duplicate-entitydef generates a warning if an entity definition is duplicated. When validation is turned on, http://apache.org/xml/features/validation/warn-on-duplicate-attdef causes Xerces to generate a warning if an attribute declaration is repeated. Similarly, http://apache.org/xml/features/validation/warn-on-undeclared-elemdef causes Xerces to generate a warning if a content model references an element that has not been declared. All three of these properties are provided to help generate more user-friendly error messages when validation fails.

DOM-Related Features and Properties

Three features or properties affect Xerces when you're using the DOM API. To understand the first one, we have to make a slight digression onto the topic of ignorable whitespace.

Ignorable whitespace is the whitespace characters that occur between the end of one element and the start of another. This whitespace is used to format XML documents to make them more readable. Here is the book example with the ignorable whitespace shown in gray:

```
<?xml version="1.0" encoding="UTF-8"?>¶
<book xmlns="http://sauria.com/schemas/apache-xml-book/book"
  xmlns:xsi="http://www.w3.org/2001/XMLSchema-instance”
  xsi:schemaLocation=
   "http://sauria.com/schemas/apache-xml-book/book
    http://www.sauria.com/schemas/apache-xml-book/book.xsd"
  version="1.0">¶
  <title>XML Development with Apache Tools</title>¶
  <author>Theodore W. Leung</author>¶
  <isbn>0-7645-4355-5</isbn>¶
  <month>December</month>¶
  <year>2003</year>¶
  <publisher>Wrox</publisher>¶
  <address>Indianapolis, Indiana</address>¶
</book>
```

An XML parser can only determine that whitespace is ignorable when it's validating. The SAX API makes the notion of ignorable whitespace explicit by providing different callbacks for characters and ignorableWhitespace. The DOM API doesn't have any notion of this concept. A DOM parser must create a DOM tree that represents the document that was parsed. The Xerces feature http://apache.org/xml/features/dom/include-ignorable-whitespace allows you control whether Xerces creates text nodes for ignorable whitespace. If the feature is false, then Xerces won't create text nodes for ignorable whitespace. This can save a sizable amount of memory for XML documents that have been pretty-printed or highly indented.

Frequently we're asked if it's possible to supply a custom DOM implementation instead of the one provided with Xerces. Doing this is a fairly large amount of work. The starting point is the property http://apache.org/xml/properties/dom/document-class-name, which allows you to set the name of the class to be used as the factory class for all DOM objects. If you replace the built-in Xerces DOM with your own DOM, then any Xerces-specific DOM features, such as deferred node expansion, are disabled, because they are all implemented within the Xerces DOM.

Xerces uses the SAX ErrorHandler interface to handle errors while parsing using the DOM API. You can register your own ErrorHandler and customize your error reporting, just as with SAX. However, you may want to access the DOM node that was under construction when the error condition occurred. To do this, you can use the http://apache.org/xml/properties/dom/current-element-node to read the DOM node that was being constructed at the time the parser signaled an error.

Other Features and Properties

Xerces uses an input buffer that defaults to 2KB in size. The size of this buffer is controlled by the property http://apache.org/xml/properties/input-buffer-size. If you know you'll be dealing with files within a certain size range, it can help performance to set the buffer size close to the size of the files you're working with. The buffer size should be a multiple of 1KB. The largest value you should set this property to is 16KB.

Xerces normally operates in a mode that makes it more convenient for users of Windows operating systems to specify filenames. In this mode, Xerces allows URIs (Uniform Resource Identifiers) to include file specifications that include backslashes (\) as separators, and allows the use of DOS drive letters and Windows UNC filenames. Although this is convenient, it can lead to sloppiness, because document authors may include these file specifications in XML documents and DTDs. The http://apache.org/xml/features/standard-uri-conformant feature turns off this convenience mode and requires that all URIs actually be URIs.

The XML 1.0 specification recommends that the character encoding of an XML file should be specified using a character set name specified by the Internet Assigned Numbers Authority (IANA). However, this isn't required. The feature http://apache.org/xml/features/allow-java-encodings allows you to use the Java names for character encodings to specify the character set encoding for a document. This feature can be convenient for an all-Java system, but it's completely non-interoperable with non-Java based XML parsers.

Turning on the feature http://apache.org/xml/features/disallow-doctype-decl causes Xerces to throw an exception when a DTD is provided with an XML document. It's possible to launch a denial-of-service attack against an XML parser by providing a DTD that contains a recursively expanding entity definition, and eventually the entity expansion overflows some buffer in the parser or causes the parser to consume all available memory. This feature can be used to prevent this attack. Of course, DTD validation can't be used when this flag is turned on, and Xerces is operating in a mode that isn't completely compliant with the XML specification.

Unfortunately, there are other ways to launch denial-of-service attacks against XML parsers, so the Xerces team has created a SecurityManager class that is part of the org.apache.xerces.util package. The current security manager can be accessed via the http://apache.org/xml/properties/security-manager property. It lets you replace the security manager with your own by setting the value of the property to an instance of SecurityManager. At the time of this writing, SecurityManager provides two JavaBean properties, entityExpansionLimit and maxOccurNodeLimit Setting entityExpansionLimit is another way to prevent the entity expansion attack. The value of this property is the number of entity expansions the parser should allow in a single document. The default value for entityExpansionLimit is 100,000. The maxOccurNodeLimit property controls the maximum number of occur nodes that can be created for an XML Schema maxOccurs. This is for the case where maxOccurs is a number, not unbounded. The default value for this property is 3,000.

Deferred DOM

One of the primary difficulties with using the DOM API is performance. This issue manifests itself in a number of ways. The DOM's representation of an XML document is very detailed and involves a lot of objects. This has a big impact on performance because of the time it takes to create all those objects, and because of the amount of memory those objects use. Developers are often surprised to see how much memory an XML document consumes when it's represented as a DOM tree.

To reduce the overhead of using the DOM in an application, the Xerces developers implemented what is called *deferred node expansion*. This is an application of lazy evaluation techniques to the creation of DOM trees. When deferred node expansion is turned on, Xerces doesn't create objects to represent the various parts of an XML document. Instead, it builds a non-object oriented set of data structures that contain the information needed to create the various types of DOM nodes required by the DOM specification. This allows Xerces to complete parsing in a much shorter time than when deferred node expansion is turned off. Because almost no objects are created, the memory used is a fraction of what would ordinarily be used by a DOM tree.

The magic starts when your application calls the appropriate method to get the DOM Document node. Deferred node expansion defers the creation of DOM node objects until your program needs them. The way it does so is simple: If your program calls a DOM method that accesses a node in the DOM tree, the deferred DOM implementation creates the DOM node you're requesting and all of its children. Obviously, the deferred DOM implementation won't create a node if it already exists. A finite amount of work is done on each access to an unexpanded node.

The deferred DOM is especially useful in situations where you're not going to access every part of a document. Because it only expands those nodes (and the fringe defined by their children) that you access, Xerces doesn't create all the objects the DOM specification says should be created. This is fine, because you don't need the nodes you didn't access. The result is a savings of memory and processor time (spent creating objects and allocating memory).

If your application is doing complete traversals of the entire DOM tree, then you're better off not using the deferred DOM, because you'll pay the cost of creating the non-object-oriented data structures plus the cost of creating the DOM objects as you access them. This results in using more memory and processor time than necessary.

The deferred DOM implementation is used by default. If you wish to turn it off, you can set the feature http://apache.org/xml/features/dom/defer-node-expansion to false. If you're using the JAXP DocumentBuilder API to get a DOM parser, then the deferred DOM is turned off.

Schema Handling

Xerces provides a number of features that control various aspects of validation when you're using XML Schema. The most important feature turns on schema validation: http://apache.org/xml/features/validation/schema. To use it, the SAX name-spaces property (http://xml.org/sax/features/namespaces) must be on (it is by default). The Xerces validator won't report schema validation errors unless the regular SAX validation feature (http://xml.org/sax/features/validation) is turned on, so you must make sure that both the schema validation feature and the SAX validation feature are set to true.

Here's the SAXMain program, enhanced to perform schema validation:

```
/*
 *
 * SchemaValidateMain.java
 *
 * Example from "Professional XML Development with Apache Tools"
 *
 */
package com.sauria.apachexml.ch1;

import java.io.IOException;

import org.apache.xerces.parsers.SAXParser;
import org.xml.sax.EntityResolver;
import org.xml.sax.SAXException;
import org.xml.sax.SAXNotRecognizedException;
import org.xml.sax.SAXNotSupportedException;
import org.xml.sax.XMLReader;

public class SchemaValidateMain {

    public static void main(String[] args) {
        XMLReader r = new SAXParser();
        try {
            r.setFeature("http://xml.org/sax/features/validation",
             true);
            r.setFeature(
                "http://apache.org/xml/features/validation/schema",
                 true);
        } catch (SAXNotRecognizedException snre) {
            snre.printStackTrace();
        } catch (SAXNotSupportedException snre) {
            snre.printStackTrace();
        }
        BookHandler bookHandler = new BookHandler();
        r.setContentHandler(bookHandler);
        r.setErrorHandler(bookHandler);
        EntityResolver bookResolver = new BookResolver();
        r.setEntityResolver(bookResolver);
        try {
            r.parse(args[0]);
            System.out.println(bookHandler.getBook().toString());
        } catch (SAXException se) {
            System.out.println("SAX Error during parsing " +
                se.getMessage());
            se.printStackTrace();
        } catch (IOException ioe) {
            System.out.println("I/O Error during parsing " +
                ioe.getMessage());
            ioe.printStackTrace();
        } catch (Exception e) {
            System.out.println("Error during parsing " +
                e.getMessage());
```

```
                e.printStackTrace();
            }
        }
}
```

Additional Schema Checking

The feature http://apache.org/xml/features/validation/schema-full-checking turns on additional checking for schema documents. This doesn't affect documents using the schema but does more thorough checking of the schema document itself, in particular particle unique attribute constraint checking and particle derivation restriction checks. This feature is normally set to false because these checks are resource intensive.

Schema-Normalized Values

Element content is also normalized when you validate with XML Schema (only attribute values were normalized in XML 1.0). The reason is that simple types can be used as both element content and attribute values, so element content must be treated the same as attribute values in order to obtain the same semantics for simple types. In Xerces, the feature http://apache.org/xml/features/validation/schema/normalized-value controls whether SAX and DOM see the Schema-normalized values of elements and attributes or the XML 1.0 infoset values of elements and attributes. If you're validating with XML Schema, this feature is normally turned on.

Reporting Default Values

In XML Schema, elements and attributes are similar in another way: They can both have default values. The question then arises, how should default values be reported to the application? Should the parser assume the application knows what the default value is, or should the parser provide the default value to the application? The only downside to the parser providing the default value is that if the application knows what the default value is, the parser is doing unnecessary work. The Xerces feature http://apache.org/xml/features/validation/schema/element-default allows you to choose whether the parser reports the default value. The default setting for this feature is to report default values. Default values are reported via the characters callback, just like any other character data.

Accessing PSVI

Some applications want to access the Post Schema Validation Infoset (PSVI) in order to obtain type information about elements and attributes. The Xerces API for accomplishing this has not yet solidified, but it exists in an experimental form in the org.apache.xerces.xni.psvi package. If your application isn't accessing the PSVI, then you should set the feature http://apache.org/xml/features/validation/schema/augment-psvi to false so you don't have to pay the cost of creating the PSVI augmentations.

Overriding schemaLocation Hints

The XML Schema specification says that the xsi:schemaLocation and xsi:noNamespaceSchemaLocation attributes are hints to the validation engine and that they may be ignored. There are at least two good reasons your application might want to ignore these hints. First, you shouldn't believe a document that purports to tell your application what schema it should use to validate the document. When you wrote your application, you had a particular version of an XML Schema in mind. The incoming document is supposed to conform to that schema. But a number of problems can crop up if you believe the incoming document when it claims to know what schema to use. The author of the incoming document may have used a different or buggy version of the schema you're using. Worse, the author of the incoming document may intentionally specify a different version of the schema in an attempt to subvert your application.

The second reason you may choose to ignore these hints is that you might want to provide a local copy of the schema so the validator doesn't have to perform a network fetch of the schema document every time it has to validate a document. If you're in a server environment processing thousands or even millions of documents per day, the last thing you want is for the Xerces validator to be doing an HTTP request to a machine somewhere on the Internet for each document it has to validate. Not only is this terrible for performance, but it makes your application susceptible to a failure of the machine hosting the schema. Fortunately, Xerces has a pair of properties you can use to override the schemaLocation hints. The first property is http://apache.org/xml/properties/schema/external-schemaLocation; it overrides the xsi:schemaLocation attribute. The value of the property is a string that has the same format as the xsi:schemaLocation attribute: a set of pairs of namespace URIs and schema document URIs. The other property is http://apache.org/xml/properties/schema/external-noNamespaceSchemaLocation; it handles the xsi:noNamespaceSchemaLocation case. Its value has the same format as xsi:noNamespaceSchemaLocation, a single URI with the location of the schema document.

Grammar Caching

If you're processing a large number of XML documents that use a single DTD, a single XML schema, or a small number of XML schemas, you should use the grammar-caching functionality built in to Xerces. You can use the http://apache.org/xml/properties/schema/external-schemaLocation or http://apache.org/xml/properties/schema/external-noNamespaceSchemaLocation properties to force Xerces to read XML schemas from a local copy, which improves the efficiency of your application. However, these properties work at an entity level (in a later section, you'll discover that you could use entity-handling techniques to accomplish what these two properties do).

Even if you're reading the grammar from a local file, Xerces still has to read the grammar file and turn it into data structures that can be used to validate an XML document, a process somewhat akin to compilation. This process is very costly. If your application uses a single grammar or a small fixed number of grammars, you would like to avoid the overhead of processing the grammar multiple times. That's the purpose of the Xerces grammar-caching functionality.

Xerces provide two styles of grammar caching: *passive caching* and *active caching*. Passive caching requires little work on the part of your application. You set a property, and Xerces starts caching grammars. When Xerces encounters a grammar that it hasn't seen before, it processes the grammar and then caches the grammar data structures for reuse. The next time Xerces encounters a reference to this grammar, it uses the cached data structures.

Here's a version of the book-processing program that uses passive grammar caching:

```
/*
 *
 * PassiveSchemaCache.java
 *
 * Example from "Professional XML Development with Apache Tools"
 *
 */
package com.sauria.apachexml.ch1;
```

```
 9: import java.io.IOException;
10:
11: import org.apache.xerces.parsers.SAXParser;
12: import org.xml.sax.SAXException;
13: import org.xml.sax.SAXNotRecognizedException;
14: import org.xml.sax.SAXNotSupportedException;
15: import org.xml.sax.XMLReader;
16:
17: public class PassiveSchemaCache {
18:
19:     public static void main(String[] args) {
20:         System.setProperty(
21:          "org.apache.xerces.xni.parser.Configuration",
22:          "org.apache.xerces.parsers.XMLGrammarCachingConfiguration");
```

Lines 20-22 contain the code that turns on passive grammar caching. All you have to do is set the Java property org.apache.xerces.xni.parser.Configuration to a configuration that understands grammar caching. One such configuration is org.apache.xerces.parsers.XMLGrammarCachingConfiguration. After that, the code is essentially the same as what you are used to seeing. This shows how easy it is to use passive grammar caching. Add three lines and you're done.

```
23:
24:         XMLReader r = new SAXParser();
25:         try {
26:             r.setFeature("http://xml.org/sax/features/validation",
27:              true);
28:             r.setFeature(
29:                 "http://apache.org/xml/features/validation/schema",
30:                  true);
31:         } catch (SAXNotRecognizedException snre) {
32:             snre.printStackTrace();
33:         } catch (SAXNotSupportedException snre) {
34:             snre.printStackTrace();
35:         }
36:         BookHandler bookHandler = new BookHandler();
37:         r.setContentHandler(bookHandler);
38:         r.setErrorHandler(bookHandler);
39:
40:         for (int i = 0; i < 5; i++)
41:             try {
42:                 r.parse(args[0]);
43:                 System.out.println(bookHandler.getBook().toString());
44:             } catch (SAXException se) {
45:                 System.out.println("SAX Error during parsing " +
46:                     se.getMessage());
47:                 se.printStackTrace();
48:             } catch (IOException ioe) {
49:                 System.out.println("I/O Error during parsing " +
50:                     ioe.getMessage());
51:                 ioe.printStackTrace();
52:             } catch (Exception e) {
53:                 System.out.println("Error during parsing " +
54:                     e.getMessage());
55:                 e.printStackTrace();
```

```
            }
        }

}
```

Although passive caching is easy to use, it has one major drawback: You can't specify which grammars Xerces can cache. When you're using passive caching, Xerces happily caches any grammar it finds in any document. If you're processing a high volume of documents, let's say purchase orders, then you probably are using only one grammar, and you probably don't want the author of those purchase order documents to be the one who determines which grammar file is used (and possibly cached).

The solution to this problem is to use active grammar caching. Active grammar caching requires you to do more work in your application, but in general it's worth it because you get complete control over which grammars can be cached, as well as control over exactly which grammar files are used to populate the grammar caches.

When you're using active caching, you need to follow two steps. First, you create a grammar cache (an instance of org.apache.xerces.util.XMLGrammarPoolImpl) and load it by pre-parsing all the grammar files you want to cache. Then you call Xerces and make sure it's using the cache you just created.

Here's a program that makes use of active caching:

```
/*
 *
 * ActiveSchemaCache.java
 *
 * Example from "Professional XML Development with Apache Tools"
 *
 */
package com.sauria.apachexml.ch1;
import java.io.IOException;

import org.apache.xerces.impl.Constants;
import org.apache.xerces.parsers.SAXParser;
import org.apache.xerces.parsers.StandardParserConfiguration;
import org.apache.xerces.parsers.XMLGrammarPreparser;
import org.apache.xerces.util.SymbolTable;
import org.apache.xerces.util.XMLGrammarPoolImpl;
import org.apache.xerces.xni.XNIException;
import org.apache.xerces.xni.grammars.Grammar;
import org.apache.xerces.xni.grammars.XMLGrammarDescription;
import org.apache.xerces.xni.parser.XMLConfigurationException;
import org.apache.xerces.xni.parser.XMLInputSource;
import org.apache.xerces.xni.parser.XMLParserConfiguration;
import org.xml.sax.SAXException;
import org.xml.sax.XMLReader;


public class ActiveSchemaCache {
    static final String SYMBOL_TABLE =
        Constants.XERCES_PROPERTY_PREFIX +
        Constants.SYMBOL_TABLE_PROPERTY;

```

```
32:     static final String GRAMMAR_POOL =
33:         Constants.XERCES_PROPERTY_PREFIX +
34:         Constants.XMLGRAMMAR_POOL_PROPERTY;
35:
36:     SymbolTable sym = null;
37:     XMLGrammarPoolImpl grammarPool = null;
38:     XMLReader reader = null;
39:
40:    public void loadCache() {
41:         grammarPool = new XMLGrammarPoolImpl();
42:         XMLGrammarPreparser preparser = new XMLGrammarPreparser();
43:         preparser.registerPreparser(XMLGrammarDescription.XML_SCHEMA,
44:             null);
45:         preparser.setProperty(GRAMMAR_POOL, grammarPool);
46:         preparser.setFeature(
47:             "http://xml.org/sax/features/validation",
48:             true);
49:         preparser.setFeature(
50:             "http://apache.org/xml/features/validation/schema",
51:             true);
52:         // parse the grammar...
53:
54:         try {
55:             Grammar g =
56:                 preparser.preparseGrammar(
57:                     XMLGrammarDescription.XML_SCHEMA,
58:                     new XMLInputSource(null, "book.xsd", null));
59:         } catch (XNIException xe) {
60:             xe.printStackTrace();
61:         } catch (IOException ioe) {
62:             ioe.printStackTrace();
63:         }
64:
65:     }
66:
```

The loadCache method takes care of creating the data structures needed to cache grammars. The cache itself is an instance of org.apache.xerces.util.XMLGrammarPoolImpl, created in line 41. The object that knows the workflow of how to preprocess a grammar file is an instance of XMLGrammarPreparser, so in line 42 you create an instance of XMLGrammarPreparser.

XMLGrammarPreparsers need to know which kind of grammar they will be dealing with. They have a method called registerPreparser that allows them to associate a string (representing URIs for particular grammars) with an object that knows how to preprocess a specific type of grammar. This means a single XMLGrammarPreparser can preprocess multiple types of grammars (for example, both DTDs and XML schemas). In this example, you're only interested in allowing XML schemas to be cached, so you register XML schemas with the preparser (lines 43-44). If you're registering either XML schemas or DTDs with a preparser, then you can pass null as the second argument to registerPreparser. Otherwise, you have to provide an instance of org,apache.xerces.xni.grammarsXMLGrammarLoader, which can process the grammar you're registering.

Now you're ready to associate a grammar pool with the preparser. This is done using the preparser's setProperty method and supplying the appropriate values (line 45). XMLGrammarPreparser provides a feature/property API like the regular SAX and DOM parsers in Xerces. The difference is that when you set a feature or property on an instance of XMLGrammarPreparser, you're actually setting the feature or property on all XMLGrammarLoader instances that have been registered with the preparser. So the next two setFeature calls (in lines 46-51) tell all registered XMLGrammarLoaders to validate their inputs and to do so using XML Schema if possible. Note that implementers of XMLGrammarLoader aren't required to implement any features or properties (just as with SAX features and properties).

Once all the configuration steps are complete, all that is left to do is to call the preparseGrammar method for all the grammars you want loaded into the cache. Note that you need to use the XMLInputSource class from org.apache.xni.parser to specify how to get the grammar file. This all happens in lines 54-63.

How do you make use of a loaded cache? It turns out to be fairly simple, but it means a more circuitous route to creating a parser. The XMLParserConfiguration interface has a setProperty method that accepts a property named http://apache.org/xml/properties/internal/grammar-pool, whose value is a grammar pool the parser configuration should use. The constructors for the various Xerces parser classes can take an XMLParserConfiguration as an argument. So, you need to get hold of a parser configuration, set the grammar pool property of that configuration to the grammar pool that loadCache created, and then create a SAX or DOM parser based on that configuration. Pretty straightforward, right?

The first thing you need is an XMLParserConfiguration. You can use the Xerces supplied org.apache.xerces.parsers.StandardParserConfiguration because you aren't doing anything else fancy:

```
67:     public synchronized Book useCache(String uri) {
68:         Book book = null;
69:         XMLParserConfiguration parserConfiguration =
70:             new StandardParserConfiguration();
```

Next you need to set the grammar pool property on the parserConfiguration to be the grammarPool created by loadCache:

```
71: 
72:         String grammarPoolProperty =
73:             "http://apache.org/xml/properties/internal/grammar-pool";
74:         try {
75:             parserConfiguration.setProperty(grammarPoolProperty,
76:                 grammarPool);
```

In this example you're using a SAX parser to process documents. The constructor for the Xerces SAX parser takes an XMLParserConfiguration as an argument, so you just pass the parserConfiguration as the argument, and now you have a SAXParser that's using the grammar cache!

```
77:             parserConfiguration.setFeature(
78:                 "http://xml.org/sax/features/validation",
79:                 true);
80:             parserConfiguration.setFeature(
81:                 "http://apache.org/xml/features/validation/schema",
82:                 true);
83:         } catch (XMLConfigurationException xce) {
84:             xce.printStackTrace();
```

```
            }

            try {
                if (reader == null)
                    reader = new SAXParser(parserConfiguration);
```

Something else is going on here: each instance of ActiveCache has a single SAXParser instance associated with it. You create an instance of SAXParser only if one doesn't already exist. This cuts down on the overhead of setting up and tearing down parser instances all the time.

One other detail. When you reuse a Xerces parser instance, you need to call the reset method in between usages. Doing so ensures that the parser is ready to parse another document:

```
                BookHandler bookHandler = new BookHandler();
                reader.setContentHandler(bookHandler);
                reader.setErrorHandler(bookHandler);
                reader.parse(uri);
                book = bookHandler.getBook();
                ((org.apache.xerces.parsers.SAXParser) reader).reset();
            } catch (IOException ioe) {
                ioe.printStackTrace();
            } catch (SAXException se) {
                se.printStackTrace();
            }
            return book;
    }

    public static void main(String[] args) {
      ActiveSchemaCache c = new ActiveSchemaCache();
      c.loadCache();
        for (int i = 0; i < 5; i++) {
            Book b = c.useCache("book.xml");
            System.out.println(b.toString());
        }

      }
}
```

The Xerces grammar-caching implementation uses hashing to determine whether two grammars are the same. If the two grammars are XML schemas, then they are hashed according to their targetNamespace. If the targetNamespaces are the same, the grammars are considered to be the same. For DTDs, it's more complicated. There are three conditions:

- If their publicId or expanded SystemIds exist, they must be identical.
- If one DTD defines a root element, it must either be the same as the root element of the second DTD, or it must be a global element in the second DTD.
- If neither DTD defines a root element, they must share a global element between the two of them.

If you're using the grammar-caching mechanism to cache DTDs, be aware that it can only cache external DTD subsets (DTDs in an external file). In addition, any definitions in an internal DTD subset (DTD within the document) will be ignored.

Entity Handling

Earlier in the chapter we mentioned that we'd be looking at a mechanism that can do the same job as the Xerces properties for xsi:schemaLocation and xsi:noNamespaceSchemaLocation. That mechanism is the SAX entity resolver mechanism. Although it isn't Xerces specific, it's very useful, because all external files are accessed as entities in XML. The entity resolver mechanism lets you install a callback that is run at the point where the XML parser tries to resolve an entity from an ID into a physical storage unit (whether that unit is on disk, in memory, or off on the network somewhere). You can use the entity resolver mechanism to force all references to a particular entity to be resolved to a local copy instead of a network copy, which simultaneously provides a performance improvement and gives you control over the actual definition of the entities.

Let's look at how to extend the example program to use an entity resolver:

```
/*
 *
 * EntityResolverMain.java
 *
 * Example from "Professional XML Development with Apache Tools"
 *
 */
package com.sauria.apachexml.ch1;

import java.io.IOException;

import org.apache.xerces.parsers.SAXParser;
import org.xml.sax.EntityResolver;
import org.xml.sax.SAXException;
import org.xml.sax.SAXNotRecognizedException;
import org.xml.sax.SAXNotSupportedException;
import org.xml.sax.XMLReader;

public class EntityResolverMain {

    public static void main(String[] args) {
        XMLReader r = new SAXParser();
        try {
            r.setFeature("http://xml.org/sax/features/validation",
                true);
            r.setFeature(
                "http://apache.org/xml/features/validation/schema",
                true);
        } catch (SAXNotRecognizedException e1) {
            e1.printStackTrace();
        } catch (SAXNotSupportedException e1) {
            e1.printStackTrace();
        }
        BookHandler bookHandler = new BookHandler();
```

```
        r.setContentHandler(bookHandler);
        r.setErrorHandler(bookHandler);
        EntityResolver bookResolver = new BookResolver();
        r.setEntityResolver(bookResolver);
```

The EntityResolver interface originated in SAX, but it's also used by the Xerces DOM parser and by the JAXP DocumentBuilder. All you need to do to make it work is create an instance of a class that implements the org.xml.sax.EntityResolver interface and then pass that object to the setEntityResolver method on XMLReader, SAXParser, DOMParser, or DocumentBuilder.

```
        try {
            r.parse(args[0]);
            System.out.println(bookHandler.getBook().toString());
        } catch (SAXException se) {
            System.out.println("SAX Error during parsing " +
                se.getMessage());
            se.printStackTrace();
        } catch (IOException ioe) {
            System.out.println("I/O Error during parsing " +
                ioe.getMessage());
            ioe.printStackTrace();
        } catch (Exception e) {
            System.out.println("Error during parsing " +
                e.getMessage());
            e.printStackTrace();
        }
    }
}
```

The real work happens in a class that implements the EntityResolver interface. This is a simple interface with only one method, resolveEntity. This method tries to take an entity that is identified by a Public ID, System ID, or both, and provide an InputSource the parser can use to grab the contents of the entity:

```
/*
 *
 * BookResolver.java
 *
 * This file is part of the "Apache XML Tools" Book
 *
 */
package com.sauria.apachexml.ch2;

import java.io.FileReader;
import java.io.IOException;

import org.xml.sax.EntityResolver;
import org.xml.sax.InputSource;
import org.xml.sax.SAXException;

public class BookResolver implements EntityResolver {
    String schemaURI =
        "http://www.sauria.com/schemas/apache-xml-book/book.xsd";

```

```
    public InputSource resolveEntity(String publicId,
        String systemId)
        throws SAXException, IOException {
        if (systemId.equals(schemaURI)) {
            FileReader r = new FileReader("book.xsd");
            return new InputSource(r);
        } else
            return null;
    }

}
```

The general flow of a resolveEntity method is to look at the publicId and/or systemId arguments and decide what you want to do. Once you've made your decision, your code then accesses the physical storage (in this case, a file) and wraps it up in an InputSource for the rest of the parser to use. In this example, you're looking for the systemId of the book schema (which is the URI supplied in the xsi:schemaLocation hint). If the entity being resolved is the book schema, then you read the schema from a local copy, wrap the resulting FileReader in an InputSource, and hand it back.

You could do a variety of things in your resolveEntity method. Instead of storing entities in the local file system, you could store them in a database and use JDBC to retrieve them. You could store them in a content management system or an LDAP directory, as well. If you were reading a lot of large text entities over and over again, you could build a cache inside your entity resolver so the entities were read only once and after that were read from the cache.

Remember, though, at this level you're dealing with caching the physical storage structures, not logical structures they might contain. Even if you use the EntityResolver mechanism in preference to Xerces' xsi:schemaLocation overrides, you still aren't getting as much bang for your buck as if you use the grammar-caching mechanism. At entity-resolver time, you're caching the physical storage and saving physical retrieval costs. At grammar-caching time, you're saving the cost of converting from a physical to a logical representation. If you're going to do logical caching of grammars, it doesn't make much sense to do physical caching of the grammar files. There are plenty of non-grammar uses of entities, and these are all fair game for speedups via the entity resolver mechanism.

Entity References

In most cases, entities should be invisible to your application—it doesn't matter whether the content in a particular section of an XML document came from the main document entity, an internal entity, or an entity stored in a separate file. Sometimes your application does want to know, particularly if your application is something like an XML editor, which is trying to preserve the input document as much as possible.

SAX provides the org.xml.sax.ext.LexicalHandler extension interface, which you can use to get callbacks about events you don't get via the ContentHandler callbacks. Among these callbacks are startEntity and endEntity, which are called at the start and end of any entity (internal or external) in the document. Ordinarily, startEntity and endEntity only report general entities and parameter entities (SAX says a parser doesn't have to report parameter entities, but Xerces does). Sometimes you'd like to know other details about the exact physical representation of a document, such as whether one of the built-in entities (&;, >;, <;, ";, or ') was used, or whether a character reference (&#XXXX) was used.

Xerces provides two features that cause startEntity and endEntity to report the beginning and end of these two classes of entity references. The feature http://apache.org/xml/features/scanner/notify-builtin-refs causes startEntity and endEntity to report the start and end of one of the built-in entities, and the feature http://apache.org/xml/features/scanner/notify-char-refs makes startEntity and endEntity report the start and end of a character reference.

The DOM has its own challenges when dealing with entities. Consider this XML file:

```
<?xml version="1.0" ?>
<!DOCTYPE a [
<!ENTITY boilerplate "insert this here">
]>
<a>
 <b>in b</b>
 <c>
  text in c but &boilerplate;
  <d/>
 </c>
</a>
```

When a DOM API parser constructs a DOM tree, it creates an Entity node under the DocumentType node. The resulting DOM tree looks like this, with the DocumentType, Entity, and Text nodes shaded in gray. The Entity node has a child, which is a text node containing the expansion text for the entity. So far, so good.

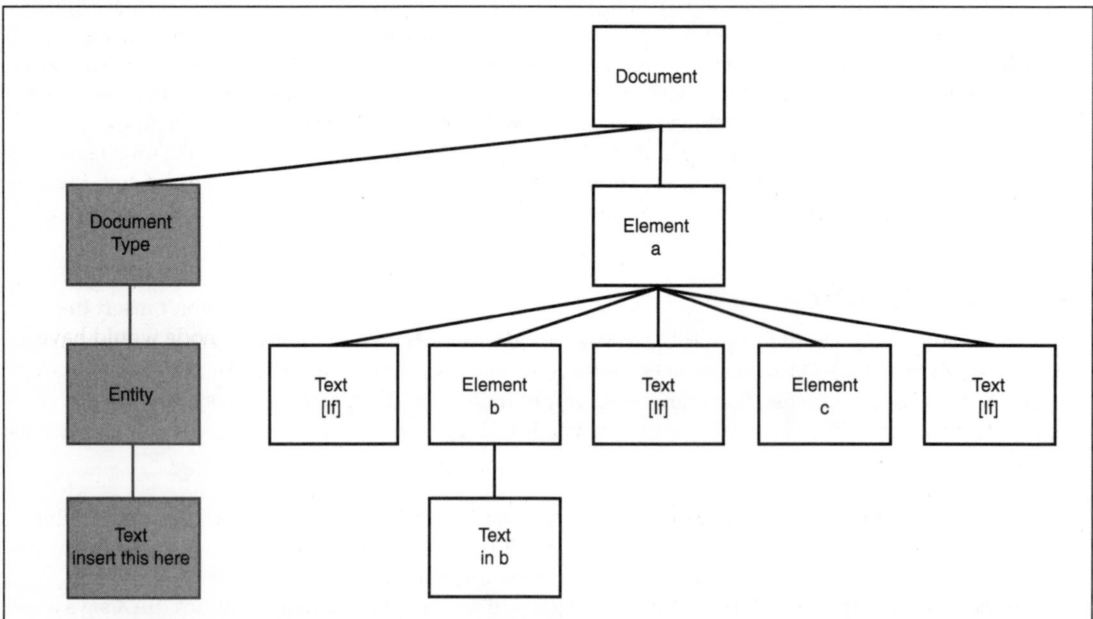

If you look closely at the diagram, you see that the part of the DOM tree for element c has been omitted. Here's the rest of it, starting at the Element node for c.

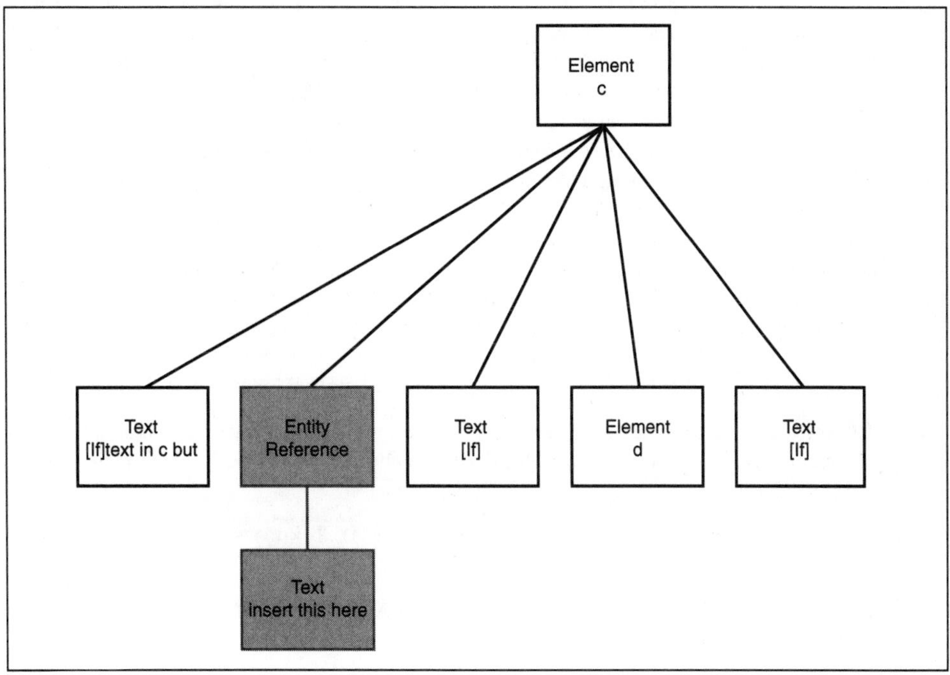

Xerces created an EntityReference node as a child of the Element node (and in the correct order among its siblings). That EntityReference node then has a child Text node that includes the text expanded from the entity. This is useful if you want to know that a particular node was an entity reference in the original document. However, it turns out to be inconvenient if you don't care whether some text originated as an entity, because your code has to check for the possibility of EntityReference nodes as it traverses the tree. If you don't care about the origin of the text, then you can set the feature http://apache.org/xml/features/dom/create-entity-ref-nodes to false, and Xerces won't insert the EntityReference nodes. Instead, it will put the Text node where the EntityReference node would have appeared, thus simplifying your application code.

Serialization

Most of the classes included with Xerces focus on taking XML documents, extracting information out of them, and passing that information on to your application via an API. Xerces also includes some classes that help you with the reverse process—taking data you already have and turning it into XML. This process is called *serialization* (not to be confused with Java serialization). The Xerces serialization API can take a SAX event stream or a DOM tree and produce an XML 1.0 or 1.1 document. One major improvement in XML 1.1 is that many more Unicode characters can appear in an XML 1.1 document; however, this makes it necessary to have a separate serializer for XML 1.1. There are also serializers that can take an XML document and serialize it using rules for HTML, XHTML, or even text files.

The org.apache.xml.serialize package includes five different serializers. All of them implement the interfaces org.apache.xml.serialize.Serializer and org.apache.xml.serialize.DOMSerializer as well as the ContentHandler, DocumentHandler, and DTDHandler classes from org.xml.sax and the DeclHandler and LexicalHandler classes from org.xml.sax.ext. The five serializers are as follows:

- **XMLSerializer** is used for XML 1.0 documents and, of course, obeys all the rules for XML 1.0.
- **XML11Serializer** outputs all the new Unicode characters allowed by XML 1.1. If the XML that you're outputting happens to be HTML, then you should use either the HTMLSerializer or the XHTMLSerializer.
- **HTMLSerializer** is used to output a document as HTML. It knows which HTML tags can get by without an end tag.
- **XHTMLSerializer** is used to output a document as XHTML, It serializes the document according to the XHTML rules.
- **TextSerializer** outputs the element names and the character data of elements. It doesn't output the DOCTYPE, DTD, or attributes.

Here are some of the differences in formatting when outputting HTML:

- The HTMLSerializer defaults to an ISO-8859-1 output encoding.
- An empty attribute value is output as an attribute name with no value at all (not even the equals sign). Also, attributes that are supposed to be URIs, as well as the content of the SCRIPT and STYLE tags, aren't escaped (embedded ", ', <, >, and & are left alone).
- The content of A and TD tags isn't line-broken.
- Most importantly, the HTMLSerializer knows that not all tags are closed in HTML. HTMLSerializer's list of the tags that do not require closing is as follows: AREA, BASE, BASEFONT, BR, COL, COLGROUP, DD, DT, FRAME, HEAD, HR, HTML, IMG, INPUT, ISINDEX, LI, LINK, META, OPTION, P, PARAM, TBODY, TD, TFOOT, TH, THEAD, and TR.

The XHTML serializer outputs HTML according to the rules for XHTML. These rules are:

- Element/attribute names are lowercase because case matters in XHTML.
- An attribute's value is always written if the value is the empty string.
- Empty elements must have a slash (/) in an empty tag (for example, <br />).
- The content of the SCRIPT and STYLE elements is serialized as CDATA.

Using the serializer classes is fairly straightforward. The serialization classes live in the package org.apache.xml.serialize. All the serializers are constructed with two arguments: The first argument is an OutputStream or Writer that is the destination for the output, and the second argument is an OutputFormat object that controls the details of how the serializer formats its input. OutputFormats are constructed with three arguments: a serialization method, which is a string constant taken from org.apache.xml.serialize.Method; a string containing the desired output character encoding; and a boolean that tells whether to indent the output. You can also construct an OutputFormat using a DOM Document object.

Before we get into the details of OutputFormat, let's look at how to use the serializers in a program. We'll look at a SAX-based version first:

```
/*
 *
 * SAXSerializerMain.java
 *
 * Example from "Professional XML Development with Apache Tools"
 *
 */
package com.sauria.apachexml.ch1;

import java.io.IOException;

import org.apache.xerces.parsers.SAXParser;
import org.apache.xml.serialize.Method;
import org.apache.xml.serialize.OutputFormat;
import org.apache.xml.serialize.XMLSerializer;
import org.xml.sax.SAXException;
import org.xml.sax.SAXNotRecognizedException;
import org.xml.sax.SAXNotSupportedException;
import org.xml.sax.XMLReader;

public class SAXSerializerMain {

    public static void main(String[] args) {
        XMLReader r = new SAXParser();
        OutputFormat format =
            new OutputFormat(Method.XML,"UTF-8",true);
        format.setPreserveSpace(true);
        XMLSerializer serializer =
            new XMLSerializer(System.out, format);
        r.setContentHandler(serializer);
        r.setDTDHandler(serializer);
        try {
            r.setProperty(
                "http://xml.org/sax/properties/declaration-handler",
                serializer);
            r.setProperty(
                "http://xml.org/sax/properties/lexical-handler",
                serializer);
        } catch (SAXNotRecognizedException snre) {
            snre.printStackTrace();
        } catch (SAXNotSupportedException snse) {
```

```
                snse.printStackTrace();
        }
        try {
            r.parse(args[0]);
        } catch (IOException ioe) {
            ioe.printStackTrace();
        } catch (SAXException se) {
            se.printStackTrace();
        }
    }
}
```

Note that you set up the serializer (in this case, an XMLSerializer) and then plug it into the XMLReader as the callback handler for ContentHandler, DTDHandler, DeclHandler, and LexicalHandler.

A SAX version of the serializers might not seem interesting at first glance. Remember that SAX allows you to build a pipeline-style conglomeration of XML processing components that implement the org.xml.sax.XMLFilter interface. The SAX version of the serializers can be the last stage in one of these pipelines. You can also write applications that accept the various SAX handlers as callbacks and that then call the callbacks as a way of interfacing to other SAX components. Combining this approach with the serializer classes is way to use SAX to generate XML from non-XML data, such as comma-delimited or tab-delimited files.

The DOM version is a little more straightforward:

```
/*
 *
 * DOMSerializerMain.java
 *
 * Example from "Professional XML Development with Apache Tools"
 *
 */
package com.sauria.apachexml.ch1;

import java.io.IOException;

import org.apache.xerces.parsers.DOMParser;
import org.apache.xml.serialize.Method;
import org.apache.xml.serialize.OutputFormat;
import org.apache.xml.serialize.XMLSerializer;
import org.w3c.dom.Document;
import org.xml.sax.SAXException;

public class DOMSerializerMain {

    public static void main(String[] args) {
        DOMParser p = new DOMParser();

        try {
            p.parse(args[0]);
        } catch (SAXException se) {
            se.printStackTrace();
        } catch (IOException ioe) {
```

```
            ioe.printStackTrace();
        }
        Document d = p.getDocument();
        OutputFormat format =
            new OutputFormat(Method.XML,"UTF-8",true);
        format.setPreserveSpace(true);
        XMLSerializer serializer =
            new XMLSerializer(System.out, format);
        try {
            serializer.serialize(d);
        } catch (IOException ioe) {
            ioe.printStackTrace();
        }
    }
}
```

Here you construct the OutputFormat and serializer and then pass the DOM Document object to the serializer's serialize method.

OutputFormat options

Now that you've seen examples of how to use the serializers, let's look at OutputFormat in more detail. A number of properties control how a serializer behaves. We'll describe some of the more important ones below in JavaBean style, so the property encoding has a getEncoding method and a setEncoding method.

Property	Description
String encoding	The IANA name for the output character encoding.
String[] cDataElements	An array of element names whose contents should be output as CDATA.
int indent	The number of spaces to indent.
boolean indenting	True if the output should be indented.
String lineSeparator	A string used to separate lines.
int lineWidth	Lines longer than lineWidth characters are too long and are wrapped/indented as needed.
String[] nonEscapingElements	An array of element names whose contents should not be output escaped (no character references are used).
boolean omitComments	True if comments should not be output.
boolean omitDocumentType	True if the DOCTYPE declaration should not be output.
boolean omitXMLDeclaration	True if the XML declaration should not be output.
boolean preserveEmptyAttributes	If false, then in HTML mode, empty attribute are output as the attribute name only, with no equal sign or empty quotes.
boolean preserveSpace	True if the serializer should preserve space that already exists in the input.

The following set of methods deals with the DOCTYPE declaration:

Method	Description
String getDoctypePublic()	Gets the public ID of the current DOCTYPE.
String getDoctypeSystem()	Gets the system ID of the current DOCTYPE.
void setDocType(String publicId, String systemID)	Sets the public ID and system ID of the current DOCTYPE.

One least caveat on the use of the serializers: serializers aren't thread safe, so you have to be careful if you're going to use them in a multithreaded environment.

At the time of this writing, the W3C DOM Working Group is working on the DOM Level 3 Load/Save specification, which includes a mechanism for saving a DOM tree back to XML. This work has not been finalized and applies only to DOM trees. It's definitely worth learning the Xerces serializers API, because they also work with SAX. It's also worthwhile because the current (experimental) implementation of DOM Level 3 serialization in Xerces is based on the org.apache.xml.serialize classes.

XNI

The first version of Xerces used a SAX-like API internally. This API allowed you to build both a SAX API and a DOM API on top of a single parser engine. For Xerces version 2, this API was extended to make it easier to build parsers out of modular components. This extended and refactored API is known as the Xerces Native Interface (XNI). XNI is based on the idea of providing a streaming information set. The XML Infoset specification describes an abstract model of all the information items present in an XML document, including elements, attributes, characters, and so on. XNI takes the streaming/callback model used by SAX and expands the callback classes and methods so that as much of the information set as possible is available to applications that use XNI. As an example, XNI retains the encoding information for external entities and passes it along to the application. It also captures the information in the XML declaration and makes it available. XNI lets you build XML processors as a pipeline of components connected by the streaming information set.

SAX was designed primarily as a read-only API. XNI provides a read-write model. This allows the streaming information set to be augmented as it passes from component to component. One important application is in validating XML schema, which causes the XML infoset to be augmented with information—such as datatypes—obtained during validation. The read/write nature of XNI is accomplished by adding an additional argument to each callback method. This argument is an instance of org.apache .xerces.xni.Augmentations, which is a data structure like a hash table that allows data to be stored and retrieved via String keys.

Most developers never look at the XNI interfaces, because they can do everything they want via the SAX, DOM, or JAXP APIs. But for those looking to exploit the full power of Xerces, digging into the details of XNI is necessary. We'll provide a basic overview of the pieces of XNI and how they fit together, and show an example based on accessing the PSVI.

XNI Basics

An XNI-based parser contains two pipelines that do all the work: the document pipeline and the DTD pipeline. The pipelines consist of instances of XMLComponent that are chained together via interfaces that represent the streaming information set. Unlike SAX, which has a single pipeline, XNI divides the pipeline in two: one pipeline for the content of the document and a separate pipeline for dealing with the information DTD. The pipeline interfaces live in org.apache.xerces.xni:

Interface	Purpose
XMLDocumentHandler	The major interface in the document content pipeline. This should be familiar to anyone familiar with SAX.
XMLDocumentFragmentHandler	The document content pipeline can handle document fragments as well. To do this, you need to connect stages using XMLDocumentFragmentHandler instead of XMLDocumentHandler.
XMLDTDHandler	The major interface in the DTD pipeline. It handles everything except parsing the content model part of element declarations.
XMLDTDContentModelHandler	Provided for applications that want to parse the content model part of element declarations.
XMLString	A structure used to pass text around within XNI. You must copy the text out of an XMLString if you want use it after the XNI method has executed. XMLStrings should be treated as read-only.
XNIException	An Exception class for use with the XNI layer.
Augmentations	A data structure like a hash table, for storing augmentations to the stream information set. The set of augmentations is an argument to almost every XNI method in the content and DTD pipelines.
QName	An abstraction of XML QNames.
XMLAttributes	An abstraction for the set of attributes associated with an element.
XMLLocator	A data structure used to hold and report the location in the XML document where processing is occurring / has failed.
XMLResourceIdentifier	A data structure representing the public ID, system ID, and namespace of an XML resource (XML Schema, DTD, or general entity).
NamespaceContext	An abstraction representing the stack of namespace contexts (like variable scopes) within an XML document.

XMLString, XNIException, Augmentations, QName, XMLAttributes, XMLLocator, XMLResourceIdentifier, and NamespaceContext are all used by one of the four major interfaces (XMLDocumentHandler, XMLDocumentFragmentHandler, XMLDTDHandler, and XMLDTDContentModelHandler).

If you look at the XMLComponent interface, you'll see that it really just defines methods for setting configuration settings on a component. Not surprisingly, it uses a feature and property interface reminiscent of SAX. The biggest addition is a pair of methods that return an array of the features/properties supported by the component. What may surprise you is that the interface doesn't say anything about the callback interfaces for the pipeline. This is intentional, because not all components are in all pipelines—that's part of the rationale for breaking up the pipeline interfaces, so that components can implement the smallest set of functionality they require.

To implement a real component that can be a part of a pipeline, you need more interfaces. These interfaces are found in org.apache.xerces.xni.parser. The callback interfaces define what it means to be a recipient or sink for streaming information set events. Components that act as sinks sit at the end of the pipeline. That means you need interfaces for components at the start of the pipeline and for components in the middle. Components at the start of the pipeline are sources of streaming information set events, so they need to be connected to an event sink. The interface for these components has a pair of methods that let you get and set the sink to which the source is connected. There are three of these source interfaces, one for each of the major pipeline interfaces (XMLDocumentFragmentHandler is considered minor because document fragments appear so infrequently):

- **XMLDocumentSource** for XMLDocumentHandler
- **XMLDTDSource** for XMLDTDHandler
- **XMLDTDContentModelSource** for XMLDTDContentModelHandler

Now, defining interfaces for components in the middle is easy. These components must implement both the source and sink (handler) interfaces for the pipeline. That gives XMLDocumentFilter, which implements XMLDocumentSource and XMLDocumentHandler. XMLDTDFilter and XMLDTDContentModelFilter are defined in a similar way.

At this point it's a little clearer what an XNI pipeline is. Using the DocumentHandler as an example, a pipeline is an instance of XMLDocumentSource connected to some number of instances of XMLDocumentFilter that are chained together. The last XMLDocumentFilter is connected to an instance of XMLDocumentHandler, which provides the final output of the pipeline. The instance of XMLDocumentSource takes the XML document as input. The next question you should be thinking about is how the pipeline is constructed, connected, and started up.

XNI Pipeline Interfaces

XNI provides interfaces you can use to take care of these matters. You aren't by any means required to do this—you could do it with custom code, but you'll probably find that you end up duplicating the functionality provided by XNI. The interfaces for managing XMLComponents are also found in org.apache.xerces.xni.parser. Let's call a pipeline of XMLComponents a *configuration*. The interface for managing a configuration is called XMLParserConfiguration. This interface extends XMLComponentManager, which provides a simple API for querying whether a set of components supports a particular feature or property. XMLParserConfiguration adds APIs that let you do several categories of tasks:

- **Configuration**—This API provides methods to tell configuration clients the set of supported features and properties. It also adds methods for changing the values of features and properties.
- **Sink management**—There are methods that allow configuration clients to register sinks for the three major pipeline interfaces in the configuration. Clients can also ask for the currently registered sink on a per-interface basis.
- **Helper services**—XMLParserConfiguration assumes that configuration-wide services and data are used by the XMLComponents in the configuration. Examples of these services include error reporting as defined by the XMLErrorHandler interface and entity resolution as defined by the XMLEntityResolver interface.
- **Parsing kickoff**—XMLParserConfiguration provides methods for starting the process of parsing XML from an XMLInputSource.

Let's look back at the diagram of Xerces. On top of the XMLParserConfiguration sits a Xerces parser class. This class is a sink for XMLDocumentHandler, XMLDTDHandler, and XMLDTDContentModelHandler. It registers itself as the sink for the various parts of the pipeline. The implementation of the various callback methods takes care of translating between the XNI callback and the parser API being implemented. For a SAX parser, the translation is pretty straightforward, consisting mostly of converting QNames and XMLStrings into Java Strings. A DOM parser is little more difficult because the callbacks need to build up the nodes of the DOM tree in addition to translating the XNI types.

Remember that we said the diagram was simplified. The Xerces SAXParser and DOMParser are actually implemented as a hierarchy of subclasses, with functionality layered between the various levels of the class hierarchy. The reason for doing this is to allow developers to produce their own variants of SAXParser and DOMParser with as little work as necessary.

There's only one part of the diagram we haven't discussed. At bottom right is a section labeled *support components*. We've already talked a little about helper components when we discussed XMLParserConfiguration. In that discussion, we were looking at components that were likely to be used by any parser configuration we could think have. Other support components are used only by a particular parser configuration. These are used internally by the parser configuration but are known by some number of the XMLComponents in the pipelines. Examples of these kinds of components include symbol tables and components dedicated to managing the use of namespaces throughout the configuration. These support components are provided to the pipeline components as properties, so they are assigned URI strings that mark them as being for internal use and then set using the configuration-wide property-setting mechanism.

Xerces2 XNI Components

XNI as we've discussed it is really a framework. The interfaces describe how the pieces of the framework interact. You can think of Xerces2 as a very useful reference implementation of the XNI framework. If you're going to build an application using XNI, you may find it useful to reuse some of the components from the Xerces2 reference implementation. These components have the advantage of being heavily tested and debugged, so you can concentrate on implementing just the functionality you need. Here are some of the most useful components from Xerces2.

Document Scanner

The document scanner knows how to take an XML document and fire the callbacks for elements (and attributes), characters, and anything else you might encounter in an XML document. This is the workhorse component for any XNI application that is going to work with an XML document. Applications that just work with the DTD or schema may end up not using this class. The document scanner is implemented by the class org,apache.xerces.impl.XMLDocumentScannerImpl and uses the URI http://apache.org/xml/properties/internal/document-scanner as its property ID. To use it, you also need the DTD scanner, entity manager, error reporter, and symbol table.

DTD Scanner

If you're processing DTDs, either directly or indirectly, you need the DTD scanner. It knows the syntax of DTDs and fires XMLDTDHandler and XMLDTDContentModelHandler events as it processes the DTD. The DTD scanner is implemented by the class org.apache.xerces.impl.XMLDTDScannerImpl and uses the URI http://apache.org/xml/properties/internal/dtd-scanner as its property ID. To use it, you also need the entity manager, error reporter, and symbol table.

DTD Validator

Scanning DTDs is different from validating with them. After the DTD pipeline has scanned the DTD and assembled the necessary definitions, the document content pipeline needs to use those definitions to validate the document. That's where the DTD validator comes in. It takes the definitions created by the DTD pipeline and uses them to validate the document. The validator is inserted into the pipeline as a filter, after the document scanner. The DTD validator is implemented by the class org.apache.xerces.impl.dtd.XMLDTDValidator and uses the URI http://apache.org/xml/properties/internal/validator/dtd as its property ID. To use it, you also need the entity manager, error reporter, and symbol table.

Namespace Binder

The process of mapping namespace prefixes to namespace URIs is called *namespace binding*. It needs to occur after DTD validation has occurred because the DTD may have provided default values for one or more namespace attributes in the document. These namespace bindings are needed for schema validation, so the namespace binder is inserted as a filter after the DTD validator and before the schema validator. The namespace binder is implemented by the class org.apache.xerces.impl.XMLNamespaceBinder and uses the URI http://apache.org/xml/properties/internal/namespace-binder as its property ID. To use it, you also need the error reporter and the symbol table.

Schema Validator

The schema validator validates the document against an XML schema. It's inserted into the pipeline as a filter after the namespace binder. As it processes the document, it may augment the streaming information set with default and normalized simple type values. It may also add items to the PSVI via the augmentations. The schema validator is implemented by the class org.apache.xerces.impl.xs.XMLSchemaValidator and uses the URI http://apache.org/xml/properties/internal/validator/schema as its property ID. To use it, you also need the error reporter and the symbol table.

Error Reporter

The parser configuration needs a single mechanism that all components can use to report errors. The Xerces2 error reporter provides a single point for all components to report errors. It also provides some support for localizing the error messages and calling the XNI XMLErrorHandler callback. Localization works as follows. Each component is given a domain designated by a URI. The component then implements the org.apache.xerces.util.MessageFormatter interface to generate and localize its own error messages. This component is used by almost all the other Xerces2 components, so you need to have one of them in your configuration if you use any of them. The error reporter is implemented by the class org.apache.xerces.impl.XMLErrorReporter and uses the URI http://apache.org/xml/properties/internal/error-reporter as its property ID.

Entity Manager

Xerces2 provides an entity manager that handles the starting and stopping of entities within an XML document. This gives its clients (primarily the document scanner and DTD scanner) the illusion that there is a single entity, not multiple entities. The entity manager is implemented by the class org.apache.xerces.impl.EntityManager and uses the URI http://apache.org/xml/properties/internal/entity-manager as its property id. To use it, you also need the error reporter and the symbol table.

Symbol Table

XML parsers look at a lot of text when processing documents. Much of that text (element and attribute names, namespaces prefixes, and so on) is repeated in XML documents. Xerces2 tries to take advantage of that fact by providing a custom symbol table for strings in order to improve performance. The symbol table always returns the same java.lang.String reference for a given string value. This means components can compare strings by comparing these references, not by comparing the string values. So, not only does the symbol table save space, it helps replace expensive calls to String#equals() with calls to ==. This component is used by all the rest of the Xerces2 components, so your configuration needs one of them if you use any Xerces2 components. The symbol table is implemented by the class org.apache.xerces.util.SymbolTable and uses the URI http://apache.org/xml/properties/internal/symbol-table as its property ID.

Using the Samples

The Xerces distribution includes a number of sample programs, some of which can be very useful when you're developing programs using Xerces—especially when you've embedded Xerces into your application. Suppose you're trying to debug an application and the problem appears to be inside Xerces itself. You may be seeing exceptions thrown or getting answers you think are incorrect. One debugging method that can save a lot of time is to capture the XML that's being input to Xerces, save it a file, and drag out one of the samples to help you see what's going on.

Before you use any of the samples, you need to get to a command-line prompt on your operating system. Make sure that xml-apis.jar, xercesImpl.jar, and xercesSamples.jar are all on your classpath.

If you're working with SAX, the first place to go is to the SAX Counter sample. This sample parses your document and prints some statistics based on what it finds. To invoke Counter, type

```
java sax.Counter <options> <filename>
```

There are command-line options to turn on and off namespace processing, validation, and schema validation, and to turn on full checking of the schema document. If you omit the options and filename, you'll get a help screen describing all the options. The key reason to start with sax.Count is that if Xerces is throwing an exception, it will probably throw that exception when you run sax.Count. From there, you can try to figure out if the problem is with the XML file, your application, or Xerces (in which case you should send mail to xerces-j-user@xml.apache.org with a bug report).

There's a pair of DocumentTracer samples, one for SAX and one for XNI. These samples are in classes named sax.DocumentTracer and xni.DocumentTracer, respectively. Their job is to print out all the SAX or XNI callbacks as they are fired for your document. Occasionally these samples can be useful to help you figure out which callbacks are being passed which data—especially when you're tired and confused after a long day of programming. They can also help you debug namespace-related problems, because all the prefixes get expanded. The output of xni.DocumentTracer is more detailed and complete than that of sax.DocumentTracer, due to the higher fidelity of the XNI callbacks, but most of the time you'll want to use sax.DocumentTracer so you can see exactly what SAX sees.

If you're using the DOM, you can use the DOM Counter sample, which lives in dom.Counter. It does the same thing as sax.Counter, but it uses the DOM and therefore will probably exercise some of the same DOM code your application does.

CyberNeko Tools for XNI

Andy Clark is one of the Xerces committers and was the driving force behind the design of XNI. He's written a suite of tools called NekoXNI to showcase some of the things you can do with XNI. Even if you aren't interested in using XNI, you might want to have a look, because some of the tools are pretty useful. In this section, we'll look at a few of these tools.

NekoHTML

NekoHTML uses XNI to allow an application to process an HTML document as if it were an XML document. There are both SAX and DOM parsers in the org.cyberneko.html.parsers package. You use org.cyberneko.html.parsers.SAXParser just like the regular Xerces SAXParser; you can plug in your own ContentHandlers and so on using the regular SAX API. The org.cyberneko.html.parsers.DOMParser works like the Xerces DOMParser with one notable twist. Instead of using the Xerces XML DOM, it uses the Xerces HTML DOM, which means you get a DOM implementation that is aware of some of the rules of HTML. To use NekoHTML, you need to have nekohtml.jar in your classpath, in addition to the regular jars you need for Xerces. But if you need to process HTML, it's worth it.

ManekiNeko

Another interesting and useful component of NekoXNI is a validator for Relax-NG called ManekiNeko. This validator is based on James Clark's Jing validator for Relax-NG, and it works by creating a wrapper that converts XNI events into the SAX events that Jing already understands. This wrapped version of Jing is then inserted into the appropriate spot in the XNI pipeline within an XMLParserConfiguration called JingConfiguration. For ease of use, Andy has again provided convenience classes that work just like the Xerces SAX and DOM parser classes. For a Relax-NG aware SAX parser, use org.cyberneko.relaxng.parsers.SAXParser; for a DOM parser, use org.cyberneko.relaxng.parsers.DOMParser. You must set the SAX validation and namespace features to true. You must also set a property that tells the Relax-NG validator where to find the Relax-NG schema to be used for validation, because Relax-NG doesn't specify a way of associating a schema with a document. This property is called http://cyberneko.org/xml/properties/relaxng/schema-location, and its value should be the URI for the schema file.

NekoPull

The last CyberNeko tool is NekoPull, the CyberNeko pull parser. The commonly used APIs for XML, SAX, and DOM are push APIs. Once your program asks the parser to parse a document, your application doesn't regain control until the parse completes. SAX calls your program code via its event callbacks, but that's about as good as it gets. With the DOM, you have to wait until the entire tree has been built before you can do anything.

The difficulty with SAX is that for any non-trivial XML grammar, you end up maintaining a bunch of stacks and a state machine that remembers where you are in the grammar at any point in the parse. It also makes it very hard to modularize your application. If you have an XML grammar where the elements are turned into objects of various classes, you have to do a lot of work to keep the event-handling code for each class associated with each class. You end up trying to create ContentHandlers that handle only the section of the grammar for a particular class, and then you have to build infrastructure to multiplex between these ContentHandlers. It can be done, but the process is tedious and error prone.

With the DOM, you can create a constructor that knows how to construct an instance of your class from an org.w3c.dom.Element node, and then you can pass the DOM tree around to instances of the various classes. You can handle contained objects by passing the right element in the DOM tree to the constructors for those contained object types. The disadvantage of the DOM is that you have to wait until the whole document is processed, even if you only need part of it. And, of course, there's the usual problem of how much memory DOM trees take up.

Pull-parsing APIs can give you the best of both worlds. In a pull-parsing API, the application asks the parser to parse the next unit in the XML document, regardless of whether that unit is an element, character data, a processing instruction, and so on. This means you can process the document in a streaming fashion, which is a benefit of SAX. You can also pass the parser instance around to your various object constructors. Because the parser instance remembers where it is in the document, the constructor can call the parser to ask for the next bits of XML, which should represent the data it needs to construct an object. Contained objects are handled just like the DOM case; you pass the parser instance (which again remembers its place) to the constructors for the contained objects. This is a much better API.

Let's walk through a pull implementation of the Book object building program:

```
/*
 *
 * NekoPullMain.java
 *
```

```
 * Example from "Professional XML Development with Apache Tools"
 *
 */
package com.sauria.apachexml.ch1;

import java.io.IOException;
import java.util.Stack;

import org.apache.xerces.xni.XMLAttributes;
import org.apache.xerces.xni.XNIException;
import org.apache.xerces.xni.parser.XMLInputSource;
import org.cyberneko.pull.XMLEvent;
import org.cyberneko.pull.XMLPullParser;
import org.cyberneko.pull.event.CharactersEvent;
import org.cyberneko.pull.event.ElementEvent;
import org.cyberneko.pull.parsers.Xerces2;

public class NekoPullMain {

    public static void main(String[] args) {
        try {
            XMLInputSource is =
                new XMLInputSource(null, args[0], null);
            XMLPullParser pullParser = new Xerces2();
            pullParser.setInputSource(is);
            Book book = makeBook(pullParser);
```

You start by instantiating an instance of the pull parser and setting it up with the input source for the document. Then you pass the parser, which is at the correct position to start reading a book, to a constructor function for the Book class.

```
            System.out.println(book.toString());
        } catch (IOException ioe) {
            ioe.printStackTrace();
        }
    }

    private static Book makeBook(XMLPullParser pullParser)
        throws IOException {
        Book book = null;
        Stack textStack = new Stack();
```

When you ask the parser for the next bit of XML, you get back an event. That event is an object (a struct, really) that contains all the information about the piece of XML the parser saw. NekoPull includes event types for the document, elements, character data, CDATA, comments, text declaration, DOCTYPE declaration, processing instructions, entities, and namespace prefix mappings. The event types are determined by integer values in the type field of XMLEvent. Some of the events are bounded; that is, they correspond to a start/end pairing and are reported twice. The bounded events are DocumentEvent, ElementEvent, GeneralEntityEvent, CDATAEvent, and PrefixMappingEvent; a boolean field called start distinguishes start events from end events.

You loop and call pullParser's nextEvent method to get events until there aren't any more (or until you break out of the loop):

```
        XMLEvent evt;
        while ((evt = pullParser.nextEvent()) != null) {
            switch (evt.type) {
                case XMLEvent.ELEMENT :
                    ElementEvent eltEvt = (ElementEvent) evt;
                    if (eltEvt.start) {
                        textStack.push(new StringBuffer());
                        String localPart = eltEvt.element.localpart;
                        if (localPart.equals("book")) {
                            XMLAttributes attrs = eltEvt.attributes;
                            String version =
                                attrs.getValue(null, "version");
                            if (version.equals("1.0")) {
                                book = new Book();
                                continue;
                            }
                            throw new XNIException("bad version");
                        }
```

If you see a starting ElementEvent for the book element, you check the version attribute to make sure it's 1.0 and then instantiate a new Book object. For all starting ElementEvents, you push a new StringBuffer onto a textStack, just like for SAX. You do this to make sure you catch text in mixed content, which will be interrupted by markup. For example, in

```
<blockquote>
    I really <em>didn't</em> like what he had to say
</blockquote>
```

the text "I really" and "like what he had to say" belongs inside the blockquote element, whereas the text "didn't" belongs inside the em element. Keeping this text together is what the textStack is all about.

The real work of building the object is done when you hit the end tag, where you get an ending ElementEvent. Here you grab the text you've been collecting for this element and, based on the tag you're closing, call the appropriate Book setter method. You should be pretty familiar with this sort of code by now:

```
                    } else if (!eltEvt.empty) {
                        String localPart = eltEvt.element.localpart;
                        StringBuffer tos =
                            (StringBuffer) textStack.pop();
                        String text = tos.toString();
                        if (localPart.equals("title")) {
                            book.setTitle(text);
                        } else if (localPart.equals("author")) {
                            book.setAuthor(text);
                        } else if (localPart.equals("isbn")) {
                            book.setIsbn(text);
                        } else if (localPart.equals("month")) {
                            book.setMonth(text);
                        } else if (localPart.equals("year")) {
                            int year = 0;
                            year = Integer.parseInt(text);
                            book.setYear(year);
```

```
                        } else if (localPart.equals("publisher")) {
                            book.setPublisher(text);
                        } else if (localPart.equals("address")) {
                            book.setAddress(text);
                        }
```

When you see a CharactersEvent, you're appending the characters in the event to the text you're keeping for this element:

```
                    }
                    break;
                case XMLEvent.CHARACTERS :
                    CharactersEvent chEvt = (CharactersEvent) evt;
                    StringBuffer tos =
                        (StringBuffer) textStack.peek();
                    tos.append(chEvt.text.toString());
                    break;
            }
        }
        return book;
    }
}
```

As you can see, the style inside the constructor method is somewhat reminiscent of a SAX content handler. The difference is that when you get to contained objects, the code is dramatically simpler. You just have a bunch of methods that look like makeBook, except that as part of the processing of certain end ElementEvents, there's a call to the constructor function of another class, with the only argument being the pull parser.

As we're writing this, the first public review of JSR-173, the Streaming API for XML, has just begun. Perhaps by the time you're reading this, NekoXNI's pull parser will be implementing what's in that JSR.

At the moment, the NekoXNI tools are separate from Xerces, but there have been some discussions about incorporating all or some of the tools into the main Xerces distribution.

Practical Usage

We've covered a lot of ways you can use Xerces to get information out of XML documents and into your application. Here are two more practical usage tips.

Xerces isn't thread safe. You can't have two threads that execute a single Xerces instance at the same time. If you're in a multithreaded situation, you should create one instance of Xerces for each thread. If for some reason you don't want to do that, make sure the access to the parser instance is synchronized, or you'll run into some nasty problems. A common solution pattern for concurrent systems is to provide the thread with a pool of parser instances that have already been created.

That leads us into the second tip. If your application is processing many XML documents, you should try to reuse parser instances. Both the Xerces SAXParser and DOMParser provide a method called reset that you can use to reset the parser's internal data structures so the instance can be used to parse another document. This saves the overhead of creating all the internal data structures for each document. When you combine this with grammar caching, you can get some nice improvements in performance relative to creating a parser instance over and over again.

Common Problems

This section addresses some common problems that people encounter when they use Xerces. Most of these issues aren't Xerces specific, but they happen so frequently that we wanted to address them.

- **Classpath problems**—It's a simple mistake but a surprisingly common one. Both xml-apis.jar and xercesImpl.jar must be on your classpath in order to use Xerces. Leaving one of them out will cause pain and suffering. If you want to use the samples, you need to include xercesSamples.jar on your classpath.

  The other thing to beware of is strange interactions between your classpath and either the JDK 1.3 Extension Mechanism or the JDK 1.4 Endorsed Standards Override Mechanism. If it looks like you aren't getting Xerces or the Xerces version that you think you're using, look for old versions of Xerces in these places. You can determine the version of Xerces by executing the following at your command line:

  ```
  java org.apache.xerces.impl.Version
  ```

  This command prints out the version of Xerces you're using. You can also call the static method org.apache.xerces.impl.Version#getVersion from inside a program to get the version string.

- **Errors not reported or always reported to the console**—If you don't provide an ErrorHandler, one of two behaviors will occur. In every version of Xerces prior to 2.3.0, if no ErrorHandler is registered, no error messages are displayed. You must register your own ErrorHandler if you want error messages to be reported. This problem confused a lot of people, so in version 2.3.0 the behavior was changed so that error messages are echoed to the console when no ErrorHandler is registered. In these versions of Xerces, you need to register your own ErrorHandler to turn off the messages to the console.

- **Multiple calls to characters**—In SAX applications, it's common to forget that the characters callback may be called more than once for the character data inside an element. Unless you buffer up the text by, say, appending it to a StringBuffer, it may look like your application is randomly throwing away pieces of character data.

- **When is ignorableWhitespace called?**—It's not enough that the definition of ignorable whitespace is confusing to people. The ignorableWhitespace callback is called for ignorableWhitespace only when a DTD is associated with the document. If there's no DTD, ignorableWhitespace isn't called. This is true even if there is an XML schema but no DTD.

- **Forgot validation switches**—Another common problem is forgetting to turn on the validation features. This is true both for DTD validation and for schema validation. A single feature must be turned on for DTD validation; but for schema validation you must have namespace support turned on in addition to the feature for schema validation. That's three properties. Make sure you have them all on.

- **Multiple documents in one file**—People like to try to put multiple XML documents into a single file. This isn't legal XML, and Xerces won't swallow it. You'll definitely see errors for that.

- **Mismatched encoding declaration**—The character encoding used in a file and the encoding name specified in the encoding declaration must match. The encoding declaration is the encoding="name" that appears after <? xml version="1.0" encoding="name"?> in an XML document. If the encoding of the file and the declared encoding don't match, you may see errors about invalid characters.
- **Forgetting to use namespace-aware methods**—If you're working with namespaces, be sure to use the namespace-aware versions of the methods. With SAX this is fairly easy because most people are using the SAX 2.0 ContentHandler, which has only the namespace-aware callback methods. If you're using DocumentHandler and trying to do namespaces, you're in the wrong place. You need to use ContentHandler. In DOM-based parsers, this is a little harder because there are namespace-aware versions of methods that have the letters *NS* appended to their names. So, Element#getAttributeNS is the namespace-aware version of the Element#getAttribute method.
- **Out of memory using the DOM**—Depending on the document you're working with, you may see out-of-memory errors if you're using the DOM. This happens because the DOM tends to be very memory intensive. There are several possible solutions. You can increase the size of the Java heap. You can use the DOM in deferred mode—if you're using the JAXP interfaces, then you aren't using the DOM in deferred mode. Finally, you can try to prune some of the nodes in the DOM tree by setting the feature http://apache.org/xml/features/dom/include-ignorable-whitespace to false.
- **Using appendChild instead of importNode across DOM trees**—The Xerces DOM implementation tries to enforce some integrity constraints on the contents of the DOM. One common thing developers want to do is create a new DOM tree and then copy some nodes from another DOM tree into it. Usually they try to do this using Node#appendChild, and then they start seeing exceptions like *DOMException: DOM005 Wrong document*, which is confusing. To copy nodes between DOM trees you need to use the Document#importNode method, and then you can call the method you want to put the node into its new home.

Applications

We've covered a lot of ground in this chapter, and yet we've hardly begun. XML parsing has so many applications that it's hard to show all the ways you might use it in your application. Here are a couple of ideas.

One place you end up directly interacting with the XML parser is in the kind of example we've been using through out this chapter: turning XML documents into domain-specific objects within your application. Although there are some proposals for tools that can do it for you, this is a task where you'll still see developers having direct interaction with the parser, at least for a little while longer.

Another application people use the parser for directly is filtering XML. When you have a very large XML document and you need only part of it, using SAX to cut out the stuff you don't want to deal with is a very viable solution.

XML parsers have a place as a document and schema development tool. They provide the means for you to create XML documents and grammars in many forms (DTDs, XML Schema, and Relax-NG) and verify that the grammars you've written do what you want and that your documents conform to those grammars.

The reality is that most developers are doing less with XML parsers directly. That's because lots of clever tool and application developers have leveraged the fundamental capability of XML parsing and used it to build tools that operate at a higher level. Although we hope you're excited about Xerces and all the cool things you can do with it, we hope you're even more excited by some of the tools that have already been built on top of it. Those tools are what the rest of this book is about.

2

Xalan

The Apache XSLT processing engine is Xalan (named after a rare musical instrument). There are both Java and C++ versions of Xalan. The current version of Xalan implements the XSLT 1.0 and XPath 1.0 Recommendations from the World Wide Web Consortium (W3C). The Xalan code base was originally donated by IBM's Lotus subsidiary, where it was known as LotusXSL. Xalan is on its second-generation code base, after some substantial changes were made from Xalan-Java 1. Since version 2.1.0, released in 2001, Xalan has also included the XSLTC compiler originally developed by Sun Microsystems.

Xalan works by interpreting the XSLT stylesheet—it translates the stylesheet as it's processing it. XSLTC compiles the stylesheet into a Java class called a *translet*. This avoids the overhead of translating the stylesheet over and over, which is particularly important in server applications where you're using the same stylesheet to transform many different XML documents.

Prerequisites

The XPath and XSLT technologies are used in a number of the xml.apache.org projects, so the next two sections of this chapter will review their key concepts. If you're proficient with XPath and XSLT, you can probably skim or skip these sections. XPath and XSLT are topics large enough for their own books, so be aware that what you're about to read is a quick review.

XPath

XPath is a language for specifying (addressing) parts of an XML document. Its data model treats an XML document as a tree of nodes. There are seven types of nodes, as shown in the following table.

Node Type	Description
Root	The root node of the XPath tree. The root element of the XML document is a child of this node.
Element	There is one element node for every element in the XML document.
Text	Character data inside elements is represented as elements. This includes data in CDATA sections. Unlike the DOM, the XPath data model puts as much character data into a text node as possible.
Attribute	There is one attribute node for every attribute of every element in the XML document. The element to which the attributes are attached is the parent of those attribute nodes. The attribute nodes aren't children of that element node.
Namespace	There is one namespace node for every namespace prefix in scope for an element. The element for which the prefixes are in scope is the parent of those namespace nodes. The namespace nodes aren't children of that element node.
Processing instruction	There is a processing instruction node for every processing instruction outside of the DTD.
Comment	There is a comment node for every comment outside of the DTD.

XPath is an expression-based language. This means every syntactically correct construct in XPath yields a value. XPath expressions can produce four different types of results: node sets (a set of nodes), booleans, numbers, and strings. The most important kinds of expressions in XPath are those that produce node sets. The type of expression used most commonly to generate a node set is a location path.

Location Paths

A *location path* is an expression that selects a node set from the XPath data model for an XML document. Location paths are rooted at a context node, which is part of the overall context used to evaluate XPath expressions. XPath was designed for use in both XSLT and XPointer, and because of the differences in what these two specifications are trying to achieve, the context for an XPath location path is different depending on whether the XPath is being used inside XSLT or XPointer. For an understanding of XPath itself, you don't need to know whether XSLT or XPointer is being used (we'll look at how XSLT defines the XPath context when we get to XSLT). For now, you need to know that all XPath expressions are evaluated in a context provided by either XSLT or XPath. The context includes a node (the context node), the context position, the context size, a set of variable bindings, a function library, and a set of namespace declarations for the expression.

There are two types of location paths. *Relative* location paths select nodes relative to the context node. *Absolute* location paths begin with the slash (/) character and select nodes relative to the root node of the document. You can think of an absolute location path as a relative location path whose context node is the root node of the document.

A location path is composed of a number of location steps, separated by a slash. The first location step selects a set of nodes relative to the context node. This node set is then used to form context nodes for the next location step. Every node in the node set obtained from the first location step is used as a context node, and the next location step is applied to those context nodes in order to select another set of nodes. This results in a set of node sets, one node set for every derived context node. This set of node sets is *unioned* together to produce a single node set. This process is repeated for each location step until there are no more location steps in the location path.

Let's look at an example to demonstrate this process. The following listing shows an XML document that represents a collection of books:

```
<?xml version="1.0" encoding="UTF-8"?>
<books xmlns="http://sauria.com/schemas/apache-xml-book/books"
  xmlns:tns="http://sauria.com/schemas/apache-xml-book/books"
  xmlns:xsi="http://www.w3.org/2001/XMLSchema-instance"
  xsi:schemaLocation=
    "http://sauria.com/schemas/apache-xml-book/books
     http://www.sauria.com/schemas/apache-xml-book/books.xsd"
  version="1.0">
  <book>
   <title>Professional XML Development with Apache Tools</title>
   <author>Theodore W. Leung</author>
   <isbn>0-7645-4355-5</isbn>
   <month>December</month>
   <year>2003</year>
   <publisher>Wrox</publisher>
   <address>Indianapolis, Indiana</address>
  </book>
  <book>
   <title>Effective Java</title>
   <author>Joshua Bloch</author>
   <isbn>0-201-31005-8</isbn>
   <month>August</month>
   <year>2001</year>
   <publisher>Addison-Wesley</publisher>
   <address>New York, New York</address>
  </book>
  <book>
   <title>Design Patterns</title>
   <author>Erich Gamma</author>
   <author>Richard Helm</author>
   <author>Ralph Johnson</author>
   <author>John Vlissides</author>
   <isbn>0-201-63361-2</isbn>
   <month>October</month>
   <year>1994</year>
   <publisher>Addison-Wesley</publisher>
   <address>Reading, Massachusetts</address>
  </book>
</books>
```

Now let's look at a simple location path: /tns:books/tns:book. This location path selects the three book elements that are children of the book element. Let's start at the beginning of the location path and see what's going on here. The initial slash tells you that this is an absolute location path. The first location step is tns:books. This location path selects any child of the root node whose name is tns:books. Here tns:books represents the namespace-qualified books element. It's important to include the tns: prefix because the books element is in a namespace—otherwise no nodes will match. The result of applying tns:books is a node set that contains the single node representing the books element in the document. Now you use that node set as a set of context nodes for the next location step, tns:book. This location step selects any child of the context node whose name is tns:book. This results in a node set with the three book elements from the document. At this point, you've run out of location steps, so this node set is the final value of the location path.

In the expression /tns:books/tns:book, you're looking at fairly simple location steps that select nodes according to their expanded names. An *expanded name* is composed of a namespace URI and a local part. Any node that can be affected by namespace declarations has an expanded name. Two expanded names are equal if they have the same local part; in addition, their namespace URIs must both be null, or, if they aren't null, they must be equal. Location steps can be quite a bit more complicated than this, though. A location step has three parts:

- **An axis**—A number of axes are defined on the XPath data model tree. These axes define sets of nodes that have a specified relationship with the context node. So far, you've just seen the use of the child axis, which includes a context node and its children. The location step only selects nodes from the axis.
- **A node test**—Node tests specify the type and expanded name of the nodes the location step should select.
- **Zero or more predicates**—Predicates filter nodes out of the node set being selected by the location step. Predicates are defined using XPath expressions.

All the location steps we'll be looking at use an abbreviated syntax that makes them easier to write. The full syntax for a location step is axis::node-test[predicate0]...[predicaten].

Now, let's look at each of these components in more detail.

Axes

Let's begin with axes. The following table describes all the XPath axes. It's important to keep in mind that everything else in a location step is done relative to the axis (unless the axis is explicitly specified in a predicate).

Axis Name	Description
child	Contains the children of the context node.
descendent	Contains the descendents of the context node—that is, the children and the children of the children, and so on. Note that attribute and namespace nodes aren't included because they aren't children.

Axis Name	Description
parent	Contains the parent of the context node if there is one.
ancestor	Contains the parent of the context node, and the parent of the parent, and so on, all the way up to and including the root node.
following-sibling	Contains all the nodes that are siblings of the context node (have the same parent) and that come after the context node in document order. If the context node is an attribute or namespace node, then this axis is empty.
preceding-sibling	Contains all the nodes that are siblings of the context node (have the same parent) and that come before the context node in document order. If the context node is an attribute or namespace node, then this axis is empty.
following	Contains all the nodes that come after the context node in document order, excluding its descendants, attribute nodes, and namespace nodes.
preceding	Contains all the nodes that come before the context node in document order, excluding its descendants, attribute nodes, and namespace nodes.
attribute	Contains the attribute nodes of the context node if the context node is an element node; otherwise this axis is empty.
namespace	Contains the namespace nodes of the context node if the context node is an element node; otherwise this axis is empty.
self	Contains the context node itself.
descendent-or-self	Contains the context node and the descendents of the context node.
ancestor-or-self	Contains the context node and the ancestors of the context node, all the way up to the root node.

Node Tests

Node tests work on the principal node type of the location step's axis. The following table shows the principal node types by axis.

Axis	Principal Node Type
attribute	Attribute
namespace	Namespace
All others	Element

There are four kinds of node tests:

- **QName**—Any node of the principal node type whose expanded name is the same as the expanded name of the QName. The location step tns:books is a QName node test.
- **NCName:***—Any node of the principal node type whose expanded name's namespace URI is the same as the namespace URI for the prefix denoted by the NCName. The location step tns:* uses an NCName node test.
- *—Selects any node of the principal node type. So, child::* selects all element children of the context node, because elements are the principal node type for the child axis.
- **NodeType**—Selects any node of type NodeType. Type tests are element, attribute, text, comment, and processing-instruction. Node matches any node of any type. The location step child::text selects all text nodes in the child axis.

Predicates

Predicates are expressions used to filter nodes out of a node set. A predicate expression is evaluated over each node in the node set. The node from the node set is used as the context node for the predicate expression. Predicate expressions are Boolean values. If the expression evaluates to true, the node is part of the result; if the expression evaluates to false, it isn't.

There's one additional twist to predicates. The predicate expression can evaluate to a number. This number is then automatically compared to the context position, yielding true if the number and the context position are the same, or false otherwise. You're probably wondering how the context position is determined. To describe this, we need to take a detour and define the proximity position of a node with respect to an axis. Axes can be either forward axes or reverse axes. A *forward axis* contains only the context node or nodes after the context node in document order (we'll define this in a minute). A *reverse axis* contains only the context node or nodes before the context node in document order. *Document order* is an ordering on the nodes in a node set that is supposed to correspond to the natural order of the content of the XML document. Element nodes occur before their children. An element's attribute and namespace nodes occur after the element node but before its children, and namespace nodes occur before the attribute nodes. *Reverse document order* is the reverse of document order. The *proximity position* of a node with respect to an axis is the position of the node when the node set is ordered in document order (for a forward axis) or reverse document order (for a reverse axis). Positions are numbered starting at 1. The *context position* of the context node in a predicate expression is the proximity position of the node with respect to the axis used by the predicate. In this setting, the context size is the size of the node set being used as input to the predicate.

Let's look at a few predicate examples:

The location path /tns:books/tns:book[tns:year='2003'] selects the tns:book children of the tns:books element (from the root) where the tns:year children of the book have the value 2003. The predicate [tns:year='2003'] narrows down the node set produced by the /tns:books/tns:book location path.

Here's an example using the context position. The XPath /tns:books/tns:book[2] selects the second tns:book child of the tns:books child of the root element.

Our last example shows how you can specify the axis to get what you're looking for. The path /tns:books[attribute::version='1.0'] asks for the tns:books child of the root node, and then asks for only those nodes whose version attribute (from the attribute axis) is equal to '1.0'.

Expressions

We're going to wind up our coverage of XPath by filling in some details related to expressions. First, we'll look at the functions XPath allows you to call, and then we'll examine the abbreviated syntax for XPath. First let's finish some details of the syntax for building expressions.

Expressions can be combined using familiar operators. The operators that work on expression are as follows, grouped in order of decreasing precedence:

- | (union of two location paths / node sets)
- **and, or**
- =, !=
- <, >, <=, >=

All XPath expressions yield one of the following four types: node-set, boolean, number, or string.

XPath Core Function Library

XPath defines a standard library of functions to be used in expressions. XSLT and XPointer extend this library with functions specific to their vocabularies. There are four groupings of functions, according to the four types available in XPath 1.0 (see the following tables).

Function	Description
number last()	Returns the context size.
number position()	Returns the context position.
number count(*node-set*)	Returns the number of nodes in the node set.
node-set id(*object*)	Returns the element whose unique ID (ID valued attribute) is *object*.
string local-name(*node-set*)	Returns the local name of the node from the node set that is first in document order.
string namespace-uri(*node-set*)	Returns the namespace URI of the node from the node set that is first in document order.
string name(*node-set*)	Returns a QName representing the expanded name of the node from the node set that is first in document order.
string string(*object*)	Returns an object as a string.
string concat(*string*, *string*, *string**)	Returns the string concatenation of all the arguments.

Function	Description
boolean starts-with(*string,string*)	Returns true if the first argument starts with the second argument.
boolean contains(*string, string*)	Returns true if the first argument contains the second argument.
string substring-before(*string, string*)	If the second string is a substring of the first string, returns the portion of the first string before the first occurrence of the second string.
string substring-after(*string, string*)	If the second string is a substring of the first string, returns the portion of the first string after the first occurrence of the second string.
string substring(*string, number, number?*)	Returns the substring of the first argument starting at the position indicated by the second argument. If the third argument is present, the substring stops at the position indicated by the third argument; otherwise it continues to the end of the string.
number string-length(*string?*)	Returns the length of the string. If no argument is provided, converts the context node to a string and returns the length of that string.
string normalize-space(*string?*)	Returns a normalized version of the string stripped of leading and trailing whitespace and with all sequences of whitespace characters replaced with a single space.
string translate(*string, string, string*)	Translates the string in the first argument by taking characters from the second argument and substituting them with the corresponding character from the third argument. See the following example.

The result of translate("characters","aeiou","AEIOU") is characters. The characters in the first argument are examined one by one. If they match a character in the second argument, they're replaced by the character at the same position (from the second argument) in the third argument.

Function	Description
boolean boolean(*object*)	Converts an object to a boolean.
	A number is true if it's neither positive nor negative zero or NAN.
	A node set is true if and only if it's non-empty.
	A string is true if and only if its length is non-zero.
boolean not(*boolean*)	Returns true if the argument is false, or false otherwise.
boolean true	Returns true.
boolean false	Returns false.
boolean lang(*string*)	Returns true if the context node's xml:lang attribute is the same as the first argument.

XPath provides some basic operators for numbers, including +, -, *, div, mod, and unary -. It also provides the functions in the following table.

Function	Description
Number number(*object*)	Converts an object to a number. Strings become numbers if they're IEEE 754 formatted. Boolean true becomes 1; false becomes 0. A node set is converted to a string, and that string is converted to a number.
Number sum(*node-set*)	Returns the sum of converting all nodes in the node set to strings and those strings into numbers.
Number floor(*number*)	Returns the largest integer that isn't greater than the number.
Number ceiling(*number*)	Returns the smallest integer that isn't less than the number.
Number round(*number*)	Returns the integer that's closest to the number. Prefers the integer closer to positive infinity if there is a tie.

Abbreviated Syntax

To make it easier to write XPath expressions, you can use the following abbreviated syntax:

- If no axis is specified, child:: is assumed.
- The attribute axis attribute:: can be abbreviated @.
- // is an abbreviation for /descendent-or-self::node()/.
- . is an abbreviation for self::node().
- .. is an abbreviation for parent::node().

Let's look at some of the examples we've used so far in this chapter, and compare abbreviated and unabbreviated forms:

- /tns:books/tns:book => /child::tns:books/child::tns:book
- /tns:books/tns:book[tns:year='2003'] => /child::tns:books/child::tns:book [child::tns:year = '2003']
- /tns:books/tns:book[2] => /child::tns:books/child::/tns:book[2]
- /tns:books[attribute::version='1.0'] => /child::tns:books[(attribute::version = "1.0")] (full)
- /tns:books[attribute::version='1.0'] => /tns:books[@version='1.0'] (fully abbreviated)

That concludes our quick review of XPath. Now we'll see how XPath fits into XSLT to give you an XML transformation system.

XSLT

XSL Transformations, or XSLT, is a language for transforming XML documents into other XML documents. It's based on a declarative programming paradigm, which means you specify what you want the results of the transformation to look like as opposed to specifying how you want the transformation to be performed. XSLT looks at XML documents as trees, using a data model that's very similar to the one used by XPath. The biggest difference between the XPath data model and the XSLT data model is that text nodes containing only whitespace are removed from the source tree and stylesheet trees after they're constructed, but prior to stylesheet processing. An XSLT transformation gives a set of rules that are used to transform a source tree into a result tree.

An XSLT transformation is expressed as an XML document. The document must be well-formed and obey the rules for namespace usage in XML. This document is also known as a *stylesheet*. The stylesheet contains XML elements that are defined by XSLT as well as elements that aren't defined by XSLT, but that appear in either the source or result document. Namespaces are used to keep the XSLT source and result elements from getting mixed up.

Templates

A stylesheet contains a number of XSLT constructs, but the most important content is a set of template rules, or templates. These templates do the job of transforming the source document. A template rule has two parts: a pattern that is matched against nodes from the source tree, and a template that can be instantiated as part of the result tree. The result tree is constructed by processing the current node list until it's empty. Initially, the current node list contains the root node of the source tree. So, the XSLT engine attempts to process the current node (in this case, the root node) from the current node list (also the root node in this case). To process a node, the engine looks for all templates whose pattern matches the current node. If there is more than one template whose pattern matches, then a conflict-resolution procedure is applied to select a single template. Once a single template has been selected, it's instantiated to create part of the result tree. As part of the template instantiation, the template may add more nodes from the source tree to the current node list. The process then repeats by selecting a new current node from the current node list until the current node list is empty.

Let's see some of this in action in a real XSLT stylesheet. You'll write a stylesheet that converts the earlier books inventory into HTML. Here's the beginning of that stylesheet:

```
1: <?xml version="1.0" encoding="UTF-8"?>
2: <xsl:stylesheet version="1.0"
3:   xmlns:xsl="http://www.w3.org/1999/XSL/Transform"
4:   xmlns:books="http://sauria.com/schemas/apache-xml-book/books">
```

The root element of the stylesheet comes from the XSLT namespace. This namespace's prefix is xsl by convention. Note that you declare the xsl prefix and the books prefix on the root element. Because the books vocabulary is in a namespace, the stylesheet needs to be able to get items in the namespace. Elements from HTML will be unprefixed.

The xsl:output element defines the output method for this stylesheet. There are output methods for XML, HTML, and text:

Lines 6-17 contain a pair of template definitions:

```
    <xsl:output method="html" indent="yes"/>
    <xsl:template match="books:books">
      <html>
        <head><title>Book Inventory</title></head>
        <body>
          <xsl:apply-templates/>
        </body>
      </html>
    </xsl:template>
    <xsl:template match="books:book">
       <xsl:apply-templates/>
      <p/>
    </xsl:template>
</xsl:stylesheet>
```

The match attribute of the xsl:template element defines the pattern that is checked against the current node. This stylesheet is processed by starting with the root node of the document and looking for a pattern that matches. The first template's pattern books:books selects any child node named books:books, which is the child of the root node in this case. (Note that you could have written the pattern as /books:books to make sure the pattern started with the root node, but making the path relative is more flexible.) The selected books:books node is now the current node. The body of the template (between the xsl:template start and end tags) contains the template that's instantiated. In this template, all elements without a namespace prefix are from HTML and are copied directly into the result tree. This creates the skeleton of an HTML document, which then needs to be filled in by the rest of the stylesheet. As the XSLT engine is instantiating this template, it encounters the xsl:apply-templates element. This element says (because it has no attributes), select all the children of the current node (now the books:books node), find the templates that match them, and instantiate those templates. This is how the rest of the source tree gets processed.

Now let's follow what happens with the xsl:apply-templates element. The books:books element has three children, each of which is a books:book element. So, xsl:apply-templates tries to find a template for each of these children. In this case it's easy, because the children are all the same kind of node and there are only two templates in the stylesheet. The XSLT engine finds the second template, which selects child nodes named books:book. The body of this template contains xsl:apply-templates and an HTML <p> (paragraph) element. Let's put off processing of xsl:apply-templates for a moment, and step back to the books:books template. The result tree now has the HTML skeleton and the result of processing the books:book template (some unknown data and a <p> element) for each of the books:book elements in the source tree. Now we can look at the processing of the xsl:apply-templates element in the books:book template. This is a bit confusing, because you don't have any additional templates in the stylesheet and none of the templates in the stylesheet match.

XSLT defines a built-in template rule for each node type in the XSLT data model. For the root node and element nodes, the built-in rule evaluates xsl:apply-templates for all the children of the current node. The built-in rule for text and attribute nodes copies the value of the text or attribute value into the result tree, while the rule for processing instructions and comments does nothing. So, when xsl:apply-templates for books:book is processed, the built-in rules are used for the children of books:book. The result of applying the stylesheet looks like this:

```
<html
  xmlns:books="http://sauria.com/schemas/apache-xml-book/books">
<head>
```

```
<META
  http-equiv="Content-Type" content="text/html; charset=UTF-8">
<title>Book Inventory</title>
</head>
<body>

   Professional XML Development with Apache Tools
   Theodore W. Leung
   0-7645-4355-5
   December
   2003
   Wrox
   Indianapolis, Indiana
  <p></p>

   Effective Java
   Joshua Bloch
   0-201-31005-8
   August
   2001
   Addison-Wesley
   New York, New York
  <p></p>

   Design Patterns
   Erich Gamma
   Richard Helm
   Ralph Johnson
   John Vlissides
   0-201-63361-2
   October
   1994
   Addison-Wesley
   Reading, Massachusetts
  <p></p>

</body>
</html>
```

You can see how the built-in templates caused the text children of books:book to be copied through unchanged.

Now let's expand the stylesheet to let you control the formatting of the children of books:book. In order to do this, you need to add a bunch of templates. Almost all of these templates select the specific child of books:book that they're supposed to format. The body of the templates includes some HTML elements to do the formatting. They use the xsl:value-of element to insert a value from the source tree into the result tree. In all of these templates, you use a dot (.) (the location path for the current node), but you could use any location path you wanted. The full stylesheet is as follows:

```
<?xml version="1.0" encoding="UTF-8"?>
<xsl:stylesheet version="1.0"
  xmlns:xsl="http://www.w3.org/1999/XSL/Transform"
  xmlns:books="http://sauria.com/schemas/apache-xml-book/books">
```

```
  <xsl:output method="xml" version="1.0" encoding="UTF-8"
      indent="yes"/>
  <xsl:template match="books:books">
    <html>
      <head><title>Book Inventory</title></head>
      <body>
        <xsl:apply-templates/>
      </body>
    </html>
  </xsl:template>
  <xsl:template match="books:book">
     <xsl:apply-templates/>
    <p />
  </xsl:template>
  <xsl:template match="books:title">
    <em><xsl:value-of select="."/></em><br />
  </xsl:template>
  <xsl:template match="books:author">
    <b><xsl:value-of select="."/></b><br />
  </xsl:template>
  <xsl:template match="books:isbn">
    <xsl:value-of select="."/><br />
  </xsl:template>
  <xsl:template match="books:month">
    <xsl:value-of select="."/>,
  </xsl:template>
  <xsl:template match="books:year">
    <xsl:value-of select="."/><br />
  </xsl:template>
  <xsl:template match="books:publisher">
    <xsl:value-of select="."/><br />
  </xsl:template>
  <xsl:template match="books:address">
    <xsl:value-of select="."/><br />
  </xsl:template>
</xsl:stylesheet>
```

Note that this stylesheet handles multiple authors with ease. The third books:book element has four books:author elements, so as xsl:apply-templates is processing the children of that element, it happily matches each of the books:author elements in the source tree and processes each one using the correct template. The fully formatted version looks like this:

```
<?xml version="1.0" encoding="UTF-8"?>
<html
 xmlns:books="http://sauria.com/schemas/apache-xml-book/books">
<head>
<title>Book Inventory</title>
</head>
<body>

   <em>Professional XML Development with Apache Tools</em>
<br/>
   <b>Theodore W. Leung</b>
```

```
<br/>
    0-7645-4355-5<br/>
    December,
    2003<br/>
    Wrox<br/>
    Indianapolis, Indiana<br/>
   <p/>
    <em>Effective Java</em>
<br/>
    <b>Joshua Bloch</b>
<br/>
    0-201-31005-8<br/>
    August,
    2001<br/>
    Addison-Wesley<br/>
    New York, New York<br/>
   <p/>
    <em>Design Patterns</em>
<br/>
    <b>Erich Gamma</b>
<br/>
    <b>Richard Helm</b>
<br/>
    <b>Ralph Johnson</b>
<br/>
    <b>John Vlissides</b>
<br/>
    0-201-63361-2<br/>
    October,
    1994<br/>
    Addison-Wesley<br/>
    Reading, Massachusetts<br/>
   <p/>
</body>
</html>
```

The xsl:apply-template element can have an attribute named select, whose value is a location path. This location path is used to select the nodes that are processed by xsl:apply-templates. Until now, you haven't seen stylesheets that use the select attribute, which means all children of the current node are used. The select attribute gives you more control over what's included in the result tree. The uses of select by xsl:value-of in the previous listing are good pointers to the way you would use select with xsl:apply-templates.

Output

XSLT uses the xsl:output element to control how the result tree is output. The xsl:output element has a number of attributes that control the output process. The most important is the method attribute, which selects the output method to use. XSLT includes three predefined output methods—one for XML, one for HTML, and one for text. The XML and HTML output methods obey the rules for XML and HTML, respectively. The HTML method has more work to do; it doesn't output end tags for certain HTML tags, such as area, br, co, hr, img, and a few others. The text output method only outputs the text nodes of a document (in document order). All other nodes are ignored. The value of the method attribute should be "xml" for XML output, "html" for HTML output, and "text" for text output. The method attribute can also be a QName, in which case the XSLT processor is responsible for supplying an output method.

The XML and HTML output methods escape the & and < characters when they appear in a text node, to ensure that the output document is well-formed XML or HTML. The xsl:value-of and xsl:text (described later) elements can have an attribute named disable-output-escaping, which you can set to "yes" to turn off this escaping.

Creating the Result Tree

XPath and xsl:apply-templates cover a lot of the details of matching parts of the source tree and instantiating templates. You need to flesh out the way the result tree is constructed. In all the examples of xsl:apply-templates that we've shown, we've used literal result elements.

A *literal result element* is an element that doesn't come from either the XSLT namespace or the namespace of any XSLT extension. When literal result elements occur in an xsl:template, they're instantiated to create an element node (with the same name as the literal result element), which is then inserted into the proper place in the result tree. This makes it somewhat natural to specify how the result tree should be built. The literal result elements inside a template can be interspersed with elements from the XSLT namespace, such as xsl:apply-templates or xsl:value-of. You saw examples of this in the previous listing. The literal result element node brings with it any attribute nodes that correspond to attributes defined on the literal result element in the stylesheet. It also brings along any namespace nodes, except those namespace URIs that are the namespace URI of either XSLT itself or a declared XSLT extension.

The uses of literal result elements that you have seen show how to compute the contents of an element from values in the source tree using either xsl:apply-templates or xsl:value-of, but we haven't shown how to do this for attribute values. XSLT uses a mechanism called *attribute value templates* to allow the values of attributes in literal result elements to be computed. To use an attribute value template, you enclose the expression that computes the necessary attribute value in curly braces ({}) inside the value of the attribute. The expression is evaluated and inserted at the point delimited by the curly braces. Here's a template that converts the books:books element to a time element. An attribute value template is used to compute the versionNumber attribute in the result tree from the version attribute in the source tree:

```
<xsl:template match="books:books">
  <tome versionNumber="{@version}"}>
    <xsl:apply-templates/>
  </tome>
</xsl:template>
```

Literal result elements are a mostly static way of specifying the result tree. XSLT also provide elements that allow you to construct any part of the result tree dynamically. To insert a dynamically generated node in the result tree, you place one of the following elements in the template at the point where you want the computed node to appear:

- **<xsl:element>**—Inserts a dynamically created element node. The name attribute is an attribute value template containing the QName to be used for the generated element. The content of xsl:element is itself a template where literal result elements or dynamically created nodes can appear. This template is for the attributes and child of the dynamically created node.

- **<xsl:attribute>**—Inserts a dynamically created attribute node. The name attribute is an attribute value template containing the QName to be used for the generated attribute; it can be specified using an attribute value template. The content of xsl:attribute is a template for the value of the attribute.
- **<xsl:text>**—Inserts a static text node. The content of the text node is the content of xsl:text. See xsl:value-of to dynamically generate text.
- **<xsl:processing-instruction>**—Inserts a dynamically created processing instruction node. The name attribute is an attribute value template that allows you to specify the name of the processing instruction. The content of xsl:processing-instruction is a template for the string value of the processing instruction.
- **<xsl:comment>**—Inserts a dynamically generated comment. The content of xsl:comment is a template for the value of the comment.
- **<xsl:value-of>**—Inserts dynamically generated text node. The text to be inserted is specified by the select attribute, which is an XSLT expression whose result is converted to a string. A text node is not created if the value of the select attribute evaluates to an empty string.
- **<xsl:copy>**—Copies the current node to the result tree, including namespace nodes but excluding attribute nodes and children. The content of xsl:copy is a template for the attributes and children of the node being copied.

XSLT allows you to sort the nodes selected by xsl:apply-templates. Sorting is accomplished by adding any number of xsl:sort elements as children of the xsl:apply-templates whose processing you want sorted. The first xsl:sort element specifies the primary sort key, the second element specifies the secondary sort key, and so on. The data to sort on is specified via the select attribute, which is expected to be an expression. You control sort order with the order attribute, whose value can be "ascending" or "descending". You can also ask for text or numerical sorting with the data-type attribute by specifying "text" or "number" for a value.

Extensions

XSLT provides two mechanisms for using extensions: extension elements and extension functions. XSLT doesn't specify how extensions are implemented, it just tells how they're specified. *Extension elements* are elements in specially designated extension namespaces. You designate extension namespaces by listing their prefixes as the value of either an extension-element prefixes attribute on xsl:stylesheet, or an xsl:extension-element-prefixes attribute on a literal result element or extension element. Both of these attributes are whitespace-separated lists of extension namespace prefixes (note that this means the prefixes need to be declared somewhere in the stylesheet).

Extension functions work a little differently. A function name that contains a colon is assumed to be a call to an extension function. The function name is expanded using the set of namespace declarations in the current context.

This concludes our brief review of XSLT. There are many topics we didn't cover, and we didn't explore any subjects in full detail. But just in case you picked up this book and don't know XSLT, at least you have a fighting chance of making it through the rest of the chapter.

Installing and Configuring Xalan

The first thing you need to do to install Xalan is to get a Xalan build. You can do this by going to http://xml.apache.org/dist/xalan-j/, which presents you with a list of the current Xalan builds. As of Xalan 2.5.1, there are two binary distributions. Let's use the Xalan 2.5.1 build as an example. The single jar distribution is named xalan-j_2_5_1-bin.*xxx*, where *xxx* is either zip or tar.gz depending on the kind of compressed archive format you need. Typically people on Windows use a .zip file, whereas people on MacOS X, Linux, and UNIX of various sorts use a .tar.gz file. There are also .*xxx*.sig files, which are detached PGP signatures of the corresponding .*xxx* file. So, xalan-j_2_5_1-bin.zip.sig contains the signature file for the xalan-j_2_5_1-bin.zip distribution file. You can use PGP and the signature file to verify that the contents of the distribution haven't been tampered with.

The single-jar distribution is called that because it includes all of Xalan (the interpretive processor and the compiled processor [XSLTC]) in single jar file. The two-jar distribution splits the two processors into separate jars: The interpretive processor is in xalan.jar, and the compiled processor is in xsltc.jar. The two-jar distribution is named xalan-j_2_5_1-bin-2jars.*xxx*.

If you want the source code for Xalan, you'll need to get the source code distribution. The source distribution for Xalan 2.5.1 is in xalan-j_2_5_1-src.*xxx*.

We'll focus on installing the binary distribution. Once you've downloaded a binary distribution, you should unpack it using a zip-file utility or tar and gzip for the .tar.gz files. Doing so creates a directory called xalan-j_2_5_1 in either the current directory or the directory you specified to your archiving utility. The key files in this directory are as follows:

- **Keys**—The PGP keys of Xalan committers.
- **License**—A text file containing the ASF license.
- **readme.html**—The jump-off point for the Xalan documentation. Open it with your Web browser.
- **bin**—A directory containing all the jar files for Xalan.
- **docs**—A directory containing the Xalan documentation.
- **samples**—A directory containing the Xalan sample applications.

You must include an XML parser in your Java classpath in order to use Xalan in your application. The standard Xalan distribution contains a copy of Xerces in the bin directory, in the xml-apis.jar and xercesImpl.jar files. If you choose not to use Xerces as your XML parser, you should be sure that the parser is on the Java classpath. In addition to Xerces, you need the Xalan jars or jars, depending on whether you downloaded the one- or two-jar distribution. This also depends on whether you plan to use only one of the Xalan processors or both of them. If you downloaded the one-jar distribution, make sure xalan.jar (which contains both processors) is on the classpath. If you downloaded the two-jar distribution, make sure the jar files for the processor(s) you plan to use are on the classpath. The interpretive processor is in xalan.jar, and the compiled processor is in xsltc.jar. There are a variety of ways to get the necessary jars onto the classpath, including setting the CLASSPATH environment variable in your DOS Command window or UNIX shell window. You can also set the CLASSPATH for the application server you're using.

Another installation option is to make Xalan the default XSLT processor for your JDK installation. This only works for JDK 1.3 and above.

JDK 1.3 introduced an Extension Mechanism for the JDK. It works like this. The JDK installation contains a special extensions directory where you can place jar files that contain extensions to Java. If JAVA_HOME is the directory where your JDK has been installed, then the extensions directory is <JAVA_HOME>\jre\lib\ext using Windows file delimiters or <JAVA_HOME>/jre/lib/ext using UNIX file delimiters.

If you're using JDK 1.4 or above, you need to use the Endorsed Standards Override Mechanism rather than the Extension Mechanism. It works like the Extension Mechanism, but it's specifically designed to allow incremental updates of packages specified by the Java Community Process (JCP). The major operational difference between the Extension Mechanism and the Endorsed Standards Override Mechanism is that the directory name is different. The Windows directory is named <JAVA_HOME>\jre\lib\endorsed, and the UNIX directory is named <JAVA_HOME>/jre/lib/endorsed.

For JDK 1.2 and above, you should ensure that <JAVA_HOME>/lib/tools.jar is on the CLASSPATH as well.

In JDK 1.4 and above, the default XSLT implementation in JAXP is Xalan 2.2D11. If you want to use a later version of Xalan, the safest thing to do is to copy xml-apis.jar, xercesImpl.jar, and xalan.jar/xsltc.jar into the endorsed standards directory.

Development Techniques

Now we'll discuss how you can use various aspects of Xalan to add XSLT processing to your application. We'll look at using the JAXP TrAX API, Xalan's own API, and the XSLTC XSLT compiler built into Xalan. We'll also cover the use of Xalan-specific XSLT extensions.

TrAX

The TrAX API is specified by the JCP as part of the Java APIs for XML processing, under JSR 63. The main abstraction we'll be using from TrAX is the *transformer*, which provides an abstraction of an XSLT processing engine. Transformers are created from a source that provides the stylesheet for the transformation. Once a transformer has been created, you can use the transform method to supply a source containing the XML to be transformed and a result that specifies the destination for the transformed XML.

Transformers are obtained via a TransformerFactory:

```
/*
 *
 * SimpleTransformerMain.java
 *
 * Example from "Professional XML Development with Apache Tools"
 *
 */
package com.sauria.apachexml.ch2;
```

```
 9:
10: import java.io.FileNotFoundException;
11: import java.io.FileOutputStream;
12:
13: import javax.xml.transform.Transformer;
14: import javax.xml.transform.TransformerConfigurationException;
15: import javax.xml.transform.TransformerException;
16: import javax.xml.transform.TransformerFactory;
17: import javax.xml.transform.stream.StreamResult;
18: import javax.xml.transform.stream.StreamSource;
19:
20: public class SimpleTransformerMain {
21:
22:     public static void main(String[] args) {
23:         TransformerFactory xFactory =
24:             TransformerFactory.newInstance();
```

A number of classes implement the Source interface. StreamSource provide a source that's derived from Java Readers or InputStreams:

```
25:         StreamSource stylesheet = new StreamSource(args[1]);
```

A transformer embodies a particular transformation (stylesheet), so it's created from a source that contains the stylesheet:

```
26:         Transformer xformer = null;
27:         try {
28:             xformer = xFactory.newTransformer(stylesheet);
```

You create a second source containing the XML to be transformed (line 32) and then create a result for the transformed XML (lines 33-39). StreamResults output their data to a Java Writer or OutputStream:

```
29:         } catch (TransformerConfigurationException tfce) {
30:             tfce.printStackTrace();
31:         }
32:         StreamSource input = new StreamSource(args[0]);
33:         StreamResult output = null;
34:         try {
35:             output =
36:                 new StreamResult(new FileOutputStream(args[2]));
37:         } catch (FileNotFoundException fnfe) {
38:             fnfe.printStackTrace();
39:         }
```

Calling the transform method transforms the input:

```
40:         try {
41:             xformer.transform(input, output);
42:         } catch (TransformerException xfe) {
43:             xfe.printStackTrace();
44:         }
45:     }
46: }
```

SAX

Xalan supports both SAX and DOM versions of the TrAX APIs. This means sources and results can be SAX event streams or DOM trees, which makes it easy to add XSLT transformation capability to your existing XML applications. You select the source and result types you need and then hook the transformer into the application. Let's look at a SAX-based version of the simple transformer program. You want a SAX-based transformation that accepts a SAX event stream for the input XML and outputs a SAX event stream for its result:

```
/*
 *
 * SAXTransformerMain.java
 *
 * Example from "Professional XML Development with Apache Tools"
 *
 */
package com.sauria.apachexml.ch2;

import java.io.FileNotFoundException;
import java.io.FileOutputStream;
import java.io.IOException;

import javax.xml.parsers.ParserConfigurationException;
import javax.xml.parsers.SAXParserFactory;
import javax.xml.transform.TransformerConfigurationException;
import javax.xml.transform.TransformerFactory;
import javax.xml.transform.sax.SAXResult;
import javax.xml.transform.sax.SAXSource;
import javax.xml.transform.sax.SAXTransformerFactory;
import javax.xml.transform.sax.TransformerHandler;
import javax.xml.transform.stream.StreamResult;
import javax.xml.transform.stream.StreamSource;

import org.xml.sax.InputSource;
import org.xml.sax.SAXException;
import org.xml.sax.XMLFilter;
import org.xml.sax.XMLReader;

public class SAXTransformerMain {

    public static void main(String[] args) {
        String input = args[0];
        String stylesheet = args[1];
        String output = args[2];

        SAXParserFactory pFactory =
            SAXParserFactory.newInstance();
        pFactory.setNamespaceAware(true);
        XMLReader r = null;

        try {
            r = pFactory.newSAXParser().getXMLReader();
        } catch (SAXException se) {
            se.printStackTrace();
```

```
46:         } catch (ParserConfigurationException pce) {
47:             pce.printStackTrace();
48:         }
```

In lines 37-48, you set up a SAX parser that provides a SAX event stream as the source for the XML you'll be transforming.

As before, you create an instance of TransformerFactory so that you can create transformers:

```
49:
50:         TransformerFactory xFactory =
51:             TransformerFactory.newInstance();
```

This time, you need to check to make sure the TransformerFactory supports using SAX both as a source and as a result. You do this by calling the getFeature method on the TransformerFactory and testing for SAXSource.FEATURE and SAXResult.FEATURE, respectively. Once you've tested for SAX compatibilty, you can downcast the TransformerFactory to a SAXTransformerFactory, which has the SAX related factory methods you need:

```
52:
53:         if (xFactory.getFeature(SAXSource.FEATURE) &&
54:             xFactory.getFeature(SAXResult.FEATURE)) {
55:             SAXTransformerFactory sxFactory =
56:                 (SAXTransformerFactory) xFactory;
57:
```

The SAX API has an interface that matches the goals for the transformation engine: XMLFilter. XMLFilter takes a SAX event stream as input (via its parent) and produces a SAX event stream as output (by calling methods on a ContentHandler, and so on). The SAXTransformerFactory has additional factory methods for constructing a transformation engine that can be used as an XMLFilter. It also has factory methods for creating a transformation engine that's only a consumer of a SAX event stream—this engine is a TransformationHandler. You'll use both of them in this example.

Calling SAXTransformer's newXMLFilter method creates the XMLFilter tFilter:

```
58:             XMLFilter tFilter = null;
59:             try {
60:                 StreamSource stylesheetSource =
61:                     new StreamSource(stylesheet);
62:                 tFilter =
63:                     sxFactory.newXMLFilter(stylesheetSource);
64:             } catch (TransformerConfigurationException tce) {
65:                 tce.printStackTrace();
66:             }
67:             tFilter.setParent(r);
```

This method takes a source containing the stylesheet as its argument. (We're using a StreamSource as a convenient way to get the stylesheet. In a later example, we'll show how to get the stylesheet using SAX.) After creating the filter, you need to set its parent, which is the XMLReader providing the input event stream. In this case, the SAX parser you created earlier is the parent.

You now have the head and body of a SAX-based XSLT pipeline. All you need now is the tail or output stage. TrAX allows you to create identity transformers—that is, transformers that copy the source to the result. They don't do any transformation (and hence have no stylesheet associated with them). Identity transformations are useful for a number of tasks, such as converting a SAX source to a DOM result and all the permutations of source and result types. You'll use an identity transform to copy a SAX event stream to a StreamResult, serializing from SAX to an output file:

```

            TransformerHandler serializer = null;
            try {
                serializer = sxFactory.newTransformerHandler();
```

Because you're working with SAX events, you want a TransformerHandler that implements an identity transform. This is easily obtained by calling the no-argument version of newTransformerHandler. You then create a StreamResult that contains a FileOutputStream and supply this as the result for the TransformerHandler:

```
                FileOutputStream fos =
                    new FileOutputStream(output);
                StreamResult result =
                    new StreamResult(fos);
                serializer.setResult(result);
            } catch (TransformerConfigurationException tce) {
                tce.printStackTrace();
            } catch (IllegalArgumentException iae) {
                iae.printStackTrace();
            } catch (FileNotFoundException fnfe) {
                fnfe.printStackTrace();
            }
```

All that's left to do is connect the serializer as the tail of the SAX pipeline by setting the filter's ContentHandler to be the serializer:

```
            tFilter.setContentHandler(serializer);

            try {
                r.parse(new InputSource(input));
            } catch (IOException ioe) {
                ioe.printStackTrace();
            } catch (SAXException se) {
                se.printStackTrace();
            }
        }
    }
}
```

Performing the transformation is as simple as telling the head of the pipeline to start parsing an input document.

DOM

As you can see, the SAX version of the program is a significant departure because of the need to fit XSLT into the SAX event-processing model. That's where all the extra interfaces came from. The DOM version of the program is much more similar to the original version:

```
/*
 *
 * DOMTransformerMain.java
 *
 * Example from "Professional XML Development with Apache Tools"
 *
 */
package com.sauria.apachexml.ch2;

import java.io.FileNotFoundException;
import java.io.FileOutputStream;
import java.io.IOException;

import javax.xml.parsers.DocumentBuilder;
import javax.xml.parsers.DocumentBuilderFactory;
import javax.xml.parsers.ParserConfigurationException;
import javax.xml.transform.Transformer;
import javax.xml.transform.TransformerConfigurationException;
import javax.xml.transform.TransformerException;
import javax.xml.transform.TransformerFactory;
import javax.xml.transform.dom.DOMResult;
import javax.xml.transform.dom.DOMSource;
import javax.xml.transform.stream.StreamResult;
import javax.xml.transform.stream.StreamSource;

import org.w3c.dom.Document;
import org.xml.sax.SAXException;

public class DOMTransformerMain {

    public static void main(String[] args) {
        String input = args[0];
        String stylesheet = args[1];
        String output = args[2];

        DocumentBuilderFactory bFactory =
            DocumentBuilderFactory.newInstance();
        bFactory.setNamespaceAware(true);
        DocumentBuilder builder = null;

        try {
            builder = bFactory.newDocumentBuilder();
        } catch (ParserConfigurationException pce) {
            pce.printStackTrace();
        }

        Document inputDoc = null;

        try {
            inputDoc = builder.parse(input);
        } catch (SAXException se) {
            se.printStackTrace();
        } catch (IOException ioe) {
            ioe.printStackTrace();
        }
```

To build a DOM-based version of the program, you need to create a DOM tree that can be used as input to the transformation engine. In lines 36-55, you create a DOM tree by using the JAXP DocumentBuilder class to create a document that will be the input to the transformation engine.

Just as in the SAX case, you need to ask the TransformerFactory whether it supports DOM trees as sources and results:

```
56:
57:         TransformerFactory xFactory =
58:             TransformerFactory.newInstance();
59:
60:         if (xFactory.getFeature(DOMSource.FEATURE) &&
61:             xFactory.getFeature(DOMResult.FEATURE)) {
```

The transformer is created using a stylesheet obtained via a StreamSource:

```
62:             Transformer xformer = null;
63:             try {
64:                 StreamSource stylesheetSource =
65:                     new StreamSource(stylesheet);
66:                 xformer =
67:                     xFactory.newTransformer(stylesheetSource);
68:             } catch (TransformerConfigurationException tce) {
69:                 tce.printStackTrace();
70:             }
```

To prepare the DOM tree for use as the source to the transformer, you need to take the extra step of setting the system ID of the DOMSource. Doing so allows any URIs in the DOM document to be resolved. The output of the transformation is also a DOM tree:

```
71:             DOMSource inputSource = new DOMSource(inputDoc);
72:             inputSource.setSystemId(input);
```

The transformer doesn't know how to create a DOM tree, so you need to get a new DocumentBuilder and use it to create an empty Document node that the transformer can use for output (lines 74-80). This empty Document node is wrapped in a DOMResult so you can pass it to the transformer (line 81). Now you can call the transform method to obtain the transformed XML as a DOM tree (lines 82-87):

```
73:
74:             builder = null;
75:             try {
76:                 builder = bFactory.newDocumentBuilder();
77:             } catch (ParserConfigurationException pce) {
78:                 pce.printStackTrace();
79:             }
80:             Document outputDoc = builder.newDocument();
81:             DOMResult outputResult = new DOMResult(outputDoc);
82:             try {
83:                 xformer.transform(inputSource, outputResult);
84:             } catch (TransformerException te) {
85:                 te.printStackTrace();
86:             }
87:
```

Once again you use an identity transformer to serialize the output DOM tree into a file, so you create an identity transformer:

```
            Transformer serializer = null;
            try {
                serializer = xFactory.newTransformer();
            } catch (TransformerConfigurationException tce) {
                tce.printStackTrace();
            }
```

The nice thing about using the DOM is that you can take the output DOM tree and wrap it as a source for input to the serializer. In SAX you had to create a TransformerHandler and hook up the event pipeline. Here you just wrap the output tree (lines 95-96), create a StreamResult around a FileOutputStream (lines 97-99), and execute the identity transformation (line 100):

```
 94:             try {
 95:                 DOMSource outputSource =
 96:                     new DOMSource(outputDoc);
 97:                 FileOutputStream fos =
 98:                     new FileOutputStream(output);
 99:                 StreamResult result = new StreamResult(fos);
100:                 serializer.transform(outputSource, result);
101:             } catch (FileNotFoundException fnfe) {
102:                 fnfe.printStackTrace();
103:             } catch (TransformerException te) {
104:                 te.printStackTrace();
105:             }
106:         }
107:     }
108: }
```

Mix and Match

In the last TrAX example, we'll show how you can use both SAX and DOM sources as inputs to a transformer. You'll take the SAX example and modify it so that the stylesheet is provided via a DOM tree. You may wonder why you'd ever want to do such a thing. Here's a scenario. You're building a system that will transform XML documents received via a network connection. The fact that the documents are coming over a network connection means you probably want to use SAX, so you get all the benefits of the streaming model. The stylesheet for these documents is generated automatically by a program that takes a DOM tree representation of a stylesheet template and customizes the stylesheet before it's used. The DOM is a good representation to use when you're modifying an XML document. This is the scenario the example shows (we'll only comment on the changes from the original SAX example):

```
/*
 *
 * SAXDOMTransformerMain.java
 *
 * Example from "Professional XML Development with Apache Tools"
 *
 */
package com.sauria.apachexml.ch2;

```

```
import java.io.FileNotFoundException;
import java.io.FileOutputStream;
import java.io.IOException;

import javax.xml.parsers.DocumentBuilder;
import javax.xml.parsers.DocumentBuilderFactory;
import javax.xml.parsers.ParserConfigurationException;
import javax.xml.parsers.SAXParserFactory;
import javax.xml.transform.TransformerConfigurationException;
import javax.xml.transform.TransformerFactory;
import javax.xml.transform.dom.DOMSource;
import javax.xml.transform.sax.SAXResult;
import javax.xml.transform.sax.SAXSource;
import javax.xml.transform.sax.SAXTransformerFactory;
import javax.xml.transform.sax.TransformerHandler;
import javax.xml.transform.stream.StreamResult;

import org.w3c.dom.Document;
import org.xml.sax.InputSource;
import org.xml.sax.SAXException;
import org.xml.sax.XMLFilter;
import org.xml.sax.XMLReader;

public class SAXDOMTransformerMain {

    public static void main(String[] args) {
        String input = args[0];
        String stylesheet = args[1];
        String output = args[2];

        SAXParserFactory pFactory =
            SAXParserFactory.newInstance();
        pFactory.setNamespaceAware(true);
        XMLReader r = null;

        try {
            r = pFactory.newSAXParser().getXMLReader();
        } catch (SAXException se) {
            se.printStackTrace();
        } catch (ParserConfigurationException pce) {
            pce.printStackTrace();
        }

        TransformerFactory xFactory =
            TransformerFactory.newInstance();

        if (xFactory.getFeature(SAXSource.FEATURE) &&
            xFactory.getFeature(SAXResult.FEATURE)) {
            SAXTransformerFactory sxFactory =
                (SAXTransformerFactory) xFactory;

```

Here's where the changes are. You need to create a DOM tree that contains the stylesheet, so you get a DocumentBuilder via DocumentBuilderFactory:

```
        DocumentBuilderFactory bFactory =
            DocumentBuilderFactory.newInstance();
        bFactory.setNamespaceAware(true);
        DocumentBuilder builder = null;

        try {
            builder = bFactory.newDocumentBuilder();
        } catch (ParserConfigurationException pce) {
            pce.printStackTrace();
        }

        Document stylesheetDoc = null;

        try {
            stylesheetDoc = builder.parse(stylesheet);
```

Now you parse the stylesheet into a DOM tree. If you were going to do updates to the DOM representation of the stylesheet, you'd do so right here:

```
        } catch (SAXException se) {
            se.printStackTrace();
        } catch (IOException ioe) {
            ioe.printStackTrace();
        }

        XMLFilter tFilter = null;
        try {
```

Once you have the DOM form of the stylesheet fully computed, you wrap it in a DOMSource and create a transformation (in this case, an XMLFilter) that uses it as the stylesheet:

```
            DOMSource stylesheetSource =
                new DOMSource(stylesheetDoc);
            stylesheetSource.setSystemId(stylesheet);
            tFilter =
                sxFactory.newXMLFilter(stylesheetSource);
        } catch (TransformerConfigurationException tce) {
            tce.printStackTrace();
        }
        tFilter.setParent(r);

        TransformerHandler serializer = null;
        try {
            serializer = sxFactory.newTransformerHandler();
            FileOutputStream fos =
                new FileOutputStream(output);
            StreamResult result =
                new StreamResult(fos);
            serializer.setResult(result);
        } catch (TransformerConfigurationException tce) {
            tce.printStackTrace();
        } catch (IllegalArgumentException iae) {
            iae.printStackTrace();
        } catch (FileNotFoundException fnfe) {
```

```
                fnfe.printStackTrace();
            }
            tFilter.setContentHandler(serializer);

            try {
                tFilter.parse(new InputSource(input));
            } catch (IOException ioe) {
                ioe.printStackTrace();
            } catch (SAXException se) {
                se.printStackTrace();
            }
        }
    }
}
```

Xalan Features

In addition to the JAXP-defined features like DOMSource.FEATURE, Xalan defines some features that only work when Xalan is the engine powering JAXP (remember that from JDK 1.4 forward, Xalan is the default XSLT engine for the JDK). These features are related to the Xalan Document Table Model (DTM).

The processing model for XSLT is defined in terms of selecting portions of trees and instantiating result elements into the result tree. Processing the document and the stylesheet both involve a lot of tree traversal operations. In order to improve the performance and memory usage of these trees, the Xalan developers created the DTM. The DTM is a non-object-oriented model of a document tree. Instead of creating objects for all the nodes in the document trees, the DTM identifies nodes via an integer handle. Integer handles are also defined and used for URIs, local names, and expanded names. The text content of nodes is left in a large string buffer and referenced by offset and length. The DTM provides a read API that looks somewhat like the DOM API, but with all node and string references replaced by integer handles. In areas where the DOM API was not a good fit for the XPath data model, the semantics of the XPath data model won out. In most cases, you won't work with the DTM directly. If you're writing your own extensions, you'll talk to the DTM via a set of proxy classes that make the DTM look like the W3C DOM.

The other benefit of the DTM is that it can be constructed incrementally. As a result, Xalan can begin to perform transformations even though the entire tree for the input document has not been constructed. This works best when Xerces is being used as the XML parser. Incremental construction is still possible with a parser besides Xerces, but it involves multithreading inside Xalan to make it work.

Now that you have a general idea of what the DTM is, let's turn back to those Xalan-specific features. You set them by calling the setAttribute method on a TransformerFactory instance. Unlike SAX features, they're booleans—this means you need to use the constants defined by the Boolean class (Boolean.TRUE and Boolean.FALSE) as values for the attributes.

The first attribute is identified by the constant TransformerFactoryImpl.FEATURE_OPTIMIZE, which is set to true by default. When the optimize feature is on, Xalan performs structural rewrites on the stylesheet in order to improve transformation performance. This is generally a good thing. However, if you're building an XSLT tool of some kind (say, an editor or debugger or something that needs direct access to the stylesheet structure), then you should set this attribute to false. Otherwise your tool will access the rewritten stylesheet, which could cause confusion for your users.

The second attribute is attached to the constant TransformerFactoryImpl.FEATURE_INCREMENTAL and controls whether transformations are performed incrementally. By default, transforms aren't done incrementally, which means stylesheet parsing and transformation are performed in the same thread. When this feature is set to true, transformation is performed incrementally. This is implemented in one of two ways depending on the XML parser in use. If Xerces is the XML parser, then Xalan uses Xerces' native pull parsing API to overlap parsing and transformation. Otherwise, Xalan creates a second thread and runs the XML parser in the second thread. Xalan takes care of multiplexing between its thread and the parsing thread. If you want to use this capability, we suggest that you use Xerces as your parser.

Xalan Specific Features

One of the most useful debugging tools in Xalan is the command-line interface to Xalan. To use this interface, you need a shell window that has the classpath properly set up for Xalan as described earlier in the chapter. One the classpath is correctly set, you can type the following:

```
java org.apache.xalan.xslt.Process –in <input file>
                                   -xsl <stylesheet>
                                   -out <output file>
                                   <flags>
```

This command transforms the input file using the stylesheet and leaves the results in the output file. You can also supply some additional flags:

Flag	Meaning
-v	Display the version number.
-xml	Use an XML formatter on output.
-html	Use an HTML formatter on output.
-TT	Trace template execution.
-TG	Trace generation events.
-TS	Trace selection events.

You should definitely use the -html flag if your output is HTML. The three trace flags (-TT, -TG, and -TS) can help you debug a stylesheet that isn't working the way you think it should. -TT will help you see the order in which templates are being applied, -TS shows what is actually being selected by various location paths, and -TG shows what's being inserted in to the result tree.

XPath API

You can also use Xalan as an XPath library so that you can retrieve pieces of documents using XPath expressions. Xalan originally implemented its own XPath API. Recently the W3C's DOM working group has produced an API for accessing a DOM tree via XPath. At the time of this writing, the DOM XPath API is a Candidate Recommendation.

Let's look at a program that uses the DOM XPath API to select a subtree of a DOM using XPath:

```
/*
 *
 * XPathMain.java
 *
 * Example from "Professional XML Development with Apache Tools"
 *
 */
package com.sauria.apachexml.ch2;

import java.io.IOException;

import javax.xml.parsers.DocumentBuilder;
import javax.xml.parsers.DocumentBuilderFactory;
import javax.xml.parsers.ParserConfigurationException;

import org.apache.xpath.domapi.XPathEvaluatorImpl;
import org.w3c.dom.Document;
import org.w3c.dom.Node;
import org.w3c.dom.xpath.XPathEvaluator;
import org.w3c.dom.xpath.XPathNSResolver;
import org.w3c.dom.xpath.XPathResult;
import org.xml.sax.SAXException;


public class XPathMain {

    public static void main(String[] args) {
        String input = args[0];
        String xpath = args[1];
        DocumentBuilderFactory bFactory =
            DocumentBuilderFactory.newInstance();
        bFactory.setNamespaceAware(true);
        DocumentBuilder builder = null;
        try {
            builder = bFactory.newDocumentBuilder();
        } catch (ParserConfigurationException pce) {
            pce.printStackTrace();
        }
        Document doc = null;
        try {
            doc = builder.parse(input);
        } catch (SAXException se) {
            se.printStackTrace();
        } catch (IOException ioe) {
            ioe.printStackTrace();
        }

```

Everything up to this point should be familiar. You're using JAXP to create the DOM tree you want to query using XPath.

Next you create an XPathEvaluator for the DOM tree using Xalan's XPathEvaluatorImpl. You also create an XPathNSResolver (more about that after we finish discussing the program):

```
        XPathEvaluator xpathEngine = new XPathEvaluatorImpl(doc);
        XPathNSResolver resolver =
            xpathEngine.createNSResolver(doc);
```

Once you have the XPathEvaluator, you call its evaluate method, passing it an XPath (in String form), the DOM tree, the XPathNSResolver, a constant telling what the result type should be, and a result node to be filled in. If the result node is null, as is the case in this example, then the XPathEvaluator should create a new node:

```
        XPathResult result = (XPathResult)
            xpathEngine.evaluate(xpath,
                                 doc,
                                 resolver,
                                 XPathResult.ANY_TYPE,
                                 null);
```

XPathResult provides a variety of methods to access the result, depending on what the actual result is. Here you're counting on the result to be a node iterator. If you supply the right input file and XPath, that will be true, but you'd want to do much more error checking in a real application. You ask for the first node from the iterator and print it out as long as it's not null:

```
        Node n = result.iterateNext();
        if (n != null) {
            System.out.println(n);
        }
    }
}
```

We need to expand on two details from the example. The first is the type of XPathResult. In the following table, an iterator produces nodes one at a time. If the document is modified during the iteration, the iteration becomes invalid. A snapshot is a list accessed by index position. Modifying the document won't invalidate the snapshot, but reevaluating the XPath may yield a different snapshot.

XPathResult Constant Field	XPathResult Accessor Method	Description
ANY_TYPE	Any + getNumberValue()	Any XPath result type.
ANY_UNORDERED_NODE_TYPE	getSingleNodeValue()	A node set accessed as a single node.
BOOLEAN_TYPE	getBooleanValue()	A boolean value.
FIRST_ORDERED_NODE_TYPE	getSingleNodeValue()	A node set accessed as a single node.
ORDERED_NODE_ITERATOR_TYPE	iterateNext()	An iterator that produces nodes in document order.

XPathResult Constant Field	XPathResult Accessor Method	Description
ORDERED_NODE_SNAPSHOT_TYPE	snapshotItem(int i)	A snapshot list of nodes in document order.
STRING_TYPE	getStringValue	A String value.
UNORDERED_NODE_ITERATOR_TYPE	iterateNext()	An iterator that produces nodes in no particular order.
UNORDERED_NODE_SNAPSHOT_TYPE	snapshotItem(int i)	A snapshot list of nodes in no particular order.

We also need to explain the role of XPathNSResolver. Here's the problem that XPathNSResolver solves. Assume you have a document that uses namespaces, such as the document in this chapter's first code listing. If you write an XPath expression over such a document, which namespace prefix should you use in the XPath expression in order to correctly match the elements in the document? XPathNSResolver maps namespace prefixes to namespace URIs. The implementation of XPathNSResolver supplied by Xalan's XPathEvaluatorImpl builds mappings for the prefixes that appear in the node used to create the XPathEvaluatorImpl. This allows you to use the prefixes that are defined in the input document. You may be in a situation where you process many documents that all use the same namespace (that is, they all use the same namespace URI) but that use different prefixes for the namespace. In this case, your XPath expressions will all fail to select any portion of the tree, because the prefixes in the documents will all be different, and therefore some won't match the prefix you're using in your XPath. You can solve this problem by providing your own implementation of the XPathNSResolver interface that provides a mapping from a namespace prefix of your choosing to the namespace URI being used by all the documents.

Xalan Applet Wrapper

One arena where XSLT can be useful is in a Java applet inside a Web browser. This approach uses the computing power of the machine running the browser instead of using up precious CPU cycles on the server machine. The Xalan developers have made it easy to use Xalan in an applet context by providing an applet that wraps Xalan. The wrapper is the class org.apache.xalan.client.XSLTProcessorApplet, and it's ready to be used in an HTML <applet> tag. XSLTProcessorApplet has three methods you need to know about:

Method	Purpose
setDocumentURL(String)	Specifies the URL of the document to be transformed.
setStyleURL(String)	Specifies the URL of the stylesheet to be used in the transformation.
getHtmlText()	Assuming the document and stylesheet URLs have been set, performs the transformation and returns the result as a String.

You can specify the input document and stylesheet using the setXXXURL methods, or you can specify them as <param> tags in the <applet> tag. Here's a simple HTML page that uses the XSLTProcessorApplet to transform the books database and render the HTML in the browser:

```
<html>
<head></head>
<body>
<applet
    name="xslapplet"\
```

JavaScript uses the name in the applet tag to help identify the applet so you can call methods on it.

You need to provide the paths to the jar files that the applet uses:

```
    code="org.apache.xalan.client.XSLTProcessorApplet.class"
    archive="bin/xalan.jar,bin/xml-apis.jar,bin/xercesImpl.jar "
    height="0"
    width"0">
```

Use the param tag method to specify the documentURL and styleURL:

```
    <param name="documentURL" value="books.xml"/>
    <param name="styleURL" value="books.xslt"/>
</applet>
<script language="JavaScript">
  document.write(document.xslapplet.getHtmlText())
</script>
</body>
```

Here you call the applet's getHtmlText method (the document and style URLs have already been set in the <param> tags) and then write the result into the document. If you used the setDocumentURL and setStyleURL methods to set the document and style URLs, then there would be additional JavaScript calls against document.xslapplet.

Debugging Xalan Problems

In this section we'll look at a few techniques for tracking down problems in applications that are using Xalan. We'll focus on three areas: making sure the Xalan configuration is correct (this is mostly the classpath), obtaining the position of transformation failures, and tracing the behavior of an embedded Xalan transformation engine.

The following program is an extended version of the simplest program that uses a Xalan transformer. We've modified the program to use Xalan's EnvironmentCheck class to confirm that the Xalan environment is correctly set up. The program also shows how to install a custom TraceListener that traces the execution of the transformation:

```
/*
 *
 * DebugMain.java
 *
 * Example from "Professional XML Development with Apache Tools"
 *
 */
package com.sauria.apachexml.ch2;

```

```
10: import java.io.FileNotFoundException;
11: import java.io.FileOutputStream;
12: import java.io.PrintWriter;
13: import java.io.StringWriter;
14: import java.util.TooManyListenersException;
15:
16: import javax.xml.transform.SourceLocator;
17: import javax.xml.transform.Transformer;
18: import javax.xml.transform.TransformerConfigurationException;
19: import javax.xml.transform.TransformerException;
20: import javax.xml.transform.TransformerFactory;
21: import javax.xml.transform.stream.StreamResult;
22: import javax.xml.transform.stream.StreamSource;
23:
24: import org.apache.log4j.BasicConfigurator;
25: import org.apache.log4j.Logger;
26: import org.apache.xalan.trace.TraceListener;
27: import org.apache.xalan.trace.TraceManager;
28: import org.apache.xalan.transformer.TransformerImpl;
29: import org.apache.xalan.xslt.EnvironmentCheck;
30:
31: public class DebugMain {
32:
33:     public static void main(String[] args) {
34:         BasicConfigurator.configure();
35:         Logger log = Logger.getLogger(DebugMain.class);
```

Lines 34-35 set up log4j, which you use to capture diagnostic output.

This is the beginning of the environment checking code. The Xalan EnvironmentCheck class has a method called checkEnvironment that dumps a status report on the environment to a PrintWriter in addition to returning a boolean that tells whether the environment is okay. You don't want this output to show up unless you need it, so you create the PrintWriter from a StringWriter. That way you capture the output and can display it if the configuration isn't right:

```
36:
37:         StringWriter sw = new StringWriter();
38:         PrintWriter pw = new PrintWriter(sw);
```

Lines 39-44 call checkEnvironment and log the environment status if the environment isn't okay:

```
39:         boolean environmentOK =
40:             (new EnvironmentCheck()).checkEnvironment(pw);
41:         if (!environmentOK) {
42:             log.error(sw);
43:             System.exit(1);
44:         }
45:
46:         TransformerFactory xFactory =
47:             TransformerFactory.newInstance();
48:         StreamSource stylesheet = new StreamSource(args[1]);
49:         Transformer xformer = null;
50:         try {
51:             xformer = xFactory.newTransformer(stylesheet);
```

Xalan provides the TraceListener interface as an aid to debugging embedded Xalan processors and as an entry point for people building XSLT tools based on Xalan. Each Xalan transformer has a TraceManager that takes care of monitoring the various events that occur as Xalan is transforming a document. You can register your own implementation of the TraceListener interface with the TraceManager to get debugging information about that Transformer instance.

The TraceListener facility isn't a part of the TrAX API, so first you check that the transformer is an instance of the Xalan implementation class and then downcast the transformer so you can access the TraceManager. Once you have the trace manager, you can create an instance of LoggingTraceListener, your custom TraceListener, and register it. We'll look at the implementation of LoggingTraceListener next. The rest of the code should be familiar.

Here you see how to use the SourceLocator interface to get information about the position of a transformation failure. The key is that you can only obtain a SourceLocator from a TransformerException. Once you have the SourceLocator, you can use it to get the SystemID, line number, and column number of the failure. Note that this information isn't always exact, but something is always better than nothing:

```
            if (xformer instanceof TransformerImpl) {
                TransformerImpl xformerImpl =
                    (TransformerImpl) xformer;
                TraceManager tMgr =
                    xformerImpl.getTraceManager();
                TraceListener logListener =
                    new LoggingTraceListener();
                tMgr.addTraceListener(logListener);
            }
        } catch (TransformerConfigurationException tfce) {
            tfce.printStackTrace();
        } catch (TooManyListenersException tmle) {
            tmle.printStackTrace();
        }
        StreamSource input = new StreamSource(args[0]);
        StreamResult output = null;
        try {
            output =
                new StreamResult(new FileOutputStream(args[2]));
        } catch (FileNotFoundException fnfe) {
            fnfe.printStackTrace();
        }
        try {
            xformer.transform(input, output);
        } catch (TransformerException xfe) {
            SourceLocator locator = xfe.getLocator();
            log.error("Transformer Exception at "+
                      locator.getSystemId()+" "+
                      locator.getLineNumber()+":"+
                      locator.getColumnNumber());
            log.error(xfe);
            xfe.printStackTrace();
        }
    }
}
```

The TraceListener interface provides a set of callbacks that are fired when Xalan performs specific actions. The callbacks are grouped around three kinds of events: TracerEvents, which are fired when a source node is matched; SelectionEvents, which are fired when a node is selected in the stylesheet tree; and GenerateEvents, which are fired when a node is generated in the result tree. You've probably noticed that these classes of events correspond to the tracing flags for the command-line interface to Xalan. This isn't a coincidence; those tracing flags are implemented via a TraceListener .LoggingTraceListener (shown in the next listing) provides a similar kind of capability, but instead of printing the tracing output to the console, it uses log4j to log important data from each event.

```
/*
 *
 * LoggingTraceListener.java
 *
 * Example from "Professional XML Development with Apache Tools"
 *
 */
package com.sauria.apachexml.ch2;

import javax.xml.transform.TransformerException;

import org.apache.log4j.Logger;
import org.apache.xalan.templates.Constants;
import org.apache.xalan.templates.ElemTemplate;
import org.apache.xalan.templates.ElemTemplateElement;
import org.apache.xalan.templates.ElemTextLiteral;
import org.apache.xalan.trace.GenerateEvent;
import org.apache.xalan.trace.SelectionEvent;
import org.apache.xalan.trace.TraceListener;
import org.apache.xalan.trace.TracerEvent;
import org.apache.xml.serializer.SerializerTrace;
import org.w3c.dom.Node;

public class LoggingTraceListener implements TraceListener {
    Logger log = Logger.getLogger(LoggingTraceListener.class);
```

In good log4j style, you obtain a logger specifically for this class so that you can turn logging on and off conveniently. In an alternate implementation, you could have three loggers, once for each event type, so that the log4j configuration could control each channel independently. In each event callback, you use a StringBuffer to build up the output that will be logged.

The logging code for GenerateEvents is straightforward; it's a switch on the various event type constants that can be present in a GenerateEvent. The GenerateEvent types are modelled after SAX's event callbacks:

```
    public void generated(GenerateEvent ge) {
        StringBuffer sb = new StringBuffer();
        String chars = null;
        switch (ge.m_eventtype) {
            case SerializerTrace.EVENTTYPE_STARTDOCUMENT :
                sb.append("STARTDOCUMENT");
                break;
```

```
34:             case SerializerTrace.EVENTTYPE_ENDDOCUMENT :
35:                 sb.append("ENDDOCUMENT");
36:                 break;
37:             case SerializerTrace.EVENTTYPE_STARTELEMENT :
38:                 sb.append("STARTELEMENT: " + ge.m_name);
39:                 break;
40:             case SerializerTrace.EVENTTYPE_ENDELEMENT :
41:                 sb.append("ENDELEMENT: " + ge.m_name);
42:                 break;
43:             case SerializerTrace.EVENTTYPE_CHARACTERS :
44:                 chars = new String(ge.m_characters, ge.m_start,
45:                                    ge.m_length);
46:                 sb.append("CHARACTERS: " + chars);
47:                 break;
48:             case SerializerTrace.EVENTTYPE_CDATA :
49:                 chars =
50:                     new String(ge.m_characters, ge.m_start,
51:                                ge.m_length);
52:                 sb.append("CDATA: " + chars);
53:                 break;
54:             case SerializerTrace.EVENTTYPE_COMMENT :
55:                 sb.append("COMMENT: " + ge.m_data);
56:                 break;
57:             case SerializerTrace.EVENTTYPE_PI :
58:                 sb.append("PI: " + ge.m_name + ", " + ge.m_data);
59:                 break;
60:             case SerializerTrace.EVENTTYPE_ENTITYREF :
61:                 sb.append("ENTITYREF: " + ge.m_name);
62:                 break;
63:             case SerializerTrace.EVENTTYPE_IGNORABLEWHITESPACE :
64:                 sb.append("IGNORABLEWHITESPACE");
65:                 break;
66:         }
67:         log.debug("Generating: " + sb);
68:     }
69:
```

For SelectionEvents, you want to know the node in the stylesheet that was selecting a portion of the source tree. In order to get all the information you need here, you have to view the SelectionEvent as an ElemTemplateElement so you can get the name of the element in the stylesheet (line 73-79). The SelectionEvent contains the rest of the information you need (the attribute name and attribute value where the XPath expression occurred). This information is output in lines 78-82:

```
70:     public void selected(SelectionEvent se)
71:         throws TransformerException {
72:         StringBuffer sb = new StringBuffer();
73:         ElemTemplateElement ete =
74:             (ElemTemplateElement) se.m_styleNode;
75:
76:         sb.append("<");
77:         sb.append(ete.getNodeName());
78:         sb.append(" ");
79:         sb.append(se.m_attributeName);
80:         sb.append("='");
```

```
81:         sb.append(se.m_xpath.getPatternString());
82:         sb.append("'> ");
```

In addition to knowing which element in the stylesheet is doing the selecting, you would also like to know which node in the source tree was selected and what its value was. This information is easy to obtain because it's avaiable from the SelectionEvent, as it should be:

```
83:         Node sourceNode = se.m_sourceNode;
84:         sb.append(" ==> { node = ");
85:         sb.append(sourceNode.getNodeName());
86:         sb.append(", content = ");
87:         sb.append(se.m_selection.str());
88:         sb.append(" }");
89:         log.debug("Selecting:  "+sb);
90:     }
91:
```

TracerEvents are fired as Xalan walks the elements in the stylesheet. You want to know what elements it's processing at any given time (lines 95-96). There are two important TracerEvent cases. The first case is when a literal result element is encountered; you want to know the name of the literal result element that was encountered (lines 98-106). In the second case, Xalan matches a template element; you want to know the pattern the template was using and the name of the template, if the template is named (lines 108-117):

```
92:     public void trace(TracerEvent te) {
93:         StringBuffer sb = new StringBuffer();
94:
95:         sb.append(te.m_styleNode.getNodeName());
96:         sb.append(" ");
97:
98:         switch (te.m_styleNode.getXSLToken()) {
99:             case Constants.ELEMNAME_TEXTLITERALRESULT:
100:                ElemTextLiteral etl =
101:                    (ElemTextLiteral) te.m_styleNode;
102:                char chars[] = etl.getChars();
103:                String charString =
104:                    new String(chars,0, chars.length).trim();
105:                sb.append(charString);
106:                sb.append(" ");
107:                break;
108:            case Constants.ELEMNAME_TEMPLATE:
109:                ElemTemplate et = (ElemTemplate) te.m_styleNode;
110:                if (et.getMatch() != null)
111:                    sb.append("match = '"+
112:                              et.getMatch().getPatternString()+
113:                              "'");
114:                if (et.getName() != null)
115:                    sb.append("name='"+et.getName()+"" +"'");
116:                sb.append(" ");
117:                break;
118:            default:
119:        }
```

After you've output the element being processed and any element-specific data, you also record the system ID of the stylesheet and the position in the stylesheet that Xalan is currently processing:

```
            sb.append("at ");
            sb.append(te.m_styleNode.getSystemId());
            sb.append(" Line ");
            sb.append(te.m_styleNode.getLineNumber());
            sb.append(", Column ");
            sb.append(te.m_styleNode.getColumnNumber());
            log.debug("Tracing:    "+sb);
        }
}
```

Using LoggingTraceListener or something like it can be a big help in resolving weird stylesheet problems in deeply embedded environments such as servlets.

One last remark about debugging techniques: You can also invoke the Xalan EnvironmentCheck functionality from within a stylesheet by using the Xalan extensions mechanism. Here's a stylesheet that lets you do that:

```
<?xml version="1.0"?>
<xsl:stylesheet
    xmlns:xsl="http://www.w3.org/1999/XSL/Transform"
    version="1.0"
    xmlns:xalan="http://xml.apache.org/xalan"
    exclude-result-prefixes="xalan">
<xsl:output indent="yes"/>

<xsl:template match="/">
  <html>]
  <head></head>
  <body>
    <xsl:copy-of select="xalan:checkEnvironment()"/>
  </body>
  </html>
</xsl:template>
</xsl:stylesheet>
```

XSLTC

Until now, we've been discussing Xalan's XSLT interpreter, which translates the XSLT stylesheet and applies the stylesheet while it's being translated. Xalan also includes an XSLT compiler, XSLTC, which compiles a stylesheet into Java bytecodes. This bytecode representation of the stylesheet is called a translet. Translets can then be executed to perform transformations. The benefit of this approach is that it skips the cost of translating the stylesheet. If you're using the same stylesheet over and over, the time spent translating the stylesheet can become significant.

Configuration Issues

To use XSLTC, you need to make sure you have all the appropriate jar files. If you chose the one-jar distribution, then you need to make sure xalan.jar, xml-apis.jar, and xercesImpl.jar are on the classpath. If you selected the two-jar distribution, make sure xsltc.jar, xml-apis.jar, and xercesImpl.jar are on the classpath. If you're using JDK 1.4 or later, then you should make sure these jar files are placed in the endorsed standards overrides directory.

Calling XSLTC from TrAX

In most of the TrAX examples, you've created Transformer objects using a TransformerFactory. Transformer objects aren't thread safe. If you have multiple threads that need XSLT transformation services, then you should create one Transformer object for each thread. The most efficient way to do this is to use the TransformerFactory to create a Templates object which you then use to create as many Transformer instances as you need. If you need multiple threads to use multiple transformers, those transformers must be created via a Templates object, regardless of whether you're using Xalan's interpretive mode or XSLTC. When you use XSLTC, both transformers and templates are compiled. There is good synergy between using templates to create transformers and using XSLTC, because the situations where you're using the same transformation on multiple threads are also situations where you're likely to benefit by compiling your stylesheets into translets.

Let's start by looking at a program that compiles an XSLT stylesheet into a translet. This program writes the translet class file into the current directory:

```
 1: /*
 2:  *
 3:  * XSLTCCompileMain.java
 4:  *
 5:  * Example from "Professional XML Development with Apache Tools"
 6:  *
 7:  */
 8: package com.sauria.apachexml.ch2;
 9: 
10: import java.util.Properties;
11: 
12: import javax.xml.transform.Templates;
13: import javax.xml.transform.TransformerConfigurationException;
14: import javax.xml.transform.TransformerFactory;
15: import javax.xml.transform.stream.StreamSource;
16: 
17: public class XSLTCCompileMain {
18: 
19:     public static void main(String[] args) {
20:         String stylesheet = args[0];
21: 
22:         String KEY = "javax.xml.transform.TransformerFactory";
23:         String VALUE =
24:             "org.apache.xalan.xsltc.trax.TransformerFactoryImpl";
25:         Properties sysProps = System.getProperties();
26:         sysProps.put(KEY,VALUE);
27:         System.setProperties(sysProps);
```

To use XSLTC, you must set the System property javax.xml.transform.TransformerFactory to org.apache.xalan.xsltc.trax.TransformerFactoryImpl (lines 22-27). After creating a TransformerFactory, you set the XSLT-specific generate-translet attribute to true. This value causes XSLT to write a class file for the translet. By default, translet class files are created in the current directory:

```

        TransformerFactory xFactory =
            TransformerFactory.newInstance();
        xFactory.setAttribute("generate-translet",Boolean.TRUE);
```

The translet is actually created when you call the TransformerFactory's newTemplates method. You pass a StreamSource containing the stylesheet to newTemplates:

```
        Templates translet = null;
        try {
            StreamSource stylesheetSource =
                new StreamSource(stylesheet);
            translet =
                xFactory.newTemplates(stylesheetSource);
        } catch (TransformerConfigurationException tce) {
            tce.printStackTrace();
        }
    }
}
```

Once you've compiled the translet, you can use it in a separate program to perform a transformation; see the following listing.

```
/*
 *
 * XSLTCRunMain.java
 *
 * Example from "Professional XML Development with Apache Tools"
 *
 */
package com.sauria.apachexml.ch2;

import java.io.FileNotFoundException;
import java.io.FileOutputStream;
import java.util.Properties;

import javax.xml.transform.Templates;
import javax.xml.transform.Transformer;
import javax.xml.transform.TransformerConfigurationException;
import javax.xml.transform.TransformerException;
import javax.xml.transform.TransformerFactory;
import javax.xml.transform.stream.StreamResult;
import javax.xml.transform.stream.StreamSource;

public class XSLTCRunMain {

    public static void main(String[] args) {
        String input = args[0];
        String translet = args[1];
        String output = args[2];
```

The translet argument is the name of the class created for the stylesheet. If the stylesheet that was compiled was called books.xslt, the default name for the translet file would be books.class. You should pass books as the value of the translet argument. We'll look at options for controlling the naming later.

Again, you need to set the system property for the TransformerFactory to use XSLTC.

```
        String KEY = "javax.xml.transform.TransformerFactory";
        String VALUE =
            "org.apache.xalan.xsltc.trax.TransformerFactoryImpl";
        Properties sysProps = System.getProperties();
        sysProps.put(KEY,VALUE);
        System.setProperties(sysProps);
```

This time you need to tell the factory that it should search the classpath for translet class files:

```
        TransformerFactory xFactory =
            TransformerFactory.newInstance();
        xFactory.setAttribute("use-classpath",Boolean.TRUE);
```

Now you resuscitate the translet from the translet class file, use it to create a template, and use that template to create a transformer:

```
        Templates templates = null;
        Transformer xformer = null;
        try {
            StreamSource transletSource =
                new StreamSource(translet);
            templates = xFactory.newTemplates(transletSource);
            xformer = templates.newTransformer();
```

All that's left is to call the transformer on the right input document:

```
        } catch (TransformerConfigurationException tce) {
            tce.printStackTrace();
        }
        try {
            StreamSource inputSource = new StreamSource(input);
            FileOutputStream fos = new FileOutputStream(output);
            StreamResult result = new StreamResult(fos);
            xformer.transform(inputSource, result);
        } catch (FileNotFoundException fnfe) {
            fnfe.printStackTrace();
        } catch (TransformerException te) {
            te.printStackTrace();
        }
    }
}
```

XSLTC TransformerFactory Attributes

In addition to the generate-translet and use-classpath attributes, XSLTC defines some attributes (shown in the following table) that can be used to tell the TransformerFactory how to generate the translet. These attributes affect the name and destination of the translet and are effective for a single call of either TransformerFactory.newTemplates or TransformerFactory.newTransfomer. They're reset to their defaults for the next call.

Attribute	Purpose	Type	Default
translet-name	Specifies the name of the translet.	String	"GregorSamsa"
destination-directory	Specifies the directory where the translet class file is to be written.	String	null
package-name	Specifies the package in which the translet class should be placed.	String	null
jar-name	Specifies a jar file where the translet class file should be written.	String	null

XSLTC also defines the following attributes that remain in force until they're turned off or the program exits.

Attribute	Purpose	Type	Default
auto-translet	If true, compares the timestamp of the translet class file with the timestamp of the stylesheet to determine whether to recompile the translet.	Boolean	Boolean.FALSE
enable-inlining	If true, inline methods generated by templates.	Boolean	Boolean.FALSE
Debug	If true, prints debugging messages.	Boolean	Boolean.FALSE

All the attributes in this section should be set on a TransformerFactory before you call newTemplates or newTransformer.

Smart Transformer Switch

The Smart Transformer Switch allows you to use Xalan interpretive mode for Transformer instances created directly from the TransformerFactory, while using XSLTC for Transformer instances created from a Templates instance. The Templates instance would be created from the same TransformerFactory. You enable this mode by setting the TrAX system property javax.xml.transform.TransformerFactory to the value org.apache.xalan.xsltc.trax.SmartTransformerFactoryImpl.

Command-Line Tools

Xalan provides command-line access to XSLT via a pair of classes, org.apache.xalan.xsltc .cmdline.Compile, and org.apache.xalan.xsltc.cmdline.Transform. These command-line tools can be useful for testing, debugging, and secure deployment. You can invoke the command-line interface to the compiler by typing

```
java org.apache.xalan.xsltc.cmdline.Compile [options] <stylesheet>
```

These are the important options to Compile:

- **-o <output>**—Specifies the name of the translet class. The default name is taken from <stylesheet>.
- **-d <directory>**—Specifies the directory where the translet class should be written.
- **-j <jarfile>**—Writes the translet class into a jar file.
- **-p <package name>**—Specifies the Java package the translet will be in.
- **-u stylesheet**—Specifies the stylesheet via URL instead of filename.

The command-line compiler can be useful for situations where you want the efficiency of translets but don't want to build compilation capability into your application. You can use the command-line compiler to build and update translets used by the running system.

You invoke the command-line translet runner by typing:

```
java org.apache.xalan.xsltc.cmdline.Transform [options]
     <doc> <translet>
```

Here are the important options to Transform:

- **-j <jarfile>**—Reads the translet from the jar file.
- **-u <document_url>**—Used in place of <doc>, specifies the input document via URL.
- -x—Turns on additional debugging output.

You can use the command-line translet runner to debug translets that have been generated by an embedded XSLTC compiler.

Xalan Extensions

XSLT provides a mechanism for extending the behavior of an XSLT processing engine. Templates in your stylesheet can contain extension elements that are taken from an extension namespace. The extension namespace is specified by the extension-element-prefixes attribute, which can appear on the <xsl:stylesheet> element, any literal result element, or on the extension element itself. The value of this attribute is a space-separated list of namespace prefixes. You must also define the namespace prefix in your stylesheet. The value of executing the extension element is inserted in the result tree.

Another useful type of extension is an extension function. Extension functions aren't defined by the XSLT specification, but most XSLT processing engines support them in one way or another. The basic idea of extension functions is to expand the set of functions that can appear in XSLT/XPath expressions. We'll look at both kinds of extensions in relation to Xalan.

Xalan allows both extension elements and extension functions. These extensions may be written in Java. They can also be written in a number of scripting languages, thanks to the use of the Bean Scripting Framework (BSF) from the Apache Jakarta project. BSF adds support for extensions written in JavaScript, NetRexx, Bean Markup Language (BML), Python, and Tool Command Language (TCL). On Windows machines, there is additional support for Win32 Active Scripting Languages (Jscript, VBScript, and PerlScript). To take advantage of BSF languages, you must put bsf.jar onto your classpath. You also need jar files or DLLs for the language you wish to use for the extension. You can find a table of languages and the components they need at http://jakarta.apache.org/bsf/projects.html.

Extension Elements

Xalan includes a few built-in extension elements. The redirect extension allows you to direct the output of a transformation to multiple files. It provides three extension elements: <write>, <open>, and <close>. The <write> extension opens a file, writes its contents to the file, and closes the file. The content of <write> is processed as a normal XSLT template body; it's just that the output goes to the file specified by the select attribute of <write>. Here's a sample stylesheet that uses <write> to take the familiar book inventory and copy the XML for each book into a file whose name is the name of the book:

```
1: <?xml version="1.0" encoding="UTF-8"?>
2: <xsl:stylesheet version="1.0"
3:   xmlns:xsl="http://www.w3.org/1999/XSL/Transform"
4:   xmlns:books="http://sauria.com/schemas/apache-xml-book/books"
5:   xmlns:redirect="http://xml.apache.org/xalan/redirect"
6:   extension-element-prefixes="redirect">
```

Lines 5-6 show the declaration of the redirect prefix and its use as an element extension prefix. Now write specifies that the filename where output is being redirected is the title of the book (line 10):

```
 7:  <xsl:output method="xml" version="1.0" encoding="UTF-8"
 8:          indent="yes"/>
 9:  <xsl:template match="books:book">
10:   <redirect:write select="books:title">
```

<xsl:copy-of> is used to make a copy of the entire book element:

```
      <xsl:copy-of select="."/>
    </redirect:write>
  </xsl:template>
</xsl:stylesheet>
```

Extension Functions

Xalan's library of extension functions is more extensive than its library of extension elements. It provides its own set of useful functions, and it provides an implementation of the EXSLT extension functions being developed by the community at www.exslt.org. This is a fairly rich set of extension functions and is the same across XSLT processors that support EXSLT, although for XSLT 1.0 processors, the details of invoking the functions may be different.

Xalan's own extension functions are written in Java, and the method for accessing them relies on a special notation. You define a namespace prefix you use to call the extension function. You can use one of three formats to bind the namespace: to a specific class, to a specific package, or to Java in general. These formats give you access to successively more functionality:

- **Class format declaration**—xmlns:extlib="xalan://com.sauria.apachexml .XalanExtensionFunctions"
- **Package format declaration**—xmlns:saurialib="xalan://com.sauria.apachexml"
- **Java format declaration**—xmlns:java="http://xml.apache.org/xalan/java"

Once you've declared the namespace, you can start calling functions. To keep things simple, let's assume you've used a class declaration. The simplest thing you can do is call a static method on the class. Here's an example:

```
<xsl:value-of select="extlib:function(arg1, arg2)"/>
```

Next you instantiate the class and call a method on it. You instantiate the class as follows:

```
<xsl:variable name="ext" select="extlib:new()"/>
```

To invoke a method you do this:

```
<xsl:variable name="value" select="extlib:method($foo,arg1, arg2)"/>
```

There are similar machinations if you choose a package format or Java format namespace. You have to supply a little more information to instantiate a class. Here's how you do it for a package format namespace:

```
<xsl:variable name="ext" select="saurialib:FooLib.new()"/>
```

The Java format version is:

```
<xsl:variable name="ext"
              select="com.sauria.apachexml.XalanExtensionFunctions"/>
```

Xalan's Functions

Xalan provides a set of functions in the org.apache.xalan.lib.NodeInfo class. These static functions allow you to retrieve the systemId, publicId, lineNumber, and columnNumber of the current node. To use these functions, you must use TransformerFactory.setAttribute to set the TransformerFactoryImpl .FEATURE_SOURCE_LOCATION attribute to true. This attribute tells Xalan to provide a SourceLocator to be filled in with the systemId, line number, and column number of nodes in the source document.

Here's the books stylesheet modified to use NodeInfo to display the line number of each book element:

```
<?xml version="1.0" encoding="UTF-8"?>
<xsl:stylesheet version="1.0"
  xmlns:xsl="http://www.w3.org/1999/XSL/Transform"
  xmlns:books="http://sauria.com/schemas/apache-xml-book/books"
  xmlns:nodeinfo="xalan://org.apache.xalan.lib.NodeInfo"
```

Here's the (class format) declaration of the nodeinfo namespace prefix:

```
  exclude-result-prefixes="books">
    <xsl:output method="html" version="4.0" encoding="UTF-8"
        indent="yes" omit-xml-declaration="yes"/>
    <xsl:template match="books:books">
      <html>
        <head><title>Book Inventory</title></head>
        <body>
          <xsl:apply-templates/>
        </body>
      </html>
    </xsl:template>
    <xsl:template match="books:book">
      <xsl:apply-templates/>
      <xsl:text>Line </xsl:text>
      <xsl:value-of select="nodeinfo:lineNumber()"/>
      <p />
    </xsl:template>
    <xsl:template match="books:title">
      <em><xsl:value-of select="."/></em><br />
    </xsl:template>
    <xsl:template match="books:author">
      <b><xsl:value-of select="."/></b><br />
    </xsl:template>
    <xsl:template match="books:isbn">
      <xsl:value-of select="."/><br />
    </xsl:template>
    <xsl:template match="books:month">
      <xsl:value-of select="."/>,
    </xsl:template>
    <xsl:template match="books:year">
      <xsl:value-of select="."/><br />
    </xsl:template>
    <xsl:template match="books:publisher">
      <xsl:value-of select="."/><br />
    </xsl:template>
    <xsl:template match="books:address">
```

```
        <xsl:value-of select="."/><br />
      </xsl:template>
</xsl:stylesheet>
```

You call NodeInfo's lineNumber method.

Xalan has a few other extension functions, but their capabilities are duplicated in the EXSLT libraries, so you're better off using the EXSLT versions.

EXSLT

The EXSLT library is actually a set of libraries of functions for use in XSLT processors. At the time of this writing, Xalan has support for the following function types:

- **Common**—Functions that convert a result tree fragment into a node set and return the XSLT type of an object.
- **Math**—Trigonometric functions, abs, log, min, max, power, random, and sqrt.
- **Set**—Functions that perform set difference and intersection, determine whether two sets have the same node in common, or find the nodes preceding or following a particular node.
- **Date and time**—Date, time, and date/time formatting functions.
- **Dynamic**— Functions that perform transitive closure of a node list, map an expression over a node list, determine the min and max of an expression over a node list, and calculate the sum of an expression over a node list.
- **String**—Alignment, concatenation, padding, splitting, and tokenizing functions.

Here's the book stylesheet modified to use the EXSLT date and time library to timestamp the report:

```
<?xml version="1.0" encoding="UTF-8"?>
<xsl:stylesheet version="1.0"
  xmlns:xsl="http://www.w3.org/1999/XSL/Transform"
  xmlns:books="http://sauria.com/schemas/apache-xml-book/books"
  xmlns:datetime="http://exslt.org/dates-and-times"
  exclude-result-prefixes="books">
    <xsl:output method="html" version="4.0" encoding="UTF-8"
        indent="yes" omit-xml-declaration="yes"/>
    <xsl:template match="books:books">
      <html>
        <head><title>Book Inventory</title></head>
        <body>
          <xsl:apply-templates/>

          <xsl:text>As of </xsl:text>
          <xsl:value-of select="datetime:dateTime()"/>
        </body>
      </html>
    </xsl:template>
    <xsl:template match="books:book">
       <xsl:apply-templates/>
```

```
      <p />
    </xsl:template>
    <xsl:template match="books:title">
      <em><xsl:value-of select="."/></em><br />
    </xsl:template>
    <xsl:template match="books:author">
      <b><xsl:value-of select="."/></b><br />
    </xsl:template>
    <xsl:template match="books:isbn">
      <xsl:value-of select="."/><br />
    </xsl:template>
    <xsl:template match="books:month">
      <xsl:value-of select="."/>,
    </xsl:template>
    <xsl:template match="books:year">
      <xsl:value-of select="."/><br />
    </xsl:template>
    <xsl:template match="books:publisher">
      <xsl:value-of select="."/><br />
    </xsl:template>
    <xsl:template match="books:address">
      <xsl:value-of select="."/><br />
    </xsl:template>
</xsl:stylesheet>
```

Writing Extensions

Writing extension elements can be a little tricky. The following version of the book stylesheet that uses a new extension element. The extension element determines how many of a given book you have on hand, based on the book's ISBN number.

Here you declare the namespace prefixes you're using. You use the class format for the declaration of the Java class, com.sauria.apachexml.ch3.InventoryExtension. You also tell Xalan that the prefix inv denotes an extension element:

```
<?xml version="1.0" encoding="UTF-8"?>
<xsl:stylesheet version="1.0"
  xmlns:xsl="http://www.w3.org/1999/XSL/Transform"
  xmlns:books="http://sauria.com/schemas/apache-xml-book/books"
  xmlns:xalan="http://xml.apache.org/xalan"
  xmlns:inv="xalan://com.sauria.apachexml.ch2.InventoryExtension"
  extension-element-prefixes="inv"
```

Now you use the <inv:onhand> extension element and include as its child the value of the isbn node in the source document. When the stylesheet is processed, you expect a count of the book inventory to be placed here:

```
  exclude-result-prefixes="books">
    <xsl:output method="xml" version="1.0" encoding="UTF-8"
        indent="yes"/>
    <xsl:template match="books:books">
      <html>
        <head><title>Book Inventory</title></head>
```

```
        <body>
          <xsl:apply-templates/>
        </body>
      </html>
    </xsl:template>
    <xsl:template match="books:book">
       <xsl:apply-templates/>
      <p />
    </xsl:template>
    <xsl:template match="books:title">
      <em><xsl:value-of select="."/></em><br />
    </xsl:template>
    <xsl:template match="books:author">
      <b><xsl:value-of select="."/></b><br />
    </xsl:template>
    <xsl:template match="books:isbn">
      <xsl:value-of select="."/><br />

      <inv:onhand>
       <xsl:value-of select="."/>
      </inv:onhand>
      <xsl:text> on hand</xsl:text><br />
    </xsl:template>
    <xsl:template match="books:month">
      <xsl:value-of select="."/>,
    </xsl:template>
    <xsl:template match="books:year">
      <xsl:value-of select="."/><br />
    </xsl:template>
    <xsl:template match="books:publisher">
      <xsl:value-of select="."/><br />
    </xsl:template>
    <xsl:template match="books:address">
      <xsl:value-of select="."/><br />
    </xsl:template>
</xsl:stylesheet>
```

Now let's look at the Java implementation of the extension element. You define a method onhand whose name is the same as the name of the extension element. Xalan says the arguments to extension element methods are an XSLProcessorContext that contains the useful state of the transformation engine and an ElemExtensionCall representing the extension element.

```
/*
 *
 * InventoryExtension.java
 *
 * Example from "Professional XML Development with Apache Tools"
 *
 */
package com.sauria.apachexml.ch2;

import javax.xml.transform.TransformerException;

import org.apache.xalan.extensions.XSLProcessorContext;
import org.apache.xalan.templates.ElemExtensionCall;
```

```
import org.w3c.dom.Node;

public class InventoryExtension {
    public String onhand(XSLProcessorContext context,
                         ElemExtensionCall extensionElt)
                throws TransformerException {
```

The logic is simple. You want to take the content of the extension element and pass it to a function that tells you how many books are on hand:

```
        Node parent = context.getContextNode();
        Node value = parent.getFirstChild();
        return lookup(value.getNodeValue());
```

The context's getContextNode method gives the current node in the source tree, which is <isbn>. When you're working with extensions, it looks like you're working with a DOM tree, so you need the Text child of the <isbn> node to pass to the business logic:

```
    }

     private String lookup(String isbn) {
        char chars[] = isbn.toCharArray();
        int sum = 0;
        for (int i = 0; i < chars.length; i++) {
            sum += Character.getNumericValue(chars[i]);
        }
        return Integer.toString(sum);
    }
}
```

In this case, the business logic breaks the string into a character array and then returns the sum of the numeric value of the characters as the number of books on hand. You can imagine your JDBC, EJB, or Web service call here.

Writing extension functions is easier than writing extension elements, because in many cases you're passing simple XSLT types to the Java code implementing the extension function. So, all you have to do is write a class that has a method that implements the functionality you need. The only trick is getting the correct arguments for that method. Xalan is very forgiving about this; it uses an approximation method to figure out whether a method can be called as an extension function. The rules for calling extension functions are complicated, but it's possible to simplify them by constraining the types you use in your Java functions. To pass an XSLT type from the left side of the following table, give the method argument the type in right column.

XSLT Type	Java Type
Node Set	org.w3c.dom.NodeList
String	java.lang.String
Boolean	java.lang.Boolean
Number	java.lang.Double
Result Tree Fragment	org.w3c.dom.NodeList

XSLTC Extensions

XSLTC doesn't offer the same level of support as Xalan when it comes to extensions. It doesn't support extension elements at all. It supports extension functions written in Java, but it doesn't support extension functions written using the Bean Scripting Framework. The interpretive redirect extension is supported. EXSLT support is also lagging a bit. Of the EXSLT modules that Xalan supports (it doesn't support them all yet), XSLTC doesn't support the dynamic functions library. Extension functions are used the same way as in interpreted Xalan.

Practical Usage

Transformation performance is one of the major areas when you're using XSLT. You should try to use XSLTC whenever possible because the performance is so good. As you've seen, though, in some areas XSLTC doesn't have as much functionality as the interpretive mode. Once you've set out to use XSLTC, you can still improve on things by trying to cache translets so they can be shared throughout your application.

The TrAX API provides a URIResolver interface and a setURIResolver method on Transformer. You can use this facility to improve the performance of your applications by mapping remote resources to local copies of those resources whenever possible. You could also build a cache for those resources using URIResolver.

Applications

In this section we'll look at a common use for Xalan. Let's say you're building a Web application, and you want to serve your data as XML. Maybe you have an XML-enabled database that spits out XML, or perhaps your content-management system generates XML. It doesn't really matter. You can use XSLT to transform that XML into something appropriate for the user agent visiting the Website. You can generate HTML specific for a particular browser, or you could generate WML if you were being visited by a cell phone.

You'll write a servlet filter that sits in front of a servlet and intercepts the servlet's request and response to augment the servlet's functionality. In this case, you intercept the request and figure out what kind of client is accessing the site. After the servlet has done its job, the filter intercepts the response, which is an XML document, and uses Xalan to transform the result in a manner appropriate to the client.

The first thing you need is a servlet you can put the filter in front of. This servlet picks up an XML file (in this case, the now-familiar book.xml file) and blasts it back out as the result:

```
/*
 *
 * XMLServlet.java
 *
 * Example from "Professional XML Development with Apache Tools"
 *
 */

```

```
import java.io.IOException;
import java.io.InputStream;
import java.io.OutputStream;
import javax.servlet.ServletException;
import javax.servlet.http.HttpServlet;
import javax.servlet.http.HttpServletRequest;
import javax.servlet.http.HttpServletResponse;

public class XMLServlet extends HttpServlet {

    protected void doGet(HttpServletRequest req,
                         HttpServletResponse res)
        throws ServletException, IOException {
        OutputStream os = res.getOutputStream();

        byte buffer[] = new byte[4096];
        InputStream is =
            getServletContext().getResourceAsStream("books.xml");
        int count = is.read(buffer);
        os.write(buffer,0,count);
    }

}
```

Here's the web.xml deployment descriptor for the Web application. It maps the servlet to a URI and also tells the Web container that a filter is attached to the servlet:

```
<?xml version="1.0" encoding="ISO-8859-1"?>

<!DOCTYPE web-app
  PUBLIC "-//Sun Microsystems, Inc.//DTD Web Application 2.3//EN"
  "http://java.sun.com/dtd/web-app_2_3.dtd">

<web-app>
  <display-name>
   Professional XML Development with Apache Tools Examples
  </display-name>
  <description>
    Examples from Professional XML Development with Apache Tools.
  </description>

  <!— Define servlet-mapped and path-mapped example filters —>
  <filter>
    <filter-name>XSLT Filter</filter-name>
    <filter-class>XSLTServletFilter</filter-class>
  </filter>

  <!— Define filter mappings for the defined filters —>
  <filter-mapping>
    <filter-name>XSLT Filter</filter-name>
    <servlet-name>XMLServlet</servlet-name>
  </filter-mapping>

  <servlet>
```

```
    <servlet-name>XMLServlet</servlet-name>
    <servlet-class>XMLServlet</servlet-class>
  </servlet>

  <servlet-mapping>
    <servlet-name>XMLServlet</servlet-name>
    <url-pattern>/servlet/*</url-pattern>
  </servlet-mapping>
</web-app>
```

Now you're ready for the filter. The filter uses Xalan in Smart Transformer mode. You need to use templates because you're in a multithreaded situation. You should also be careful about the amount of stylesheet compilation and loading, so you implement an application-wide cache for all the templates you use:

```
/*
 *
 * XSLTServletFilter.java
 *
 * Example from "Professional XML Development with Apache Tools"
 *
 */
import java.io.CharArrayWriter;
import java.io.IOException;
import java.io.PrintWriter;
import java.io.StringReader;
import java.util.Collections;
import java.util.HashMap;
import java.util.Map;
import java.util.Properties;

import javax.servlet.Filter;
import javax.servlet.FilterChain;
import javax.servlet.FilterConfig;
import javax.servlet.ServletContext;
import javax.servlet.ServletException;
import javax.servlet.ServletRequest;
import javax.servlet.ServletResponse;
import javax.servlet.http.HttpServletRequest;
import javax.servlet.http.HttpServletResponse;
import javax.xml.transform.Source;
import javax.xml.transform.Templates;
import javax.xml.transform.Transformer;
import javax.xml.transform.TransformerConfigurationException;
import javax.xml.transform.TransformerFactory;
import javax.xml.transform.stream.StreamResult;
import javax.xml.transform.stream.StreamSource;

public class XSLTServletFilter implements Filter {
    FilterConfig config = null;
    Map transletCache = null;

    public void init(FilterConfig fc) throws ServletException {
        config = fc;
```

```
40:
41:         ServletContext ctx = fc.getServletContext();
42:
43:         transletCache =
44:             (Map) ctx.getAttribute("transletCache");
45:
46:         if (transletCache == null) {
47:             transletCache =
48:                 Collections.synchronizedMap(new HashMap());
49:             ctx.setAttribute("transletCache", transletCache);
50:         }
```

In lines 41-50, the filter looks for the application-wide translet cache. If it doesn't exist, the filter creates one. You use a synchronized HashMap for the cache. In lines 52-57, you set up Xalan for Smart Transformer mode:

```
51:
52:         String KEY = "javax.xml.transform.TransformerFactory";
53:         String VALUE =
54:     "org.apache.xalan.xsltc.trax.SmartTransformerFactoryImpl";
55:         Properties sysProps = System.getProperties();
56:         sysProps.put(KEY,VALUE);
57:         System.setProperties(sysProps);
58:     }
59:
```

All the action happens in doFilter:

```
60:     public void doFilter(
61:         ServletRequest req,
62:         ServletResponse res,
63:         FilterChain chain)
64:         throws IOException, ServletException {
65:         String contentType;
66:         String styleSheet;
67:
68:         HttpServletRequest httpReq = (HttpServletRequest) req;
69:         String userAgent = httpReq.getHeader("User-Agent");
70:         contentType = selectContentType(userAgent);
71:         res.setContentType(contentType);
```

You intercept the request and find out what the user agent (browser) is. Then you pass that information to a function that figures out the right content type for the data the filter/servlet combination returns.

The BufferedReponseWrapper class looks like a ServletResponse. It captures all the data written into the wrapper in a buffer so the filter can manipulate it after the servlet has generated it:

```
72:
73:         PrintWriter out = res.getWriter();
74:
75:         BufferedResponseWrapper wrappedResponse =
76:             new BufferedResponseWrapper((HttpServletResponse)res);
```

Here's where the filter calls the servlet to do its job. The servlet executes in complete ignorance of the filter:

```
 77:
 78:            chain.doFilter(req, wrappedResponse);
```

Now you get the buffer from the response wrapper and use it to create a StreamSource that can be used as input to a transformer:

```
 79:
 80:            String s = new String(wrappedResponse.getBuffer());
 81:            StringReader sr =
 82:                new StringReader(s);
 83:            Source xmlSource = new StreamSource(sr);
```

You also select the right translet based on what the user agent was:

```
 84:
 85:            try {
 86:                Templates translet = selectTemplates(userAgent);
```

The next two lines (87-88) solve some impedance mismatch problems between the transformer and the filter:

```
 87:                CharArrayWriter caw = new CharArrayWriter();
 88:                StreamResult result = new StreamResult(caw);
 89:                Transformer xformer = translet.newTransformer();
 90:                xformer.transform(xmlSource, result);
```

Now that the result is set up, you create a transformer from the translet/templates and perform the transformation. Then you compute the length of the output (line 91) and blast the results out to the user agent:

```
 91:                res.setContentLength(caw.toString().length());
 92:                out.write(caw.toString());
 93:            } catch (Exception ex) {
 94:                out.println(ex.toString());
 95:                out.write(wrappedResponse.toString());
 96:            }
 97:        }
 98:
 99:        private String selectContentType(String ua) {
100:            String contentType = "";
101:            if (ua.indexOf("MSIE") != -1) { // IE
102:                contentType = "text/html";
103:            } else if (ua.indexOf("Firebird") != -1) { // Firebird
104:                contentType = "text/html";
105:            } else if (ua.indexOf("Gecko") != -1) { // Mozilla
106:                contentType = "text/html";
107:            }
108:            return contentType;
109:        }
```

For the sake of example, you hard-coded the conditional selection of the contentType. For a production system, you'd probably put this information in a table and do a lookup. The same is true for selectStylesheet, which figures out the filename for the stylesheet to be used:

```

    private String selectStylesheet(String ua) {
        String stylesheet = "";
        if (ua.indexOf("MSIE") != -1) { // IE
            stylesheet = "books-ie.xslt";
        } else if (ua.indexOf("Firebird") != -1) { // Firebird
            stylesheet = "books-firebird.xslt";
        } else if (ua.indexOf("Gecko") != -1) { // Mozilla
            stylesheet = "books-mozilla.xslt";
        }
        return stylesheet;
    }

    private Templates selectTemplates(String ua) {
        Templates translet = null;

        TransformerFactory xFactory =
            TransformerFactory.newInstance();
        String styleSheet = selectStylesheet(ua);

        translet = (Templates) transletCache.get(styleSheet);
        if (translet != null) {
            return translet;
        }
```

After you determine which stylesheet should be used, you check the cache to see whether you already have a translet for it. If so, you're done. Otherwise you have to compile it:

```

        try {
            String stylePath =
             config.getServletContext().getRealPath(styleSheet);
            Source styleSource = new StreamSource(stylePath);
            translet =
                xFactory.newTemplates(styleSource);
        } catch (TransformerConfigurationException e) {
            e.printStackTrace();
        }
        transletCache.put(styleSheet, translet);
```

After you compile the translet, you put it in the cache and then hand it back so it can be used:

```
        return translet;
    }

    public void destroy() {
    }
}
```

BufferedResponseWrapper is an HttpServletResponseWrapper that contains a ByteArrayOutputStream that's used to buffer the results of the servlet so the filter can get them. The getBuffer method is the only addition to the HttpServletResponseWrapper API:

```
/*
 *
 * BufferedResponseWrapper.java
 *
 * Example from "Professional XML Development with Apache Tools"
 *
 */

import java.io.ByteArrayOutputStream;
import java.io.IOException;
import java.io.PrintWriter;

import javax.servlet.ServletOutputStream;
import javax.servlet.http.HttpServletResponse;
import javax.servlet.http.HttpServletResponseWrapper;

public class BufferedResponseWrapper
    extends HttpServletResponseWrapper {

    ByteArrayOutputStream bufferedStream =
        new ByteArrayOutputStream();

    public BufferedResponseWrapper(HttpServletResponse res) {
        super(res);
    }

    public ServletOutputStream getOutputStream()
        throws IOException {
        return new ServletByteArrayOutputStream(bufferedStream);
    }


    public PrintWriter getWriter() throws IOException {
        return new PrintWriter(bufferedStream);
    }

    public byte[] getBuffer() {
        return bufferedStream.toByteArray();
    }
}
```

ServletByteArrayOutputStream is necessary because you must implement the getOutputStream method of HttpServletResponseWrapper. You want to make sure the ServletByteArrayOutputStream shares the same ByteArrayOutputStream used by the BufferedResponseWrapper:

```
/*
 *
 * ServletByteArrayOutputStream.java
 *
```

```
 * Example from "Professional XML Development with Apache Tools"
 *
 */

import java.io.ByteArrayOutputStream;
import java.io.IOException;

import javax.servlet.ServletOutputStream;

public class ServletByteArrayOutputStream
    extends ServletOutputStream {

    ByteArrayOutputStream baos = null;

    public ServletByteArrayOutputStream() {
        baos = new ByteArrayOutputStream();
    }

    public ServletByteArrayOutputStream(ByteArrayOutputStream
                                                baos) {
        this.baos = baos;
    }

    public void write(int i) throws IOException {
        baos.write(i);
    }

    public byte[] getBuffer() {
        return baos.toByteArray();
    }

}
```

There you have it—a servlet filter that takes XML output from a servlet and transforms it for the type of client visiting the servlet. This example should give you some ideas about how to incorporate Xalan into your own applications.

FOP

XSLT is part one of a two-part specification for an extensible stylesheet language. XSLT takes care of rearranging trees of XML into different trees of potentially different kinds of XML. That's very useful by itself, and that's one of the reasons (the other being the sheer size of the specifications) that XSLT was broken out into its own specification. The second part of the specification is called Extensible Stylesheet Language (XSL) and focuses on formatting XML once the tree transformations have been applied. XSL defines a concept known as *formatting objects*, which is an XML vocabulary that serves as input to a formatter; the formatter then formats the data contained in the formatting objects for presentation. You may also see XSL referred to as XSL-FO (XSL-formatting objects). The two acronyms refer to the same pieces of technology.

The Apache XML Project has an XSL formatting object formatter called FOP (Formatting Object Processor). The processor was originally written by James Tauber and was one of the seed projects for the Apache XML Project. Since then a number of other developers have joined the development team for FOP.

FOP is a worthwhile piece of software if your interest in XML is more from the publishing side. You can use XSLT to take XML and put it into XML-derived online formats like HTML and SVG, but you reach the limit when you need to output something that isn't XML. FOP and XSL formatting objects are the way you can use XML to deliver the same content in multiple presentations, especially in the area of printing. The general way this works is that you use XSLT to convert your XML into XSL formatting objects, and then you use FOP and the appropriate output target to produce output in the format of your choice. FOP has support for PDF, PCL, PostScript, SVG, some of FrameMaker MIF, and some text. If you need to dynamically generate any of these output formats, then FOP should be able to help. In addition to the publishing uses for FOP, applications that generate billing statements, invoices, and similar documents can use FOP to produce their output.

Prerequisites

An XSL document is an XML document whose elements are taken from the namespace http://www.w3.org/1999/XSL/Format, which is normally given the prefix *fo*. The XSL document becomes a tree of elements, and that tree of elements is converted into a tree of formatting objects. Each formatting object in the tree describes an output area. A tree of geometric areas is built using the semantics of the corresponding formatting object. These output areas are spread over a series of pages. Areas have a position on the page and a specification of what to display (from the formatting object) and may also have a background, padding, and borders. The following diagram shows an area with background, padding, and borders inside.

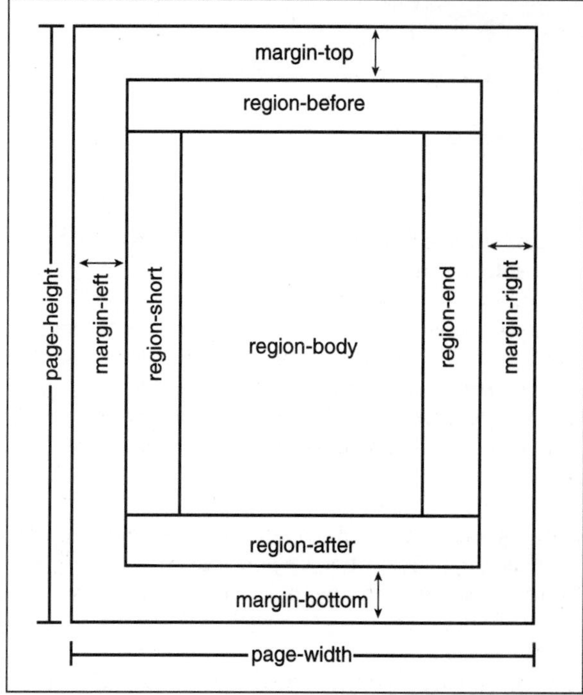

The area tree is then rendered onto a specific output medium such as PDF or HTML.

XSL's most significant new component is the notion of pages (or frames). Many features in XSL are related to controlling the usage of space within a page, whether the space is between lines, words, or letters. These features have to work equally well when the pages will be rendered on the Web. Parts of the XSL formatting model are based on CSS2, such as property/trait names and selectors. This provides some transfer of skill and concepts for people who are already familiar with CSS.

Another innovation in XSL is the use of a relative frame of reference for describing the direction of writing. This means XSL can accommodate writing systems where the writing is from left to right, top to bottom; right to left, top to bottom; or top to bottom, right to left. These directions are specified as start to end, before to after, in that order. So for a left to right, top to bottom system, start is the left edge, end is the right edge, before is the top edge, and after is the bottom edge. For a top to bottom, right to left system, start is the top edge, end is the bottom edge, before is the right edge, and after is the left edge.

Basic XSL

Let's look at a simple XSL document and examine its components. The root element of the XSL document is fo:root, using the fo prefix according to convention:

```
1: <?xml version="1.0" encoding="UTF-8"?>
2: <fo:root xmlns:fo="http://www.w3.org/1999/XSL/Format">
```

The XSL document begins with a set of name layout masters, one for each different kind of page layout to be used in the output document. Here you define a single page master using the fo:simple-page-master element. The definition specifies the margins all around from the edge of the page and also specifies a separate uniform margin around the region body:

```
3:  <fo:layout-master-set>
4:   <fo:simple-page-master margin-right="0.5in" margin-left="0.5in"
5:       margin-bottom="0.5in" margin-top="0.5in" page-width="8.5in"
6:       page-height="11in" master-name="book-page">
7:    <fo:region-body margin="1in"/>
8:   </fo:simple-page-master>
9:  </fo:layout-master-set>
```

Flows

Page sequences contain flows. There are two types of flows, <fo:flow> flows and <fo:static-content> flows. <fo:flow> flows contain content that's distributed across a sequence of pages. <fo:static-content> flows are used for text that will be repeated on many pages, like a header or footer. In this example, a single <fo:flow> is connected to the region-body section of the page (see figure 4.1) by using "xsl-region-body" as the value of the flow-name attribute on <fo:flow> (line 11):

```
10:  <fo:page-sequence master-reference="book-page">
11:   <fo:flow flow-name="xsl-region-body">
12:    <fo:block>
```

You can also specify flows to be connected to region-before, region-after, region-start, or region-end, by specifying a different flow name for the flow-name attribute of <fo:flow>. The flow names are xsl-region-before, xsl-region-after, xsl-region-start, and xsl-region-end. Attaching flows to the other regions allows you to do things like headers, footers, and sidebars.

The contents of a flow are a series of flow objects. There are two primary classes of flow objects: block-level flow objects, such as <fo:block>, <fo:list-block>, and <fo:table>; and inline flow objects, such as <fo:inline>, <fo:external-graphic>, and <fo:page-number>. The block-level flow objects are for formatting blocks of text, such as paragraphs, titles, captions, and so on, whereas inline flow objects are for formatting text without starting a new block. The flow objects can have attributes that control various aspects of formatting. For block flow objects, you can control line height, text alignment, indentation, font style and size, color, borders, and many other aspects. Specifying fonts can be done very flexibly;

you can have separate attributes such as font-family, font-style, font-weight, and color. You can also use the font attribute and write shorthand specifications that look like this: font="bold 16pt Helvetica". Unfortunately, FOP 20.5 doesn't support the font="" style shortcuts, so you must use the separate attributes to specify font information. For inline flow objects, some of the aspects you can control are line height, font style and size, and color.

List Blocks

The example XSL document uses a list block to present the books in the books inventory file. In XSL, an <fo:list-block> does more than create bulleted or numbered lists; it provides a way to place two blocks side by side. Both the <fo:list-item-label> and the <fo:list-item-body> contain blocks that are placed side by side inside the block for the <fo:list-block>:

```
<fo:list-block provisional-label-separation="3pt"
    provisional-distance-between-starts="18pt">
 <fo:list-item>
  <fo:list-item-label>
   <fo:block space-after.optimum="15pt">
    <fo:inline font-size="14pt">
     ?—¢ Professional XML Development with Apache Tools
    </fo:inline>
   </fo:block>
  </fo:list-item-label>
  <fo:list-item-body>
   <fo:block space-after.optimum="15pt">
    <fo:inline
        font-weight="bold">Theodore W. Leung</fo:inline>
    <fo:inline>0-7645-4355-5</fo:inline>
    <fo:inline>December, </fo:inline>
    <fo:inline>2003</fo:inline>
    <fo:inline>Wrox</fo:inline>
    <fo:inline>Indianapolis, Indiana</fo:inline>
   </fo:block>
  </fo:list-item-body>
```

Inside the <fo:list-item-label> is an explicit block you use to control the spacing of the text after the label. You also use an <fo:inline> to control the font size of the item label. Like the <fo:list-item-label>, the <fo:list-item-body> includes an <fo:block> that controls the spacing after the block. Within the block, you again use <fo:inline>s to control the formatting of different parts of the block content.

The rest of the document is as follows:

```
 </fo:list-item>
 <fo:list-item>
  <fo:list-item-label>
   <fo:block space-after.optimum="15pt">
    <fo:inline font-size="14pt">
    ?—¢ Effective Java</fo:inline>
   </fo:block>
  </fo:list-item-label>
  <fo:list-item-body>
   <fo:block space-after.optimum="15pt">
```

```
          <fo:inline font-weight="bold">Joshua Bloch</fo:inline>
          <fo:inline>0-201-31005-8</fo:inline>
          <fo:inline>August, </fo:inline>
          <fo:inline>2001</fo:inline>
          <fo:inline>Addison-Wesley</fo:inline>
          <fo:inline>New York, New York</fo:inline>
         </fo:block>
        </fo:list-item-body>
       </fo:list-item>
       <fo:list-item>
        <fo:list-item-label>
         <fo:block space-after.optimum="15pt">
          <fo:inline font-size="14pt">
          ?—¢ Design Patterns</fo:inline>
         </fo:block>
        </fo:list-item-label>
        <fo:list-item-body>
         <fo:block space-after.optimum="15pt">
          <fo:inline font-weight="bold">Erich Gamma</fo:inline>
          <fo:inline font-weight="bold">Richard Helm</fo:inline>
          <fo:inline font-weight="bold">Ralph Johnson</fo:inline>
          <fo:inline font-weight="bold">John Vlissides</fo:inline>
          <fo:inline>0-201-63361-2</fo:inline>
          <fo:inline>October, </fo:inline>
          <fo:inline>1994</fo:inline>
          <fo:inline>Addison-Wesley</fo:inline>
          <fo:inline>Reading, Massachusetts</fo:inline>
         </fo:block>
        </fo:list-item-body>
       </fo:list-item>
      </fo:list-block>
     </fo:block>
    </fo:flow>
   </fo:page-sequence>
  </fo:root>
```

Generating XSL with XSLT

Let's look at how the XSL document was generated from the book inventory. A common method of generating XSL documents is to use XSLT, which makes sense because the two specifications were designed to work together. This isn't the only method, of course. You could write an application that generated the XSL file directly and sent it to FOP; if you were concerned about performance, you might consider doing this. However, you'd give up a lot of flexibility. Taking XML data and using XSLT to convert it to XSL gives you much more flexibility because you can do other things with that XML. If you generate XSL directly, you lose the ability to repurpose the data at some later point. Here is an XSLT stylesheet that generates an XSL file based on the books.xml datafile.

```
<?xml version="1.0" encoding="UTF-8"?>
<xsl:stylesheet version="1.0"
  xmlns:xsl="http://www.w3.org/1999/XSL/Transform"
  xmlns:books="http://sauria.com/schemas/apache-xml-book/books"
  xmlns:fo="http://www.w3.org/1999/XSL/Format"
  exclude-result-prefixes="books">
```

Note that you declare the fo namespace prefix for use in the rest of the stylesheet.

The template for the root of the books document creates the shell of the XSL document and then allows templates for the child elements of the <books:books> element to do their job:

```
<xsl:output method="xml" version="1.0" encoding="UTF-8"
    indent="yes"/>

<xsl:template match="books:books">
 <fo:root>
  <fo:layout-master-set>
   <fo:simple-page-master master-name="book-page"
    page-height="11in" page-width="8.5in"
    margin-top="0.5in" margin-bottom="0.5in"
    margin-left="0.5in" margin-right="0.5in">
    <fo:region-body margin="1in"/>
   </fo:simple-page-master>
  </fo:layout-master-set>

  <fo:page-sequence master-reference="book-page">
   <fo:flow flow-name="xsl-region-body">
    <fo:block>
     <fo:list-block
         provisional-distance-between-starts="18pt"
         provisional-label-separation="3pt">
      <xsl:apply-templates/>
     </fo:list-block>
    </fo:block>
   </fo:flow>
  </fo:page-sequence>
 </fo:root>
</xsl:template>
```

In this template, you use the | operator from XPath to apply templates to a subset of the children of <books:book>. This is a nice, flexible approach, and it uses only a little more space than listing the elements you want selected:

```
<xsl:template match="books:book">
 <fo:list-item>
  <xsl:apply-templates select="books:title"/>
  <fo:list-item-body>
   <!-- need this to prevent garbling -->
   <fo:block space-after.optimum="15pt">
    <xsl:apply-templates
      select="books:author | books:isbn | books:month |
              books:year | books:publisher | books:address"/>
   </fo:block>
  </fo:list-item-body>
 </fo:list-item>
</xsl:template>
```

The remainder of the stylesheet looks similar to what you saw in Chapter 2, "Xalan," except you're generating XSL instead of HTML. So, you're seeing a demonstration of the versatility of XSLT in action:

```
    <xsl:template match="books:title">
     <fo:list-item-label>
      <fo:block space-after.optimum="15pt">
       <fo:inline font-size="14pt">
        &#x2022; <xsl:value-of select="."/>
       </fo:inline>
      </fo:block>
     </fo:list-item-label>
    </xsl:template>
    <xsl:template match="books:author">
      <fo:inline font-weight="bold">
       <xsl:value-of select="."/>
      </fo:inline>
    </xsl:template>
    <xsl:template match="books:isbn">
      <fo:inline><xsl:value-of select="."/></fo:inline>
    </xsl:template>
    <xsl:template match="books:month">
      <fo:inline><xsl:value-of select="."/>, </fo:inline>
    </xsl:template>
    <xsl:template match="books:year">
      <fo:inline><xsl:value-of select="."/></fo:inline>
    </xsl:template>
    <xsl:template match="books:publisher">
      <fo:inline><xsl:value-of select="."/></fo:inline>
    </xsl:template>
    <xsl:template match="books:address">
      <fo:inline><xsl:value-of select="."/></fo:inline>
    </xsl:template>
</xsl:stylesheet>
```

Tables

Let's look at one other XSL document that includes a table. Lists and tables are two important items you need to be familiar with in order to format business information. (Those of you who are more interested in publishing types of applications will need much more detail on XSL than we can present in this chapter.) The key thing is that you must specify all the table columns explicitly using <fo:table-column>, including their width (the column-width attribute):

```
<?xml version="1.0" encoding="UTF-8"?>
<fo:root xmlns:fo="http://www.w3.org/1999/XSL/Format">
 <fo:layout-master-set>
  <fo:simple-page-master margin-right="0.5in" margin-left="0.5in"
      margin-bottom="0.5in" margin-top="0.5in" page-width="8.5in"
```

```
        page-height="11in" master-name="book-page">
     <fo:region-body margin="1in"/>
    </fo:simple-page-master>
  </fo:layout-master-set>
  <fo:page-sequence master-reference="book-page">
    <fo:flow flow-name="xsl-region-body">
     <fo:block>
      <fo:table>
       <fo:table-column column-width="2.0in"/>
       <fo:table-column column-width="1.5in"/>
       <fo:table-column column-width="0.5in"/>
       <fo:table-column column-width="2.0in"/>
```

Once you've specified the columns, you can specify a header for the table (<fo:table-header>), which contains one table cell for each column. Note that the content of each table cell is a block:

```
       <fo:table-header>
        <fo:table-row>
         <fo:table-cell>
          <fo:block>Title</fo:block>
         </fo:table-cell>
         <fo:table-cell>
          <fo:block>ISBN</fo:block>
         </fo:table-cell>
         <fo:table-cell>
          <fo:block>Year</fo:block>
         </fo:table-cell>
         <fo:table-cell>
          <fo:block>Publisher</fo:block>
         </fo:table-cell>
        </fo:table-row>
       </fo:table-header>
```

The body of the table (enclosed in <fo:table-body>) is composed of rows (<fo:table-row>) that contain table cells, one for each column in the row:

```
       <fo:table-body>
        <fo:table-row>
         <fo:table-cell>
          <fo:block>Professional XML Development with Apache Tools</fo:block>
         </fo:table-cell>
         <fo:table-cell>
          <fo:block>0-7645-4355-5</fo:block>
         </fo:table-cell>
         <fo:table-cell>
          <fo:block>2003</fo:block>
         </fo:table-cell>
         <fo:table-cell>
          <fo:block>Wrox </fo:block>
         </fo:table-cell>
        </fo:table-row>
        <fo:table-row>
         <fo:table-cell>
```

```
        <fo:block>Effective Java</fo:block>
       </fo:table-cell>
       <fo:table-cell>
        <fo:block>0-201-31005-8</fo:block>
       </fo:table-cell>
       <fo:table-cell>
        <fo:block>2001</fo:block>
       </fo:table-cell>
       <fo:table-cell>
        <fo:block>Addison-Wesley</fo:block>
       </fo:table-cell>
      </fo:table-row>
      <fo:table-row>
       <fo:table-cell>
        <fo:block>Design Patterns</fo:block>
       </fo:table-cell>
       <fo:table-cell>
        <fo:block>0-201-63361-2</fo:block>
       </fo:table-cell>
       <fo:table-cell>
        <fo:block>1994</fo:block>
       </fo:table-cell>
       <fo:table-cell>
        <fo:block>Addison-Wesley</fo:block>
       </fo:table-cell>
      </fo:table-row>
     </fo:table-body>
    </fo:table>
   </fo:block>
  </fo:flow>
 </fo:page-sequence>
</fo:root>
```

The XSLT stylesheet for generating the table version of the XSL file is shown here:

```
<?xml version="1.0" encoding="UTF-8"?>
<xsl:stylesheet version="1.0"
  xmlns:xsl="http://www.w3.org/1999/XSL/Transform"
  xmlns:books="http://sauria.com/schemas/apache-xml-book/books"
  xmlns:fo="http://www.w3.org/1999/XSL/Format"
  exclude-result-prefixes="books">
    <xsl:output method="xml" version="1.0" encoding="UTF-8"
        indent="yes"/>

    <xsl:template match="books:books">
     <fo:root>
      <fo:layout-master-set>
       <fo:simple-page-master master-name="book-page"
        page-height="11in" page-width="8.5in"
        margin-top="0.5in" margin-bottom="0.5in"
        margin-left="0.5in" margin-right="0.5in">
        <fo:region-body margin="1in"/>
       </fo:simple-page-master>
      </fo:layout-master-set>
```

```

    <fo:page-sequence master-reference="book-page">
     <fo:flow flow-name="xsl-region-body">
      <fo:block>
       <fo:table>
        <fo:table-column column-width="2.0in"/>
        <fo:table-column column-width="1.5in"/>
        <fo:table-column column-width="0.5in"/>
        <fo:table-column column-width="2.0in"/>
        <fo:table-header>
         <fo:table-row>
         <fo:table-cell>
         <fo:block>Title</fo:block>
         </fo:table-cell>
         <fo:table-cell>
         <fo:block>ISBN</fo:block>
         </fo:table-cell>
         <fo:table-cell>
         <fo:block>Year</fo:block>
         </fo:table-cell>
         <fo:table-cell>
         <fo:block>Publisher</fo:block>
         </fo:table-cell>
      </fo:table-row>
      </fo:table-header>
        <fo:table-body>
         <xsl:apply-templates/>
        </fo:table-body>
       </fo:table>
      </fo:block>
     </fo:flow>
    </fo:page-sequence>
   </fo:root>
  </xsl:template>

  <xsl:template match="books:book">
   <fo:table-row>
    <xsl:apply-templates select="books:title | books: author |
    books:isbn | books:year | books:publisher"/>
   </fo:table-row>
  </xsl:template>

  <xsl:template match="books:title">
   <fo:table-cell>
    <fo:block>
     <xsl:value-of select="."/>
    </fo:block>
   </fo:table-cell>
  </xsl:template>

  <xsl:template match="books:author"/>

  <xsl:template match="books:isbn">
   <fo:table-cell>
```

```
      <fo:block><xsl:value-of select="."/></fo:block>
    </fo:table-cell>
    </xsl:template>

    <xsl:template match="books:month">
     <fo:table-cell>
      <fo:block><xsl:value-of select="."/></fo:block>
     </fo:table-cell>
    </xsl:template>

    <xsl:template match="books:year">
     <fo:table-cell>
      <fo:block><xsl:value-of select="."/></fo:block>
    </fo:table-cell>
    </xsl:template>

    <xsl:template match="books:publisher">
     <fo:table-cell>
      <fo:block><xsl:value-of select="."/></fo:block>
     </fo:table-cell>
    </xsl:template>

    <xsl:template match="books:address">
     <fo:table-cell>
      <fo:block><xsl:value-of select="."/></fo:block>
     </fo:table-cell>
    </xsl:template>
</xsl:stylesheet>
```

The XSL specification is large, and at the time of this writing FOP doesn't support everything in the specification. Every FOP distribution contains a documentation page that includes a large table showing which XSL features are supported in that version of FOP. The safest way to proceed is to look at that page for the FOP distribution you're using. You can also consult the FOP user's mailing list (directions for finding this are in the documentation) if you're unsure whether a particular feature is supported.

Installing and Configuring FOP

FOP requires at least a JDK 1.3 installation in order to operate. Before you can do anything with FOP, you need to download and install a build. You can obtain an FOP build by going to http://xml.apache.org/dist/fop, where you'll see a list of the current official FOP builds. The build for a particular version of FOP is divided into two parts. Let's use FOP 0.20.5 as an example. The binary distribution of FOP 0.20.5 is in a file named fop-0.20.5-bin..*xxx*, where *xxx* is either .zip or .tar.gz, depending on which kind of compressed archive format you need. Typically, people on Windows use a .zip file, whereas people on Mac OS X, Linux, and UNIX of various sorts use a .tar.gz file. There are also .*xxx*.asc files, which are detached PGP signatures of the corresponding .*xxx* files. So, fop-0.20.5-bin.asc contains the signature file for the fop-0.20.5-bin.zip distribution file. You can use PGP and the signature file to verify that the contents of the distribution haven't been tampered with. In addition to the binary distribution, you can download a source distribution, fop-0.20.5-src.zip, if you want to look at or modify the sources.

We'll focus on installing the binary distribution. Once you've downloaded a binary distribution, you should unpack it using either WinZip or tar as discussed in the previous paragraph. Doing so creates a directory called fop-0.20.5 in either the current directory or the directory you specified to your archiving utility. The key files in this directory are as follows:

- **build**—A directory containing fop.jar and the FOP site documentation (in build/site).
- **conf**—A directory containing the configuration files for FOP.
- **examples**—The FOP sample programs.
- **lib**—A directory containing the jar files FOP needs. FOP includes versions of jars that have been tested with that version of FOP. In particular, versions of Xerces, Xalan, and Batik are included in the distribution. You may have more recent versions of these libraries on your system. We'll discuss this issue more in a moment.
- **fop.bat**—A Windows batch file for running FOP from the command line.
- **fop.sh**—A UNIX/Linux shell script for running FOP from the command line.

You must include all the jars in the lib directory in your Java classpath in order to use FOP in your application. There are a variety of ways to accomplish this, including setting the CLASSPATH environment variable in your DOS Command window or UNIX shell window. You can also set the CLASSPATH for the application server you're using. The issue is complicated a bit by the fact that FOP includes copies of the Xerces, Xalan, and Batik jars. Depending on what your application does, you may need specific versions of these jars that differ from the versions provided with FOP. In most cases, you can use the jars you need, but in some cases you may run into conflicts because of bugs that have been fixed or worked around in the different versions of Xerces, Xalan, or Batik.

Hyphenation

FOP provides hyphenation on a per-language basis. The standard FOP installation comes with support for English, Spanish, Finnish, Hungarian, Italian, Polish, Portuguese, and Russian. If you need hyphenation support for a language that isn't in this list, you'll need to create a new hyphenation pattern file.

FOP's hyphenation rules use an XML-based pattern scheme based on the hyphenation rules found in TeX. TeX is a powerful document-formatting system popular in academia, particularly in math and the sciences. If TeX has a hyphenation file for the language you're interested in, you can use it to help generate a file that FOP can use.

FOP's hyphenation file is an XML file that looks like this:

```
1: <hyphenation-info>
2:   <hyphen-char value="-"/>
3:   <hyphen-min before="3" after="2"/>
4:   <classes>aA bB cC — zZ</classes>
5:   <exceptions>as-so-ciate present ta-ble</exceptions>
6:   <patterns>.custom5 .di4al. a5tel.</patterns>
7: </hyphenation-info>
```

The root element is <hyphenation-info>. The <hyphen-char> element is used to say which character is used as a hyphen. In this example, the character is the expected "-" character (line 2). The <hyphen-min>

element specifies the minimum number of characters that must appear on a line before and after a hyphenated word break. In this example file, there must be three characters before the hyphen and two characters after the hyphen (line 3).

Lines 4-6 are shortened versions of what would appear in a real hyphenation file. They are there to show you the order in which the <classes>, <exceptions>, and <patterns> elements must appear. The <classes> element contains sets of characters separated by whitespace. The hyphenation engine treats all characters in a set as equivalent for hyphenation purposes. So, sets like aA, bB, cC, and so on tell the engine to treat the uppercase and lowercase versions of the same letter as equivalents for the purpose of hyphenation. We'll skip the <exceptions> element for now and come back to it after we describe what the <patterns> element contains.

The <patterns> element contains pattern strings separated by whitespace. Within a pattern, each non-numeric character is a character that may appear in a word. The period (.) character represents a word boundary—either the beginning or end of a word, depending on where it appears. If a number appears in the pattern, it's a score indicating the desirability of a hyphen at the position where the number appears. The scoring system is a bit complicated. If the number is odd, then the location is desirable for a hyphen; 5 is the score for most desirable and 1 is the score for least desirable. If the number is even, then the location is undesirable for a hyphen; 0 (which is assumed if no number is present) isn't desirable, whereas 4 is *extremely* undesirable. In the sample file, the patterns say "it's very desirable to have a hyphen after *custom*, when *custom* is the start of the word," "it's extremely undesirable to hyphenate *dial* between the *i* and the *a*," and "if a word ends in *atel*, then the best place for the hyphen is between the *a* and the *t*."

The <exceptions> element contains a list of words separated by whitespace. This list overrides the rules in the <patterns> element. Two kinds of words appear in the list: Words containing hyphens should only be broken at the point where the hyphen appears, and words containing no hyphens should never be hyphenated.

Development Techniques

Now we'll look at techniques that will help you use FOP in your applications. We'll start by looking at how to embed FOP in your program using the FOP Driver API, SAX, and DOM. FOP supplies an XML schema you can use to validate your XSL documents, and we'll discuss how to do that as well. Then we'll cover the various output formats FOP can produce and how to use fonts and graphics, and we'll conclude by looking at FOP extensions, which are similar to Xalan extensions.

Embedding

Let's begin with the simplest program that uses FOP from inside. The following program reads an XSL file from a file and creates a PDF file as its output. The two files are specified on the command line. (More sophisticated usages of FOP embedding will follow.)

```
/*
 *
 * FOPMain.java
 *
 * Example from "Professional XML Development with Apache Tools"
```

```
 *
 */
package com.sauria.apachexml.ch3;

import java.io.BufferedOutputStream;
import java.io.FileNotFoundException;
import java.io.FileOutputStream;
import java.io.IOException;
import java.io.OutputStream;

import org.apache.avalon.framework.logger.ConsoleLogger;
import org.apache.avalon.framework.logger.Logger;
import org.apache.fop.apps.Driver;
import org.apache.fop.apps.FOPException;
import org.apache.fop.apps.FormattingResults;
import org.apache.fop.messaging.MessageHandler;
import org.xml.sax.InputSource;

public class FOPMain {
    public static void main(String[] args) {
        String xslFile = args[0];
        String pdfFile = args[1];

        OutputStream outFile = null;

        try {
            outFile = new FileOutputStream(pdfFile);
            outFile = new BufferedOutputStream(outFile);
        } catch (FileNotFoundException fnfe) {
            fnfe.printStackTrace();
        }
```

For efficiency, you wrap the FileOutputStream in a BufferedOutputStream. Doing so is particularly important if you're formatting large documents.

You construct the FOP Driver class and pass it an InputSource containing the XSL file and the output stream where the PDF is to be written:

```

        Driver fopDriver = new Driver(new InputSource(xslFile),
                                      outFile);
```

FOP uses the Apache Jakarta Avalon project's logging framework to handle logging. If you want to see the log of messages as FOP is processing the input document, then you need to create the appropriate Logger subclass and then pass it to the FOP MessageHandler as well as the FOP Driver. Here you use a ConsoleLogger, but you can use any Logger the Avalon logging framework provides.

```
        Logger logger =
            new ConsoleLogger(ConsoleLogger.LEVEL_WARN);
        MessageHandler.setScreenLogger(logger);
        fopDriver.setLogger(logger);
```

This line tells the Driver that you want to render the output as PDF:

```
        fopDriver.setRenderer(Driver.RENDER_PDF);
```

You have to call the Driver's run method to process the document:

```
        try {
            fopDriver.run();
        } catch (IOException ioe) {
            ioe.printStackTrace();
        } catch (FOPException fe) {
            fe.printStackTrace();
        }
```

After formatting is complete, you can get a FormattingResults object from the Driver and ask it for statistics about the processing. Here you ask for the number of pages that were formatted:

```

        FormattingResults results = fopDriver.getResults();
        System.out.println("Pages Formatted: "+
                           results.getPageCount());
    }
}
```

Using the Configuration Files and Options

FOP can read its configuration settings from a file. This is a version of the embedded FOP program that shows how to tell FOP to use a configuration file:

```
/*
 *
 * FOPConfigMain.java
 *
 * Example from "Professional XML Development with Apache Tools"
 *
 */
package com.sauria.apachexml.ch3;

import java.io.BufferedOutputStream;
import java.io.File;
import java.io.FileNotFoundException;
import java.io.FileOutputStream;
import java.io.IOException;
import java.io.OutputStream;

import org.apache.avalon.framework.logger.ConsoleLogger;
import org.apache.avalon.framework.logger.Logger;
import org.apache.fop.apps.Driver;
import org.apache.fop.apps.FOPException;
import org.apache.fop.apps.FormattingResults;
```

```
import org.apache.fop.apps.Options;
import org.apache.fop.messaging.MessageHandler;
import org.xml.sax.InputSource;

public class FOPConfigMain {

    public static void main(String[] args) {
        String configFile = args[0];
        String xslFile = args[1];
        String pdfFile = args[2];

        OutputStream outFile = null;

        try {
            outFile = new FileOutputStream(pdfFile);
            outFile = new BufferedOutputStream(outFile);
        } catch (FileNotFoundException fnfe) {
            fnfe.printStackTrace();
        }

        File config = new File(configFile);
        Options options = null;

```

This part of the FOP API is a bit inconsistent. To read the configuration file, you need to create an instance of java.io.File. Everything else relies on either InputSource or OutputStream, so you have to remember that you need a File here, not some kind of InputStream.

You specify the configuration by instantiating an instance of org.apache.fop.apps.Options and passing to it the File containing the configuration file. After that, you're done—FOP takes care of the rest. (The Options constructor creates a static configuration instance under the covers. Note that this can be a problem if you try to use FOP in a multithreaded environment. If you're going to use FOP in a threaded environment, you need to synchronize access to the FOP Driver.)

```
        try {
            options = new Options(config);
        } catch (FOPException fe) {
            fe.printStackTrace();
        }

        Driver fopDriver = new Driver(new InputSource(xslFile),
                                      outFile);
        Logger logger =
            new ConsoleLogger(ConsoleLogger.LEVEL_WARN);
        MessageHandler.setScreenLogger(logger);
        fopDriver.setLogger(logger);
        fopDriver.setRenderer(Driver.RENDER_PDF);
        try {
            fopDriver.run();
        } catch (IOException ioe) {
            ioe.printStackTrace();
        } catch (FOPException fe) {
            fe.printStackTrace();
```

```
        }

        FormattingResults results = fopDriver.getResults();
        System.out.println("Pages Formatted: "+
                               results.getPageCount());
    }
}
```

The FOP user configuration file allow you to control a number of different things. It consists of some key-value pairs and then some element related to fonts. In this section we'll cover the key value pairs and defer the font-related information to the "Fonts" section. You can look at conf/userconfig.xml in the FOP distribution directory for an example. Key value pairs in the configuration file look like this:

```
<entry>
 <key> key </key>
 <value> value for key </value>
</entry>
```

The following table lists the possible keys and the meanings of their values:

Key	Value
baseDir	A URL specifying the directory containing the input files. Defaults to the current working directory if embedded, or the directory containing the input files if command line.
fontBaseDir	A URL specifying a directory where fonts can be found. Defaults to the same value as baseDir.
hyphenation-dir	A URL specifying a directory where custom hyphenation files can be found. No default.
strokeSVGText	For the PDF renderer only: False to force text in an SVG document to be converted to text. Default is true, which means some text may be converted to SVG shapes.

SAX

Sometimes your application will generate XSL directly, without placing the formatting objects into a file in the filesystem. In these cases, you should process the XSL via a stream of SAX events or a DOM tree your application creates. In this section, we'll look at how to feed the FOP Driver from a SAX event stream:

```
/*
 *
 * FOPSAXMain.java
 *
 * Example from "Professional XML Development with Apache Tools"
 *
 */
package com.sauria.apachexml.ch3;
```

```
 9:
10: import java.io.BufferedOutputStream;
11: import java.io.FileNotFoundException;
12: import java.io.FileOutputStream;
13: import java.io.IOException;
14: import java.io.OutputStream;
15:
16: import javax.xml.parsers.ParserConfigurationException;
17: import javax.xml.parsers.SAXParserFactory;
18:
19: import org.apache.avalon.framework.logger.ConsoleLogger;
20: import org.apache.avalon.framework.logger.Logger;
21: import org.apache.fop.apps.Driver;
22: import org.apache.fop.apps.FormattingResults;
23: import org.apache.fop.messaging.MessageHandler;
24: import org.xml.sax.SAXException;
25: import org.xml.sax.XMLReader;
26:
27: public class FOPSAXMain {
28:
29:     public static void main(String[] args) {
30:         String xslFile = args[0];
31:         String pdfFile = args[1];
32:         OutputStream outputFile = null;
33:
34:         try {
35:             outputFile = new FileOutputStream(pdfFile);
36:             outputFile = new BufferedOutputStream(outputFile);
37:         } catch (FileNotFoundException fnfe) {
38:             fnfe.printStackTrace();
39:         }
40:
41:         Driver fopDriver = new Driver();
42:         fopDriver.setOutputStream(outputFile);
43:
44:         Logger logger =
45:             new ConsoleLogger(ConsoleLogger.LEVEL_WARN);
46:         MessageHandler.setScreenLogger(logger);
47:         fopDriver.setLogger(logger);
48:         fopDriver.setRenderer(Driver.RENDER_PDF);
```

This time you set up the FOP Driver using the default constructor. This means no input or output file is associated with the Driver. For this example, you send the output to a PDF file, so the code to set up the buffered FileOutputStream is the same (lines 34-39). After you construct the FOP Driver, you have to explicitly set the Driver's output stream (line 42).

You finish setting up the FOP Driver as in the previous examples, but you don't call its run method. Instead you create a namespace-aware SAX parser (XMLReader, actually) using the JAXP SAXParserFactory. You ask the driver to give you its SAX ContentHandler. You register this ContentHandler with the SAX parser instance you created (line 56) so the FOP-provided callbacks are called when the parser processes the documents. You then format the document by asking the SAX parser to parse the XSL document (line 57):

```

    XMLReader r = null;
    SAXParserFactory spf = SAXParserFactory.newInstance();
    spf.setNamespaceAware(true);

    try {
      r = spf.newSAXParser().getXMLReader();
      r.setContentHandler(fopDriver.getContentHandler());
      r.parse(xslFile);
    } catch (SAXException se) {
      se.printStackTrace();
    } catch (ParserConfigurationException pce) {
      pce.printStackTrace();
    } catch (IOException ioe) {
      ioe.printStackTrace();
    }

    FormattingResults results = fopDriver.getResults();
    System.out.println("Pages Formatted: "+
                         results.getPageCount());
  }
}
```

DOM

Using a DOM tree as input to FOP requires another slightly different style of invoking FOP:

```
/*
 *
 * FOPDOMMain.java
 *
 * Example from "Professional XML Development with Apache Tools"
 *
 */
package com.sauria.apachexml.ch3;

import java.io.BufferedOutputStream;
import java.io.FileNotFoundException;
import java.io.FileOutputStream;
import java.io.IOException;
import java.io.OutputStream;

import javax.xml.parsers.DocumentBuilder;
import javax.xml.parsers.DocumentBuilderFactory;
import javax.xml.parsers.ParserConfigurationException;

import org.apache.avalon.framework.logger.ConsoleLogger;
import org.apache.avalon.framework.logger.Logger;
import org.apache.fop.apps.Driver;
import org.apache.fop.apps.FOPException;
import org.apache.fop.apps.FormattingResults;
import org.apache.fop.messaging.MessageHandler;
import org.w3c.dom.Document;
```

```
import org.xml.sax.SAXException;

public class FOPDOMMain {

    public static void main(String[] args) {
        String xslFile = args[0];
        String pdfFile = args[1];

        DocumentBuilderFactory dbf =
            DocumentBuilderFactory.newInstance();
        dbf.setNamespaceAware(true);
```

You use the JAXP DocumentBuilderFactory to create a namespace-aware DOM parser. Then you call the DocumentBuilder to parse the XSL document and create a DOM tree:

```

        DocumentBuilder builder = null;
        try {
            builder = dbf.newDocumentBuilder();
        } catch (ParserConfigurationException pce) {
            pce.printStackTrace();
        }

        Document doc = null;
        try {
            doc = builder.parse(xslFile);
```

Again, you have to set up the FOP Driver using the default constructor and then set the output stream to be a buffered FileOutputStream:

```
        } catch (SAXException se) {
            se.printStackTrace();
        } catch (IOException ioe) {
            ioe.printStackTrace();
        }

        OutputStream outputFile = null;

        try {
            outputFile = new FileOutputStream(pdfFile);
            outputFile = new BufferedOutputStream(outputFile);
        } catch (FileNotFoundException fnfe) {
            fnfe.printStackTrace();
        }

        Driver fopDriver = new Driver();
        fopDriver.setOutputStream(outputFile);
```

You finish setting up the FOP driver as before:

```

        Logger logger =
            new ConsoleLogger(ConsoleLogger.LEVEL_WARN);
```

```
        MessageHandler.setScreenLogger(logger);
        fopDriver.setLogger(logger);
        fopDriver.setRenderer(Driver.RENDER_PDF);
```

You process the XSL document by calling the render method on the Driver and passing the DOM tree as an argument:

```

        try {
            fopDriver.render(doc);
        } catch (FOPException fe) {
            fe.printStackTrace();
        }

        FormattingResults results = fopDriver.getResults();
        System.out.println("Pages Formatted: "+
                               results.getPageCount());
    }
}
```

Note that for each of the three input styles for the Driver, you use a different method name to invoke FOP. This seems like an area for improvement in the FOP APIs.

XSLT

The last example with an embedded FOP driver involves the use of XSLT. Your application might use XSLT and a stylesheet to convert an XML file into an XSL formatting objects document. This example shows how to chain together a JAXP-compliant XSLT processor, such as Xalan, and FOP:

```
/*
 *
 * XSLTFOPMain.java
 *
 * Example from "Professional XML Development with Apache Tools"
 *
 */
package com.sauria.apachexml.ch3;

import java.io.BufferedOutputStream;
import java.io.FileNotFoundException;
import java.io.FileOutputStream;
import java.io.OutputStream;

import javax.xml.transform.Result;
import javax.xml.transform.Source;
import javax.xml.transform.Transformer;
import javax.xml.transform.TransformerConfigurationException;
import javax.xml.transform.TransformerException;
import javax.xml.transform.TransformerFactory;
import javax.xml.transform.sax.SAXResult;
import javax.xml.transform.stream.StreamSource;

```

```
import org.apache.avalon.framework.logger.ConsoleLogger;
import org.apache.avalon.framework.logger.Logger;
import org.apache.fop.apps.Driver;
import org.apache.fop.apps.FormattingResults;
import org.apache.fop.messaging.MessageHandler;

public class XSLTFOPMain {

    public static void main(String[] args) {
        String xmlFile = args[0];
        String xsltFile = args[1];
        String pdfFile = args[2];

        OutputStream outFile = null;

        try {
            outFile = new FileOutputStream(pdfFile);
            outFile = new BufferedOutputStream(outFile);
        } catch (FileNotFoundException fnfe) {
            fnfe.printStackTrace();
        }

        Driver fopDriver = new Driver();

        Logger logger =
            new ConsoleLogger(ConsoleLogger.LEVEL_WARN);
        MessageHandler.setScreenLogger(logger);
        fopDriver.setLogger(logger);
        fopDriver.setRenderer(Driver.RENDER_PDF);
        fopDriver.setOutputStream(outFile);
```

The setup for FOP should be familiar by now. You use the default constructor for the Driver and set the output stream explicitly. All the real work in this example has to do with where the FOP engine gets its input.

The key piece is that the result of the XSLT processor is the input to the FOP engine. So, you create a SAXResult that's set to the Driver's ContentHandler:

```

        Source xmlSource = new StreamSource(xmlFile);
        Source xsltSource = new StreamSource(xsltFile);
        Result result =
            new SAXResult(fopDriver.getContentHandler());
```

A SAXResult produces a SAX event stream to be consumed via a ContentHandler, so this is a perfect fit for what you're trying to do. If for some reason you wanted to do this using DOM trees, you could create a DOMResult and then call the FOP Driver with it as you did in the DOM example.

Because you're using SAX, asking the first stage in the SAX pipeline to do the work causes the entire pipeline to do its job. Calling the Transformer's transform method is all you need to get the job done:

```

        TransformerFactory xformFactory =
```

```
            TransformerFactory.newInstance();
        Transformer xformer = null;

        try {
            xformer = xformFactory.newTransformer(xsltSource);
        } catch (TransformerConfigurationException tce) {
            tce.printStackTrace();
        }

        try {
            xformer.transform(xmlSource, result);
        } catch (TransformerException te) {
            te.printStackTrace();
        }

        FormattingResults results = fopDriver.getResults();
        System.out.println("Pages Formatted: "+
                               results.getPageCount());
    }
}
```

Validating XSL

Sometimes it can be difficult to find problems in your XSL documents. One way to locate problems is to validate your XSL document against FOP's XML Schema grammar. This grammar is included in the FOP source distribution in the file src/foschema/fop.xsd. If you've never used XML Schema to validate an XML document, you'll need to add some attributes to the <fo:root> element in your XSL document. You need a namespace declaration for the XML Schema Instance namespace: xmlns:xsi="http://www.w3.org/2001/XMLSchema-instance". You also need to add an xsi:schemaLocation attribute to tell the schema validator where to find the schema file. This will look something like xsi:schemaLocation= "http://www.w3.org/1999/XSL/Format <URI path to>/fop.xsd". Be sure the path to fop.xsd is a URI (relative URIs are okay). Once you've added these attributes to your XSL document, you can use an XML Schema–aware validating XML parser to check your document for syntactic correctness.

Command-Line Usage

When you have embedded FOP in your application, it may be difficult to track down problems in the output. You can also run FOP as a command-line tool from your operating system's command line. When you run FOP this way, you can play with the XSL input file and see how doing so changes the output file. In some situations, this can help you figure out how to generate XSL that produces the formatted output you want.

The FOP distribution provides a Windows batch file and a UNIX shell script file you use to invoke FOP from the command line. Before you use them, you need to edit them to make sure they point at the directory where you installed FOP. Under Windows, set the variable LOCAL_FOP_HOME in the fop.bat file. The variable is called FOP_HOME in the UNIX fop.sh script.

Once you've edited the batch or shell script file, you can execute it from the command line (UNIX users may need to set execute permissions on the shell script first). The syntax of the command is:

```
fop [options] [input options] [output options]
```

The following table describes the FOP options:

Option	Description
-d	Debug mode.
-x	Dump configuration settings.
-q	Quiet mode.
-c cfg.xml	Use configuration file cfg.xml.
-l *<lang>*	Language for user information.
-s	If outputting an area tree (see -at), omit the tree below block areas.
-txt.encoding	If using -txt encoding, the encoding should be used for the output file; the encoding must be valid Java encoding.
-o *<password>*	Encrypt the PDF file with the option owner password.
-u *<password>*	Encrypt the PDF file with the option user password.
-noprint	Encrypt the PDF file without printing permission.
-nocopy	Encrypt the PDF file without copy content permission.
-noedit	Encrypt the PDF file without edit content permission.
-noannotations	Encrypt the PDF file without edit annotation permission.

The following table describes the FOP input options:

Option	Description
-fo *<infile>*	XSL formatting objects file.
-xml *<infile>*	XML input file, used in conjunction with -xsl.
-xsl <stylesheet>	XSLT stylesheet that converts the XML input file specified with -xml to XSL with formatting objects.

The following table describes the FOP output options:

Option	Description
-pdf *<outfile>*	Render output as PDF and save it in *<outfile>*.
-awt	Display output on the screen.
-mif *<outfile>*	Render output as MIF and save it in *<outfile>*.
-pcl *<outfile>*	Render output as PCL and save it in *<outfile>*.

Option	Description
-ps *<outfile>*	Render output as PostScript and save it in <outfile>.
-txt *<outfile>*	Render output as text (according to the text encoding) and save it in *<outfile>*.
-svg *<outfile>*	Render output as an SVG slides file and save it in *<outfile>*.
-at *<outfile>*	Render output as an area tree in XML and save it in *<outfile>*.
-print	Render output and send it to the printer.

The following table describes the sub-options for the -print option:

Print option	Description
-Dstart=*i*	Start printing at page *i*.
-Dend=*i*	Stop printing at page *i*.
-Dcopies=*i*	Print *i* copies.
-Deven=true | false	Print only even pages if true, only odd pages if false.

Ant Task

A third way of using FOP is as an Ant task. Ant is a very popular XML-based build tool for Java. You may want to use FOP to generate PDF, or FrameMaker MIF documentation for the project you're building. The FOP Ant task allows you to easily integrate FOP functionality into your Ant-based build. Ant can be extended using new tasks that reside in jars besides the Ant jar file. To do this, you must place a <taskdef> element in the build file before you try to use the FOP task. The code for the FOP <taskdef> looks like this:

```
<property name="fop.dir"
          value="....path to your FOP jar files..."/>

<taskdef name="fop"
        classname="org.apache.fop.tools.anttasks.Fop">
        <classpath>
           <pathelement location="${fop.dir}\build\fop.jar"/>
           <pathelement location="${fop.dir}\lib\avalon.jar"/>
           <pathelement location="${fop.dir}\lib\batik.jar"/>
        </classpath>
</taskdef>
```

Now that the FOP task is accessible to Ant, you can create Ant tasks that call FOP. You do this by including an <fop> element inside a target. The parameters to FOP are specified as attributes of the <fop> element. The FOP task is able to use Ant's <fileset> element to operate on directories of files at once. The following table lists the attributes you can use and their meaning:

Task Attribute	Description	Required
fofile	XSL file to be rendered.	Yes, unless a nested fileset element is used.
outfile	Output filename.	Yes, if fofile is used.
outdir	Output directory.	Yes, if a nested fileset element is used. Also specifies the directory if outfile is used.
format	Available output formats are application/pdf, application/postscript, application/vnd.mif, application/rtf, application/vnd.hp-PCL, text/plain, and text/xml.	No; defaults to application/pdf.
userconfig	Name of the user configuration file.	No.
messagelevel	Logging level values are error, warn, info, verbose, and debug.	No; defaults to verbose.
logfiles	Log the names of files that are processed (if true).	No; defaults to true.

Here's a simple Ant target that uses FOP to generate a PDF file for each .fo file in the myxsldir directory. The PDFs are placed in the directory mypdfdir. Both directories are in the current directory at the time the task is executed:

```
<target name="generate-multiple-pdfs"
        description="Generates multiple PDF files">
 <fop format="application/pdf"
      outdir="mypdfdir" messagelevel="debug">
  <fileset dir="myxsldir">
   <include name="*.fo"/>
  </fileset>
 </fop>
</target>
```

Fonts

FOP provides its own system for registering fonts. Most of the time this won't cause a problem, but a few of the output renderers don't use the FOP font system. In particular, the AWT and print renderers use Java's AWT package to do their work, and the AWT gets its information from the underlying operating system. Differences can result, depending on the operating system. These may include different font metrics or completely different fonts. You sure you use renderers that use the same font model.

FOP starts with a built-in set of 14 fonts taken from the Adobe PDF specification: Helvetica (normal, bold, italic, and bold italic), Times (normal, bold, italic, and bold italic), Courier (normal, bold, italic, and bold italic), Symbol, and ZapfDingbats. FOP also has support for custom fonts beyond this set. The current version of FOP (0.20.5) can add Type 1 and Truetype fonts; this is done by creating font metric files in XML format.

You generate the font metrics for a Type 1 font using the PFMReader class, which understands the PFM files that usually come with a Type 1 font. PFMReader looks at the PFM file and generates an XML font metrics file FOP can understand. The usage of PFMReader looks something like this:

```
java org.apache.fop.fonts.apps.PFMReader <pfm-file> <xml-file>
```

In order for PFMReader to work, fop.jar, avalon-framework.jar, and the Xerces and Xalan jars must be in the classpath.

In a similar fashion, The TTFReader class can generate a compatible font metrics file by reading a .ttf font file. Its usage looks similar to that of PFMReader:

```
java org.apache.fop.fonts.apps.TTFReader <ttf-file> <xml-file>
```

Again, fop.jar, avalon-framework.jar, and the Xerces and Xalan jars must be in the classpath. TrueType also allows for collections of fonts. Running TTFReader on a TrueType font collection causes TTFReader to list all the font names in the collection and then exit with an exception. You can use this fact to obtain the name of the specific TrueType font you need and then run TTFReader with the -ttcname "font-name" option, which generates the metrics file for the font you named.

Once you have generated font metrics files that FOP can understand, you still need to register these fonts with FOP. This brings us back to the FOP configuration file. Let's assume you've generated a font metrics file for Arial in arialfm.xml and the font itself is in Arial.ttf, both in the directory specified by fontBaseDir.

The last section in the configuration file looks like this:

```
<fonts>
 <font metrics-file="arialfm.xml" kerning="yes"
       embed-file="Arial.ttf">
  <font-triplet name="Arial" style="italic" weight="bold" />
 </font>
</fonts>
```

The options for <font-triplet>'s style attribute are normal and italic, and the options for its weight attribute are normal and bold. <font>'s kerning attribute can be either yes or no. The embed-file attribute is optional. When you're using Type 1 fonts, be sure you give the name of the font file, not the metrics file, for <font>'s embed-file attribute.

If you supply the embed-file attribute on <font>, the font is embedded in the output document rather than being referenced. When you use Type 1 fonts, the entire font is embedded. When you use TrueType fonts (or collections), a new font that contains only the glpyhs that were actually used is embedded. This behavior can cause problems with searching, indexing, and cut and paste, because the output document contains indexes of the glyphs in the fonts, not the actual characters.

Output

FOP is all about rendering XSL documents in different formats. FOP provides a collection of classes that perform the job of rendering. In this section we'll take a closer look at the renderers that come with FOP.

PDF

Adobe's Portable Document Format (PDF) is the best-supported output format. FOP supports PDF version 1.3, which corresponds to the version implemented in Acrobat Reader 4.0. There are some PDF features that FOP doesn't support at the moment; these include tagged PDF, document properties, and watermarks. You can use the open-source program iText (http://sourceforge.net/projects/itext) to add these features to PDF files generated by FOP. Starting with version 0.20.5, FOP has built-in support for PDF encryption. Here's a program that shows how to encrypt a PDF file:

```
/*
 *
 * FOPEncryptionMain.java
 *
 * Example from "Professional XML Development with Apache Tools"
 *
 */
package com.sauria.apachexml.ch3;

import java.io.BufferedOutputStream;
import java.io.FileNotFoundException;
import java.io.FileOutputStream;
import java.io.IOException;
import java.io.OutputStream;
import java.util.Map;

import org.apache.avalon.framework.logger.ConsoleLogger;
import org.apache.avalon.framework.logger.Logger;
import org.apache.fop.apps.Driver;
import org.apache.fop.apps.FOPException;
import org.apache.fop.apps.FormattingResults;
import org.apache.fop.messaging.MessageHandler;
import org.xml.sax.InputSource;

public class FOPEncryptionMain {

    public static void main(String[] args) {
        String xslFile = args[0];
        String pdfFile = args[1];

        OutputStream outFile = null;

        try {
            outFile = new FileOutputStream(pdfFile);
            outFile = new BufferedOutputStream(outFile);
        } catch (FileNotFoundException fnfe) {
            fnfe.printStackTrace();
        }

```

```
        Driver fopDriver = new Driver(new InputSource(xslFile),
                                      outFile);
        Logger logger =
            new ConsoleLogger(ConsoleLogger.LEVEL_WARN);
        MessageHandler.setScreenLogger(logger);
        fopDriver.setLogger(logger);
        fopDriver.setRenderer(Driver.RENDER_PDF);

        Map rendererOptions = new java.util.HashMap();
        rendererOptions.put("ownerPassword", "ownerpassword");
        rendererOptions.put("userPassword", "userpassword");
        rendererOptions.put("allowCopyContent", "FALSE");
        rendererOptions.put("allowEditContent", "FALSE");
        rendererOptions.put("allowPrint", "FALSE");
        rendererOptions.put("allowEditAnnotations","FALSE");
        fopDriver.getRenderer().setOptions(rendererOptions);

        try {
            fopDriver.run();
        } catch (IOException ioe) {
            ioe.printStackTrace();
        } catch (FOPException fe) {
            fe.printStackTrace();
        }

        FormattingResults results = fopDriver.getResults();
        System.out.println("Pages Formatted: "+
                           results.getPageCount());
    }
}
```

To encrypt a PDF document, you create a java.util.Map that contains a set of rendering options and pass it to the setOptions method of the Driver's renderer (assuming you've selected the PDF renderer). In this example, you set all the available PDF encryption options. If you look carefully, you'll see that these correspond to options that can be set from the FOP command line. Setting any one of these options causes the PDF file to be encrypted.

The Driver constant for the PDF renderer is Driver.RENDER_PDF.

PostScript

The PostScript renderer generates PostScript level 3 with most DSC comments. As of FOP 0.20.5, there are still a number of limitations in the PostScript renderer:

- Images and SVG may not display correctly.
- SVG support is very incomplete.
- No image transparency is available.
- Character spacings may be wrong.
- Font embedding and multibyte characters aren't supported.
- PPD support is missing.

The Driver constant for the PostScript renderer is Driver.RENDER_PS.

PCL

The PCL renderer generates the Hewlett-Package Page Control Language (PCL) used in HP printers. The printed PCL output should be as close to identical as possible when compared to the printed output of the PDF renderer, subject to the limitations of the renderer and output device. The list of limitations is as follows:

- Text or graphics outside the top or left of the printable aren't rendered properly.
- Helvetica is mapped to Arial, and Times is mapped to Times New.
- Custom fonts aren't supported.
- Symbols are used for the non-symbol fonts ISO-8859-1.
- Multibyte characters aren't supported.
- SVG support is limited to lines, rectangles, circles, ellipses, text, simple paths, and images. Colors (dithered black and white) are supported, but gradients aren't. SVG clipping isn't supported.
- Images print black and white only. To print a non-monochrome image, it should be dithered first.
- Image scaling is accomplished by modifying the effective resolution of the image data. Available resolutions are 75, 100, 150, 300, and 600 DPI.
- Color printing isn't supported. Colors are rendered by mapping the color intensity to one of the PCL fill shades (nine steps from white to black).

The Driver constant for the PCL renderer is Driver.RENDER.PCL.

SVG

The SVG renderer creates an SVG document that has links between the pages. This renderer is most useful for rendering slides and SVG images of pages. Large document create SVG documents that are too large for current SVG viewers to display. SVG font information is obtained from the Java VM, so there is the possibility of font mismatches when compared to the other renderers.

The Driver constant for the SVG renderer is Driver.RENDER_SVG.

MIF

The MIF renderer produces the Maker Interchange Format used by Adobe's FrameMaker. This renderer isn't fully implemented.

The Driver constant for the MIF renderer is Driver.RENDER_MIF.

TXT

The Text renderer produces ASCII text that tries to approximate the output of the PDF renderer. It's most useful for getting an idea what the PDF document will look like. When you use this renderer, there are often extra or missing spaces between characters and lines due to the way FOP lays out text. You can reduce the number of spacing problems by adding the following attributes to your XSL document: font-family="Courier", font-size="7.3pt", line-height="10.5pt".

The Driver constant for the Text renderer is Driver.RENDER_TXT.

XML

The XML renderer produces an XML description of the area tree for the document. It's primarily used for testing.

The Driver constant for the XML renderer is Driver.RENDER_XML.

AWT

The AWT renderer displays the pages one at a time in an AWT window. Each page is displayed inside a Java graphic. This renderer uses the Java VM font model, so there is the possibility of font mismatches compared to the other renderers.

The Driver constant for the AWT renderer is Driver.RENDER_AWT.

Graphics

FOP supports a number of different graphics file formats. This support is either built into FOP or provided via a separate library that must be downloaded.

Graphics Resolution

There is a mismatch between most of the FOP output formats (including PDF) and some bitmapped image file formats. The bitmap formats store some notion of the resolution of the image (most often dots per inch [dpi]), whereas the output formats have no notion of resolution. FOP ignores any resolution specified by the image file and uses the dimensions specified by the <fo:external-graphic> element when rendering the image:

- If no dimensions are specified, FOP uses a 72dpi resolution to convert image dots to inches in the output.
- If only one dimension is specified, FOP again uses the 72dpi resolution to convert image dots to images for the specified dimension. The other dimension is computed by preserving the image's aspect ratio.
- If both dimensions are specified, FOP renders the image in the space specified by the dimensions and adjusts the image's resolution to fit all of the image's pixels into the dimensions.

Image Caching

FOP caches images between multiple runs of FOP in the same JVM. Ordinarily this is a good performance-enhancing technique. However, if you're dynamically generating images, this can be a problem, because FOP uses the URL of the image as the key to its cache. If you're dynamically generating images, then you must make your URL change each time the image is regenerated. One way to do this is to add a dummy parameter to the image URL. You can then change the value of the parameter each time, to fool FOP's cache.

The other problem with the FOP cache is that it can cause an OutOfMemoryError. To prevent this problem, you need to manually empty the cache before it happens. You can do this by calling org.apache.fop.image.FopImageFactory.resetCache.

Natively Supported Formats

FOP has built-in support for BMP, EPS, GIF, JPEG, and TIFF files:

- **BMP**—FOP's support for Microsoft Windows Bitmap (BMP) files is limited to the RGB color space. BMPs are supported for all renderers.
- **EPS**—FOP supports Encapsulated Postscript (EPS) metafiles in both bitmap and vector modes. It provides full support for the PostScript renderer but only partial support for the PDF renderer. FOP doesn't have a built-in PostScript interpreter, so it can only embed an EPS file into the PDF file. The problem is that the Adobe Acrobat reader, which also lacks a built-in PostScript interpreter, can't display the EPS image. When you print the PDF using a PostScript device (GhostScript counts as a PostScript interpreter), the EPS image will print properly.
- **GIF**—FOP supports GIF files without any problems and for all renderers.
- **JPEG**—FOP's native JPEG support works for the grayscale, RGB, and CMYK color spaces. It has trouble with unusual color lookup tables and color profiles. If a JPEG image isn't displaying properly, you may be able to correct the problem by opening the image in a graphics program such as PhotoShop or the Gimp and saving it back out (specifying 24-bit color output before you save can also help).
- **TIFF**—FOP's native TIFF support only works for the PDF and PostScript renderers. In addition, the TIFF images must be single-channel images (bi-level or grayscale) that use white-is-zero in the TIFF PhotometricInterpretation tag. The TIFF images must also either be uncompressed or use CCITT (T.4, T.6) or JPEG compression.

Jimi

Jimi is a library developed by Sun for managing images. It can handle a number of formats including GIF, JPEG, TIFF, PNG, PICT, Photoshop, BMP, Targa, ICO, CUR, Sunraster, XBM, XPM, and PCX files. Due to Sun's binary licensing for Jimi, the ASF is unable to provide downloadable Jimi jars for use with FOP. If you want to use a graphics format supported through Jimi (PNG at the moment), then you'll need to go to Sun's Website (http://java.sun.com/products/jimi), agree to the Sun binary license, download your own copy, and install it. The standard FOP distribution has been compiled with support for Jimi, so all you need to do is place the Jimi libraries in the Java classpath. The FOP documentation suggests that you do this by taking the JimiProClasses.zip file from the Jimi distribution and copying it to the FOP lib directory as jimi-1.0.jar.

Jimi's biggest limitation is that it's only compatible with JDK 1.1. Users of JDK 1.3 and above will need to use JAI.

FOP uses Jimi to provide support for PNG files. There are no limitations on FOP renderers or PNG images.

JAI

The Java Advanced Imaging API is compatible with JDK versions 1.3 and above and provides support for the BMP, JPEG, JPEG 2000, PNG, PNM, Raw, TIFF, and WBMP image formats. Supported JAI platforms include Win32, Solaris, Linux, AIX, Mac OS X, and Digital Linux. FOP uses JAI to provide support for PNG and TIFF files but is limited to the RGB and RGBA color spaces for both formats.

Batik

Batik is another xml.apache.org project that provides an SVG renderer and viewer. XSL allows non-XSL data, such as SVG, to be incorporated into documents. There are two ways to do this. You can place the SVG data in the XSL document using the <fo:instream-foreign-object> element or place it in a separate file referenced via <fo:external-graphic>. FOP uses Batik to render SVG images in the PDF renderer. SVG images are rendered according to the dimensions specified in the SVG file, but inside the viewport specified by the <fo:external-graphic> element. For best results, the dimensions and the viewport should be equal. You need to be aware of two issues when using SVG images with the PDF renderer: how SVG graphics are incorporated into the PDF file and how SVG text is placed into the PDF file.

Batik uses PDF commands to draw graphics objects such as lines and curves when rendering SVG files as PDF. However, some SVG constructs don't map directly to PDF drawing commands. An SVG graphic may specify effects, patterns, or images, which don't have PDF analogs. Therefore, these constructs are rendered as raster graphics and are influenced by FOP's 72dpi resolution. The current version of FOP (0.20.5) doesn't support PDF transparency, so SVG images with transparency effects render incorrectly.

Batik tries to use PDF text to render SVG whenever possible. But if the font isn't supported or the text can't be drawn normally, then Batik converts the text to a set of SVG curves and draws all the curves. One side effect is that the PDF document will contain the curves and not the characters, which means text-searching won't work.

FOP Extensions

FOP provides a namespace-based extensions mechanism that allows extensions to XSL. Of course, these extensions won't be compatible with other XSL formatters. Three extensions are provided with FOP: an extension for SVG, an extension for bookmarks in PDF, and an extension for placing a label in a page header/footer when a table spans multiple pages.

The PDF bookmark extension allows you to create outlines that contain links (bookmarks) to other parts of the document (identified via ID attributes). To use the extension, you need to declare the FOP extension namespace (line 2):

```
1: <fo:root xmlns:fo="http://www.w3.org/1999/XSL/Format"
2:          xmlns:fox="http://xml.apache.org/fop/extensions">
3:  <fox:outline internal-destination="ch1">
4:   <fox:label>Chapter 1</fox:label>
5:  </fox:outline>
6: </fo:root>
```

Once you've declared the extension namespace, you place <fox:outline> elements to indicate where the bookmark points and <fox:label> elements to specify the label for the bookmark.

The continued-label extension allows you to print a custom table header or footer when a table is too big to fit on a single page and overflows across page boundaries. This extension also uses the FOP extension namespace. You place a <fox:continued-label> element inside the table cell in the table header or footer where you want the continuation label to appear. You can use <fo:inline> to format the label. The label will appear only when the table has overflowed onto a second (or subsequent) page.

The current version of FOP (0.20.5) lets you write your own extensions by subclassing org.apache.fop .extensions.ExtensionObj. The FOP developers are in the middle of a major architectural overhaul of FOP, and it's likely that this extension API will change because it depends on the internals of the FOP implementation.

Practical Usage

Most of the practical issues you'll run into using FOP are related to rendering support. You should be aware of the limitations of the renderer you've chosen, what fonts that renderer supports, and, if you're using images, which image formats work well with your renderer.

The operation of FOP is relatively straightforward. You set it up and tell it which renderer you want, and FOP should produce a result. There aren't many configuration settings you need to be aware of.

Keep the following performance tip in mind. The FOP Driver has a method called reset that you can call after running the Driver. This method clears the internal data structures of the Driver so you can use the same Driver instance again. This saves the time spent in creating the Driver and the creation of the internal data structures. If you're doing multiple FOP runs (and any serious application will), you should call reset between Driver invocations instead of allocating new Driver objects all the time.

Applications

Let's revisit the mini-application we discussed at the end of Chapter 2. In that example, you wanted to build a Website that was using Xalan/XSLT to format the output of an XML file and produce HTML customized for the browser a person was using to visit the site. Now let's say you want to replace the HTML output with PDF. You don't have to tear down the entire system and rebuild it. Instead, you can modify the XSLT servlet filter and create a second filter that takes the output of the XSLT filter and runs it through FOP. Then you can replace the original XSLT filter with the filter chain containing the XSLT/FOP filters. We'll only cover the classes that are new or have changed (there is one of each).

Here's the updated XSLT filter:

```
/*
 *
 * XSLTServletFilter.java
 *
 * Example from "Professional XML Development with Apache Tools"
 *
 */
package com.sauria.apachexml.ch3;
import java.io.IOException;
```

```
import java.io.PrintWriter;
import java.io.StringReader;
import java.io.Writer;
import java.util.Collections;
import java.util.HashMap;
import java.util.Map;

import javax.servlet.Filter;
import javax.servlet.FilterChain;
import javax.servlet.FilterConfig;
import javax.servlet.ServletContext;
import javax.servlet.ServletException;
import javax.servlet.ServletRequest;
import javax.servlet.ServletResponse;
import javax.servlet.http.HttpServletRequest;
import javax.servlet.http.HttpServletResponse;
import javax.xml.transform.Source;
import javax.xml.transform.Templates;
import javax.xml.transform.Transformer;
import javax.xml.transform.TransformerConfigurationException;
import javax.xml.transform.TransformerFactory;
import javax.xml.transform.stream.StreamResult;
import javax.xml.transform.stream.StreamSource;

public class XSLTFOPServletFilter implements Filter {
    FilterConfig config = null;
    Map transletCache = null;

    public void init(FilterConfig fc) throws ServletException {
        config = fc;

        ServletContext ctx = fc.getServletContext();

        transletCache =
            (Map) ctx.getAttribute("transletCache");

        if (transletCache == null) {
            transletCache =
                Collections.synchronizedMap(new HashMap());
            ctx.setAttribute("transletCache", transletCache);
        }
    }
```

The code in init is almost the same as in Chapter 2. The code for the Xalan SmartTransformerFactory has been omitted because XSLTC isn't quite up to processing the stylesheets you're using to generate XSL. So, you revert to using the standard Xalan interpreted mode.

The doFilter method is a little shorter than the one in Chapter 2. Instead of creating a CharacterArrayWriter, you place the output of the XSLT transformation directly onto the OutputStream of the servlet response object passed to the XSLT filter. As you'll see, this is the response object provided by the FOP filter. By writing the XSLT into the FOP filter's response, you make the result of the transformation available to the FOP filter:

```

    public void doFilter(
        ServletRequest req,
        ServletResponse res,
        FilterChain chain)
        throws IOException, ServletException {
        String contentType;
        String styleSheet;

        HttpServletRequest httpReq = (HttpServletRequest) req;

        PrintWriter out = res.getWriter();

        BufferedResponseWrapper wrappedResponse =
         new BufferedResponseWrapper((HttpServletResponse)res);

        chain.doFilter(req, wrappedResponse);
        res.setContentType("application/xml");

        String s = new String(wrappedResponse.getBuffer());
        StringReader sr =
            new StringReader(s);
        Source xmlSource = new StreamSource(sr);

        try {
            Templates translet = getTemplates();
            Writer w = res.getWriter();
            StreamResult result = new StreamResult(w);
            Transformer xformer = translet.newTransformer();
            xformer.transform(xmlSource, result);
        } catch (Exception ex) {
            out.println(ex.toString());
            out.write(wrappedResponse.toString());
        }
    }
```

The getTemplates method replaces the selectTemplates method because you aren't selecting the stylesheet based on the user-agent accessing the site. For the sake of brevity, we're showing the stylesheet hardwired, but you could easily modify it to select the stylesheet based on the URI being accessed in the browser; doing so would allow you to use different stylesheets for different pages on the Website:

```

    private Templates getTemplates() {
        Templates translet = null;

        TransformerFactory xFactory =
            TransformerFactory.newInstance();
        String styleSheet = "books-table.xslt";

        translet = (Templates) transletCache.get(styleSheet);
        if (translet != null) {
            return translet;
        }
```

```
        try {
            String stylePath =
             config.getServletContext().getRealPath(styleSheet);
            Source styleSource = new StreamSource(stylePath);
            translet =
                xFactory.newTemplates(styleSource);
        } catch (TransformerConfigurationException e) {
            e.printStackTrace();
        }

        transletCache.put(styleSheet, translet);
        return translet;
    }

    public void destroy() {}
}
```

This XSLT filter can be used with any XML and any XSLT stylesheet. Taking out the user agent logic makes that a bit clearer.

Now let's look at the FOP filter. This filter expects the servlet response it receives (whether from a servlet or another filter) to contain an XSL document. The filter then runs the XSL document through FOP and puts the rendered output on its own response object for processing:

```
package com.sauria.apachexml.ch3;
import java.io.ByteArrayInputStream;
import java.io.IOException;
import java.io.InputStream;
import java.io.OutputStream;

import javax.servlet.Filter;
import javax.servlet.FilterChain;
import javax.servlet.FilterConfig;
import javax.servlet.ServletException;
import javax.servlet.ServletRequest;
import javax.servlet.ServletResponse;
import javax.servlet.http.HttpServletResponse;

import org.apache.avalon.framework.logger.ConsoleLogger;
import org.apache.avalon.framework.logger.Logger;
import org.apache.fop.apps.Driver;
import org.apache.fop.apps.FOPException;
import org.apache.fop.apps.FormattingResults;
import org.apache.fop.messaging.MessageHandler;
import org.xml.sax.InputSource;

/*
 *
 * FOPServletFilter.java
 *
 * Example from "Professional XML Development with Apache Tools"
 *
 */
```

```

public class FOPServletFilter implements Filter {
    static Driver fopDriver = new Driver();

    public void init(FilterConfig fc) throws ServletException {
    }

    public void doFilter(
        ServletRequest request,
        ServletResponse response,
        FilterChain chain)
        throws IOException, ServletException {

        BufferedResponseWrapper wrappedResponse =
            new BufferedResponseWrapper((HttpServletResponse)
                                            response);

```

Again, you need a BufferedResponseWrapper to grab the data the previous servlet/filter in the chain wrote to its response.

In this example you hardwire the output format to be PDF. You could look at the URI or headers of the request to select the renderer you want. You also need to set the response's content-type to the appropriate value:

```
        chain.doFilter(request, wrappedResponse);
        response.setContentType("application/pdf");

```

Recall that FOP uses some static configuration variables within its implementation. This makes using it problematic in multithreaded environments such as a servlet. The filter solves this problem by allocating a static instance of the FOP Driver and then synchronizing access to it using the filter itself as a lock:

```
        synchronized (this) {
            fopDriver.reset();
```

Threading issues aside, you don't want to create a new instance of the FOP Driver every time the filter runs, because of the cost of instantiating a new Driver object. Instead you call the Driver's reset method so you can use the single instance over and over.

The wrappedResponse (the response from the previous servlet or filter in the chain) is used as the input to the FOP Driver. You get the byte array buffer and then create the necessary wrapper classes to convert that byte array into a suitable InputSource for FOP. You set the InputSource and OutputStream explicitly because you're reusing the FOP Driver instance, so supplying these via a constructor won't work:

```

            byte buf[] = wrappedResponse.getBuffer();
            InputStream bais = new ByteArrayInputStream(buf);

            InputSource is = new InputSource(bais);
            fopDriver.setInputSource(is);
```

The remainder of the driver setup should be familiar. You set the OutputStream, turn on any logging you need, set the renderer, and run FOP:

```

            OutputStream outFile = response.getOutputStream();
            fopDriver.setOutputStream(outFile);

            Logger logger =
               new ConsoleLogger(ConsoleLogger.LEVEL_WARN);
            MessageHandler.setScreenLogger(logger);
            fopDriver.setLogger(logger);
            fopDriver.setRenderer(Driver.RENDER_PDF);
            try {
                fopDriver.run();
            } catch (IOException ioe) {
                ioe.printStackTrace();
            } catch (FOPException fe) {
                fe.printStackTrace();
            }

            FormattingResults results = fopDriver.getResults();
            logger.info("Pages Formatted: " +
                         results.getPageCount());
        }
    }

    public void destroy() {
    }
}
```

The last piece of the servlet filter chain is the Web Application deployment descriptor (web.xml), which is shown here:

```
<?xml version="1.0" encoding="ISO-8859-1"?>

<!DOCTYPE web-app
  PUBLIC "-//Sun Microsystems, Inc.//DTD Web Application 2.3//EN"
  "http://java.sun.com/dtd/web-app_2_3.dtd">

<web-app>
  <display-name>
   Professional XML Development with Apache Tools Examples
  </display-name>
  <description>
    Examples from Professional XML Development with Tools.
  </description>

  <!-- Define servlet-mapped and path-mapped example filters -->
  <filter>
    <filter-name>XSLT Filter</filter-name>
    <filter-class>
     com.sauria.apachexml.ch4.XSLTFOPServletFilter
    </filter-class>
  </filter>
```

```
  <filter>
    <filter-name>FOP Filter</filter-name>
    <filter-class>
     com.sauria.apachexml.ch4.FOPServletFilter
    </filter-class>
  </filter>
```

You have two filter definitions instead of one:

```

  <!-- Define filter mappings for the defined filters -->
  <filter-mapping>
    <filter-name>FOP Filter</filter-name>
    <servlet-name>XMLServlet</servlet-name>
  </filter-mapping>

  <filter-mapping>
    <filter-name>XSLT Filter</filter-name>
    <servlet-name>XMLServlet</servlet-name>
  </filter-mapping>

```

The order of the filters in the chain is determined by the order of the <filter-mapping> elements. According to web.xml, the order of the chain is FOP filter, XSLT filter, XML servlet. This looks backward, but it's exactly what you want. When the browser makes a request, the request is processed by the FOP filter, and then the XSLT filter and after that it is finally allowed to get to the XML servlet. The filter chain doesn't do anything with the requests. The responses are processed in the reverse order of the requests. So, the response from the XML servlet (a document containing books in the books schema) is passed to the XSLT filter, which processes that response and generates its own response (a document containing XSL formatting objects). The XSLT filter's response then goes to the FOP filter that takes the XSL document from the XSLT filter and runs FOP over it to produce the final response, which contains a PDF file. You can see that the mapping is exactly what you wanted in order to produce the result:

```
  <servlet>
    <servlet-name>XMLServlet</servlet-name>
    <servlet-class>
     com.sauria.apachexml.ch3.XMLServlet
    </servlet-class>
  </servlet>

  <servlet-mapping>
    <servlet-name>XMLServlet</servlet-name>
    <url-pattern>/ch3/*</url-pattern>
  </servlet-mapping>

</web-app>
```

We'll leave the problem of integrating the user-agent-specific HTML system and the FOP-based system as an exercise for you to think about. Consider the fact that you need to execute the FOP filter only in certain circumstances.

Using servlet filters this way shows off the power and flexibility of XML's approach to layered data manipulation. In this example we see three levels of layering: 1) XML data, 2) an XSLT stylesheet that turns the XML data into XSL, and 3) an XSL document that contains the data and describes how to render the data. This layering is a perfect fit for the Java servlet filter API which allows you to build a generic reusable filter for each layer in the XML architecture. Once You've built the filters, you can build systems by combining the filters and updating date structures that tell you which stylesheets and renderers to use. In the example, the stylesheets and renderers have been hardwired into the filter, but you could just as easily perform a lookup in a Java properties file or a SQL database.

FOP provides a way for you to bridge between XML content and a number of non-XML-based publishing formats. If your application publishes documents of some kind, it's obvious why you need a solution like FOP. If you're writing business applications, FOP gives you a way to enable your applications for the physical, by providing you with ways to easily generate documents that can be printed.

4

Batik

Scalable Vector Graphics (SVG) is a W3C Recommendation for encoding vector graphics drawing instructions as XML. You may wonder why SVG exists—after all, we've been using HTML and the <img> tag for a number of years and have gotten along fine. SVG provides some interesting capabilities that using images doesn't. If your browser is SVG enabled, then all the drawing takes place in the browser. This is where the scalable part of SVG comes into play. You can send an SVG file to a device, and the device can scale and render it according to its own display characteristics—something that's hard to do with images. Because the file sits in the browser, scaling, panning, and zooming can be performed by the SVG browser. This is possible with images, but the results are often ugly to look at. SVG images solve this problem.

SVG uses a vector drawing model, which can have advantages over a bitmapped model. In particular, doing something like drawing text along a curve or producing line-oriented drawings is easier with a vector model. The vector model allows the scaling mentioned in the last paragraph.

SVG drawings can be dynamic and interactive. This is a big change from bitmapped images. In practice, this means you can use drawings to provide a visually rich and interactive user interface. Dynamic SVG can do most of the things you'd do using a tool like Flash. The benefit of SVG is that it's a standard being developed by the W3C, whereas Flash is a proprietary technology. Although it's true that Macromedia has opened the Flash file format (SWF), there's still a difference between an open file format controlled by a single company and a standardized language controlled by an international standards body. Advocates of Flash will point out that SWF files are binary and very small, which is a concern in the Web environment. However, SVG mandates the use of gzip compression on its files, which helps to reduce the size of SVG documents.

Support for SVG is limited but improving. Adobe provides an SVG Viewer plugin that works with all major Web browsers. (You can obtain this plugin at www.adobe.com/svg.) In addition, the open-source Mozilla browser plans to include built-in SVG support in a future release. As we'll see in this chapter, Batik provides a stand-alone open-source SVG browser written in Java. On the authoring front, a number of commercial drawing packages support SVG, including Adobe Illustrator, Jasc WebDraw, and CorelDRAW. The Sodipodi program provides open-source drawing tools for creating SVG.

The Batik project at xml.apache.org started because several teams that were working on SVG wanted to pool their efforts. The initial set of contributors came from CSIRO, ILOG, Eastman Kodak, and Sun Microsystems. Here's what the Batik site say about the origin of the name *Batik*:

> **Batik is a highly evolved art tradition that developed in Java (one of the islands comprising what is now called Indonesia). Batik is generally thought of as the quintessentially Indonesian textile. Motifs of flowers, twining plants, leaves, buds, birds, butterflies, fish, insects and geometric forms are rich in symbolic association and variety; there are about three thousand recorded batik patterns.**

We think Batik gracefully evokes Java, graphics, and high quality, terms that constitute the core of the toolkit.

Prerequisites

Next we'll look at SVG. The SVG 1.0 spec, which Batik supports, is over 600 pages long, so we can only give you a flavor of what you'll be able to do with it. SVG is limited to two-dimensional graphics, but it includes some elements for incorporating raster (bitmapped) graphics as well. We'll look at the static aspects of SVG first (the drawing stuff) and then look at the dynamic aspects.

Static SVG

We'll start our tour of SVG with the following picture. It was described using SVG and rendered as a JPEG using Batik's SVG renderer functionality. It shows some of the basic shape functionality that's part of SVG.

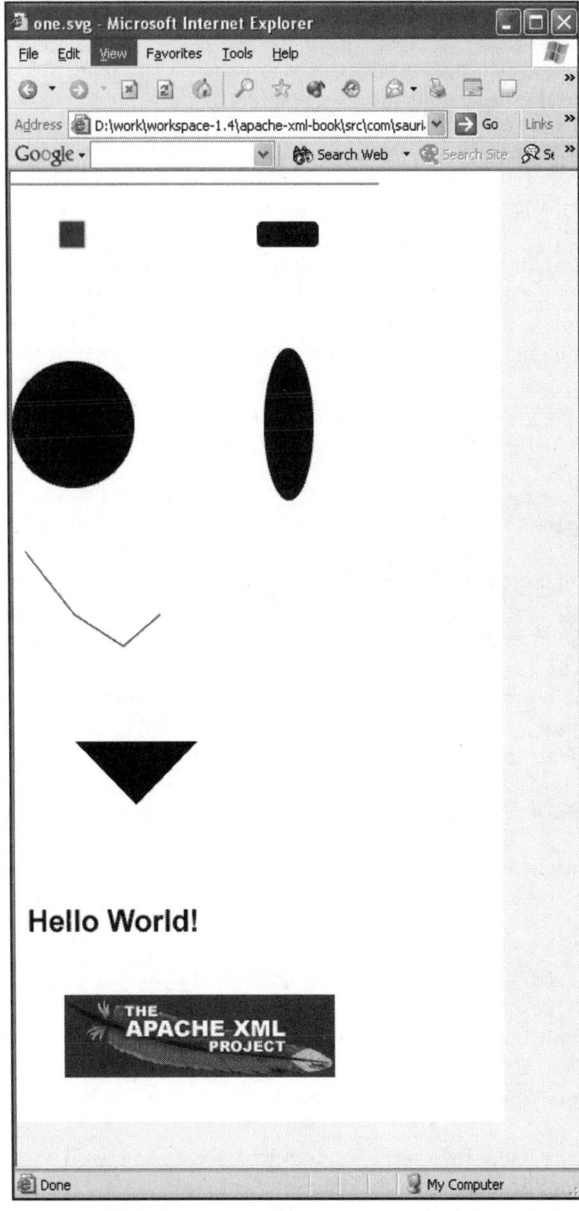

The SVG that created this image is as follows. The elements appear in the order (top to bottom, left to right) that they appear in the SVG document:

```
<?xml version="1.0" encoding="UTF-8"?>
<!DOCTYPE svg PUBLIC "-//W3C//DTD SVG 1.0//EN"
"http://www.w3.org/TR/2001/REC-SVG-20010904/DTD/svg10.dtd">
```

You can obtain the SVG DTD via the W3C's Website and use it to validate SVG documents.

The root element of an SVG document is <svg>. The width and height attributes specify the width and height of the SVG relative to the surrounding context (if any):

```
4: <svg xmlns="http://www.w3.org/2000/svg"
5:      xmlns:xlink="http://www.w3.org/1999/xlink"
6:      width="400" height="750">
```

You can specify the values for width and height using a unit of measure such as px (pixels), em, cm, or any other unit dimension defined by CSS. If no unit is specified (as is the case in this example), then the unit is the unit of measure in the current user coordinate system. Note that SVG namespace is the default namespace for this document. You also declare the xlink prefix for use later on.

The <title> and <desc> elements allow you to provide additional documentation for your SVG. These elements may appear in many SVG elements:

```
7:  <title>one.svg</title>
8:  <desc>Sample SVG File</desc>
```

Generally, the contents of these elements aren't rendered by an SVG user agent, although they may provide information the user-agent can use. An example would be using the contents of <title> to produce tooltip-style documentation as the user moves the cursor over various parts of an SVG document.

The <g> element is used to group related graphics elements. It's useful because you can give a group a name using the id attribute. The name is needed for some of the SVG animation elements and allows groups of graphics elements to be reused within a document:

```
9:  <g id="line">
```

The <line> element draws a line between two points. The coordinates for the first point are described by the x1 and y1 attributes, and the coordinates for the second point are described by the x2 and y2 attributes:

```
10:   <line x1="0" y1="10" x2="300" y2="10" stroke="black"/>
```

A number of additional attributes control various aspects of a graphics element's appearance. The stroke attribute controls the color of the pen used to make a drawing stroke. You can use simple color names, or you can use any CSS2 color specification.

Lines 12-15 show examples using the <rect> element to draw rectangles. The x attribute specifies the x coordinate of the side of the rectangle that has the smallest x-coordinate in the current user coordinate system. Similarly, the y attribute specifies the y coordinate of the side of the rectangle that has the smallest y-coordinate in the current user coordinate system. The values of the x and y attributes default to zero. Note that you're specifying the coordinates of a single side, so the x and y attributes together specify two sides of the rectangle. The width and height attributes must specify positive offsets (in the current user coordinate system) for the width (x-axis) and height (y-axis) of the rectangle. A width or height value of zero prevents the rectangle from being drawn:

```
11:  </g>
12:  <g id="rects">
13:   <rect x="40" y="40" width="20" height="20"
14:         style="stroke:red; fill:blue"/>
15:   <rect x="200" y="40" width="50" height="20" rx="5" ry="5"/>
```

The style attribute in line 14 shows an alternate method of controlling the formatting of a graphics element. Instead of using a separate attribute for each presentation property (such as stroke="" fill=""), you can specify a style attribute and use CSS notation to do the same thing. The names of the CSS properties and the presentation attributes are the same. The advantage of doing it this way is that it may be more familiar to people using CSS, and it saves a few keystrokes. The disadvantages fall to the implementor of SVG processors. Having separate attributes means the XML processor does the work of digging out the presentation attribute values. If you use the style attribute approach, then your code must take the style attribute and parse its contents in order to get the presentation values. Here, stroke specifies the color of the pen strokes (red) and fill specifies the color (blue) used to fill the rectangle.

The <rect> example in line 15 adds one more twist. By specifying the rx and ry attributes, you can create a rectangle with rounded corners. The rx and ry attributes control the x-axis and y-axis radii, respectively, of the ellipse that's used to round off the corners of the rectangle.

The <circle> element draws a circle centered at the point specified by the cx and cy attributes. The radius of the circle is controlled by the r attribute. The <ellipse> element is very similar, except that it has two radius attributes: rx for the x-axis radius and ry for the y-axis radius:

```
16:  </g>
17:  <g id="round">
18:   <circle cx="50" cy="200" r="50"/>
19:   <ellipse cx="225" cy="200" rx="20" ry="60"/>
```

<polyline> and <polygon> both rely on the points attribute, which contains a list of points. The x and y coordinates of the points are separated by commas, and the coordinate pairs themselves are separated by spaces. <polyline> starts with the first coordinate pair and then draws a line to the next coordinate pair. Generally, you use <polyline> when you want an open shape, because a closed shape is really a polygon. <polygon> does what <polyline> does, except that it also draws a line from the last coordinate pair to the first coordinate pair, creating a closed figure:

```
20:  </g>
21:  <g id="polys">
22:   <polyline fill="none" stroke="black"
23:             points="10,300 50,350 90,375 120,350"/>
24:   <polygon points="50,450 100,500 150,450"/>
```

The penultimate graphics element in this file is <text>, which draws its content as a text string. The x and y attributes determine the position of the text. Again, you use the style attribute and CSS2 property names to control the font attributes to be applied to the text:

```
25:  </g>
26:  <g id="text">
27:   <text x="10" y="600"
28:    style="font-family:Arial; font-size:24; font-weight:bold;">
29:    Hello World!
```

```
</text>
```

The last example shows the use of the SVG <a> and <image> elements. The <image> element allows you to include a raster image file in your SVG output. The x and y attribute specify the position of one corner of the rectangle where the image will appear, and the height and width attributes control the size of the rectangle:

```
</g>
<g id="image-link">
 <a xlink:href="http://xml.apache.org">
 <image x="40" y="650" width="220px" height="65px"
         xlink:href="http://xml.apache.org/images/group-logo.gif"/>
 </a>
</g>
</svg>
```

<image> uses XLink's href attribute to specify the location of the image file. Actually, SVG uses XLink to specify all linking type behavior. The <image> element appears as the content of an <a> element. This usage of the SVG <a> element works just like the HTML usage, except that it uses XLink's href attribute. The target of the link may be any resource, not just an SVG resource. The one caveat is that the user agent displaying the SVG document where the link is clicked must be able to display the resource the link points to. In addition, any number of SVG graphics elements may appear as the contents of the <a>; an XLink simple link is created for each graphics element.

Container Elements

Some SVG elements fall into one of two special categories: *container elements* or *graphics elements*. The container elements you've seen so far are <svg>, <g>, and <a>. The <line> <rect>, <circle>, <ellipse>, <polyline>, <polygon>, <text>, and <image> elements are graphics elements. The <title> and <desc> elements may appear inside any container or graphics element. This capability can be useful for documenting various aspects of your drawing inside the SVG file.

In sophisticated documents, you'd like to be able to define and use sets of graphics elements. Reusable elements can be defined by attaching an id attribute to any <svg>, <symbol>, <g>, or graphics element. These elements can then be inserted into your document via the <use> element. Let's look at a simple example:

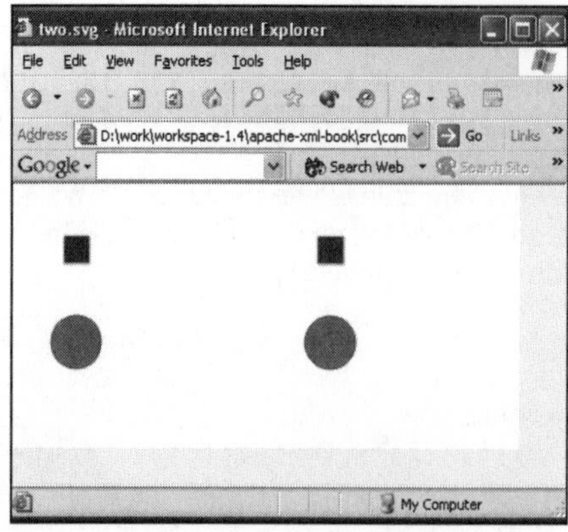

In this figure, you want to define the blue square and grey circle as reusable visual elements. The following code shows how to do this:

```
<?xml version="1.0" encoding="UTF-8"?>
<!DOCTYPE svg PUBLIC "-//W3C//DTD SVG 1.0//EN"
  "http://www.w3.org/TR/2001/REC-SVG-20010904/DTD/svg10.dtd">
<svg xmlns="http://www.w3.org/2000/svg"
     xmlns:xlink="http://www.w3.org/1999/xlink"
     width="400" height="200">
 <title>two.svg</title>
 <desc>Sample SVG file showing reuse</desc>
 <defs>
  <g id="group">
   <rect x="40" y="40" width="20" height="20"
         style="stroke:red; fill:blue"/>
   <circle cx="50" cy="120" r="20"
            style="stroke:green; fill:gray"/>
  </g>
 </defs>
```

You begin by defining a <g> containing your rectangle and circle. The id for the <g> is group, which is how you'll refer to the combination later in the document. The <g> is placed inside a <defs> element. The convention in SVG is to place elements that will be referenced by other elements inside a <defs>. You can think of a <defs> as a <g> that isn't rendered by an SVG renderer. The <defs> and its children appear in the source document and the SVG DOM for the source document.

Now you insert the combination with the <use> element. XLink's href is used for maximum flexibility:

```
 <g>
  <use xlink:href="#group" />
 </g>
```

In order to place the second combination in the right location, you create a <g> that translates the coordinate system of its children by adding 200 to the x-coordinate. Now the elements referenced by the <use> element will all be translated and will appear to the right of the first instance of the combination:

```
 <g transform="translate(200,0)">
  <use xlink:href="#group" />
 </g>
</svg>
```

The Transform Attribute

The last section introduced the transform attribute. This attribute can be attached to the <g>, <defs>, <use>, or any graphics element. The value of a transform attribute is a space-separated list of transforms:

- **matrix(a b c d e f)**—Apply the transformation matrix specified by the vector [a, b, c, d, e, f], which corresponds to the following 3x3 transformation matrix:
    - a b c
    - d e f
    - 0 0 1

- **translate(*tx,ty*)**—Translate all coordinates by adding *tx* to the x coordinate and *ty* to the y coordinate.
- **scale(*sx, sy*)**—Scale all coordinates by multiplying each x coordinate by *sx* and each y coordinate by *sy*.
- **rotate(*angle, cx, cy*)**—Rotate all coordinates by *angle*, with the center of rotation at *cx, cy*.
- **skewX(*angle*)**—Skew all x coordinates by the angle.
- **skewY(*angle*)**—Skew all y coordinates by the angle.

Transformations in the list are applied in the order they appear.

The Path Element

The last major SVG topic we'll look at is the <path> element. This element lets you specify the outline of a shape. In fact, the function of all the graphics elements can be accomplished by using <path>. However, in many cases it's more convenient to use a specific graphics element. As you'll see, though, <path> can do some things that none of the other elements can do, so when you need to use <path>, you really need to use it.

The following figure shows <path> in action:

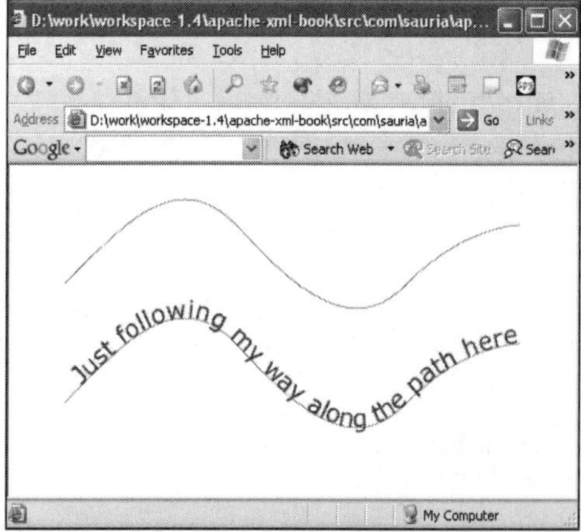

This SVG element uses the viewBox attribute to indicate that the area specified by the width and height attributes is mapped to a coordinate system range. So, the 5-inch by 3-inch drawing area will be covered by a viewBox that has a minimum x coordinate of 0, a minimum y coordinate of 0, a width of 800 pixels, and a height of 600 pixels:

```
<?xml version="1.0" standalone="no"?>
<!DOCTYPE svg PUBLIC "-//W3C//DTD SVG 20010904//EN"
  "http://www.w3.org/TR/2001/REC-SVG-20010904/DTD/svg10.dtd">
<svg width="5in" height="3in" viewBox="0 0 800 600"
     xmlns="http://www.w3.org/2000/svg"
         xmlns:xlink="http://www.w3.org/1999/xlink">
```

The <path> element takes a d attribute that contains a list of path commands. The M command sets the current point to an absolute x and y position without drawing. The C command takes a sets of three coordinate pairs (x1, y1, x2, y2, x, y) and draws a cubic Bézier curve using the current point as the start of the curve; x1, y1 as the control point of the beginning of the curve; x2, y2 as the control point of the end of the curve; and x, y as the end of the curve. After the curve has been drawn, the current point is at x, y:

```
<g id="plainPath">
 <path style="stroke:black; fill:none"
       d="M 0 200
          C 100 100 200   0 300 100
          C 400 200 500 300 600 200
          C 700 100 800 100 800 100"/>
```

The <textPath> element must appear inside a <text> element. Here you use the enclosing <text> element to control the font properties of the text. The content of the <textPath> element is drawn along a path specified using an XLink href attribute. The startOffset attribute specifies where along the path to begin drawing the text. Its value is an offset from the beginning of the path:

```
</g>

<g id="labelledPath" transform="translate(0,200)">
 <path id="followMe" style="stroke:blue; fill:none"
       d="M 0 200
          C 100 100 200   0 300 100
          C 400 200 500 300 600 200
          C 700 100 800 100 800 100"/>
 <text font-family="Verdana" font-size="42.5" fill="blue" >
  <textPath xlink:href="#followMe" startOffset="40">
   Just following my way along the path here
  </textPath>
 </text>
</g>
</svg>
```

The <path> element has a rich set of drawing commands. There are two versions of every command—an uppercase version that uses absolute coordinates and a lowercase version that uses relative coordinates:

- **M/m(x, y)**—Start a new subpath at (x, y).
- **Z/z**—Close the current path by drawing a line to the starting point.
- **L/l(x, y)+**—Draw a line from the current point to (x, y). If there are multiple (x, y) pairs, then go on drawing lines from one pair to the next.
- **H/h(x)**—Draw a line from the current point (curX, curY) to (x, curY).
- **V/v(y)**—Draw a line from the current point (curX, curY) to (curX, y).
- **C/c(x1 y1 x2 y2 x y)**—Draw a cubic Bézier curve using the current point as the start of the curve, (x1, y1) as the control point for the start of the curve, (x2, y2) as the control point for the end of the curve, and (x, y) as the end of the curve.

- **S/s(x2 y2 x y)**—Draw a cubic Bézier curve from the current point to (x, y), using (x2, y2) as the second control point. Assume that the first control point is a reflection of the second control point on the previous point (relative to the current point) or the current point if the last command was not C, c, S, or s.
- **Q/q(x1 y1 x y)**—Draw a quadratic Bézier curve from the current point to (x, y), using (x1, y1) as the control point.
- **T/t(x y)**—Draw a quadratic Bézier curve from the current point to (x, y), assuming the control point is a reflection of the control point for the previous command relative to the current point. If the previous command was not a Q, q, T, or t, the use the current point as the control point.
- **A/a(rx ry x-axis-rotation large-arc-flag sweep-flag x y)**—Draw an elliptical arc from the current point to (x, y). The size and orientation of the ellipse are controlled by rx (x axis radius), ry (y axis radius), and x-axis-rotation. The center of the ellipse is calculated automatically. The large-arc flag and sweep-flag are used to select which of the four possible arc segments are drawn. If large-arc-flag is 1 then the arc drawn will be one of the two arcs that sweep out more than 180 degrees. If the sweep flag is 1 then the arc that follows the positive angle direction will be drawn.

This has been a quick primer on the features of static SVG. There are a host of things we couldn't cover, but we've given you a feel for the types of things you can do with SVG.

Dynamic SVG

Now that you have static SVG under your belt, we can turn to dynamic SVG. *Dynamic SVG* means the SVG image isn't static. You can take static SVG drawings and cause them to come to life. There are two ways to do this: You can use what we'll call an *imperative style*, or you can use a *declarative style*.

Imperative Dynamic SVG

The imperative style of doing dynamic SVG will remind you of Dynamic HTML (DHTML). It combines the SVG document, a representation of the DOM for the SVG document, and a scripting language. The scripts interact with the SVG DOM and with event handlers specified on SVG elements. By updating elements and attributes in the SVG DOM, the scripts cause the SVG being displayed to change without reloading the document.

It's hard to show a dynamic SVG application on paper, but here is a picture of the starting point of a simple imperative SVG file, imperative-dynamic.svg:

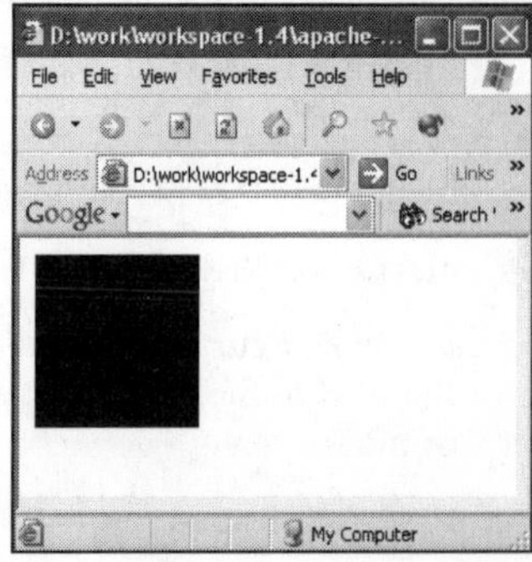

The first part is normal—just what you're used to seeing:

```
<?xml version="1.0" standalone="no"?>
<!DOCTYPE svg PUBLIC "-//W3C//DTD SVG 20010904//EN"
  "http://www.w3.org/TR/2001/REC-SVG-20010904/DTD/svg10.dtd">
<svg width="300" height="150"
     xmlns="http://www.w3.org/2000/svg"
     xmlns:xlink="http://www.w3.org/1999/xlink">
```

Next you see a script element that contains a script written in the language specified by the type attribute. In this case you're using ECMAScript (JavaScript). The function randomColor generates three random numbers between 0 and 256 (it uses parseInt to convert them to integers because ECMAScript treats everything as a floating-point number) and converts them to hexadecimal. (The 16 argument to toString is the number base.) The three numbers are then concatenated and prefixed with # to generate a color value:

```
<script type="text/ecmascript">
 function randomColor(){
  var r = parseInt(Math.random() * 256).toString(16);
  var g = parseInt(Math.random() * 256).toString(16);
  var b = parseInt(Math.random() * 256).toString(16);
  var color = "#"+r+g+b;
  return color;
 }
</script>
```

The <rect> element has an onclick attribute. This is an event handler attribute containing a piece of script code that's executed when the event click occurs (that is, when a mouse click is detected inside the <rect>). The code takes the event (evt) and finds its target, which is the <rect> element. The setAttribute method on this element is called to change the value of the fill attribute to be the result of calling the randomColor method defined earlier. The net result is that every time you click the mouse on the rectangle, it changes to a new color:

```
<rect x="10" y="10" width="100" height="100"
      onclick="evt.target.setAttribute('fill', randomColor())"/>
</svg>
```

In this example, you specify the scripting language on the <script> tag. Alternatively, you could specify it for the entire document by placing a contentScriptType attribute on the root <svg> element. Because the default for that attribute is text/ecmascript, you could omit the type attribute altogether.

By attaching event handlers to various objects in your SVG drawing, you can create a nice interactive user interface for an application. The event handlers can update various parts of the document to animate various aspects of the interface. You can also use scripting to generate animations. To do this effectively, you need to know what event handlers are available. Here's a group of event handlers that can be attached to any container or graphics element:

- **onfocusin**—Fires when the element receives the focus.
- **onfocusout**—Fires when the element loses the focus.
- **onactivate**—Fires when the element is activated.

- **onclick**—Fires when the mouse is clicked (up and down) over the element.
- **onmouseup**—Fires when the mouse button is released over the element.
- **onmousedown**—Fires when mouse button is pressed down over the element.
- **onmouseover**—Fires when the mouse is moved into/over the element.
- **onmousemove**—Fires when the mouse is moved inside the element.
- **onmouseout**—Fires when the mouse leaves the element.
- **onload**—Fires when the document is loaded.

The following events are fired only at the document level:

- **onunload**—Fires when the document is removed from the user-agent window or frame. This event applies only to the outermost <svg> element.
- **onabort**—Fires when page loading is interrupted.
- **onerror**—Fires when the page doesn't load correctly, or when an error occurs during script execution.
- **onresize**—Fires when the document window is resized. This event applies only to the outermost <svg> element.
- **onscroll**—Fires when the document window is scrolled. This event applies only to the outermost <svg> element.
- **onzoom**—Fires when the document window is zoomed. This event applies only to the outermost <svg> element.

Imperative dynamic SVG gives you the most control over the dynamic behavior of your document because you can attach any behavior to any element, and because you can replace elements in the SVG DOM tree with elements of your choosing (subject to the grammar rules of SVG). Sometimes you don't need all the power and flexibility of this approach. In particular, there are times when you want relatively simple animations of SVG elements. These situations are candidates for the use of declarative dynamic SVG.

Declarative Dynamic SVG

In imperative dynamic SVG, you tell the user agent exactly how to implement dynamic behavior: You write a program or series of programs in a scripting language. You don't have to do this in declarative dynamic SVG. Under this model, you tell SVG what animation you'd like to see, and the implementation of the SVG engine or user agent is responsible for figuring out how to make the animation come to life.

Let's look at a simple animation example. This figure shows the initial state of the animation—a simple green rectangle. The animation should make the green box move from the left end of the viewable area to the right end, jump back to the left end, and repeat the movement.

Here's an SVG document that produces the animation:

```
<?xml version="1.0" encoding="UTF-8"?>
<!DOCTYPE svg PUBLIC "-//W3C//DTD SVG 1.0//EN"
  "http://www.w3.org/TR/2001/REC-SVG-20010904/DTD/svg10.dtd">
<svg xmlns="http://www.w3.org/2000/svg"
     xmlns:xlink="http://www.w3.org/1999/xlink"
     width="5in" height="1in" viewBox="0 0 800 200">
 <defs>
  <symbol id="box">
   <rect x="0" y="50" height="20" width="50" fill="green"/>
  </symbol>
 </defs>
```

You define the <rect> as a <symbol> so that you can use it in the animation. Think of a <symbol> as a <g> that doesn't get rendered.

Now you use the <rect> that causes it to render. The <animate> element does all the work. In this case the animation is of the x attribute. The animation takes 2 seconds and is repeated twice. The fill attribute says to freeze the animation at the end:

```
 <use xlink:href="#box">
  <animate attributeName="x" dur="2s" repeatCount="2"
      fill="freeze"
      values="0; 100; 200; 300; 400; 500; 600; 700; 800;"/>
 </use>
</svg>
```

The animation works by taking the values from the values attribute and updating the x attribute (attributeName) with them. The animate tag figures out when each value should be used by dividing the duration by the number of values. It then interpolates intermediate values for the x attribute and time so that the animation looks smooth. To change multiple attributes at the same time, you specify multiple <animate>elements. These elements are copies of the original <animate> but update a different attributeName and have a different set of values.

You can attach two other important attributes to <animate>. The keyTimes attribute lets you specify a list of times. Each entry in keyTimes corresponds to a value in the values attribute. The time values are specified as floating-point numbers between 0 and 1, as a proportional offset into the total duration of the animation.

The calcMode attribute determines how the SVG engine does the interpolation. The values include:

- **discrete**—No interpolation.
- **linear**—Simple linear interpolation between the values.
- **paced**—A constant pace of motion in the animation.
- **spline**—Interpolation from one value to the next using a cubic Bézier spline. The control points for each spline are specified in the keySplines attribute, one per entry in the keyTimes attribute. Each control point entry includes four values.

SMIL Animation Elements

The declarative animation features of SVG were done in collaboration with the developers of the W3C's Synchronized Multimedia Integration Language (SMIL). This means SVG is a host language for SMIL animation. SVG has extended the set of animation elements from SMIL with some SVG-specific elements. The elements that came from SMIL include <animate>, <animateColor>, and <animateMotion>. <animateColor> allows you to animate the color of an element in the same style as <animate>. The <animateMotion> element allows you to animate the motion of an element along a path. Here's an example using <animateMotion> that uses the same green rectangle but animates it along a path:

```
<?xml version="1.0" encoding="UTF-8"?>
<!DOCTYPE svg PUBLIC "-//W3C//DTD SVG 1.0//EN"
  "http://www.w3.org/TR/2001/REC-SVG-20010904/DTD/svg10.dtd">
<svg xmlns="http://www.w3.org/2000/svg"
     xmlns:xlink="http://www.w3.org/1999/xlink"
     width="5in" height="2in" viewBox="0 0 800 400">
 <defs>
  <symbol id="box">
   <rect x="0" y="50" height="20" width="50" fill="green"/>
  </symbol>
 </defs>
 <use xlink:href="#box">
  <animateMotion dur="3s" repeatCount="2"
      fill="freeze"
          rotate="auto"
      path="M 0 200
            C 100 100 200   0 300 100
            C 400 200 500 300 600 200
            C 700 100 800 100 800 100"/>
 </use>
</svg>
```

<animateMotion> shares some of the same attributes as <animate>, but it adds a couple of its own: rotate, and path. The path attribute specifies a path the animation is to follow. The rotate attribute allows you to control how the animated object rotates. Specifying auto means the object rotates by the angle of the direction of the motion path (directional tangent vector of the path at each point). You can also specify auto-reverse, which means the same thing as auto except the angle is 180 degrees minus the angle of the direction of the motion path. Specifying a number gives you a one-time rotation relative to the x-axis of the current coordinate system.

The major SVG extension to the SMIL animation elements is <animateTransform>. It allows you to animate an object using SVG transforms. Again, we'll use an example with the now-familiar green rectangle:

```
<?xml version="1.0" encoding="UTF-8"?>
<!DOCTYPE svg PUBLIC "-//W3C//DTD SVG 1.0//EN"
  "http://www.w3.org/TR/2001/REC-SVG-20010904/DTD/svg10.dtd">
<svg xmlns="http://www.w3.org/2000/svg"
     xmlns:xlink="http://www.w3.org/1999/xlink"
     width="5in" height="2in" viewBox="0 0 800 400">
 <defs>
  <symbol id="box">
   <rect x="0" y="50" height="20" width="50" fill="green"/>
  </symbol>
 </defs>
 <use xlink:href="#box" transform="translate(50,100)">
```

The translation on the <use> moves the box so that the entire rotation is visible.

The type attribute specifies that this is a rotation transformation. The values for the rotation angle go from 0 degrees to 720 degrees. The additive attribute specifies that this transformation is added to any other transformations that come before it (in particular the translate on the <use> element). Otherwise, the transformation ignores any transformations coming before it:

```
  <animateTransform attributeName="transform" attributeType="XML"
     dur="2s" repeatCount="2"
  type="rotate" from="0" to="720"
     additive="replace" fill="freeze"/>
 </use>
</svg>
```

In addition to the additive attribute, there is an accumulate attribute on <animateTransform> that controls whether each iteration replaces the previous one (value is "replace") or builds on it (value is "sum").

There are also event handlers associated with the animation elements:

- **onbegin**—Fires at the beginning of the animation.
- **onend**—Fires at the end of the animation.
- **onrepeat**—Fires when the animation repeats itself.

This quick overview of declarative dynamic SVG has given you an idea of the capabilities available to you.

Installing and Configuring Batik

You need JDK 1.3 or above to use Batik. The released distributions of Batik are found at http://xml.apache.org/batik/dist. For the sake of example, let's assume you'll be using Batik 1.5. The distribution of Batik is contained in three zip files: batik-1.5.zip (the binary distribution), batik-docs-1.5.zip (the Javadoc documentation), and batik-src-1.5.zip (the source distribution). You should get at least the binary distribution and the Javadoc documentation in order to do development with Batik. The source distribution can be useful if you want to customize Batik, or if you want to use a source-level debugger to debug in Batik itself.

The binary distribution of Batik contains the following directories and files:

- **docs**—A directory containing the Batik documentation (not including Javadoc).
- **lib**—A directory containing all the jar files you might use in an application. There are more than 20 jar files in this directory.
- **samples**—A directory containing sample SVG files.
- **batik.jar**—A jar file that fills in the classpath with the Batik jar files.
- **batik-rasterizer.jar**—The application jar file for the Batik SVG Rasterizer.
- **batik-slideshow.jar**—The application jar file for the Batik SVG Slide Show application.
- **batik-squiggle.jar**—The application jar file for Batik's SVG Browser, Squiggle.
- **batik-ttf2svg.jar**—The application jar file for Batik's TrueType font to SVG Converter.

If you're doing development, the easiest thing to do is to set your classpath to include batik.jar. Doing so includes all the Batik jar files, so it can increase the disk footprint of your application. You can use the diagram in the Batik documentation to see which jar files depend on other jar files. In order for the convenience jars like batik.jar to work, you must preserve the structure of the directory tree, because the directory tree specified in the convenience jar file is specified relative to the convenience jar. This means you need a directory called lib in the same directory as the convenience jar.

If you're just using the Batik applications, you need to place the application/convenience jar on the classpath. The manifest of the application jar will include whichever jar files are needed from the lib directory.

Development Techniques

In this section, we'll look a ways to use the libraries and applications Batik provides. On the library side, we'll see how to use Batik to generate an SVG document using a more graphics-minded way of thinking. We'll also discuss how to take an SVG document and present it, both on screen and as an image file. After that we'll look at scripting support in the Batik library components and deal with some security-related issues for Batik applications.

Once we've finished with the libraries, we'll look at Batik's stand-alone applications for rasterizing SVG files and browsing them interactively. We'll examine the Batik SVG pretty-printer, which can be useful when you're trying to debug a large SVG file. Finally, we'll use the ttf2svg application to generate SVG font information from TrueType files.

SVGGraphics2D

Let's turn our attention now to the problem of how to generate SVG documents easily. Of course, you can always start up a copy of your favorite text or XML editor and create SVG documents that way, but ideally we'd like something a little closer to the problem domain. Batik provides a class called SVGGraphics2D that is derived from the Graphics2D class in the Java2D API. This class allows you to execute Java2D drawing commands and generate an equivalent SVG document:

```
/*
 *
 * SVGGeneratePrint.java
 *
 * Example from "Professional XML Development with Apache Tools"
 *
 */
package com.sauria.apachexml.ch4;

import java.awt.Color;
import java.awt.Dimension;
import java.awt.Font;
import java.awt.Shape;
import java.awt.geom.Ellipse2D;
import java.awt.geom.Rectangle2D;
import java.io.FileNotFoundException;
import java.io.FileOutputStream;
import java.io.OutputStream;
import java.io.OutputStreamWriter;
import java.io.UnsupportedEncodingException;
import java.io.Writer;

import org.apache.batik.dom.svg.SVGDOMImplementation;
import org.apache.batik.svggen.SVGGraphics2D;
import org.apache.batik.svggen.SVGGraphics2DIOException;
import org.w3c.dom.DOMImplementation;
import org.w3c.dom.svg.SVGDocument;

public class SVGGeneratePrint {

    public static void main(String[] args) {
        DOMImplementation impl =
            SVGDOMImplementation.getDOMImplementation();
        String svgNS = SVGDOMImplementation.SVG_NAMESPACE_URI;
        SVGDocument doc =
            (SVGDocument)impl.createDocument(svgNS, "svg", null);

```

You need an instance of an SVGDocument, which is the SVG DOM's equivalent of the Document interface from the regular DOM. You get an instance of SVGDocument by using the SVGDOMImplementation to get a DOMImplementation that understands SVG. Now you can pass the SVGDocument instance to SVGGraphics2D's constructor (line 38). Lines 40-49 are a series of Java 2D method calls to generate the visuals you want your SVG document to reproduce:

```
38:         SVGGraphics2D g = new SVGGraphics2D(doc);
39:
40:         Shape circle = new Ellipse2D.Double(0,0,50,50);
41:         g.setPaint(Color.red);
42:         g.fill(circle);
43:         Shape rect = new Rectangle2D.Double(60,0,40,60);
44:         g.setPaint(Color.green);
45:         g.fill(rect);
46:         g.setPaint(Color.blue);
47:         Font font = new Font("Helvetica",Font.BOLD,24);
48:         g.setFont(font);
49:         g.drawString("Hello World",0f,90f);
```

In Line 50, you set the size of the SVG document to be 300x100 pixels:

```
50:         g.setSVGCanvasSize(new Dimension(300,100));
```

You want to generate an SVG file as the output, so you create a FileOutputStream for the output file and then use OutputStreamWriter to obtain a writer:

```
51:
52:         Writer out = null;
53:         try {
54:             OutputStream s =
55:                new FileOutputStream("SVGGeneratePrint.svg");
56:             out = new OutputStreamWriter(s, "UTF-8");
```

Once you have the writer, you can call the stream method on SVGGraphics2D to generate the SVG document. The boolean useCSS argument determines whether SVGGraphics2D generates SVG that has individual attributes for the various SVG styling properties. Setting it to true means to use a single style attribute with CSS style properties as the contents. Setting it to false means to generate attributes:

```
57:         } catch (UnsupportedEncodingException use) {
58:             use.printStackTrace();
59:         } catch (FileNotFoundException fnfe) {
60:             fnfe.printStackTrace();
61:         }
62:         try {
63:             boolean useCSS = true;
64:             g.stream(out,useCSS);
65:         } catch (SVGGraphics2DIOException sioe) {
66:             sioe.printStackTrace();
67:         }
68:     }
69: }
```

The following listing, styled-boxes.svg, shows the resulting SVG file. You can see that SVGGraphics2D has generated all the style properties and their values (even when the values are the defaults:

```
<?xml version="1.0" encoding="UTF-8"?>

<!DOCTYPE svg PUBLIC '-//W3C//DTD SVG 1.0//EN'
 'http://www.w3.org/TR/2001/REC-SVG-20010904/DTD/svg10.dtd'>
<svg style="stroke-dasharray:none; shape-rendering:auto;
     font-family:&apos;sansserif&apos;; text-rendering:auto;
     fill-opacity:1; color-rendering:auto;
     color-interpolation:auto; font-size:12; fill:black;
     stroke:black; image-rendering:auto; stroke-miterlimit:10;
     stroke-linecap:square;
     stroke-linejoin:miter; font-style:normal; stroke-width:1;
     stroke-dashoffset:0; font-weight:normal;
     stroke-opacity:1;" xmlns="http://www.w3.org/2000/svg"
     width="300" contentScriptType="text/ecmascript"
     preserveAspectRatio="xMidYMid meet"
     xmlns:xlink="http://www.w3.org/1999/xlink"
     zoomAndPan="magnify" version="1.0"
     contentStyleType="text/css" height="100">
```

The Java2D commands mapped nicely into SVG elements. You can easily see the correspondence between the Ellipse2D, Rectangle2D, and DrawString commands in the Java program and the <circle>, <rect>, and <text> elements in the SVG:

```
  <!--Generated by the Batik Graphics2D SVG Generator-->
  <defs id="genericDefs" />
  <g>
    <g style="fill:red; stroke:red;">
      <circle r="25" style="stroke:none;" cx="25" cy="25" />
      <rect x="60" y="0" width="40"
            style="fill:lime; stroke:none;" height="60" />
    </g>
    <g style="fill:blue; font-size:24; font-weight:bold;
              stroke:blue;">
      <text xml:space="preserve" x="0" y="90"
            style="stroke:none;">
       Hello World
      </text>
    </g>
  </g>
</svg>
```

The following figure shows the result of rendering the SVG document.

Setting Options on SVGGraphics2D

Now let's look at some options you can set on the SVGGraphics2D class. Most of these options are set via the SVGGeneratorContext class. We'll discuss changing the default comment generated in the SVG document and customizing the way images are stored. Changing the default comment is easy; doing so requires a method call on the SVGGeneratorContext.

The image storing is a little harder to explain. First you need to know that when you call one of the drawImage methods on SVGGraphics2D, it creates an image in a raster format and writes it into a file on disk so that the generated SVG can reference the image in the file. By default, SVGGraphics2D uses a Base64 encoding of the image. You can change the format by creating an instance of ImageHandlerJPEGEncoder (to create JPEGs) or ImageHandlerPNGEncoder (to create PNGs) and passing it to the setImageHandler method on SVGGeneratorContext. Both of these classes have constructors that take two string arguments. The first argument is the directory where the image files should be written; the second is the URI prefix that should be placed in front of the image filename so the SVG document can find the images. So far so good. But what you'd really like to do is remember whether you've already generated an image file for an image and, if you have, use the existing image file rather than generate a new one. This process is handled by the CachedImageHandlerBase64Encoder, CachedImageHandlerJPEGEncoder, and CachedImageHandlerPNGEncoder for Base64, JPEG, and PNG, respectively.

The following example shows how to use these classes. It creates two SVG documents that both use the same image, and uses one of the CachedImageHandlers to prevent the creation of duplicate image files:

```
/*
 *
 * SVGGenerateCustom.java
 *
 * Example from "Professional XML Development with Apache Tools"
 *
 */
package com.sauria.apachexml.ch4;

import java.awt.Component;
import java.awt.Dimension;
import java.awt.Frame;
import java.awt.Graphics2D;
import java.awt.Image;
import java.awt.MediaTracker;
import java.awt.RenderingHints;
import java.awt.image.BufferedImage;
import java.awt.image.BufferedImageOp;
import java.awt.image.RescaleOp;
import java.io.FileNotFoundException;
import java.io.FileOutputStream;
import java.io.OutputStream;
import java.io.OutputStreamWriter;
import java.io.UnsupportedEncodingException;
import java.io.Writer;

import org.apache.batik.dom.svg.SVGDOMImplementation;
import org.apache.batik.svggen.CachedImageHandlerJPEGEncoder;
import org.apache.batik.svggen.GenericImageHandler;
```

```
import org.apache.batik.svggen.SVGGeneratorContext;
import org.apache.batik.svggen.SVGGraphics2D;
import org.apache.batik.svggen.SVGGraphics2DIOException;
import org.w3c.dom.DOMImplementation;
import org.w3c.dom.svg.SVGDocument;

public class SVGGenerateCustom {

```

The getImage method exists to read an image from a JPEG file and turn it into an Image you can pass to a Graphics2D (and hence SVGGraphics2D) drawImage method:

```
    public static BufferedImage getImage() {
        Component c = new Frame();
        Image i = c.getToolkit().getImage("one.jpg");
```

You get the initial Image by calling the getImage method on the toolkit of the current Component. The Frame you create is used exclusively in this function—it's never meant to be visible.

Before you can use the image you have to wait for it to load, so you enlist the MediaTracker to slow you down until the image has loaded:

```
        MediaTracker t = new MediaTracker(c);
        t.addImage(i,0);
        try {
            t.waitForAll();
        } catch (InterruptedException ie) {}
```

Now you can create a Java2D-compatible image and get it rendered and ready for use in the rest of the program:

```
        BufferedImage bi =
            new BufferedImage(i.getWidth(c), i.getHeight(c),
                              BufferedImage.TYPE_INT_RGB);
        Graphics2D big = bi.createGraphics();
        big.drawImage(i,0,0,c);
        return bi;
    }

```

The makeSVG function creates an SVG document by calling getImage. It's passed a GenericImageHandler (the interface for the CachedImageHandlers) that it uses to handle the images, and a number that is the number of the copy of the image and resulting SVG document:

```
    public static void makeSVG(GenericImageHandler ih, int n) {
        DOMImplementation impl =
            SVGDOMImplementation.getDOMImplementation();
        String svgNS = SVGDOMImplementation.SVG_NAMESPACE_URI;
        SVGDocument doc =
            (SVGDocument)impl.createDocument(svgNS, "svg", null);
```

Once again, you need an SVGDocument to get started. This time, you don't use it to create an SVGGraphics2D directly. Instead, you use it to create an SVGGeneratorContext.

Once you have the context, you can use it to perform your customizations. First you change the default comment, and then you register the GenericImageHandler that you were passed:

```
60:
61:         SVGGeneratorContext ctx =
62:             SVGGeneratorContext.createDefault(doc);
63:         ctx.setComment(
64:          "Generated for XML Professional Development with Apache Tools");
65:         ctx.setGenericImageHandler(ih);
```

The context is used to create the SVGGraphics2D:

```
66:
67:         SVGGraphics2D g = new SVGGraphics2D(ctx, false);
```

In lines 69-71, you do the setup required to draw an image using Java2D:

```
68:
69:         g.setSVGCanvasSize(new Dimension(400,750));
70:         RenderingHints rh = new RenderingHints(null);
71:         BufferedImageOp bio = new RescaleOp(1f,0f, rh);
72:         g.drawImage(getImage(), bio, 0,0);
```

The output file now has a version number appended to the end so you can tell which SVG file goes with which copy of the image. The rest of makeSVG is devoted to calling the SVGGraphics2D stream method to generate the SVG file:

```
73:
74:         Writer out = null;
75:         try {
76:             OutputStream s =
77:               new FileOutputStream("SVGGenerateCustom"+n+".svg");
78:             out = new OutputStreamWriter(s, "UTF-8");
79:         } catch (UnsupportedEncodingException use) {
80:             use.printStackTrace();
81:         } catch (FileNotFoundException fnfe) {
82:             fnfe.printStackTrace();
83:         }
84:         try {
85:             boolean useCSS = true;
87:             g.stream(out, useCSS);
88:         } catch (SVGGraphics2DIOException sioe) {
89:             sioe.printStackTrace();
90:         }
91:     }
92:
93:     public static void main(String[] args) {
94:
95:         GenericImageHandler ih = null;
96:         try {
97:             ih = new CachedImageHandlerJPEGEncoder("images",
98:                                                     "images");
99:         } catch (SVGGraphics2DIOException sioe) {
100:            sioe.printStackTrace();
101:        }
```

When the program runs, you create an instance of CachedImageHandlerJPEGEncoder, which causes images to be stored as JPEGs and enables the cached image handling functionality. The arguments to the CachedImageHandlerJPEGEncoder constructor are the same as for the ImageHandlerJPEGEncoder: the first String is the name of the directory where image files (JPEGs in this case) are to be stored, and the second String is the URI prefix prepended to the image file when it's referenced in the SVG document.

You then make two calls to makeSVG, which would normally cause two image files to be generated. By passing your instance of CachedImageHandlerJPEGEncoder, Batik notices that it has seen this image before and reuses the image file it previously stored in the images directory:

```
            makeSVG(ih,0);
            makeSVG(ih,1);
        }
}
```

One of the resulting SVG files follows. They are both identical, which is what you'd expect. If you hadn't used image caching, they would differ in the reference to the image:

```
<?xml version="1.0" encoding="UTF-8"?>

<!DOCTYPE svg PUBLIC '-//W3C//DTD SVG 1.0//EN'
  'http://www.w3.org/TR/2001/REC-SVG-20010904/DTD/svg10.dtd'>
<svg style="stroke-dasharray:none; shape-rendering:auto;
            font-family:&apos;sansserif&apos;;
            text-rendering:auto; fill-opacity:1;
            color-rendering:auto; color-interpolation:auto;
            font-size:12; fill:black; stroke:black;
            image-rendering:auto; stroke-miterlimit:10;
            stroke-linecap:square; stroke-linejoin:miter;
            font-style:normal; stroke-width:1;
            stroke-dashoffset:0; font-weight:normal;
            stroke-opacity:1;"
            xmlns="http://www.w3.org/2000/svg" width="400"
            contentScriptType="text/ecmascript"
            preserveAspectRatio="xMidYMid meet"
            xmlns:xlink="http://www.w3.org/1999/xlink"
            zoomAndPan="magnify" version="1.0"
            contentStyleType="text/css" height="750">
  <!--Generated for Professional XML Development with Apache Tools-->
```

You can see that the comment has been replace with your comment.

The image tag is quite busy because of the required and default attributes. Most important for the purposes of this example is the xlink:href attribute, whose value is "images/jpegImage1.jpg". The images part of the URI comes from the images that you passed as the second argument to the CachedImageHandlerJPEGEncoder constructor:

```
  <defs id="genericDefs" />
  <g>
    <g>
      <image x="0" y="0" width="400"
             xmlns:xlink="http://www.w3.org/1999/xlink"
             xlink:href="images/jpegImage1.jpg"
```

```
                   xlink:type="simple" xlink:actuate="onRequest"
                   height="750"
                   preserveAspectRatio="xMidYMid meet"
                   xlink:show="replace" />
         </g>
       </g>
</svg>
```

Handling SVG styles

The last example of customization is a bit longer than you've seen so far. SVGGraphics2D allows you to change the way SVG styling is done. This is accomplished via the StyleHandler interface and the setStyleHandler method on the SVGGeneratorContext. The setStyle method on the StyleHandler interface is called for every SVG element that can be styled. So, if you want to change how style information is handled, you can provide your own implementation of StyleHandler.

Recall that SVG has two options for handling styles: creating a separate attribute for each style property or creating a CSS style attribute and filling it with CSS style properties. The most common way of dealing with CSS in HTML is to attach a class to various elements in the HTML document and then provide CSS definitions for those classes in a stylesheet, which can either be part of the same document or reside in a separate document. In this example, you'll use the StyleHandler API to implement this variation on styling. You'll use an embedded stylesheet (not a separate one) that contains definitions for classes attached to the SVG elements.

This implementation of StyleHandler is called StyleSheetStyleHandler. It's responsible for building up the embedded stylesheet as it processes elements in the document. It's also responsible for annotating elements in the document with the correct class attribute:

```
/*
 *
 * StyleSheetStyleHandler.java
 *
 * Example from "Professional XML Development with Apache Tools"
 *
 */
package com.sauria.apachexml.ch4;

import java.util.Iterator;
import java.util.Map;

import org.apache.batik.svggen.SVGGeneratorContext;
import org.apache.batik.svggen.StyleHandler;
import org.w3c.dom.CDATASection;
import org.w3c.dom.Element;

public class StyleSheetStyleHandler implements StyleHandler {
    private CDATASection styleSheet;

    public StyleSheetStyleHandler(CDATASection styleSheet) {
        this.styleSheet = styleSheet;
    }
```

The embedded stylesheet is a CDATASection that is passed to StyleSheetStyleHandler when it's constructed.

When you encounter an element that needs styling, you generate a new ID that starts with C. This is the class identifier for this element and is used to link the element with the stylesheet definitions:

```
24:     public void setStyle(Element element, Map styleMap,
25:                          SVGGeneratorContext context) {
26:
27:         String id = context.getIDGenerator().generateID("C");
```

Once you have the ID, you can add a set of style instructions to the stylesheet for that ID (line 28):

```
28:         styleSheet.appendData("."+id+" {");
29:
30:         for (Iterator iter = styleMap.keySet().iterator();
31:              iter.hasNext();) {
32:             String key = (String) iter.next();
33:             String value = (String) styleMap.get(key);
34:             styleSheet.appendData(key+":"+value+";");
35:         }
```

The style information is passed to the setStyle method as a Map. You can build the required stylesheet instructions by iterating over all the keys in the map and creating the key/value pairs using correct CSS syntax (line 34).

Once you've processed all the style properties, you can close the definition for this class:

```
36:         styleSheet.appendData("}\n");
```

The last thing you do is create a class attribute on the element with the current ID, thus establishing the link between the SVG element and the stylesheet definition:

```
37:
38:         element.setAttribute("class", id);
39:     }
40: }
```

Now let's look at what's going on in the main program that uses StyleSheetStyleHandler:

```
/*
 *
 * SVGStyleSheetGenerator.java
 *
 * Example from "Professional XML Development with Apache Tools"
 *
 */
package com.sauria.apachexml.ch4;

import java.awt.Color;
import java.awt.Dimension;
import java.awt.Font;
import java.awt.Shape;
import java.awt.geom.Ellipse2D;
import java.awt.geom.Rectangle2D;
```

```
16: import java.io.FileNotFoundException;
17: import java.io.FileOutputStream;
18: import java.io.OutputStream;
19: import java.io.OutputStreamWriter;
20: import java.io.UnsupportedEncodingException;
21: import java.io.Writer;
22:
23: import org.apache.batik.dom.svg.SVGDOMImplementation;
24: import org.apache.batik.svggen.DefaultExtensionHandler;
25: import org.apache.batik.svggen.ImageHandlerBase64Encoder;
26: import org.apache.batik.svggen.SVGGeneratorContext;
27: import org.apache.batik.svggen.SVGGraphics2D;
28: import org.apache.batik.svggen.SVGGraphics2DIOException;
29: import org.apache.batik.svggen.SVGSyntax;
30: import org.apache.batik.svggen.StyleHandler;
31: import org.w3c.dom.CDATASection;
32: import org.w3c.dom.DOMImplementation;
33: import org.w3c.dom.Element;
34: import org.w3c.dom.svg.SVGDocument;
35:
36: public class SVGStyleSheetGenerator {
37:
38:     public static void main(String[] args) {
39:         DOMImplementation impl =
40:             SVGDOMImplementation.getDOMImplementation();
41:         String svgNS = SVGDOMImplementation.SVG_NAMESPACE_URI;
42:         SVGDocument doc =
43:             (SVGDocument)impl.createDocument(svgNS, "svg", null);
44:
45:         SVGGeneratorContext ctx =
46:             SVGGraphics2D.buildSVGGeneratorContext(doc,
47:                 new ImageHandlerBase64Encoder(),
48:                 new DefaultExtensionHandler());
```

You create an instance of SVGDocument and use it to create an SVGGeneratorContext, which you need in order to register the StyleHandler. You have to provide an ImageHandler and an ExtensionHandler to the context factory method.

Here you create the CDATASection that will contain the stylesheet for the document:

```
49:
50:         CDATASection styleSheet = doc.createCDATASection("");
```

In lines 52-53 you create the StyleSheetStyleHandler instance, passing it the empty stylesheet. Then you register the instance as the style handler for the document in line 54. That gives you a context object with all the customizations you wanted; now you can create the SVGGraphics2D instance (line 56) and draw shapes into it (lines 58-68):

```
51:
52:         StyleHandler styleHandler =
53:             new StyleSheetStyleHandler(styleSheet);
54:         ctx.setStyleHandler(styleHandler);
55:
```

```
56:         SVGGraphics2D g = new SVGGraphics2D(ctx, false);
57:
58:         Shape circle = new Ellipse2D.Double(0,0,50,50);
59:         g.setPaint(Color.red);
60:         g.fill(circle);
61:         Shape rect = new Rectangle2D.Double(60,0,40,60);
62:         g.setPaint(Color.green);
63:         g.fill(rect);
64:         g.setPaint(Color.blue);
65:         Font font = new Font("Helvetica",Font.BOLD,24);
66:         g.setFont(font);
67:         g.drawString("Hello World",0f,90f);
68:         g.setSVGCanvasSize(new Dimension(300,100));
69:
70:
71:         Element docElt = doc.getDocumentElement();
72:         Element root = g.getRoot(docElt);
```

You call g.getRoot for a side effect here: You want the SVGGraphics to generate the SVG DOM tree for the SVGGraphics2D. You need to do a little DOM tree modification before you can write out the SVG document. At this point the SVG document contains SVG elements that have been annotated by StyleSheetStyleHandler as they've been created, and StyleSheetStyleHandler has finished writing all the CSS instructions into the stylesheet. But the stylesheet itself isn't yet embedded in the SVG document. That's the work that you have to do next.

You splice the stylesheet into the document this way:

```
73:
74:         Element defs =
75:             doc.getElementById(SVGSyntax.ID_PREFIX_GENERIC_DEFS);
76:         Element style =
77:             doc.createElementNS(SVGSyntax.SVG_NAMESPACE_URI,
78:                                 SVGSyntax.SVG_STYLE_TAG);
79:         style.setAttributeNS(null, SVGSyntax.SVG_TYPE_ATTRIBUTE,
80:                              "text/css");
81:         style.appendChild(styleSheet);
82:         defs.appendChild(style);
```

Every SVG document that SVGGraphics2D generates contains a <defs> element with the id genericDefs. You want to attach your stylesheet as a child of this <defs> element. So, you call getElementById to find that <defs> element (line 74-75). Then you create an SVG <style> element (lines 76-78) and set its type attribute to "text/css" (lines 79-80). You make the stylesheet a child of this <style> element (line 81) and make the <style> element a child of the <defs> element (line 82). Now everything is hooked up the way it's supposed to be, and you can write the SVG file out to a file:

```
83:
84:         Writer out = null;
85:         try {
86:             OutputStream s =
87:                new FileOutputStream("SVGStyleSheetGenerator.svg");
88:             out = new OutputStreamWriter(s, "UTF-8");
89:         } catch (UnsupportedEncodingException use) {
90:             use.printStackTrace();
```

```
        } catch (FileNotFoundException fnfe) {
            fnfe.printStackTrace();
        }
        try {
            g.stream(root, out);
        } catch (SVGGraphics2DIOException sioe) {
            sioe.printStackTrace();
        }
    }
}
```

The resulting SVG file is as follows:

```
<?xml version="1.0" encoding="UTF-8"?>

<!DOCTYPE svg PUBLIC '-//W3C//DTD SVG 1.0//EN'
 'http://www.w3.org/TR/2001/REC-SVG-20010904/DTD/svg10.dtd'>
<svg contentScriptType="text/ecmascript" width="300"
     xmlns:xlink="http://www.w3.org/1999/xlink"
     zoomAndPan="magnify" class="C6"
     contentStyleType="text/css" height="100"
     preserveAspectRatio="xMidYMid meet"
     xmlns="http://www.w3.org/2000/svg" version="1.0">
```

Notice that the contents of the <svg> element's style attribute has been reduced substantially.

Here you can see the results of your SVG DOM surgery. There's the CSS stylesheet for the document, right where it should be. You can check to see that the various class definitions are attached to the same elements—this document should be equivalent styled-boxes.svg.

```
  <!--Generated by the Batik Graphics2D SVG Generator-->
  <defs id="genericDefs">
    <style type="text/css" xml:space="preserve">
      <![CDATA[.C1 {stroke:red;fill:red;}
.C2 {stroke:none;}
.C3 {stroke:none;fill:lime;}
.C4 {font-size:24;font-weight:bold;stroke:blue;fill:blue;}
.C5 {stroke:none;}
.C6 {stroke-width:1;stroke-dashoffset:0;font-size:12;
stroke-dasharray:none;color-rendering:auto;font-weight:normal;
color-interpolation:auto;stroke-linejoin:miter;fill:black;
image-rendering:auto;font-family:'sansserif';stroke-opacity:1;
stroke-miterlimit:10;stroke:black;text-rendering:auto;
font-style:normal;stroke-linecap:square;fill-opacity:1;
shape-rendering:auto;}
]]>
    </style>
  </defs>
  <g>
    <g class="C1">
      <circle r="25" class="C2" cx="25" cy="25" />
      <rect width="40" x="60" height="60" y="0" class="C3" />
    </g>
```

```
    <g class="C4">
      <text xml:space="preserve" x="0" y="90" class="C5">
       Hello World
      </text>
    </g>
  </g>
</svg>
```

That completes our coverage of SVGGraphics2D. Most of the richness of this class comes from its ability to leverage the Java2D API, making it easier for you to think about doing the graphics while allowing the class to carry the burden of converting the drawing commands to SVG.

JSVGCanvas

Now that you know how to generate an SVG document using Batik, let's look at how you can use the Batik libraries to display an SVG document on the screen. Batik provides a Swing component called JSVGCanvas that does exactly this. You create an instance of JSVGCanvas and insert it into your Swing component hierarchy. When you're ready to display an SVG document in the canvas, you call the setURI method and pass it the URI of the SVG document you want to display. Once you do that, the canvas handles the rest. During the course of rendering and displaying the document, JSVGCanvas fires some events you may be interested in. You can register event listeners for these events on the canvas.

Let's look at how to use JSVGCanvas to build a simple SVG browser/viewer:

```
/*
 *
 * SimpleBrowser.java
 *
 * Example from "Professional XML Development with Apache Tools"
 *
 */
package com.sauria.apachexml.ch4;

import java.awt.BorderLayout;
import java.awt.FlowLayout;
import java.awt.event.ActionEvent;
import java.awt.event.ActionListener;
import java.awt.event.WindowAdapter;
import java.awt.event.WindowEvent;
import java.io.File;
import java.io.IOException;

import javax.swing.JComponent;
import javax.swing.JFileChooser;
import javax.swing.JFrame;
import javax.swing.JLabel;
import javax.swing.JMenu;
import javax.swing.JMenuBar;
import javax.swing.JMenuItem;
import javax.swing.JPanel;

import org.apache.batik.swing.JSVGCanvas;
```

```
29: import org.apache.batik.swing.gvt.GVTTreeRendererAdapter;
30: import org.apache.batik.swing.gvt.GVTTreeRendererEvent;
31: import org.apache.batik.swing.svg.GVTTreeBuilderAdapter;
32: import org.apache.batik.swing.svg.GVTTreeBuilderEvent;
33: import org.apache.batik.swing.svg.SVGDocumentLoaderAdapter;
34: import org.apache.batik.swing.svg.SVGDocumentLoaderEvent;
35: import org.apache.batik.swing.svg.SVGLoadEventDispatcherAdapter;
36: import org.apache.batik.swing.svg.SVGLoadEventDispatcherEvent;
37:
38: public class SimpleBrowser {
39:     JFrame frame;
40:     JLabel label = new JLabel("Status: ");
41:     JSVGCanvas canvas = new JSVGCanvas();
42:     JMenuBar menuBar;
43:
44:     public SimpleBrowser(JFrame f) {
45:         frame = f;
46:     }
47:
```

The simple browser class has a number of Swing components in it: a JFrame for the entire browser, a JLabel where you can display status information, a JMenuBar for controlling the browser, and, of course, an instance of JSVGCanvas that does all the real work.

The addMenuBar method sets up the menu bar for use with the rest of the applications. You set up the menu bar (lines 49-50) with a single menu, File (lines 51-52), and you create the Open... item for the menu (lines 53-54):

```
48:     public void addMenuBar() {
49:         menuBar = new JMenuBar();
50:         frame.setJMenuBar(menuBar);
51:         JMenu menu = new JMenu("File");
52:         menuBar.add(menu);
53:         JMenuItem item = new JMenuItem("Open...");
54:         menu.add(item);
55:
```

Next you define the action to be taken when the item is selected. You want to use a JFileChooser to select a file from the current directory (line 58). If the use selects a file and clicks the Open button (lines 59-61), then you want to read and display the SVG file by calling the setURI method on the JSVGCanvas (line 63):

```
56:         item.addActionListener(new ActionListener() {
57:             public void actionPerformed(ActionEvent ae) {
58:                 JFileChooser fc = new JFileChooser(".");
59:                 int choice = fc.showOpenDialog(frame);
60:                 if (choice == JFileChooser.APPROVE_OPTION) {
61:                     File f = fc.getSelectedFile();
62:                     try {
63:                         canvas.setURI(f.toURL().toString());
64:                     } catch (IOException ex) {
65:                         ex.printStackTrace();
66:                     }
```

```
                }
            }
        });
```

After the Open… item is done, you create a Quit item, add it to the menu, and install its action:

```
        item = new JMenuItem("Quit");
        menu.add(item);
        item.addActionListener(new ActionListener () {
            public void actionPerformed(ActionEvent ae) {
                System.exit(0);
            }
        });
    }

```

createComponents sets up the layout of the components inside the JFrame content pane:

```
    public JComponent createComponents() {
        final JPanel panel = new JPanel(new BorderLayout());

```

The labelPanel is a space for the JSVGCanvas event handlers to report their activities to the user:

```
        JPanel labelPanel =
            new JPanel(new FlowLayout(FlowLayout.LEFT));
        labelPanel.add(label);
        labelPanel.add(new JLabel(" "));
```

The labelPanel goes in the North position, and the JSVGCanvas goes in the Center position:

```

        panel.add("North", labelPanel);
        panel.add("Center", canvas);

        return panel;
    }

```

You use addListeners to create and register event listeners for the various events that JSVGCanvas reports. Understanding the operation phases of JSVGCanvas will help you understand what the event listeners are for. When the setURI method is called, the XML/SVG document is parsed and an SVG DOM tree is constructed. The SVGDocumentLoaderListener is concerned with this phase. It can report the start and end (either successful or unsuccessful) of the phase. The SVG DOM tree is used to construct a Graphics Vector Toolkit (GVT) tree. This phase is monitored by the GVTTreeBuilderListener. Once the GVT tree is built, you can render the document. If the document is dynamic, then the code that processes the onload event is called. SVGLoadEventDispatcherListener monitors the progress of the onload dispatching code. After this, the GVT tree is used to render the document, and the rendering is monitored by GVTTreeRendererListener.

You use the addSVGDocumentLoaderListener method on the canvas to register a listener, and you use the SVGDocumentLoaderAdaptor class so that you only have to provide the event callbacks you're interested in:

```
    public void addListeners() {
        canvas.addSVGDocumentLoaderListener(
            new SVGDocumentLoaderAdapter() {
            public void documentLoadingStarted(
                SVGDocumentLoaderEvent e) {
                label.setText("SVG Document Loading...");
            }
            public void documentLoadingCompleted(
                SVGDocumentLoaderEvent e) {
                label.setText("SVG Document Loaded.");
            }
        });

```

For the sake of space, you're only tracking the start and completed events for the various event listeners. There are also callbacks that tell whether the phase failed or was cancelled. The code for all the listener registrations is basically the same—it's the usual tedious Swing event-registration code:

```
        canvas.addGVTTreeBuilderListener(
            new GVTTreeBuilderAdapter() {
            public void gvtBuildStarted(
                GVTTreeBuilderEvent e) {
                label.setText("GVT Build Started...");
            }
            public void gvtBuildCompleted(
                GVTTreeBuilderEvent e) {
                label.setText("GVT Build Complete.");
                frame.pack();
            }
        });

        canvas.addGVTTreeRendererListener(
            new GVTTreeRendererAdapter() {
            public void gvtRenderingPrepare(
                GVTTreeRendererEvent e) {
                label.setText("GVT Rendering Started...");
            }
            public void gvtRenderingCompleted(
                GVTTreeRendererEvent e) {
                label.setText("GVT Rendering Complete.");
            }
        });

        canvas.addSVGLoadEventDispatcherListener(
            new SVGLoadEventDispatcherAdapter () {
            public void svgLoadEventDispatchStarted(
                SVGLoadEventDispatcherEvent e) {
                label.setText("OnLoad Processing Started...");
            }
```

```
137:
138:                public void svgLoadEventDispatchCompleted(
139:                    SVGLoadEventDispatcherEvent e) {
140:                    label.setText("OnLoad Processing Complete.");
141:                }
142:            });
143:        }
144:
```

It all comes together in the main function. You create a JFrame (line 145) that you use to create the browser (line 146). Then you add the menu bar (line 148), the panel of components (line 149), and the event listeners (line 150):

```
145:        public static void main(String[] args) {
146:            JFrame f = new JFrame("Batik");
147:            SimpleBrowser app = new SimpleBrowser(f);
148:            app.addMenuBar();
149:            f.getContentPane().add(app.createComponents());
150:            app.addListeners();
151:
```

You attach a window close event handler for completeness (152-156), size up the frame, and make it visible:

```
152:            f.addWindowListener(new WindowAdapter() {
153:                public void windowClosing(WindowEvent e) {
154:                    System.exit(0);
155:                }
156:            });
157:            f.setSize(400, 400);
158:            f.setVisible(true);
159:        }
160: }
```

Now you're ready to open SVG files and render them.

In addition to event handling, JSVGCanvas also has built-in interactors that provide functionality for zooming, panning, and rotating the contents of the canvas. If your application is going to use Java to manipulate the document, you'll need to call the getSVGDocument method on JSVGCanvas in order to get it.

Image Transcoding

Our next piece of Batik library functionality has to do with transcoding SVG files into images. These images can be written to disk, or they can be written to Java2D BufferedImage objects. Batik provides transcoders for three formats: JPEG, PNG, and TIFF. The transcoders for each format are named with the file format in their name: JPEGTranscoder, PNGTranscoder, and TIFFTranscoder.

Transcoding from an SVG File

In this example, we'll look at how to take an area within an SVG document and transcode it to an image file. The example uses the PNGTranscoder, but the code works equally well with any of the transcoders:

```
1: /*
2:  *
3:  * TranscodeFileArea.java
4:  *
5:  * Example from "Professional XML Development with Apache Tools"
6:  *
7:  */
8: package com.sauria.apachexml.ch4;
9:
10: import java.awt.Color;
11: import java.awt.Rectangle;
12: import java.io.FileNotFoundException;
13: import java.io.FileOutputStream;
14: import java.io.IOException;
15: import java.io.OutputStream;
16:
17: import org.apache.batik.transcoder.TranscoderException;
18: import org.apache.batik.transcoder.TranscoderInput;
19: import org.apache.batik.transcoder.TranscoderOutput;
20: import org.apache.batik.transcoder.image.ImageTranscoder;
21: import org.apache.batik.transcoder.image.PNGTranscoder;
22:
23: public class TranscodeFileArea {
24:
25:     public static void main(String[] args) {
26:         int width = 50;
27:         int height = 50;
28:         Rectangle areaRect = new Rectangle(10,10,width,height);
```

First you set up an AWT Rectangle that specifies the area you want to transcode.

After instantiating the PNGTranscoder (line 30), you add a series of transcoding hints to the transcoder. You set the background color to white (line 32), and then you set the width (lines 33-34) and height (lines 35-36) of the output image. You also give the transcode the Rectangle with the area you want transcoded (lines 37-38):

```
29:
30:         PNGTranscoder xcoder = new PNGTranscoder();
31:         xcoder.addTranscodingHint(
32:             ImageTranscoder.KEY_BACKGROUND_COLOR, Color.white);
33:         xcoder.addTranscodingHint(PNGTranscoder.KEY_WIDTH,
34:                                   new Float(width));
35:         xcoder.addTranscodingHint(PNGTranscoder.KEY_HEIGHT,
36:                                   new Float(height));
37:         xcoder.addTranscodingHint(PNGTranscoder.KEY_AOI,
38:                                   areaRect);
```

The transcoders use a TranscoderInput to specify their input source and a TranscoderOutput to specify their output destination. The TranscoderInput constructor expects an absolute URI. Filenames hoping to pass as relative URIs are rejected:

```
39:
40:         String uri = args[0];
41:
42:         TranscoderInput in = new TranscoderInput(uri);
```

You create the TranscoderOutput from a FileOutputStream (lines 44-50) and then call the transcode method on the transcoder (line 53):

```
43:
44:         OutputStream os = null;
45:         try {
46:             os = new FileOutputStream(args[1]);
47:         } catch (FileNotFoundException fnfe) {
48:             fnfe.printStackTrace();
49:         }
50:         TranscoderOutput out = new TranscoderOutput(os);
51:
52:         try {
53:             xcoder.transcode(in,out);
54:         } catch (TranscoderException te) {
55:             te.printStackTrace();
56:         }
57:         try {
58:             os.flush();
59:         } catch (IOException ioe) {
60:             ioe.printStackTrace();
61:         }
62:     }
63: }
```

Transcoding from an SVG DOM

The next example shows how to transcode an SVG DOM tree into an image file:

```
/*
 *
 * TranscodeDOM.java
 *
 * Example from "Professional XML Development with Apache Tools"
 *
 */
package com.sauria.apachexml.ch4;

import java.awt.Color;
import java.awt.Dimension;
import java.awt.Font;
import java.awt.Shape;
import java.awt.geom.Ellipse2D;
import java.awt.geom.Rectangle2D;
```

```
import java.io.FileNotFoundException;
import java.io.FileOutputStream;
import java.io.IOException;
import java.io.OutputStream;

import org.apache.batik.dom.svg.SVGDOMImplementation;
import org.apache.batik.svggen.SVGGraphics2D;
import org.apache.batik.transcoder.TranscoderException;
import org.apache.batik.transcoder.TranscoderInput;
import org.apache.batik.transcoder.TranscoderOutput;
import org.apache.batik.transcoder.image.ImageTranscoder;
import org.apache.batik.transcoder.image.PNGTranscoder;
import org.w3c.dom.DOMImplementation;
import org.w3c.dom.Element;
import org.w3c.dom.svg.SVGDocument;

public class TranscodeDOM {

    public static void main(String[] args) {
        DOMImplementation impl =
            SVGDOMImplementation.getDOMImplementation();
        String svgNS = SVGDOMImplementation.SVG_NAMESPACE_URI;
        SVGDocument doc =
            (SVGDocument)impl.createDocument(svgNS, "svg", null);

        SVGGraphics2D g = new SVGGraphics2D(doc);

        Shape circle = new Ellipse2D.Double(0,0,50,50);
        g.setPaint(Color.red);
        g.fill(circle);
        Shape rect = new Rectangle2D.Double(60,0,40,60);
        g.setPaint(Color.green);
        g.fill(rect);
        g.setPaint(Color.blue);
        Font font = new Font("Helvetica",Font.BOLD,24);
        g.setFont(font);
        g.drawString("Hello World",0f,90f);
        g.setSVGCanvasSize(new Dimension(300,100));
```

The code up to this point should look familiar. You're just creating an SVG DOM tree that you can use as input to the transcoder.

The next two lines are very important, because the SVG DOM isn't created until these methods are called:

```
        Element root = doc.getDocumentElement();
        g.getRoot(root);
```

Instead of constructing the TranscoderInput from a URI, this time you construct it with an SVG DOM. Nothing could be easier:

```
        PNGTranscoder xcoder = new PNGTranscoder();
        xcoder.addTranscodingHint(
            ImageTranscoder.KEY_BACKGROUND_COLOR, Color.white);

        TranscoderInput in = new TranscoderInput(doc);
        OutputStream os = null;
        try {
            os = new FileOutputStream("svgDOM.png");
        } catch (FileNotFoundException fnfe) {
            fnfe.printStackTrace();
        }
        TranscoderOutput out = new TranscoderOutput(os);

        try {
            xcoder.transcode(in, out);
        } catch (TranscoderException te) {
            te.printStackTrace();
        }
        try {
            os.flush();
        } catch (IOException ioe) {
            ioe.printStackTrace();
        }

    }
}
```

If you want generate a Java2D BufferedImage, you can call the createImage method on any of the transcoders. You'll need to pass the width and height of the image (in pixels) to this method.

SVG Scripting

As you saw in the section on imperative dynamic SVG, you can do a lot with an SVG document when you combine it with a scripting language such as ECMAScript. The SVG scripting capabilities of Batik come into play when you're rendering an SVG document using the JSVGCanvas. The SVG DOM being manipulated by the scripting language is the SVG DOM that the JSVGCanvas generates in order to render the document.

JSVGCanvas ECMAScript API

To use scripting in JSVGCanvas, you need to know what properties and methods it supports. Here's a brief description. All these names are available as global variable and function names because the global object in an SVG document is the window object.

The properties are as follows:

- **document**—The current SVG document.
- **event (or evt)**—The last event that was fired.
- **window**—The current global object.

These are the methods:

- **alert(*message*)**—Show an alert dialog containing *message*.
- **confirm(*question*)**—Show a confirm dialog that presents the *question* and provides OK and Cancel buttons. Return true if the user clicks OK and false otherwise.
- **prompt(*message* [, *defaultValue*])**—Show an input dialog box that displays a prompt message. If defaultValue is supplied, it's displayed in the input box. Return whatever string the user types (including the *defaultValue*) or null.
- **setInterval(*script, interval*)**—Schedule the *script* to be executed over and over with an *interval* (in milliseconds) between executions. The *script* is a string containing the script body. The current script continues to execute. Return an object that can be used as an *intervalID*.
- **setInterval(*function, interval*)**—Schedule the *function* to be executed over and over with an *interval* (in milliseconds) between executions. The current script continues to execute. Return an object that can be used as an *intervalID*.
- **clearInterval(*intervalID*)**—Unschedule the script or function associated with *intervalID*.
- **setTimeout(*script, timeout*)**—Wait *timeout* milliseconds and then execute the *script*. The *script* is a string containing the script body. The current script continues to execute. Return an object that can be used as a *timeoutID*.
- **setTimeout(*function, timeout*)**—Wait *timeout* milliseconds and then execute the *function*. The current script continues to execute. Return an object that can be used as a *timeoutID*.
- **clearTimeout(*timeoutID*)**—Cancel the delayed execution associated with *timeoutID*.
- **parseXML(*text, document*)**—Given a text string containing an XML document fragment, and also give *document* (a DOM document object to be used as a DOM factory object), parse the XML document fragment and return an instance of org.w3c.dom.DocumentFragment that represents the XML document fragment.
- **getURL(*uri, function*[, *encoding*])**—Download some data located at *uri* and pass it to *function*. *Function* should take as an argument an ECMAScript object with three properties:
    - **success**—True if the data was retrieved, false otherwise.
    - **contentType**—The content type of the data.
    - **content**—A string representing the data.

If the encoding argument is specified, the data file is assumed to use that encoding; otherwise UTF-8 is assumed.

Alternate Scripting Languages

Batik allows you to use scripting languages besides ECMAScript to perform imperative dynamic SVG tasks. Let's modify the simple browser to use Jython (a Java implementation of Python 2.1) as your scripting language. (You can get a copy of Jython via www.jython.org.) The Batik developers have provided a Batik InterpreterFactory subclass for doing this. Unfortunately, it's still a decent amount of work. You need to register the JPythonInterpreterFactory with the InterpreterPool that's in the BridgeContext object inside the JSVGCanvas. The only way you can get access to all the things you need is by subclassing JSVGCanvas:

```
 1: /*
 2:  *
 3:  * JSVGJythonCanvas.java
 4:  *
 5:  * Example from "Professional XML Development with Apache Tools"
 6:  *
 7:  */
 8: package com.sauria.apachexml.ch4;
 9:
10: import org.apache.batik.bridge.BridgeContext;
11: import org.apache.batik.bridge.DocumentLoader;
12: import org.apache.batik.bridge.UserAgent;
13: import org.apache.batik.script.InterpreterPool;
14: import org.apache.batik.script.jpython.JPythonInterpreterFactory;
15: import org.apache.batik.swing.JSVGCanvas;
16:
17: public class JSVGJythonCanvas extends JSVGCanvas {
18:     public class JythonBridgeContext extends BridgeContext {
```

Actually, the problem is a little worse than we told you. You need to create a subclass of the BridgeContext class. (You'll see why in a minute.) The BridgeContext is the glue between the SVG DOM, the GVT tree used for rendering, and the drawing part of the JSVGCanvas. Fortunately, all the work can be done in the constructor of this new BridgeContext subclass. Because this context is being used only to enable Python scripting, you make it an inner class of the JSVGJythonCanvas.

After calling the parent constructor, you call setDynamic to make sure the canvas knows you're in dynamic SVG mode and that things will be updated:

```
19:         public JythonBridgeContext(UserAgent ua,
20:                                    DocumentLoader loader) {
21:             super(ua, loader);
22:
23:             setDynamic(true);
```

You create an empty interpreter pool (line 25). The pool isn't really empty—it already has an interpreter for ECMAScript installed, because SVG mandates ECMAScript support for scripting. Next, you tell the interpreter pool that scripts with MIME type "text/python" will use an instance of JPythonInterpreterFactory (line 26-27). After that, you call the setInterpreterPool method on the context with your Jython-enhanced InterpreterPool, and you're all set (line 28):

```
24:
25:             InterpreterPool ipool = new InterpreterPool();
26:             ipool.putInterpreterFactory("text/python",
27:                 new JPythonInterpreterFactory());
28:             setInterpreterPool(ipool);
```

This call to setInterpreterPool is why you needed to subclass BridgeContext—setInterpreterPool is protected. The Batik jars don't include built versions of JythonInterpreterFactory or JythonInterpreter, so you'll need to build them and make sure that they and a copy of jython.jar are on your classpath.

JSVGJythonCanvas' createBridgeContext method creates a new instance of JythonBridgeContext and returns it:

```

          }
      }
      public BridgeContext createBridgeContext() {
          BridgeContext ctx =
              new JythonBridgeContext(userAgent, loader);

          return ctx;
      }

  }
```

You can modify the SimpleBrowser.java from earlier in the chapter by removing the addListeners method and the call to it. Because you're using a subclass of JSVGCanvas, you need to tell the browser which class you're using. Line 33 does all the work of turning your simple SVG browser into a simple browser that understands Python scripts:

```
 1: /*
 2:  *
 3:  * JythonBrowser.java
 4:  *
 5:  * Example from "Professional XML Development with Apache Tools"
 6:  *
 7:  */
 8: package com.sauria.apachexml.ch4;
 9:
10: import java.awt.BorderLayout;
11: import java.awt.FlowLayout;
12: import java.awt.event.ActionEvent;
13: import java.awt.event.ActionListener;
14: import java.awt.event.WindowAdapter;
15: import java.awt.event.WindowEvent;
16: import java.io.File;
17: import java.io.IOException;
18:
19: import javax.swing.JComponent;
20: import javax.swing.JFileChooser;
21: import javax.swing.JFrame;
22: import javax.swing.JLabel;
23: import javax.swing.JMenu;
24: import javax.swing.JMenuBar;
25: import javax.swing.JMenuItem;
26: import javax.swing.JPanel;
27:
28: import org.apache.batik.swing.JSVGCanvas;
29:
30: public class JythonBrowser {
31:     JFrame frame;
32:     JLabel label = new JLabel("Status: ");
33:     JSVGCanvas canvas = new JSVGJythonCanvas();
```

```
    JMenuBar menuBar;

    public JythonBrowser(JFrame f) {
        frame = f;
    }

    public void addMenuBar() {
        menuBar = new JMenuBar();
        frame.setJMenuBar(menuBar);
        JMenu menu = new JMenu("File");
        menuBar.add(menu);
        JMenuItem item = new JMenuItem("Open...");
        menu.add(item);

        item.addActionListener(new ActionListener() {
            public void actionPerformed(ActionEvent ae) {
                JFileChooser fc = new JFileChooser(".");
                int choice = fc.showOpenDialog(frame);
                if (choice == JFileChooser.APPROVE_OPTION) {
                    File f = fc.getSelectedFile();
                    try {
                        canvas.setURI(f.toURL().toString());
                    } catch (IOException ex) {
                        ex.printStackTrace();
                    }
                }
            }
        });
        item = new JMenuItem("Quit");
        menu.add(item);
        item.addActionListener(new ActionListener () {
            public void actionPerformed(ActionEvent ae) {
                System.exit(0);
            }
        });
    }

    public JComponent createComponents() {
        final JPanel panel = new JPanel(new BorderLayout());

        JPanel labelPanel =
            new JPanel(new FlowLayout(FlowLayout.LEFT));
        labelPanel.add(label);
        labelPanel.add(new JLabel(" "));

        panel.add("North", labelPanel);
        panel.add("Center", canvas);

        return panel;
    }

    public static void main(String[] args) {
        JFrame f = new JFrame("Batik");
        JythonBrowser app = new JythonBrowser(f);
```

```
        app.addMenuBar();
        f.getContentPane().add(app.createComponents());

        f.addWindowListener(new WindowAdapter() {
            public void windowClosing(WindowEvent e) {
                System.exit(0);
            }
        });
        f.setSize(400, 400);
        f.setVisible(true);
    }
}
```

The following listing shows a version of imperative-dynamic.svg that has been converted to use Python instead of ECMAScript:

```
<?xml version="1.0" standalone="no"?>
<!DOCTYPE svg PUBLIC "-//W3C//DTD SVG 20010904//EN"
  "http://www.w3.org/TR/2001/REC-SVG-20010904/DTD/svg10.dtd">
<svg width="300" height="150"
     xmlns="http://www.w3.org/2000/svg"
     xmlns:xlink="http://www.w3.org/1999/xlink"
         contentScriptType="text/python">
 <script type="text/python">
<![CDATA[
import random
def randomColor():
  return "#"+hex(int(random.random() * 16777216))[2:]
]]>
 </script>
```

The big difference here is in the content of the <script> element, which now contains Python code rather than ECMAScript.

The function-calling syntaxes of Python and ECMAScript are similar enough that no change was required in the onclick event handler:

```
 <rect x="10" y="10" width="100" height="100"
       onclick="evt.target.setAttribute('fill', randomColor())"/>
</svg>
```

You can use a similar technique if you want to use TCL as your scripting language. The Batik developers also provided support for using Jacl, a Java implementation of TCL.

You can also use a Java program to manipulate the contents of the SVG DOM and achieve imperative dynamic SVG effects. You can do this via regular W3C DOM API calls. There are two major areas where you may have trouble. The first is attaching event listeners written in Java to elements in the SVG document. The only good way to do this is to attach id attributes to the various elements and then supply Java EventListeners to process the various events. If you have more than a few elements and events, this can quickly add up to a lot of code. The second area where you may run into trouble is the fact that Java operations on the SVG DOM must take place in the (Swing) canvas update thread. This means you need to use org.apache.batik.bridge.UpdateManager to transfer control from your thread to the canvas update thread.

Because of these two issues, you're much better off using a scripting language to do imperative dynamic SVG tasks. The scripting languages are pretty powerful, and unless you need some Java functionality, the scripting languages are more than up to the job. In fact, if you use Jython, it can call just about any function on any Java object; in many cases you can get the job done using Jython, which is much more convenient than trying to go the full Java bridge route. In this case, the only thing you need to watch out for is performing SVG DOM operations in the Java code you're calling from Jython. But you should be able to keep all that code in Jython and only call out for non-DOM operations.

Security

There are two security areas you may need to be aware of when you're using Batik: Java-level application security and controlling access to external resources.

Application Security

Batik provides org.apache.batik.util.ApplicationSecurityEnforcer, which you can use in your applications to control application security. ApplicationSecurityEnforcer lets you install a Java2 SecurityManager and a security policy. This is a helper class that makes dealing with security managers a little easier. You still have to write a Java2 security policy file that grants your application permission to perform actions and access resources.

Accessing External Resources

You'll have to deal with this area when you use JSVGCanvas. SVG documents can reference documents anywhere on the Internet, thanks to the use of XLink linking in the specification. Depending on your application, this may not be something you wish to promote.

The JSVGCanvas class uses a UserAgent class that contains various pieces of information about the UserAgent connected to the canvas. The UserAgent interface provides two methods that work together to control access to external resources: getScriptSecurity, which controls access to scripts; and getExternalResourceSecurity, which controls access to external resources besides scripts.

Let's look at how you can use these methods to build a restricted version of the SimpleBrowser that can only load scripts and resources from approved URIs. Once again, you must subclass JSVGCanvas. This time you need to do it so that you can override the protected createUserAgent method:

```
/*
 *
 * JSVGRestrictedCanvas.java
 *
 * Example from "Professional XML Development with Apache Tools"
 *
 */
package com.sauria.apachexml.ch4;

import org.apache.batik.bridge.DefaultExternalResourceSecurity;
import org.apache.batik.bridge.DefaultScriptSecurity;
import org.apache.batik.bridge.ExternalResourceSecurity;
import org.apache.batik.bridge.RelaxedExternalResourceSecurity;
import org.apache.batik.bridge.RelaxedScriptSecurity;
import org.apache.batik.bridge.ScriptSecurity;
```

```
import org.apache.batik.bridge.UserAgent;
import org.apache.batik.swing.JSVGCanvas;
import org.apache.batik.util.ParsedURL;

public class JSVGRestrictedCanvas extends JSVGCanvas {

```

You want to supply your own implementation of UserAgent, but you don't want to supply a full implementation of the entire interface. The UserAgent that JSVGCanvas normally uses is fine, except that you want to override getExternalResourceSecurity and getScriptSecurity. It's fortunate, then, that you're subclassing JSVGCanvas anyway, because the default UserAgent it uses is an inner class. So, you create an inner class in JSVGRestrictedCanvas that subclasses JSVGCanvas.CanvasUserAgent and override the methods you need.

getExternalResourceSecurity returns an implementor of ExternalResourceSecurity:

```
    protected class RestrictedUserAgent
        extends JSVGCanvas.CanvasUserAgent {

        public ExternalResourceSecurity
            getExternalResourceSecurity(
                ParsedURL resourceURL,
                ParsedURL docURL) {
            if (resourceURL.getHost().endsWith("apache.org") ||
                resourceURL.getHost().endsWith("sauria.com"))
                return
                  new RelaxedExternalResourceSecurity(
                      resourceURL, docURL);
            else
                return
                  new DefaultExternalResourceSecurity(
                      resourceURL, docURL);
        }
```

The various security policies are implemented by classes that implement this interface. The list of available classes looks like this:

- **NoLoadExternalResourceSecurity**—No external resources may be loaded.
- **EmbededExternalResourceSecurity**—Only resources embedded in the current document may be loaded.
- **DefaultExternalResourceSecurity**—Embedded resources and resources coming from the same location as the document referencing them (the current document) are allowed.
- **RelaxedExternalResourceSecurity**—Any external resource may be loaded.

The security policy for external resources is this: If the URL is going to the apache.org or sauria.com domain, then you can load resources from there without any problem. Otherwise, the default security policy should be used. You want this general rule to apply to scripts as well.

getScriptSecurity works much the same as getExternalResourceSecurity, but the names of the security policy classes are different:

- **NoLoadScriptResourceSecurity**—Don't load any scripts.
- **EmbededScriptSecurity**—Only load scripts that are embedded in the current document.
- **DefaultScriptSecurity**—Load the script if it's embedded in the current document or if it's coming from the same location as the current document.
- **RelaxedScriptSecurity**—Scripts from any location can be loaded.

```

        public ScriptSecurity getScriptSecurity(
            String scriptType,
            ParsedURL scriptURL,
            ParsedURL docURL) {
            if (scriptURL.getHost().endsWith("apache.org") ||
                scriptURL.getHost().endsWith("sauria.com"))
                return
                  new RelaxedScriptSecurity(scriptType,
                                                    scriptURL, docURL);
            else
                return
                  new DefaultScriptSecurity(scriptType,
                                                    scriptURL, docURL);
        }
```

You supply your own createUserAgent factory method that returns an instance of the custom UserAgent:

```
    }

    protected UserAgent createUserAgent() {
        return new JSVGRestrictedCanvas.RestrictedUserAgent();
    }
}
```

Once you have the JSVGCanvas, you just need to plug it into the simple browser, and you have an access-controlled SVG browser. In line 33 you plug in the JSVGRestrictedCanvas and turn on access control:

```
 1: /*
 2:  *
 3:  * RestrictedBrowser.java
 4:  *
 5:  * Example from "Professional XML Development with Apache Tools"
 6:  *
 7:  */
 8: package com.sauria.apachexml.ch4;
 9:
10: import java.awt.BorderLayout;
```

```
import java.awt.FlowLayout;
import java.awt.event.ActionEvent;
import java.awt.event.ActionListener;
import java.awt.event.WindowAdapter;
import java.awt.event.WindowEvent;
import java.io.File;
import java.io.IOException;

import javax.swing.JComponent;
import javax.swing.JFileChooser;
import javax.swing.JFrame;
import javax.swing.JLabel;
import javax.swing.JMenu;
import javax.swing.JMenuBar;
import javax.swing.JMenuItem;
import javax.swing.JPanel;

import org.apache.batik.swing.JSVGCanvas;

public class RestrictedBrowser {
    JFrame frame;
    JLabel label = new JLabel("Status: ");
    JSVGCanvas canvas = new JSVGRestrictedCanvas();
    JMenuBar menuBar;

    public RestrictedBrowser(JFrame f) {
        frame = f;
    }

    public void addMenuBar() {
        menuBar = new JMenuBar();
        frame.setJMenuBar(menuBar);
        JMenu menu = new JMenu("File");
        menuBar.add(menu);
        JMenuItem item = new JMenuItem("Open...");
        menu.add(item);

        item.addActionListener(new ActionListener() {
            public void actionPerformed(ActionEvent ae) {
                JFileChooser fc = new JFileChooser(".");
                int choice = fc.showOpenDialog(frame);
                if (choice == JFileChooser.APPROVE_OPTION) {
                    File f = fc.getSelectedFile();
                    try {
                        canvas.setURI(f.toURL().toString());
                    } catch (IOException ex) {
                        ex.printStackTrace();
                    }
                }
            }
        });
        item = new JMenuItem("Quit");
        menu.add(item);
        item.addActionListener(new ActionListener () {
```

```
                public void actionPerformed(ActionEvent ae) {
                    System.exit(0);
                }
            });
        }

        public JComponent createComponents() {
            final JPanel panel = new JPanel(new BorderLayout());

            JPanel labelPanel =
                new JPanel(new FlowLayout(FlowLayout.LEFT));
            labelPanel.add(label);
            labelPanel.add(new JLabel(" "));

            panel.add("North", labelPanel);
            panel.add("Center", canvas);

            return panel;
        }

        public static void main(String[] args) {
            JFrame f = new JFrame("Batik");
            RestrictedBrowser app = new RestrictedBrowser(f);
            app.addMenuBar();
            f.getContentPane().add(app.createComponents());

            f.addWindowListener(new WindowAdapter() {
                public void windowClosing(WindowEvent e) {
                    System.exit(0);
                }
            });
            f.setSize(400, 400);
            f.setVisible(true);
        }
    }
```

The following listing shows an SVG file that references resources from the apache.org, sauria.com, and sun.com domains. If you open this file in the RestrictedBrowser, you'll see that the first two images render properly and that you get a security exception instead of the third image:

```
<?xml version="1.0" encoding="UTF-8"?>
<!DOCTYPE svg PUBLIC "-//W3C//DTD SVG 1.0//EN"
  "http://www.w3.org/TR/2001/REC-SVG-20010904/DTD/svg10.dtd">
<svg xmlns="http://www.w3.org/2000/svg"
     xmlns:xlink="http://www.w3.org/1999/xlink"
     width="400" height="750">
 <title>one.svg</title>
 <desc>Sample SVG File</desc>
 <g id="image-link">
  <a xlink:href="http://xml.apache.org">
   <image x="10" y="10" width="220px" height="65px"
    xlink:href="http://xml.apache.org/images/group-logo.gif"/>
  </a>
  <a xlink:href="http://www.sauria.com">
```

```
    <image x="10" y="200" width="200px" height="213"
       xlink:href="http://www.sauria.com/images/twl4.jpg"/>
   </a>
   <a xlink:href="http://java.sun.com">
    <image x="10" y="100" width="38px" height="66px"
       xlink:href="http://java.sun.com/images/v4_java_logo.gif"/>
   </a>
  </g>
</svg>
```

SVG Rasterizer

Batik's SVG Rasterizer is an application you can use to convert one or more SVG files into raster file format. Doing so allows you to use SVG to describe images that can be viewed without requiring SVG rendering capabilities. You can use the rasterizer two ways: as a command-line application or as an Ant build task.

Command Line

To use the rasterizer as a command-line tool, you need to execute the following command:

```
java –jar batik-rasterizer.jar [options] [files]
```

This assumes that the batik-rasterizer.jar is in the current directory, but you can specify the path to the jar file if necessary. The possible options for the rasterizer are

- **-d <*dir* | *file*>**—Output directory, which can be an output file if there is a single input file.
- **-m <*mimeType*>**—Output mime type: image/png, image/jpeg, image/tiff, or application/pdf (requires FOP to be installed).
- **-w <*width*>**—Output width (floating point).
- **-h <*height*>**—Output height (floating point).
- **-maxw <*width*>**—Maximum output width (floating point).
- **-maxh <*height*>**—Maximum output height (floating point).
- **-a <*x,y,w,h*>**—Output area: *x* and *y* followed by *w*(idth) and *h*(eight).
- **-bg <*a.r.g.b*>**—Output color (*a*, *r*, *g*, and *b* are integer values).
- **-cssMedia <*media*>**—Convert the SVG file for this CSS media type.
- **-cssAlternate <*alternate*>**—Alternate CSS stylesheet URI to use when converting SVG documents.
- **-cssUser <*userStylesheet*>**—Apply the CSS stylesheet specified by this URI in addition to any other stylesheets.
- **-lang <*userLanguage*>**—The language to use when converting SVG documents.

- **-q *<quality>***—For image/jpeg only: the JPEG quality.
- **-dpi *<resolution>***—Output resolution.
- **-validate**—Validate the SVG documents against the SVG DTD.
- **-onload**—Execute the onload event handler before rasterizing.
- **-scriptSecurityOff**—Don't do any security checks on scripts that run due to execution of the onload event handler.
- **-scripts *<listOfAllowedScriptTypes>***—List script types that should not be loaded. The list of valid types is the set of valid values for the <script> tag's type attribute.

ANT Task

Using the Batik rasterizer as an Ant task is less straightforward than it should be, because the ANT task doesn't come pre-built in the Batik binary distribution. Here are the steps you need to go through to build the rasterizer task:

1. Download the Batik source distribution and unpack it.
2. Go to the directory xml-batik/contrib/rasterizertask.
3. Make sure batik-rasterizer.jar, batik-transcoder.jar, and batik-util.jar are on the classpath.
4. Type "ant-jar".
5. RasterizerTask.jar will be in xml-batik/contrib/rasterizertask/build/lib.

Once you've built the rasterizer task, you need to set up the classpath for Ant with both RasterizerTask.jar and batik-rasterizer.jar. Here's a sample Ant build file that uses the rasterizer.

The first thing that you need is to define the rasterizer task:

```
<project name="Batik Rasterizer Task" default="rasterize"
          basedir=".">
 <taskdef name="rasterize"
classname="org.apache.tools.ant.taskdefs.optional.RasterizerTask"
  />
```

You want JPEG files:

```
 <target name="rasterize">
  <rasterize
   result="image/jpeg"
```

They're stored in /tmp:

```
   destdir="/tmp">
```

The input to the rasterizer is a fileset that includes all files in /tmp that end with .svg:

```
   <fileset dir="/tmp">
    <include name="**/*.svg" />
```

```
      </fileset>
    </rasterize>
  </target>
</project>
```

The rasterizer task takes most of the same options as the command-line task, but they're specified using attributes of the rasterize task:

- **result**—The result image type. Must be image/jpeg, image/png, image/tiff, or application/pdf (FOP must be installed).
- **height**—Height of the result image in pixels. The height will be calculated if this attribute isn't set. The rasterizer preserves the aspect ratio of the SVG file no matter what.
- **width**—Width of the result image in pixels. The width will be calculated if this attribute isn't set. The rasterizer preserves the aspect ration of the SVG file no matter what.
- **maxheight**—Maximum height of the image in pixels. The image can't be taller than this value.
- **maxwidth**—Maximum width of the image in pixels. The image can't be wider than this value.
- **quality**—For JPEG images only. A quality value between 0 an 1, where larger numbers mean better quality.
- **area**—An area within the SVG file to be rasterized. The area is specified via "*x*, *y*, *w*, *h*", where *x* and *y* are the coordinates of the upper-left corner of the area, and *w* and *h* are the width and height.
- **bg**—The background color of the result. You can specify three or four values, all of which are integers between 0 and 255 and separated by commas. If you specify four values, they'e alpha channel, red, green, and blue. If you specify three values, they're red, green, and blue (the alpha channel is set to 255).
- **media**—CSS media type used to select a CSS stylesheet. The default value is screen.
- **dpi**—Resolution for the result image. The default value is 96.
- **lang**—Language used to select language-specific areas of the SVG file during rasterization. Valid values are defined in RFC 3066. The default value is en.
- **src**—Name of a single input file. Must be used with dest.
- **dest**—Name of a single output file, including the directory if desired. Must be used with src.
- **srcdir**—Name of the input directory. Optional if you use a <fileset>; otherwise must be used if src isn't used.
- **destdir**—Name of the output directory. Use this with srcdir or an embedded <fileset>.
- **classname**—Java class name of the XML parser being used to parse the SVG. You can also specify "jaxp" to indicate any JAXP-compatible parser in the classpath. The default value is org.apache.xerces.parsers.SAXParser.

As you've seen in the example, the rasterizer task can use nested Ant <fileset> elements to specify the set of SVG files to rasterize. This gives you the ability to specify multiple files and include or exclude specific files.

SVG Browser

Batik includes a full-featured SVG Browser called Squiggle. Squiggle can load and display SVG documents. It can display multiple documents at once, display the source of the document, and save the content of the document as a JPEG, PNG, or TIFF. It can also print SVG documents to a printer and generate thumbnail images. To run Squiggle, you need to execute the following command:

```
java –jar batik-squiggle.jar [-font-size ] [ SVG URL ]
```

As usual, this command assumes that batik-squiggle.jar is in the current directory. If it isn't, supply the full path to the jar file. If you like, you can specify the size of fonts using the -font-size option. You can also supply the URL of an SVG document, although this isn't necessary. Squiggle provides a number of different ways for you to open an SVG document using the File menu. You can open files from the filesystem or from the Internet without any problems.

Squiggle also allows you to manipulate the image in the browser. You can zoom the document in or out (hold Ctrl and use the left mouse button to drag out a rectangle of the area you want to zoom into) and pan it left or right (by holding down the Shift key and dragging with the mouse). You can also rotate the document by holding the Ctrl key and dragging with the right mouse button. The following figure shows the effect of rotating an SVG file. You can also specify a transform very precisely by opening the transform dialog (with Ctrl-E), where you can type the exact values you want for a transformation.

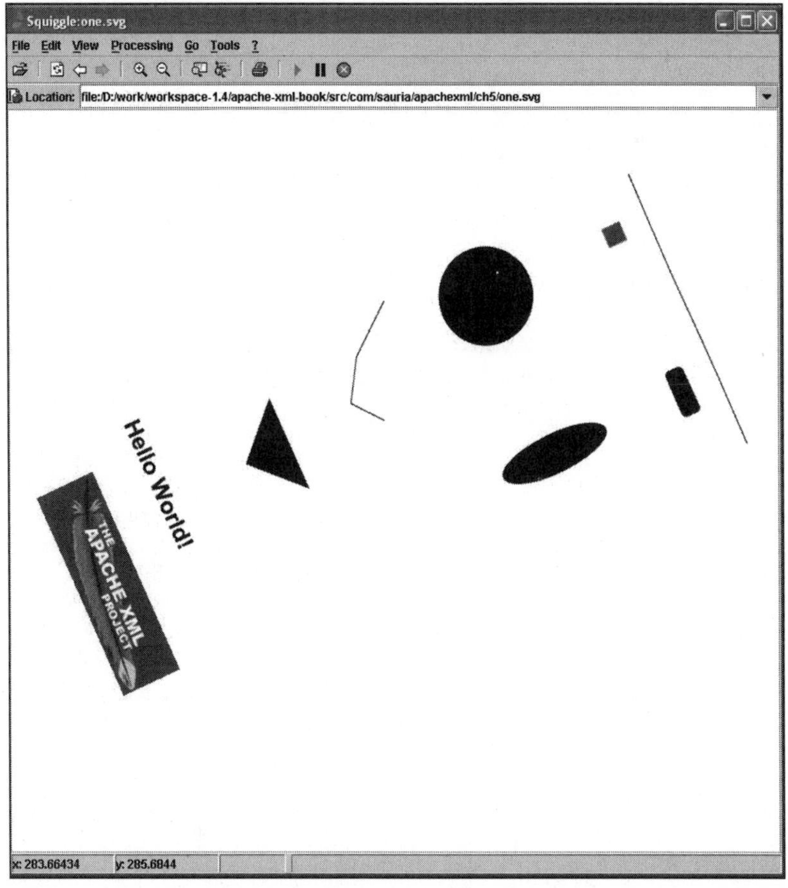

As an aid to debugging, Squiggle lets you view the source of the SVG document you are currently working with. The text editor view is similar to the view you'd get if you did a View Source in your favorite Web browser. Squiggle also provides a structured DOM tree inspector that lets you examine the SVG DOM tree your document is using. The inspector shows a tree control that represents the structure of the DOM, and panels that show all the attributes attached to the particular element you're looking at. This is easier to use when you need to make sure the correct values were set on the correct attributes. This figure shows the DOM inspector in action:

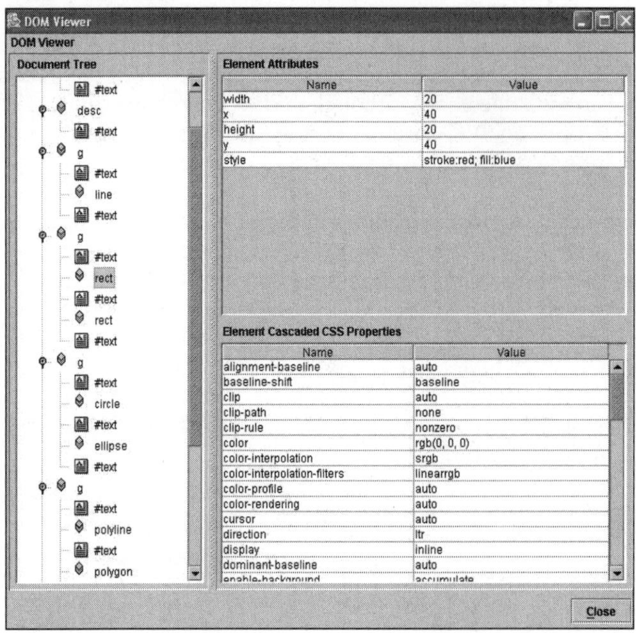

SVG Pretty-Printer

Batik comes with a command-line tool you can use to pretty-print SVG files. It can help the readability of the file substantially and can be a help if you're trying to debug a broken SVG file. To run the pretty-printer, execute the following command:

```
java –jar batik-svgpp.jar [options] [input file] [output file]
```

This command assumes that batik-svgpp.jar is present in the current directory, but you can supply the full path to the jar file and things will work fine. If you omit the output filename, then the pretty-printed output will appear on the standard output instead of being written to a file.

The pretty-printer is controlled by a number of option flags:

- **-newline <cr | cr-lf | lf>**—Specifies the character to use for line endings. The default is lf, the UNIX newline character. The DOS/Windows newline character is cr-lf, and the Macintosh uses cr.

- **-tab-width <*number*>**—Sets the number of spaces in a tab. Defaults to 4.
- **-doc-width <*number*>**—Sets the number of columns in the document. Defaults to 80.
- **-no-format**—Doesn't perform any indentation. You can still change newlines or change the DOCTYPE.
- **-xml-decl <*string*>**—Supplies a string for the XML declaration.
- **-doctype <change | remove>**—Either removes or changes the DOCTYPE of the document. If change is selected, uses one or both of -public-id and -system-id to supply new values for the DOCTYPE.
- **-public-id <*string*>**—Supplies a new string for the document's public identifier. Must be used with -doctype change.
- **-system-id <string>**—Supplies a new string for the document's system identifier. Must be used with -doctype change.

SVG Font Converter

If you want your SVG documents to be as portable as possible, you'll run into the issue of fonts. If you're going to generate SVG documents that will be displayed in an environment where the fonts in the document aren't available, you must embed the font characters you use in the SVG document. Batik provides the ttf2svg application to help you to do this. You run ttf2svg by executing

```
java –jar batik-ttf2svg.jar <ttf-path> [options]
```

The jar file batik-ttf2svg.jar must be in the current directory for this command to work. If it isn't, then you need to supply the full path to the jar file.

ttf2svg takes several options:

- **-l <*range-begin*>**—Specifies the low value of the range of characters to be converted.
- **-h <*range-end*>**—Specifies the high value of the range of characters to be converted.
- **-ascii**—Forces usage of the ASCII character map.
- **-id <*id*>**—Attaches an id="<*id*>" attribute to the generated <font> element.
- **-o <*output file*>**—Specifies the destination file for the SVG font information. If this is omitted, output goes to the standard output.
- **-testcard**—Generates an SVG <text> element that uses the characters in the font as a test for the conversion.

Here's the test card generated by converting the Windows Arial font:

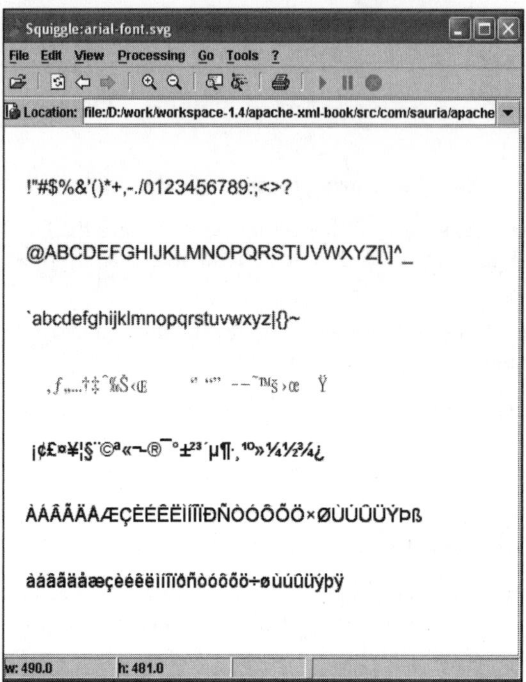

Practical Usage

By now your eyes may be crossed from trying to read the SVG for some of the simple pictures we've been using. As you can see, these documents can get complicated pretty fast. Those of you in the basic text editor camp may want to consider using a tool that gives you more support for dealing with SVG. The best is an SVG-aware editor that keeps you from making grammar mistakes. Some of the XML editors can do this if you supply them with a DTD. SVG is really just an intermediate representation for the visual image you're working on. The next step up is one of the SVG-aware graphics tools we mentioned at the beginning of the chapter: Adobe Illustrator, Jasc WebDraw, CorelDRAW, or the open source Sodipodi. If you have to work on the XML file level, at a minimum you should be using the SVG DTD to validate the documents and the Batik pretty-printer to help you sort out what's what.

SVG is still in its early days, so there are some compatibility problems. You'd do well to cross-check your SVG documents by rendering them in as many SVG engines as you can. The major ones to try are the Adobe SVG plugin (probably the most widespread), Batik's Squiggle, and the SVG-enabled builds of Mozilla.

You should use the <defs> and <symbol> elements to produce libraries of SVG symbols you can use. You can stick these libraries in XML external entities so they can be shared among multiple documents. In the same vein, use the fact that SVG is leveraging CSS to separate styling information from the SVG elements. By attaching classes to the elements and then defining the styling for the classes in an external stylesheet, you give yourself more flexibility when you need to modify style aspects of your document.

If you're working in Java, then it's definitely worth the effort to learn to use SVGGraphics2D. It allows you to think drawing and shapes while still producing SVG as the output. This relieves you of the burden of SVG syntax and property names.

Dynamic SVG is one of the most interesting areas in SVG. You should try to get as far as you can with the built-in animation elements before you switch over to scripting. At some point, though, you'll need to do some scripting, because that's how event-handling is done. Again, modularity is important—find ways to place your scripts and animations in external libraries so they can be reused. You should try to do much of your scripting in ECMAScript, because that's the only scripting language you can expect to have available in every SVG implementation.

Try to resist the urge to drop down into Java to manipulate the document. It won't be portable, so your application will only work in Squiggle or a JSVGCanvas-based application. Not only that, but it's a lot more work to drop down into Java, and ECMAScript is good enough for many of the DOM tree manipulations you might want to do. If your SVG application needs to connect with non-DOM Java functionality, then we encourage you to see if you can access that functionality from Jython.

Applications

There are many possible applications for SVG. As a portable vector graphics format, it has a lot to offer to applications in many problem domains. The Batik team has done a reasonable job of making it easy to generate and display SVG from Java programs. They've made it easy to retrofit existing Java2D applications to generate SVG documents. We'll discuss two applications for SVG/Batik; one is more immediate and short term, and the other is longer term.

In the short term, SVG provides a great way to dynamically generate complicated graphics visuals for Web applications. We'll present a short application that illustrates this point. BatikServlet is designed to display an input form that prompts the user for the number of graphs in a bar graph. When the user clicks the Submit button in the form, the form action causes an HTTP POST to occur. BatikServlet's POST behavior is to take the form argument and draw an increasing bar graph with the number of bars requested in the form. Although the example is simple, it illustrates the point that an SVG-enabled Web application can interact with the browser user, collect some data, combine that data with data of its own (probably obtained from a database in a more realistic example), and render it into SVG that is then displayed by the browser:

```
/*
 *
 * BatikServlet.java
 *
 * Example from "Professional XML Development with Apache Tools"
 *
 */
package com.sauria.apachexml.ch4;

import java.awt.Color;
import java.awt.Shape;
import java.awt.geom.Rectangle2D;
import java.io.IOException;
import java.io.PrintWriter;
```

```
import java.io.Writer;

import javax.servlet.ServletException;
import javax.servlet.http.HttpServlet;
import javax.servlet.http.HttpServletRequest;
import javax.servlet.http.HttpServletResponse;

import org.apache.batik.dom.svg.SVGDOMImplementation;
import org.apache.batik.svggen.SVGGraphics2D;
import org.w3c.dom.DOMImplementation;
import org.w3c.dom.svg.SVGDocument;

public class BatikServlet extends HttpServlet {

```

BatikServlet's doGet method presents the HTML form used to collect information from the user:

```
    protected void doGet(HttpServletRequest request,
                         HttpServletResponse response)
        throws ServletException, IOException {
            response.setContentType("text/html");
            PrintWriter w = response.getWriter();

            w.println("<html><head></head>");
            w.println("<body>");
            w.println("Enter number of bars:");
            w.println("<form action=\"ch4\" method=\"post\">");
            w.println("<input type=\"text\" name=\"bars\"><br>");
            w.println("<input type=\"submit\">");
            w.println("</form>");
            w.println("</body>");
            w.println("</html>");
            w.flush();
    }

```

The doPost method extracts the data from the form parameter and uses it to generate an SVG document. The form parameter, bars, is retrieved and converted to an integer:

```
    protected void doPost(HttpServletRequest request,
                          HttpServletResponse response)
        throws ServletException, IOException {
            String numStr = request.getParameter("bars");
            int bars = 10;
            bars = Integer.parseInt(numStr)+1;
            DOMImplementation impl =
                SVGDOMImplementation.getDOMImplementation();
            String svgNS =
                SVGDOMImplementation.SVG_NAMESPACE_URI;
            SVGDocument doc =
                (SVGDocument)impl.createDocument(svgNS,
                                                 "svg", null);

```

Here's the setup code for SVGGraphics2D. Lines 61-67 show the loop that renders the bar graph:

```
61:             SVGGraphics2D g = new SVGGraphics2D(doc);
62:             for (int i = 0; i < bars; i++) {
63:                 Shape rect =
64:                     new Rectangle2D.Double(10+20*i,
65:                                            100-10*i,10,10*i);
66:                 g.setPaint(Color.green);
67:                 g.fill(rect);
68:             }
```

You have to properly set the HTTP content type so the browser will know it's about to receive SVG data:

```
69:             response.setContentType("image/svg+xml");
70:
```

After that, you get the writer from the HttpServletResponse and write the SVG directly to it:

```
71:             Writer w = response.getWriter();
72:
73:             boolean useCSS = true;
74:             g.stream(w, useCSS);
75:             w.flush();
76:     }
77:
78: }
```

On the user's end, they see a nice bar graph in their Web browser. Depending on the SVG functionality in their browser, they may be able to do simple manipulation of the graph.

To complete the example, the following listing shows the web.xml file that's used to configure the servlet engine for BatikServlet:

```
<?xml version="1.0" encoding="ISO-8859-1"?>

<!DOCTYPE web-app
  PUBLIC "-//Sun Microsystems, Inc.//DTD Web Application 2.3//EN"
  "http://java.sun.com/dtd/web-app_2_3.dtd">

<web-app>
  <display-name>Professional XML Development with Apache Tools Examples
  </display-name>
  <description>
    Examples from Professional XML Development with Apache Tools.
  </description>

  <!-- Define servlet-mapped and path-mapped example filters -->

  <!-- Define filter mappings for the defined filters -->

  <servlet>
    <servlet-name>BatikServlet</servlet-name>
    <servlet-class>com.sauria.apachexml.ch5.BatikServlet
```

```
    </servlet-class>
  </servlet>

  <servlet-mapping>
    <servlet-name>BatikServlet</servlet-name>
    <url-pattern>/ch5/*</url-pattern>
  </servlet-mapping>

</web-app>
```

Rich Client User Interfaces

Just over the horizon is another application for SVG, one that you should keep your eye on. Some Web developers have used Macromedia's Flash as a method for producing visually rich and interactive user interfaces for Web applications. We believe SVG has the potential to take on this role. SVG has some important advantages over Flash in this regard. It's specified by open standards, both for SVG and for ECMAScript, the scripting language recommended for producing dynamic SVG. The techniques for producing dynamic SVG are the same as for producing DHTML, so Web developers won't have to learn a new set of concepts as they do for Flash.

There are at least two major obstacles to this happening. First, SVG isn't supported in all Web browsers and requires users to download a plugin. This isn't as big an obstacle as it might seem, because recent versions of Flash need to be downloaded as well. The other obstacle is that SVG needs a richer set of libraries for doing things like calling Web services. This API needs to be standardized somehow, perhaps via a standardized SVG extension mechanism. This will make the glue layer between SVG and the client browser/platform strong enough to build rich applications on the client side.

We hope you can see many possibilities for including SVG functionality in your applications—perhaps providing great illustrations for a publishing project or highly interactive client-side user interfaces for Web applications. SVG is just getting started, and the Batik libraries provide a great way for you to begin taking advantage of SVG in your applications.

5

Cocoon Concepts

Cocoon is an XML-based Web publishing framework. It focuses on solving the problem of separation of concerns. The objective is to keep content, style, logic, and management functions separated from each other so that changes in one area don't lead to code changes in another area. This is achieved by creating component pipelines in which reusable components can be connected in a fashion that is reminiscent of UNIX's pipes facility.

Cocoon is unlike most of the other tools we have discussed because no standard defines how it operates. Cocoon uses multiple standards, including XML, XSLT, and others, but its behavior and operation aren't defined by a standard. You may decide that this is a liability. On the other hand, you may decide that it's a strength.

The Cocoon project was one of the projects used to seed the Apache XML project in 1999. It's on its second major version and is regarded as very successful. Cocoon has been a great testing ground for many Apache projects because it uses a large number of them, from the XML, Web Services, and Jakarta projects.

Prerequisites

Using Cocoon requires that you have a good understanding of XML and XSLT (and therefore XPath). The areas of Cocoon that we'll explore call for a few other technologies: It will be helpful if you're familiar with SAX and a bit of SQL, and the coverage of XSP will be easier to follow if you're familiar with a templating system like JSP. Other areas of Cocoon involve the use of SVG or SOAP, so these technologies would also be good to have in your tool bag.

Concepts

Cocoon is a very large system. Each concept alone is easy to deal with, but the difficulty comes in trying to understand how all the pieces fit together. So, before we dive in to the individual concepts and their implementations, let's step back and get a sense of the big picture.

In a normal Web application, the application receives a request from some user agent, usually a Web browser. The contents of that request are passed to a CGI script or, in Java, to a servlet. The servlet is responsible for performing a computation on the request and returning a response to the user agent. This is the familiar interaction pattern for Web applications.

With Cocoon we have the same pattern, but you can think of Cocoon as a way of structuring the computation performed by the servlet. Cocoon processes requests using pipelines of components. Its job is to look at the request, figure out which pipeline will process it, and hand the request over to that pipeline. Cocoon needs to be able to describe how to match a request to a pipeline, and it must be able to specify the set of components that are in a pipeline and the sequence in which the requests will flow through the pipeline. Cocoon itself is implemented as a servlet that performs the processing we just described. The following figure gives a conceptual view of how Cocoon processes a request and introduces some of the terms Cocoon uses for the request-processing and pipeline-processing steps.

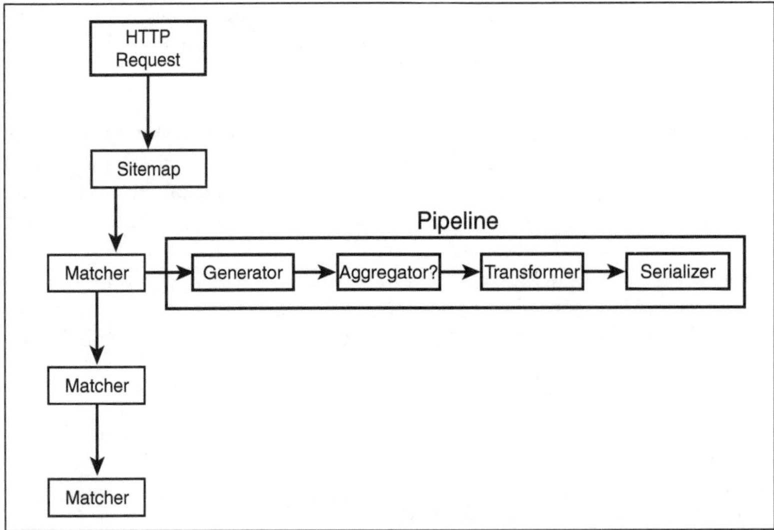

Sitemap

In Cocoon, an XML document called the *sitemap* holds descriptions of pipelines and the components in those pipelines. The sitemap also contains definitions of matchers that are used to perform pattern-matching against a request to determine whether a particular pipeline will process the request.

The pipelines are made up of components. These components are named after the functions they perform: generators, aggregators, transformers, and serializers. (More on that in a moment.)

Following is a sitemap that describes a very simple site. The site takes the contents of an XML file in the filesystem, transforms it with an XSLT stylesheet, and outputs it as XHTML. The order of the sections in a sitemap is important, and the first two sections of the sitemap describe the set of <components> that are available for use in the rest of the sitemap:

```
<?xml version="1.0" encoding="UTF-8"?>
<map:sitemap xmlns:map="http://apache.org/cocoon/sitemap/1.0">

 <map:components>

  <map:generators default="file">
    <map:generator logger="sitemap.generator.file"
         name="file" pool-grow="4" pool-max="32"
         pool-min="8"
         src="org.apache.cocoon.generation.FileGenerator"/>
  </map:generators>

  <map:transformers default="xslt">
    <map:transformer
         logger="sitemap.transformer.xslt" name="xslt"
         pool-grow="2" pool-max="32" pool-min="8"
         src="org.apache.cocoon.transformation.TraxTransformer">
     <use-request-parameters>false</use-request-parameters>
     <use-session-parameters>false</use-session-parameters>
     <use-cookie-parameters>false</use-cookie-parameters>
     <xslt-processor-role>xalan</xslt-processor-role>
    </map:transformer>
  </map:transformers>

  <map:serializers default="html">
   <map:serializer logger="sitemap.serializer.xhtml"
        mime-type="text/html" name="xhtml" pool-grow="2"
        pool-max="64" pool-min="2"
        src="org.apache.cocoon.serialization.XMLSerializer">
    <doctype-public>
     -//W3C//DTD XHTML 1.0 Strict//EN
    </doctype-public>
    <doctype-system>
     http://www.w3.org/TR/xhtml1/DTD/xhtml1-strict.dtd
    </doctype-system>
    <encoding>UTF-8</encoding>
   </map:serializer>
  </map:serializers>

  <map:matchers default="wildcard">
   <map:matcher logger="sitemap.matcher.wildcard" name="wildcard"
       src="org.apache.cocoon.matching.WildcardURIMatcher"/>
   <map:matcher logger="sitemap.matcher.regexp" name="regexp"
       src="org.apache.cocoon.matching.RegexpURIMatcher"/>
  </map:matchers>

  <map:selectors default="browser">
   <map:selector logger="sitemap.selector.exception"
       name="exception"
```

```
      src="org.apache.cocoon.selection.ExceptionSelector">
   <exception
       class="org.apache.cocoon.ResourceNotFoundException"
       name="not-found"/>
   <exception class="java.lang.Throwable" unroll="true"/>
  </map:selector>
 </map:selectors>

</map:components>

<map:pipelines>

 <map:pipeline>

   <map:match pattern="">
    <map:generate src="books.xml"/>
    <map:transform src="books.xslt">
     <map:parameter name="contextPath"
                    value="{request:contextPath}"/>
    </map:transform>
    <map:serialize type="xhtml"/>
   </map:match>

   <map:match pattern="images/*.gif">
     <map:read mime-type="images/gif"
         src="resources/images/{1}.gif"/>
   </map:match>

   <map:match pattern="styles/*.css">
     <map:read mime-type="text/css"
         src="resources/styles/{1}.css"/>
   </map:match>

   <map:handle-errors>
     <map:select type="exception">

       <map:when test="not-found">
         <map:generate type="notifying"/>
         <map:transform
             src="stylesheets/system/error2html.xslt">
           <map:parameter name="contextPath"
               value="{request:contextPath}"/>
           <map:parameter name="pageTitle"
               value="Resource not found"/>
         </map:transform>
         <map:serialize status-code="404"/>
       </map:when>

       <map:otherwise>
         <map:generate type="notifying"/>
         <map:transform
             src="stylesheets/system/error2html.xslt">
           <map:parameter name="contextPath"
               value="{request:contextPath}"/>
```

```
104:           </map:transform>
105:           <map:serialize status-code="500"/>
106:         </map:otherwise>
107:
108:       </map:select>
109:     </map:handle-errors>
110:
111:   </map:pipeline>
112:
113:  </map:pipelines>
114:
115: </map:sitemap>
```

After the views element (which is empty in this example) is the <pipelines> element, which contains as many <pipeline> elements as needed. In this case, there is only one pipeline. Let's look at how this pipeline is constructed and what it does.

The <components> element contains all the component declarations for the sitemap. For a single, small pipeline, such as the one shown in this example, all the declarations can seem overwhelming. But once you have multiple pipelines, each containing multiple components, you start to see the benefit of declaring all the components. Cocoon comes with a large set of prebuilt components that makes it easy for you to construct pipelines from a rich palette. Not every sitemap will use every component—hence the need to declare components.

The first child element of <components> is <generators> (lines 6-11), which contains a sequence of <generator> elements. Generators start pipelines and generate a SAX event stream that can then be processed by other components in the pipeline. The <generators> element (and all component container elements) takes an optional default attribute whose value is the generator to use if no generator is specified in a pipeline. For the sake of simplicity, this sitemap contains a single <generator> (lines 7-10) named file. This is an instance of the Cocoon File Generator component. The File Generator reads an XML document from the local filesystem or a URL and generates a SAX event stream from it. The attributes of this generator are logger, which identifies a LogKit log target; name, which assigns a name that can be used to refer to the component; and src, which specifies the Java class that implements the functionality of the component. The attributes pool-min, pool-max, and pool-grow are parameters that tell Cocoon's object-pooling system how to pool instances of this component. For the generator file, the pool starts at four instances and grows in four-instance increments until it reaches 32 instances.

The next component section is <transformers> (lines 13-23). Again, an optional default attribute specifies the name of a transformer to use in a pipeline if no transformers are specified. The example specifies a single transformer (lines 14-22), which uses an XSLT processor (via JAXP's TrAX API) to transform an input SAX event stream into an output SAX event stream. There can be more than one transformer in a pipeline; in this case they are usually daisy-chained to each other, the output of one into the input of the next. The input to the first transformer in the chain is the generator for the pipeline, and the output of the last generator is a serializer. The default TrAX processor is used according to the JAXP rules. The attributes that appear here are the same attributes you saw for generator and have the same meaning, although the values are a little different. The <transformer> element also has children elements (lines 18-21) that provide additional configuration information. The first three elements—<use-request-parameters>, <use-session-parameters>, and <use-cookie-parameters>—control whether information in HTTP request parameters, servlet sessions, and HTTP cookies is available to the stylesheet. If it is, then it's available as variables whose names are those of the parameters, sessions, or cookies.

After the <transformers> section is a <serializers> section (lines 25-38). A serializer takes a SAX event stream and turns it into a binary or character stream for final output. The serializer defined here (lines 26-37) converts a SAX event stream into an XHTML document. In addition to the component attributes, a mime-type attribute (line 27) specifies the MIME type of the output. This is important because the class being used to do the serialization is org.apache.cocoon.serialization.XMLSerializer (that isn't a typo). The difference between XHTML mode and XML mode is in the value of the mime-type attribute. If the attribute is set to "text/html", then the output is XHTML; but if the attribute is set to "text/xml", then output is XML, which may or may not happen to be XHTML. This serializer also has some child elements (line 30-36) that are used to specify the variant of XHTML (there's a choice of Strict XHTML, Transitional XHTML, or Frameset XHTML, and each has different public and system IDs) to produce (lines 30-35). The <encoding> element controls which character encoding is used for the XHTML document.

The <matchers> section (lines 40-45) defines the matchers available to the rest of the sitemap. When a sitemap contains more than one pipeline, as most do, the question of which pipeline to execute is answered by the matchers. This sitemap defines two matchers: one named wildcard (lines 41-42) and one named regexp. Both matchers are implemented by classes that are already part of Cocoon, and each has its own log target. The wildcard matcher matches wildcards (* and **), whereas the regexp matcher accepts a complete regular expression. Matchers can be used for other flow-of-control tasks, but their primary task is to select the pipeline that will execute.

Selectors are different from matchers. Whereas matchers pick which pipeline to execute, selectors conditionally execute parts of the same pipeline. This sitemap defines a single <selector> (lines 48-55) in its <selectors> section (lines 47-56). This selector, named exception, allows the sitemap to respond to Java exceptions that are thrown during the execution of the pipeline. The child elements of the selector are <exception> elements that map a symbolic name like not-found to a Java exception class like org.apache.cocoon.ResourceNotFoundException. When the selector is executed, these symbolic names of a thrown exception are available for the sitemap to make a decision. The second <exception> element (line 54) also has an unroll attribute whose value is true. If an exception marked as unrolled is nested as the cause of another exception, then the processing for the enclosing exception is executed, rather than the processing for the nested exception. The enclosing exception must have been declared with an <exception> element.

After all those component definitions, you're ready to define a pipeline and get some work done. The next section of this sitemap is the <pipelines> container element, which contains all the pipelines defined for the sitemap (lines 60-113). A pipeline is defined by a <pipeline> element (line 62).

At the beginning of the pipeline is a <match> element (lines 64-71). This element determines whether the pipeline that it encloses gets executed. This particular match uses the default matcher, which is the wildcard matcher. The wildcard matcher uses wildcard characters to match against the request URI. Here the pattern being matched is "", the empty string. Let's assume the Cocoon Servlet is mapped to the url-pattern /, that this sitemap file resides in the directory that is the root of your Web application, and that the Web application's name is simple. The URI http://hostname:port/simple matches this pattern because by the time Cocoon gets the URI, the protocol, hostname, port, and Web application name will have been consumed by the Cocoon servlet.

The children of this <match> element are a <generate> element (line 65), a <transform> element (lines 66-69), and a <serialize> element (line 70). This is a typical minimal pipeline. The generator specified by the <generate> element generates a SAX event stream, the transformer specified by the <transform> element transforms the event stream into another event stream, and the serializer takes the resulting event stream and produces some output. In this short pipeline, the <generate> element uses the default generator, which you defined in the components section (line 6) to be the file generator. So, the SAX event stream is generated by means of the file generator reading the file books.xml (via a relative URI to the sitemap file) and parsing it using SAX. That SAX stream is the input to the transformer specified by the <transform> element, which happens to also be the default transformer (line 13). The default transformer is the XSLT transformer, so the incoming SAX stream is fed to the XSLT engine, along with the stylesheet books.xslt (again retrieved via a relative URI). In addition, the child <parameter> element passes the contextPath of the request as a parameter named contextPath. The transformed event stream is then passed to the serializer specified by <serialize>. This element doesn't use the default serializer, but uses the type attribute to specify the serializer it wants. The value of the type attribute is the name given to the serializer (line 27) in the <components> section. The serializer is the last element in the <match>, so the XHTML output is written to the result and processing concludes. After all the definitions were out of the way, it took only eight lines in the sitemap to run XSLT over an XML file and present the output as XHTML.

You're not done with the sitemap—you're actually not even finished with the <pipeline> element. There are two more <match> elements to look at. The first one (lines 73-77) matches URIs that start with *images/*, match some number of non-path-separator characters (that's what the * means), and end with *.gif*—in short, any .gif file under images. If the URI matches, then the sitemap invokes a reader using the <map:read> element. A reader is a single-unit pipeline—it combines the function of a generator, transformer, and serializer all at once. Readers are used to call out to functionality that doesn't return XML data. The reader calls out, possibly passing some parameter values, and then returns the result. The default reader (the Resource Reader) is called here (lines 74-75). The Resource Reader is used to copy binary data to the output. By default in Cocoon, the Resource Reader is the default reader for a sitemap, (all the other default components are predefined).

The mime-type attribute tells the Resource Reader the MIME type of the data being copied to the output. The src attribute specifies how the Resource Reader gets the data it will copy. In this case, the src is relative to the URI for the sitemap. Notice that although the pattern matched is images/*.gif, the src is resources/images/{1}.gif, which demonstrates that the Resource Reader can do some dereferencing in order to get to the src data. The {1} that appears in the value of the src attribute is related to the use of wildcards by the <match>'s pattern attribute. When you use wildcards, there are three special characters:

- * means to match any characters except a path separator.
- ** means to match any characters including a path separator.
- \ is used as an escape character so that * and \ can appear in the pattern as literals rather than wildcards: * matches an asterisk (*) in the URI, and \\ matches a backslash (\) in the URI.

Each use of a wildcard in the pattern is given a number. By specifying that number inside curly braces, you let the children of the <match> element access the text that was matched by the appropriately numbered wildcard. If you wrote {2} in the content of a wildcard match whose pattern was images/*/**.gif, you would get the text matched by the **, because it's the second wildcard used. You're trying to retrieve the correctly named GIF file from the resources/images directory and copy it to the output.

The second <match> element (lines 78-81) does essentially the same thing; the only difference is that the mime-type and wildcard pattern are different. This time, the data being copied through is CSS stylesheets, which are also not XML data.

The final element in this pipeline is a <handle-errors> element (lines 83-109). This element controls how errors are handled when they occur. We'll see how selectors are used in the sitemap as we look at this element. The first element you encounter inside <handle-errors> is a <select> element. This is a selector, and like other components, the name of the selector being used is the value of the type attribute—in this case, exception (a selector you defined in the <selectors> section). When the sitemap executes the <handle-errors> section, the exception selector is executed. If an exception has been thrown, the selector leaves that information available to the sitemap. The sitemap can use a <when> element to test whether an exception has been thrown. This is the reason for naming the <exception> elements used in the definition of the selector. The <when> and <otherwise> elements are used to test the value produced by the selector. <when> allows you to specify a test condition and acts like an if statement. <otherwise> acts like an else statement. You can use as many <when> elements are you need.

This example has a single <when> element and an <otherwise> element. The <when> element (lines 86-96) tests to see if the value left by the selector is "not-found", which indicate that the ResourceNotFoundException was thrown. If this exception has been thrown, then the value is available, and the <when> element executes. The content of the <when> element is a pipeline. It includes a <generate>, a <transform>, and a <serialize>. The <generate> (line 87) uses a built-in generator known as the Notifying generator, whose job is to take error information and turn it into XML. Usually the error information is extracted from a Java Throwable object. The <transform> element (lines 88-94) uses an XSLT stylesheet from a site-wide stylesheet library to format the error information into a human-readable error page. It passes some parameters to the XSLT processor: the value of the contextPath (lines 90-91) and a title for the XHTML page being produced. The <serialize> element uses the default HTML serializer and uses the status-code attribute to set the HTTP status code (to 404—resource not found).

The <otherwise> element uses basically the same pipeline. The differences are that its <transform> doesn't pass a title for the page being generated, and it sets the status code to 500 instead of 404.

That concludes our tour of a short (!) Cocoon example. We hope you have a good idea of the basic Cocoon components and how they fit together. It should be clear that pipelines are the key to doing everything in Cocoon. The last part of the sitemap, the <handle-error> section, should drive that point home.

For the sake of completeness, here is the books.xml file that served as input:

```
<?xml version="1.0" encoding="UTF-8"?>
<books xmlns="http://sauria.com/schemas/apache-xml-book/books"
  xmlns:tns="http://sauria.com/schemas/apache-xml-book/books"
  xmlns:xsi="http://www.w3.org/2001/XMLSchema-instance"
  xsi:schemaLocation=
    "http://sauria.com/schemas/apache-xml-book/books
     http://www.sauria.com/schemas/apache-xml-book/books.xsd"
  version="1.0">
  <book>
   <title>Professional XML Development with Apache Tools</title>
   <author>Theodore W. Leung</author>
   <isbn>0-7645-4355-5</isbn>
   <month>December</month>
```

```
   <year>2003</year>
   <publisher>Wrox</publisher>
   <address>Indianapolis, Indiana</address>
  </book>
  <book>
   <title>Effective Java</title>
   <author>Joshua Bloch</author>
   <isbn>0-201-31005-8</isbn>
   <month>August</month>
   <year>2001</year>
   <publisher>Addison-Wesley</publisher>
   <address>New York, New York</address>
  </book>
  <book>
   <title>Design Patterns</title>
   <author>Erich Gamma</author>
   <author>Richard Helm</author>
   <author>Ralph Johnson</author>
   <author>John Vlissides</author>
   <isbn>0-201-63361-2</isbn>
   <month>October</month>
   <year>1994</year>
   <publisher>Addison-Wesley</publisher>
   <address>Reading, Massachusetts</address>
  </book>
</books>
```

This is the books.xslt stylesheet:

```
<?xml version="1.0" encoding="UTF-8"?>
<xsl:stylesheet version="1.0"
  xmlns:xsl="http://www.w3.org/1999/XSL/Transform"
  xmlns:books="http://sauria.com/schemas/apache-xml-book/books"
  exclude-result-prefixes="books">
    <xsl:output method="html" version="4.0" encoding="UTF-8"
        indent="yes" omit-xml-declaration="yes"/>
    <xsl:template match="books:books">
      <html>
        <head><title>Book Inventory</title></head>
        <body>
          <xsl:apply-templates/>
        </body>
      </html>
    </xsl:template>
    <xsl:template match="books:book">
       <xsl:apply-templates/>
      <p />
    </xsl:template>
    <xsl:template match="books:title">
      <em><xsl:value-of select="."/></em><br />
    </xsl:template>
    <xsl:template match="books:author">
      <b><xsl:value-of select="."/></b><br />
    </xsl:template>
```

```
    <xsl:template match="books:isbn">
      <xsl:value-of select="."/><br />
    </xsl:template>
    <xsl:template match="books:month">
      <xsl:value-of select="."/>,
    </xsl:template>
    <xsl:template match="books:year">
      <xsl:value-of select="."/><br />
    </xsl:template>
    <xsl:template match="books:publisher">
      <xsl:value-of select="."/><br />
    </xsl:template>
    <xsl:template match="books:address">
      <xsl:value-of select="."/><br />
    </xsl:template>
</xsl:stylesheet>
```

The following figure shows the output of the pipeline:

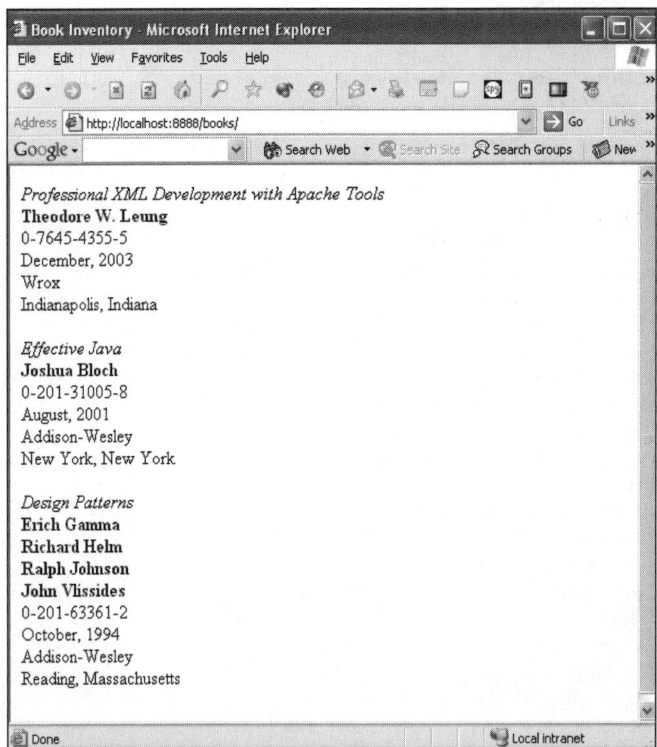

Now that you have a general idea of the things that go into a sitemap, let's explore the various component types in greater detail. As we do this, we'll explain some of Cocoon's many component types as well as introduce a few new component types and concepts that weren't in the example sitemap.

Generators

As you've already seen, generators are used to start the processing of a Cocoon pipeline. They represent a source of data that can be represented as a stream of SAX events. Let's say you have some data, like an event log of some kind. A generator based on the event log would conceptually operate by converting the event log into an XML document and then running that document through a SAX parser to emit a SAX event stream. The generator might not actually be implemented that way, but conceptually that's how it works.

When you're working with Cocoon, you need to think about where the data in your application will come from and whether one of the generators supplied with Cocoon will be able to provide it. Of course, to do that you need to have an idea of what generators are available in Cocoon and their capabilities. The list that follows is intended to give you an overview of what each of these built-in generators can do. You'll probably want to consult the components appendix of the Cocoon user manual to learn about these generators in detail:

- **Directory generator**—This generator produces an event stream that represents an XML representation of a file system directory. The document has a <directory> element as the root element, with children that are either <directory> or <file> elements. These elements contain attributes for the name, last modified time, and size of the file. The elements use the namespace URI http://apache.org/cocoon/directory/2.0 and the prefix dir. When you use this generator in the sitemap, you can control how deep the directory traversal goes, the format used for dates, the sort order, and a number of other options. This generator is in org.apache.coccon. generation.DirectoryGenerator and is named directory.
- **File generator**—You've already seen the use of the file generator. It simply reads an XML document from a URL and produces the SAX event stream for it. The namespace URI and prefix are determined by the document that is read. This is the default generator for Cocoon. It's in org.apache.org.cocoon.generation.FileGenerator and is named file.
- **Image directory generator**—This is a subclass of the directory generator, which ensures that all the files in the directory are images. It adds attributes containing the image dimensions to the event stream and uses the same namespace URI and prefix as the directory generator. This generator is in org.apache.cocoon.generation.ImageDirectoryGenerator and is available with the name imagedirectory.
- **Linkstatus generator**—The linkstatus Generator takes a URL as its src attribute and recursively traverses all the links embedded in the HTML found at that URL. The event stream contains <link> elements whose attributes contain the URL for the link, the content-type of the link (if traversal was successful), and the HTTP status code. The elements provided by the linkstatus generator use the namespace URI http://apache.org/cocoon/linkstatus/2.0 and the prefix linkstatus. This generator is useful for forcing a traversal of all pages in a Cocoon site. You can use it to preload pages into the Cocoon cache or to precompile eXstensible Server Pages (XSPs). The linkstatus generator is in org.apache.cocoon. generation.LinkStatusGenerator and is assigned the name linkstatus.
- **Notifying generator**—You've seen the use of this generator in the <handle-errors> section of the sample sitemap. When an error occurs in the pipeline, the error (which is usually a Java Throwable object) is passed to the notifying generator. Nothing further happens until you access the notifying generator from a pipeline. When you do that, the information in the Throwable object is placed into the event stream. You get a <notify> element as the root

element, and there will be a <title> element whose content gives the title of the error notification, a <source> element whose content gives the name of the class of the error object, a <message> element whose content is the result of calling getMessage on the error object, and a <description> element whose content is the result of calling toString on the error object. These elements use the namespace URI http://apache.org/cocoon/error/2.0 and the prefix error. The notifying generator is in org.apache.coccon.sitemap.NotifyingGenerator and is named notifier.

- **Request generator**—This generator takes information in the HttpServletRequest and converts it to XML. The namespace URI for the elements is http://apache.org/cocoon/request/2.0. The root element is <request>, and it has four children. The <requestHeaders> element contains a sequence of <header> elements that represent the HTTP headers. Each <header> has a name attribute that contains the header name, and the content of the element is the value of the header. After that a <requestParameters> element that contains the parameters to the request. These are represented by a sequence of <parameter> elements. Again, a name attribute supplies the name of the parameter. However, because parameters can have multiple values, the content of a <parameter> element is a <value> element whose content is the parameter value. The next child element is <requestAttributes>. This element is supplied only if the sitemap parameter generate-attributes is set to true in the <generator> or <generate> element. The content of <requestAttributes> is a sequence of <attribute> elements. Each has a name attribute, and the attribute values appear as child <value> elements, just as for <requestParameters>. The last child element is <configurationParameters>, which contains a sequence of <parameter> elements, one for each parameter specified in the <generate> or <generator> element. These <parameter> elements are different from the <parameter> elements for the <requestParameter> elements. They use a name attribute for the parameter name, but the value is the content of the <parameter> element. No child <value> element is needed. The request generator is available under the name request and is in org.apache.cocoon.generation.RequestGenerator.

- **Server pages generator**—The server pages generator uses an XSP page as the generator for the event stream. We'll talk about this in more detail when we discuss XSPs. For now, you need to know that the generator is in org.apache.cocoon.generation.ServerPagesGenerator and uses the name serverpages.

- **Status generator**—The status generator takes Cocoon's internal status and renders it as a SAX event stream. It uses the namespace URI http://apache.org/cocoon/status/2.0. The root element is called <statusinfo>, and it can have two kinds of children: <group>s and <value>s. <statusinfo> has attributes that give the date and hostname of the server. A <group> can have another <group> or a <value> as a child. A <value> can have a sequence of <line>s as a child, and each line's content is character data. Both <group> and <value> have a name attribute. This generator is in org.apche.cocoon.generation.StatusGenerator under the name status.

- **Stream generator**—The stream generator generates a SAX event stream from an HttpRequest's InputStream. It can deal with either GET or POST requests. When you use it in a pipeline, it uses the HttpRequest that caused the pipeline to execute. The stream generator is available under the name stream and is in org.apache.cocoon.generation.StreamGenerator.

- **XPath directory generator**—The XPath directory generator works the like the directory generator, but it allows you to specify two additional parameters. If you specify an xmlFiles parameter with a regular expression value, then the files that match the regular expression are treated as XML files. If you specify an xpath parameter, then the XPath you provide as the parameter value is used to filter XML files (as specified by the xmlFiles parameter). Only those portions of each XML file that match the XPath expression are in the event stream. This generator is in org.apche.cocoon.generation.XPathDirectoryGenerator and is assigned the name xpathdirectory.

Transformers

Transformers are the components that get the job done. Without them, a pipeline could only generate some SAX events and serialize them back out. You'd get a little functionality, but not much. The standard Cocoon distribution includes a number of transformers; the following list gives you an overview of those that are built in. Some of these transformers are quite sophisticated, so we'll provide a general description of how the transformers work. You'll need to look at the components appendix of the Cocoon manual to learn about all the features of a particular transformer:

- **XSLT transformer**—We've already looked at this transformer in the example sitemap. The transformer is in org.apache.cocoon.transformation.TraxTransformer and uses the name xslt.
- **Fragment extractor transformer**—This transformer assumes that the incoming event stream represents an XML document that contains embedded SVG images. The transformer replaces those embedded images with an XLink locator that points to the image. This transformer is in org.apche.cocoon.transformation.FragmentExtractorTransfomer. It uses the name extractor.
- **I18N transformer**—This transformer provides support to make it easier to internationalize your Web application. It does this by providing the ability to translate text content and attribute values into various languages. It lets you use parameters in those translations, similar to the functionality you get in a java.text.MessageFormat. Support for formatting dates, numbers, and currency is provided via the functionality provided in the java.text package.

  The I18N transformer assumes there are elements and attributes from the namespace http://apache.org/cocoon/i18n/2.1. The <text> element indicates text that is supplied from a message catalog. The content of the <text> element is used as the key to the catalog—the message catalog is queried with this key, and the resulting text replaces the <text> element in the output event stream. The attr attribute contains a space-separated list of attribute names. The values of these attributes are also assumed to be keys into the message catalog and are replaced with the text obtained from the catalog. Parameter substitution is done by enclosing the <text> element in a <translate> element and using {n} notation to indicate the placeholders to be filled in. Placeholders are numbered starting at 0 and are filled in by <param> elements the follow the <text> element inside the <translate> element, one for each placeholder. The content of a <param> element is the value of the parameter. The parameters may also be translated by enclosing the content of the <param> elements in a <text> element.

  You can format dates, times, or dates and times according to the current locale using the <date>, <time>, or <datetime> elements. Each of these elements takes a value attribute that contains the value to be formatted. A src-pattern attribute tells the transformer how to parse the value, and a pattern attribute tells the transformer how to format the value into the output event stream. You can also specify a locale and source-local attribute to indicate the current locale and the locale for the value. The patterns use the syntax of the java.text.SimpleDateFormat.

  The <number> element is used to format numbers. To format numbers only, you can specify a pattern attribute and a value attribute. The patterns follow the syntax of java.text.DecimalFormat. You can also use <number> to format currency values or percentages by specifying a type attribute with the value "currency" or "percent" instead of pattern.

  The message catalogs used by the I18n transformer are XML files whose root element is <catalogue> and whose child elements are <message> elements. The content of the <message> element is the text to be replaced. A key attribute associates a key with each <message> element. Each message catalog is given a name when the transformer is defined. This name is used as the base name for the message catalog file. The I18n transformer allows for a hierarchy of message catalogs that looks like the hierarchy allowed by java.util.ResourceBundle. The hierarchy search proceeds by trying basename.xml followed by basename_langauge.xml, followed by basename_language_country.xml, and ending with basename_language_country_variant.xml.

The message catalogs are configured in the <transformer> element. Three configuration elements appear as children of the <transformer> element. The <catalogues> element contains a sequence of <catalogue> elements, one for each catalog. Each <catalogue> has an id element for identification, a name element that provides the base name for the catalog file, and a location attribute that specifies the location of the catalog files. After the <catalogues> element, an optional <untranslated-text> element contains the text that's returned if a key can't be translated (by default, the key name is output instead). The optional <cache-at-startup> element contains the value "true" or "false" as its content ("false" is the default). If the value is "true", then Cocoon tries to cache the messages in that catalog when it starts up.

The I18n transformer is in org.apache.cocoon.transformation.I18nTransformer and is known by the name i18n.

- **Log transformer**—The log transformer prints all the events that pass through it into a file. When you use the log transformer in a <transform> tag, you can supply two parameters: logfile, which tells the transformer which file to write the events into; and append, which tells the transformer whether it should append to the logfile or start the log over. If you don't specify a value for logfile, the events are logged to the servlet engine's standard output. This transformer is primarily used for debugging. It uses the name log and is available in org.apache.cocoon.transformation.LogTransformer.

- **SQL transformer**—This transformer is one way of interacting with a SQL database in Cocoon. It assumes that some special XML elements in the input stream are destined for it. These elements are taken from http://apache.org/cocoon/SQL/2.0. The way it works is a little tricky. The input stream must contain a <page> element from the SQL namespace. There also must be an <execute-query> element as a child of the <page> element. Here's the difficult part: There may be other elements from other namespaces as children of the <page> element, and the <execute-query> may be a child of one of these elements or their children. This is necessary because you want be able to position the results of the SQL query in the correct place in the document/event stream. The <execute-query> element has a single child element called <query>. The content of the <query> element is a SQL query. You can use simple SQL statements like select, insert, and update. You can also use a SQL stored procedure. If you use a stored procedure, then you must supply an isstoredprocedure attribute on <query>, and its value must be "true". The <query> element also takes a name attribute that's used to name the result set.

  After the transformer has executed, the output event stream contains a <rowset> element where the <execute-query> element was. If a name attribute was supplied for the <query> element, then the <rowset> has a name attribute with the same value. If you set the show-nr-of-rows parameter in the <transform> element, then there is an attribute named nrofrows whose value is the number of rows in the <rowset> The content of the <rowset> is a sequence of <row> elements. Each <row> element contains an element for each column in the result set, and the content of that element is the value of the column in the appropriate row.

  When you specify the SQL transformer in a <transform> element, you need to supply a parameter called use-connection. The value of this parameter is the name of a datasource connection defined in the Cocoon configuration file cocoon.xconf. You can supply a parameter called show-nr-of-rows, which adds a nrofrows attribute containing the number of rows to the <rowset>.

You can also supply a parameter called clob-encoding that specifies the character encoding to be used when reading data out of CLOB columns.

The SQL transformer is available under the name sql and is in the class org.apache.cocoon .transformation.SQLTransformer.

- **Filter transformer**—The filter transformer allows you to reduce the number of elements in a sequence in order to avoid processing them. It assumes that the incoming event stream contains a sequence of the same element. The parameters for the transformer allow you to specify which element should be filtered (the parameter name is element-name), how many elements should be passed through (the parameter name is count), and what block number to start at (the parameter name is blocknr). When the transformer executes, it breaks the sequence into blocks whose size is determined by the count parameter. The output event stream takes the elements in the sequence and wraps them up in a <block> element. There are count elements per <block>, and each block is given an id attribute whose value starts at 1. The blocknr parameter specifies the id of the <block> that is to be filled in. That's the only <block> that has elements from the sequence in it; all the other <block> elements are empty. This transformer is useful for producing paged output, because you can use variables to provide the values for the parameters. The name assigned to this transformer is filter, and the class is org.apache.cocoon.transformation.FilterTransformer.

- **Write DOM session transformer**—This transformer converts the input event stream into a DOM tree and stores that DOM tree in the servlet session. There are two parameters to this transformer: dom-name is the name used to store the DOM tree in the servlet session, and dom-root-element allows you to specify the name of the element in the input event stream that's used as the root of the DOM tree. You use the name writeDOMsession to use this transformer, and the class is org.apache.cocoon.transformation.WriteDOMSessionTransformer.

- **Read DOM session transformer**—This transformer retrieves a DOM tree from the servlet session and converts it back into a SAX event stream. The dom-name parameter is the name of the DOM tree that's retrieved from the session. The trigger-name parameter is the name of the element in the input event stream that triggers the transformer to start generating events. The position parameter determines how the events from the DOM tree are placed relative to the trigger element. If position is "before", then the events from the tree appear before the trigger element. If position is "in", then the transformer generates a startElement for the trigger element, generates all the events for the DOM tree, and then resumes generating events from the input event stream. If the position is "after", then the events for the DOM tree are generated right after the endElement event for the trigger element. In all cases, the events from the DOM tree are added to the stream coming from the transformer input. It's just a question of where. This transformer is available via the name readDOMsession, and the class is org.apache.cocoon.transformation.ReadDOMSessionTransformer.

- **XInclude transformer**—The XInclude transformer expects the input event stream to contain at least one XInclude element. XInclude provides a way to merge one or more XML documents into another. The transformer performs the inclusion specified by the XInclude element or elements and outputs an event stream containing the merged document. The class for the XInclude transformer is org.apache.cocoon.transformation.XIncludeTransformer, and the name is xinclude.

- **CInclude transformer**—In addition to using XInclude to combine documents, Cocoon has defined its own inclusion mechanism. This is available via the CInclude transformer. It expects the input event stream to contain elements from the namespace http://apache.org/cocoon/include/1.0. The simplest form of include is an <include> element, which has a src attribute that indicates the document to include. You can also specify an element attribute that defines the name of an element used to wrap the included XML. If the wrapper element is specified, the <include> element in the input stream is replaced by the wrapper element, and the child of the wrapper element is the contents of the included document; otherwise, the <include> element is replaced by the document contents. The namespace and prefix of the wrapper element are controlled by the ns and prefix attributes of the <include> element.

The CInclude transform also allows you to include XML from an external HTTP via either the GET or POST method. The GET method is relatively simple. Instead of <include>, you use <includexml>, which has no attributes and a single child element <src>. The content of the <src> element is the URL that should be accessed using the GET method. If an error occurs, then the input event stream is lost. If you wish to proceed anyway, you can set the ignoreErrors attribute of <includexml> to "true".

To use the CInclude transform to do a POST to request a document, you again use the <includexml> element, but this time it has three child elements. In addition to the <src> element, it contains a <configuration> element that contains a <parameter> element. <parameter> elements have two children—<name> and <value>—and store the name and value as their content. To perform a POST, the <parameter> is named method and the value is POST. After the <configuration> element is a <parameters> element. This element contains a sequence of <parameter> elements (just like the one used in <configuration>), one for each parameter to the POST method.

The CInclude transformer is in org.apache.cocoon.transformation.CIncludeTransformer and is available under the name cinclude.

- **EncodeURL transformer**—The EncodeURL transformer takes care of encoding URLs that appear in the input event stream. This is much easier that trying to call encodeURL at all the right points. By making the EncodeURL transformer the last transformer in your pipeline (before the serializer), you can ensure that all URLs in the output event stream are properly encoded. The transformer takes two configuration options as children of the <transformer> element where it's defined. The <include-name> option allows you to specify a regular expression that's used to determine which attributes are treated as URLs to be encoded. The regular expressions are of the form element-name/@attribute-name. The default value for <include-name> is ./*@href | .*/@action | frame/@src, which covers any href attribute, any action attribute, and any src attribute of a <frame> element. The <exclude-name> option allows you to exclude attributes that should not be treated as URLs. Its default value is img/@src, which means the src attributes of <img> elements won't be encoded. This transformer is in the class org.apache.cocoon.trasnformation.EncodeURLTrasnformer and is assigned the name encodeURL.
- **Augment transformer**—This transformer looks at all href attributes in the input event stream and converts any relative URLs to absolute URLs. The transformer normally makes relative URLs absolute in relation to the request URI. If you specify the mount parameter as a child of the <transform> element, then URLs are made absolute relative to the servlet context appended with the value mount. For example, if the value of mount is "resources" and the Cocoon Web application has been installed as http://localhost:8080/cocoon, then URLs are made absolute against http://localhost:8080/cocoon/resources. This means the relative URL icon.gif becomes http://localhost:8080/cocoon/resources/icon.gif. This transformer is in org.apache.cocoon.transformation.AugmentTransformer and uses the name augment.

Serializers

As you've already seen in the sample sitemap, serializers transform a SAX event stream into binary or character streams for output. If a pipeline contains a generator, it should also contain a serializer. We'll take you through the set of available serializers so you'll have an idea of the kind of functionality that's available. You can get full details on any serializer in the components appendix of the Cocoon user manual:

- **XML serializer**—This Serializer serves as the basis for a number of the other serializers. It generates an XML document from the input SAX event stream. This serializer is in the class org.apache.cocoon.serialization.XMLSerializer under the name xml. You can provide a number of configuration parameters when you use the serializer from a <serialize> tag:
    - **cdata-section-elements**—A whitespace-separated list of elements whose text content should be enclosed in CDATA sections for output.
    - **doctype-public**—The public ID to be placed in the DTD of the output document.
    - **doctype-system**—The system ID to be placed in the DTD of the output document.
    - **encoding**—The character encoding to be supplied for the encoding declaration in the output document.
    - **indent**—"yes" if some elements should trigger a line break, or "no" otherwise (the default value is "yes").
    - **media-type**—The MIME content type of the document.
    - **method**—The output method that should be used. The method names are the XSLT output method names.
    - **omit-xml-declaration**—"yes" to omit the XML declaration.
    - **standalone**—"yes" to output a standalone document declaration.
    - **version**—The version of the output method. The defaults are 1.0 for the XML output method and 4.0 for the HTML output method.
- **HTML serializer**—The HTML serializer is the default for Cocoon pipelines. It's in the class org.apache.cocoon.serialization.HtmlSerializer and available under the name html. This serializer accepts the same configuration parameters as the XML serializer.
- **XHTML serializer**—This is a use of the XML serializer for serializing the event stream as XHTML. There are some differences. When defining the XHTML serializer, you must supply some configuration parameters. These appear as child elements of the <serializer> element. The elements are doctype-public and doctype-system. The meaning of these elements corresponds to the XML serializer configuration parameters of the same name. You should supply the public and system ID of one of the three XHTML DTDs as the values of doctype-public and doctype-system, respectively. You also need to provide a mime-type attribute on the <serializer> element. The value of the mime-type should be "text/html". The XHTML serializer uses the same class as the XML serializer, org.apache.cocoon.serialization.XMLSerializer, but is named xhtml.
- **Text serializer**—The Text serializer is built on the XML serializer but in a different way than the XHTML serializer. When you define the text serializer, you need to supply a mime-type

attribute on the <serializer> element. The value of this attribute should be "text/plain". After that, you're all set. The class for the text serializer is org.apache.cocoon.serialization.TextSerializer (not XMLSerializer). The name is text.

- **WAP/WML serializer**—The WML serializer is also built on the XML serializer. You need to supply the mime-type attribute on the <serializer> when you define it, and you need to provide <doctype-public> and <doctype-system> children. The mime-type attribute should be set to "text/vnd.wap.wml". The value for <doctype-public> is -//WAPFORUM//DTD WML 1.1//EN, and the value for <doctype-system> is http://www.wapforum.org/DTD/wml_1.1.xml. You should name the serializer wml and use the class org.apache.cocoon.serialization.XMLSerializer.

- **SVG/XML serializer**—This is the last of the serializers based on the XML serializer. You need to set the mime-type attribute of the <serializer> element to "text/xml" when you define the serializer. You also need to set the value of the <doctype-public> child element to -//W3C//DTD SVG 1.0//EN and the value of the <doctype-system> child element to http://www.w3.org/TR/2001/REC-SVG-20010904/DTD/svg10.dtd. This serializer is named svgxml and is in org.apache.cocoon.serialization.XMLSerializer.

- **SVG/JPEG serializer**—This serializer expects the event stream to contain an SVG document. It serializes that document by using Batik to convert it into a JPEG image. This serializer uses the class org.apache.cocoon.serialization.SVGSerializer and is available under the name svg2jpeg. When you define it, it needs a mime-type attribute on the <serializer> element. The value for the attribute should be "image/jpeg". This causes SVGSerializer to select the correct Batik transcoder.

  You can supply some configuration parameters using <parameter> children of the <serializer> element. The SVG/JPEG serializer has its own specific parameter named quality; it's a float that specifies the JPEG quality as a value between 0.0 and 1.0, with 1.0 being the best quality. There are also some parameters used by any serializer that uses SVGSerializer:

  - **width**—The width of the rasterized image. If no height is specified, the aspect ratio is preserved.
  - **height**—The height of the rasterized image. If no width is specified, the aspect ratio is preserved.
  - **background_color**—The background color. The value is of the form RRGGBB or #RRGGBB. The default background color is white.
  - **language**—The language to use. The default is English (en).
  - **user_stylesheet_uri**—The URI of a user stylesheet.
  - **pixel_to_mm**—The pixel to millimeter conversion factor. By default it's 0.264583, which yields 96dpi.

- **SVG/PNG serializer**—This serializer works just like the SVG/JPEG serializer. When you define it, you supply "image/png" as the mime-type attribute value instead of "image/jpeg". You also use the name svg2png instead of svg2jpeg. In addition to the shared parameters for SVGSerializer (see the SVG/JPEG serializer), this serializer defines two parameters useful for PNG files. The parameter force_transparent_white controls the color of fully transparent pixels. If the parameter is "true", they're white. If it's "false", they're black (the default). The other parameter is named gamma and controls the gamma correction of the PNG. The default value of gamma is about 2.22.

- **SVG/TIFF serializer**—This serializer is also based on SVGSerializer. Set the value of the mime-type attribute to "image/tiff". The name for this serializer is svg2tiff. It uses all the shared SVGSerializer parameters (see SVG/JPEG serializer), and it also uses the force_transparent _white parameter defined by the SVG/PNG serializer.
- **Link serializer**—The link serializer is the companion to the LinkStatus generator. It's in the class org.apache.cocoon.serialization.LinkSerializer and can be accessed via the name links. The MIME type of the output is application/x-cocoon-links. You also need a views section in your site map (we'll talk about views later):

```
<map:views>
 <map:view from-position="last" name="links">
  <map:serialize type="links" />
 </map:view>
<map:views>
```

- **Zip archive serializer**—The zip archive serializer generates a zip archive as its output. It expects the input event stream to contain elements from the namespace http://apache.org/cocoon /zip-archive/1.0. The root element is an <archive> element that contains a sequence of <entry> elements. Each <entry> contains a name attribute for the entry. If the entry refers to out-of-line data, then a src attribute appears, and its value is a URL to the data to be archived. URLs can use the cocoon: protocol. Inline XML data can be archived as well. In this case, there is no src attribute, but there is a serializer attribute whose value is the name of a serializer. The XML data to be serialized appears as the child of the <entry> element. The zip archive serializer is in org.apache.cocoon.serialization.ZipArchiveSerializer and uses the name zip.
- **PDF serializer (optional)**—Cocoon's PDF serializer uses FOP to serialize XML to PDF. The code for the serializer is part of the Cocoon distribution, but you need to install the FOP fop.jar in Cocoon's lib directory. Once you've done that, you can specify fo2pdf as the name of the serializer, which is in org.apache.cocoon.serialization.FOPSerializer. The PDF serializer expects the input event stream to contain an XSL FO document. You can use the FOP tools to generate a PDF with embedded fonts.
- **PS serializer (optional)**—The PostScript serializer also uses FOP to do its job, so you need to do the same setup as for the PDF serializer. The serializer is in org.apache.cocoon.serialization .PSSerializer, and you can use the name fo2ps to access it. Like the PDF serializer, it expects an XSL FO document in the input event stream.
- **PCL serializer (optional)**—This serializer is like the PostScript and PDF serializers. It's in org.apache.cocoon.serialization.PCLSerializer, and the name is fo2pcl.

Matchers

Matchers are the way Cocoon assigns portions of its virtual URI space to instructions in the sitemap. The <match> element uses a matcher and a pattern to determine whether it should handle a particular request. The body of the <match> element contains the sitemap instructions that should be executed if the pattern is matched.

Cocoon uses a first-match approach when looking at the matchers. It's not hard to come up with a set of matchers where more than one matcher will match the request. In this case, Cocoon uses the matcher that appears earliest in the sitemap. The result is that you must order your matchers from most specific to least specific. (This is similar to the way you order catch clauses in a Java try-catch block.)

When you use a wildcard or regular expression pattern, Cocoon remembers the text that was matched by the pattern. You can reference it later in the pipeline if you need it. You reference it by placing an {n} expression in the sitemap. The n refers to the number of the pattern. Patterns are numbered starting from one, and each time you use a pattern, the number is increased.

Cocoon includes quite a few built-in matchers. As with the other components, this list is designed to give you an overview of some of the more useful matchers:

- **Wildcard URI matcher**—This matcher uses wildcards to match against the request URI. As a reminder, the legitimate wildcard characters are * (matches zero or more characters excluding the path separator /), ** (matches zero or more characters including the path separator), and \ (escapes the * and \ characters). This syntax is used for all wildcard matching in the Cocoon matchers. The wildcard URI matcher can be found with the name wildcard and uses the class org.apache.cocoon.matching.WildcardURIMatcher.
- **Regexp URI matcher**—The Regexp URI matcher uses a regular expression to match against the request URI. The matcher is in org.apache.cocoon.matching.RegexpURIMatcher and can be found via the name regexp. The regular expression syntax used is taken from the Jakarta Regexp project (http://jakarta.apache.org/regexp/index.html). In the following descriptions, A and B stand for regular expressions. These are some of the most frequently used characters—check the Jakarta Regexp page for the full syntax:
    - Any non-special character \, [,], (,), ^, $, *, +, ? matches itself.
    - . matches any character except newline.
    - A* matches A zero or more times.
    - A+ matches A one or more times.
    - A? matches A zero or one times.
    - AB matches A followed by B.
    - A|B matches A or B.
    - ^ matches the beginning of a line.
    - $ matches the end of a line.
    - [abc] matches a, b, or c (characters).
    - [a-zA-Z] matches a character in the range a-z or A-Z.
    - [^abc] matches any character but a, b, or c.
    - \b matches a word boundary.
    - \B matches a non-word boundary.
    - \w matches a word (alphanumeric plus underscore [_]) character.
    - \W matches a non-word character.
    - \s matches a whitespace character.
    - \S matches a non-whitespace character.

  - \d matches a digit character.
  - \D matches a non-digit character.

- **Wildcard header matcher**—This matcher allows you to do a wildcard match against the HTTP request headers. To specify the header you want to match, you need to supply a <header-name> element as a child element of the <matcher> element when you define the matcher. The content of the <header-name> element should be the name of the header you want to match. Because you have to define a new matcher for each header, we suggest that you name the matcher by taking the name of the HTTP header and appending -match. So, if you're matching the referrer header, you would name the matcher referrer-match. The wildcard header matcher is in org.apache.cocoon.matching.WildcardHeaderMatcher.

Selectors

Selectors implement basic conditional logic inside a pipeline. They can evaluate simple conditions that involve various parts of the request environment, such as the URI, the headers, the parameters, or the host name.

They are different from matchers in a number of ways. First, matchers control the execution of entire pipelines, whereas selectors control the execution of portions of pipelines. Matchers make binary decisions—either they match, or they don't. Selectors can test values for equality, much like an if, if-else, or switch statement.

When you use a selector, you create a <select> element in the pipeline. This element has two kinds of children. The <when> element includes a test attribute that provides a value to be tested by the selector. You may have as many of these as you like. The children of a <when> element are components in the pipeline like <transform> or <serialize>. They can even be an entire pipeline. The other child of <select> is <otherwise>, which acts like an <else> clause. If none of the <when> elements has a match for its test attribute, then the children of <otherwise> are executed. <otherwise> can have the same children as <when>.

It's important to know when the selectors are executed: They're executed when the pipeline is set up, not during pipeline execution. This means they appear to execute before any regular components that lexically precede them in the sitemap. So, you can't make a selector dependent on the output of a generator or transformer, because the selector executes before the generator or transformer.

Let's look at some of the selectors that are available in Cocoon:

- **Browser selector**—This selector lets you make decisions based on the HTTP User-Agent header. When you define the selector in the <selectors> section, you must define a list of agent names to be used as the values of the test attribute in the selector's <when> statements. You do this by creating <browser> elements as children of the <selector> element you're using to define the selector. A <browser> element has two attributes: name is the name you're going to use in the test attributes of <when> elements, and useragent is the string that should appear somewhere in the User-Agent header. You can have multiple <browser> elements with the same name but different useragent strings. This allows you to consolidate browsers that are really the same under a single name. The browser selector is available via the class org.apache.cocoon .selection.BrowserSelector and uses the name browser.

- **Host selector**—The host selector works in a similar fashion to the browser selector, but instead of testing the User-Agent header, it tests the Host header. This allows Cocoon to perform host-specific sitemap processing. The primary application is in multihomed or virtual hosted environments. Like the browser selector, the host selector requires you to add child elements to the <selector> element as you're defining the selector. The difference is that the child elements are <host> elements. The <host> element has two attributes: name, which is the value to be tested against the value of a <when> element's test attribute; and value, which contains the name of the host as carried by the HTTP Host header. Just as with the browser selector, you can have multiple <host> elements that have the same value for the name attribute but different values for the value attribute. The host selector is available in the class org.apache.cocoon.selection .HostSelector and is normally associated with the name host.
- **Parameter selector**—This selector takes the value to be tested from a Cocoon sitemap parameter. You can set this parameter a few ways: from within a <match> element, via a <parameter> element, or by an action (more on actions in the next section). This selector can also test against a matched wildcard or regular expression value. The test that's performed is a case-sensitive String comparison.

  When you use the parameter selector, the first child element of the <select> element must be a <parameter> element whose name attribute is set to "parameter-selector-test". The value of that parameter is either the sitemap parameter "{sitemapParameterName}" or a reference to a matched wildcard or regular expression "{n}", where n is the number of the wildcard or regular expression. After that, you can supply your <when> and <otherwise> clauses. The parameter selector is in the class org.apache.cocoon.selection.ParameterSelector and uses the name parameter.
- **Request attribute selector**—This selector lets you select on the value of an attribute in the servlet request. To do this, you supply a <parameter> element as the first child of the <select> element. This parameter is named attribute-name, and its value is the name of the attribute that you want to select on. The Request Attribute selector uses the name request-attribute and is in the class org.apache.cocoon.selection.RequestAttributeSelector.
- **Request parameter selector**—The request parameter selector works like the Request Attribute selector, except that the name of the <parameter> element is parameter-name. This selector is available in org.apache.cocoon.selection.RequestParameterSelector and uses the name request-parameter.

Actions

Up until now, all the Cocoon components we have looked at produced some kind of display data. Serializers generate data to be displayed, and they are fed by transformers, which are fed by generators. The data that is displayed originates with the generator. Sometimes you need to adjust the pipeline while it's running. Actions provide a way to do this without polluting the display data with information needed to control the pipeline.

An action is a Cocoon component that can both receive values from the sitemap and provide values to the Sitemap. This allows it to control the behavior of a pipeline at runtime. You should use actions to handle form processing and dynamic navigation.

When an action executes, it receives any attributes of the <act> element, as well as any parameters defined by child <parameter> objects. The action also has access to the request and application state.

When the action completes, it provides a set of values that can be accessed via the {name} notation. These values are provided as a Java Map object. The action can also return null instead of returning a Map. If this happens, then any statements inside the <act> element aren't executed.

Defining an action looks much like defining any other Cocoon component. The <actions> section goes after the <selections> section and contains a sequence of <action> elements. The <actions> element might look like this:

```
<map:actions>
 <map:action name="action" logger="logtarget"
   src="classname"/>
</map:actions>
```

The definition of an action uses an <action> element, which looks much like the other elements for defining components. There are attributes for naming the action to be defined, assigning a LogKit log target, and specifying the class that implements the functionality of the action.

When you use an action in a pipeline, you create an <act> element as a child of a <match> element. The type attribute of the <act> element is the name of the action you wish to execute. Any parameters you want to pass to the action appear as the initial children of the <act> element. After that come any statements that need to use the values passed back by the action. The values to be used are enclosed in {}. A <match> element that uses an action might look like this:

```
<map:match pattern="uri">
 <map:act type="action-name">
  <map:parameter name="parameter" value="value"/>

  <map:generate src="{returnValue}"/>
  <map:serializer/>
 </map:act>
</map:match>
```

Most of the actions that are predefined in Cocoon are related to big tasks like database access or session handling. The following list makes you aware that these tasks can be accomplished using actions, and we'll cover the actions when we talk about each of these subjects in detail:

- **Database actions**—Cocoon provides two sets of actions for dealing with database access, which we'll cover in Chapter 6, "Cocoon Development," when we talk about database access.
- **Sendmail action**—The sendmail action is in the class org.apache.cocoon.acting.Sendmail and is normally given the name sendmail. This action allows your application to send e-mail. The parameters you can pass into the sendmail action via <parameter> elements are as follows:
    - **smtphost**—The IP address or name of the host that should deliver the mail (optional).
    - **to**—The destination address of the message.
    - **cc**—Carbon copy recipients of the message, separated by commas (optional).
    - **bcc**—Blind carbon copy recipients of the message, separated by commas (optional).

- from—The address of the sender of the message.
- subject—The subject line for the message (optional).
- body—The text of the message body (optional).
- charset—The character encoding of the message (optional).
- attachment—The attachments for this message, separated by blanks (optional).

These parameters are passed back to the sitemap and are accessible via {name}:

- **status**—One of three values: "success", "user-error", or "server-error". "Success" means the message was sent, "user-error" means the user-made an error (probably in addressing—to, from, cc, bcc), and "server-error" means the message couldn't be delivered to the smtphost.
- **message**—A text explanation of why the message couldn't be delivered. This isn't present if the message was sent successfully.

- **Session action**—The session action allows you to create or destroy a session context. Session-handling will be covered in detail in a separate section later in this chapter.

Action Sets

You place a sequence of actions into an *action set*. This is a named set of actions that are executed as one action by the sitemap. The actions in the action set are executed in the order they appear. Only the last action that appears in the action set is allowed to return values to the sitemap.

Defining action sets is easy. The <action-sets> element goes right before the <pipeline> element in the sitemap. It contains a sequence of <action-set> elements. Each <action-set> has a name attribute and contains a sequence of <map:act> elements as its children.

Using an action set is also easy. You use a <map:act> element, but instead of giving a type attribute, you give a set attribute whose value is the name of the action set to execute. Everything else is done just like a regular <map:act> element.

Readers

Cocoon is an XML-centric system. All the components you have seen so far rely on getting XML as input and generate XML as output. But not everything in a Web application will be XML—there will be images, binary data from databases, and other non-XML data that you wish to incorporate into your application. This is where readers come into the picture. *Readers* are components that implement a self-contained pipeline—at least, that's how you can visualize them in Cocoon terms. One way to think of them is as pass-throughs for various kinds of data. Some of the Cocoon readers are as follows:

- **Resource reader**—This reader is used to copy binary data to the output of the pipeline. Any kind of binary (and text data as well) can be copied by a reader. It's the most general of all the readers. To define the resource reader, you use the name resource and the class name org.apache.cocoon.reading.ResourceReader. To use it, you need to supply a src attribute that specifies the resources to be read (and copied to the output) and a mime-type attribute that specifies the MIME type to be passed to the result. You can also specify some optional parameters as children of the <read> element. These parameters are defined using the <parameter> tag, and work as follows:

- **expires**—The time in milliseconds that the resource can be cached. (Optional.)
- **quick-modified-test**—If the value is "true", only the last modified time of the current source is tested, but not if the current source is the same as the source that was just used. This defaults to "false". (Optional.)
- **byte-ranges**—If the value is "true", support for byte ranges is turned on. The default is "true". (Optional.)
- **buffer-size**—The size of the buffer used to read a resource. The default value is "8192". (Optional.)

- **Image reader**—This reader is an extension of the resource reader and works the same way. It uses the same attributes and all the configuration parameters of the Resource reader. The class name for the reader is org.apache.cocoon.reading.ImageReader and the usual name for the reader is image. This reader defines some configuration parameters beyond those defined by the resource reader:
    - **width**—Image width in pixels. If no height is specified, the aspect ratio is preserved. (Optional.)
    - **height**—Image height in pixels. If no width is specified, the aspect ratio is preserved. (Optional.)
    - **allow-enlarging**—If the value is "yes" and the image is smaller than that specified by the width and height parameters, then the image is enlarged. If the value is "no", those images are reduced in size. This parameter defaults to "yes". (Optional.)
- **JSP reader**—The JSP reader allows you to pass the Cocoon request to a JavaServer Page (JSP) and have the page process the request. The result of processing the page is passed to the result. To define the JSP reader, use the class org.apache.cocoon.reading.JSPReader and the name jsp. When you use the JSP reader in a <read> element, you should set the mime-type attribute to be the MIME type of the JSP result.
- **Database reader (optional)**—This reader allows you to take data out of a column in a database and pass it through to the result. A common application for it is to retrieve images that are stored in BLOB columns. To define the Database reader, use the class org.apache.cocoon .reading.DatabaseReader and make the name databasereader. A few configuration options are available when you define the reader. These options are child elements of the <reader> element. The <use-connection> element takes the name of a database selector (as defined in the cocoon.xconf file) as its content. The <invalidate> element has two values for its content: "never" and "always". If the last-modified parameter (discussed in a moment) is -1, then the content of <invalidate> determines the caching behavior. Otherwise the caching behavior is defined by the last-modified time retrieved from the database.

    When you use the database reader, the attributes of the <read> element have additional meaning. In particular, the value of the src attribute should be a key value from the key column in the database. You should also take care to set the mime-type attribute to the appropriate type. You also need to supply some parameters. As usual, you do so via <parameter> children of the <read> element. Here are the parameter names:

- **table**—The name of the database table to be queried.
- **image**—The name of the column containing the data to retrieve.
- **key**—The name of the key column for the data in the image column.
- **where**—A string containing a SQL WHERE expression, but without the word WHERE. (Optional.)
- **order-by**—A string containing a SQL ORDER BY expression but without the words ORDER BY. (Optional.)
- **last-modified**—The name of a column that must a SQL TIMESTAMP, which is interpreted as the last-modified time of the data.
- **content-type**—The name of a column that contains a string. The value of this string is used to override the setting of the mime-type attribute. This allows different media types to be stored in the same column.

The Database reader combines the values of all these parameters into a SQL query that looks like this:

```
SELECT {image} [, last-modified] [, {order-by-column} ]
FROM {table}
WHERE {key} = {src} [ AND {where} ] [ORDER BY {order-by}]
```

Views

Remember that one of the goals of Cocoon is to separate the various concerns: content, style, logic, and management. The view mechanism allows you to reuse the content portion of a pipeline while changing the style and presentation of it. Cocoon's view mechanism lets you divert the content of a pipeline into a sequence of instructions that are contained in a view. You could accomplish this diversion using selectors, but the advantage of views over selectors is that a single view can be used to divert any number of pipelines.

How is this diversion accomplished? Views are attached to exit points in pipelines. At these exit points, the pipeline content is diverted into the view. Of course, you now need to ask how the exit points defined. Some of the elements in a sitemap take a label attribute. The label attribute takes a list of labels names, separated by either spaces or commas (you can mix the separators in a single attribute value). This defines an exit point that can be referred to by any of the label names. Here is the list of sitemap elements you can label: <map:generator>, <map:generate>, <map:transformer>, <map:transform>, <map:aggregate>, and <map:part>. If one of these elements possesses a label, and a view references that label, then the XML content of that element is diverted to the referencing view, and execution picks up with the instructions in that view. In the case of a <part> element, the content that's diverted is only the content produced by that <part>.

Cocoon also defines two special view names, first and last. They are automatically defined for every pipeline. The first label defines an exit point after the first component of that pipeline (the generator); last defines an exit point after the last component in the pipeline, but before the serializer (otherwise there would be no point to the view, because the serializer is responsible for the final output and you want the view to take over that job).

You define a view by using the <views> section of the sitemap. The <views> section comes right after the <components> section. It contains a sequence of <view> elements as its content. A <view> element contains a sequence of sitemap instructions as its child content. The allowable elements are <transform>, <call>, and <serialize>. The <view> element must have a name attribute that names the view.

Views are attached to exit points using one of two attributes. The from-label attribute contains the name of a label where the view should be attached. The output of the component with that label is diverted to the instructions in the view. The from-position attribute uses the special view names. If its value is "first", then the output of the generator is sent to the view. If the value is "last", the event stream that would have been the input to the serializer is diverted to the view instead. When from-position is used, the view is defined for every pipeline in the sitemap.

Once views are set up in the sitemap, you need to access them. All processing in Cocoon is based on properties of the request, the URI, the headers, or parameters. Cocoon currently selects a view via a special URI query parameter named cocoon-view. So, to select a view named fancy-pdf, the URI should look like http://localhost:8080/cocoon/mydocument.html?cocoon-view=fancy-pdf. Cocoon uses its regular request-processing to look at this URL (without the cocoon-view parameter) and select a pipeline to execute. The fancy-pdf view is then hooked up to the exit point defined when the view was defined.

Resources

Often you'll find that a pipeline (or pipelines) appears repeatedly throughout a sitemap. Cocoon's resources give you a way to define a name for a pipeline so that it can be used multiple times. The <resources> section of the sitemap appears after the <views> section and before the <action-sets> section. Its content is a sequence of <resource> elements. A <resource> element has a name attribute that defines the name used to refer to the resource elsewhere in the sitemap. The children of the <resource> element are the elements that make up the pipeline. You should put the statements that appear inside a <pipeline> element inside the <resource> element. Resources can also use parameters that are passed to them via the <call> element. To use a parameter value, you use the {*parameterName*} notation.

<pipeline> elements

Now we're ready for an exhaustive list of all the elements that can appear in a Cocoon pipeline. You've seen some of them, but a few new ones also in this section:

- **<map:match>**—This element contains a sequence of pipeline elements that are executed if the matcher succeeds.
- **<map:generate>**—The <map:generate> element designates the generator that provides the initial XML content for a pipeline. The particular generator is selected via the type attribute.
- **<map:transform>**—This element can appear multiple times between a <map:generate> and <map:serialize> element. It's used to select a component that transforms the XML event stream from one form to another. The transform is specified via the type attribute.
- **<map:serialize>**—The <map:serialize> element specifies the serializer that takes the XML content of the pipeline and sends it to the result. The specific serializer is designated via the type attribute.

- **<map:select>**—This element contains a sequence of <map:when> elements followed by an optional <map:otherwise> element. The <map:when> elements are tested against the value of a selector, and the children of the <map:when> element whose test attribute equals the selector value are executed. If no <map:when> element matches the selector value, then the children of the <map:otherwise> element are executed (if there is a <map:otherwise> element).
- **<map:act>**—The <map:act> element is used to cause an action to execute. The action is specified by the value of the type attribute, and the values returned by the action are available to the elements that are the children of the <map:act> element.
- **<map:redirect-to>**—The <map:redirect-to> element allows you to perform an HTTP redirect. An attribute named target specifies the destination URI for the redirect. If this URI is within Cocoon's virtual URI space, the usual URI processing occurs, including matching and pipeline execution. There is also a session attribute that determines whether the redirect preserves the session. If your Web application uses an HTTP session, then you should set the value of the session attribute to "true".
- **<map:call>**—The <map:call> element invokes a resource (a reusable pipeline). The element takes a single attribute, resource, whose value is the name of the resource to invoke. You can pass parameters to the resource by creating child <map:parameter> elements to define the parameters and their values.
- **<map:parameter>**—This element appears as a child of other pipeline elements. It provides a standard way of passing parameters to pipeline components. It takes a name attribute whose value is the name of the parameter and a value parameter that contains the value of the parameter.
- **<map:handle-errors>**—The <handle-errors> section of the pipeline defines what happens when an error occurs in that pipeline. The content of <handle-errors> is just a pipeline. There is one special twist, though: If you don't define a generator, Cocoon defines one for you, based on the notifying generator. Other than that, you can use all the constructs you can use in any other pipeline. A type attribute lets you specify which HTTP error codes are handled. The default value for this attribute is "500".
- **<map:mount>**—It's not hard to imagine that the sitemap for a large site will be long, complicated, and hard to debug. Cocoon provides a way for you to modularize your sitemaps in order to keep them understandable, maintainable, and debuggable. The idea is to use sub-sitemaps that have their own sitemap file and that are responsible for a subspace of the URI space of the parent.

  Let's suppose your Web application has an administrative section that occupies the URI space under /admin. You create a sitemap for that application and have it deal with URIs that are under /admin, but the matchers should assume that the /admin has been stripped off. This way, you can move the URI space handled by the sub-sitemap with minimal effort if you decide to reorganize the site. Once you've defined the sub-sitemap, you use a <map:mount> element to attach the sub-sitemap to the root sitemap and notify the root sitemap that certain URIs will be handled by the sub-sitemap. Here's the use of <map:mount>:

  ```
  <map:match pattern="admin/*">
   <map:mount uri-prefix="admin" check-reload="no"
              src="admin/sitemap.xmap"/>
  </map:match>
  ```

The <map:match> element assigns the admin URI space to the sitemap, just as with any other pipeline. No new syntax is needed for this part. The <map:mount> element does all its work with three attributes. The uri-prefix attribute tells the root sitemap what to strip from the URI before handing the URI to the sub-sitemap. In this case, *admin* is stripped off the front of the URI. The check-reload attribute should be set to "yes" if you want the sub-sitemap to be reloaded if its sitemap file is modified (done by checking the file modification time). The src attribute tells the root sitemap where the sub-sitemap file is located. If the URI admin/editData was passed to the root sitemap, it would match this pipeline. The admin uri-prefix would be stripped, and the remaining URI, editData, would be passed to the sub-sitemap in admin/sitemap.xmap.

Any component defined in a sitemap is accessible from its sub-sitemaps. The sub-sitemap can reference components in the parent sitemap by name.

- **<map:aggregate>**—You can use the <map:aggregate> element anywhere you can use the <map:generate> element. This element defines an aggregator, which allows you to combine a number of XML sources into a single source and use that as the initial XML content for the pipeline. The content of the <map:aggregate> element is a sequence of <map:part> elements. A <map:part> element has a single attribute src that's used to specify the source of the XML data for that part. The aggregator combines the parts by wrapping them in an element. The elements from each part become the children of the wrapper element. Their order in the wrapper element is determined by the order of the parts. The <map:aggregate> element has an attribute named element that specifies the name of the wrapper element. The values that can go into the src attributes are Cocoon URIs.

Cocoon URIs

To give you flexibility in where you place resources that you might need in Cocoon, Cocoon adds some URL schemes to the commonly available ones:

- **http://hostname:port/resource**—This is a standard HTTP URL. A sample URL is http://localhost:8080/myxml.xml.
- **context://servlet-context-path/resource**—This scheme allows you to retrieve a resource relative to the servlet context on the current servlet engine. The URL context:///stylesheets/format.xsl refers to a resource stylesheets/format.xsl, relative to the current servlet context.
- **cocoon:/resource**—This scheme allows you to refer to a resource produced by the current Cocoon sitemap. The URL cocoon:/mydata.xml passes the string mydata.xml to the current sitemap as the request URI. The current sitemap then processes that URI to obtain a resource that is returned.
- **cocoon://resource**—This scheme is like the previous scheme except it uses the root sitemap for the Web application; this is indicated by two slashes (//) instead of one. For the URL cocoon://mydata.xml, Cocoon passes mydata.xml as the request URI to the root sitemap. The root sitemap processes the URI and returns a resource. Note that you can use this to access any sub-sitemaps because a sub-sitemap handles a subspace of the URI space.
- **resource://class-path-context/resource**—This scheme allows you to obtain resources relative to the class loader for the current context. The class-path-context must be a path through the class-path to the data; when you've stored XML files side by side with the class files, this is the URI scheme you want to use. An example of this kind of URL is resource://org/apache/cocoon/components/language/markup/xsp/java/xsp.xsl.

- **jar://http://hostname:port/resource.jar!/path/in/jar**—This scheme allows you to obtain resources that are contained in a Jar file. You need to specify the URI to the Jar file and the path inside the jar that leads to the resource. These two components are separated by an exclamation point (!).
- **file:///resource**—This is a standard file URL. An example is file:///mydata.xml.

You can use these additional schemes anywhere a URI is called for.

XSP

Cocoon provides eXtensible Server Pages (XSPs) as a way of generating XML content for a Cocoon pipeline. At their simplest, XSPs are XML documents that allow you to include code in some programming language. When the XSP page is requested, the XSP engine executes the code and replaces the code with the result of that execution. If you're familiar with JavaServer Pages (JSPs), you'll have a good idea of how basic XSPs work. XSPs give you a way to bridge into a programming language to access data that would otherwise be inaccessible via the standard Cocoon generator mechanism.

All the examples in this section are based on Java as the programming language, but you should be aware that Cocoon supports a large number of programming languages for use in XSPs. This is accomplished via the Bean Scripting Framework, an Apache Jakarta project (http://jakarta.apache.org/bsf).

Simple XSPs

Let's look at a very simple XSP page, just to get acquainted with the concepts and syntax:

```
 1: <?xml version="1.0"?>
 2: <?cocoon-process type="xsp"?>
 3:
 4: <xsp:page
 5:   language="java"
 6:   xmlns:xsp="http://apache.org/xsp">
 7:
 8:  <date>
 9:   <xsp:expr>new java.util.Date().toString()</xsp:expr>
10:  </date>
11: </xsp:page>
```

This XSP is named date.xsp. As you can see from line 1, it's an XML document. All XSP pages must include a Cocoon processing instruction that invokes the XSP processor. This appears in line 2. The root element of an XSP document is named page and is in the XSP namespace, which uses the URI http://apache.org/xsp. In lines 4-6, you see the start tag for <xsp:page>, the signal to Cocoon that the language embedded in the XSP is Java (line 5), and the declaration of the xsp namespace prefix (line 6).

When the XSP is processed, all the elements from the XSP namespace are removed by the XSP processor. In line 8, you introduce the root element of the XML to be generated by the XSP, <date>. There is only one piece of XSP code in this example, and it's in line 9. The <xsp:expr> element allows you to specify an expression in the language defined by <xsp:page>'s language attribute. The expression provided creates a new instance of java.util.Date and then converts it to a String so that it can be output. Lines 10 and 11 close all the remaining elements.

Now that you have your XSP, you need to connect it to a pipeline in a Cocoon application. To do that, you need to add some entries to a sitemap. Here's a simple sitemap that makes that connection:

```
 1: <?xml version="1.0" encoding="UTF-8"?>
 2: <map:sitemap xmlns:map="http://apache.org/cocoon/sitemap/1.0">
 3:
 4:  <map:pipelines>
 5:
 6:   <map:pipeline>
 7:
 8:     <map:match pattern="*.xsp">
 9:      <map:generate type="serverpages" src="{1}.xsp"/>
10:      <map:transform src="{1}.xslt">
11:       <map:parameter name="contextPath"
12:                      value="{request:contextPath}"/>
13:      </map:transform>
14:      <map:serialize type="html"/>
15:     </map:match>
16:
17:   </map:pipeline>
18:
19:  </map:pipelines>
20:
21: </map:sitemap>
```

This sitemap is much shorter than the initial sitemap we showed you in this chapter. In that sitemap, we were trying to introduce Cocoon concepts and show you how to define various kinds of components. This sitemap relies on the fact that Cocoon comes with a number of predefined and default components, and we're taking advantage of that to keep the sitemap short so you can focus on the parts related to XSPs.

This pipeline is set up so that the pipeline processes all URIs that end in .xsp in lines 8-15. This is because of the <match> element in line 8. The pipeline uses the serverpages generator to process an XSP file that has the same name as the wildcarded portion of the request URI. After the appropriate XSP has been processed, its output is sent to an XSLT stylesheet that's named to match the XSP file. The <transform> element in lines 10-13 uses Cocoon's default transformer, which is the TrAX-based XSLT engine. The pipeline assumes that this stylesheet will convert the output of the XSP into HTML for rendering in a browser, so the HTML serializer is selected to produce the output.

The result of executing the XSP is a piece of XML that looks like this:

```
<date>Thu Sep 18 16:22:13 PDT 2003</date>
```

The stylesheet you use to convert this XML into HTML looks like this:

```
<?xml version="1.0" encoding="UTF-8"?>
<xsl:stylesheet version="1.0"
 xmlns:xsl="http://www.w3.org/1999/XSL/Transform">
 <xsl:output method="html" version="4.0" encoding="UTF-8"
             indent="yes" omit-xml-declaration="yes"/>
 <xsl:template match="date">
  <html>
```

```
    <head><title>Today's date</title></head>
    <body>
     Today is <b> <xsl:apply-templates/> </b>
    </body>
  </html>
 </xsl:template>
</xsl:stylesheet>
```

It's all pretty simple, but we wanted you to understand how the flow goes before we dive into additional features.

XSP Details

Now let's look at how to write the same XSP using more of XSP's features:

```
<?xml version="1.0"?>
<?cocoon-process type="xsp"?>

<xsp:page
  language="java"
  xmlns:xsp="http://apache.org/xsp">

 <xsp:structure>
  <xsp:include>java.util.Date</xsp:include>
 </xsp:structure>

 <xsp:logic>
  String getDate() {
    Date d = new Date();
       return d.toString();
  }
 </xsp:logic>

 <date>
  <xsp:expr>getDate()</xsp:expr>
 </date>
</xsp:page>
```

The big difference here has to do with handling all the Java artifacts that can appear in an XSP. In the original page, you use fully qualified classnames and don't use any variables or functions. This page does the same thing, but in a more scalable fashion. The first change is to import the classes that are used in the page instead of using fully qualified names. To import classes, you add an <xsp:structure> element that contains a sequence of <xsp:include> elements. The content of an <xsp:include> is either a fully qualified classname (as in this example) or a wildcarded import of an entire package, something like java.util.*. That takes care of the fully qualified classname issue.

Next, you define a function that performs the date computation. To do that, you add an <xsp:logic> element. Any variables or functions defined inside this element are defined at the class level in Java. XSP pages are compiled into Java classes, and the <xsp:logic> element lets you add fields and methods to the class. Here you define a method getDate that creates the Date object and then returns its string representation.

All of these changes propagate down to the original <xsp:expr> element, which now just contains a method invocation of getDate. The page has gotten a bit longer, and for a simple page like the original page it seems a little like overkill; but for larger pages, these facilities make it much easier to write the logic and the expressions.

Now we're ready to look at the full set of XSP <elements>, so you can get an idea of what you can do:

- **<?cocoon-process?>**—This processing instruction (PI) tells Cocoon how to process this file. You may have multiple cocoon-process PIs because Cocoon can process an XSP page in two different ways. It can process the document as an XSP file, causing the language code to be executed. To indicate this style of processing, specify "xsp" as the value of the type pseudo-attribute. Cocoon can also use an XSL stylesheet to transform the document. This can occur either before or after the XSP processing. The processing order is determined by the order in which the PIs appear in the document. To use a stylesheet with an XSP document, specify "xslt" as the value of the type pseudo-attribute. If you use a stylesheet with the document, you need to supply an XML stylesheet processing instruction that tells where to find the stylesheet. (See the next item.)
- **<?xml-stylesheet?>**—This PI is defined by the W3C's Associating Style Sheets with XML Documents recommendation. Associating a stylesheet is easy; you supply two pseudo-attributes. The href pseudo-attribute contains the URI for the stylesheet, and the type pseudo-attribute contains the MIME type of the stylesheet, which should be "text/xsl" for XSLT stylesheets.
- **<xsp:page>**—The root element of an XSP page is <xsp:page>. It takes a language attribute that allows you to specify the programming language being used in the XSP. You'll probably also define some namespace prefixes on this element. The minimum would be for you to define the xsp prefix. The <xsp:page> must contain at least one user-defined element that's used as the root element of the XSP result.
- **<xsp:structure>**—This element is a container for <xsp:include> elements.
- **<xsp:include>**—XSP uses the <xsp:include> element to import type definitions that are needed by the rest of the XSP. In Java, these are specified either as fully qualified classnames or in wild-carded package style, like java.util.*.
- **<xsp:logic>**—The implementation of the logic of an XSP should be the content of the <xsp:logic> element. For Java-based XSPs, this includes member fields and methods.
- **<xsp:expr>**—An <xsp:expr> element invokes logic in the <xsp:logic> to return a string valued expression. In Java, this is through method calls, field accesses, or string literals. Java string literals that appear as the content of an <xsp:expr> tag must be inside double quotes ("").
- **<xsp:element>**—This element allows you to dynamically create an element in the output XML. The <xsp:element> element takes a name attribute whose value is the name of the element to be created. You can nest these elements to create element subtrees dynamically. You can also insert literal XML elements and character data as part of the content of this element.
- **<xsp:attribute>**—The <xsp:attribute> element should appear as the child of either an <xsp:element> element or a literal XML element. It allows you to dynamically create an attribute by supplying a name attribute for the name of the new attribute. The value of the new attribute is the content of the <xsp:attribute> element.

- **<xsp:comment>**—To create a comment in the XSP output, use the <xsp:comment> element and make the content of the element the text of your comment.

- **<xsp:pi>**—The <xsp:pi> element allows you to create processing instructions. You supply a target attribute that defines the PI target name. If you wish to create pseudo-attributes, you do so via <xsp:expr> elements in the content of the <xsp:pi> element. So, to create a PI that looks like <?xml-stylesheet href="sheet.xsl" type="text/xsl"?>, your <xsp:pi> element would look like this:

```
<xsp:pi target="xml-stylesheet">
 <xsp:expr>"href=\"sheet.xsl\" type=\"text/xsl\""</xsp:expr>
</xsp:pi>
```

- **<xsp:content>**—You can use the <xsp:content> element inside an <xsp:logic> element to insert the Java code for an XSP fragment at that point on the program. This is particularly useful for inserting an XSP fragment that is to be output as the body of a loop.

Logicsheets

If you're familiar with JSP, you're probably looking at what we've shown you so far with a mixture of fear and horror. That's because a lot of programming language code is sprinkled throughout those XSPs, so XSP authors need to understand the code in order to perform certain tasks. JSP provides a solution called *taglibs* that allows you to define a new tag and implement the functionality of the tag in a separate Java file. This returns the JSP page to being (mostly) tags.

Cocoon solves this problem in a slightly different way. Cocoon's solution is to use something called a *logicsheet*. A logicsheet is simply an XSLT stylesheet that produces an XSP page as output. So, Cocoon separates the logic from the XSP by placing all the code parts into an XSLT stylesheet. The page author writes a page that includes tags that are matched by templates in the stylesheet and replaced by the Java code that produces the results the tag calls for. This page is transformed using the logicsheet, resulting in an XSP like the ones you've seen, including all the Java. This is done without much extra effort on the part of the page author.

To see how this works, let's take the previous example and turn it into a logicsheet-based example. Here's a revised version of date.xsp that uses a logicsheet:

```
 1: <?xml version="1.0"?>
 2: <?cocoon-process type="xsp"?>
 3: <?xml-logicsheet href="logicsheet.now.xsl"?>
 4:
 5: <xsp:page
 6:  language="java"
 7:  xmlns:xsp="http://apache.org/xsp"
 8:  xmlns:now="http://sauria.com/cocoon/logicsheets/now">
 9:
10:  <date><now:time/></date>
11: </xsp:page>
```

What has changed since the previous versions? In line 3, there is now an xml-logicsheet processing instruction, which signals the XSP engine to apply the logicsheet referenced by the href pseudo-attribute. On line 8, you introducing a new namespace for the elements that are handled by the logicsheet. You've removed all the other XSP elements from the page. In line 10, instead of <xsp:expr>, there is a single element <now:time/> that's drawn from the namespace handled by the logicsheet. All the code that used to be in the page has now moved to the file logicsheet.now.xsl, which is shown here:

```
 1: <?xml version="1.0"?>
 2: <xsl:stylesheet
 3:   xmlns:xsl="http://www.w3.org/1999/XSL/Transform"
 4:   xmlns:xsp="http://apache.org/xsp"
 5:   xmlns:now="http://sauria.com/cocoon/logicsheets/now"
 6:   version="1.0">
 7:
 8:  <xsl:template match="xsp:page">
 9:   <xsl:copy>
10:    <xsl:apply-templates select="@*"/>
11:
12:    <xsp:structure>
13:     <xsp:include>java.util.Date</xsp:include>
14:    </xsp:structure>
15:
16:    <xsp:logic>
17:   String getDate() {
18:     Date d = new Date();
19:     return d.toString();
20:   }
21:    </xsp:logic>
22:
23:    <xsl:apply-templates/>
24:
25:   </xsl:copy>
26:  </xsl:template>
27:
28:  <xsl:template match="now:time">
29:   <xsp:expr>getDate()</xsp:expr>
30:  </xsl:template>
31:
32:  <xsl:template match="@*|node()" priority="-1">
33:   <xsl:copy>
34:    <xsl:apply-templates select="@*|node()"/>
35:   </xsl:copy>
36:  </xsl:template>
37:
38: </xsl:stylesheet>
```

As promised, the logicsheet is an XSLT stylesheet, so the beginning lines should look familiar: they declare all the namespaces, xsl, xsp, and now. There are three templates in the stylesheet. The first one, starting at line 8, matches the <xsp:page> element. It's the root stylesheet; it copies the <xsp:page> element and its attributes to the output XSP page. It also inserts the <xsp:structure> and <xsp:logic> elements from the previous version of date.xsp. After it inserts them, it applies the templates to the children of <xsp:page> (line 23). The second template, starting at line 28, handles the now:time element when it appears. This template replaces <now:time/> with the <xsp:expr> element that calls the getDate method defined in the <xsp:logic> element. The final template in the logicsheet is a catch-all template rule that recursively copies elements and their attributes, unless there is a more specific template for the element. In this logicsheet, the second template, which handles <now:time>, is more specific when the <now:time/> element is encountered. For every other descendent of <xsp:page>, this stylesheet copies what's there to the output XSP.

Applying Logicsheets to XSPs

You can use two methods to apply a logicsheet to an XSP. One is via the xml-logicsheet processing instruction you used in the previous example. The drawback to this approach is that every XSP that uses the logicsheet must include the PI. If an XSP uses more than one logicsheet, then you need two PIs. It starts to get hard to manage.

The other method of applying a logicsheet is to register it in Cocoon's list of built-in logicsheets. You do this by adding a <builtin-logicsheet> element to the proper section of the <markup-languages> element in the Cocoon configuration file, cocoon.xconf (which is usually in the WEB-INF directory of your Web application). The declaration for your logicsheet would look like this:

```
<builtin-logicsheet>
 <parameter name="prefix" value="now"/>
 <parameter name="uri"
            value=" http://sauria.com/cocoon/logicsheets/now "/>
 <parameter name="href"
            value="file:///logicsheets/logicsheet.now.xsl"/>
</builtin-logicsheet>
```

There are definitely some differences between the two approaches. When you register as a built-in logicsheet, you have to restart Cocoon if the contents of the logicsheet change. With the PI, Cocoon automatically notices that the logicsheet has changed and recompiles your XSPs. The other big difference is that you don't have any control over the order in which logicsheets are applied when you register as a built-in logicsheet. If you need to control the order, then you need to use the processing instruction.

Standard Logicsheets

Cocoon includes five major built-in logicsheets. We'll defer covering the session logicsheet until the next section on session handling, and we'll leave the treatment of the ESQL database logicsheet until the next chapter, which has a larger section on interacting with SQL databases. That leaves us with three logicsheets to discuss: The request logicsheet, the forms logicsheet, and the sendmail logicsheet.

Request Logicsheet

The request logicsheet allows you to access various aspects of the current request. You have access to most of the data in a Java HttpServletRequest object. To use the request logicsheet, you need to define a prefix for it. The suggested prefix is xsp-request, and the namespace uri is http://apache.org/xsp/request/2.0.

Each element in the request logicsheet can return data in at least two ways. The method used is controlled by an as attribute that can be used on any element from the logicsheet. If you leave out the as attribute, the logicsheet places the result inside an <xsp:expr> element so that the result can be used in a Java expression. If you provide the value "xml" for the as attribute, then the logicsheet makes the result the content of an element from the xsp-request namespace, according to the element you used.

Elements in the request logicsheet may accept or need additional information. The logicsheet allows you to provide this information either as an attribute or a child element. This does not apply to the as attribute you just learned about.

This logicsheet has a very large number of elements, due to the amount of information in an HttpServletRequest object. Rather than list them all here, we'll show you some of the most common ones:

- **<xsp-request:get-attribute>**—Lets you get the attribute with a specific name. As we mentioned earlier, you can supply this name as a name attribute or a <name> child element.
- **<xsp-request:get-header>**—Lets you get the HTTP header with a particular name. Use a name attribute or <name> element to specify the name.
- **<xsp-request:get-locale>**—Gives the preferred locale being advertised by the user agent.
- **<xsp-request:get-parameter>**—Lets you get named request parameters. If the parameter has more than one value, it returns only the first. If you want all the values, you need to use <xsp-request:get-parameter-values>. You specify the name via a name attribute or <name> child element.
- **<xsp-request:remove-attribute>**—Lets you remove an attribute from the request. You specify the name of the attribute via a name attribute or <name> child element.
- **<xsp-request:set-attribute>**—Lets you set a value for an attribute. You give the name of the attribute via a name attribute or <name> child element, and you supply the value as the content of the <xsp-request:set-attribute> element.

That should give you a flavor for the kinds of information you can get via the request logicsheet.

Forms Logicsheet

The forms logicsheet works together with the FormValidator action to let you validate the input values from an HTML form. To tell you how to use the logicsheet, we have to start with the FormValidator action.

The FormValidator action is in the class org.apache.cocoon.acting.FormValidatorAction and typically uses the name form-validator. To use this action with XSP, you need to make the XSP pipeline the child of a <map:act> element that uses the FormValidator action as its action. This ensures that the FormValidator executes and makes the results of its checking available to the XSP, and therefore the Forms logicsheet.

The FormValidator action uses a descriptor file to validate the contents of an HTML form. When you create a <map:act> element that uses the FormValidator, you also need to supply two parameters as its children. The first parameter is named descriptor, and its value is the URI of the descriptor file. The second parameter is named validate-set, and it specifies the name of the constraint set inside the descriptor file. This constraint set is used to perform the validation. Let's assume that the HTML form you're interested in looks like this—a form for entering the information related to a book:

```
<html>
 <head>
  <title>Book Input form</title>
 </head>
 <body>
  <form action="">
 Title <input type="text" name="title" /> <br />
 Author <input type="text" name="author" /> <br />
```

```
ISBN <input type="text" name="isbn" /> <br />
Month <input type="text" name="month" /> <br />
Year <input type="text" name="year" /> <br />
Publisher <input type="text" name="publisher" /> <br />
Address <input type="text" name="address" /> <br />
<input type="submit" value="Add Book" /> <br />
 </form>
</body>
</html>
```

The descriptor file for validating that form looks something like this:

```
<?xml version="1.0"?>
<root>
 <parameter name="title" type="string" nullable="no" />
 <parameter name="author" type="string" nullable="no" />
 <parameter name="isbn" type="string" nullable="no"
  matches-regex="\d{3}-\d{10}" />
 <parameter name="month" type="string" nullable="no"
  one-of="Jan|Feb|Mar|Apr|May|Jun|Jul|Aug|Sep|Oct|Nov|Dec" />
 <parameter name="year" type="long" nullable="no"
  min="1900" max="2100" />
 <parameter name="publisher" type="string" nullable="no" />
 <parameter name="address" type="string" nullable="no" />

 <constraint-set name="books">
  <validate name="title"/>
  <validate name="author"/>
  <validate name="isbn" />
  <validate name="month"/>
  <validate name="year"/>
  <validate name="publisher"/>
  <validate name="address"/>
 </constraint-set>
</root>
```

The entire descriptor is enclosed in a <root> element, which is divided into two sections. The first section isn't explicitly defined, but it consists of a sequence of <parameter> elements. The next section consists of one or more <constraint-set> elements.

The <parameter> elements are different from other parameter elements you've seen in Cocoon. These elements have a name attribute that's used to specify the name of a form parameter and a type attribute that's used to specify the type of data in the parameter. Acceptable values for the type attribute are "string", "long", and "double". You can also specify whether the parameter value may be null by using the nullable attribute (values are "yes" and "no"). If the value of the form parameter is null and you have provided a default attribute, then the value of that attribute becomes the value of the parameter.

In addition to controlling the type of the form parameters, you can also specify constraints on the values. You can use six constraint attributes on the values of parameters:

- **matches-regex**—The value of the form parameter must match the regular expression that is the value of this attribute.

- **one-of**—The value of the form parameter is one of the elements in the list of values that make up the value of this attribute. The items in the list are separated by the vertical bar (|).
- **min-len**—The value of this attribute specifies the minimum length of the form parameter.
- **max-len**—The value of this attribute specifies the maximum length of the form parameter.
- **min**—The value of this attribute specifies the minimum value of the form parameter.
- **max**—The value of this attribute specifies the maximum value of the form parameter.

Once you've defined all the parameters for a form, you can then create a <constraint-set> element that the FormValidator action uses to figure out which parameters to validate when it's invoked. A <constraint-set> element has a name attribute that's used to assign the name used by the FormValidator action. The content of a <constraint-set> is a sequence of <validate> elements. You must give a name attribute that specifies the name of a parameter to be validated. You can also specify one of the six constraint attributes. If you choose to do this, the value you supply overrides any constraint attributes specified by the <parameter> element that defined this parameter.

When the FormValidator action is executed, it returns null if the form parameters don't match the constraints in the specified <constraint-set>. Otherwise, it makes the value of the form parameters available to the sitemap. To access a form parameter from the sitemap, you use the {parameterName} notation.

You may be wondering what any of this has to do with XSP logicsheets. The form logicsheet knows how to interact with the results provided by the FormValidator action, so that your XSPs can do something intelligent based on the results of the validation. The namespace URI for the form logicsheet is http://apache.org/xsp/form-validator/2.0, and it's normally associated with the prefix xsp-formval.

There are varying levels at which you can use the elements from the FormValidator. If you're only interested in the results of the validation, you can use the <xsp-formval:on-ok> element. The content of the element is copied to the output XSP page if the form validated properly. You can supply a name attribute whose value is the name of a form parameter. In this case, the content of the element is copied through if the parameter named by the name attribute validated correctly. This allows you finer-grained control over the processing.

The next level of form logicsheet support allows you to ask questions about a particular parameter. The logicsheet defines a number of elements with the form <xsp-formval:is-??>, where the ?? stands for one of the constraint attribute tests. You need to specify a name attribute on these elements to indicate which parameter should be checked. These elements can be used where ever a boolean might appear in an <xsp:logic> tag. This means they can be used as the values for the conditional part of if/then/else statements. The <xsp-formval:is-??> elements are as follows:

- **<xsp-formval:is-ok>**—Return true if the parameter was validated successfully.
- **<xsp-formval:is-error>**—Return true if some error occurred.
- **<xsp-formval:is-null>**—Return true if the parameter was null but wasn't allowed to be.
- **<xsp-formval:is-toosmall>**—Return true if a numerical value was too small or the length of a string was too short.

- **<xsp-formval:is-toolarge>**—Return true if a numerical value was too large or the length of a string was too long.
- **<xsp-formval:nomatch>**—Return true if the string value didn't match the regular expression constraint.
- **<xsp-formval:is-notpresent>**—Return true if the named parameter didn't exist in the request.

At this level, you can also gain access to the Map of values returned by the action. The element <xsp-formval:results> gives the XSP a java.util.Map with the result values in it.

There is one last level involved in using the form logicsheet. The logicsheet allows you to query the contents of the descriptor file used by the FormValidator action. Among other things, this lets you access the actual constraint values specified in the parameter file so you can tell the user what the constraints on a particular parameter are. As a result, you can give an error message like *The year must be between 1900 and 2100.* To query the descriptor file, you use the <xsp-formval:descriptor> element. This element takes two attributes that correspond to the parameters passed to the FormValidator action. The name attribute contains the URI of the descriptor file you want to query, whereas the constraint-set attribute specifies the constraint set you're interested in. In the body of the <xsp-formval:descriptor> element, you can use the <xsp-formval:get-attribute> element to get any attribute of any parameter in the descriptor file. Use the parameter attribute to specify which parameter you're interested in, and use the nameattribute to specify the attribute of that parameter. To access the one-of attribute of the month parameter in the descriptor file you saw earlier, you'd use <xsp-formval:get-attribute parameter="month" name="one-of"/>.

Sendmail Logicsheet

The sendmail logicsheet allows you to send mail from an XSP using elements. Elements from the sendmail logicsheet use the namespace URI http://apache.org/cocoon/sendmail/1.0. The usual namespace prefix used for this logicsheet is sendmail.

You use the sendmail logicsheet by wrapping a series of sendmail elements inside a <sendmail :send-mail> element. The elements that are available are as follows:

- **<sendmail:smtphost>**—The host that's delivering the mail for you.
- **<sendmail:from>**—The e-mail address of the sender.
- **<sendmail:to>**—The e-mail address(es) of the recipient(s). May be a comma-separated list of e-mail addresses.
- **<sendmail:cc>**—The e-mail address(es) for the cc recipient(s). May be a comma-separated list of e-mail addresses.
- **<sendmail:bcc>**—The e-mail address(es) of the blind cc recipient(s). May be a comma-separated list of e-mail addresses.
- **<sendmail:subject>**—The subject of the message.
- **<sendmail:body>**—The body of the message.
- **<sendmail:charset>**—The character set for encoding the message (takes effect only if there are no attachments).

- **<sendmail:attachment>**—You may have zero or more of these elements. The <sendmail :attachment> element takes three attributes: name, which is the name of the attachment; mime-type, which gives the MIME media type of the attachment; and url, which gives a reference to the attachment content.
- **<sendmail:on-success>**—XML that is to be output if mail delivery is successful.
- **<sendmail:on-error>**—XML that is to be output if mail delivery fails. You can use the <sendmail:error-message/> element to obtain the text of the error message.

Sessions

Session management is an important part of Web applications. Because HTTP is a stateless protocol, there needs to be a way for the application to relate accesses from a particular user agent into a session. Cocoon's session functionality leverages the functionality of the Java Servlet API. Cocoon gives you different ways to handle session information in your Web application. In this section, we'll show you how to deal with sessions from XSPs and actions.

Sessions in XSP

You can work with sessions in XSPs by using the session logicsheet. This logicsheet provides you with access to the servlet HttpSession in an XSP-friendly manner. The namespace URI for this logicsheet is http://apache.org/xsp/session/2.0, and the usual prefix for it is xsp-session.

A session-aware XSP should declare the prefix for the session logicsheet and should also provide the create-session attribute on the <xsp:page> element. The value of this attribute should be set to "true", meaning that either an existing session should be retrieved or a new session should be created if no session exists. In addition, you can create a session at the sitemap level by setting the session attribute of the <map:redirect-to> element to "true".

Once you have set up the logicsheet and set the create-session attribute, you can use any of the elements from the session logicsheet to query or update values in the session. You can provide parameters to these elements via either an attribute or a child element of the same name. So, a name parameter can appear as either a name attribute or as a child <name> element. Elements that retrieve data from the session can retrieve it in one of two forms. By default, it's returned in a form suitable for embedding in an <xsp:expr> element. If you supply an as attribute whose value is set to "xml", then the data is marked up as elements from the xsp-session namespace. We refer to this as *asking for XML output*. Here are the elements you can use:

- **<xsp-session:get-attribute>**—Return the value of a session attribute. You specify a name parameter to tell which attribute to retrieve. If you ask for XML output, you get an <xsp-session:attribute> element with the attribute value as the content.
- **<xsp-session:get-attribute-names>**—Return the names of all the session attributes. If you ask for XML output, you get an <xsp-session:attribute-names> element that contains a sequence of <xsp-session:attribute-name> elements. The <xsp-session:attribute-name> elements contain a single attribute name as their content.
- **<xsp-session:set-attribute>**—Set or update the value of a session attribute. You supply a name parameter and supply the value as the content of the element.

- **<xsp-session:remove-attribute>**—Remove the named attribute from the session. You supply a name parameter whose value is the name of the attribute to remove.
- **<xsp-session:is-new>**—Return true if the session was just created. If you ask for XML output, you get an <xsp-session:is-new> element with the value as the content.
- **<xsp-session:invalidate>**—Invalidate the current session. Any data stored in the session is lost.
- **<xsp-session:get-id>**—Get the ID of the session. If you ask for XML output, you get an <xsp-session:id> element with the ID as the content.
- **<xsp-session:get-creation-time>**—Get the creation time of the session. If you ask for XML output, you get an <xsp-session:creation-time> element with the time as the content.
- **<xsp-session:get-last-accessed-time>**—Get the last time the session was accessed. If you ask for XML output, you get an <xsp-session:last-accessed-time> element with the time as the content.
- **<xsp-session:get-max-inactive-interval>**—Get the minimum time (in seconds) in between session requests before the server will cause the session object to expire. If you ask for XML output, you get an <xsp-session:max-inactive-interval> element with the time as the content.
- **<xsp-session:set-max-inactive-interval>**—Set the minimum time (in seconds) between session requests before the server will cause the session object to expire. You specify the new value via an interval attribute.
- **<xsp-session:encode-url>**—Encode a URL with the session ID. You supply an href attribute that contains the URL to be encoded.

As you can see, these elements allow you to manipulate most aspects of the session state.

Session Action

You can also use the session action to help manage the session state. The session action is in the class org.apache.cocoon.webapps.session.acting.SessionAction. It's normally named session. In comparison to the session logicsheet, the session action has fairly limited functionality: It's limited to creating and destroying sessions. To create a session, you create a <map:act type="session"/> element. That's it. This is equivalent to creating the following <map:act> element:

```
1: <map:act type="session">
2:  <map:paramater name="action" value="create"/>
3: </map:act>
```

To destroy a session, you change the value of the action parameter (in line 2) to "terminate" (by changing the value of the value attribute. You have some additional options when destroying a session: You can choose to destroy the session immediately, which is the default, or you can choose to destroy the session only if it's unused. This second option is selected by providing another <map:parameter> element:

```
<map:act type="session">
 <map:paramater name="action" value="create"/>
 <map:parameter name="mode" value="if-unused"/>
</map:act>
```

Cocoon Development

In this chapter, we'll take the Cocoon concepts you learned about in the previous chapter and apply them. We'll begin by looking at how to install and configure Cocoon. From there we'll go on to build a small database-driven Web application. We'll talk briefly about what is necessary to extend Cocoon with your own generators, transformers, and serializers. The chapter concludes with some practical tips and a few words on applications for Cocoon.

Installing and Configuring Cocoon

Starting with Cocoon 2.1, the Cocoon developers have decided to produce only a source code distribution. So, you have to download a source distribution and build it yourself. Fortunately, it's a pretty painless process. The first thing you need, as always, is a Cocoon build. These can be found at http://cocoon.apache.org/mirror.cgi. Click the link for the latest source distribution in the archive format of your choice (for the sake of keeping things concrete, we'll assume you're working with a Cocoon 2.1.1 build). There is a .zip file format for Windows-based machines and a .tar.gz format for Linux, UNIX, and Mac OS X.

Once you've downloaded the distribution, unpack it using an appropriate archiving tool. This should leave a directory called cocoon-2.1.1 in either the current directory or the directory you specified as the target for your archiving program. The contents of this directory are as follows:

- **Credits.txt**—Credits for included software.
- **DESKTOP.INI**—Folder icon customization file (for Microsoft Windows).
- **INSTALL.txt**—Basic installation instructions.
- **KEYS**—PGP Keys file.
- **README.txt**—Initial README file.

- **blocks.properties**—Prototype blocks configuration file.
- **build.bat**—Windows batch file for building Cocoon.
- **build.properties**—Prototype Ant build properties file.
- **build.sh**—Bourne shell script for building Cocoon.
- **build.xml**—Ant build file.
- **cli.xconf**—Configuration file for the Cocoon command-line processor.
- **cocoon.bat**—Windows batch file for running Cocoon with the embedded Jetty servlet engine.
- **cocoon.sh**—Bourne shell script for running Cocoon with embedded Jetty Servlet engine.
- **forrest.properties**—Build properties used by the Forrest system when building the Cocoon documentation.
- **gump.xml**—Gump build descriptor. Gump is the ASF's system for testing the dependencies between various Java projects.
- **legal**—Directory containing the license files for all third-party software incorporated into Cocoon.
- **lib**—Directory and subdirectories containing all the jars needed for Cocoon. The subdirectories are worth knowing about:
    - **core**—The core libraries needed by Cocoon.
    - **endorsed**—The libraries that need to go in the JDK 1.4 or Tomcat 4.1 endorsed directory.
    - **optional**—Optional libraries.
- **src**—The source code for Cocoon.
- **status.xml**—The Cocoon status file in XML format.
- **tools**—The tools needed to build and run Cocoon.

Now you're ready to begin the process of building Cocoon. The first step is to open a command prompt or shell window. You need to set the JAVA_HOME environment variable to be the path to your Java Development Kit (JDK). If you're using JDK 1.4, you need to upgrade the XML parser and XSLT engine that come with JDK 1.4. You need to create the %JAVA_HOME%\jre\lib\endorsed directory. (If you're using Tomcat, you should create the directory %TOMCAT_HOME%\common\endorsed, instead). Now, copy the files Xerces*.jar, xalan-*.jar, and xml-apis.jar from the lib/endorsed directory under the cocoon-2.1.1 directory into the directory you just created.

If you're an advanced user of Cocoon, you may want to alter the set of blocks (optional modules) that are compiled into Cocoon, or you may wish to change some of the build settings. You alter the set of blocks by copying the file blocks.properties into a file called local.blocks.properties and making the necessary changes. You change the build settings in a similar way by copying the file build.properties into a file named local.build.properties. The build properties control whether some modules get built; if this is your first time compiling Cocoon, you should leave these files alone and build all of Cocoon.

Next you'll build Cocoon from sources. Change your current working directory to the cocoon-2.1.1 directory and type "build" (Windows) or "./build.sh" (UNIX). Depending on how fast your machine is, you have time for a nice cup of coffee. The results of the build will be in a new subdirectory of cocoon-2.1.1 called build. This in turn contains two directories: The cocoon-2.1.1 directory contains all the jar and war files you need to install Cocoon, and the webapp directory contains a Java Web application that is set to run. It includes the Cocoon documentation and samples.

When you come back from your coffee break (and the compile has finished), you should be ready to run Cocoon. The easiest way to do this is to type "cocoon servlet" (Windows) or "./cocoon.sh servlet" (UNIX). Cocoon comes prepackaged with the Jetty servlet engine, so when you type this command, Jetty will start up and you'll be ready to go with Cocoon. To verify that things are working, point your Web browser at http://localhost:8888 to go to the beginning of the Cocoon documentation.

To install Cocoon in the application server of your choice, refer to the Cocoon documentation—there are too many configurations to discuss here. In general, you'll need to install the Cocoon Web application. You can do this either by taking the cocoon.war file from the build/cocoon-2.1.1 directory or by taking the build/webapp directory, depending on how your application server handles war files and Web application installations. The other major issue you'll run into when installing Cocoon is making sure you install the correct versions of Xerces and Xalan. These versions will be affected by the version of the JDK you're running as well as your application server's class-loading policy.

Configuring Cocoon

Cocoon's configuration is kept in configuration files. When you install Cocoon as a Web application, some aspects of the configuration (like initial URI mappings and various configuration variables) are controlled by the Web application deployment descriptor, which is found in the Web applications as WEB-INF/web.xml. This includes the location of the Cocoon configuration files, cocoon.xconf and logkit.xconf.

Cocoon uses Apache's Avalon component framework heavily. This is apparent in the use of Avalon's logging facility LogKit. The values of the logger attributes in a sitemap are the names of LogKit log targets. The names and behavior of these log targets are controlled in the file logkit.xconf. By default, this file is in the WEB-INF directory of the Cocoon Web application.

The primary Cocoon configuration file is cocoon.xconf, which usually resides in the WEB-INF directory of the Cocoon Web application. In this file, you specify sitemap input and output modules, source factories, entity resolution catalogs, XML and XSLT processor parameters, XSP configuration parameters, XSP logicsheets, database modules, database datasources, and configuration parameters for many Cocoon blocks and modules. If there is a configuration setting for it, it's probably in cocoon.xconf.

Cocoon uses the file cocoon.roles to separate the implementation of a role (like XML processor) from the class that implements it. The mapping of roles to actual Java classes is defined by the content of cocoon.roles. You can find this file in the directory src/java/org/apache/cocoon, under the main Cocoon distribution directory.

The last thing that you should remember about Cocoon configuration is that everything in Cocoon is driven by sitemaps. This means you'll almost certainly need to modify the top-level sitemap file once you begin working on your own applications on earnest.

Development Techniques

In this section, we'll focus on two major topics: how to get Cocoon to interact with a relational database, and how to tie together all the concepts we've discussed to get a Web application.

Database Access

Most interesting Web applications interact with a database system. The data retrieved from the database is used to generate the Web pages dynamically, and this data, which changes as users interact with it, makes the Web application interesting.

Cocoon provides two mechanisms for interacting with relational databases. First, you can use XSPs to generate XML data from a relational database by using the ESQL logicsheet, which allows you to embed SQL commands into your XSP pages. This allows you to generate reports and fill out forms with data from the database so that the data can be edited. Second, you can use actions. Cocoon contains two sets of database actions—you'll hear them referred to as the *original* database actions and the *modular* database actions. We'll focus on the modular database actions, because the Cocoon developers recommend that all new applications begin with them.

Getting a Connection

The first thing you need to do to work with a database in Cocoon is get a database connection. Cocoon leverages the Java DataBase Connectivity (JDBC) APIs and drivers to access the database. You need to download a JDBC driver for your database in order to get going. You should install the jar file(s) for this driver in the WEB-INF/lib directory of the Cocoon Web application. Cocoon needs to be told to load the database driver. You can do this by adding a load-class init-param entry to the Web application deployment descriptor (web.xml) found in WEB-INF/web.xml. The entry looks like this:

```
<init-param>
 <param-name>load-class</param-name>
 <param-value>org.hsqldb.jdbcDriver</param-value>
</init-param>
```

Supply the fully qualified name of your JDBC driver class as the init-param value. Here we're showing you the name of the driver for the Hypersonic SQL database that's included in the Cocoon distribution.

ESQL

Cocoon provides database access to XSPs via the built-in ESQL logicsheet. If you're going to use ESQL, you need to perform one additional database configuration step. The Cocoon configuration file cocoon.xconf deals with databases in the <datasources> element. You need to add a datasource entry for the database you want to access via ESQL. A datasource entry is a child of the <datasources> element called <jdbc>. Here's what a datasource entry might look like:

```
<jdbc name="hsql">
  <pool-controller max="10" min="5"/>
  <dburl>jdbc:hsqldb:hsql://localhost:9002</dburl>
  <user>johndoe</user>
  <password>sekret</password>
</jdbc>
```

You need to supply a name attribute for the <jdbc> element. This is the name of the connection and is the name you should give to ESQL when it needs a connection. The <pool-controller> element uses the max and min elements to specify the maximum and minimum number of JDBC driver connections to maintain using Cocoon's object pooling services. The <dburl> element gives the JDBC URL for accessing the machine, database, and database instance you're interested in. (Consult the documentation for your JDBC driver to find the correct value to place here.) The last two elements are the username and password required to access the database. Once you've created this entry and restarted Cocoon, you should be ready to go. Of course, this assumes you've already created the database tables you need and that you've inserted any data necessary for your application.

To use the ESQL logicsheet in your XSPs, you need its namespace URI, which is http://apache.org/cocoon/SQL/v2. You should define this on the <xsp:page> element and use the prefix esql. By default, the ESQL logicsheet is defined as a built-in logicsheet, so you shouldn't need an xml-stylesheet processing instruction to associate the logicsheet with your XSP.

To execute a SQL command in your XSP, insert an <esql:connection> element. This element contains all the information you need to execute a command. You can think of it as being divided into two sections: The first section describes how to get the database connection, and the second section executes the command.

Setting the Connection

There are two ways to specify the connection for an <esql:connection> element. If you've defined a datasource for your database in cocoon.xconf, you can use the <esql:pool> element and supply the name of the datasource as the content of the element. Otherwise, you can give all the information for the connection as the following sequence of elements:

- **<esql:driver>**—The fully qualified classname of the JDBC driver for the connection.
- **<esql:dburl>**—The JDBC URL that leads to the database you want to access.
- **<esql:username>**—The username needed to log in to the database.
- **<esql:password>**—The password needed to log in to the database.

With either method of describing the connection, you can control the commit behavior of the connection with an <esql:autocommit> element. If you set it to true (the default), the statement in the connection will be treated as a single transaction and committed. If you set it to false, the statement will be executed without the commit. This element is a direct child of <esql:connection>.

Specifying the SQL Statement

After you've specified the connection, you specify the statement you want executed. You do so with the <esql:execute-query> element. This element is a container for a sequence of elements. First, an <esql:query> element is used to specify the SQL statement. If the statement returns a result set, then you should provide an <esql:results> element. If the statement is an update, then you should provide an <esql:update-result> element instead of the <esql:results> element. If the statement is a stored procedure, then you should provide an <esql:call-results> element. You can provide an optional <esql:error-results> element to produce output if an error occurs. Let's look at each of these elements in detail.

The <esql:query> element takes a SQL statement as its content. If you want to have dynamically generated queries (let's say you want to generate the ORDER BY potion of a query), you can use the <esql:parameter> element to mark out a dynamic value. The content of the <esql:parameter> is then an <xsp:expr> element containing the code that computes the value for that portion of the query. When you use the <esql:parameter> element, the ESQL logicsheet uses JDBC PreparedStatements to execute the statement, which provides better protection against SQL injection attacks. If you need to dynamically generate portions of the query, then you can use <xsp:expr> to append a string to the content of <esql:query>; but be aware that this approach can post a security risk, especially if the data used in the <xsp:expr> element originated in the user agent.

Query Results

Once you've specified the statement to be executed, you need to describe what to do about the results. There are a number of choices. If the statement you executed is a query, then one possible result is a result set. The ESQL logicsheet provides you with the <esql:results> element as a way of formatting the result set. The child of <esql:results> is a mix of your own application-specific elements and elements taken from the <esql:namespace>. The ESQL elements let you mark the beginning and end of a row in the rowset as well as access the columns within a row. You enclose the elements that should make up a single row in the start and end tags of an <esql:row-results> element. Within this element are type-specific elements you use to retrieve the value of a column. Here's a list of those elements—each takes an attribute named column that specifies the column being accessed:

- **<esql:get-string>**—Get the column value as a string.
- **<esql:get-int>**—Get the column value as an integer.
- **<esql:get-short>**—Get the column value as a short.
- **<esql:get-long>**—Get the column value as a long.
- **<esql:get-double>**—Get the column value as a double.
- **<esql:get-float>**—Get the column value as a float.
- **<esql:get-boolean>**—Get the column value as a boolean.
- **<esql:get-date>**—Get the column value as a date. If there is a format attribute, use its value as a java.text.SimpleDateFormat format string and format the value with it.
- **<esql:get-time>**—Get the column value as a time. If there is a format attribute, use its value as a java.text.SimpleDateFormat format string and format the value with it.
- **<esql:get-timestamp>**—Get the column value as a timestamp. If there is a format attribute, use its value as a java.text.SimpleDateFormat format string and format the value with it.
- **<esql-get-ascii>**—Get the column value as a CLOB.
- **<esql:get-object>**—Get the column value as an object.
- **<esql:get-array>**—Get the column value as a java.sql.Array.
- **<esql:get-struct>**—Get the column value as a java.sql.Struct.
- **<esql:get-xml>**—Get the column value as XML.
- **<esql:is-null>**—Return true if the column value is null.

Other elements you can use as children of the <esql:row-result> element are as follows:

- **<esql:get-columns>**—Return a sequence of elements. Each element's name is the name of a column in the table.
- **<esql:get-column-name>**—Return the name of the column. The column attribute must be a number, not a name.
- **<esql:get-column-label>**—Return the label of the column. The column attribute must be a number, not a name.
- **<esql:get-column-type-name>**—Return the data type of the column. The column attribute must be a number, not a name.

You should also provide an <esql:no-results> element (at the same level as <esql:results>). The content of this element is output if the statement produces no results.

If your statement was an update statement, you need to provide <esql:update-results>. You provide your own content for this element. You can use the <esql:get-update-count> element as a child of <esql:update-results>. Doing so puts the number of updated rows into your XSP.

Errors

If an error occurs, the output is produced via an <esql:error-results> element. As usual, the child content of this element becomes the output for your XSP. You can use a few ESQL elements as children of <esql:error-result>:

- **<esql:get-message>**—Get the message from the exception that was thrown.
- **<esql:to-string>**—Convert the thrown exception to a String and insert that string in the output.
- **<esql:get-stacktrace>**—Copy the stacktrace of the thrown exception into the output.

Stored Procedures

The ESQL logicsheet also lets you call stored procedures. Doing this changes the contents of the <esql:execute-query> element. Instead of an <esql:query> child, you'll have an <esql:call> element. The content of this element is the stored procedure call. Some JDBC drivers use executeQuery rather than execute to invoke a stored procedure. If this is true of your JDBC driver, then you need to add a needs-query attribute to the <esql:call> element and set its value to "true".

You still use the <esql:parameter> element to supply the parameters for the stored procedure. Because stored procedure parameters have a direction (in, out, or inout), you can supply a direction attribute on an <esql:parameter> element. The value of this attribute is "in", "out", or "inout".

Stored procedures can return their results in a variety of ways. They can return a result set as the return parameter of the procedure invocation, or they can return several out parameter. If the procedure returns a result set via the return parameter, then you need to set the resultset-from-object attribute on <esql:call> to the value "1". You can then use the <esql:results> element to work with the results. You need to set the from-call attribute to the value "yes" on all the <esql:get-<type>/> elements. This tells them to get their values from the JDBC CallableStatement rather than the usual ResultSet.

If the stored procedure returns multiple out parameters, then you have two options for processing the results. If you only supply a single <esql:results> element, it will be reused for each out parameter, but this assumes that all the out parameters are result sets. If the output parameters are a sequence whose elements can be either result sets or update counts, then you can supply multiple <esql:results> and <esql:update-results> elements. You place them in the same order as the out parameters, so that an <esql:results> corresponds to a resultset out parameter and an <esql:update-results> corresponds to an update count out parameter. You can pair the <esql:results> or <esql:update-results> with an <esql:no-results> element. This functionality works only if you create a child element of <esql:connection> named <esql:allow-multiple-results> and set its content to "yes".

Example

Here's an example of the ESQL logicsheet in action. Let's assume you have a database of information on book publishers and you want to extract all the names and addresses:

```
 1: <?cocoon-process type="xsp"?>
 2:
 3: <xsp:page
 4:   language="java"
 5:   xmlns:xsp="http://apache.org/xsp"
 6:   xmlns:esql="http://apache.org/cocoon/SQL/v2">
 7:  <page>
 8:   <esql:connection>
 9:    <esql:pool>books</esql:pool>
10:    <esql:execute-query>
11:     <esql:query>SELECT name, address FROM publishers</esql:query>
12:     <esql:results>
13:      <table>
14:       <esql:row-results>
15:        <tr>
16:         <td><esql:get-string column="name"/></td>
17:         <td><esql:get-string column="address"/></td>
18:        </tr>
19:       </esql:row-results>
20:      </table>
21:     </esql:results>
22:     <esql:no-results>
23:      <table/>
24:     </esql:no-results>
25:    </esql:execute-query>
26:   </esql:connection>
27:  </page>
28: </xsp:page>
```

In line 9, you use <esql:pool> to set up the JDBC connection. The query you're executing is simple and straightforward (line 11). The real meat is in lines 12-21, where the results are described, and lines 22-24, where the non-results are described. Notice how the content for <esql:results> has elements like <table>, <tr>, and <td> interspersed with elements like <esql:row-results> and <esql:get-string>. For the non-results in lines 22-24, you output an empty table element.

The XML produced by this XSP looks like this:

```
<?xml version="1.0" encoding="UTF-8"?>
<page xmlns:xsp="http://apache.org/xsp"
      xmlns:xspdoc="http://apache.org/cocoon/XSPDoc/v1"
      xmlns:esql="http://apache.org/cocoon/SQL/v2">
    <table>
      <tr>
       <td>Addison-Wesley</td>
       <td>New York, New York</td>
      </tr>
      <tr>
       <td>Addison-Wesley</td>
       <td>Reading, Massachusetts</td>
      </tr>
      <tr>
       <td>John Wiley and Sons</td>
       <td>New York, New York</td>
      </tr>
    </table>
</page>
```

The only editing we performed on the file was to format the namespace declarations so they fit nicely onto lines.

Database Actions

Now let's look at the other way of dealing with a SQL database from Cocoon: the modular database actions. The database actions in general work on a simple proposition. They look for parameters via an input module and use a descriptor table to map the parameter values onto a SQL table or tables. Each database action represents a single operation on a database table: an add (insert), delete, or update. So, once the parameter mapping is done, you already know what operation is to be performed, and you execute the appropriate SQL statement.

The modular database actions use Cocoon's input and output modules to decouple the handling of input and output parameters from the processing of the mapped parameters and the SQL statement. Cocoon provides input modules that let you obtain data from an HttpServletRequest, which makes it easy to pick the parameter values out of a request and pass them to the action for execution. We'll look at the mapping descriptor file, examine the supported actions, and work through a simple example.

The Descriptor File

The descriptor file for the database is an XML file that has three sections. The root element of the file is named <root> by convention, but you can name it anything you choose. The first section of the file is the single element <connection>, whose content is the name of a database source that has been defined in the cocoon.xconf file.

The second section of the file is a sequence of <table> elements. The table element has a name attribute and an optional alias attribute. The name attribute is the name of the database table to which this element corresponds. The alias attribute allows you to specify an additional name for this table, and you can use this additional name anywhere you can use the name. You can create a shorter name for the table or use the alias only for certain operations on the table.

The <table> element has two children: <keys> and <values>. The <keys> element contains a sequence of <key> elements, which are supposed to represent the key columns in the table. A <key> element has three attributes: name is the name of the column in the table, type is the type of the column in the table, and autoincrement is true if the column is an autoincrement column. You can use the following types as values of the type attribute:

- string
- big-decimal, byte, double, float, int, long, short
- boolean
- date, time, time-stamp
- ascii, blob, binary, clob
- array, object, row

Each <key> element can have zero or more child <mode> elements. A <mode> element has a name attribute that specifies the name of the input module to consult in order to handle this <key>. The <mode> element also takes a type attribute. There are two mode types: autoincr (autoincrement) and others (for all other operations). There is also a universal mode name, all, which matches any mode.

The <values> element contains a <value> element for each column of the table that isn't a key column. A <value> element takes a name attribute that determines the column in the table and a type element that specifies the type of the column. It uses the same type names as the <key> element. <value> elements can also have nested <mode> elements.

The third and final section of the descriptor file is a sequence of <table-set> elements. A <table-set> element has a sequence of <table> elements as children. This list of tables specifies a group of tables to be operated on as a unit. Each <table> element has a name attribute whose value must be a table that was declared by a <table> element in the second section. A <table> element can also have an others-mode attribute, which can take the value of any <mode> type that was used in a <key> or <value> element for that table. It signifies that the table is using that mode, and that only those elements with child <mode> elements corresponding to that mode type will be affected.

Here's a simple descriptor file:

```
 1: <?xml version="1.0"?>
 2: <root>
 3:  <connection>books</connection>
 4:
 5:  <table name="publishers" alias="publishers">
 6:   <keys>
 7:    <key name="id" type="int" autoincrement="true">
 8:     <mode name="auto" type="autoincr"/>
 9:    </key>
10:   </keys>
11:   <values>
12:    <value name="name" type="string"/>
13:    <value name="address" type="string"/>
14:   </values>
15:  </table>
16:
17:  <table-set name="publishers">
18:    <table name="publishers"/>
19:  </table-set>
20: </root>
```

You can see the <connection> element in line 3, the <table> element in lines 5-15, and the <table-set> element in lines 17-20. Notice that in line 8, you use a <mode> element to mark the id column as being an autoincrementing column.

The Modular Actions

The modular database actions are all in the package org.apache.cocoon.acting.modular. There are five actions:

- **DatabaseAddAction**—This action inserts one or more new rows into one or more tables.
- **DatabaseDeleteAction**—This action deletes one or more rows from one or more tables.
- **DatabaseQueryAction**—This action executes an arbitrary query, including update queries. You associate the queries with tables by adding a <queries> child to the <table> element before the <keys> element. The children of <queries> are <query> elements. These elements take a mode attribute whose value is used to select the query when the action is executed. The query is the content of the <query> element. You can use the ? placeholder for a PreparedStatement in the query. The data that's retrieved is available to the sitemap as parameters.
- **DatabaseSelectAction**—This action selects one or more rows from one or more tables. The data that's retrieved is available to the sitemap as parameters.
- **DatabaseUpdateAction**—This action updates one or more row in one or more tables.

You need to declare the modular database actions in the <map:actions> section of your sitemap before you can use them. When you use one of the modular database actions, you need to supply a <map:parameter> child element that specifies the table-set the action should operate on. The actual input parameters for the action are delivered by a Cocoon input module. By default, this data comes from the request parameters.

Example

Here's a simple example that combines the list-pubs.xsp you saw as the ESQL example with the use of the modular database actions to perform insertion on the database. It's a common strategy to use an ESQL XSP to generate listings of data (using SELECT and so forth) and to use the modular database actions to process the modification operations such as insertion, deletion, and updates. The modular actions make it easy to take form parameters and use them to modify the contents of database tables.

Everything in Cocoon starts with the sitemap, so here's the sitemap file:

```
<?xml version="1.0" encoding="UTF-8"?>
<map:sitemap xmlns:map="http://apache.org/cocoon/sitemap/1.0">
 <map:components>
  <map:actions>
   <map:action name="mod-db-add"
    src="org.apache.cocoon.acting.modular.DatabaseAddAction">
    <descriptor>database.xml</descriptor>
    <throw-exception>true</throw-exception>
   </map:action>

   <map:action name="req-params"
    src="org.apache.cocoon.acting.RequestParameterExistsAction"/>
  </map:actions>
 </map:components>

 <map:pipelines>

  <map:pipeline>

    <map:match pattern="list-pubs.xsp">
     <map:generate type="serverpages" src="list-pubs.xsp"/>
      <map:transform src="form.xslt">
      <map:parameter name="contextPath"
                     value="{request:contextPath}"/>
     </map:transform>
     <map:serialize/>
    </map:match>

    <map:match pattern="add-pub">
     <map:generate type="file" src="add-pub.xml"/>
     <map:transform src="form.xslt"/>
     <map:serialize/>
    </map:match>

    <map:match pattern="form">
     <map:act type="req-params">
      <map:parameter name="parameters"
       value="add-publisher publishers.name publishers.address"/>
      <map:act type="mod-db-add">
       <map:parameter name="table-set" value="publishers"/>
      </map:act>
     </map:act>
     <map:redirect-to uri="list-pubs.xsp" />
    </map:match>
```

```
45:
46:    </map:pipeline>
47:
48:  </map:pipelines>
49:
50: </map:sitemap>
```

In the <map:actions> section (lines 4-13), you declare two actions. The first (lines 5-9) is the modular database action for adding rows to tables, org.apache.cocoon.acting.modular.DatabaseAction. This action needs a few parameters, which appear as child elements. The <descriptor> element tells the action where to find the database descriptor file used by all the modular actions. This example uses the descriptor file we showed you in the section on the descriptor file. To make debugging a little easier, you set the <throw-exception> parameter to true.

In lines 11-12, you also declare the org.apache.cocoon.acting.RequestParameterExistsAction. This action checks to make sure a particular set of request parameters exists. This is a concise stand-in for using the FormValidation action.

After the components are declared, all you have left is the pipelines. You're declaring multiple pipelines within a single <map:pipeline> element using multiple <map:match> elements. Each <map:match> element controls a distinct pipeline. By looking at the pattern attributes of the <map:match> elements, you can see how the sitemap's URI space is partitioned. This sitemap processes three URIs: list-pubs.xml, add-pub, and form.

The pipeline for list-pubs.xsp (lines 20-27) is straightforward. It uses the XSP serverpages generator to make list-pubs.xsp the generator for the pipeline. The XSLT stylesheet form.xslt is used to convert the output of list-pubs.xsp into HTML, which is then serialized by the default (HTML) serializer.

The URI add-pub takes the user's browser to a form they can use to add a new publisher to the database (the pipeline is on lines 29-33). This form is described by an XML file, add-pub.xml, that lives in the same directory as the sitemap. You use the file generator to scoop up this file and send it into the pipeline. The XML file goes through form.xslt to become HTML, which again is output using the default serializer.

The last URI, form, is the URI for the input form's action. When the user clicks the Add Publisher button in the HTML version of add-pub.xml, they are sent to this pipeline (lines 35-44). The first thing that happens in this pipeline is that the req-param action is executed. The <map:parameter> for this action says that the parameters add-publisher, publishers.name, and publishers.address must all be present in the request. If they are, then the mod-db-add action is executed. This is the modular database action for adding to the database. Its <map:parameter> says that it should use the publishers table-set, which is defined in the database.xml file. The request parameters publishers.name and publishers.address contain the values for the corresponding columns in that table-set and are used to perform an insert on the database. After the insert has been performed, the pipeline redirects the user's browser to the list-pubs.xsp URI so they can see a display of the new publisher entry.

Let's look at a few pieces of glue. Here's the content of add-pub.xml. You can see that it looks like a subset of HTML. There's not a lot of point in defining a completely new vocabulary when most of what you're doing involves HTML—it's easier to be able to insert HTML elements into the page's XML form and let the stylesheet take care of doing the formatting of the HTML:

```
<page>
 <p>
  Please enter the name and address of the new publisher:
 </p>
 <form action="form">
Name:  <input type="text" name="publishers.name"/>
  <br />
Publisher:  <input type="text" name="publishers.address"/>
  <br />
  <br />
  <input type="submit"
   name="add-publisher" value="Add publisher"/>
 </form>
</page>
```

The big thing going on in add-pub.xml is the <form>. Here's where you see all the pieces of the sitemap tied together. The action attribute of the <form> element directs the user's browser to the pipeline that does the work of adding the new publisher to the database. The text <input> elements are named to match the columns in the table to be inserted into, so that the modular database add action can pick up the values from the form submit request. The name attribute of the <submit> element provides the final form parameter the req-param action is looking for.

Here's form.xslt, the simple stylesheeet we're using:

```
 1: <?xml version="1.0"?>
 2:  <xsl:stylesheet version="1.0"
 3:    xmlns:xsl="http://www.w3.org/1999/XSL/Transform">
 4:
 5:   <xsl:template match="page">
 6:    <html>
 7:     <head></head>
 8:     <body>
 9:      <xsl:apply-templates/>
10:     </body>
11:    </html>
12:   </xsl:template>
13:
14:   <xsl:template match="@*|node()" priority="-1">
15:    <xsl:copy>
16:     <xsl:apply-templates select="@*|node()"/>
17:    </xsl:copy>
18:   </xsl:template>
19:
20: </xsl:stylesheet>
```

A default template (lines 14-18) copies the contents and attributes of an element into the output document unless there's a more specific template in the stylesheet. The stylesheet includes only one other template (lines 5-12), and that's for handling the <page> element, which is the root element of the add-forms.xml file. This template rule creates an HTML template and then invokes <xsl:apply-templates/> to process the children of <page>, which are copied into the output HTML document verbatim thanks to the default template.

Simple Application

In this section we'll look at using Cocoon to create a database-driven application. We won't use every Cocoon concept we've talked about, but we'll use quite a few. The application provides the following functionality:

- Add a new book.
- Add a new book.publisher.
- List all the books. From the listing, you can edit a book or delete a book.
- List all the book publishers. From the listing, you can edit a publisher or delete a publisher.

Database Table Definitions

This application is based on the books schema we've been using throughout this book. This time, you'll translate it into a set of database tables and build a simple book list management program. The first thing you need, then, is a set of database tables. Let's use the Hypersonic SQL database that comes built into the Cocoon distribution, for convenience. Because publishers publish many books, you'll break out the publisher information from the book information and refer to it via a foreign key. That leaves you with the following two tables; both use Hypersonic SQL's IDENTITY keyword to obtain autoincrementing behavior for row IDs:

```
CREATE TABLE publishers(
 id IDENTITY,
 name VARCHAR,
 address VARCHAR
)

CREATE TABLE books(
 id IDENTITY,
 author VARCHAR,
 title VARCHAR,
 isbn VARCHAR,
 month VARCHAR,
 year INTEGER,
 pub_id INTEGER
)
```

Sample Data Set

You also need some data, so you'll execute the following set of SQL statements against the database. You can do this by obtaining a standalone Hypersonic SQL distribution (http://hsqldb.sourceforge.net) and using the DatabaseManager class to get a command-line interface to the database. Be sure to connect with the correct server parameters (you can get them from the JDBC entry, explained later):

```
INSERT INTO publishers
VALUES(1,'Addison-Wesley','New York, New York')

INSERT INTO publishers
VALUES(2,'Addison-Wesley','Reading, Massachusetts')

INSERT INTO publishers
```

```
VALUES(3,'Wrox','Indianapolis, Indiana')

INSERT INTO books
VALUES(1,'Theodore W. Leung', Professional XML Development with
Apache Tools',
'0-7645-4355-5','October',2003,3)

INSERT INTO books
VALUES(2,'Joshua Bloch','Effective Java','0-201-31005-
8','August',2001,1)

INSERT INTO books
VALUES(3,' Erich Gamma, Richard Helm, Ralph Johnson, John Vlissides
','Design Patterns','0-201-63361-2','October',1994,2)
```

cocoon.xconf

Once you've created the tables, you're ready to tell Cocoon about the database. To do this, you need to create a <jdbc> element that's a child of the <datasources> element in WEB-INF/cocoon.xconf. Here's the entry to add (assuming you haven't altered your Cocoon configuration too much):

```
<jdbc name="books">
 <pool-controller max="10" min="5"/>
 <dburl>jdbc:hsqldb:hsql://localhost:9002</dburl>
 <user>sa</user>
 <password/>
</jdbc>
```

database.xml

You'll use a combination of ESQL logicsheets and the modular database actions to get the job done. The ESQL XSPs query information from the database and format it into HTML forms, while the modular database actions take care of all insert, update, and delete behaviors. To use the modular actions, you need a database descriptor file, database.xml. This file is an extension of the one you used in the example for the modular actions. The <table> and <table-set> elements for publishers are unchanged from that version, but the <table> and <table-set> elements for the books table are new. Nothing fancy is going on in either set of entries, though. The mode of the ID columns is set for autoincrement, but that's about all:

```
<?xml version="1.0"?>
<root>
 <connection>books</connection>

 <table name="publishers" alias="publishers">
  <keys>
   <key name="id" type="int" autoincrement="true">
    <mode name="auto" type="autoincr"/>
   </key>
  </keys>
  <values>
   <value name="name" type="string"/>
   <value name="address" type="string"/>
  </values>
```

```
  </table>

  <table name="books" alias="books">
   <keys>
    <key name="id" type="int" autoincrement="true">
      <mode name="auto" type="autoincr"/>
    </key>
   </keys>
   <values>
    <value name="author" type="string"/>
    <value name="title" type="string"/>
    <value name="isbn" type="string"/>
    <value name="month" type="string"/>
    <value name="year" type="int"/>
    <value name="pub_id" type="int"/>
   </values>
  </table>

  <table-set name="publishers">
   <table name="publishers"/>
  </table-set>

  <table-set name="books">
   <table name="books"/>
  </table-set>
</root>
```

sitemap.xmap

As always, understanding the sitemap is essential to understanding how the application works. In the <components> section of this sitemap, you define three of the modular database actions: add, delete, and update. You also use the RequestParameterExistsAction (lines 23-25) to verify that the necessary parameters are passed to the database actions. The remainder of the sitemap is the pipeline section, which is devoted to splitting out responsibility for the Web application's URI space. Four match clauses are used to partition the URI space:

- ""—The empty URI, which corresponds to accessing the top of the space for this sitemap, redirects to the URI index.xml (lines 32-34).
- ***.xml**—Any URI that ends with XML is processed by looking for a file whose name matches the *.xml part of the URI, processing that file with the XSLT stylesheet form.xslt, and serializing the results as HTML. There are such files: index.xml and add-pub.xml. The file index.xml creates a top-level menu that can be used to perform some of the application functions. The file add-pub.xml implements the form that's used to add a new publisher.
- ***.xsp**—Any URI that ends with .xsp is an XSP and is processed using the serverpages generator. The resulting XML is also transformed using form.xslt and rendered as HTML. The application includes five XSPs:
    - add-book.xsp implements the form used to add a new book.
    - list-books.xsp generates a listing of all the books in the database.
    - list-publishers.xsp generates a listing of all the publishers in the database.

- ❑ edit-books.xsp implements the form used to edit a book.
- ❑ edit-publisher.xsp implements the form used to edit a publisher.

- ❑ **.*book.* | .*publisher.***—Any URI that contains the word book or publisher is directed into this pipeline (lines 51-104). The pipeline uses the regexp matcher instead of the wildcard matcher to accomplish this.

The pipeline consists of a guarded set of database action invocations. Each invocation is guarded by a call to the req-params action, which is used to ensure that the correct set of parameters for each action is present. This allows all the actions to go through the pipeline, but only the one that is relevant is executed. The key is to note that the first parameter in every request parameter check is the name of the operation being performed. If the guard is triggered (by having the right operation name and all the table parameters), then the modular database action executes. The actions are told which table set to use in order to perform the right operation. The pipeline ends by returning the user to the main menu via a redirect (line 103).

Here's the code for the sitemap:

```
 1: <?xml version="1.0" encoding="UTF-8"?>
 2: <map:sitemap xmlns:map="http://apache.org/cocoon/sitemap/1.0">
 3:  <map:components>
 4:   <map:actions>
 5:    <map:action name="mod-db-add"
 6:     src="org.apache.cocoon.acting.modular.DatabaseAddAction">
 7:     <descriptor>database.xml</descriptor>
 8:     <throw-exception>true</throw-exception>
 9:    </map:action>
10:
11:    <map:action name="mod-db-delete"
12:     src="org.apache.cocoon.acting.modular.DatabaseDeleteAction">
13:     <descriptor>database.xml</descriptor>
14:     <throw-exception>false</throw-exception>
15:    </map:action>
16:
17:    <map:action name="mod-db-update"
18:     src="org.apache.cocoon.acting.modular.DatabaseUpdateAction">
19:     <descriptor>database.xml</descriptor>
20:     <throw-exception>false</throw-exception>
21:    </map:action>
22:
23:    <map:action name="req-params"
24:     src="org.apache.cocoon.acting.RequestParameterExistsAction"/>
25:   </map:actions>
26:  </map:components>
27:
28:  <map:pipelines>
29:
30:   <map:pipeline>
31:
32:    <map:match pattern="">
33:     <map:redirect-to uri="index.xml"/>
34:    </map:match>
```

```

    <map:match pattern="*.xml">
     <map:generate type="file" src="{1}.xml"/>
     <map:transform src="form.xslt"/>
     <map:serialize/>
    </map:match>

    <map:match pattern="*.xsp">
     <map:generate type="serverpages" src="{1}.xsp"/>
      <map:transform src="form.xslt">
      <map:parameter name="contextPath"
                     value="{request:contextPath}"/>
     </map:transform>
     <map:serialize/>
    </map:match>

    <map:match type="regexp" pattern=".*book.*|.*publisher.*">
     <map:act type="req-params">
      <map:parameter name="parameters"
       value="add-publisher publishers.name publishers.address"/>
      <map:act type="mod-db-add">
       <map:parameter name="table-set" value="publishers"/>
      </map:act>
     </map:act>

     <map:act type="req-params">
      <map:parameter name="parameters"
       value="add-book books.author books.title books.isbn
              books.month books.year books.pub_id"/>
      <map:act type="mod-db-add">
       <map:parameter name="table-set" value="books"/>
      </map:act>
     </map:act>

     <map:act type="req-params">
      <map:parameter name="parameters"
       value="delete-publisher publishers.id"/>
      <map:act type="mod-db-delete">
       <map:parameter name="table-set" value="publishers"/>
      </map:act>
     </map:act>

     <map:act type="req-params">
      <map:parameter name="parameters"
       value="delete-book books.id"/>
      <map:act type="mod-db-delete">
       <map:parameter name="table-set" value="books"/>
      </map:act>
     </map:act>

     <map:act type="req-params">
      <map:parameter name="parameters"
       value="update-publisher publishers.name
              publishers.address"/>
```

```
      <map:act type="mod-db-update">
       <map:parameter name="table-set" value="publishers"/>
      </map:act>
     </map:act>

     <map:act type="req-params">
      <map:parameter name="parameters"
       value="update-book books.author books.title books.isbn
              books.month books.year books.pub_id"/>
      <map:act type="mod-db-update">
       <map:parameter name="table-set" value="books"/>
      </map:act>
     </map:act>

     <map:redirect-to uri="index.xml"/>
    </map:match>

  </map:pipeline>

 </map:pipelines>

</map:sitemap>
```

index.xml

The form.xslt stylesheet assumes that most of the content of the input XML is close to HTML and that most of it will pass right through. In the case of index.xml, a message gives the user instructions, and some links lead to forms for performing operations. The <page> element is transformed into the HTML boilerplate:

```
<page>
 <p>
  Please select the operation you want to perform:
 </p>
 <a href="add-book.xsp">Add a book</a> <br />
 <a href="add-pub.xml">Add a publisher</a> <br />
 <a href="list-books.xsp">Show books</a> <br />
 <a href="list-publishers.xsp">Show publishers</a> <br />
</page>
```

add-pub.xml

This is a simple form that allows the user to enter the name and address of a publisher. Note that the form action is add-publisher-action, which doesn't refer to a file. It's a URI that falls into the URI space handled by the action pipeline. The names of the text <input> elements correspond to columns in the publishers table, and the name of the submit <input> element provides the operation name for the action pipeline. When the user clicks Submit, the operation name and the table parameter are sent to the action pipeline, where they're picked up by the correct action (the operation name check ensures this):

```
<page>
 <p>
  Please enter the name and address of the new publisher:
 </p>
```

```
 <form action="add-publisher-action">
Name:  <input type="text" name="publishers.name"/>
  <br />
Publisher:  <input type="text" name="publishers.address"/>
  <br />
  <br />
  <input type="submit"
   name="add-publisher" value="Add publisher"/>
 </form>
</page>
```

list-publishers.xsp

List-publishers.xsp uses ESQL to return a result table that includes all the publisher entries in the database. It's a straightforward application of the ESQL logicsheet. The one tricky thing going on is the use of an extra table column (lines 23-42) to handle the edit and delete functionality:

```
 1: <?cocoon-process type="xsp"?>
 2:
 3: <xsp:page
 4:   language="java"
 5:   xmlns:xsp="http://apache.org/xsp"
 6:   xmlns:esql="http://apache.org/cocoon/SQL/v2">
 7:  <page>
 8:   <esql:connection>
 9:    <esql:pool>books</esql:pool>
10:    <esql:execute-query>
11:     <esql:query>
12:      SELECT id, name, address FROM publishers
13:     </esql:query>
14:     <esql:results>
15:      <table border="1" cellspacing="0">
16:       <tr>
17:        <td>Name</td><td>Address</td>
18:       </tr>
19:       <esql:row-results>
20:        <tr>
21:         <td><esql:get-string column="name"/></td>
22:         <td><esql:get-string column="address"/></td>
23:         <td>
24:          <form action="edit-publisher.xsp">
25:           <input type="hidden" name="publishers.id">
26:            <xsp:attribute name="value">
27:             <esql:get-int column="id"/>
28:            </xsp:attribute>
29:           </input>
30:           <input type="submit"
31:            name="edit-publisher" value="edit"/>
32:          </form>
33:          <form action="delete-publisher-action">
34:           <input type="hidden" name="publishers.id">
35:            <xsp:attribute name="value">
36:             <esql:get-int column="id"/>
37:            </xsp:attribute>
```

```
            </input>
            <input type="submit"
             name="delete-publisher" value="delete"/>
           </form>
          </td>
         </tr>
        </esql:row-results>
       </table>
      </esql:results>
      <esql:no-results>
       <table/>
      </esql:no-results>
     </esql:execute-query>
    </esql:connection>
   </page>
  </xsp:page>
```

The editing function is handled by embedding a form that has a hidden input field whose value is the ID of the publisher in that row of the result table. When the user submits the edit form, the publisher ID is sent to edit-publisher.xsp, which takes care of the user interface for changing the form data.

The deleting function is implemented much the same way, but the form action doesn't go to another page the way it does for editing. Instead, the delete form action is another of the URIs, delete-publisher-action, that matches the action pipeline. The publisher's ID is passed to the action along with the delete-publisher command name.

edit-book.xsp

The edit-book.xsp file is a combination of ESQL and modular actions. The page uses the ESQL logicsheet to bring up a form whose values are already filled in, so the user can edit them. To do this, it takes the publisher ID that was passed as a form parameter (line 20) and uses it in the WHERE clause of the SQL query (lines 18-20). The ESQL elements are mixed in with the form elements to produce the filled-in form; you use the <xsp:attribute> element to generate the value attribute on the <input> elements, which is how the filled-in values get into the form:

```
 1: <?cocoon-process type="xsp"?>
 2:
 3: <xsp:page
 4:   language="java"
 5:   xmlns:xsp="http://apache.org/xsp"
 6:   xmlns:esql="http://apache.org/cocoon/SQL/v2"
 7:   xmlns:xsp-request="http://apache.org/xsp/request/2.0">
 8:
 9:  <page>
10:   <p>
11:    Please change the name and address of the publisher:
12:   </p>
13:   <form action="update-publisher-action">
14:    <esql:connection>
15:     <esql:pool>books</esql:pool>
16:     <esql:execute-query>
17:      <esql:query>
18: SELECT name, address
```

```
FROM publishers
WHERE id = <xsp-request:get-parameter name="publishers.id"/>
     </esql:query>
     <esql:results>
      <esql:row-results>
       <input type="hidden" name="publishers.id">
        <xsp:attribute name="value">
         <xsp-request:get-parameter name="publishers.id"/>
        </xsp:attribute>
       </input>

Name:
       <input type="text" name="publishers.name">
        <xsp:attribute name="value">
         <esql:get-string column="name"/>
        </xsp:attribute>
       </input>
       <br />
Publisher:
       <input type="text" name="publishers.address">
        <xsp:attribute name="value">
         <esql:get-string column="address"/>
        </xsp:attribute>
       </input>
       <br />
       <br />
       <input type="submit"
        name="update-publisher" value="Edit publisher"/>
      </esql:row-results>
     </esql:results>
    </esql:execute-query>
   </esql:connection>
  </form>
 </page>
</xsp:page>
```

This form has been somewhat pretty-printed for presentation in the book, which has introduced some spaces into the <xsp:attribute> elements. The real versions of these files don't contain those spaces.

The form's fields have the same names as the corresponding columns in the publishers table. The submit <input> element provides an operation name, and the form action (update-publisher-action) is set up to funnel that information to the action pipeline in the sitemap to perform the update.

The pages for the publisher side show the basic idea of how ESQL logicsheet elements, form actions, modular database actions, and the sitemap collaborate to make adding, listing, editing, and deleting data quite easy. The pages for the book side show how to achieve more complicated user interface effects using the same approach.

add-book.xsp

This form is similar to the add form for publishers. There are <input> fields for every column in the book table, except pub_id. The user interface for this form presents a drop-down list of all the publishers so the user can select one and have the interface figure out which ID to put in the pub_id column.

So, in addition to the regular form logic, an ESQL logicsheet query (lines 31-46) retrieves the ID and name for each publisher in the database and uses that information to build a drop-down menu of publisher names. The <option> element's value attribute is set to the publisher's ID (lines 38-40), and its content is the name of the publisher.

Note again the name of the form action (add-book-action) and the name of the submit <input> element (add-book), which are used to direct the form submission through the action pipeline to add the book:

```
 1: <?cocoon-process type="xsp"?>
 2:
 3: <xsp:page
 4:   language="java"
 5:   xmlns:xsp="http://apache.org/xsp"
 6:   xmlns:esql="http://apache.org/cocoon/SQL/v2">
 7:
 8:  <page>
 9:   <p>
10:   Please enter the information on the new book:
11:   </p>
12:   <form action="add-book-action">
13: Author:
14:    <input type="text" name="books.author"/>
15:    <br />
16: Title:
17:    <input type="text" name="books.title"/>
18:    <br />
19: ISBN:
20:    <input type="text" name="books.isbn"/>
21:    <br />
22: Month:
23:    <input type="text" name="books.month"/>
24:    <br />
25: Year:
26:    <input type="text" name="books.year"/>
27:    <br />
28:    <br />
29: Publisher:
30:    <select name="books.pub_id">
31:     <esql:connection>
32:      <esql:pool>books</esql:pool>
33:      <esql:execute-query>
34:       <esql:query>SELECT id, name FROM publishers</esql:query>
35:       <esql:results>
36:        <esql:row-results>
37:         <option>
38:          <xsp:attribute name="value">
39:           <esql:get-int column="id"/>
```

```
            </xsp:attribute>
            <esql:get-string column="name"/>
           </option>
          </esql:row-results>
         </esql:results>
        </esql:execute-query>
       </esql:connection>
      </select>
      <br />
      <input type="submit"
       name="add-book" value="Add book"/>
     </form>
   </page>
 </xsp:page>
```

list-books.xsp

The file list-books.xsp is almost identical to list-publishers.xsp in concept. The only real difference is in the SQL query that's used to get the books and the obvious changes to column names and so forth. The SQL query is a little more complicated because the name of the publisher is displayed in the listing:

```
<?cocoon-process type="xsp"?>

<xsp:page
  language="java"
  xmlns:xsp="http://apache.org/xsp"
  xmlns:esql="http://apache.org/cocoon/SQL/v2">
 <page>
  <esql:connection>
   <esql:pool>books</esql:pool>
   <esql:execute-query>
    <esql:query>
SELECT books.*, publishers.name
FROM books, publishers
WHERE books.pub_id = publishers.id</esql:query>
    <esql:results>
     <table border="1" cellspacing="0">
      <tr>
       <td>Author</td><td>Title</td><td>ISBN</td><td>Month</td>
       <td>Year</td><td>Publisher</td>
      </tr>
      <esql:row-results>
       <tr>
        <td><esql:get-string column="author"/></td>
        <td><esql:get-string column="title"/></td>
        <td><esql:get-string column="isbn"/></td>
        <td><esql:get-string column="month"/></td>
        <td><esql:get-string column="year"/></td>
        <td><esql:get-string column="name"/></td>
        <td>
         <form action="edit-book.xsp">
          <input type="hidden" name="books.id">
           <xsp:attribute name="value">
            <esql:get-int column="id"/>
```

```
           </xsp:attribute>
          </input>
          <input type="submit"
           name="edit-book" value="edit"/>
         </form>
         <form action="delete-book-action">
          <input type="hidden" name="books.id">
           <xsp:attribute name="value">
            <esql:get-int column="id"/>
           </xsp:attribute>
          </input>
          <input type="submit"
           name="delete-book" value="delete"/>
         </form>
        </td>
       </tr>
      </esql:row-results>
     </table>
    </esql:results>
    <esql:no-results>
     <table/>
    </esql:no-results>
   </esql:execute-query>
  </esql:connection>
 </page>
</xsp:page>
```

edit-book.xsp

The edit-book.xsp file is a bit more complicated than edit-publishers.xsp. The complexity arises from having to keep track of the publisher for a particular book. The publisher is shown in a drop-down menu, so when the edit page comes up, you want the drop-down menu to be set to the correct value for the book being displayed. This involves creating a selected attribute on the appropriate <option> element. A few <xsp:logic> sections (lines 10-12, lines 69-71, and lines 85-89) declare, initialize, and use the variable thePubId to accomplish this task. The menu selection is performed in the last <xsp:logic> section, lines 85-89:

```
 1: <?cocoon-process type="xsp"?>
 2:
 3: <xsp:page
 4:   language="java"
 5:   xmlns:xsp="http://apache.org/xsp"
 6:   xmlns:esql="http://apache.org/cocoon/SQL/v2"
 7:   xmlns:xsp-request="http://apache.org/xsp/request/2.0">
 8:
 9:  <page>
10: <xsp:logic>
11: int thePubId = -1;
12: </xsp:logic>
13:   <p>
14:   Please change the information on the book:
15:   </p>
16:   <form action="update-book-action">
17:    <esql:connection>
```

```
    <esql:pool>books</esql:pool>
    <esql:execute-query>
     <esql:query>
SELECT author, title, isbn, month, year, pub_id
FROM books
WHERE id = <xsp-request:get-parameter name="books.id"/>
     </esql:query>
       <esql:results>
      <esql:row-results>
       <input type="hidden" name="books.id">
        <xsp:attribute name="value">
         <xsp-request:get-parameter name="books.id"/>
        </xsp:attribute>
       </input>

Author:
    <input type="text" name="books.author">
     <xsp:attribute name="value">
      <esql:get-string column="author"/>
     </xsp:attribute>
    </input>
    <br />
Title:
    <input type="text" name="books.title">
     <xsp:attribute name="value">
      <esql:get-string column="title"/>
     </xsp:attribute>
    </input>
    <br />
ISBN:
    <input type="text" name="books.isbn">
     <xsp:attribute name="value">
      <esql:get-string column="isbn"/>
     </xsp:attribute>
    </input>
    <br />
Month:
    <input type="text" name="books.month">
     <xsp:attribute name="value">
      <esql:get-string column="month"/>
     </xsp:attribute>
    </input>
    <br />
Year:
    <input type="text" name="books.year">
     <xsp:attribute name="value">
      <esql:get-string column="year"/>
     </xsp:attribute>
    </input>
    <br />
    <br />
<xsp:logic>
thePubId = <esql:get-int column="pub_id"/>;
</xsp:logic>
```

```
            </esql:row-results>
        </esql:results>
     </esql:execute-query>
Publisher:
     <select name="books.pub_id">
      <esql:execute-query>
       <esql:query>SELECT id, name FROM publishers</esql:query>
       <esql:results>
        <esql:row-results>
         <option>
          <xsp:attribute name="value">
           <esql:get-int column="id"/>
          </xsp:attribute>
<xsp:logic>
 if (<esql:get-int column="id"/> == thePubId) {
  <xsp:attribute name="selected"/>;
 }
</xsp:logic>
          <esql:get-string column="name"/>
         </option>
        </esql:row-results>
       </esql:results>
      </esql:execute-query>
    </select>
    <br />
    <input type="submit"
     name="update-book" value="edit book"/>
    </esql:connection>
   </form>
  </page>
</xsp:page>
```

form.xslt

This is a slightly modified version of the form.xslt used in the modular database actions example. The only change is to add a navigational link back to the main menu (lines 10-11):

```
 1: <?xml version="1.0"?>
 2:  <xsl:stylesheet version="1.0"
 3:    xmlns:xsl="http://www.w3.org/1999/XSL/Transform">
 4:
 5:   <xsl:template match="page">
 6:    <html>
 7:     <head></head>
 8:     <body>
 9:      <xsl:apply-templates/>
10:      <p />
11:      <a href="index">Back to main menu</a>
12:     </body>
13:    </html>
14:   </xsl:template>
15:
16:   <xsl:template match="@*|node()" priority="-1">
17:    <xsl:copy>
```

```
      <xsl:apply-templates select="@*|node()"/>
    </xsl:copy>
  </xsl:template>

</xsl:stylesheet>
```

So there you have it—a simple example that shows how to query, insert, update, and delete data from a database.

Practical Usage

Cocoon is a vast system, which makes it hard to learn what it offers and how to use it. One of the best resources for Cocoon help is the Cocoon Wiki at http://wiki.cocoondev.org. This Wiki has more documentation than the regular Cocoon documentation set, and, most important, it has a search engine. There are tutorials, how-to documents, collections of Cocoon best practices, and more.

Performance

There are some important things you should know about Cocoon performance:

- The logging has a big impact on performance, so you should turn off as much of it as possible.
- The sizing of the various Cocoon pools makes a big difference in performance. You can tune pool sizes in your sitemap file and in cocoon.xconf.
- If you have static content mixed in with your dynamic content, consider using Apache to relieve Cocoon of the burden of serving static content.
- Be careful about the performance of your XSLT stylesheets if you're using a lot of them. Here are a couple of things you can do:
    - Keep stylesheets small, with a small number of templates. From this point of view, it's better to have more little stylesheets rather than fewer large stylesheets.
    - Consider using Xalan's XSLTC compiled mode.
- XSPs can be slow if they're being recompiled. Cocoon compiles XSPs into Java files. You can create generators that use those compiled classes instead of recompiling them. These files are located in the directory where your servlet engine compiles pages (including JSPs), in the path org/apache/cocoon/www/<*name of XSP*>.class. You can create a generator from the compiled class by using <map:generator type="compiledXSP" src="org.apache.cocoon.www.<name of XSP>.class/>. You then use the generator normally via <map:generate type="compiledXSP"/>.
- Use the Cocoon profiler to tell you how much time is being spent in the SAX event pipeline.

Applications

Cocoon is a complete system for building Web applications. It's a good candidate for Web applications that have multiple formats or multiple language requirements. Cocoon's sitemap facility makes it easy to break your application into separate sections or modules. The rich set of Cocoon components saves you time by providing the building blocks you need to assemble an application rapidly.

The Apache XML project has created the Forrest project (http://xml.apache.org/forrest), which is a Cocoon-based system for generating project documentation Websites. Forrest leverages Cocoon's functionality to make it easy to generate documentation and keep it up to date. It also provides support for generating offline and printed versions of documentation Websites.

7

Xindice

One of the most important things you can do with data of any kind is store it persistently so you can retrieve it later. Most people store their XML data as files in a filesystem or as text or Character/Binary Large OBject (CLOB/BLOB) fields in relational databases. Files are great, but when you get a lot of files, it can become unwieldy to manage them or find the information you're looking for. Relational databases aren't really a good fit for XML documents, which are hierarchically structured. Using a text or CLOB field in a relational database lets you store the data and in some cases perform full-text indexing, but it doesn't allow you to query the structure of the XML document that has been stored.

What we need is a database that understands XML and can use that understanding to make it easier to store and retrieve XML data. The XML:DB initiative is working to foster the development of databases that understand XML. The initiative has four goals:

- Development of technology specifications for managing the data in XML databases.
- Contribution of reference implementations of those specifications under an open source license.
- Formation of a community where XML database vendors and users can ask questions and exchange information to learn more about XML database technology and applications.
- Evangelism of XML database products and technologies to raise the visibility of XML databases in the marketplace.

The XML:DB initiative has broken up the space of XML databases like this (taken from http://xmldb.org/faqs.html):

> *The XML:DB initiative has defined three different types of XML database.*
>
> *Native XML Database (NXD)*
>
> a) *Defines a (logical) model for an XML document -- as opposed to the data in that document -- and stores and retrieves documents according to that model. At a minimum, the model must include elements, attributes, PCDATA, and document order. Examples of such models are the XPath data model, the XML Infoset, and the models implied by the DOM and the events in SAX 1.0.*
>
> b) *Has an XML document as its fundamental unit of (logical) storage, just as a relational database has a row in a table as its fundamental unit of (logical) storage.*
>
> c) *Is not required to have any particular underlying physical storage model. For example, it can be built on a relational, hierarchical, or object-oriented database, or use a proprietary storage format such as indexed, compressed files.*
>
> *XML Enabled Database (XEDB)--A database that has an added XML mapping layer provided either by the database vendor or a third party. This mapping layer manages the storage and retrieval of XML data. Data that is mapped into the database is mapped into application specific formats and the original XML meta-data and structure may be lost. Data retrieved as XML is NOT guaranteed to have originated in XML form. Data manipulation may occur via either XML specific technologies(e.g. XPath, XSL-T, DOM or SAX) or other database technologies(e.g. SQL). The fundamental unit of storage in an XEDB is implementation dependent. The XML solutions from Oracle and Microsoft as well as many third party tools fall into this category.*
>
> *Hybrid XML Database (HXD)--A database that can be treated as either a Native XML Database or as an XML Enabled Database depending on the requirements of the application. An example of this would be Ozone.*

The Xindice project is a Native XML Database (NXD) as defined by the XML:DB initiative. It originated when the dbXML group decided to donate its XML:DB implementation, dbXML Core, to the Apache Software Foundation in December 2001.

Prerequisites

The XML:DB initiative has defined an abstract API for interacting with an NXD. This API has two parts. A programmatic API lets programs talk to the database. This API serves the same function as the JDBC API: It provides a vendor-neutral API for applications that need to use a database. The initiative also defined an XML vocabulary, XUpdate, for describing updates to be performed on XML data in an NXD. Both the XML:DB API and XUpdate rely on XPath. If you aren't familiar with XPath (and you ought to be, because it's so useful), you should skip back to Chapter 2 on Xalan and XSLT; that chapter includes a brief overview of XPath syntax and functionality.

XML:DB

The XML:DB API is broken into a series of modules. These modules are combined to form Core Levels of the API. Because the NXD area is new, and because the required functionality is changing, the authors of the XML:DB API felt that breaking the API into modules was the best way to allow flexibility while providing a guarantee of a particular level of database functionality for a given Core Level. At the moment there are two Core Levels, 0 and 1.

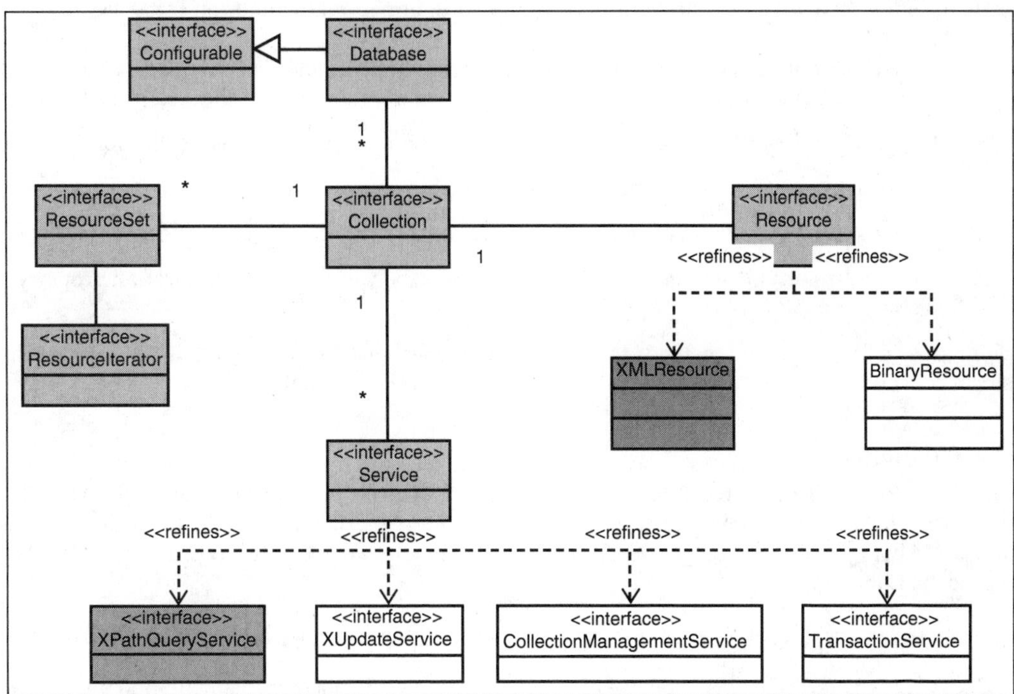

This figure gives an overview of the interfaces defined by XML:DB. The API is designed to be platform neutral, so it's specified using CORBA IDL types. For our discussion, we'll look at the Java bindings, but you should know that the intent is for the same API to be used across multiple languages. There are two modules in Core Level 0: API Base and XMLResource.

Core Level 0

The API Base module contains the Configurable, Database, Collection, Resource, ResourceSet, ResourceIterator, and Service interfaces (shown in blue in the previous figure). The XMLResource module contains the XMLResource interface (shown in red). All the interfaces in the API throw XMLDBException to indicate errors. XMLDBException wraps integer error codes in ErrorCodes.

Database

Let's look at the interfaces in the API Base module. The Database interface is an abstraction of the NXD you want to use. The specification doesn't specify how you obtain an object that implements Database, so this aspect of using XML:DB is vendor specific and nonportable. Database extends the Configurable interface, which is patterned on the SAX2 Configurable interface, but differs from the SAX version because property values can only be Strings, not Objects. The major functionality of Database is to give you a Collection you can work on. Collections are identified with URIs and can be access-controlled via username and password authentication. Here are the most important methods on Database:

- **Collection getCollection(String *uri*, String *username*, String *password*)**—Returns a Collection instance using the *uri* parameter as a key. *Username* and *password* are checked if they aren't null.
- **boolean acceptsURI(String *uri*)**—Returns true if this database contains a collection for the *uri*.
- **String getName()**—Returns the name of the database instance.
- **String getProperty(String *name*)**—Gets the value of the configuration property name.
- **void setProperty(String *name*, String *value*)**—Sets the value of the configuration property name to *value*.

You'll notice that there are no methods to create/delete collections. These operations must be performed using a collection manager service. We'll talk more about services in a bit.

DatabaseManager

In the Java implementation of XML:DB, the DatabaseManager class is the glue between the XML:DB interfaces and the database vendors' implementation of those interfaces. You need to create a DatabaseManager in order to be able to do anything useful with an NXD and the XML:DB APIs. All the methods of DatabaseManager are static:

- **Database[] getDatabases()**—Returns a list of all available databases.
- **void registerDatabase(Database *db*)**—Registers a new database implementation instance with the Database Manager. This implementation instance is obtained by using reflection to create an instance of a vendor-supplied database implementation class.
- **void deregisterDatabase(Database *db*)**—Unregisters the database implementation instance. Once deregistered, the implementation instance can no longer handle requests.
- **Collection getCollection(String *uri*)**—Retrieves the Collection instance corresponding to the URI. The URI has the format xmldb:*<vendor-id>*://*<host>*:*<port>*/path/to/collection. The *<host>* and *<port>* values are optional. The colon between *<host>* and *<port>* is needed only if *<port>* is supplied.
- **Collection getCollection(String *uri*, String *username*, String *password*)**—Retrieves the Collection instance corresponding to the URI. The URI has the format xmldb:*<vendor-id>*://*<host>*:*<port>*/path/to/collection. The *<host>* and *<port>* values are optional. The colon between *<host>* and *<port>* is needed only if *<port>* is supplied. If *username* and *password* are supplied (not null), they must be correct.

Collection

Resources in the database are stored in collections, represented by the Collection interface. Collection is where you'll get access to most of the functionality of an NXD. All the methods for creating, retrieving/querying, updating, and deleting resources are found on Collection. Database vendors can implement the contents of the database as a hierarchy of collections, but this isn't required (although it may impact your ability to retrieve data, especially if queries can't traverse child collections). Some of the key methods on Collection are as follows:

- **String getName()**—Returns the name of the collection.
- **String createId()**—Creates a unique identifier (within the collection). You need this to create a resource.
- **Resource createResource(String *id*, String *type*)**—Creates an empty resource with the *id*. The valid values for *type* are "XMLResource" and "BinaryResource". If the *id* is null, a new ID is created by calling createId.
- **Resource getResource(String *id*)**—Retrieves the resource associated with the *id*.
- **int getResourceCount()**—Returns the number of resources in the collection.
- **String[] listResources()**—Returns a list of all the resource IDs for all the resources in the collection.
- **void removeResource(Resource *res*)**—Removes the resource.
- **void storeResource(Resource *res*)**—Stores the resource. If the resource doesn't exist yet, it's created; if it already exists, it's updated.
- **boolean isOpen()**—Returns true if the collection is open.
- **Service getService(String *name*, String *version*)**—Returns the service named *name* with version *version*.
- **Service[] getServices()**—Returns a list of the names of all the available services.
- **Collection getParentCollection()**—If the database supports hierarchical collections, returns the parent collection of this collection or null if there is no parent.
- **Collection getChildCollection(String *name*)**—Gets the child connection named *name*.
- **int getChildCollectionCount()**—Returns the number of child collections for this collection.
- **String[] listChildCollections()**—Returns a list of the names of all child collections for this collection.

Resource

All resources have a String identifier and a type. *Resources* are the actual containers for data stored within a database. You need a concrete implementation of the Resource interface to do anything useful. The interface identifies a common set of operations:

- **String getId()**—Returns the String used to identify the Resource.
- **String getResourceType()**—Returns the String that tells what type the Resource is. The valid values are "XMLResource" and "BinaryResource".

- **Collection getParentCollection()**—Returns the collection that contains this resource.
- **Object getContent()**—Returns the content of the resource as an Object.
- **void setContent(Object *o*)**—Sets the content of the resource to be the Object.

XMLResource

XMLResource is a specialization of the Resource interface. It adds operations that allow you to put XML data into the resource and get it back out again. The methods of XMLResource don't deal with XML documents, but rather with either a SAX event stream or a DOM tree:

- **boolean getSAXFeature(String *feature*)**—Gets the value of a SAX2 configurable feature on the underlying SAX processor.
- **void setSAXFeature(String *feature*, boolean *value*)**—Sets the value of a SAX2 configurable feature on the underlying SAX processor. This is particularly important so you can turn on validation.
- **void getContentAsSAX(ContentHandler *handler*)**—Retrieves the XML data in the resource from the database and feeds it to the SAX ContentHandler *handler*.
- **ContentHandler setContentAsSAX()**—Asks the database to provide a SAX ContentHandler you can give to your application. As your application fires SAX events, they are detected by the database and stored.
- **Node getContentAsDOM()**—Returns a W3C DOM node that's the root of the XML data.
- **void setContentAsDOM(Node *content*)**—Sets the stored XML data to be the W3C DOM tree rooted at *content*.
- **String getDocumentId()**—If this document has a parent document (Resource), returns its ID; otherwise, returns null.

BinaryResource

BinaryResource is the other specialization of the Resource interface. It allows you to store data as a byte array. It adds no methods to the Resource interface. Instead, it specifies that the getContent and setContent methods are working on byte[] as opposed to Object. When you're working with a BinaryResource, you should be able to safely downcast the Object arguments and return values of setContent and getContent to byte[].

ResourceSet

We haven't talked about queries yet; we'll get to them after we introduce services. But the XML:DB Core Level 0 does include interfaces for dealing with query results. In XML:DB, queries return ResourceSets, which are sets of resources. The name of this interface should really be ResourceList, because the access model for the contents of the ResourceSet is integer indices. This, of course, means that order within the set is important. The other major feature of ResourceSets is that they can produce a ResourceIterator, which you can use to process the contents of the set. Here are the methods on ResourceSet:

- **Resource getResource(long *index*)**—Gets the Resource at *index*.
- **void removeResource(long *index*)**—Removes the Resource at *index*.

- **long getSize()**—Returns the number of Resources in the set. This may cause all Resources in the set to be retrieved, depending on the implementation.
- **void addResource(Resource *res*)**—Adds *res* to the set.
- **void clear()**—Removes all Resources from the set.
- **ResourceIterator getIterator()**—Returns a ResourceIterator that produces every Resource in the set.
- **Resource getMembersAsResource()**—Return an XMLResource containing a representation of all Resources in the set.

ResourceIterator

A ResourceIterator implements the Iterator design pattern. The interface defines Resource-specific methods in the general form of the Java2 collections iterators. We believe the authors of XML:DB wanted to spare the clients of ResourceIterator from having to cast from Object to Resource, so they created a type-specific interface. Unfortunately, it's one more piece of information that you need to keep around and be aware of. Fortunately, the interface is short and sweet:

- **boolean hasMoreResources()**—Returns true if there are more Resources left in the iterator.
- **Resource nextResource()**—Returns the next available resource.

Service

The last interface in the API Base is Service, which provides an extension mechanism for collection implementations. Implementations can provide as many or as few services as they wish. The higher levels of the XML:DB Core APIs define some services, and vendors are free to define their own. The Service interface provides a generic interface that all services should provide:

- **String getName()**—Returns the name of the service.
- **String getVersion()**—Returns the version of the service.
- **void setCollection(Collection *c*)**—Sets the collection that the service will operate on.

Services also implement the Configurable interface, allowing for customization.

Core Level 1

XML:DB Core Level 1 contains all the functionality in Core Level 0 and adds the XPathQueryService interface.

XPathQueryService

The XPathQueryService provides a query capability for XML:DB. Because it's defined as a service, there's room for multiple query capabilities, each implemented as a separate service. You can imagine a more SQL-like query interface, or an XQuery based interface, when the W3C finalizes XQuery as a recommendation. At the moment, though, XPathQueryService is the only query capability for XML:DB-compliant databases.

XPathQueryService gets all of its expressive power from the XPath expression language. In Chapter 2, you saw how XSLT uses XPath to select portions of an XML document. That style of usage is supported by XPathQueryService. One issue with XPath queries is that they rely on namespace prefixes to select nodes belonging to namespaces. XPathQueryService provides a number of methods to set up a group of namespace prefix bindings that are used as the context for any XPath queries executed by the service:

- **void clearNamespaces()**—Clears the current set of namespace bindings.
- **String getNamespace(String *prefix*)**—Returns the URI associated with the namespace prefix.
- **void removeNamespace(String *prefix*)**—Removes the namespace prefix from the current set of namespace bindings.
- **void setNamespace(String *prefix*, String *uri*)**—Adds a namespace binding for *prefix* and *uri* to the current set of namespace bindings.
- **ResourceSet query(String *query*)**—Executes the XPath query on the Collection, using the current set of namespace bindings, and returns the results as a ResourceSet.
- **ResourceSet queryResource(String *id*, String *Query*)**—Executes the XPath query on the resource with identifier *id*, using the current set of namespace bindings, and returns the results as a ResourceSet.

Other Services

At the moment, only Core Levels 0 and 1 are defined by XML:DB. However, the XML:DB initiative has defined a few other services, although they aren't assigned to any level in the Core API. These services provide facilities for updating and managing collections and for transaction management.

XUpdateQueryService

The XUpdateQueryService allows you to execute XUpdate commands against a collection or a resource in a collection. We'll cover the details of XUpdate in the next section. For now, you need to know that XUpdate commands take the form of an XML document:

- **long update(String *document*)**—Executes an XUpdate document on the collection. All updated documents should be written back to the database. Returns the number of documents updated.
- **long updateResource(String *id*, String *document*)**—Executes an XUpdate document against the resource with identifier *id*. All updated documents should be written back to the database. Returna the number of documents updated.

CollectionManagementService

The CollectionManagementService provides the facilities you need to create and remove collections:

- **Collection createCollection(String *name*)**—Creates a collection named *name*.
- **void removeCollection(String *name*)**—Removes the collection named *name*.

TransactionService

XML:DB defines a TransactionService to allow basic transaction capabilities. These capabilities allow you to mark transaction boundaries and control transaction commit and abort:

- **void begin()**—Marks the beginning of a new transaction.
- **void commit()**—Commits the results of the current transaction.
- **void rollback()**—Aborts the current transaction and rolls back any updates performed because the begin method was called.

The current release of Xindice doesn't support the transaction service, but it does support all the other API's that we've discussed in this section.

XUpdate

The XML:DB initiative has defined XUpdate, an XML vocabulary that specifies how to update all or part of an XML document. In the context of an XML:DB database, XUpdate documents are used as commands to the XUpdateQueryService; but XUpdate is useful any time you need to describe an update to an XML document. XUpdate relies on XPath for selecting the parts of the document to be updated and uses XPath expressions for conditional processing of updates. XUpdate is broken into two pieces: a set of elements for describing the contents of the update operation and a set of attributes for describing the kind of update operation that should be performed. For the examples in this section, we'll return to the simple inventory of books (books.xml):

```
<?xml version="1.0" encoding="UTF-8"?>
<books xmlns="http://sauria.com/schemas/apache-xml-book/books"
  xmlns:tns="http://sauria.com/schemas/apache-xml-book/books"
  xmlns:xsi="http://www.w3.org/2001/XMLSchema-instance"
  xsi:schemaLocation=
    "http://sauria.com/schemas/apache-xml-book/books
     http://www.sauria.com/schemas/apache-xml-book/books.xsd"
  version="1.0">
  <book>
   <title>Professional XML Development with Apache Tools</title>
   <author>Theodore W. Leung</author>
   <isbn>0-7645-4355-5</isbn>
   <month>December</month>
   <year>2003</year>
   <publisher>Wrox</publisher>
   <address>Indianapolis, Indiana</address>
  </book>
  <book>
   <title>Effective Java</title>
   <author>Joshua Bloch</author>
   <isbn>0-201-31005-8</isbn>
   <month>August</month>
   <year>2001</year>
   <publisher>Addison-Wesley</publisher>
   <address>New York, New York</address>
  </book>
  <book>
   <title>Design Patterns</title>
   <author>Erich Gamma</author>
   <author>Richard Helm</author>
   <author>Ralph Johnson</author>
   <author>John Vlissides</author>
```

```
    <isbn>0-201-63361-2</isbn>
    <month>October</month>
    <year>1994</year>
    <publisher>Addison-Wesley</publisher>
    <address>Reading, Massachusetts</address>
  </book>
</books>
```

Update Contents

XUpdate provides elements for creating elements, attributes, and processing constructions with computed names. It also provides elements for creating text and comments, so that all the major components of XML documents can be created and used for updates:

- **<xupdate:element name="*elementName*">elementContent</xupdate:element>**—<xupdate :element> allows you to create an element that can be used as part of an update. To make it more convenient to work with elements, the content of <xupdate:element> can be elements and text. Here's an example:

```
<xupdate:element name="book">
 <title>Refactoring</title>
 <author>Martin Fowler</author>
 <isbn>0-201-48567-2</isbn>
 <month>September</month>
 <year>2000</year>
 <publisher>Addison-Wesley</publisher>
 <address>Reading, Massachusetts</address>
 <xupdate:comment>Added 8/2003</xupdate:comment>
</xupdate:element>
```

This creates a new book element that you can use to update your book inventory. That book element looks like this:

```
<book>
 <title>Refactoring</title>
 <author>Martin Fowler</author>
 <isbn>0-201-48567-2</isbn>
 <month>September</month>
 <year>2000</year>
 <publisher>Addison-Wesley</publisher>
 <address>Reading, Massachusetts</address>
 <!-- Added 8/2003 -->
</book>
```

- **<xupdate:attribute name="*attributeName*">attribute value</xupdate:attribute>**—In a similar fashion, <xupdate:attribute> allows you to create an attribute. This example

```
<xupdate:element name="printing">
 <xupdate:attribute name="year">
  1996
 </update:attribute>
 <xupdate:text>5</xupdate:text>
</xupdate:element>
```

produces an element that looks like this:

```
<printing year="1996>5</printing>
```

- **<xupdate:processing-instruction name="*piName*">instructions</xupdate:processing -instruction>**—<xupdate:processing instruction> creates a processing instruction named piName. The arguments to the processing instruction come from the content of the <xupdate:processing-instruction> element. This example

```
<xupdate:processing-instruction name="xsl-stylesheet">
 type="text/xsl" href="books.xslt"
</xupdate:processing-instruction>
```

produces a processing instruction that looks like this:

```
<?xsl-stylesheet type="text/xsl" href="books.xslt" ?>
```

- **<xupdate:text>*text*</xupdate:text>**—<xupdate:text> inserts text content into the update under construction.

- **<xupdate:comment>*comment text*</xupdate:comment>**—<xupdate:comment> inserts a comment into the update under construction.

Update Operations

Now that you can construct fragments of XML documents, you can use those fragments to update the contents of a document in the database. An XUpdate update consists of an <xupdate:modifications> element that contains one or more of the following update command elements:

- **<xupdate:insert-before select="*xpath-expression*">*update*</xupdate:insert-before>**—Inserts the update elements before the node selected by the select *xpath-expression*. In XPath terms, the inserted node becomes the preceding sibling of the selected node:

```
<xupdate:insert-before select="tns:books/tns:book[1]">
 <xupdate:processing-instruction name="xsl-stylesheet">
  type="text/xsl" href="books.xslt"
 </xupdate:processing-instruction>
</xupdate:insert-before>
```

- **<xupdate:insert-after select="*xpath-expression*">*update*</xupdate:insert-after>**—Inserts the update elements after the node selected by the select *xpath-expression*. In XPath terms, the inserted node becomes the following sibling of the selected node:

```
<xupdate:insert-after
 select='/tns:books/tns:book[tns:title="Effective Java"]'>
<xupdate:element name="book">
  <title>Refactoring</title>
  <author>Martin Fowler</author>
  <isbn>0-201-48567-2</isbn>
  <month>September</month>
  <year>2000</year>
  <publisher>Addison-Wesley</publisher>
  <address>Reading, Massachusetts</address>
  <xupdate:comment>Added 8/2003</xupdate:comment>
 </xupdate:element>
</xupdate:insert-after>
```

- **<xupdate:append select="*xpath-expression*" child ="*child- xpath-expression*">*update*</xupdate:append>**—The select *xpath-expression* selects a node that's used as the parent of the node to be appended. The child attribute is optional. If it's provided, it specifies the integer position of the new child node. If it's omitted, the new child is appended as the last child of the selected node:

```
<xupdate:append select="/tns:books">
 <xupdate:element name="book">
  <title>Refactoring</title>
  <author>Martin Fowler</author>
  <isbn>0-201-48567-2</isbn>
  <month>September</month>
  <year>2000</year>
  <publisher>Addison-Wesley</publisher>
  <address>Reading, Massachusetts</address>
  <xupdate:comment>Added 8/2003</xupdate:comment>
 </xupdate:element>
</xupdate:append>
```

- **<xupdate:update select="*xpath-expression*">*update*</xupdate:update>**—Updates/replaces the node selected by the select *xpath-expression* with the update:

```
<xupdate:update
 select='/tns:books/tns:book/tns:author[text()="Ted Leung"]'>
 Theodore W. Leung
</xupdate:update>
```

- **<xupdate:remove select="*xpath-expression*"/>**—Removes the node selected by the select *xpath-expression*:

```
<xupdate:remove select='//tns:book[tns:year="2001"]'/>
```

- **<xupdate:rename select="*xpath-expression*">*name*</xupdate:rename>**—Renames the node (element or attribute node) selected by the select *xpath-expression* to *name*:

```
<xupdate:rename select='/tns:book'>book-
inventory</xupdate:rename>
```

- **<xupdate:variable name="*var*" select="*xpath-expression*"/>**—Defines a variable *var* whose value is the node selected by the select *xpath-expression*:

```
<xupdate:variable name="twlbook"
 select='//tns:book[tns:author="Ted Leung"]'/>
```

- **<xupdate:value-of select="*xpath-expression*"/>**—Replaces the <xupdate:value-of> element with the value selected by the select *xpath-expression*:

```
<xupdate:value-of select="$twlbook"/>
<xupdate:value-of select='//tns:book[tns:author="Ted Leung"]'/>
```

Let's look at a few examples of how this works. We'll take the earlier book inventory and apply a few XUpdates to it to see what we get. Apply this insert-before:

```
<?xml version="1.0"?>
<xupdate:modifications version="1.0"
 xmlns:xupdate="http://www.xmldb.org/xupdate">
 <xupdate:insert-after
```

```
    select='/tns:books/tns:book[tns:title="Effective Java"]'>
   <xupdate:element name="book">
    <title>Refactoring</title>
    <author>Martin Fowler</author>
    <isbn>0-201-48567-2</isbn>
    <month>September</month>
    <year>2000</year>
    <publisher>Addison-Wesley</publisher>
    <address>Reading, Massachusetts</address>
    <xupdate:comment>Added 8/2003</xupdate:comment>
   </xupdate:element>
  </xupdate:insert-after>
 </xupdate:modifications>
```

Your document looks like this:

```
<?xml version="1.0"?>
<books xmlns="http://sauria.com/schemas/apache-xml-book/books"
 xmlns:tns="http://sauria.com/schemas/apache-xml-book/books"
 xmlns:xsi="http://www.w3.org/2001/XMLSchema-instance"
 xsi:schemaLocation="
   http://sauria.com/schemas/apache-xml-book/books
   http://www.sauria.com/schemas/apache-xml-book/books.xsd"
 version="1.0">
  <book>
   <title>Professional XML Development with Apache Tools</title>
   <author>Theodore W. Leung</author>
   <isbn>0-7645-4355-5</isbn>
   <month>December</month>
   <year>2003</year>
   <publisher>Wrox</publisher>
   <address>Indianapolis, Indiana</address>
  </book>
  <book>
   <title>Effective Java</title>
   <author>Joshua Bloch</author>
   <isbn>0-201-31005-8</isbn>
   <month>August</month>
   <year>2001</year>
   <publisher>Addison-Wesley</publisher>
   <address>New York, New York</address>
  </book>
  <book>
   <title>Refactoring</title>
   <author>Martin Fowler</author>
   <isbn>0-201-48567-2</isbn>
   <month>September</month>
   <year>2000</year>
   <publisher>Addison-Wesley</publisher>
   <address>Reading, Massachusetts</address>
   <!--Added 8/2003-->
  </book>
  <book>
   <title>Design Patterns</title>
```

```
   <author>Erich Gamma</author>
   <author>Richard Helm</author>
   <author>Ralph Johnson</author>
   <author>John Vlissides</author>
   <isbn>0-201-63361-2</isbn>
   <month>October</month>
   <year>1994</year>
   <publisher>Addison-Wesley</publisher>
   <address>Reading, Massachusetts</address>
  </book>
</books>
```

Here is an XUpdate document which renames the books element to book-inventory.

```
<?xml version="1.0"?>
<xupdate:modifications version="1.0"
  xmlns:xupdate="http://www.xmldb.org/xupdate">
 <xupdate:rename select="/tns:books">book-inventory</xupdate:rename>
</xupdate:modifications>
```

The updated document looks like this:

```
<?xml version="1.0"?>
<book-inventory
 xmlns="http://sauria.com/schemas/apache-xml-book/books"
 xmlns:tns="http://sauria.com/schemas/apache-xml-book/books"
 xmlns:xsi="http://www.w3.org/2001/XMLSchema-instance"
 xsi:schemaLocation="
   http://sauria.com/schemas/apache-xml-book/books
   http://www.sauria.com/schemas/apache-xml-book/books.xsd"
 version="1.0">
  <book>
   <title>Professional XML Development with Apache Tools</title>
   <author>Theodore W. Leung</author>
   <isbn>0-7645-4355-5</isbn>
   <month>December</month>
   <year>2003</year>
   <publisher>Wrox</publisher>
   <address>Indianapolis, Indiana</address>
  </book>
  <book>
   <title>Effective Java</title>
   <author>Joshua Bloch</author>
   <isbn>0-201-31005-8</isbn>
   <month>August</month>
   <year>2001</year>
   <publisher>Addison-Wesley</publisher>
   <address>New York, New York</address>
  </book>
  <book>
   <title>Refactoring</title>
   <author>Martin Fowler</author>
   <isbn>0-201-48567-2</isbn>
   <month>September</month>
```

```
    <year>2000</year>
    <publisher>Addison-Wesley</publisher>
    <address>Reading, Massachusetts</address>
    <!--Added 8/2003-->
  </book>
  <book>
    <title>Design Patterns</title>
    <author>Erich Gamma</author>
    <author>Richard Helm</author>
    <author>Ralph Johnson</author>
    <author>John Vlissides</author>
    <isbn>0-201-63361-2</isbn>
    <month>October</month>
    <year>1994</year>
    <publisher>Addison-Wesley</publisher>
    <address>Reading, Massachusetts</address>
  </book>
</book-inventory>
```

Installing and Configuring Xindice

The latest Xindice builds can be found via http://xml.apache.org/xindice/download.html. Two builds are available: a xml-xindice-*.zip file for Windows and an xml-xindice-*.tar.gz file for UNIX, Linux, and Mac OS X. You only need a single distribution file; there are no separate source and binary distributions.

For the sake of example, we'll assume you're unpacking the Xindice 1.0 distribution. Once you unpack the distribution (by unzipping on Windows or by using gzip and tar on the other platforms), you'll have a directory called xml-xindice-1.0, either in the current directory or in the directory you specified to your archiving utility. The contents of that directory look like this:

- **bin**—Windows batch files and UNIX shell scripts for the Xindice command-line programs. Also contains similar files for running Ant (to build Xindice).
- **config**—Various Xindice configuration files.
- **db**—Xindice database files (stored here by default).
- **docs**—HTML documentation for Xindice.
- **icons**—Icons used by Xindice.
- **idl**—The CORBA IDL description of the XML:DB API.
- **java**—Java-related files:
    - **examples**—Source code for the Xindice examples.
    - **lib**—Prebuilt jar files needed by Xindice.
    - **src**—Java source code for Xindice.
    - **tests**—JUnit unit tests for Xindice.
- **logs**—Server log files.

When you're writing Xindice applications, you need to place the Xindice jar files in your classpath. You need the following jars: openorb-1.2.0.jar, openorb_tools-1.2.0.jar, xindice.jar, xmldb.jar, xmldb-sdk.jar, and xmldb-xupdate.jar. You also need the Xerces and Xalan jars provided in the Xindice java/lib directory. This last requirement can cause you some headaches on JDK 1.4 because JDK 1.4 provides its own XML parser and a different version of Xalan, all via the Java Endorsed Standards mechanism. You need to use the Java Endorsed Standards Override Mechanism (see Chapter 1, "Xerces" or Chapter 2, "Xalan") to override the versions of Xerces and Xalan being used by JDK 1.4. Some of these problems will probably be addressed in a newer version of Xindice, but at the time of this writing, the production version of Xindice (1.0) is subject to these sorts of problems.

Command-Line Tools

Before we can explore how to develop applications using Xindice, let's take a tour through the Xindice command-line tools. These are the tools that allow you to do administration and to access the database via a command-line processor.

Runtime Environment

Some additional setup is required so you can run the command-line tools. You need to create a command/shell window (depending on your operating system type) and set the value of the environment variable XINDICE_HOME to the directory where Xindice is installed. You may also wish to add the XINDICE_HOME/bin directory to the PATH variable, so you can execute the Xindice commands no matter where you are in the directory hierarchy.

If you're going to use JDK 1.4, then you'll need to modify the batch (or shell) scripts in XINDICE_HOME/bin to use the Java Endorsed Standards Override Mechanism to get the proper versions of Xerces and Xalan into the classpath.

The first thing you need to be able to do is start the Xindice server. To do this, go to your shell window, change to the XINDICE_HOME directory, and execute either the batch or shell script file named startup. It will start the Xindice server. If you don't execute this command in the background, you'll need a second window to execute the Xindice command-line parsers. In the sections that follow, we'll look at the commands available from the xindiceadmin command. The xindice command is for regular users and allows a subset of these commands.

Adding to the Database

Four subcommands let you add information to a Xindice database.

add_collection

The add_collection subcommand (you can use ac for brevity) allows you to add/create a new collection. The collection can be specified as a top-level collection by providing / for the collection argument or as a child collection by specifying /parent-collection for the collection argument. This command is only available in xindiceadmin:

```
xindiceadmin add_collection —c collection —n name [—v]
```

- **-c** ***collection***—Collection to add a collection to.
- **-n** ***name***—Name for the new collection.
- **-v**—Verbose mode (optional).

This example creates a new top-level collection called books:

```
xindiceadmin add_collection —c /db -n books
```

This example creates a computers as a child collection of /db/books:

```
xindiceadmin add_collection —c /db/books —n computers
```

add_document

The add_document subcommand (you can use ad for brevity) allows you to add a document to a collection. The collection must already exist:

```
xindiceadmin add_document —c collection —f file_path —n name [—v]
```

- **-c** ***collection***—Collection to add the document to.
- **-f** ***file_path***—File containing the document to add.
- **-n** ***name***—Name/ID for the document.
- **-v**—Verbose mode (optional).

This example adds the document books.xml to the collection /db/books/computer. The document is retrievable by the IDinventory:

```
xindiceadmin add_document —c /db/books/computer
 —f books.xml —n inventory
```

add_multiple

The add_multiple command lets you add the contents of an entire directory to a collection. You can filter the directory contents by filename extension:

```
xindiceadmin add_multiple —c collection
 —f directory [—e extension] [—v]
```

- **-c** ***collection***—Collection to add the documents to.
- **-f** ***directory***—Directory containing the files you wish to add.
- **-e** ***extension***—Filename extension of the files you wish to add (optional).
- **-v**—Verbose mode (optional).

This example adds all the .xml files in the current directory to the /db/books/computer collection:

```
xindiceadmin add_multiple —c /db/books/computer —f . —e .xml
```

import

The import command lets you add the contents of a directory tree to a collection. Unlike with add_multiple, any directories in the directory being imported are created as collections, and suitable files in those directories are imported into the corresponding collections. This command is available only in xindiceadmin:

```
xindiceadmin import –c collection –f directory [–e extension] [–v]
```

- **-c** *collection*—Collection to add the documents and directories to.
- **-f** *directory*—Root of the directory hierarchy to import.
- **-e** *extension*—Filename extension of the files you want to import (optional)
- **-v**—Verbose mode (optional).

This example adds all .xml files in the directory tree rooted at the current directory into a matching hierarchy of collections rooted at /books:

```
xindiceadmin import –c /db/books –f . –e .xml
```

Retrieval

The retrieval commands allow you to find out what collections there are, retrieve the contents of a document from a collection, and issue an XPath query over the contents of the collection.

list_collections

The list_collections command (you can use lc for brevity) displays a listing of all the collections contained in the collection you specify. The root collection is called /db:

```
xindiceadmin list_collections –c collection [–v]
```

- **-c** *collection*—The collection to list.
- **-v**—Verbose mode (optional).

This example lists the collections in the root collection:

```
xindiceadmin list_collections –c /db
```

list_documents

The list_documents command (you can use ld for brevity) displays a listing of all the documents contained in the collection you specify:

```
xindiceadmin list_documents –c collection -v
```

- **-c** *collection*—The collection to list.
- **-v**—Verbose mode (optional).

This example lists the documents in the books collection:

```
xindiceadmin list_documents -c /db/books
```

retrieve_document

The retrieve_document command (you can use rd for brevity) retrieves the document named *name* from the collection. If you specify the -f option, the retrieved document is stored in the *file-path* argument:

```
xindiceadmin retrieve_document -c collection
 -n name [-f file-path] [-v]
```

- **-c** ***collection***—Collection from which to retrieve the document.
- **-n** ***name***—Name of the of document to retrieve.
- **-f** ***file-path***—File to retrieve into (optional). If omitted, the document is sent to the standard output.
- **-v**—Verbose mode (optional).

This example retrieves the document named inventory from the collection /db/books and stores it in a file called mybooks.xml:

```
xindiceadmin -c /db/books -n inventory -f mybooks.xml
```

xpath

The xpath command allows you to retrieve elements from documents in a collection that match an XPath expression:

```
xindiceadmin xpath -c context -q query [-v]
```

- **-c** ***collection***—Collection to query.
- **-q** ***query***—XPath expression.
- **-v**—Verbose mode (optional).

This example retrieves entire documents using XPath. There's a problem using the xpath command with documents that use namespaces, because there is no way to bind the namespace prefixes in the command-line tool:

```
xindiceadmin xpath -c /db/books -q /
```

Deleting

Of course, there are command for deleting collections and documents.

delete_collection

The delete_collection command (you can use dc for brevity) deletes the named collection from a collection. This command is available only in xindiceadmin:

```
xindiceadmin delete_collection —c collection —n name —y [—v]
```

- **-c** *collection*—The collection containing the collection to be deleted.
- **-n** *name*—The name of the collection to be deleted.
- **-y**—Don't ask for confirmation.
- **-v** —Verbose mode (optional).

This example shows how to delete the books collection:

```
xindiceadmin delete_collection —c /db —n books
```

delete_document

The delete_document command (you can use dd for brevity) deletes the named document from the collection:

```
xindiceadmin delete_document —c collection —n name [—v]
```

- **-c** *collection*—The collection containing the document to delete
- **-n** *name*—The name of the document to delete.
- **-v**—Verbose mode (optional).

This example shows how to delete the inventory document from the books collection:

```
xindiceadmin delete_document —c /db/books —n inventory
```

Indexing

In order to speed access to documents stored in Xindice, you can create indexes.

add_indexer

The add_indexer command (you can use ai for brevity) allows you to index a collection for a particular pattern. To index more than one pattern, create multiple indices. This command is available only in xindiceadmin:

```
xindiceadmin add_indexer —c collection —n name —p pattern
 [—pagesize pagesize] [—maxkeysize max-key-size]
 [—t index-type] [—v]
```

- **-c** *collection*—The collection to index.
- **-n** *name*—The name of the index being created.
- **-p** *pattern*—The pattern used to create the index; the syntax of the pattern looks like this:
    - element-name indexes the value of the named element.
    - element-name@attribute-name indexes the value of the named attribute on the named-element.

- * indexes the values of all elements.
- *@attribute-name indexes the value of the named attribute on any element.
- element-name@* indexes the value of all the attributes of the named element.
- *@* indexes the value of all attributes for all elements.
- To specify elements that are in a namespace, you write the name of the element like this: [namespace-uri]element-name. So, [http://sauria.com/schemas/apache-xml-book/books]book is the book element from the book inventory.

- **-maxkeysize** ***max-key-size***—The maximum key size for the index (defaults to 0) (optional).
- **-pagesize** ***pagesize***—The size of pages in the index (defaults to 4096 bytes) (optional).
- **-t** ***index-type***—The type of index (optional). If the -t option is omitted, then the type is either string or trimmed. If the pattern contains @, then the type is string; otherwise it's trimmed. Possible values for *index-type* are:
  - string
  - trimmed
  - short
  - int
  - long
  - float
  - double
  - byte
  - char
  - boolean
  - name
- **-v**—Verbose mode (optional).

This example shows how to build an index for the author elements of the book inventory schema:

```
xindiceadmin add_indexer -c /db/books -n authorIndex
 -p [http://sauria.com/schemas/apache-xml-book/books]author
```

list_indexers

The list_indexers command (you can use li for brevity) displays all the indexers in use for a given collection. This command is available only in xindiceadmin:

```
xindiceadmin list_indexers –c context [–v]
```

- **-c** *collection*—The collection for which to list indexers.
- **-v**—Verbose mode (optional).

This example shows how to list all the indexers on the books collection:

```
xindiceadmin list_indexers -c /db/books
```

delete_indexer

The delete_indexer command (you can use di for brevity) allows you to remove an index from a collection. This command is available only in xindiceadmin:

```
xindiceadmin delete_indexer -c collection -n name [-v]
```

- **-c** *collection*—The collection from which to delete the indexer .
- **-n** *name*—The name of the indexer to delete.
- **-v**—Verbose mode (optional).

This example shows how to remove the author index from the books collection:

```
xindiceadmin delete_indexer -c /db/books -n authorIndex
```

Other

The next two commands don't really fit into any of the categories that we've seen up to this point. The first deals with backing up the contents of the database, while the second is used to shut down the Xindice server.

export

The export command allows you to export the contents of a collection (including child collections and their children) to a directory:

```
xindiceadmin export (export) –c collection –f directory-path [–v]
```

- **-c** *collection*—The collection to be exported.
- **-f** *directory-path*—The directory where the exported data should go; the directory must already exist.
- **-v**—Verbose mode (optional).

This example shows how to export the books collection to a directory called archive:

```
xindiceadmin export –c /db/books –f archive
```

shutdown

The shutdown command is used to shut down the Xindice server. This command is available only in xindiceadmin:

```
xindiceadmin shutdown —c collection [-v]
```

- **-c** *collection*—The root collection of the database.
- **-v**—Verbose mode (optional).

This example shows how to shut down the current xindice server:

```
xindiceadmin shutdown —c /db
```

Development Techniques

Now that you can create collections and populate them with data, let's look at how you gain access to that data from a Java program. We'll do this by looking at the way Xindice implements the various features of the XML:DB API. Remember that in order to run any of these examples, you need to start a copy of the Xindice server.

XML:DB API

First we'll look at how you can create a new Collection using the XML:DB APIs and the Xindice database driver.

Creating Collections

CreateCollectionTree creates a tree of Collections rooted at /db (the Xindice database root). You specify the tree by providing a UNIX-style directory path that corresponds to the Collection tree. The string "product/inventory/books" causes the creation of three Collections: books, nested inside inventory, nested inside product, which is under the Xindice root /db. This example demonstrates the basics of creating a Collection and using a service:

```
/*
 *
 * CreateCollectionTree.java
 *
 * Example from "Professional XML Development with Apache Tools"
 *
 */
package com.sauria.apachexml.ch7;

import org.xmldb.api.DatabaseManager;
import org.xmldb.api.base.Collection;
import org.xmldb.api.base.Database;
import org.xmldb.api.base.XMLDBException;
import org.xmldb.api.modules.CollectionManagementService;

public class CreateCollectionTree {
```

```
    public static void main(String[] args) {
        String driver =
            "org.apache.xindice.client.xmldb.DatabaseImpl";
        Class c = null;
        try {
            c = Class.forName(driver);
        } catch (ClassNotFoundException cnfe) {
            cnfe.printStackTrace();
        }

        Database db = null;
        try {
            db = (Database) c.newInstance();
        } catch (InstantiationException ie) {
            ie.printStackTrace();
        } catch (IllegalAccessException iae) {
            iae.printStackTrace();
        }
```

The usage model for Xindice is similar to the usage model for JDBC, version one. First, you supply the fully qualified classname of an NXD database driver (as a String). The documentation of the database will tell you the name of this class. For Xindice, the class is org.apache.xindice.client.xmldb .DatabaseImpl. You then use reflection to load the driver by calling Class.forName to get the java.lang.Class object for the database driver. Finally, you get a class that implements the Database interface by calling the Class.newInstance method on the database driver Class object.

Before you can perform any database operations, you need to register the Database object with the XML:DB Database manager. Once the database is registered, you can obtain the root Collection by calling the DatabaseManager's getCollection method with an XML:DB URI:

```

        Collection root = null;
        try {
            DatabaseManager.registerDatabase(db);
            root = DatabaseManager.getCollection(
                        "xmldb:xindice:///db");
        } catch (XMLDBException xde) {
            xde.printStackTrace();
        }

```

The format of an XML:DB is the URI scheme (xmldb) followed by a colon, followed by a vendor string (in this case, "xindice"), followed by ://. The next position in the URI allows you to specify a hostname and portname, just like an HTTP URI. This allows you to access a database running on a different machine and/or port than the current machine. If you want to use the default values (as you're doing in this example), you can omit the hostname:portname—the host will default to the localhost, and the port will default to 4080. After the hostname:portname (even if it's empty), you provide a / and the path to the Collection you're interested in.

Next you split the supplied pathname into an array that contains the Collections that need to be created:

```
        String collections[] = args[0].split("/");

```

You're ready to iterate over the array of Collections:

```
        Collection currentCollection = root;

```

To create or remove Collections, you need to use a CollectionManagementService. If you recall, the XML:DB Core API doesn't provide a standard facility for creating or removing Collections, but it does provide a standard service for the purpose. The service manages the child Collections for a particular Collection. Because you're creating a hierarchy of Collections, you need to obtain the CollectionManagementService instance for each Collection that you create in order to create children in that Collection:

```
        for (int i = 0; i < collections.length; i++) {
            CollectionManagementService cms = null;
            try {
                cms =
                    (CollectionManagementService)
                     currentCollection.getService(
                        "CollectionManagementService",
                        "1.0");
            } catch (XMLDBException xde) {
                xde.printStackTrace();
            }

```

Here you get all the children of the current Collection to check whether a Collection with the desired name is already a child of the current Collection. If it is, you make that child the current Collection and proceed.

```
            Collection child = null;
            try {
                child =
                    currentCollection.getChildCollection(
                        collections[i]);
            } catch (XMLDBException xde) {
                xde.printStackTrace();
            }
            if (child != null) {
               currentCollection = child;
               continue;
            }
```

If a child Collection with the requested name doesn't exist, then you use the createCollection method on the CollectionManagementService to create one with the right name:

```

            try {
                currentCollection =
```

```
                    cms.createCollection(collections[i]);
            } catch (XMLDBException xde) {
                xde.printStackTrace();
            }

        }
    }
}
```

Navigating Collections

The next example finds the first Collection that has a particular name. It does this by performing a recursive depth-first search of the entire tree of Collections, starting at the database root. This example shows how to perform navigation within the Collection tree:

```
/*
 *
 * FindCollection.java
 *
 * Example from "Professional XML Development with Apache Tools"
 *
 */
package com.sauria.apachexml.ch7;

import org.xmldb.api.DatabaseManager;
import org.xmldb.api.base.Collection;
import org.xmldb.api.base.Database;
import org.xmldb.api.base.XMLDBException;

public class FindCollection {
    public static void main(String[] args) {
        String driver =
            "org.apache.xindice.client.xmldb.DatabaseImpl";
        Class c = null;
        try {
            c = Class.forName(driver);
        } catch (ClassNotFoundException cnfe) {
            cnfe.printStackTrace();
        }

        Database db = null;
        try {
            db = (Database) c.newInstance();
        } catch (InstantiationException ie) {
            ie.printStackTrace();
        } catch (IllegalAccessException iae) {
            iae.printStackTrace();
        }

        Collection root = null;
        try {
            DatabaseManager.registerDatabase(db);
            root = DatabaseManager.getCollection(
                    "xmldb:xindice:///db");
```

```
        } catch (XMLDBException xde) {
            xde.printStackTrace();
        }
```

Before you can perform any database operations, you need to load the database driver and initialize the DatabaseManager. After that has been completed, you're ready to go searching for the Collection. The name of the Collection to find is taken from the command-line arguments.

The work of finding the desired connection is the findCollection method's job. It checks to see whether its Collection argument has the desired name. If not, it searches the children of its argument to see if one of them matches. This process continues recursively until all the Collections have been checked or a match is found:

```

        try {
            Collection result = findCollection(root, args[0]);
            if (result != null)
                System.out.println("Found: "+result.getName());
        } catch (XMLDBException xde) {
            xde.printStackTrace();
        }
    }

```

This is the base case of the recursion. If the current Collection has the desired name, then it's returned as the result of findCollection. If it doesn't match, you proceed:

```
    public static Collection findCollection(Collection c,
                                            String name)
        throws XMLDBException {
        if (c.getName().equals(name))
            return c;
```

In preparation for searching the children, you call listChildCollections to obtain an array containing the names of all the child Collections:

```
        String collectionIds[] = c.listChildCollections();
```

You then loop over the array of child names, obtain the corresponding Collection via getChildCollection, and call findCollection using the child Collection as the argument to findCollection. If a Collection with the right name is found by searching a child Collection, then it's returned as the result of findCollection:

```
        for (int i = 0; i < collectionIds.length; i++) {
            String childName = collectionIds[i];
            Collection child = c.getChildCollection(childName);
            Collection result= findCollection(child, name);
            if (result != null)
                return result;
        }
        return null;
    }
}
```

Deleting Collections

In the next example, we'll tackle the problem of deleting a subtree of the Collection tree. In addition to deleting Collections, we'll also see how to enumerate and delete the resources stored in a Collection:

```
/*
 *
 * DeleteCollectionTree.java
 *
 * Example from "Professional XML Development with Apache Tools"
 *
 */
package com.sauria.apachexml.ch7;

import org.xmldb.api.DatabaseManager;
import org.xmldb.api.base.Collection;
import org.xmldb.api.base.Database;
import org.xmldb.api.base.Resource;
import org.xmldb.api.base.XMLDBException;
import org.xmldb.api.modules.CollectionManagementService;

public class DeleteCollectionTree {

    public static void main(String[] args) {
        String driver =
            "org.apache.xindice.client.xmldb.DatabaseImpl";
        Class c = null;
        try {
            c = Class.forName(driver);
        } catch (ClassNotFoundException cnfe) {
            cnfe.printStackTrace();
        }

        Database db = null;
        try {
            db = (Database) c.newInstance();
        } catch (InstantiationException ie) {
            ie.printStackTrace();
        } catch (IllegalAccessException iae) {
            iae.printStackTrace();
        }

        Collection root = null;
        try {
            DatabaseManager.registerDatabase(db);
            root = DatabaseManager.getCollection(
                    "xmldb:xindice:///db");
        } catch (XMLDBException xde) {
            xde.printStackTrace();
        }
```

As usual, you begin with the database driver initialization and registration.

The subtree to delete is specified as a UNIX like path, separated by /. You split this into an array of pathnames so the XML:DB methods can use it. To delete a Collection, you need to use the CollectionManagementService. As you've already seen, this service provides methods that operate on the current Collection, so you need to navigate to the Collection that's the root of the subtree you're interested in deleting:

```
46:
47:         String collections[] = args[0].split("/");
48:         Collection current = root;
49:
```

You iterate over the list of Collection names and call getChildCollection on the Collection names to get to the correct location:

```
50:         for (int i = 0; i < collections.length; i++) {
51:             try {
52:                 current = current.getChildCollection(
53:                             collections[i]);
54:             } catch (XMLDBException xde) {
55:                 xde.printStackTrace();
56:             }
57:         }
```

Once you've reached that location, you can call the deleteChildren method on that Collection, which does the work of deleting the subtree:

```
58:
59:         deleteChildren(current);
60:     }
61:
```

Before you can delete a Collection, you need to delete any child Collections and delete any resources the Collection contains. In line 65, you get an array containing the names of each child Collection, and in lines 69-78 you iterate over that array and remove all the child collections:

```
62:     public static void deleteChildren(Collection c) {
63:         String children[] = null;
64:         try {
65:             children = c.listChildCollections();
66:         } catch (XMLDBException e) {
67:             e.printStackTrace();
68:         }
69:         for (int i = 0; i < children.length; i++) {
70:             String childName = children[i];
71:             Collection child = null;
72:             try {
73:                 child = c.getChildCollection(childName);
74:             } catch (XMLDBException e1) {
75:                 e1.printStackTrace();
76:             }
77:             deleteChildren(child);
78:        }
79:
```

Once all the child Collections have been removed, you can remove any documents in the Collections:

```
        deleteDocuments(c);
```

Now the Collection is completely empty, and you can remove it. To remove the Collection itself, you need to get the CollectionManagementService for its parent and then remove the Collection from the parent by supplying its name:

```
        try {
            CollectionManagementService cms;
            Collection parent = c.getParentCollection();
            cms =
                (CollectionManagementService) parent.getService(
                    "CollectionManagementService",
                    "1.0");
            cms.removeCollection(c.getName());
        } catch (XMLDBException e2) {
            e2.printStackTrace();
        }
```

To remove all the documents in a Collection, you call listResources to get a list of the names of all the Resources in the Collection. Then you iterate over that list and remove each Resource by name:

```
    }

    private static void deleteDocuments(Collection c) {
        String docs[];
        try {
            docs = c.listResources();
            for (int i = 0; i < docs.length; i++) {
                Resource r;
                r = c.getResource(docs[i]);
                c.removeResource(r);
            }
        } catch (XMLDBException e) {
            e.printStackTrace();
        }

    }
}
```

Working with Resources

In the last example, you got your first taste of working with Resources—they're what you want to work with, because they contain the XML data. In the next few examples, we'll look at how to create Resources from existing XML data and how to retrieve the contents of Resources in the database.

String-based I/O

The first of these examples loads the XML data from a file into a Resource and then prints the data from that Resource onto the standard output. It takes three command-line arguments: a UNIX style path that specifies the Collection in which the Resource should be created, the name of a file containing the XML data you want to put into the Resource, and the name you want to give the newly created Resource:

```
/*
 *
 * LoadDumpMain.java
 *
 * Example from "Professional XML Development with Apache Tools"
 *
 */
package com.sauria.apachexml.ch7;

import java.io.BufferedReader;
import java.io.FileNotFoundException;
import java.io.FileReader;
import java.io.IOException;

import org.xmldb.api.DatabaseManager;
import org.xmldb.api.base.Collection;
import org.xmldb.api.base.Database;
import org.xmldb.api.base.Resource;
import org.xmldb.api.base.XMLDBException;

public class LoadDumpMain {

    public static void main(String[] args) {
        String driver =
            "org.apache.xindice.client.xmldb.DatabaseImpl";
        Class c = null;
        try {
            c = Class.forName(driver);
        } catch (ClassNotFoundException cnfe) {
            cnfe.printStackTrace();
        }

        Database db = null;
        try {
            db = (Database) c.newInstance();
        } catch (InstantiationException ie) {
            ie.printStackTrace();
        } catch (IllegalAccessException iae) {
            iae.printStackTrace();
        }

        Collection root = null;
        try {
            DatabaseManager.registerDatabase(db);
            root = DatabaseManager.getCollection(
                      "xmldb:xindice:///db");
        } catch (XMLDBException xde) {
            xde.printStackTrace();
        }

        String collections[] = args[0].split("/");
        Collection current = root;

        for (int i = 0; i < collections.length; i++) {
```

```
55:             try {
56:                 current =
57:                     current.getChildCollection(collections[i]);
58:             } catch (XMLDBException xde) {
59:                 xde.printStackTrace();
60:             }
61:         }
```

The code up to this point should be familiar; it initializes the database and navigates to the correct Collection. Next you call a pair of methods that do the work of loading and dumping the document:

```
62:
63:         loadDocument(current, args[1], args[2]);
64:         dumpDocument(current, args[2]);
65:     }
66:
67:     private static void loadDocument(
68:         Collection c,
69:         String file,
70:         String name) {
71:         Resource document = null;
72:         try {
73:             document = c.createResource(name, "XMLResource");
```

You need to create an XMLResource (in the right Collection) with the right name so that you can store your XML data in it. You have to specify the type of resource as a String argument to the createResource method ("XMLResource" in this case).

In lines 78-94 you create a FileReader to access the XML file and use the readLine method of BufferedReader to read all the lines of the XML file into a StringBuffer:

```
74:         } catch (XMLDBException xde) {
75:             xde.printStackTrace();
76:         }
77:
78:         BufferedReader br = null;
79:         try {
80:             br = new BufferedReader(new FileReader(file));
81:         } catch (FileNotFoundException fnfe) {
82:             fnfe.printStackTrace();
83:         }
84:
85:         StringBuffer data = new StringBuffer();
86:         String line;
87:
88:         try {
89:             while ((line = br.readLine()) != null) {
90:                 data.append(line);
91:             }
92:         } catch (IOException ioe) {
93:             ioe.printStackTrace();
94:         }
95:
```

The setContent method on XMLResource is happy to accept a String containing an XML document, which you can easily provide by calling toString on the StringBuffer. After that, you call the storeResource method on your Collection and pass it the filled-in XMLResource to make the data persistent:

```
        try {
            document.setContent(data.toString());
            c.storeResource(document);
```

The contents of dumpDocument are straightforward. Given the correct Collection and the name of a Resource, you call getResource with the name to get the Resource you want. As long as the Resource exists, you can call the getContent method. The getContent method on XMLResource returns the contents of the Resource as a String. All you have to do is print that String on the standard output:

```
        } catch (XMLDBException xde) {
            xde.printStackTrace();
        }
    }

    private static void dumpDocument(Collection c,
                                     String name) {
        try {
            Resource document = c.getResource(name);

            if (document != null)
                System.out.println(document.getContent());
        } catch (XMLDBException xde) {
            xde.printStackTrace();
        }

    }

}
```

SAX-based I/O

The standard getContent and setContent methods are convenient if you have XML data lying around in files or if you construct XML data as character strings. However, you'll probably want to use Xindice as part of a much larger system that is processing XML data. If this is the case, it's quite likely that some other part of the system will already have parsed the XML data, which means your system is probably dealing with an internal representation of XML as either a SAX event stream or a DOM tree. It would be horribly inefficient to convert a SAX event stream or a DOM tree back into an XML document so that you could store it in Xindice, and then have to parse documents stored in Xindice back into a SAX event stream or a DOM tree. In the next two examples, you'll take LoadDumpMain and modify it to work in a system where either SAX or DOM is the preferred representation for XML. Let's start with the SAX version:

```
/*
 *
 * LoadDumpSAXMain.java
 *
 * Example from "Professional XML Development with Apache Tools"
```

```
 *
 */
package com.sauria.apachexml.ch7;

import java.io.IOException;

import javax.xml.parsers.ParserConfigurationException;
import javax.xml.parsers.SAXParserFactory;
import javax.xml.transform.TransformerConfigurationException;
import javax.xml.transform.TransformerFactory;
import javax.xml.transform.sax.SAXResult;
import javax.xml.transform.sax.SAXTransformerFactory;
import javax.xml.transform.sax.TransformerHandler;
import javax.xml.transform.stream.StreamResult;

import org.xml.sax.ContentHandler;
import org.xml.sax.SAXException;
import org.xml.sax.XMLReader;
import org.xmldb.api.DatabaseManager;
import org.xmldb.api.base.Collection;
import org.xmldb.api.base.Database;
import org.xmldb.api.base.XMLDBException;
import org.xmldb.api.modules.XMLResource;

public class LoadDumpSAXMain {

    public static void main(String[] args) {
        String driver =
            "org.apache.xindice.client.xmldb.DatabaseImpl";
        Class c = null;
        try {
            c = Class.forName(driver);
        } catch (ClassNotFoundException cnfe) {
            cnfe.printStackTrace();
        }

        Database db = null;
        try {
            db = (Database) c.newInstance();
        } catch (InstantiationException ie) {
            ie.printStackTrace();
        } catch (IllegalAccessException iae) {
            iae.printStackTrace();
        }

        Collection root = null;
        try {
            DatabaseManager.registerDatabase(db);
            root = DatabaseManager.getCollection(
                      "xmldb:xindice:///db");
        } catch (XMLDBException xde) {
            xde.printStackTrace();
        }

```

```
60:         String collections[] = args[0].split("/");
61:         Collection current = root;
62:
63:         for (int i = 0; i < collections.length; i++) {
64:             try {
65:                 current =
66:                     current.getChildCollection(collections[i]);
67:             } catch (XMLDBException xde) {
68:                 xde.printStackTrace();
69:             }
70:         }
71:
72:         loadDocument(current, args[1], args[2]);
73:         dumpDocument(current, args[2]);
74:     }
75:
```

The differences from LoadDumpMain are in the implementation of the loadDocument and dumpDocument methods. First you create your XML resource, in line 83:

```
76:     private static void loadDocument(
77:         Collection c,
78:         String file,
79:         String name) {
80:         XMLResource document = null;
81:         try {
82:             document = (XMLResource)
83:                 c.createResource(name, "XMLResource");
84:         } catch (XMLDBException xde) {
85:             xde.printStackTrace();
86:         }
87:
```

If you're familiar with SAX, the only mildly trick part is at line 90:

```
88:
89:         try {
90:             ContentHandler h = document.setContentAsSAX();
```

To set the contents of an XMLResource using SAX, you call the method setContentAsSax. This method takes no arguments, which isn't typical of a method that's supposed to set the contents of an object. But that's because of the way SAX works. In SAX, all the work is done by event handlers, which means the work of putting XML data into the XMLResource has to be done by an event handler. So, setContentAsSAX returns a SAX event handler, which you can then plug into a SAXParser or XMLReader. When you tell that instance to parse, the event handler populates the Resource.

In lines 92-97, that's exactly what you do. You use the JAXP SAXParserFactory to get a SAXParser, which you treat as an XMLReader. The content handler you got from setContentHandlerAsSAX is set as this parser's content handler. After that, you call parse, and the XMLResource is loaded:

```
91:
92:             SAXParserFactory spf = SAXParserFactory.newInstance();
```

```
93:             spf.setNamespaceAware(true);
94:
95:             XMLReader r = spf.newSAXParser().getXMLReader();
96:             r.setContentHandler(h);
97:             r.parse(file);
```

You call storeResource to finish the process and make the XMLResource persistent:

```
98:
99:             c.storeResource(document);
100:        } catch (XMLDBException xde) {
101:            xde.printStackTrace();
102:        } catch (ParserConfigurationException pce) {
103:            pce.printStackTrace();
104:        } catch (SAXException se) {
105:            se.printStackTrace();
106:        } catch (IOException ioe) {
107:            ioe.printStackTrace();
108:        }
109:    }
110:
```

The internals of dumpDocument have undergone a major overhaul as well:

```
111:    private static void dumpDocument(Collection c,
112:                                     String name) {
113:        try {
114:            XMLResource document = (XMLResource)
115:                c.getResource(name);
116:
```

After you get the XMLResource, the code starts to look different. Again, things may seem a little backward due to SAX's event handling model. You need to display the XML stored in the Resource on the standard output. So, your content handler needs to be able to do that. You leverage the serialization /identity transformations available via JAXP's Transformer (XSLT library) to get a SAX event handler that serializes a SAX event stream into an XML document. The Resource will call the content handler.

You create the JAXP TransformerFactory in lines 118-120 and downcast it to a SAXTransformerFactory (which you need in order to obtain handlers that you can plug into SAX). You use that factory to create a TransformerHandler, which you can use as a content handler for the Resource:

```
117:            if (document != null){
118:                TransformerFactory xf =
119:                    TransformerFactory.newInstance();
120:                SAXTransformerFactory sxf = null;
121:
122:                if (!xf.getFeature(SAXResult.FEATURE)) {
123:                    System.out.println("Bad factory");
124:                    return;
125:                }
126:                sxf = (SAXTransformerFactory) xf;
127:                TransformerHandler serializer =
128:                    sxf.newTransformerHandler();
```

Because the output of the TransformerHandler goes to the standard output, you create a JAXP StreamResult around System.out and make that StreamResult the destination for the TransformerHandler:

```
                    StreamResult result =
                        new StreamResult(System.out);
                    serializer.setResult(result);
```

Calling the getContentAsSAX method and supplying your serializer causes the Resource to generate SAX events and invoke the callback methods on the TransformerHandler, which prints the document to standard output:

```

                    document.getContentAsSAX((ContentHandler)
                                                    serializer);
                }
            } catch (XMLDBException e) {
                e.printStackTrace();
            } catch (TransformerConfigurationException tce) {
                tce.printStackTrace();
            }

        }

}
```

There appear to be a few bugs with the SAX functionality of XMLResource in Xindice 1.0. Some fixes for these bugs have been checked into the Xindice CVS, but they haven't been rolled into a 1.0 series release. At the time of this writing, the Xindice developers are putting together a 1.1 series release.

DOM-based I/O

As you might expect from your previous examinations of SAX versus DOM, the DOM version is more straightforward:

```
/*
 *
 * LoadDumpDOMMain.java
 *
 * Example from "Professional XML Development with Apache Tools"
 *
 */
package com.sauria.apachexml.ch7;

import java.io.IOException;

import javax.xml.parsers.DocumentBuilder;
import javax.xml.parsers.DocumentBuilderFactory;
import javax.xml.parsers.ParserConfigurationException;
import javax.xml.transform.Transformer;
import javax.xml.transform.TransformerConfigurationException;
import javax.xml.transform.TransformerException;
import javax.xml.transform.TransformerFactory;
```

```
import javax.xml.transform.dom.DOMResult;
import javax.xml.transform.dom.DOMSource;
import javax.xml.transform.stream.StreamResult;

import org.w3c.dom.Document;
import org.w3c.dom.Node;
import org.xml.sax.SAXException;
import org.xmldb.api.DatabaseManager;
import org.xmldb.api.base.Collection;
import org.xmldb.api.base.Database;
import org.xmldb.api.base.XMLDBException;
import org.xmldb.api.modules.XMLResource;

public class LoadDumpDOMMain {

    public static void main(String[] args) {
        String driver =
            "org.apache.xindice.client.xmldb.DatabaseImpl";
        Class c = null;
        try {
            c = Class.forName(driver);
        } catch (ClassNotFoundException cnfe) {
            cnfe.printStackTrace();
        }

        Database db = null;
        try {
            db = (Database) c.newInstance();
        } catch (InstantiationException ie) {
            ie.printStackTrace();
        } catch (IllegalAccessException iae) {
            iae.printStackTrace();
        }

        Collection root = null;
        try {
            DatabaseManager.registerDatabase(db);
            root = DatabaseManager.getCollection(
                    "xmldb:xindice:///db");
        } catch (XMLDBException xde) {
            xde.printStackTrace();
        }

        String collections[] = args[0].split("/");
        Collection current = root;

        for (int i = 0; i < collections.length; i++) {
            try {
                current =
                    current.getChildCollection(collections[i]);
            } catch (XMLDBException xde) {
                xde.printStackTrace();
            }
        }
```

```

        loadDocument(current, args[1], args[2]);
        dumpDocument(current, args[2]);
    }

    private static void loadDocument(
        Collection c,
        String file,
        String name) {
        XMLResource document = null;
        try {
            document = (XMLResource)
                c.createResource(name, "XMLResource");
        } catch (XMLDBException xde) {
            xde.printStackTrace();
        }

```

After creating the XMLResource, you're ready to load the document. You use the JAXP DocumentBuilderFactory to get a namespace-aware DocumentBuilder. Asking this DocumentBuilder to parse the file gives you a document you can pass to the setContentsAsDOM method, which is expecting a Node:

```

        try {
            DocumentBuilderFactory dbf =
                DocumentBuilderFactory.newInstance();
            dbf.setNamespaceAware(true);

            DocumentBuilder b = dbf.newDocumentBuilder();
            Document d = b.parse(file);
```

Once the content of the Resource has been set from the DOM tree, you invoke storeResource to write the Resource to disk:

```

            document.setContentAsDOM(d);
            c.storeResource(document);
        } catch (XMLDBException xde) {
            xde.printStackTrace();
        } catch (ParserConfigurationException pce) {
            pce.printStackTrace();
        } catch (SAXException se) {
            se.printStackTrace();
        } catch (IOException ioe) {
            ioe.printStackTrace();
        }
    }

```

Dumping the document is also easier. You obtain a DOM tree from the XMLResource and then use a JAXP identity transform to serializer the DOM tree to standard output:

```
    private static void dumpDocument(Collection c,
                                      String name) {
        try {
            XMLResource document = (XMLResource)
                c.getResource(name);

            if (document != null){
                TransformerFactory xf =
                    TransformerFactory.newInstance();

                if (!xf.getFeature(DOMResult.FEATURE)) {
                    System.out.println("Bad factory");
                    return;
                }
                Transformer serializer = xf.newTransformer();
```

You can use the regular TransformerFactory to get a regular Transformer for use as a serializer. Now you have to set up the arguments for the transformer.

You obtain the DOM tree from the XMLResource and use it to create a DOMSource that serves as the input for the Transformer. A StreamResult wrapped around System.out serves as the output for the Transformer. Calling the Transformer's transform method displays the XML content of the Resource on the standard output:

```
                Node root = document.getContentAsDOM();
                DOMSource outputSource = new DOMSource(root);
                StreamResult result =
                    new StreamResult(System.out);
                serializer.transform(outputSource, result);
            }
        } catch (XMLDBException e) {
            e.printStackTrace();
        } catch (TransformerConfigurationException tce) {
            tce.printStackTrace();
        } catch (TransformerException te) {
            te.printStackTrace();
        }

    }

}
```

XPath-based Querying

The XML:DB API doesn't mandate a particular language for querying an NXD, although it does provide for an XPath-based query service (XPathQueryService) as part of the XML:DB Core Level 1 specification. Depending on your point of view, this is a good or bad thing. The positive point of view says that it's too early in the evolution of querying XML documents to settle on a single language for querying them. The negative point of view says that having multiple query languages is harder for developers because they may have to learn several languages. This point of view also says that the presence of multiple query languages makes it confusing for those trying to select a technology to work with.

The next example shows how to use XML:DB's Core Level 1 XPath-based query service, XPathQueryService. Most of the hard work is done by the XPath engine, which leaves you to get the service and use it. XPathQueryMain takes two command-line arguments: a collection to query and the XPath expression for the query. If you need to use namespaces, for now you need to change the values hardwired in the code. We leave the exercise of parsing namespace prefix and URI pairs from the command line up to you.

```
/*
 *
 * XPathQueryMain.java
 *
 * Example from "Professional XML Development with Apache Tools"
 *
 */
package com.sauria.apachexml.ch7;

import org.xmldb.api.DatabaseManager;
import org.xmldb.api.base.Collection;
import org.xmldb.api.base.Database;
import org.xmldb.api.base.Resource;
import org.xmldb.api.base.ResourceIterator;
import org.xmldb.api.base.ResourceSet;
import org.xmldb.api.base.XMLDBException;
import org.xmldb.api.modules.XPathQueryService;

public class XPathQueryMain {

    public static void main(String[] args) {
        String driver =
            "org.apache.xindice.client.xmldb.DatabaseImpl";
        Class c = null;
        try {
            c = Class.forName(driver);
        } catch (ClassNotFoundException cnfe) {
            cnfe.printStackTrace();
        }

        Database db = null;
        try {
            db = (Database) c.newInstance();
        } catch (InstantiationException ie) {
            ie.printStackTrace();
        } catch (IllegalAccessException iae) {
            iae.printStackTrace();
        }

        Collection root = null;
        try {
            DatabaseManager.registerDatabase(db);
            root = DatabaseManager.getCollection(
                      "xmldb:xindice:///db");
        } catch (XMLDBException xde) {
```

```
46:                 xde.printStackTrace();
47:             }
48:
49:             String collections[] = args[0].split("/");
50:             Collection current = root;
51:
52:             for (int i = 0; i < collections.length; i++) {
53:                 try {
54:                     current =
55:                         current.getChildCollection(collections[i]);
56:                 } catch (XMLDBException xde) {
57:                     xde.printStackTrace();
58:                 }
59:             }
60:
61:             ResourceSet result = query(current, args[1]);
```

The query method executes the XPath query (in args[1]) against the current Collection. The result of the query is an XML:DB ResourceSet. You access it using a ResourceIterator. Here you just print out the content of each matching resource:

```
62:
63:             try {
64:                 for (ResourceIterator ri = result.getIterator();
65:                       ri.hasMoreResources();) {
66:                     Resource r = ri.nextResource();
67:                     System.out.println(r.getContent());
```

After you've obtained the XPathQueryService, you need to do some work to support namespaces if they will be used in the XPath query (lines 81-87). First you clear any namespace mappings in the service instance. Next you use setNamespace to establish a mapping between namespace prefixes (the first argument) and namespace URIs (the second element). When you call the query method on the service instance, any namespace prefixes in the XPath query are resolved using the mappings installed by setNamespace. Here you include all the namespaces defined for the book inventory schema. The last call to setNamespace, with "" as the first argument, sets the default namespace (lines 86-87):

```
68:                 }
69:             } catch (XMLDBException xde) {
70:                 xde.printStackTrace();
71:             }
72:
73:         }
74:
75:         private static ResourceSet query(Collection c,
76:                                          String queryString) {
77:             ResourceSet rs = null;
78:             try {
79:                 XPathQueryService qs = (XPathQueryService)
80:                     c.getService("XPathQueryService","1.0");
81:                 qs.clearNamespaces();
82:                 qs.setNamespace("tns",
83:                    "http://sauria.com/schemas/apache-xml-book/books");
84:                 qs.setNamespace("xsi",
```

```
                "http://www.w3.org/2001/XMLSchema-instance");
            qs.setNamespace("",
                "http://sauria.com/schemas/apache-xml-book/books");
            rs = qs.query(queryString);
        } catch (XMLDBException xde) {
            xde.printStackTrace();
        }
        return rs;
    }
}
```

Using XUpdate

The last example with the XML:DB API demonstrates how to use XUpdate. The Updater class shows how to use the XUpdateQueryService to modify a document in the database using an XUpdate document. Update takes three command-line arguments: the collection containing the document to update, the name of the document in the collection, and the name of an XUpdate file:

```
/*
 *
 * Updater.java
 *
 * Example from "Professional XML Development with Apache Tools"
 *
 */
package com.sauria.apachexml.ch7;

import java.io.BufferedReader;
import java.io.FileNotFoundException;
import java.io.FileReader;
import java.io.IOException;

import org.xmldb.api.DatabaseManager;
import org.xmldb.api.base.Collection;
import org.xmldb.api.base.Database;
import org.xmldb.api.base.XMLDBException;
import org.xmldb.api.modules.XMLResource;
import org.xmldb.api.modules.XUpdateQueryService;

public class Updater {
    public static void main(String[] args) {
        String id = args[2];
        String driver =
            "org.apache.xindice.client.xmldb.DatabaseImpl";
        Class c = null;
        try {
            c = Class.forName(driver);
        } catch (ClassNotFoundException cnfe) {
            cnfe.printStackTrace();
        }

        Database db = null;
        try {
            db = (Database) c.newInstance();
        } catch (InstantiationException ie) {
            ie.printStackTrace();
```

```
39:         } catch (IllegalAccessException iae) {
40:             iae.printStackTrace();
41:         }
42:
43:         Collection root = null;
44:         try {
45:             DatabaseManager.registerDatabase(db);
46:             String uri = "xmldb:xindice:///db";
47:             if (args[0] != null)
48:                 uri += "/"+args[0];
49:             root = DatabaseManager.getCollection(uri);
50:         } catch (XMLDBException xde) {
51:             xde.printStackTrace();
52:         }
```

You use a different way of getting to the starting collection in this example. Rather than parse the path provided on the command line, you modify the URI given to the DatabaseManager. This works just as well as the approach you've been using.

In lines 54-69, you read the contents of the XUpdate document into a StringBuffer because the XUpdateQueryService needs a String containing the XUpdate command:

```
53:
54:         StringBuffer updateBuffer = new StringBuffer();
55:         BufferedReader br;
56:         try {
57:             br = new BufferedReader(new FileReader(args[1]));
58:             String line;
59:
60:             while ((line = br.readLine()) != null) {
61:                 updateBuffer.append(line);
62:             }
63:         } catch (FileNotFoundException fnfe) {
64:             fnfe.printStackTrace();
65:         } catch (IOException ioe) {
66:             ioe.printStackTrace();
67:         }
68:
69:         String update = updateBuffer.toString();
```

When you're at the correct collection, you can get an instance of the XQueryUpdateService for that collection and pass the document ID and the XUpdate command as arguments to the updateResource method. This method returns a count of the modified nodes:

```
70:         try {
71:             XUpdateQueryService s = (XUpdateQueryService)
72:                 root.getService("XUpdateQueryService", "1.0");
73:             long count = s.updateResource(id, update);
```

As a form of sanity checking, you print out the update count and the content of the updated Resource:

```
74:             System.out.println(count);
75:             XMLResource document =
```

```
                    (XMLResource) root.getResource(id);
                System.out.println(document.getContent());
            } catch (XMLDBException xde) {
                xde.printStackTrace();
            }
        }
}
```

This concludes our tour of examples through the XML:DB APIs. They include quite a bit of functionality. Xindice supports the XML:DB Core Level 1 API and some additional services: the CollectionManagerService and the XUpdateQueryService.

Practical Usage

Practically speaking, Xindice works best on JDK 1.3. You should definitely run the Xindice server under JDK 1.3. On the client side, you can use JDK 1.4 for most of the XML:DB Core Level 0 and Level 1 APIs. If you see odd unexplainable errors, you can try running your client application under JDK 1.3 to see if that solves the problem. If you need to run your client application on JDK 1.4, then you'll need to use the Java Endorsed Standards mechanism to override the JDK 1.4 built-in XML and XSL processors with the versions of Xerces and Xalan distributed with Xindice. Applications that use XUpdate will be affected by the versions of Xerces and Xalan that are available. The easiest way to deal with the Endorsed Standards Mechanism is to make your own copies of the Xindice batch or shell script file and edit it to do the override for you. You should also create a script that sets up the override for your own applications (see http://home1.gte.net/greno/Updated_Batch_Files_for_Xindice_1_0.htm).

When you create resources in an Xindice collection, it's better to supply the names for the resources. It's true that Xindice generates IDs for you; but often during development you'll want refer to specific resources, and it's easier to do this if you control the system used to name them.

You need to keep in mind that Xindice is a database system. One of the keys to good performance in database systems is building the right indices. When you create a collection, you should think carefully about the kinds of queries you're going to make on that collection and create indices that will help the common cases.

Applications

Let's look at how you can use Xindice in the context of the book inventory program you've been building up. In the simplest version of that program, you had a servlet that somehow produced XML, which was then processed by a Java servlet filter to perform an XSLT transform to HTML. The XMLServlet worked by reading a known XML file and returning it as the servlet response. The obvious thing to do is to replace the internal logic of XMLServlet with logic that performs a query against an Xindice database, and then return the results of the query as XML. After that, the processing flow will be as before.

Before we look at the code, let's talk about what you need to have running on the Xindice side. Of course, you need to have the Xindice server running. The default collection used by these programs is /db/books, so you need to create a collection in Xindice. You can do that as follows:

```
xindiceadmin ac –c /db –n books
```

Next you need some data. You can put in as much as you want, but for now, it all has to obey the schema you're using for the books inventory (books.xml). You can add the sample file like this:

```
xindiceadmin  ad –c /db –n inventory –f <path to books.xml>/books.xml
```

XMLServlet: Accessing Xindice

Now that you have a running Xindice database containing some data, you're ready to modify the XMLServlet class. You'll change the servlet to behave as follows. An HTTP GET causes a default query to be executed over the books collection. The default query is the XPath /, which returns the entire document. An HTTP POST is allowed to supply two parameters: a collection that's the name of the collection under /db; and query, which is an XPath query. The response is an XML document whose root element is <result>. Each immediate child of <result> is an XMLResource from the Xindice ResultSet:

```
 1: /*
 2:  *
 3:  * XMLServlet.java
 4:  *
 5:  * Example from "Professional XML Development with Apache Tools"
 6:  *
 7:  */
 8:
 9: package com.sauria.apachexml.ch7;
10: import java.io.IOException;
11: import java.io.PrintWriter;
12:
13: import javax.servlet.ServletException;
14: import javax.servlet.http.HttpServlet;
15: import javax.servlet.http.HttpServletRequest;
16: import javax.servlet.http.HttpServletResponse;
17:
18: import org.xmldb.api.DatabaseManager;
19: import org.xmldb.api.base.Collection;
20: import org.xmldb.api.base.Database;
21: import org.xmldb.api.base.Resource;
22: import org.xmldb.api.base.ResourceIterator;
23: import org.xmldb.api.base.ResourceSet;
24: import org.xmldb.api.base.XMLDBException;
25: import org.xmldb.api.modules.XPathQueryService;
26:
27: public class XMLServlet extends HttpServlet {
28:     String DEFAULT_COLLECTION="books";
29:     String DEFAULT_QUERY="/";
```

In lines 28-29, you set the default values for the collection and query, which are used by doGet.

The initDB method contains the usual Xindice database driver setup:

```
30:
31:     public Database initDB() {
```

```
        String driver =
            "org.apache.xindice.client.xmldb.DatabaseImpl";
        Class c = null;
        try {
            c = Class.forName(driver);
        } catch (ClassNotFoundException cnfe) {
            cnfe.printStackTrace();
        }

        Database db = null;
        try {
            db = (Database) c.newInstance();
        } catch (InstantiationException ie) {
            ie.printStackTrace();
        } catch (IllegalAccessException iae) {
            iae.printStackTrace();
        }

        try {
            DatabaseManager.registerDatabase(db);
        } catch (XMLDBException xde) {
            xde.printStackTrace();
        }
        return db;
    }
```

The doGet method initializes an Xindice database client and then calls the xindiceQuery method that does all the work. doGet passes the default collection and query values to xindiceQuery. Once the query is complete and the response has been sent, destroyDB is called to unregister the database. These two methods could be beefed up to provide a connection pool for Xindice, but you don't do that here:

```
    protected void doGet(HttpServletRequest req,
                         HttpServletResponse res)
        throws ServletException, IOException {
        Database db = initDB();
        xindiceQuery(db, res, DEFAULT_COLLECTION, DEFAULT_QUERY);
        destroyDB(db);
    }
```

In preparation for sending output to the response, you obtain a PrintWriter on the HttpServletResponse and set the content type of the response to be XML ("text/xml"):

```

    private void xindiceQuery(Database db,
                              HttpServletResponse response,
                              String collection, String query) {
        PrintWriter out = null;
        try {
            out = response.getWriter();
            response.setContentType("text/xml");
        } catch (IOException ioe) {
            ioe.printStackTrace();
        }
```

The code in lines 77-98 disassembles the collection path and sets up the correct Collection. Once you're using the right Collection, you can call the query method to perform the XPath query and obtain an XML:DB ResourceSet. Now you have to iterate through the ResourceSet and produce XML. This process would be easy, except that each XMLResource in the ResourceSet is given back to you as an XML document, complete with an XML declaration. So, you need to combine all these XML documents into a single document that can be used as the HTTP servlet response. You do this by stripping the XML declaration from each XMLResource and making the remainder of each XMLResource (a root element) a child of a new root element. The root element of the result document is <result>:

```
 76:
 77:            Collection root = null;
 78:            try {
 79:                root = DatabaseManager.getCollection(
 80:                           "xmldb:xindice:///db");
 81:            } catch (XMLDBException xde) {
 82:                xde.printStackTrace();
 83:            }
 84:
 85:            String collections[] = collection.split("/");
 86:            if (collection.equals(""))
 87:                collections = new String[0];
 88:
 89:            Collection current = root;
 90:
 91:            for (int i = 0; i < collections.length; i++) {
 92:                try {
 93:                    current =
 94:                        current.getChildCollection(collections[i]);
 95:                } catch (XMLDBException xde) {
 96:                    xde.printStackTrace();
 97:                }
 98:            }
 99:
100:            ResourceSet result = query(current, query);
101:
```

Before you can process any of the Resources from the ResourceSet, you need to output the start tag of the root element (line 103):

```
102:            try {
103:                out.println("<result>");
```

Next you loop through all the Resources from the ResourceSet and write them to the response. Because each Resource (XMLResource, really) is turned into an XML document, you need to strip the XML declaration from the content returned by the Resource. You do this by looking for the <?xml part of the XML declaration (line 109), looking for the matching ?> (line 110), grabbing everything after the ?> as your real content (line 111), and writing that to the response (line 113).

```
104:                for (ResourceIterator ri = result.getIterator();
105:                    ri.hasMoreResources();
106:                    ) {
107:                    Resource r = ri.nextResource();
```

```
108:                 String content = (String) r.getContent();
109:                 if (content.startsWith("<?xml")) {
110:                     int pos=(content.indexOf("?>"));
111:                     content = content.substring(pos+3);
112:                 }
```

After all the Resources have been written, you close the <result> element and flush the entire thing to the response:

```
113:                 out.println(content);
114:             }
115:             out.println("</result>");
116:             out.flush();
```

The doPost method works like doGet, except it tries to get values for the collection and query from the parameters of the HttpServletRequest (lines 127-132). After that, the code that's executed (lines 134-136) is the same as for doGet:

```
117:         } catch (XMLDBException xde) {
118:             xde.printStackTrace();
119:         }
120:
121:     }
122:
123:     protected void doPost(HttpServletRequest req,
124:                           HttpServletResponse res)
125:         throws ServletException, IOException {
126:
127:         String collection = req.getParameter("collection");
128:         collection = (collection != null) ?
129:                          collection : DEFAULT_COLLECTION;
130:
131:         String query = req.getParameter("query");
132:         query = (query != null) ? query : DEFAULT_QUERY;
133:
134:         Database db = initDB();
135:         xindiceQuery(db, res, collection, query);
136:         destroyDB(db);
137:     }
138:
```

The query method should be familiar from the earlier example on XPath queries. It obtains the XPathQueryService, sets up the namespace mappings, and executes the query:

```
139:     private ResourceSet query(Collection c,
140:                               String queryString) {
141:         ResourceSet rs = null;
142:         try {
143:             XPathQueryService qs = (XPathQueryService)
144:                 c.getService("XPathQueryService","1.0");
145:             qs.clearNamespaces();
146:             qs.setNamespace("tns",
147:              "http://sauria.com/schemas/apache-xml-book/books");
```

```
                qs.setNamespace("xsi",
                 "http://www.w3.org/2001/XMLSchema-instance");
                qs.setNamespace("",
                 "http://sauria.com/schemas/apache-xml-book/books");
                rs = qs.query(queryString);
            } catch (XMLDBException xde) {
                xde.printStackTrace();
            }
            return rs;
        }

```

The destroyDB method unregisters the Database from the DatabaseManager. It's just cleaning up nicely:

```
        public void destroyDB(Database db) {
            try {
                DatabaseManager.deregisterDatabase(db);
            } catch (XMLDBException xmldb) {
                xmldb.printStackTrace();
            }
        }
    }
```

At last you have an XMLServlet that's talking to a real XML datasource, not just delivering the contents of a single file. The new improved XMLServlet is also able to process queries, due to Xindice's XPath querying capabilities. However, those very query capabilities necessitate some additional changes in your application. The original application presented in Chapter 2 could rely on the fact that the schema of the data being returned by the XMLServlet was unchanging. You always got back an instance of your book schema. With the Xindice-powered XMLServlet, that has changed. The reason is that XPath queries can return elements that aren't top-level elements from the book schema. You get results that are a bunch of <author> elements, or <isbn> elements, or <year> elements. Any program that processes the response from XMLServlet must be able to deal with these varying elements in the result.

XSLTServletFilter

In Chapter 2, the XSLTServletFilter processed the response from XMLServlet using XSLT to transform the XML into HTML. You need to modify XSLTServletFilter so that it can deal with different XML documents. You'll handle this in a pretty straightforward fashion. The filter gets to look at the request before it's passed to a servlet and can modify the response after the servlet has produced it. You'll take advantage of this privilege to peek at the parameters in the request. In particular, the filter will look at the query parameter in the request and do some simple pattern-matching to select an XSLT spreadsheet based on the contents of the query string. The code is fairly simple in that it only looks for a single string in the XPath query. You could build code that takes apart an XPath query so it could perform more precise selection of stylesheets based on the contents of the query. The tradeoff is that you might end up having a large number of stylesheets to choose from (and to write and maintain). An alternative approach would be to generate the stylesheet to be used. This would reduce the number of stylesheets but introduce additional complexity because you want a human to be able to specify a portion of the stylesheet and have the filter generate the rest. You could do this using XSLT on a programmer-provided stylesheet. The approach demonstrated here illustrates the point that the filter needs to be able to accommodate multiple XML result documents:

```java
/*
 *
 * XSLTServletFilter.java
 *
 * Example from "Professional XML Development with Apache Tools"
 *
 */
package com.sauria.apachexml.ch7;
import java.io.IOException;
import java.io.PrintWriter;
import java.io.StringReader;
import java.io.Writer;
import java.util.Collections;
import java.util.HashMap;
import java.util.Map;

import javax.servlet.Filter;
import javax.servlet.FilterChain;
import javax.servlet.FilterConfig;
import javax.servlet.ServletContext;
import javax.servlet.ServletException;
import javax.servlet.ServletRequest;
import javax.servlet.ServletResponse;
import javax.servlet.http.HttpServletRequest;
import javax.servlet.http.HttpServletResponse;
import javax.xml.transform.Source;
import javax.xml.transform.Templates;
import javax.xml.transform.Transformer;
import javax.xml.transform.TransformerConfigurationException;
import javax.xml.transform.TransformerFactory;
import javax.xml.transform.stream.StreamResult;
import javax.xml.transform.stream.StreamSource;

public class XSLTServletFilter implements Filter {
    FilterConfig config = null;
    Map transletCache = null;

    public void init(FilterConfig fc) throws ServletException {
        config = fc;

        ServletContext ctx = fc.getServletContext();

        transletCache =
            (Map) ctx.getAttribute("transletCache");

        if (transletCache == null) {
            transletCache =
                Collections.synchronizedMap(new HashMap());
            ctx.setAttribute("transletCache", transletCache);
        }
    }
```

The init method is unchanged from the version you saw in Chapter 2. It sets up the translet cache for efficiency.

Here the filter grabs a copy of the query parameter so it can be used for stylesheet selection:

```

    public void doFilter(
        ServletRequest req,
        ServletResponse res,
        FilterChain chain)
        throws IOException, ServletException {
        String contentType;
        String styleSheet;

        HttpServletRequest httpReq = (HttpServletRequest) req;
        String query = httpReq.getParameter("query");
        query = (query != null) ? query : "";

        PrintWriter out = res.getWriter();

        BufferedResponseWrapper wrappedResponse =
          new BufferedResponseWrapper((HttpServletResponse)res);

        chain.doFilter(req, wrappedResponse);
        res.setContentType("text/html");

        String s = new String(wrappedResponse.getBuffer());
        StringReader sr =
            new StringReader(s);
        Source xmlSource = new StreamSource(sr);

        try {
            Templates translet = selectTemplates(query);
            Writer w = res.getWriter();
            StreamResult result = new StreamResult(w);
            Transformer xformer = translet.newTransformer();
            xformer.transform(xmlSource, result);
        } catch (Exception ex) {
            out.println(ex.toString());
            out.write(wrappedResponse.toString());
        }
    }

    private Templates selectTemplates(String query) {
        Templates translet = null;

        TransformerFactory xFactory =
            TransformerFactory.newInstance();
        String styleSheet = selectStyleSheet(query);

        translet = (Templates) transletCache.get(styleSheet);
        if (translet != null) {
            return translet;
        }

        try {
            String stylePath =
```

```
                config.getServletContext().getRealPath(styleSheet);
            Source styleSource = new StreamSource(stylePath);
            translet =
                xFactory.newTemplates(styleSource);
        } catch (TransformerConfigurationException e) {
            e.printStackTrace();
        }

        transletCache.put(styleSheet, translet);
        return translet;
    }
```

You modify the selectStyleSheet method to look at the query and return the appropriate stylesheet. If the query contains a reference to the author element, then the filter selects the xindice-author.xslt stylesheet. If it references the isbn element, the filter selects the xindice-isbn.xslt stylesheet. Otherwise, the filter selects the xindice-full.xslt stylesheet:

```

    private String selectStyleSheet(String query) {
        if (query.indexOf("author") >= 0)
            return "xindice-author.xslt";
        if (query.indexOf("isbn") >= 0)
            return "xindice-isbn.xslt";
        return "xindice-full.xslt";
    }

    public void destroy() {}
}
```

Deployment Descriptors

Here's the Web container deployment descriptor (web.xml) for this Web application:

```
<?xml version="1.0" encoding="ISO-8859-1"?>

<!DOCTYPE web-app
  PUBLIC "-//Sun Microsystems, Inc.//DTD Web Application 2.3//EN"
  "http://java.sun.com/dtd/web-app_2_3.dtd">

<web-app>
  <display-name>Professional XML Development with Apache Tools Examples
  </display-name>
  <description>
    Examples from Professional XML Development with Apache Tools.
  </description>
```

You define the XSLTServletFilter as a filter name XSLT Filter:

```

  <!-- Define servlet-mapped and path-mapped example filters -->
  <filter>
    <filter-name>XSLT Filter</filter-name>
```

```
    <filter-class>
      com.sauria.apachexml.ch7.XSLTServletFilter
    </filter-class>
  </filter>
```

Here you tell the container that XSLT Filter is used on XMLServlet:

```
  <!-- Define filter mappings for the defined filters -->
  <filter-mapping>
    <filter-name>XSLT Filter</filter-name>
    <servlet-name>XMLServlet</servlet-name>
  </filter-mapping>
```

Next you define XMLServlet and XindiceXSLTServlet, which we'll discuss in a little while:

```
  <servlet>
    <servlet-name>XMLServlet</servlet-name>
    <servlet-class>
      com.sauria.apachexml.ch7.XMLServlet
    </servlet-class>
  </servlet>
  <servlet>
    <servlet-name>XindiceXSLTServlet</servlet-name>
    <servlet-class>
      com.sauria.apachexml.ch7.XindiceXSLTServlet
    </servlet-class>
  </servlet>
```

Last, you provide URL mappings for the servlets you've defined:

```
  <servlet-mapping>
    <servlet-name>XMLServlet</servlet-name>
    <url-pattern>/filter/*</url-pattern>
  </servlet-mapping>
  <servlet-mapping>
    <servlet-name>XindiceXSLTServlet</servlet-name>
    <url-pattern>/xindice/*</url-pattern>
  </servlet-mapping>
</web-app>
```

XSLT Stylesheets

Next we'll show you the three XSLT stylesheets so you can get feel for how to deal with the different results. The first stylesheet is xindice-author.xslt, which expects an XML document whose content is a <result> root element containing children <author> elements from the book inventory namespace. This stylesheet produces an HTML document that contains an ordered list of the authors' names (the content of the <author> element):

```
 1: <?xml version="1.0" encoding="UTF-8"?>
 2: <xsl:stylesheet version="1.0"
 3:   xmlns:xsl="http://www.w3.org/1999/XSL/Transform"
 4:   xmlns:books="http://sauria.com/schemas/apache-xml-book/books">
 5:   <xsl:output method="html" version="1.0" encoding="UTF-8"
 6:               indent="yes"/>
 7:
 8:   <xsl:template match="result">
 9:     <html>
10:     <head>
11:       <title></title>
12:     </head>
13:     <body>
14:       <ol>
15:       <xsl:apply-templates/>
16:       </ol>
17:     </body>
18:     </html>
19:   </xsl:template>
```

The template in lines 8-19 matches the result element and sets up the HTML skeleton. It uses <apply-templates/> to process its children (<author> elements).

This template generates the HTML <li> items for each author name:

```
20:
21:   <xsl:template match="books:author">
22:     <li>
23:       <xsl:value-of select="."/>
24:     </li>
25:   </xsl:template>
26: </xsl:stylesheet>
```

The second stylesheet is the xindice-isbn.xslt stylesheet. This stylesheet deals with queries regarding ISBN numbers and produces an unordered list of ISBN numbers in the HTML document from a <result> element that has <isbn> elements from the books inventory namespace as children. This stylesheet has the same form as xindice-author.xslt. The difference is the use of <ul> versus <ol>:

```
<?xml version="1.0" encoding="UTF-8"?>
<xsl:stylesheet version="1.0"
  xmlns:xsl="http://www.w3.org/1999/XSL/Transform"
  xmlns:books="http://sauria.com/schemas/apache-xml-book/books">
  <xsl:output method="html" version="1.0" encoding="UTF-8"
              indent="yes"/>
  <xsl:template match="result">
    <html>
      <head>
        <title></title>
      </head>
      <body>
```

```
          <ul>
            <xsl:apply-templates/>
          </ul>
        </body>
      </html>
    </xsl:template>

    <xsl:template match="books:isbn">
      <li>
        <xsl:value-of select="."/>
      </li>
    </xsl:template>
  </xsl:stylesheet>
```

xindice-full.xslt is the third stylesheet, which is used when the children of the <result> element are <book> elements from the book inventory namespace. In this case, you create a description list using <dl>, make the titles <dt> of the descriptions the <author> children of <book>, and make the descriptions <dd> the <title> children of the <book>. Here you use <dl> instead of <ol>:

```
<?xml version="1.0" encoding="UTF-8"?>
<xsl:stylesheet version="1.0"
  xmlns:xsl="http://www.w3.org/1999/XSL/Transform"
  xmlns:books="http://sauria.com/schemas/apache-xml-book/books">
  <xsl:output method="html" version="1.0" encoding="UTF-8"
              indent="yes"/>
  <xsl:template match="result">
   <html>
    <head>
     <title></title>
    </head>
    <body>
     <dl>
      <xsl:apply-templates/>
     </dl>
    </body>
   </html>
  </xsl:template>
```

You don't want to process all the children of <books:book>, so you use <apply-templates> with select attributes to control which children templates are applied to:

```

  <xsl:template match="books:book">
    <xsl:apply-templates select="books:author"/>
    <xsl:apply-templates select="books:title"/>
  </xsl:template>
```

The rest of the stylesheet contains template definitions to generate <dt> elements for the <author> children and <dd> elements for the title children:

```

  <xsl:template match="books:title">
    <dd>
```

```
        <xsl:value-of select="."/>
      </dd>
    </xsl:template>

    <xsl:template match="books:author">
      <dt>
        <xsl:value-of select="."/>
      </dt>
    </xsl:template>
  </xsl:stylesheet>
```

The following listing shows a simple HTML form you can use to enter the collection name and an XPath query, so you can verify that the POST behavior is correct:

```
<html>
 <head></head>
 <body>
 <form name="queryForm" method="POST" action="filter">
  Enter name of collection to query:<br>
  <input type="text" name="collection"><br>
  Enter a XPath Query<br>
  <input type="text" name="query"><br><br>
  <input type="submit" name="submit">
 </form>
 <body>
</html>
```

When you combine all the artifacts that we've seen in this section, you get a system that can issue XPath queries against an Xindice database and product HTML output as a result of using XSLT transforms on the Xindice results.

A SAX-based Version

It's good to see that you can build a modular system using something like XMLServlet and XSLTServletFilter. The problem with a system like this from an XML point of view is that the servlet filter API only allows you to move text results through the filter chain. This is inefficient because each filter needs text as input and must provide text as output. You know you can do better than that in the XML world, either by using a set of SAX filters as a pipeline or by passing a DOM tree between methods. So, let's look at how you can implement the same solution using a SAX filter technique. This should remove most of the additional parsing and serialization that happens with the filter approach. Start by adding functionality to the XMLServlet:

```
/*
 *
 * XindiceXSLTServlet.java
 *
 * Example from "Professional XML Development with Apache Tools"
 *
 */

package com.sauria.apachexml.ch7;
import java.io.IOException;
```

```
import java.io.PrintWriter;

import javax.servlet.ServletContext;
import javax.servlet.ServletException;
import javax.servlet.http.HttpServlet;
import javax.servlet.http.HttpServletRequest;
import javax.servlet.http.HttpServletResponse;
import javax.xml.transform.Source;
import javax.xml.transform.TransformerConfigurationException;
import javax.xml.transform.TransformerFactory;
import javax.xml.transform.sax.SAXResult;
import javax.xml.transform.sax.SAXTransformerFactory;
import javax.xml.transform.sax.TransformerHandler;
import javax.xml.transform.stream.StreamResult;
import javax.xml.transform.stream.StreamSource;

import org.xmldb.api.DatabaseManager;
import org.xmldb.api.base.Collection;
import org.xmldb.api.base.Database;
import org.xmldb.api.base.ResourceIterator;
import org.xmldb.api.base.ResourceSet;
import org.xmldb.api.base.XMLDBException;
import org.xmldb.api.modules.XMLResource;
import org.xmldb.api.modules.XPathQueryService;

public class XindiceXSLTServlet extends HttpServlet {
    String DEFAULT_COLLECTION="books";
    String DEFAULT_QUERY="//tns:author";

    public Database initDB() {
        String driver =
            "org.apache.xindice.client.xmldb.DatabaseImpl";
        Class c = null;
        try {
            c = Class.forName(driver);
        } catch (ClassNotFoundException cnfe) {
            cnfe.printStackTrace();
        }

        Database db = null;
        try {
            db = (Database) c.newInstance();
        } catch (InstantiationException ie) {
            ie.printStackTrace();
        } catch (IllegalAccessException iae) {
            iae.printStackTrace();
        }

        try {
            DatabaseManager.registerDatabase(db);
        } catch (XMLDBException xde) {
            xde.printStackTrace();
        }
        return db;
```

```
65:     }
66:
67:     protected void doGet(HttpServletRequest req,
68:                          HttpServletResponse res)
69:         throws ServletException, IOException {
70:
71:         Database db = initDB();
72:         xindiceQuery(db, res, DEFAULT_COLLECTION, DEFAULT_QUERY);
73:         destroyDB(db);
74:     }
75:
76:     private void xindiceQuery(Database db,
77:                               HttpServletResponse response,
78:                               String collection, String query) {
79:         PrintWriter out = null;
80:         response.setContentType("text/html");
81:
82:         Collection root = null;
83:         try {
84:             String uri = "xmldb:xindice:///db";
85:             uri += "/"+collection;
86:             root = DatabaseManager.getCollection(uri);
87:         } catch (XMLDBException xde) {
88:             xde.printStackTrace();
89:         }
90:
91:         ResourceSet result = query(root, query);
92:
```

The initDB, destroyDB, doGet, doPost, and selectStylesheet methods are the same as in XMLServlet. The difference sets in after you've processed the query and need to transform the results. You need to iterate over the Resources in the ResourceSet and obtain their content. Because you're trying to avoid extra serialization and parsing, you get the content as a SAX event stream. This means you iterate over a set of SAX event streams, which you'll output to the servlet response. The challenge is finding a way to take multiple SAX streams and merge them into a single stream.

Because you know you'll be using SAX, you need to use a JAXP SAXTransformer and associated classes like SAXTransformerFactory. In lines 94-104, you create a TransformerFactory and downcast it to obtain a SAXTransformerFactory:

```
 93:         try {
 94:             TransformerFactory xf =
 95:                 TransformerFactory.newInstance();
 96:             SAXTransformerFactory sxf = null;
 97:
 98:             if (!xf.getFeature(SAXResult.FEATURE)) {
 99:                 System.out.println("Bad factory");
100:                 return;
101:             }
102:
103:             sxf = (SAXTransformerFactory) xf;
104:             TransformerHandler serializer = null;
```

You need a Transformer (actually, a TransformerHandler) that uses a stylesheet to transform the Xindice output and then writes the transformed output into the servlet response:

```
105:
106:            try {
107:                Source styleSheet = selectStyleSheet(query);
108:                serializer =
109:                    sxf.newTransformerHandler(styleSheet);
```

In lines 114-121, you set up the output stage of the transformer. You create a new StreamResult that wraps the Servlet's response OutputStream (line 117) and sets the Result of the serializer to go to this StreamResult (line 121):

```
110:            } catch (TransformerConfigurationException e) {
111:                e.printStackTrace();
112:            }
113:
114:            StreamResult output = null;
115:            try {
116:                output =
117:                    new StreamResult(response.getOutputStream());
118:            } catch (IOException ioe) {
119:                ioe.printStackTrace();
120:            }
121:            serializer.setResult(output);
```

You solve the problem of merging multiple SAX streams into a single SAX stream by defining an XMLFilter to do the work for you. The tricky part about merging is that each of the input SAX streams will try to fire all the SAX events for an XML document. In particular, it will fire events for startDocument and endDocument, which will cut off the ability to merge any additional streams. You need a filter that swallows the startDocument and endDocument callbacks, so that even though they're fired by the input SAX stream, they aren't output by the serializer. You also need a way to manually fire the startDocument and endDocument events on the serializer; otherwise, you'll have a non-well-formed XML document. The class XPathResultHandler takes care of this for you. In line 124, you set the destination of the XPathResultHandler to be the TransformerHandler:

```
122:
123:            XPathResultHandler filter = new XPathResultHandler();
124:            filter.setContentHandler(serializer);
```

XPathResultHandler's start method causes a startDocument event to be fired on the destination of the filter. Now the TransformationHandler thinks you have started parsing a new XML document:

```
125:            filter.start();
```

As you iterate over the XMLResources in the ResourceSet, you obtain the content of each as a SAX stream, passing in the XPathResultHandler as the ContentHandler to use. This allows Xindice to fire all the SAX events for the XMLResource without the problematic startDocument and endDocument events being passed to the TransformerHandler:

```
126:
127:            for (ResourceIterator ri = result.getIterator();
```

```
                ri.hasMoreResources();
                ) {
                XMLResource r = (XMLResource) ri.nextResource();
                r.getContentAsSAX(filter);
```

The end method of XPathResultHandler causes an endDocument event to be fired on the destination of the filter, telling the TransformationHandler that you're done parsing the XML document:

```
            }

            filter.end();
        } catch (XMLDBException xde) {
            xde.printStackTrace();
        }
    }

    private Source selectStyleSheet(String query) {
        String file = "xindice-full.xslt";
        if (query.indexOf("author") >= 0)
            file = "xindice-author.xslt";
        if (query.indexOf("isbn") >= 0)
            file = "xindice-isbn.xslt";

        ServletContext ctx = getServletContext();
        Source result = new StreamSource(ctx.getRealPath(file));
        return result;
    }

    protected void doPost(HttpServletRequest req,
                            HttpServletResponse res)
        throws ServletException, IOException {

        String collection = req.getParameter("collection");
        collection = (collection != null) ?
                         collection : DEFAULT_COLLECTION;

        String query = req.getParameter("query");
        query = (query != null) ? query : DEFAULT_QUERY;

        Database db = initDB();
        xindiceQuery(db, res, collection, query);
        destroyDB(db);
     }

    private ResourceSet query(Collection c,
                               String queryString) {
        ResourceSet rs = null;
        try {
            XPathQueryService qs = (XPathQueryService)
                c.getService("XPathQueryService","1.0");
            qs.clearNamespaces();
            qs.setNamespace("tns",
             "http://sauria.com/schemas/apache-xml-book/books");
            qs.setNamespace("xsi",
```

```
               "http://www.w3.org/2001/XMLSchema-instance");
            qs.setNamespace("",
             "http://sauria.com/schemas/apache-xml-book/books");
            rs = qs.query(queryString);
        } catch (XMLDBException xde) {
            xde.printStackTrace();
        }
        return rs;
    }

    public void destroyDB(Database db) {
        try {
            DatabaseManager.deregisterDatabase(db);
        } catch (XMLDBException xmldb) {
            xmldb.printStackTrace();
        }
    }
}
```

XPathResultHandler

Here's the code for XPathResultHandler. It's very short because it extends the SAX XMLFilterImpl helper class, which by default passes every event from one side of the filter to the other:

```
/*
 *
 * XPathResultHandler.java
 *
 * Example from "Professional XML Development with Apache Tools"
 *
 */
package com.sauria.apachexml.ch7;

import org.xml.sax.ContentHandler;
import org.xml.sax.SAXException;
import org.xml.sax.helpers.AttributesImpl;
import org.xml.sax.helpers.XMLFilterImpl;

public class XPathResultHandler extends XMLFilterImpl {


    public void endDocument() throws SAXException {
    }

    public void startDocument() throws SAXException {
    }
```

Overriding endDocument and startDocument provides the event-swallowing behavior you need for this application. All other events are passed straight through.

In the start method, you need to get the ContentHandler that's been registered as the destination of the filter and call startDocument. You also need to provide the wrapping <result> element for all the children (XMLResources), so you call startElement manually as well. Note that you have to supply an instance of AttributesImpl in order for this to work:

```

    public void start() {
        try {
            ContentHandler h = super.getContentHandler();
            h.startDocument();
            h.startElement(null,"result","result",
                           new AttributesImpl());
```

Likewise, in the end element, you get the destination ContentHandler, call endElement to close the <result> element, and then fire endDocument to signal that you're done:

```
        } catch (SAXException se) {
            se.printStackTrace();
        }
    }

    public void end() {
        try {
            ContentHandler h = super.getContentHandler();
            h.endElement(null,"result","result");
            h.endDocument();
        } catch (SAXException se) {
            se.printStackTrace();
        }
    }
}
```

Storing XML data is still a relatively new area, and there are lots of proposals for how it should be done. We hope this tour of Xindice and Native XML Databases has given you some ideas for ways you can use native XML storage capabilities in your own applications. Xindice's ability to query more than a single document at once and its use of XPath as an XML-aware query language make it a good fit for applications when you're planning to store your data as XML.

8

XML-RPC

In this section of the book, we'll look at uses for XML that are more commonly associated with application-level plumbing. The first two, XML-RPC and Axis, let you invoke functionality across the Internet. This is a powerful ability that will change the way many kinds of applications are constructed. XML security, which we'll discuss in Chapter 10, is also part of this infrastructure level; it provides a way to embed security constraints into XML documents.

XML-RPC is a remote procedure call (RPC) protocol based on encoding the information needed to make the call as XML. HTTP is used to transport this XML document to a remote server, which parses the document, invokes the procedure, and returns the result of executing the procedure. This return result is also marked up as XML and is returned as the HTTP response.

The XML-RPC protocol was invented early in 1998 by Dave Winer of Userland Software, Don Box of DevelopMentor, and Bob Atkinson and Mohsen Al-Ghosein of Microsoft. At the time, this group was working on a very early version of SOAP. Winer had already published a specification for an RPC scheme using XML, and the group formed when the Microsoft folks invited Winer to collaborate with them. Userland already had customers of its Frontier product who were starting to use an XML-RPC format, so Winer released a version of the group's spec as XML-RPC. The group continued on to develop SOAP, which is a much richer (and, some would say, more complicated) method of invoking remote functionality using XML.

Because it was very simple, a large number of developers working in many languages implemented XML-RPC protocol stacks. Today you can find XML-RPC implementations in AppleScript, ASP, C, Delphi, Eiffel, Flash, Java, JavaScript, Lisp, Objective-C, Perl, PHP, Python, RealBasic, Rebol, Ruby, Scheme, Squeak, and Tcl. These implementations run on platforms that include the Apache Web server, Java, the .NET framework, Mac OS X, WebObjects, and Zope (we're stretching the definition of a platform in this case). This means you can find an XML-RPC implementation for just about any software system you might be using. This is very important, because the goal of XML-RPC is to allow applications written in different languages, running on different platforms, to integrate with each other. By using XML and HTTP as the building blocks for XML-RPC, you get a solution that is relatively easy to implement and usable wherever the basic infrastructure of the Internet is available.

The people working on the Helma object publisher developed an XML-RPC stack in Java as part of their development. In early 2002, the Helma XML-RPC stack was donate to the Apache Software Foundation and became a project under the Apache XML project. In early 2003, the Apache Software Foundation decided to create a new top-level project devoted to Web services technologies. This project was seeded with a number of projects from the Apache XML project, including the XML-RPC project.

Prerequisites

The prerequisites for working with XML-RPC are simple. XML-RPC lets you invoke procedures on another computer. In order for this to work, you need to know what data types may be passed as the arguments to this procedure. You need to know how your XML-RPC library maps data types in your programming language into the types allowed by XML-RPC. It's helpful to understand the basics of XML, although you'll never see any XML unless you try to debug your application at the XML-RPC level. It's also helpful to understand HTTP and issues related to HTTP, such as SSL, Web proxies/firewalls, and so forth. A good XML-RPC library shields you from most of these details and allows you to focus on calling or implementing a procedure.

Concepts

Let's go a little deeper into the details of XML-RPC. The following figure shows the call side flow of an XML-RPC remote procedure call:

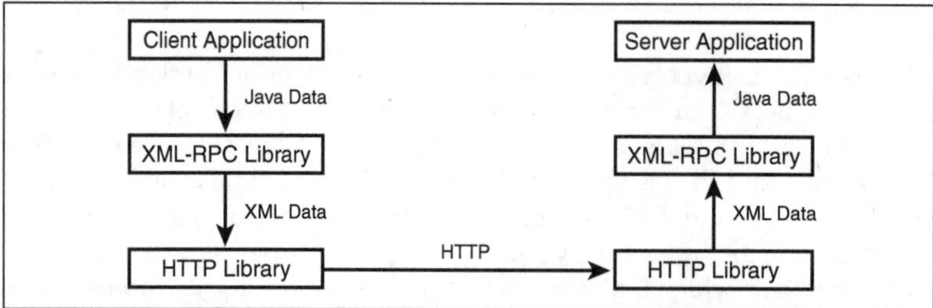

Your client application calls some functions in an XML-RPC library in order to make the RPC. These functions have arguments that use the native data types of the programming language you're using—in this case, Java. The job of the XML-RPC library is to take those Java data values and convert them to elements in an XML document. That XML document can then be passed to an HTTP library, which is used to POST that XML data to the server machine's HTTP port. On the server side, the server's HTTP library receives the POSTed XML data and passes it to an XML-RPC library on the server. This library takes the XML data and converts it into data in the appropriate programming language—again, Java in this case—and then calls the server method by passing it the converted data as arguments. The entire process then reverses itself to get the return value of the server procedure from the server back over to the client.

Note that the word *object* doesn't appear in the last paragraph. XML-RPC is about invoking procedures. There's no notion of invoking methods on objects, polymorphic/virtual method dispatch, or any of those sorts of concepts. You can use XML-RPC in an object-oriented language, but you can also use it with languages that don't support objects. This is in keeping with XML-RPC's target usage as a way of integrating functionality.

XML Encoding RPCs

What does an XML-RPC document look like? It depends on whether you're calling the procedure or returning a result from the procedure. Calling a procedure looks like this:

```
1: <?xml version="1.0" encoding="UTF-8"?>
2: <methodCall>
```

The root element of an XML-RPC procedure call document is called <methodCall>. It has one immediate child, <methodName>, which specifies the procedure to be called:

```
3:  <methodName>createBook</methodName>
```

The next child of <methodCall> is <params>, which is a container element containing enough <param> elements to supply all the arguments needed by the procedure:

```
4:  <params>
5:   <param>
6:    <value>
7:     <string>Professional XML Development with Apache Tools/string>
8:    </value>
9:   </param>
```

A <param> element contains a <value> element, which in turn contains an element that describes the type of the parameter value. The content of the type element is the value of the parameter. We'll discuss the type elements in more detail later. In this document, most of the values are Strings, so you see <string> as the type element. The one exception is in line 27, where you see <i4>, a 4-byte integer:

```
10:   <param>
11:    <value>
12:     <string>Theodore W. Leung</string>
13:    </value>
14:   </param>
15:   <param>
16:    <value>
17:     <string>0-7645-4355-5</string>
18:    </value>
19:   </param>
20:   <param>
21:    <value>
22:     <string>December</string>
23:    </value>
24:   </param>
25:   <param>
```

```
      <value>
        <i4>2003</i4>
      </value>
    </param>
    <param>
      <value>
        <string>Wrox </string>
      </value>
    </param>
    <param>
      <value>
        <string>Indianapolis, Indiana</string>
      </value>
    </param>
  </params>
</methodCall>
```

There are two forms for an RPC response document—one for successful RPCs and one for unsuccessful RPCs. The XML document for a successful RPC looks like this:

```
<?xml version="1.0" encoding="UTF-8"?>
<methodResponse>
 <params>
  <param>
   <value>
    <i4>1</i4>
   </value>
  </param>
 </params>
</methodResponse>
```

In this case, the root <methodResponse> element contains a <params> element with a single <param> element. This corresponds to a single-valued function return value. As you'll see, XML-RPC lets you encode structs, so it's possible to return composite results from XML-RPC calls.

The second case, for a faulty procedure call, looks like this:

```
<?xml version="1.0" encoding="UTF-8"?>
<methodResponse>
 <fault>
  <value>
   <struct>
    <member>
     <name>faultCode</name>
     <value><int>1</int></value>
    </member>
    <member>
     <name>faultString</name>
     <value><string>Illegal argument</string></value>
    </member>
   </struct>
  </value>
 </fault>
</methodResponse>
```

Instead of <methodResponse> containing a <params> element, it contains a <fault> element. The <fault> element contains a <struct> that has two values: an integer faultCode and a faultString describing a human-readable description of the error that occurred.

Here are descriptions of all the type elements available in XML-RPC:

- **<i4> /<int>**—The value is a 4-byte signed integer.
- **<string>**—The value is a string, which may contain NULL bytes. There has been some confusion over whether XML-RPC strings are ASCII strings or Unicode strings. At the time of this writing, the specification has been updated to allow Unicode strings, based on the use of Unicode in XML. Be aware that not all XML-RPC implementations may support Unicode strings.
- **<boolean>**—The value is a boolean, with allowable values of 0 (false) and 1 (true).
- **<double>**—The value is a double-precision signed floating-point number.
- **<dateTime.iso8601>**—The value is a time and date according to the ISO 8601 standard for time and date formats. The problem is that the value of the time zone is dependent on the server you're contacting. This makes it difficult to use <dateTime.iso8601> in a portable fashion.
- **<base64>**—The value is a base64-encoded binary value.
- **<array>**—The value is a heterogeneous array (not all the values must be of the same type). An <array> element contains a <data> element that's a container for an unlimited number of <value> elements. A sample array might be as follows:

  ```
  <array>
   <data>
    <value><string>John Doe</string></value>
    <value><i4>26</i4></value>
    <value><double>492.36</double></value>
   </data>
  </array>
  ```

  The value of a <value> element may itself be an <array> or <struct>.

- **<struct>**—The value is a struct, a set of <member> elements. A <member> element has <name> and <value> as children. The named value aspect of <struct>s is what differentiates them from <array>s. The <name> element is a string, whereas the <value>element can contain any XML-RPC value, including <array> or <struct>. Here's a sample struct:

  ```
  <struct>
   <member>
    <name></name>
    <value></value>
   </member>
  <member>
    <name></name>
    <value></value>
   </member>
  <member>
    <name></name>
    <value></value>
   </member>
  ```

```
        <member>
          <name></name>
          <value></value>
        </member>
      </struct>
```

The XML-RPC specification doesn't say how the server should interpret the <methodName> element. The server can use this as a procedure name, or it can use it as the name of a shell script to execute. It doesn't matter, as long as the server can take the request document and produce a response document. If you'd like more details about XML-RPC, you can find the specification at www.xmlrpc.com/spec.

Using HTTP as an RPC Transport

XML-RPC uses HTTP to perform the task of getting the procedure call document from one machine to another. XML-RPC calls use the HTTP POST method to move the data to the remote machine. The return value of the procedure call is the HTTP response to the POST method. Here's a wire dump of the POST for a procedure call:

```
1: POST /RPC2 HTTP/1.0
2: User-Agent: Apache XML-RPC 1.0
3: Host: 127.0.0.1
4: Content-Type: text/xml
5: Content-Length: 665
```

All the HTTP headers you would expect to find are present. Line 1 shows the HTTP method (POST), the URI on the server being POSTed to (/RPC2), and the version of HTTP (1.0). Line 2 shows the user agent, in this case the Apache XML-RPC client. Line 3 says which host made the request. The HTTP Content-Type and Content-Length headers appear in lines 4 and 5 just like any other HTTP POST request. The remainder of the POST is the XML document that represents the procedure call:

```
 6:
 7: <?xml version="1.0" encoding="UTF-8"?>
 8: <methodCall>
 9:  <methodName>createBook</methodName>
10:  <params>
11:   <param>
12:    <value>
13:     <string>Professional XML Development with Apache Tools</string>
14:    </value>
15:   </param>
16:   <param>
17:    <value>
18:     <string>Theodore W. Leung</string>
19:    </value>
20:   </param>
21:   <param>
22:    <value>
23:     <string>0-7645-4355-5</string>
24:    </value>
25:   </param>
26:   <param>
27:    <value>
```

```
      <string>December</string>
     </value>
    </param>
    <param>
     <value>
      <i4>2003</i4>
     </value>
    </param>
    <param>
     <value>
      <string>Wrox</string>
     </value>
    </param>
    <param>
     <value>
      <string>Indianapolis, Indiana</string>
     </value>
    </param>
  </params>
</methodCall>
```

As you might expect, the response from an XML-RPC server looks like a normal HTTP response:

```
1: HTTP/1.0 200 OK
2: Server: Apache XML-RPC 1.0
3: Connection: close
4: Content-Type: text/xml
5: Content-Length: 154
```

Line 1 shows the version of HTTP (1.0), the HTTP return code (200), and the explanation (OK) for that return code. Line 2 identifies the server you're interacting with, Apache XML-RPC 1.0. The HTTP 1.1 keep-alive header, Connection, appears in line 3 and says the client can close its connection. The response must also provide a Content-Type and Content-Length, as shown in lines 4 and 5. After that, the server returns the actual response data in the form of an XML-RPC response document:

```
 6:
 7: <?xml version="1.0" encoding="UTF-8"?>
 8: <methodResponse>
 9:  <params>
10:   <param>
11:    <value>
12:     <i4>1</i4>
13:    </value>
14:   </param>
15:  </params>
16: </methodResponse>
```

Support for using HTTP is available via libraries written in many languages. This makes it easy to implement XML-RPC, assuming you have access to such a library. This is a key design goal of XML-RPC: to make it easy to implement and to leverage as much existing infrastructure as possible. By using

HTTP as the transport mechanism, XML-RPC gains the benefit of all the work that has been done to make HTTP secure. All the tricks you know for Web security translate to XML-RPC. So, your knowledge of SSL, proxy servers, and firewalls all transfers over to using XML-RPC, because you're using the same transport protocol, HTTP.

Installing and Configuring XML-RPC

Obtaining an XML-RPC build is simple. Point your Web browser at http://ws.apache.org/xmlrpc and click the Download link to get to the XML-RPC downloads. You can click your way down into the distribution directory and look at the releases. There are source and binary distributions in two formats: .zip files for Windows users and .tar.gz files for UNIX, Linux, and Mac OS X users. Using version 1.1 of XML-RPC as an example, the binary distribution for Windows is named xmlrpc-1.1.zip, and the source distribution is named xmlrpc-1.1-src.zip. In some of the version directories, you'll find .md5 files that contain MD5 checksums of the corresponding .zip or .tar.gz files. So, the MD5 file for the Windows binary distribution is in xmlrpc-1.1.zip.md5.

At a minimum, you need the binary distribution for the platform of your choice. If you want the source distribution, you need to download that as well. After you've downloaded the distribution, unpack it using a zip-file utility or tar and gzip for the .tar.gz files. Doing so creates a directory called xmlrpc-1.1 either in the current directory or in the directory you specified to your archiving utility. The important files in this directory are as follows:

- **LICENSE**—A copy of the Apache Software License.
- **README.txt**—A brief file containing getting-started instructions.
- **build.xml**—The Ant build file for XML-RPC.
- **build.properties**—An Ant properties file containing configuration variables for the build.
- **xmlrpc-1.1.jar**—The jar file containing the XML-RPC 1.1 classes.
- **xmlrpc-1.1-applet.jar**—A jar file containing the XML-RPC 1.1 classes needed for applet applications.
- **src** (if you downloaded and unpacked the source distribution)—The source code for XML-RPC 1.1.

Once you've unpacked the distribution, add the xmlrpc-1.1.jar to your classpath. XML-RPC includes the MinML XML parser. If you're using an XML parser in other parts of your application, you may need to place the XML parser jar files before the xmlrpc-1.1.jar. The exception would be on JDK 1.4, which uses the Endorsed Standards Mechanism to determine which SAX parser is used.

Development Techniques

We're ready to start looking at the details of the Apache XML-RPC library. One of the design goals for the XML-RPC library is to be simple as possible for developers to use—and, as you'll see, the XML-RPC API is straightforward to use. You'll write a series of XML-RPC clients and servers that implement a service that allows you to create books. You won't use your book schema directly, but you'll use it as a guide to help you design the service. When you create a book, you need the author, title, ISBN number, month, year, publisher, and publisher's address. This information will be passed to the XML-RPC client-side libraries as RPC arguments, and the information will also be extracted from the RPC arguments delivered on the server side. We'll cover the latest stable release, Apache XML-RPC 1.1. Let's begin by looking at a client program for calling the book service.

A Simple Client

Apache XML-RPC provides two classes you can use to invoke a remote procedure: org.apache.xmlrpc.XmlRpcClient and org.apache.xmlrpc.XmlRpcClientLite. Let's start with XmlRpcClientLite, just to keep thing simple. It doesn't really make things much simpler from the point of view of writing an application, because XmlRpcClient and XmlRpcClientLite share the same API:

```
/*
 *
 * BasicClient.java
 *
 * Example from "Professional XML Development with Apache Tools"
 *
 */
package com.sauria.apachexml.ch8;

import java.io.IOException;
import java.net.MalformedURLException;
import java.util.Vector;

import org.apache.xmlrpc.XmlRpcClientLite;
import org.apache.xmlrpc.XmlRpcException;

public class BasicClient {

    public static void main(String[] args) {
```

Because you're just calling a method to demonstrate the API, you do it from the class's main method.

The first thing you need is a class that lets you invoke the procedure. In this case, that's an instance of XmlRpcClientLite. The instance serves as a proxy for the remote server you want to use. When you're creating an instance of XmlRpcClientLite, you need to pass the information about the server to the constructor. This information can be specified as a String, as a hostname and port number, or as a java.net.URL. In this example, you're talking to a server that's running on the same machine as the client, and the server is listening on port 8080. Because XML-RPC leverages the HTTP infrastructure, you can expect to see HTTP and HTTPS URLs frequently:

```
        XmlRpcClientLite s = null;

        try {
            s = new XmlRpcClientLite("http://localhost:8080");
```

The key to keeping the client-side API simple is right here. XmlRpcClientLite uses a java.util.Vector to create a vector of the arguments to the RPC. Note that the contents of the Vector can be any types necessary for the RPC. In particular, they don't all have to be the same type:

```
24:         } catch (MalformedURLException mue) {
25:             mue.printStackTrace();
26:         }
27:
28:         Vector params = new Vector();
29:         params.addElement("Theodore W. Leung");
30:         params.addElement(
31:             "Professional XML Development with Apache Tools");
32:         params.addElement("0-7645-4355-5");
33:         params.addElement("December");
34:         params.addElement(new Integer(2003));
35:         params.addElement("Wrox");
36:         params.addElement("Indianapolis, Indiana");
```

You invoke the RPC by calling the execute method on XmlRpcClientLite. This method takes a String argument containing the name of the procedure and the Vector of arguments. When you make an XML-RPC call that talks to the Apache XML-RPC library, you have to prefix the method name with the name of the handler registered with the Apache XML-RPC server. In this example, you're invoking the function createBook that's defined by the handler registered under the name books. If you were using XML-RPC to call a procedure being exposed by a different XML-RPC runtime, then you'd need to obey whatever conventions that system had for method names:

```
37:
38:         try {
39:             Boolean result = (Boolean)
40:                 s.execute("books.createBook", params);
```

The result of calling execute is an Object representing the XML-RPC result. The createBook function returns a Boolean value, so you need to cast the return value to the correct type before you display it (line 41):

```
41:             System.out.println(result);
42:         } catch (XmlRpcException xre) {
43:             xre.printStackTrace();
44:         } catch (IOException ioe) {
45:             ioe.printStackTrace();
46:         }
47:     }
48: }
```

Those are the basics of using the Apache XML-RPC client APIs to invoke an XML-RPC procedure.

Mapping to Java Types

One of the big issues in using XML-RPC is understanding how the XML-RPC types are represented by the language and XML-RPC runtime library you're using. Recall that XML-RPC defines a limited set of types that can be passed as arguments or returned as results. The right column in the following table shows which Java types correspond to the various XML-RPC types when you're making an RPC. These are the types you can put into the Vector of parameters. Putting some other type into the Vector will cause an error.

XML-RPC Type	RPC Handler Argument Type
<i4> or <int>	Int
<boolean>	Boolean
<string>	java.lang.String
<double>	Double
<dateTime.iso8601>	java.util.Date
<struct>	java.util.Hashtable
<array>	java.util.Vector
<base64>	byte[]

The next table shows the values returned from the execute method. Note that all the Java primitive types have been replaced with their Object wrappers.

XML-RPC Type	RPC Result Type
<i4> or <int>	java.lang.Integer
<boolean>	java.lang.Boolean
<string>	java.lang.String
<double>	java.lang.Double
<dateTime.iso8601>	java.util.Date
<struct>	java.util.Hashtable
<array>	java.util.Vector
<base64>	byte[]

A Simple Server

Next, let's look at a simple implementation of a server using the Apache XML-RPC APIs:

```
/*
 *
 * BasicServer.java
 *
 * Example from "Professional XML Development with Apache Tools"
 *
 */
```

```
package com.sauria.apachexml.ch8;

import java.io.FileWriter;
import java.io.IOException;
import java.io.PrintWriter;

import org.apache.xmlrpc.WebServer;

public class BasicServer {

    public Boolean createBook(String author, String title,
                                String isbn, String month,
                                int year, String publisher,
                                String address) {
        try {
            PrintWriter w =
                new PrintWriter(new FileWriter(isbn+".txt"));
            w.println(author);
            w.println(title);
            w.println(isbn);
            w.println(month);
            w.println(year);
            w.println(publisher);
            w.println(address);
            w.close();
        } catch (IOException e) {
            e.printStackTrace();
            return Boolean.FALSE;
        }
        return Boolean.TRUE;
    }
```

The createBook method is the procedure you want to make available remotely. Note that XML-RPC has no notion of objects—only calling procedures. When you make a procedure available to remote callers, you should keep this in mind. Remote procedures are exposed via XML-RPC more like the doGet or doPost methods in a servlet. Your procedure shouldn't rely on instance variables except for things like statistics. The types of the arguments to the procedure and the type of the return value must be taken from the lists in the tables in the previous section.

The Apache XML-RPC library provides a few classes to make it easy to implement an XML-RPC server. The simplest is org.apache.xmlrpc.WebServer, which includes a simple HTTP server that does just what's needed for XML-RPC. You create a WebServer that listens on port 8080 on the current machine:

```

    public static void main(String[] args) {
        BasicServer handler = new BasicServer();

        WebServer s = null;

        try {
            s = new WebServer(8080);
```

Once the WebServer instance is running (it starts up when it's constructed), all you need to do is tell it how to handle RPC requests. This is easily accomplished using the addHandler method. This method takes a String that's the handler name and a Java object:

```
        } catch (IOException ioe) {
            ioe.printStackTrace();
        }

        s.addHandler("books", handler);
    }
}
```

As we mentioned earlier, to call a procedure on the handler object, you must prefix the method name with the handler name and a period. Here you use the BasicServer class as the handler, so the name you supply to invoke createBook is books.createBook. When a client invokes an RPC on the WebServer, the Apache XML-RPC runtime takes the handler class and looks for a method with the right name on the right handler (you can register multiple handlers). It then looks at the method's argument list and tries to match the types of the parameters in the XML-RPC document with the types of the parameters in the method. It uses the rules from the earlier table to do this. If the types match up, then the runtime calls the method and returns the result.

Asynchronous Clients

Let's go back to the client side and look at some of the other options you have for writing XML-RPC clients. In the next example, we'll explore the full XmlRpcClient as well as writing an asynchronous client using AsyncCallback.

The full XmlRpcClient provides the same API as the lighter XmlRpcClientLite class. The major difference is that XmlRpcClient uses the built-in java.net.URLConnection class, whereas XmlRpcClientLite implements its own, less functional HTTP support. In particular, if you need support for HTTP proxies, cookies, or HTTP redirection, you need to use XmlRpcClient. The advantage of using XmlRpcClientLite is that it can be much faster than XmlRpcClient, particularly if HTTP keep-alive support is turned on (you'll see this in the example).

The other approach we'll demonstrate in this example is the use of an asynchronous processing model in the client. Instead of the client code waiting for the RPC return, you'll allow that client code to proceed after invoking the RPC. When the RPC returns, processing is handled by a callback function that's been registered for that RPC invocation. This event-driven style of programming should be familiar from SAX programming or AWT/Swing programming. The major benefit of the asynchronous style is that it allows the application to continue processing while a (potentially) long-running RPC executes.

In order to use asynchronous processing, you need a callback class that implements the org.apache.xmlrpc.AsyncCallback interface. Here you use the client class as the client callback handler:

```
/*
 *
 * AsyncClient.java
 *
 * Example from "Professional XML Development with Apache Tools"
 *
```

```
 */
package com.sauria.apachexml.ch8;

import java.net.MalformedURLException;
import java.net.URL;
import java.util.Vector;

import org.apache.xmlrpc.AsyncCallback;
import org.apache.xmlrpc.XmlRpc;
import org.apache.xmlrpc.XmlRpcClient;

public class AsyncClient implements AsyncCallback {
```

You must implement two methods from the AsyncCallback interface: handleResult and handleError. The handleResult method is called if the RPC returned a good result. The arguments are an Object representing the result of the RPC, a URL representing the URL for the XML-RPC, and a String containing the method that was invoked. The url and method arguments are necessary because a handler can provide more than one method, so you may need to use the value of method to determine how to process the results. Here you display the values of the RPC. The AsyncCallbackHandler methods run in a separate thread from the main application, so depending on your application, you may need to perform some thread synchronization in this method:

```

    public void handleResult(Object result, URL url,
                             String method) {
        System.out.println(result);
        System.out.println(url);
        System.out.println(method);
    }
```

The handleError method is called if the RPC fails. The url and string arguments are the same as for handleResult and serve the same purpose. The difference is that the first argument is an Exception that represents the XML-RPC fault:

```

    public void handleError(Exception exc, URL url,
                            String method) {
        System.out.println(exc);
        System.out.println(url);
        System.out.println(method);
    }
```

The XmlRpc class contains a pair of static methods that control the configuration of XmlRpcClient (and XmlRpcClientLite) instances. The setDebug method turns on debug logging that displays the name of the procedure being called and its arguments. It also prints the names of the XML elements in the XML-RPC response as it receives them. HTTP's keep-alive feature can improve the performance of repeated XML-RPC calls to the same handler. Calling setKeepAlive turns this feature on (true) and off (false):

```

    public static void main(String[] args) {
        XmlRpc.setDebug(true);
        XmlRpc.setKeepAlive(true);
```

Creating an instance of XmlRpcClient (line 40) is the same as creating an instance of XmlRpcClientLite, and so is preparing the Vector of parameters:

```
37:
38:         XmlRpcClient s = null;
39:         try {
40:             s = new XmlRpcClient("http://localhost:8080");
41:         } catch (MalformedURLException mue) {
42:             mue.printStackTrace();
43:         }
44:
45:         Vector params = new Vector();
46:         params.addElement("Theodore W. Leung");
47:         params.addElement(
48:             "Professional XML Development with Apache Tools");
49:         params.addElement("0-7645-4355-5");
50:         params.addElement("December");
51:         params.addElement(new Integer(2003));
52:         params.addElement("Wrox");
53:         params.addElement("Indianapolis, Indiana");
```

Apache XML-RPC also provides support for HTTP BASIC authentication, which requires a username and password. The setBasicAuthentication method allows you to specify the username and password that are presented to the XML-RPC server:

```
54:
55:         s.setBasicAuthentication("twl","password");
```

Making an asynchronous call is a little harder than making a synchronous call. You need an instance of AsyncCallback (line 57) that you can pass as the last argument of the executeAsync method (line 58). The first and second arguments to executeAsync are the same as for execute. The call returns immediately, and when the XML-RPC returns, the handler specified in the executeAsync call is used to process the results. The executeAsync method is also available on the XmlRpcClientLite class:

```
56:
57:         AsyncCallback handler = new AsyncClient();
58:         s.executeAsync("books.createBook", params, handler);
59:
60:         System.out.println("finished.");
61:     }
62: }
```

Getting More Control Over Server Processing

The Apache XML-RPC library gives you a way to write a server that has complete control over how to process an XML-RPC call. It does this by providing an interface called org.apache.xmlrpc .XmlRpcHandler. Your handler then implements XmlRpcHandler to get control of the RPC processing. This is a big change from the way you implemented the basic server earlier—in that case, an RPC handler was just a class that had a method with the right name and signature.

The HandlerServer class implements XmlRpcHandler so you can keep everything in a single class, in the interest of brevity:

```
/*
 *
 * HandlerServer.java
 *
 * Example from "Professional XML Development with Apache Tools"
 *
 */
package com.sauria.apachexml.ch8;

import java.io.FileWriter;
import java.io.IOException;
import java.io.PrintWriter;
import java.util.Vector;

import org.apache.xmlrpc.WebServer;
import org.apache.xmlrpc.XmlRpcHandler;

public class HandlerServer implements XmlRpcHandler {
```

The XmlRpcHandler interface defines only a single method: execute. Execute takes the name of the method the client wants to invoke and a Vector containing the arguments after they've been parsed out of the XML-RPC document, according to the rules from the earlier table. If you were hoping to get your hands on the actual XML for the XML-RPC call, you're out of luck. You can put any code you like in the body of execute. Your handler's don't have to be methods on an object. You're free to implement the XML-RPC processing any way you like.

```

    public Object execute(String method, Vector params)
        throws Exception {
        try {
            PrintWriter w =
                new PrintWriter(
                    new FileWriter(params.elementAt(2)+".txt"));

            for (int i = 0; i < params.size(); i++) {
                w.println(params.elementAt(i));
            }
            w.close();
        } catch (IOException e) {
            e.printStackTrace();
            return Boolean.FALSE;
        }
        return Boolean.TRUE;
    }
```

Creating the server and registering the handler proceed the same as before; you just change the handler to implement the XmlRpcHandler interface:

```

    public static void main(String[] args) {
```

```
        HandlerServer handler = new HandlerServer();

        WebServer s = null;
        try {
            s = new WebServer(8080);
        } catch (IOException ioe) {
            ioe.printStackTrace();
        }
        s.addHandler("books", handler);
    }
}
```

Handling BASIC Authentication on the Server

The most common (albeit not the safest) method of performing authentication at the HTTP level is to use HTTP's BASIC authentication method. It involves providing the HTTP server with a base64-encoded username and password. You've already seen how Apache XML-RPC client libraries provide support for specifying the username and password via the setBasicAuthentication method. On the server side, you get support for BASIC authentication by implementing the org.apache.xmlrpc.AuthenticatedXMLRpcHandler interface.

Using AuthenticatedXmlRpcHandler is very similar to using XmlRpcHandler, except the signature of the execute method is different. In addition to the method name and Vector of parameters, execute also expects a pair of Strings containing the username and password supplied to the BASIC authentication method. You can then check these values in the body of the execute method:

```
/*
 *
 * AuthHandlerServer.java
 *
 * Example from "Professional XML Development with Apache Tools"
 *
 */
package com.sauria.apachexml.ch8;

import java.io.FileWriter;
import java.io.IOException;
import java.io.PrintWriter;
import java.util.Vector;

import org.apache.xmlrpc.AuthenticatedXmlRpcHandler;
import org.apache.xmlrpc.WebServer;

public class AuthHandlerServer
    implements AuthenticatedXmlRpcHandler {

    public Object execute(String method, Vector params,
                          String user, String password)
                          throws Exception {
        if (!user.equals("user") || !password.equals("password"))
            throw
                new IllegalArgumentException(
```

```
                        "Authentication failed");

        try {
            PrintWriter w =
                new PrintWriter(
                  new FileWriter(params.elementAt(2) + ".txt"));

            for (int i = 0; i < params.size(); i++) {
                w.println(params.elementAt(i));
            }
            w.close();
        } catch (IOException e) {
            e.printStackTrace();
            return Boolean.FALSE;
        }
        return Boolean.TRUE;
    }

    public static void main(String[] args) {
        AuthHandlerServer handler = new AuthHandlerServer();

        WebServer s = null;

        try {
            s = new WebServer(8080);
        } catch (IOException ioe) {
            ioe.printStackTrace();
        }

        s.addHandler("books", handler);
    }
}
```

XML-RPC in Existing Servers

Up to now you've been working with the Apache XML-RPC library's stand-alone Web server. But what do you do when you need to provide services via XML-RPC and you already have a Web server? One answer would be to use the stand-alone Web server but have it listen on a different port. This approach may work in some situations but may not work in others. Firewall administrators will probably be unwilling to open a new port to allow XML-RPC services. In these cases, you need a way to provide XML-RPC services using your existing Web server. If you're using a Java-based Web server like Tomcat, Jetty, or the Web container of a J2EE application server, then the Apache XML-RPC libraries provide a way for you to offer XML-RPC services without using the stand-alone server.

This capability is provided by the class org.apache.xmlrpc.XmlRpcServer, which operates on a java.io.InputStream that's assumed to contain an XML-RPC request. Let's examine how to use this class in the context of a servlet:

```
/*
 *
 * XMLRPCServlet.java
 *
```

```
 5:  * Example from "Professional XML Development with Apache Tools"
 6:  *
 7:  */
 8: package com.sauria.apachexml.ch8;
 9: 
10: import java.io.IOException;
11: import java.io.OutputStream;
12: 
13: import javax.servlet.ServletException;
14: import javax.servlet.http.HttpServlet;
15: import javax.servlet.http.HttpServletRequest;
16: import javax.servlet.http.HttpServletResponse;
17: 
18: import org.apache.xmlrpc.XmlRpcServer;
19: 
20: public class XMLRPCServlet extends HttpServlet {
21:     XmlRpcServer s = null;
22: 
23:     public void init() throws ServletException {
24:         s = new XmlRpcServer();
25: 
26:         s.addHandler("books", new BasicServer());
```

You use the init method to avoid creating instances of XmlRpcServer over and over. After you create an instance of XmlRpcServer (line 24), you set it up by registering handlers for the procedures you want to expose via XML-RPC. You can use any of the handler implementations you've seen so far. You can supply a Java object and let Apache XML-RPC find the right method to call (as you do here in line 26), or you can supply an object that implements either XmlRpcHandler or AuthenticatedXmlRpcHandler. Once all the handlers are registered, you're ready to open the servlet for business.

Because XML-RPC is defined to use the HTTP POST method for its transport, you only have to implement the doPost method in your servlet:

```
27:     }
28: 
29:     protected void doPost(HttpServletRequest req,
30:                           HttpServletResponse res)
31:         throws ServletException, IOException {
32:         byte[] result = s.execute(req.getInputStream());
```

Line 32 does all the work. XmlRpcServer provides two methods for executing XML-RPC calls. The version you see here takes an InputStream containing the XML-RPC request document. This request is processed according to the handlers registered with the server instance, and the response XML-RPC document is returned as a byte array. The other execute method takes an additional pair of string arguments that should contain a username and password for authentication purposes. If you're using XML-RPC inside a J2EE Web container, you're probably better off using the J2EE declarative security mechanisms, especially if they're used in other parts of your application. For this purpose, treat the XML-RPC code like any other servlet that needs protection.

The rest of the code in the servlet is devoted to setting up the servlet response. You have to set the response's content type to "text/xml" (line 34) and provide the correct value for the HTTP

Content-Length header (line 35). After you've done this, you can take the byte array you obtained from the execute method and send its contents to the servlet's response stream:

```
33:
34:             res.setContentType("text/xml");
35:             res.setContentLength(result.length);
36:
37:             OutputStream out = res.getOutputStream();
38:             out.write(result);
39:             out.flush();
40:         }
41: }
```

The following listing shows the web.xml file you need to provide to a servlet container in order to make the servlet available to the world. Note that clients need to use the full URL for the servlet, which typically contains the name of the Web application. For example, on our test server, clients need to specify the URL http://localhost:8080/apache-xml-book-web-xmlrpc/RPC2/ as the URL of the XML-RPC server:

```
<?xml version="1.0" encoding="ISO-8859-1"?>
<!DOCTYPE web-app
  PUBLIC "-//Sun Microsystems, Inc.//DTD Web Application 2.3//EN"
  "http://java.sun.com/dtd/web-app_2_3.dtd">
<web-app>
  <display-name>Professional XML Development with Apache Tools Examples
  </display-name>
  <description>
    Examples from Professional XML Development with Apache Tools.
  </description>
  <servlet>
    <servlet-name>XMLServlet</servlet-name>
    <servlet-class>
      com.sauria.apachexml.ch8.XMLRPCServlet
    </servlet-class>
  </servlet>
  <servlet-mapping>
    <servlet-name>XMLServlet</servlet-name>
    <url-pattern>/RPC2/*</url-pattern>
  </servlet-mapping>
</web-app>
```

Using SSL

XML-RPC is wonderful because it lets you invoke functionality over the Internet. This is also potentially a problem from a security point of view. Fortunately, many of the same techniques that apply to secure Web applications also apply to XML-RPC applications. You've already seen that the Apache XML-RPC libraries provide support for HTTP BASIC authentication. Unfortunately, BASIC authentication is weak because it encrypts the username and password pair using base64 encoding. If you combine BASIC authentication with Secure Sockets Layer (SSL) encryption, you get something that's a little more workable. You also need SSL because the XML payload of XML-RPC is much more approachable by human beings, which increases the need to protect the data via encryption. Binary RPC protocols make a little work necessary to dig out the contents of an RPC payload; doing RPC with XML makes doing so downright easy.

The developers of the Apache XML-RPC libraries have built classes to make it easier to implement an SSL-based XML-RPC solution. By creating secure versions of the WebServer and XmlRpcClient classes, they've taken some of the pain out of dealing with SSL—at least within the Java code for your application.

We won't give a tutorial on SSL here, so we assume you already know what SSL is for and basically how it works. We'll cover enough of the setup that you can use SSL with your XML-RPC applications. The first thing you need in order to use SSL is an SSL certificate for the server that's providing XML-RPC procedures. Throughout this example, we'll assume that you're using Java 1.4.x (we're using JDK 1.4.2) SSL implementation and tools. This is the easiest way to demonstrate SSL capability because the Java Secure Sockets Extension (JSSE) is built into JDK 1.4 (it's a separate download and jar for earlier versions). You use the JDK keytool program to generate a private key and self-signed certificate (signed public key) for your XML-RPC server:

```
keytool -genkey -dname "cn=localhost, ou=Book, o=Sauria, c=US"
  -alias server -keypass password -keystore keystore
  -storepass password -validity 90
```

This keytool command generates a private key for the server. The key is stored in the file *keystore* with password *password*. It uses the alias server and is valid for 90 days. The arguments to the -dname flag provide the organization information needed by the certificate.

Next you use keytool to export the certificate for the key whose alias is server into server.cer:

```
keytool -export -alias server -keystore keystore -keypass password
  -storepass password -rfc -file server.cer
```

You need to provide the *keystore* and keystore *password* to get access to the key you created in the previous step. You also need to export the certificate in RFC 1421 format (the -rfc flag).

The last thing that you need to do is import the certificate into a file that a client JSSE program can use as a truststore. The *truststore* is a list of certificates that the application should trust. Once again, keytool does the job. You import the certificate from the server.cer file you created earlier into a keystore file called *truststore*. As usual, you supply the necessary password:

```
keytool -import -alias server -file server.cer -keystore truststore
  -storepass password
```

When keytool asks you

```
Trust this certificate? [no]:
```

you answer yes. Now a client can use this truststore and know that the certificate you generated is trustworthy.

Now let's look at an XML-RPC server that uses SSL. This server is a modification of the earlier BasicServer example. The createBook procedure is the same as in BasicServer:

```
/*
 *
 * BasicSecureServer.java
 *
 * Example from "Professional XML Development with Apache Tools"
 *
 */
package com.sauria.apachexml.ch8;

import java.io.FileWriter;
import java.io.IOException;
import java.io.PrintWriter;

import org.apache.xmlrpc.secure.SecureWebServer;
import org.apache.xmlrpc.secure.SecurityTool;

public class BasicSecureServer {

    public Boolean createBook(String author, String title,
                              String isbn, String month,
                              int year, String publisher,
                              String address) {
        try {
            PrintWriter w =
                new PrintWriter(new FileWriter(isbn+".txt"));
            w.println(author);
            w.println(title);
            w.println(isbn);
            w.println(month);
            w.println(year);
            w.println(publisher);
            w.println(address);
            w.close();
        } catch (IOException e) {
            e.printStackTrace();
            return Boolean.FALSE;
        }
        return Boolean.TRUE;
    }
```

Here you use the new server class as the handler:

```

    public static void main(String[] args) {
        BasicSecureServer handler = new BasicSecureServer();
```

The big task is using the org.xml.apache.xmlrpc.secure.SecurityTool class to set up the parameters for using SSL. The server needs to be told which security protocol it's using, where to find the server keystore, and what the password for that keystore is. This information is used to set up SSL for the server's connection:

```

        SecurityTool.setSecurityProtocol("SSL");
        SecurityTool.setKeyStore("./keystore");
        SecurityTool.setKeyStorePassword("password");
```

You replace the use of the org.apache.xmlrpc.WebServer class with org.apache.xmlrpc.SecureWebServer, and everything looks as it did before:

```

        SecureWebServer s = null;

        try {
            s = new SecureWebServer(8080);
        } catch (IOException ioe) {
            ioe.printStackTrace();
        }

        s.addHandler("books", handler);
    }
}
```

To use SSL, you use the org.apache.xmlrpc.secure.SecureXmlRpcClient:

```
/*
 *
 * BasicSecureClient.java
 *
 * Example from "Professional XML Development with Apache Tools"
 *
 */
package com.sauria.apachexml.ch8;

import java.io.IOException;
import java.net.MalformedURLException;
import java.util.Vector;

import org.apache.xmlrpc.XmlRpcException;
import org.apache.xmlrpc.secure.SecureXmlRpcClient;
import org.apache.xmlrpc.secure.SecurityTool;

public class BasicSecureClient {

    public static void main(String[] args) {
        SecureXmlRpcClient s = null;
```

Before you create the SecureXmlRpcClient instance, you use SecurityTool to tell the client to use SSL, as well as the location and password for the keystore and truststore. The truststore is the important piece here, because it determines whether the client decides to trust the certificate presented by the server. The

SecurityTool setup method wants values for the keystore as well, so you supply the empty string to keep SecurityTool happy:

```

        try {
            SecurityTool.setSecurityProtocol("SSL");
            SecurityTool.setKeyStore("");
            SecurityTool.setKeyStorePassword("");
            SecurityTool.setTrustStore("./truststore");
            SecurityTool.setTrustStorePassword("password");
```

After you instantiate the SecureXmlRpcClient, you need to call its setup method to set everything up for using SSL. After that, the rest of the code is identical to what you saw in BasicClient:

```
            s = new SecureXmlRpcClient("https://localhost:8080");
            try {
                s.setup();
            } catch (Exception e) {
                e.printStackTrace();
            }
        } catch (MalformedURLException mue) {
            mue.printStackTrace();
        }

        Vector params = new Vector();
        params.addElement("Theodore W. Leung");
        params.addElement(
            "Professional XML Development with Apache Tools");
        params.addElement("0-7645-4355-5");
        params.addElement("December");
        params.addElement(new Integer(2003));
        params.addElement("Wrox");
        params.addElement("Indianapolis, Indiana");

        try {
            Boolean result = (Boolean)
                s.execute("books.createBook", params);
            System.out.println(result);
        } catch (XmlRpcException xre) {
            xre.printStackTrace();
        } catch (IOException ioe) {
            ioe.printStackTrace();
        }
    }
}
```

Using the JSSE isn't the only option you have on the server side. If you're running XML-RPC services via a servlet inside a J2EE Web container, you may be able to benefit from the container's handling of SSL. If you're using something like Tomcat, Jetty, or Resin, this probably won't help much, because more likely than not they're using JSSE to do their SSL processing—although we've seen Tomcat installations that sat behind hardware SSL accelerators. If you're using Tomcat with an Apache Web connector, WebSphere, or WebLogic, then you may benefit from a C implementation of SSL. In this case, the SSL-encrypted content will already be decrypted by the time it reaches your XML-RPC servlet, and you won't have to worry about dealing with SSL.

Practical Usage

XML-RPC depends on the types in the client call and the server call matching exactly. You need to use the tables from earlier in the chapter to check that all the types match. Otherwise you'll get exceptions saying that methods could not be found. This is particularly difficult on the client side because there is no checking on the Vector of parameters that's passed to the execute method. If you leave out an argument or reverse the order, it can be a frustrating experience to debug.

You can debug these sorts of problems by using an HTTP monitoring program such as the tcpmon utility included with Axis. This program sits between you and the HTTP server and displays the contents of the HTTP request and response as they're generated. The only trick is that you need to change the port in either your client or server program so you can interpose the monitor program. An alternate solution is to use an Ethernet packet sniffer like Ethereal (www.ethereal.com) to look at the network packets as they go by. If you're on a switched network, you may not be able to use Ethereal.

If you're on a network with a firewall, the firewall may interfere with your ability to use XML-RPC, particularly if you specify an unusual port number. You can check to see if this is happening by using the telnet command. By typing

```
telnet <host> <port>
```

you can determine whether you can make a network connection to the particular port on the host. The host can be a domain name or an IP address. If telnet can't connect and you know the server is up and running on that host and port, then there may be a firewall between you.

Applications

XML-RPC is a technology that makes it possible to invoke procedures located on another machine, possibly across the Internet. The applications for XML-RPC are the same ones that exist for regular procedure calls, with a few caveats.

You should be careful not to make your RPCs too fine grained, or your application will spend more time invoking the procedure with XML than it will spend executing the actual procedure on the remote machine. This is a recipe for bad performance. You should also try to design your application so that you minimize the number of RPC calls your application needs to make.

One of the most popular applications for XML-RPC is in the emerging field of social software. Because it's easy to use and implement, XML-RPC is undergoing significant deployment by the creators of Weblogging software systems. XML-RPC is used to notify aggregation servers about Weblog updates. It's also used as the basis for APIs that allow rich Weblogging client programs to update Weblogs that reside on hosted Web servers.

Simplifying XML-RPC

We'll leave you with a program that's not an application; but, depending on your philosophical bent, it demonstrates a technique that can be helpful when you're building applications. When you're using Apache XML-RPC, you can mess up the arguments you pass to XmlRpcClient's execute method. We'll show you a way to use Java dynamic proxies along with an interface to make things a bit easier. You'll define an interface that contains the procedures you want to use via XML-RPC (shown in the following listing). Instead of dealing directly with XML-RPC, you'll deal with a Java dynamic proxy that implements this interface. The dynamic proxy takes care of translating a call on the interface methods into an XML-RPC call. You'll use the same interface on the server side to help define the server-side handler. By using the interface, you can eliminate errors that occur due to problems setting up the parameter Vector:

```
/*
 *
 * BookHandler.java
 *
 * Example from "Professional XML Development with Apache Tools"
 *
 */
package com.sauria.apachexml.ch8;

public interface BookHandler {
    public Boolean createBook(String author, String title,
                              String isbn, String month,
                              int year, String publisher,
                              String address);
}
```

The real work is done by the XmlRpcProxy class shown next. A *dynamic proxy* is a class that acts as a proxy for another class. (Dynamic proxies are available only in JDK 1.3 and above.) The proxied class must implement some number of interfaces. The dynamic proxy can intercept the invocation of those interfaces' methods. The neat thing about dynamic proxies is that the proxy relationship can be set up at runtime, not compile time. When a dynamic proxy is created, it needs an object that implements the InvocationHandler interface, because this is how the proxy describes the interception behavior. To keep things neat, the class that implements InvocationHandler normally provides a factory method that creates a dynamic proxy that uses that InvocationHandler. The dynamic proxy usually wraps the methods of the class it's proxying.

The newInstance method is the factory method used to obtain an XmlRpcProxy. The obj argument is the class that will be proxied, the String url is the URL of the XML-RPC server, and the String handler is the name of the XML-RPC handler on which the proxy will invoke methods:

```
/*
 *
 * XmlRpcProxy.java
 *
 * Example from "Professional XML Development with Apache Tools"
 *
 */
package com.sauria.apachexml.ch8;

import java.lang.reflect.InvocationHandler;
import java.lang.reflect.Method;
import java.lang.reflect.Proxy;
import java.util.Vector;

import org.apache.xmlrpc.XmlRpcClient;
```

```

public class XmlRpcProxy implements InvocationHandler {
    String url = null;
    String handler = null;
    Object obj;
    XmlRpcClient xmlProxy;

    public static Object newInstance(Object obj,
                                     String handler,
                                     String url) {
        return Proxy.newProxyInstance(
            obj.getClass().getClassLoader(),
            obj.getClass().getInterfaces(),
            new XmlRpcProxy(obj, handler, url));
    }
```

Instances of XmlRpcProxy save the object being proxied, the URL of the XML-RPC server, and the XML-RPC handler to invoke. This is more information than you need. You don't need to save the object being proxied—the method you're invoking is just a type-safe template you're using to protect against errors in using XML-RPC. All the real work is done by the remote method. You can see that in the invoke method; you never use obj (the object being proxied):

```

    public XmlRpcProxy(Object o, String u, String h) {
        obj = o;
        url = u;
        handler = h;
    }

    public Object invoke(Object proxy, Method method,
                         Object[] args)
        throws Throwable {
```

The body of the invoke method is responsible for invoking the XML-RPC procedure. Invoke is called when any proxied method is called. In this example, when someone calls the createBook method on the dynamic proxy, invoke is called to handle it.

Invoke first builds up XML-RPC's Vector of parameters by iterating over the args[] array. This is how you convert from the type-safe signature method createBook in the BookHandler interface to the non-type-safe Vector of parameters needed by XML-RPC. All you have to do is copy the argument values into the Vector. The type-checking has been done at compile time:

```
        Object result = null;
        Vector params = new Vector();

        for (int i = 0; i < args.length; i++) {
            params.add(args[i]);
        }
```

Now you create an instance of XmlRpcClient so you can invoke the method:

```

        xmlProxy = new XmlRpcClient(url);
```

Finally, the proxy executes the XML-RPC call and returns the result:

```
            result = xmlProxy.execute(handler+"."+method.getName(),
                                          params);

            return result;
        }
}
```

XmlRpcProxyTest is the test class that shows off how this technique works. Lines 10-21 show how you implement the BookHandler interface, and the main method shows how you use it:

```
 1: /*
 2:  *
 3:  * XmlRpcProxyTest.java
 4:  *
 5:  * Example from "Professional XML Development with Apache Tools"
 6:  *
 7:  */
 8: package com.sauria.apachexml.ch8;
 9:
10: public class XmlRpcProxyTest implements BookHandler {
11:
12:     public Boolean createBook(
13:         String author,
14:         String title,
15:         String isbn,
16:         String month,
17:         int year,
18:         String publisher,
19:         String address) {
20:         return null;
21:     }
22:
23:     public static void main(String[] args) {
24:         Object o = XmlRpcProxy.newInstance(
25:                         new XmlRpcProxyTest(),
26:                         "http://localhost:8080",
27:                         "books");
28:
29:         BookHandler h = (BookHandler) o;
```

You call the factory method on XmlRpcProxy to create a proxy instance that uses the XML-RPC server at http://localhost:8080 and dispatches to the handler named books that's registered on that serer. You also need to cast the proxy class to the BookHandler interface.

All that's left to do is call the createBook method and print the result. Note that the call to createBook is a regular Java method invocation, which is type-checked at compile time:

```
30:
31:         Boolean b = h.createBook(
32:             "Theodore W. Leung",
33:             "Professional XML Development with Apache Tools",
```

```
            "0-7645-4355-5",
            "December",
            2003,
            "Wrox",
            "Indianapolis, Indiana");
        System.out.println(b);
    }
}
```

To round out the picture, here's a version of BasicServer that uses the BookHandler interface. It ensures that changes to BookHandler's methods are reflected on both the client side and the server side:

```
/*
 *
 * BasicHandlerServer.java
 *
 * Example from "Professional XML Development with Apache Tools"
 *
 */
package com.sauria.apachexml.ch8;

import java.io.FileWriter;
import java.io.IOException;
import java.io.PrintWriter;

import org.apache.xmlrpc.WebServer;

public class BasicHandlerServer implements BookHandler {
```

The only change needed to BasicServer is to make it implement BookHandler, which "coincidentally" already has the proper createBook method:

```

    public Boolean createBook(String author, String title,
                              String isbn, String month,
                              int year, String publisher,
                              String address) {
        try {
            PrintWriter w =
                new PrintWriter(new FileWriter(isbn+".txt"));
            w.println(author);
            w.println(title);
            w.println(isbn);
            w.println(month);
            w.println(year);
            w.println(publisher);
            w.println(address);
            w.close();
        } catch (IOException e) {
            e.printStackTrace();
            return Boolean.FALSE;
        }
        return Boolean.TRUE;
    }
```

```

    public static void main(String[] args) {
        BasicHandlerServer handler = new BasicHandlerServer();

        WebServer s = null;

        try {
            s = new WebServer(8080);
        } catch (IOException ioe) {
            ioe.printStackTrace();
        }

        s.addHandler("books", handler);
    }
}
```

This concludes our tour of XML-RPC. If you need something simple and lightweight to connect a client and a server, or if you need to talk to minority languages like Python or Ruby, then XML-RPC is a good choice. For larger applications in an enterprise context, you might consider XML-RPC's bigger cousin, SOAP. We'll look at Apache Axis, the ASF SOAP and WSDL engine, in Chapter 9.

Axis

You've probably heard the term *Web services* being tossed around. In this chapter we'll talk about Apache Axis, which is the Apache project that's implementing some of the base Web services specifications. Let's begin by explaining what Web services are. The idea behind Web services is to create modular applications that communicate with each other using Internet standards such as XML and HTTP. The Web services area is growing a lot of specifications that cover everything from workflow to security. But at their simplest, Web services are about breaking applications into pieces. Each self-contained piece is called a *service*. Examples of services include charging a purchase to a credit card, performing an address check, computing a loan balance, processing a loan application, and so on. By using Internet standards to tie these services together, the hope is that we can build reusable applications that can interoperate across operating system and programming language boundaries. It's a tall order, but we already have the lowest level infrastructure that lets you describe a service, publish that description, and invoke functionality on the service based on that description. That's the functionality in Apache Axis.

We need to discuss two important XML-based technologies—WSDL and SOAP—in order for you to use Axis to describe and invoke services. The Web Services Description Language (WSDL) lets you describe a Web service using an XML document. If you're familiar with CORBA's IDL (Interface Description Language) or Microsoft's IDL or MIDL, then the idea of WSDL will be familiar to you. As you'll see, the concepts have been recast using services terminology, and XML is used as the syntax for the service description. SOAP is the other technology we'll look at; it provides the mechanism for invoking service functionality using XML.

The Web services area is generating a lot of excitement, some of it deserved and some of it undeserved (at least at the moment). There's so much activity that in early 2003, the Apache Software Foundation decided to create a new top-level project dedicated to Web services. A few projects in the XML project already were Web-services related, and the people working in those projects wanted a closer sense of community with each other and a more focused Web site and governance.

One of the projects that moved from the XML project to the Web Services project was Axis. Unfortunately, the situation is a little confusing. There are multiple SOAP projects at the ASF, for historical reasons. The original SOAP project was called Apache SOAP and was based on a code base donated to Apache by IBM. Apache SOAP targeted SOAP 1.1, but it had issues with efficiency and its internal architecture, and it was quickly decided that a major overhaul was needed. At the same time, a number of people were already using Apache SOAP in production. Apache Axis is best understood as Apache SOAP 2.0. (Conceptually, that's what it is.) Most of the Apache SOAP committers went on to work on Axis and only worked on Apache SOAP as a maintenance project. Today Apache Axis has so many benefits over Apache SOAP (better SOAP 1.1 compliance, better interoperability with other SOAP stacks, WSDL support, support for the JAX-RPC API) that there's no reason to use Apache SOAP if you're starting a new project. Axis is where it's at, for now and the foreseeable future.

Prerequisites

In order to follow the material in this chapter, you need to know about XML, including namespaces, and you need to know a little about HTTP and Java servlets. You also need to understand XML Schema, because the current type system for WSDL is based on it. In the next section we'll give an overview and limited introduction to SOAP, WSDL, and JAX-RPC (the Java API for XML-based RPC), but we expect that you're already somewhat familiar with them.

Concepts

We'll cover WSDL and SOAP in an odd order. When you're developing a Web service, the best way to do it is to work with WSDL and let tools generate skeleton code that you then fill in. For the most part, the skeleton code will keep you from having to know about the gory details of SOAP. At least, that's the theory. Unfortunately, to write the WSDL description, you need to understand some things about SOAP. So, although we should be talking about WSDL first, we'll discuss SOAP first and then WSDL. Once we've finished with these two, we'll go on to JAX-RPC.

SOAP

You'll recall from Chapter 8 that development of SOAP continued after XML-RPC was created. There have been three versions of SOAP: 0.9, 1.1, and, most recently, 1.2. SOAP has grown from its beginnings as an informal collaboration between Userland Software, DevelopMentor, and Microsoft, adding IBM/Lotus as collaborators, and finally moving to the W3C. At the time of this writing (August 2003), SOAP 1.1 is the version that's most widely deployed. SOAP 1.2 was the first version of SOAP to be standardized by the W3C (in June 2003).

SOAP can be described many ways. One way to look at SOAP is that it's a bigger brother to XML-RPC, meaning that it combines XML and HTTP to provide a mechanism for invoking functionality on remote machines. That was the original understanding of what SOAP was about, and it shows if you read the SOAP 0.9 or 1.1 specifications—a large chunk of the specification is devoted to rules for encoding types in XML, which is necessary for remote procedure call semantics. It's also evident in Sun's naming of JAX-RPC—the Java API for XML-based RPC.

At its simplest, SOAP is an XML vocabulary for describing one-way messages. The SOAP specification says that a message is an <Envelope>, which can contain an optional <Header> and a mandatory

<Body> as its children. Everything else SOAP can be used for is built on that basic concept. This includes messaging modes (one-way versus request-response) and type-encoding rules. The key thing to remember is that you can put anything you want into either the <Header> or <Body> of a SOAP message (you should use namespaces to keep things tidy). What happens to the message is determined by a set of conventions.

SOAP RPC Request

To make this discussion more concrete, let's look at a SOAP message that represents a remote procedure invocation transported using HTTP. As you can see, this is a normal HTTP request (a POST):

```
 1: POST /apache-xml-book-web-axis/services/BookService HTTP/1.0
 2: Content-Type: text/xml; charset=utf-8
 3: Accept: application/soap+xml, text/*
```

In order to get the listing to fit in this space, we removed two entries from the list of Accept: headers: application/dime and multipart/related. Taken together, they allow SOAP attachments to be returned as the result of the procedure call, using either the DIME or SOAP with Attachments specification.

The next few lines are just regular HTTP headers. We're most interested in the SOAP message, which starts at line 11:

```
 4: User-Agent: Axis/1.1
 5: Host: 127.0.0.1
 6: Cache-Control: no-cache
 7: Pragma: no-cache
 8: SOAPAction: ""
 9: Content-Length: 840
10:
11: <?xml version="1.0" encoding="UTF-8"?>
```

This is plain XML, so you have an XML declaration with version and encoding attributes.

The message consists of a single root element named Envelope, which is taken from the namespace associated with the soapenv namespace prefix. (You'll see lots of namespaces when you're working with SOAP, so get used to it.) Here, there are declarations for the soapenv prefix, which is bound to the URI for the SOAP 1.1 envelope namespace. The xsd and xsi namespaces are bound to the XML Schema and XML Schema Instance namespaces, per convention:

```
12: <soapenv:Envelope
13:  xmlns:soapenv="http://schemas.xmlsoap.org/soap/envelope/"
14:  xmlns:xsd="http://www.w3.org/2001/XMLSchema"
15:  xmlns:xsi="http://www.w3.org/2001/XMLSchema-instance">
```

Note that no header is attached to this Envelope. If there were a Header element or elements, they would have to be in a namespace. That's not true of elements in the Body of the message—they don't have to be in a namespace.

Turning to the Body of the Envelope, you find a single element: a createBook element taken from the ns1 namespace, which is bound to a URI that looks oddly like a reversed fully qualified Java classname.

The createBook element also has a soapenv:encodingStyle attribute, which is set to the URI for the SOAP encoding:

```
<soapenv:Body>
 <ns1:createBook
  soapenv:encodingStyle=
   "http://schemas.xmlsoap.org/soap/encoding/"
  xmlns:ns1="http://BookService.ch9.apachexml.sauria.com">
```

What's going on here? The answer is that you're seeing a usage convention at work. When you use SOAP for a procedure call, the convention says that a SOAP strut is used as the content of the Body. In SOAP, a *struct* is an element with child elements, one per element of the struct. The name of the struct element is the name of the struct type, and the child elements are called *accessor elements*. The type name of the struct is the name of the procedure to be executed. The accessors of the procedure struct are the arguments to the procedure. The soapenv:encodingStyle attribute specifies the rules used to convert programming language types into SOAP data types. The ns1 namespace is a way to clearly define where the values of the procedure call struct are taken from. You know that namespace URIs must be unique values and don't need any special meaning.

From here on, you see a sequence of accessor elements. Each accessor corresponds to a parameter of the method being called. The xsi:type attribute is used to tell the SOAP runtime what the type of the data is. In this example, all the types are drawn from the XML Schema data types. There you have it, a full SOAP message.

```
  <author xsi:type="xsd:string">Theodore W. Leung</author>
  <title
   xsi:type="xsd:string">
   Professional XML Development with Apache Tools
  </title>
  <isbn xsi:type="xsd:string">0-7645-4355-5</isbn>
  <month xsi:type="xsd:string">December</month>
  <year xsi:type="xsd:int">2003</year>
  <publisher
   xsi:type="xsd:string">
   Wrox
  </publisher>
  <address xsi:type="xsd:string">Indianapolis, Indiana</address>
 </ns1:createBook>
</soapenv:Body>
</soapenv:Envelope>
```

SOAP RPC Response

Just to complete the picture, let's look at what happens when the called procedure returns. Because you're using HTTP to transport the XML messages, a reasonable route for the procedure return value is the HTTP response that corresponds to the HTTP request used to transport the invocation message. And sure enough, that's what you find.

```
HTTP/1.1 200 OK
Content-Type: text/xml; charset=utf-8
```

The HTTP 200 status code means that everything went ok, and the Content-Type: tells you that you're getting XML as the response payload.

```
Date: Fri, 22 Aug 2003 23:53:27 GMT
Server: Apache Coyote/1.0
Connection: close

```

Once again, after the HTTP headers, you see an XML document, which contains a SOAP envelope.

```
<?xml version="1.0" encoding="UTF-8"?>
<soapenv:Envelope
 xmlns:soapenv="http://schemas.xmlsoap.org/soap/envelope/"
 xmlns:xsd="http://www.w3.org/2001/XMLSchema"
 xmlns:xsi="http://www.w3.org/2001/XMLSchema-instance">
 <soapenv:Body>
```

Everything looks the same as the Envelope from the procedure invocation. The Envelope element declares a bunch of namespaces that are used by the rest of the Envelope. The difference shows up when you get to the body. Once again, you're looking at a SOAP struct, which is interpreted by convention. The struct element, <createBookReturn> contains as single accessor <createBookReturn> which is the return value. If the called procedure defined input/output arguments, then they would appear as accessors after the return value.

```
  <ns1:createBookResponse
   soapenv:encodingStyle=
    "http://schemas.xmlsoap.org/soap/encoding/"
   xmlns:ns1="http://BookService.ch9.apachexml.sauria.com">
   <createBookReturn
    xsi:type="xsd:boolean">false</createBookReturn>
  </ns1:createBookResponse>
 </soapenv:Body>
</soapenv:Envelope>
```

SOAP RPC Fault

If a remote invocation doesn't go well, you get error feedback both from the HTTP response and from the XML returned in the response. You get an HTTP 500 error status instead of a 200. You also get some content in the response, again, as XML:

```
HTTP/1.1 500 Internal Server Error
Content-Type: text/xml; charset=utf-8
Date: Sat, 23 Aug 2003 02:18:00 GMT
Server: Apache Coyote/1.0
Connection: close

```

The designers of SOAP tried to keep things uniform, so the XML that comes back in the response is also a SOAP envelope. This time, it's a SOAP fault envelope:

```
<?xml version="1.0" encoding="UTF-8"?>
<soapenv:Envelope
```

```
 xmlns:soapenv="http://schemas.xmlsoap.org/soap/envelope/"
 xmlns:xsd="http://www.w3.org/2001/XMLSchema"
 xmlns:xsi="http://www.w3.org/2001/XMLSchema-instance">
 <soapenv:Body>
```

The difference between a SOAP fault envelope and the other envelopes you've seen is that the child element of the SOAP Body element is a SOAP Fault element:

```
  <soapenv:Fault>
   <faultcode>soapenv:Server.userException</faultcode>
   <faultstring>java.lang.IllegalArgumentException</faultstring>
   <detail/>
  </soapenv:Fault>
 </soapenv:Body>
</soapenv:Envelope>
```

The Fault element contains three elements: <faultcode>, which is an error code meant for processing by a program; <faultstring>, which is a text string meant for processing by a human; and an optional <detail> element, which can be use to return application-specific fault information.

As you can see, it takes two SOAP messages—one for the request and one for the response—to accomplish a remote procedure invocation. SOAP is all about messages, and these messages can be combined to accomplish more complicated tasks such as remote procedure invocation. All that SOAP provides is a way to describe the contents of messages and breaking them into a header and a body. The SOAP encoding is used to convert programming language types into XML schema types. The encoding isn't required; you can easily specify your own encoding by changing the value of the soapenv:encodingStyle attribute. If you're going to use an encoding, you should probably stick to the SOAP encoding. For the types defined by the SOAP encoding, this gives you a way to invoke procedures on services, regardless of the language in which the requestor and provider are written.

As long as the types being used can be encoded using the SOAP encoding, you should be able to interoperate. It's this last sentence where things get a little difficult. The SOAP encoding doesn't cover every type available in every programming language. In Java, it doesn't really cover objects, although the JAX-RPC specification tries to fill this hole. The problem is that if you want to transfer types that aren't covered by the SOAP encoding, you have to make up your own. And now you have an interoperability problem, because you can't guarantee that anyone else can understand your encoding unless you tell them how.

For this reason, people are starting to shift away from using the SOAP encoding and are moving toward making the contents of SOAP Body elements be XML elements that are specified by an XML Schema definition. Because XML Schema can express relatively rich types, this gives a much larger palette of types (and combination rules) to work from. You'll hear this referred to a *literal mode* SOAP.

WSDL

The Web Services Description Language (WSDL) uses XML to describe Web services. The original specification was authored by IBM and Microsoft, and version 1.1 was submitted to the W3C for standardization. The first W3C version will be WSDL 1.2, which is currently a W3C Working Draft. WSDL 1.1 is deployed in the field and is supported by a number of Web services toolkits, including Axis.

You need to be familiar with a number of concepts in order to work with WSDL. A *port type* is an abstract description of a Web service. It's a set of operations. Conceptually, these are the operations a service requestor requests in order to access the service's functionality. Operations rely on *messages* to get their work done. An operation can have an input message and/or an output message. A service requestor causes an input message to be sent to the service when it invokes an operation on the service. Messages are composed of parts—the individual pieces. In the case of an input message, which represents the operation name and arguments, a part is associated with each argument. WSDL maps parts onto the XML Schema type system.

You can begin to see the relationship between WSDL and SOAP. The messages described by WSDL could be SOAP messages. It's important to understand that WSDL doesn't say the message is a SOAP message. All the concepts we've talked about to this point are abstract and could be implemented using SOAP messages over HTTP or ASN.1 messages over UDP. WSDL doesn't care. It just defines the operations available on a port type, the messages that make up the operations, and the parts that make up the messages. The following figure illustrates these concepts in a graphical manner:

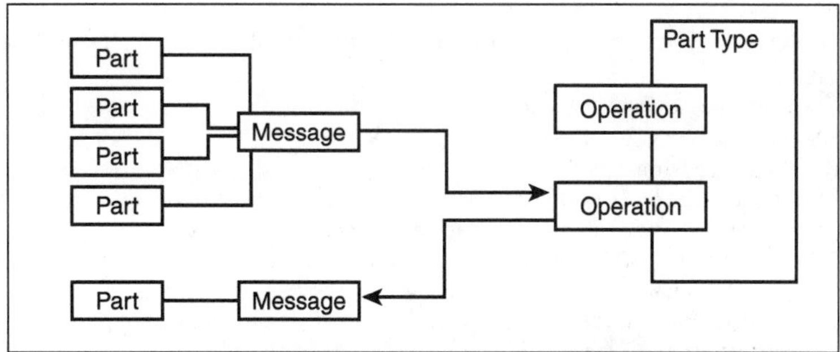

Fortunately, that's not all WSDL does. WSDL has a notion of *bindings*. A binding allows you to connect WSDL operations and port types to wire protocols and data formats to obtain a description of a service that can be invoked by real computers. When you combine a binding with a port type you get a *port*, which is a thing that can be invoked by a program. A collection of such ports is called a *service*. The relationship between port types, bindings, ports, and services is shown in this figure:

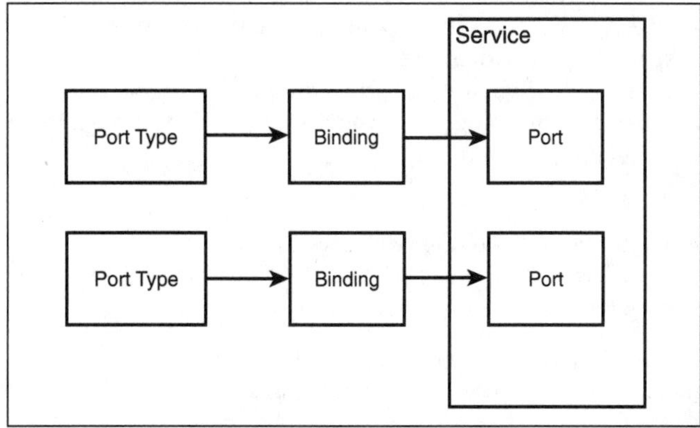

WSDL specifies a binding for SOAP over HTTP, for HTTP GET and POST, and for MIME. Other bindings are under development. Given a WSDL description that uses the SOAP over HTTP binding, you can write tools that generate SOAP-based Web services from the WSDL file. This is much easier than trying to write all the code by hand, and if the tools are consistent in their interpretation of the WSDL specification, then there should be good interoperability between services created this way. At the WSDL 1.1 level, there are still some interoperability problems. Many of these issues will be addressed in WSDL 1.2. In the meantime, the Web Services Interoperability Organization (WS-I) has issued a Basic Profile that includes a number of guidelines for using SOAP 1.1 and WSDL 1.1 in an interoperable manner. You can find the WS-I at www.ws-i.org.

A Real WSDL File

Let's dive into a real WSDL file. This WSDL file describes a Web service that represents a book service. The service supports one operation at the moment, createBook, which takes as arguments the information needed for a book record. Invoking the operation creates a book record in the Web service. The signature of the createBook method might look like this in Java:

```
public boolean createBook(String author, String title, String isbn,
    String month, int year, String publisher, String address)
```

Now, on to the WSDL file. The root element of a WSDL document is a <definitions> element taken from the wsdl namespace:

```
<?xml version="1.0" encoding="UTF-8"?>
<wsdl:definitions
 targetNamespace="http://BookService.ch9.apachexml.sauria.com"
 xmlns="http://schemas.xmlsoap.org/wsdl/"
 xmlns:impl="http://BookService.ch9.apachexml.sauria.com"
 xmlns:wsdl="http://schemas.xmlsoap.org/wsdl/"
 xmlns:wsdlsoap="http://schemas.xmlsoap.org/wsdl/soap/"
 xmlns:xsd="http://www.w3.org/2001/XMLSchema">
```

As you can see from the number of namespace declarations on the <definitions> element, you'll be using a lot of namespaces. Most of these uses are self evident, but we'll point out anything relevant as we go. The order of the elements in a WSDL document is significant. It starts with messages and parts and builds up until it gets to services. This allows WSDL processing tools to work in a single pass:

Next is a pair of message declarations. As you can see, each message has a name and is composed of one or more parts. The parts are named, and the order in which they appear in the message is significant. Each message part is also associated with a type. In this example, you're using the type attribute to associate a message part with an XML Schema type (either complex or simple types are allowed). You can also associate parts with elements by using the element attribute. In this case, the type associated with the element is the type of the message part:

```

 <wsdl:message name="createBookResponse">
  <wsdl:part name="createBookReturn" type="xsd:boolean"/>
 </wsdl:message>

 <wsdl:message name="createBookRequest">
  <wsdl:part name="author" type="xsd:string"/>
  <wsdl:part name="title" type="xsd:string"/>
  <wsdl:part name="isbn" type="xsd:string"/>
  <wsdl:part name="month" type="xsd:string"/>
```

```
    <wsdl:part name="year" type="xsd:int"/>
    <wsdl:part name="publisher" type="xsd:string"/>
    <wsdl:part name="address" type="xsd:string"/>
  </wsdl:message>
```

Once you've defined all the messages you need, you can use those messages to create operations. Because operations are tied to port types, you need a <portType> element. The <portType> is named and contains a sequence of operations. This example contains a single operation named createBook. The createBook operation has an input message and an output message. The input message is bound to the createBookRequest message, and the output message is bound to the createBookResponse message. Note that each of the message names is namespace-prefixed with *impl*. The impl prefix is bound to the same namespace URI as the targetNamespace of the WSDL document. Because you created the two messages with unprefixed names, they are in the targetNamespace and require prefixing when used as the value of the message attribute.

The <operation> element also has a parameterOrder attribute. This optional attribute provides a way to record the original RPC signature if the operation corresponds to an RPC invocation. It specifies the order of the parts in terms of their order in the RPC signature:

```
  <wsdl:portType name="BookHandler">
   <wsdl:operation
    name="createBook"
    parameterOrder=
     "author title isbn month year publisher address">
    <wsdl:input message="impl:createBookRequest"
     name="createBookRequest"/>
    <wsdl:output message="impl:createBookResponse"
     name="createBookResponse"/>
   </wsdl:operation>
  </wsdl:portType>
```

One other note about the parts involved in input and output messages: Nothing about the way messages are defined prevents the same part from appearing in both an input and output message. This gives you a convenient way to represent in/out parameters. If a part appears only in an input message, it's an in parameter. If it appears only in an output message, it's an out parameter. When a part appears in both the input and output messages of an operation, then it's an in/out parameter.

The <binding> element creates a binding between a WSDL port type and a message format and transport protocol. Here you're creating a binding to SOAP of HTTP:

```
  <wsdl:binding
   name="BookServiceSoapBinding" type="impl:BookHandler">
   <wsdlsoap:binding style="rpc"
    transport="http://schemas.xmlsoap.org/soap/http"/>
```

The <binding> element looks a lot like the <portType> element. It establishes a name for the binding, and the type attribute give the name of the portType (again, namespace qualified) the binding is for. The first child of the <binding> element is another <binding> element, but this one is taken from the wsdlsoap namespace, which is the namespace for the WSDL SOAP binding. The <wsdlsoap:binding>

element specifies that the transport being used is HTTP (via the transport attribute). Elements like <wsdlsoap:binding> are known as *extensibility elements*.

The style attribute on <wsdlsoap> binding determines the mode for the operation. There are two modes: rpc and document. (The default value is "document".) The rpc mode signals that the usage pattern of the messages is RPC-oriented (request and response message), whereas document means the usage is XML document oriented (possibly request and response, possibly request only or response only). In practice, this difference confuses a lot of people because there's no reason you can't use the document style to perform remote procedure calls. In fact, the Microsoft .NET tools do this, and the WS-I basic profile mandates document-literal mode for interoperability (we're talking about the document part now—we'll get to the literal part in a moment). The use of rpc versus document style does have one concrete effect. When WSDL is bound to SOAP, each WSDL message part appears as an element in the Body of the SOAP envelope. In rpc style, the Body of a SOAP message is defined to be a single wrapper (or struct) element that contains the part elements as children, whereas in document style, the message parts appear directly as children of the SOAP Body element. So, if you see a SOAP message that has multiple children of the <Body> element, you can be fairly sure it was generated from document-style WSDL. If you see only a single child, you can't always tell, because a SOAP message generated from WSDL document style may follow the structural rules (wrapper element around message part elements) used by rpc style.

The <wsdlsoap:operation> extensibility element allows you to supply a value for the SOAPAction header. Some SOAP engines use the value of this header to route the service request:

```
   <wsdl:operation name="createBook">
    <wsdlsoap:operation soapAction=""/>
```

The <wsdlsoap:body> extensibility elements tell how to interpret the message associated with an input or output message. The namespace attribute determines the namespace to use for the message. The use attribute determine whether the message's parts are encoded. This attribute has two possible values: "encoded" and "literal". If the value is "encoded", then the message parts represent abstract types, and each message part is encoded using the encoding specified by the encodingStyle attribute. If the value is "literal", then the message parts aren't encoded, but each message part is associated with an XML Schema complex or simple type:

```
    <wsdl:input name="createBookRequest">
     <wsdlsoap:body
       encodingStyle="http://schemas.xmlsoap.org/soap/encoding/"
       namespace="http://BookService.ch9.apachexml.sauria.com"
       use="encoded"/>
```

This is the other half of the document-literal mode mentioned earlier. As you can see, there are four possible combinations of style and use: rpc-encoded, rpc-literal, document-encoded, and document-literal. It's important to be aware of rpc-encoded (popular on Java-based SOAP implementations) and document-literal (the future of Web services as mandated by the WS-I).

A <wsdlsoap:body> extensibility element is needed for each <input> or <output> element in each <operation>:

```
    </wsdl:input>
    <wsdl:output name="createBookResponse">
```

```
    <wsdlsoap:body
     encodingStyle="http://schemas.xmlsoap.org/soap/encoding/"
     namespace="http://BookService.ch9.apachexml.sauria.com"
     use="encoded"/>
   </wsdl:output>
  </wsdl:operation>
 </wsdl:binding>
```

Once you have a complete binding, you're ready to put the pieces together. A WSDL <port> is a combination of a <portType> with a binding. The way WSDL documents are written, a WSDL binding element already names the portType it's associated with. You can see this via the binding attribute on <port>. All that's left to do is connect the binding to a location that provides the service. Because this process is binding specific, you do it with an extensibility element from the wsdlsoap namespace, <wsdlsoap:address>, which specifies the service location via the location attribute. Here you see a URI that handles service requests for this service:

```

 <wsdl:service name="BookHandlerService">
  <wsdl:port
   binding="impl:BookServiceSoapBinding"
   name="BookService">
   <wsdlsoap:address
    location="http://localhost:8080/apache-xml-book-web-axis/
services/BookService"/>
   </wsdl:port>
 </wsdl:service>

</wsdl:definitions>
```

A WSDL service is just a collection of ports. There's no reason you can't specify multiple ports that use the same binding but have different addresses.

A Document-Literal WSDL File

This WSDL description is for an rpc-encoded Web service. Many of the currently deployed Java Web services use the rpc-encoded style. The introduction of the WS-I Basic Profile will shift usage toward a document-literal encoding style, so document-literal is the future of interoperable Web services. With that in mind, let's look at a WSDL file for a document-literal Web service:

```
<?xml version="1.0" encoding="UTF-8"?>
<wsdl:definitions
 targetNamespace="http://SBookService.ch9.apachexml.sauria.com"
 xmlns="http://schemas.xmlsoap.org/wsdl/"
 xmlns:impl="http://SBookService.ch9.apachexml.sauria.com"
 xmlns:wsdl="http://schemas.xmlsoap.org/wsdl/"
 xmlns:wsdlsoap="http://schemas.xmlsoap.org/wsdl/soap/"
 xmlns:xsd="http://www.w3.org/2001/XMLSchema"
 xmlns:book="http://sauria.com/schemas/apache-xml-book/book" >

 <wsdl:types>
  <xsd:schema
   targetNamespace=
     "http://sauria.com/schemas/apache-xml-book/book"
```

```
    xmlns:book="http://sauria.com/schemas/apache-xml-book/book"
    elementFormDefault="qualified">
    <xsd:element name="address" type="xsd:string"/>
    <xsd:element name="author" type="xsd:string"/>
    <xsd:element name="book">
     <xsd:complexType>
      <xsd:sequence>
       <xsd:element ref="book:title"/>
       <xsd:element ref="book:author"/>
       <xsd:element ref="book:isbn"/>
       <xsd:element ref="book:month"/>
       <xsd:element ref="book:year"/>
       <xsd:element ref="book:publisher"/>
       <xsd:element ref="book:address"/>
      </xsd:sequence>
      <xsd:attribute name="version" type="xsd:string"
                     use="required"/>
     </xsd:complexType>
    </xsd:element>
    <xsd:element name="isbn" type="xsd:string"/>
    <xsd:element name="month" type="xsd:string"/>
    <xsd:element name="publisher" type="xsd:string"/>
    <xsd:element name="title" type="xsd:string"/>
    <xsd:element name="year" type="xsd:short"/>
   </xsd:schema>
  </wsdl:types>
```

The <types> element wasn't present in the first WSDL file we looked at. The content of the <types> element is an XML schema. The schema you're using here is the same schema you've used for books throughout the examples in previous chapters.

The types in a <types> element are meant to be used to define message parts. Here's the difference from the previous WSDL file: Instead of the createBookRequest consisting of a sequence of message parts, one per piece of information needed to create a book, in this version of the file there's only a single message part, which takes its type from the <book> element of the XML schema in the <types> element. Note that the <part> element uses the element attribute to get the type of the <book> element:

```

  <wsdl:message name="createBookResponse">
   <wsdl:part name="createBookReturn" type="xsd:boolean"/>
  </wsdl:message>

  <wsdl:message name="createBookRequest">
   <wsdl:part name="book" element="book:book"/>
  </wsdl:message>

  <wsdl:portType name="SBookHandler">
   <wsdl:operation name="createBook" parameterOrder="book">
    <wsdl:input message="impl:createBookRequest"
                name="createBookRequest"/>
    <wsdl:output message="impl:createBookResponse"
                 name="createBookResponse"/>
   </wsdl:operation>
  </wsdl:portType>
```

The remainder of the changes are in the <binding> for the service. The binding style is "document", as required for a document-literal Web service:

```

<wsdl:binding name="SBookServiceSoapBinding"
              type="impl:SBookHandler">
 <wsdlsoap:binding style="document"
            transport="http://schemas.xmlsoap.org/soap/http"/>
```

Because you're using document-literal style, the use attribute on <body> is set to "literal" and the encodingStyle attribute has been removed, because it's no longer needed:

```

  <wsdl:operation name="createBook">
   <wsdlsoap:operation soapAction=""/>

   <wsdl:input name="createBookRequest">
    <wsdlsoap:body
         namespace="http://SBookService.ch9.apachexml.sauria.com"
         use="literal"/>
   </wsdl:input>

   <wsdl:output name="createBookResponse">
    <wsdlsoap:body
         namespace="http://SBookService.ch9.apachexml.sauria.com"
         use="literal"/>
   </wsdl:output>
  </wsdl:operation>
 </wsdl:binding>

 <wsdl:service name="SBookHandlerService">
  <wsdl:port binding="impl:SBookServiceSoapBinding"
              name="SBookService">
   <wsdlsoap:address
      location="http://localhost:8080/apache-xml-book-web-axis/
services/SBookService"/>
  </wsdl:port>
 </wsdl:service>
</wsdl:definitions>
```

As you can see, not many changes are needed to convert a WSDL file to document-literal style. The introduction of the <types> element isn't necessary, but we wanted to give you some exposure to how it's used.

To give you an idea of how switching to document-literal affects the SOAP messages, here are the SOAP request and response messages for the earlier WSDL file. For comparison, the messages from earlier in the chapter were generated by a service generate from the following WSDL file. Notice that the book element in lines 7-15 looks exactly like a book element from Chapter 1:

```
1: <?xml version="1.0" encoding="UTF-8"?>
2: <soapenv:Envelope
```

```
 xmlns:soapenv="http://schemas.xmlsoap.org/soap/envelope/"
 xmlns:xsd="http://www.w3.org/2001/XMLSchema"
 xmlns:xsi="http://www.w3.org/2001/XMLSchema-instance">
 <soapenv:Body>
  <book xmlns="http://sauria.com/schemas/apache-xml-book/book">
   <title>Professional XML Development with Apache Tools</title>
   <author>Ted Leung</author>
   <isbn>0-7645-4355-5</isbn>
   <month>December</month>
   <year>2003</year>
   <publisher>Wrox</publisher>
   <address>Indianapolis, Indiana</address>
  </book>
 </soapenv:Body>
</soapenv:Envelope>
```

The response message hasn't changed much:

```
<?xml version="1.0" encoding="UTF-8"?>
<soapenv:Envelope
 xmlns:soapenv="http://schemas.xmlsoap.org/soap/envelope/"
 xmlns:xsd="http://www.w3.org/2001/XMLSchema"
 xmlns:xsi="http://www.w3.org/2001/XMLSchema-instance">
 <soapenv:Body>
  <createBookReturn xsi:type="xsd:boolean"
                    xmlns="">false</createBookReturn>
 </soapenv:Body>
</soapenv:Envelope>
```

JAX-RPC

The last important standard supported by Axis is JAX-RPC, the Java API for XML-based RPC. JAX-RPC provides a layer over a SOAP/WSDL runtime and is supposed to insulate applications from the vendor-specific aspects of the stack. This API is developed as part of the Java Community Process and is currently in Version 1.0.

The JAX-RPC model is based on trying to make Web services calls as similar to RMI calls as possible. The programming model is based on mapping WSDL concept to Java concepts. The concepts start in the middle of the WSDL constructs and work their way out. In JAX-RPC, the thing that corresponds to a portType is a Service Endpoint Interface (SEI). The methods on the SEI correspond to WSDL operations, with messages and ports being subsumed into the arguments to the SEI methods. Working in the other direction, there are three different client-side representations of a port: stub objects generated by tools from WSDL, a dynamic proxy-based calling interface, and a completely dynamic call interface that should be familiar to users of the CORBA Dynamic Invocation Interface (DII). On the server side, services are programmed to implement the Service interface.

JAX-RPC also defines a standardizes set of mappings from XML schema/WSDL types to Java types, so it's easy to generate Java classes from a WSDL document. It also defines the reverse mapping, from Java types to XML/WSDL types. One feature of this mapping is the notion of Holder classes, which are used when an operation has an in/out parameter. Holder classes are wrappers that allow the in/out parameter-passing semantics to be preserved. The JAX-RPC specification defines holders for every Java type that can be mapped to by an XML/WSDL type. The JAX-RPC type mapping also includes a definition for mapping Java Bean-like Java objects (which must implement the java.io.Serializable interface and public default constructor) to XML. We'll cover this information in more detail when we look at Axis's tools for working with WSDL. The important thing to know is that two different Java implementations using JAX-RPC should be able to interoperate as long as they're using the type mappings for JAX-RPC. This interoperability doesn't automatically extend to SOAP runtimes written in other languages.

On the server/service side, JAX-RPC provides a simple API for managing the life cycle of a service, via the ServletLifeCycleInterface. This assumes that the JAX-RPC implementation is based on a servlet container. A service implementer can use this interface to gain access to data available only from the servlet container.

The last piece of functionality that JAX-RPC provides is the ability to install handlers into the SOAP message path, on both the service requestor and the service provider. Handlers are pieces of code that are allowed to perform operations on a SOAP message before they reach their destination. Handlers perform computations based on the values of headers in the messages or provide features such as message logging, encryption, or digital signatures.

In Axis, you'll primarily deal with JAX-RPC via the various schemes for creating service requestors. We'll take you through each of the schemes, explaining the differences along the way. All the schemes implement a request to a service defined by the last WSDL document we showed you.

Using JAX-RPC Stubs

The most static way of writing a service provider is to use a JAX-RPC-compliant tool to generate a set of stub classes from the WSDL document. The class BookHandlerServiceLocator is generated by the WSDL2Java tool and is a factory class you can use to get a BookService class, which represents a port. That port implements the interface BookHandler, which is the SEI for the service:

```
/*
 *
 * BookServiceStubMain.java
 *
 * Example from "Professional XML Development with Apache Tools"
 *
 */
package com.sauria.apachexml.ch9;

import java.rmi.RemoteException;

import com.sauria.apachexml.ch9.BookService.BookHandlerServiceLocator;

import com.sauria.apachexml.ch9.BookService.BookHandler;

public class BookServiceStubMain {

    public static void main(String[] args) {

        BookHandler port = null;

        try {
```

```
            port = (BookHandler)
                new BookHandlerServiceLocator().getBookService();
```

Once you've obtained an object that implements the SEI, it becomes straightforward to invoke an operation on the service by calling the appropriate method on the SEI:

```
        }
        catch (javax.xml.rpc.ServiceException jre) {
            if(jre.getLinkedCause()!=null)
                jre.getLinkedCause().printStackTrace();
        }

        boolean result = false;
        try {
            result = port.createBook(
                "Ted Leung",
                "Professional XML Development with Apache Tools",
                "0-7645-4355-5",
                "December",
                2003,
                "Wrox",
                "Indianapolis, Indiana");
        } catch (RemoteException re) {
            re.printStackTrace();
        }
        System.out.println(result);
    }
}
```

Using a JAX-RPC Dynamic Proxy

The advantages of the stub approach are that everything is pretty type safe, there are no performance impacts from dynamic behavior, and the classes can be generated from a tool. The next approach we'll look at, the dynamic proxy approach, is a bit more flexible. With the dynamic proxy, you need to supply an SEI and, optionally, a WSDL file, and the dynamic proxy takes care of producing a usable object that implements the SEI:

```
/*
 *
 * BookServiceDynProxyMain.java
 *
 * Example from "Professional XML Development with Apache Tools"
 *
 */
package com.sauria.apachexml.ch9;

import java.net.MalformedURLException;
import java.net.URL;
import java.rmi.RemoteException;

import javax.xml.namespace.QName;
import javax.xml.rpc.Service;
```

```
16: import javax.xml.rpc.ServiceException;
17: import javax.xml.rpc.ServiceFactory;
18:
19: import com.sauria.apachexml.ch9.BookService.BookHandler;
20:
21: public class BookServiceDynProxyMain {
22:     static String router =
23:        "http://localhost:8080/apache-xml-book-web-axis/services";
24:     static String service = "BookService";
```

Lines 23-24 are just to help keep the lines short enough to fit on a book page.

You use the static newInstance method on the ServiceFactory class to get a new ServiceFactory:

```
25:
26:     public static void main(String[] args) {
27:         try {
28:             ServiceFactory sf = ServiceFactory.newInstance();
```

Before you can use the ServiceFactory to get a service, you need to tell it the URL of a WSDL file and the QName of the service you're interested in using. The way Axis is implemented, accessing the URI of a Web service via get and with the parameter wsdl (written ?wsdl in the URI) causes Axis to return a WSDL description of the service. Line 29 takes advantage of that functionality to provide the WSDL file you need. The QName of the service is obtained from the WSDL document by creating a QName out of the targetNamespace for the WSDL document and the name of the Service element:

```
29:             URL u = new URL(router+"/"+service+"?wsdl");
30:             QName serviceName =
31:                 new QName(
32:                   "http://BookService.ch9.apachexml.sauria.com",
33:                   "BookHandlerService");
34:             Service s = sf.createService(u, serviceName);
```

Once you've obtained a service object, you need to ask for the appropriate port. To do this, you need the QName of the port (constructed from the WSDL document just like the service name) and the Class object of the SEI. The resulting port implements the SEI, so after you get it, it's just a matter of calling the correct method:

```
35:
36:             QName portName =
37:                 new QName(
38:                   "http://BookService.ch9.apachexml.sauria.com",
39:                   "BookHandlerService");
40:             BookHandler h =
41:                 (BookHandler) s.getPort(portName,
42:                                         BookHandler.class);
43:
44:             boolean value = h.createBook(
45:                 "Theodore W. Leung",
46:                 "Professional XML Development with Apache Tools",
47:                 "0-7645-4355-5",
```

```
                      "December",
                      2003,
                      "Wrox",
                      "Indianapolis, Indiana");
                  System.out.println(value);
              } catch (RemoteException re) {
                  re.printStackTrace();
              } catch (MalformedURLException mue) {
                  mue.printStackTrace();
              } catch (ServiceException se) {
                  se.printStackTrace();
              }
          }
      }
```

Using the JAX-RPC Dynamic Invocation Interface

The final scheme for creating a service requestor is the Dynamic Invocation Interface (DII). When you're using the DII, you create the entire invocation of the Web service at runtime. This includes the location and name of the service and port as well as the name of the operation and its arguments. This is the most flexible of the methods but also the most computationally expensive:

```
 1: /*
 2:  *
 3:  * BookServiceDIIMain.java
 4:  *
 5:  * Example from "Professional XML Development with Apache Tools"
 6:  *
 7:  */
 8: package com.sauria.apachexml.ch9;
 9:
10: import java.rmi.RemoteException;
11:
12: import javax.xml.namespace.QName;
13: import javax.xml.rpc.Call;
14: import javax.xml.rpc.ParameterMode;
15: import javax.xml.rpc.Service;
16: import javax.xml.rpc.ServiceException;
17: import javax.xml.rpc.ServiceFactory;
18: import javax.xml.rpc.encoding.XMLType;
19:
20: public class BookServiceDIIMain {
21:     static String router =
22:        "http://localhost:8081/apache-xml-book-web-axis/services";
23:     static String service = "BookService";
```

You need an empty call object to begin with, so you create a ServiceFactory instance (line 28) and then use that factory instance to create an empty Service (line 30). Using that empty Service, you finally create your empty Call object (line 32):

```
24:
25:     public static void main(String[] args) {
26:         Call call = null;
27:         try {
```

```
            ServiceFactory sf = ServiceFactory.newInstance();
            Service s = sf.createService(null);
            call = s.createCall();
```

You set the target endpoint address to be the URI for the service and set the operation name to be the namespace-qualified name of the operation:

```
        } catch (ServiceException se) {
            se.printStackTrace();
        }
        call.setTargetEndpointAddress(router+"/"+service);
        call.setOperationName(
            new QName(
                "http://BookService.ch9.apachexml.sauria.com",
                "createBook"));
```

After you set the endpoint address and operation name, you need to tell the Call object about the parameters for the operation as well as the return type. Each parameter requires the name of the parameter, its type, and whether it's an IN, OUT, or INOUT parameter:

```
        ParameterMode in = ParameterMode.IN;
        call.addParameter("author", XMLType.XSD_STRING, in);
        call.addParameter("title", XMLType.XSD_STRING,  in);
        call.addParameter("isbn", XMLType.XSD_STRING, in);
        call.addParameter("month", XMLType.XSD_STRING, in);
        call.addParameter("year", XMLType.XSD_INT, in);
        call.addParameter("publisher", XMLType.XSD_STRING, in);
        call.addParameter("address", XMLType.XSD_STRING, in);
        call.setReturnType(XMLType.XSD_BOOLEAN);
```

Because you're composing the Call at runtime, there's no way to specify the arguments in a type-safe manner. The best that you can do is to put the arguments into an Object array:

```
        Object params[] = new Object[] {
            "Theodore W. Leung",
            "Professional XML Development with Apache Tools",
            "0-7645-4355-5",
            "December",
            new Integer(2003),
            "Wrox",
            "Indianapolis, Indiana"
        };
```

Once you have the arguments, you can invoke the service using the call object and the parameter array:

```
        try {
            Object result = call.invoke(params);
            System.out.println(result);
```

```
        } catch (RemoteException re) {
            re.printStackTrace();
        }
    }
}
```

Using DII from WSDL

A variation of the DII scheme uses information from a WSDL file to provide the type information about the arguments and return type of the operation being invoked:

```
/*
 *
 * BookServiceDIIWSDLMain.java
 *
 * Example from "Professional XML Development with Apache Tools"
 *
 */
package com.sauria.apachexml.ch9;

import java.net.MalformedURLException;
import java.net.URL;
import java.rmi.RemoteException;

import javax.xml.namespace.QName;
import javax.xml.rpc.Call;
import javax.xml.rpc.Service;
import javax.xml.rpc.ServiceException;
import javax.xml.rpc.ServiceFactory;

public class BookServiceDIIWSDLMain {
    static String router =
       "http://localhost:8080/apache-xml-book-web-axis/services";
    static String service = "BookService";

    public static void main(String[] args) {
        Call call = null;
        try {
            ServiceFactory sf = ServiceFactory.newInstance();

            URL u = new URL(router+"/"+service+"?wsdl");
            QName serviceName =
                new QName(
                   "http://BookService.ch9.apachexml.sauria.com",
                   "BookHandlerService");
            Service s = sf.createService(u, serviceName);
```

Instead of creating a blank service, you create one using a WSDL file, supplying the qualified name of the Service you wish to access.Then you use a different version of the createCall method to create a Call object that's preconfigured with the parameter and return types for a particular operation. The operation is specified using its namespace-qualified name:

```

      QName portName =
        new QName(
         "http://BookService.ch9.apachexml.sauria.com",
         "BookService");
      call = s.createCall(portName, "createBook");
```

After you've obtained your customized Call object, the invocation of the service is just as in the other variation. You build up an Object array of the arguments and pass this array to the invoke method on the Call object:

```
    } catch (MalformedURLException mue) {
      mue.printStackTrace();
    } catch (ServiceException se) {
      se.printStackTrace();
    }

    Object params[] = new Object[] {
      "Theodore W. Leung",
      "Professional XML Development with Apache Tools",
      "0-7645-4355-5",
      "December",
      new Integer(2003),
      "Wrox",
      "Indianapolis, Indiana"
    };

    try {
      Object result = call.invoke(params);
      System.out.println(result);
    } catch (RemoteException re) {
      re.printStackTrace();
    }
  }
}
```

We want to show you an example of using the JAX-RPC handlers. Unfortunately, the usage has some areas that are Axis specific, so we'll wait until we've covered all the necessary Axis-related information.

Installing and Configuring Axis

The installation procedure for Axis can be a little intimidating because potentially you need to do a lot of things. The first step, as always, is to obtain a current Axis build via http://ws.apache.org/axis. For the sake of example, we'll assume you want to work with an Axis 1.1 build. You can click the Release link in the bar on the left to display a list of official releases, including betas. Clicking the link for Axis 1.1 takes you to a page that displays the available files. There's an Axis binary distribution in a file named axis-1.1.*xxx*, where .*xxx* is either .zip or .tar.gz. If you're using Windows, you'll probably want to get the zip version of the distribution. UNIX, Linux, and Mac OS X users will probably want to get the .tar.gz version. The source distribution is in a file named axis-1.1-src.*xxx*, where the values of .*xxx* are the same as for the binary distribution. You can use a regular archiving utility such as Winzip (on Windows) or GNU tar (on UNIX, Linux, and Mac OS X) to unpack the binary (and source) distribution files. After you do this, you'll have a directory called axis-1_1 in the current directory (or the directory you specified when unpacking the files).

Here are the important contents of axis-1_1:

- **docs**—Contains all the Axis documentation, including Javadoc.
- **lib**—Contains the jar files needed to use Axis.
- **samples**—The Axis sample applications.
- **webapps**—The sample Axis Web application.
- **xmls**—Ant task files.
- **LICENSE**—The Apache Software License.
- **README**—A basic README (start with docs/index.html).

You need to set up two environments to work with Axis. If you want to write Web service providers, then you need to set up Axis so that it can provide Web services. Doing so typically means installing into a Web container like Tomcat, Jetty, Resin, or the Web container of a J2EE application server. You need this environment to test the services you write.

You also need to set up an environment where you can write the service provider and service requester (client) code. Doing so involves setting your classpath, either on the command line or in your Java development environment. If you're writing service requestors that need to be deployed in a Web container or EJB container, then you also need the deployment environment we talked about in the last paragraph.

Deployment Environment Setup

We'll cover setting up an Axis deployment environment using Tomcat. For this example, we assume you're using Tomcat 4.1.24 as the Web container and JDK 1.4. Axis provides Web services by using a servlet that takes SOAP requests over HTTP and routes them to the appropriate Web services code, performing needed SOAP processing along the way. To set up Axis inside a Web container, you need the relevant Axis jar files, and you need entries in your web.xml file that provide servlet mappings for the Axis servlet. Let's call the directory where Tomcat is installed CATALINA_HOME, and let's call the directory where Axis is unpacked AXIS_HOME. We'll use Windows filename conventions, but you can reverse the slashes for UNIX without any problems.

Follow these steps:

1. If you're starting from scratch, then you should copy the directory AXIS_HOME\webapps \axis to CATALINA_HOME\webapps and skip to step 6.
2. If you have an existing Web application, the process is a little more difficult. You have to copy some files piecemeal from AXIS_HOME to your application. Let's call the root directory for your Web application (the one inside CATALINA_HOME\webapps) MY_APP.

3. Copy the jar files from AXIS_HOME\webapps\axis\WEB-INF\lib to MY_APP\WEB-INF\lib.
4. Copy the JSP file happyaxis.jsp from AXIS_HOME\webapps\axis to MY_APP.
5. Edit the file MY_APP\WEB_INF\web.xml and copy the <servlet> and <servlet-mapping> elements for AxisServlet and AdminServlet from AXIS_HOME\webapps\axis\WEB-INF\lib. You'll probably also want to copy the <mime-mapping> elements so your browser knows how to display .wsdl and .xsd files.
6. Restart Tomcat.
7. From your Web browser, try to access the happyaxis.jsp file. It's at the top level of the Web application. If you started from scratch, the URL is http://<server:port>/axis/happyaxis.jsp. If you started with your own Web application, the URL is http://<server:port>/mywebapp /happyaxis.jsp. The happyaxis.jsp attempts to check that all the required Axis libraries are present.
8. You may want to use Xerces instead of the default JDK 1.4 XML parser. If you decide to do this, follow the directions in Chapter 1 for installing Xerces on JDK 1.4 via the Endorsed Standards Mechanism.

Development Environment Setup

The environment for building Axis service providers and service requestors must contain the same set of jar files you used in step 3 of the previous section:

- **axis.jar**—The main Axis classes.
- **axis-ant.jar**—Ant tasks to make it easier to work with Axis.
- **commons-discovery.jar**—Jakarta library for discovering pluggable interfaces.
- **commons-logging.jar**—Jakarta library for abstracting logging functionality.
- **jaxrpc.jar**—JAX-RPC APIs.
- **log4j-1.2.8.jar**—Jakarta logging library.
- **saaj.jar**—SAAJ APIs.
- **wsdl4j.jar**—WSDL4J (classes for working with WSDL files).

You'll need to add most of these to your classpath. If you aren't going to use the Ant tasks, you can leave out axis-ant.jar. Likewise, if you aren't using the WSDL tools, you can leave out wsdl4j.jar. The easiest way to do this is to define some environment variables to help you. In the following code, replace AXIS_HOME with the value of AXIS_HOME:

```
set AXIS_LIB=AXIS_HOME\lib
set AXISCLASSPATH=%AXIS_LIB%\axis.jar;%AXIS_LIB%\axis-ant.jar;
    %AXIS_LIB%\commons-discovery.jar;%AXIS_LIB%\commons-logging.jar;
    %AXIS_LIB%\jaxrpc.jar;%AXIS_LIB%\log4j-1.2.8.jar;
    %AXIS_LIB%\saaj.jar;%AXIS_LIB%\wsdl4j.jar
```

Development Techniques

Now we're ready to look at how to use Axis to build Web services applications. We'll begin by giving you a conceptual model of what's going on inside Axis, which will help you understand how the pieces fit together. From there, we'll look at how to write Axis deployment descriptors and the administration tools you'll need in order to deploy a Web service. Then we'll tackle how to work with WSDL using the tools provided by Axis, so you can be prepared to write the kind of code you saw in the JAX-RPC examples. You'll have the necessary knowledge to write code for a basic Web service both on the requestor and provider sides, and you'll know how to deploy it into Axis so it can be called.

We'll also cover some other techniques. In particular, we'll revisit the notion of SOAP message handlers and demonstrate how to put them into action. We'll also look at Axis's facilities for doing custom type mapping, should you ever need to do that. We'll wind up this section with a look at some useful tools that are included in the Axis distribution.

Axis Conceptual Model

This section is purposely not called "Axis Architecture." The goal of this section is to help you understand conceptually what's going on when Axis processes a SOAP message. It isn't our intent to give you a blow-by-blow rundown on the details of the Axis architecture, although you'll find that many similarities exist between the model we describe here and the actual architecture of Axis.

When a service requestor invokes an operation on a Web service, the data provided as arguments to the invocation is encoded using the appropriate encoding rules. Most commonly, this is either SOAP encoding for rpc-encoded Web services or no encoding for document-literal Web services. Once this process is complete, you have a complete SOAP envelope that's ready for delivery to the service provider. Before the envelope is sent to the provider, it must first traverse a pair of handler chains. A *handler chain* is a list of handlers, each of which is given a chance to process the message in whatever way it sees fit. There are two of these chains, one specific to the particular service (requestor) and one that's global for the entire Axis runtime on that requestor node. After the envelope has been processed by the two chains, it's sent to a transport that takes care of delivering the message to the service provider. In many cases, the transport uses HTTP, but the Axis development team is working on support for using a Java Message Service (JMS) package as a transport. SOAP over JMS is a very promising solution for scenarios that involve application integration inside the firewall.

The transport takes care of delivering the SOAP envelope to the provider host. Assuming Axis is also the SOAP runtime being used on the provider, the Axis engine on the provider gets the envelope out of the transport and passes it through a pair of handler chains. This time the order of the handler chains is reversed—that is, the envelope goes through the provider's global handler chain followed by a service-specific handler chain. After the envelope exits the service-specific chain, the contents of the message undergo type decoding, which creates Java objects that correspond to the data in the envelope. These objects are then passed to the code that implements the service. Once the service code has executed and produced a result, the entire process reverses itself. If you look carefully at the following diagram, you'll see that the request and response paths are identical if you follow each path from its beginning to its end. This makes sense when you recall that SOAP is a one-way message system.

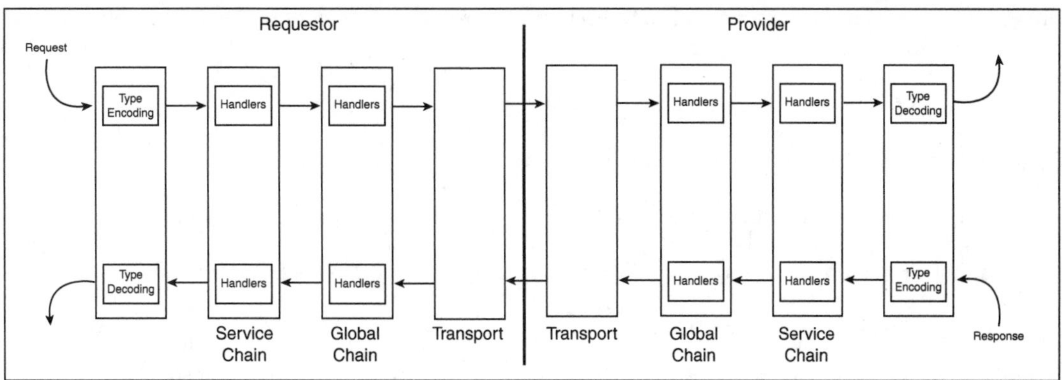

Inside the Axis runtime engine, information describes how to perform the type encoding and decoding, which transport to use, and the configuration of the service-specific and global handler chains. You tell Axis this information via deployment descriptors.

Deployment Descriptors

If you 've worked at all with a servlet or J2EE container, then the deployment descriptors you've used are XML files that control various aspects of how your application deploys into the container environment. The Axis deployment descriptors continue in this tradition. The primary configuration for Axis is stored in a file called server-config.wsdd, which is typically found in the WEB-INF directory of the Web application that contains the Axis dispatching servlet, AxisServlet. This file is written using Axis's Web service deployment descriptor (WSDD) format, which is an XML vocabulary. We'll teach you about Axis deployment descriptors by walking through this file:

```
<?xml version="1.0" encoding="UTF-8"?>
<deployment xmlns="http://xml.apache.org/axis/wsdd/"
  xmlns:java="http://xml.apache.org/axis/wsdd/providers/java">
```

The root element of a WSDD document is a <deployment> element. As usual, you have a gaggle (okay, two) of namespace declarations. The next element, <globalConfiguration>, contains elements that affect an entire Axis engine. The adminPassword parameter is the password used to secure the AdminService. The administration interface for an Axis engine is itself a Web service:

```
 <globalConfiguration>
  <parameter name="adminPassword" value="admin"/>
```

If you're sending messages with attachments using either DIME or SOAP with Attachments, the attachments.Directory specifies the directory where these attachments are stored while being processed:

```
  <parameter name="attachments.Directory"
    value="D:\workspace\apache-xml-book\WEB-INF\attachments"/>
```

attachments.implementation should contain the name of a class that implements attachments support:

```
  <parameter name="attachments.implementation"
    value="org.apache.axis.attachments.AttachmentsImpl"/>
```

If sendXsiTypes is true, an xsi:type attribute is added to every part element in the message. If it's false, no xsi:type attributes are generated:

```
10:    <parameter name="sendXsiTypes" value="true"/>
```

If sendMultiRefs is true, then multiref items are sent:

```
11:    <parameter name="sendMultiRefs" value="true"/>
```

If sendXMLDeclaration is true, then an XML declaration is included in the SOAP message:

```
12:    <parameter name="sendXMLDeclaration" value="true"/>
```

The axis.sendMinimizedElements parameter provides compatibility with .NET. If your .NET client can't handle a service that returns an empty array inside another object, then set this to "false":

```
13:    <parameter name="axis.sendMinimizedElements" value="true"/>
```

This <requestFlow> establishes a set of handlers that are invoked when a request is processed. Because it's nested inside the <globalConfiguration>, it applies to all requests processed by this Axis engine:

```
14:    <requestFlow>
```

By default, two handlers are installed in the global request processing flow (<requestFlow>). Both handlers use the class org.apache.axis.handlers.JWSHandler to define their behavior. The first handler takes care of processing .jws Web services (described in detail later), which are handled on a per-session basis. The second handler processes .jwr Web services, which are identical to .jws services except that they're processed on a per-request basis. Here the <handler> elements are used both to define the existence of the handlers and to indicate the use of the handlers in the <requestFlow>:

```
15:     <handler type="java:org.apache.axis.handlers.JWSHandler">
16:      <parameter name="scope" value="session"/>
17:     </handler>
18:     <handler type="java:org.apache.axis.handlers.JWSHandler">
19:      <parameter name="scope" value="request"/>
20:      <parameter name="extension" value=".jwr"/>
21:     </handler>
```

The three <handler> elements in lines 24-29 simply declare the existence of each of the three handlers and provide a name that can be used to reference them in other parts of the deployment descriptor. All that's happening here is the predefinition of names for some built-in handlers:

```
22:    </requestFlow>
23:   </globalConfiguration>
24:   <handler name="LocalResponder"
25:    type="java:org.apache.axis.transport.local.LocalResponder"/>
26:   <handler name="URLMapper"
27:    type="java:org.apache.axis.handlers.http.URLMapper"/>
28:   <handler name="Authenticate"
29:    type=
30:   "java:org.apache.axis.handlers.SimpleAuthenticationHandler"/>
```

As we mentioned, the Axis administration service is implemented as a Web service. The <service> element in lines 31-37 contains the complete description of the service. In line 31, the service is given a name (the same name that would appear in the name attribute of the WSDL <service> element), and Axis is told that it should use the MSG provider from the java namespace. A *provider* is a handler that implements the dispatching to the actual service code. The MSG provider implements message-style services (more on message style in a little bit). The first of the three parameter items specifies which methods can be invoked—in this case, the AdminService method. The second parameter specifies that administration requests can only be made from the same machine the Axis engine is running on. The third parameter specifies the name of the class that implements the service. The <namespace> element specifies the namespace the service is in:

```
31:  <service name="AdminService" provider="java:MSG">
32:   <parameter name="allowedMethods" value="AdminService"/>
33:   <parameter name="enableRemoteAdmin" value="false"/>
34:   <parameter name="className"
35:     value="org.apache.axis.utils.Admin"/>
36:   <namespace>http://xml.apache.org/axis/wsdd/</namespace>
37:  </service>
```

The Version service is described in lines 38-41. This service uses the java:RPC provider, which is the provider that understands how to perform SOAP encoding to and from Java objects. The only method that can be invoked is getVersion, and the class implementing the service is org.apache.axis.Version:

```
38:  <service name="Version" provider="java:RPC">
39:   <parameter name="allowedMethods" value="getVersion"/>
40:   <parameter name="className" value="org.apache.axis.Version"/>
41:  </service>
```

Your first transport, for http, appears in lines 42-48. Transports are also allowed to specify <requestFlow>s and <responseFlow>s. The HTTP transport <requestFlow> uses the handler named URLMapper that was defined earlier in the descriptor, as well as the handler in org.apache.axis .handlers.http.HTTPAuthHandler. URLMapper tries to use any extra path information in the request URI as the service name. HTTPAuthHandler makes authentication information from the HTTP authentication headers available to a service:

```
42:  <transport name="http">
43:   <requestFlow>
44:    <handler type="URLMapper"/>
45:    <handler
46:       type="java:org.apache.axis.handlers.http.HTTPAuthHandler"/>
47:   </requestFlow>
48:  </transport>
```

The last entry in the descriptor is the local transport, which can be useful for testing. It defines a <responseFlow> that uses the LocalResponder defined earlier in the descriptor:

```
49:  <transport name="local">
50:   <responseFlow>
51:    <handler type="LocalResponder"/>
52:   </responseFlow>
53:  </transport>
```

```
54: </deployment>
```

When you write a Web service, you create a pair of deployment descriptors. One is used for deploying the service into Axis, and the other is used for undeploying the service. By convention, the deployment file is named deploy.wsdd and the undeployment file is named undeploy.wsdd (but that's just a convention). The root element of the undeployment descriptor is <undeployment>. Typically, your deployment and undeployment descriptors contain only a <service> element as a child of the <deployment> or <undeployment> element.

Deploying Web Services

Once you've written your Web service code and created a deployment descriptor, you need a way to perform deployment and undeployment operations. The normal way to do this is to use the AdminClient program that resides in org.apache.axis.client.AdminClient. Your classpath must be set as discussed previously in order to use AdminClient. Typically, you invoke AdminClient by running java, so the command looks like this:

```
java org.apache.axis.client.AdminClient [options] <descriptor file>
```

The options available on AdminClient are as follows:

- **-l<*url*>**—AdminClient talks to the AxisServlet. You may need to change the URL to the AxisServlet, depending on how you have installed Axis in your Web application. By default, AdminClient thinks AxisServlet is accessible via http://localhost:8080/axis/servlet/AxisServlet. You can use the -l option to change the URL in one place, or you can use -h, -p, and -s to change the pieces individually.
- **-h<*hostname*>**—Change the hostname part of the default AxisServlet URL.
- **-p<*portNumber*>**—Change the port number part of the default AxisServlet URL.
- **-s<*servletPath*>**—Change the path to the servlet part of the default AxisServlet URL.
- **-f<*filename*>**—Use a simple file-based protocol to talk to the admin service.
- **-u<*username*>**—If the Axis servlet is protected by BASIC authentication, the username is needed to access the Axis servlet.
- **-w<*password*>**—If the Axis servlet is protected by BASIC authentication, the password is needed to access the Axis servlet.
- **-d**—Turn on debugging.
- **-t<*transport-name*>**—Communicate with the AdminService using the transport name.

You can also supply one of three commands instead of the descriptor file:

- **list**—Display the current contents of the server-config.wsdd file.
- **quit**—If talking to the AxisSimpleServer, tell the simple server to shut down.
- **passwd <*new-passwd*>**—Change the administrative password to *new-passwd*.

You can also use deployment descriptors on the service requestor side. The typical use is to install a requestor-side handler. Once you've written the requestor-side deployment descriptor, you can use the org.apache.axis.utils.Admin program to install it. The command looks like this:

```
java org.apache.axis.utils.Admin client <client-descriptor>
```

Admin can also be used to install provider-side descriptors by changing the first argument from client to server. Typically, you'll use AdminClient to work with descriptors on the provider side.

Axis and WSDL

It's much easier to develop a Web service application using WSDL than without WSDL. If you have a WSDL description of the service, then tools can use that description to help you in various ways. Using a WSDL file allows Axis's tools to generate requestor-side stubs, provider-side skeleton implementations, and deployment descriptors for the provider side. Axis also provides tools for generating a WSDL file from an existing Java class, so you can gain the benefits of using WSDL even if you aren't starting from scratch.

Document Styles

Before we get into the tools, we need a bit of discussion regarding the way Axis interprets the WSDL style and use attributes. Recall that the combination of style and use attributes yields four possibilities: rpc-encoded, rpc-literal, document-encoded, and document-literal. We'll only concern ourselves with how to handle rpc-encoded and document-literal services.

Axis understands four styles of services: RPC, document, wrapped, and message services. This is controlled by the style attribute of the <service> element in a WSDD descriptor for the service. You need to know the relationship between these four styles and the rpc-encoded and document-literal schemes described by WSDL.

The easiest to understand is Axis RPC services. RPC services implement the WSDL rpc-encoded scheme. This means the SOAP body looks like the following listing, where there is a single child element whose name corresponds to the operation to be invoked, and the children of this element are the arguments to the operation. The SOAP encoding is used to encode the arguments:

```
<?xml version="1.0" encoding="UTF-8"?>
<soapenv:Envelope
 xmlns:soapenv="http://schemas.xmlsoap.org/soap/envelope/"
 xmlns:xsd="http://www.w3.org/2001/XMLSchema"
 xmlns:xsi="http://www.w3.org/2001/XMLSchema-instance">
 <soapenv:Body>
  <ns1:createBook
   soapenv:encodingStyle=
    "http://schemas.xmlsoap.org/soap/encoding/"
   xmlns:ns1="http://BookService.ch9.apachexml.sauria.com">
   <author xsi:type="xsd:string">Theodore W. Leung</author>
   <title
    xsi:type="xsd:string">
    Professional XML Development with Apache Tools
   </title>
   <isbn xsi:type="xsd:string">0-7645-4355-5</isbn>
```

```
    <month xsi:type="xsd:string">December</month>
    <year xsi:type="xsd:int">2003</year>
    <publisher
     xsi:type="xsd:string">
     Wrox
    </publisher>
    <address xsi:type="xsd:string">Indianapolis, Indiana</address>
   </ns1:createBook>
  </soapenv:Body>
</soapenv:Envelope>
```

When you use an Axis RPC service, Axis automatically uses the JAX-RPC rules to convert Java objects into the XML for the arguments on the requestor; it reverses the process on the provider to turn the XML back into Java objects that can be passed to the code that implements the service. RPC services set the style attribute of the <service> element to "rpc".

The document, wrapped, and message styles all have to do with handling SOAP messages that aren't using the SOAP encoding. To see how Axis deals with the different styles, let's look at a sample literal message. Looking at it, you can't tell whether it's using WSDL document or RPC style, because the SOAP Body has only a single child:

```
<?xml version="1.0" encoding="UTF-8"?>
<soapenv:Envelope
 xmlns:soapenv="http://schemas.xmlsoap.org/soap/envelope/"
 xmlns:xsd="http://www.w3.org/2001/XMLSchema"
 xmlns:xsi="http://www.w3.org/2001/XMLSchema-instance">
 <soapenv:Body>
  <book xmlns="http://sauria.com/schemas/apache-xml-book/book">
   <title>Professional XML Development with Apache Tools</title>
   <author>Theodore W. Leung</author>
   <isbn>0-7645-4355-5</isbn>
   <month>December</month>
   <year>2003</year>
   <publisher>Wrox</publisher>
   <address>Indianapolis, Indiana</address>
  </book>
 </soapenv:Body>
</soapenv:Envelope>
```

For Axis document and wrapped style services, Axis still tries to help you as much as it can. It uses the JAX-RPC type mapping rules to try to automatically convert the elements in the SOAP Body into Java objects. The difference between the two services is in how they try to do this. An Axis document-style service looks at each child of the Body and creates a Java object for each child. So, for the previous listing, a document-style service will create a Book class that contains all the children of the <book> element as fields (Java Bean properties, really) of the class. A wrapped-style service assumes the real data is wrapped up inside a wrapper element (which would be <book> in this example). The wrapped style unwraps the data from inside the wrapper element and deals with it directly. Instead of producing a Book class, a wrapped service will produce an argument list consisting of the title, author, isbn, month, year, publisher, and address data for the book. This is important because the Axis WSDL2Java tool uses the WSDL file to generate stub classes and skeleton implementation classes, and the difference between document and wrapped style services shows up in the argument lists of methods that implement a service's operations. You might wonder why you have to bother about wrapped services. The answer is that the Microsoft .NET Web services default to a wrapped style of use. The setting for the style attribute of <service> in the WSDD file is "document" for document style and "wrapped" for wrapped style.

The last kind of service is a message-style service. When you specify a message-style service, Axis doesn't do any type mapping for you. Instead, you get objects corresponding to the actual XML of the SOAP Envelope. When you choose to use a message-style service, you're asking for full manual control of the process; you don't get any support from WSDL. On the provider side, there are four possible signatures for a service method. If your operation is called createBook, then here are the four variations:

```
public Element[] createBook(Element[] bodies);
```

You're passed an array of DOM Elements, one Element for each child element of the SOAP body. You must return the result as an array of DOM Elements.

```
public SOAPBodyElement[] createBook(SOAPBodyElement[] bodies);
```

You're passed an array of SOAPBodyElements, one SOAPBodyElement for each child element of the SOAP body. A SOAPBodyElement implements the SOAP Element interface from the Java API for XML Messaging (JAXM/SAAJ). You must return the result as an array of SOAPBodyElements.

```
public Document createBook(Document body);
```

You're passed a DOM Document element containing the entire SOAP body. You must return a DOM Document element containing the SOAP body as the result.

```
public void createBook(SOAPEnvelope request, SOAPEnvelope response);
```

You're passed two SOAPEnvelopes: one for the request and one for the response. You need to fill in the response envelope. This is the only one of the four signatures that gives you access to the header portion of the SOAP Envelope. So, if you need to access or modify the headers, this is the signature you should implement.

WSDL2Java

There are a couple of scenarios in which WSDL2Java can be very helpful. Let's say you're writing a program that needs to use an existing Web service. If that Web service has a WSDL description, then your job is pretty easy. You can point WSDL2Java at the WSDL file (even across the Internet) and generate the requestor-side stubs that will allow your application to call the Web service. After you've compiled the generated classes, you need to write your code to use them. It doesn't take long for this to work. This will only get tricky if the WSDL file uses types that can't be mapped by the JAX-RPC XML-to-Java mapping.

If you're building a Web service provider from scratch, then the best way to develop it is to start by creating a WSDL file and then generating the code artifacts that implement the service. Once you have those code artifacts, you can fill in the template for the implementation, write some requestor code, and be on your way.

WSDL2Java is a command-line tool that takes a WSDL file as input and produces a set of Java classes and, potentially, a set of deployment descriptors. When all the code-generation options are turned on, WSDL2Java generates classes for the service requestor side and the service provider side. The classes are generated based on a correspondence between WSDL elements and Java classes. We'll discuss the correspondence and assume that all the code-generation options are turned on.

WSDL2Java generates a Java class for each top-level type declaration element that appears in the <types> section of the WSDL document. If the type or element is used as an in/out parameter, then WSDL2Java generates a JAX-RPC Holder class as well. All these classes are usable on both the requestor and provider sides. Axis can also generate helper classes for each type. These helper classes take the serialization and deserialization code and move them into separate classes. This process allows you to use Axis's serialization mechanism to easily convert the Java classes back and forth to XML.

A WSDL port type is compiled into a Java interface. In JAX-RPC terms, this is the Service Endpoint Interface (SEI). The name of the interface is taken from the name attribute of the <portType> element.

Each WSDL binding element is translated into several classes. On the requestor side, the binding is used to generate a stub class. The stub class's name is constructed by concatenating the name attribute of the <service> element that uses the binding and the word *SOAPBindingStub*. The SOAPBindingStub class implements the SEI. You'll rarely deal with this class, because you'll be dealing with the SEI it implements. On the provider side, two possible sets of classes are generated, depending on the value of the --skeletonDeploy flag. Without this flag, WSDL2Java generates an implementation template class that implements the SEI and contains method stubs you can fill in with the code that does the work. This class's name is constructed from the name attribute of the <service> element using the binding and the word *SOAPBindingImpl*. If you specify the --skeletonDeploy flag to be true, then WSDL2Java generates an additional skeleton class. The skeleton class implements the SEI and forwards all its methods to the implementation template class. When you're using a skeleton class, the Axis runtime calls the methods on the skeleton class in order to do its work. The skeleton file is named by taking the name of the <service> and appending the word *SOAPBindingSkeleton*.

There are a couple of scenarios around the provider-side stubs. In the easy scenario, you starting from scratch and don't have any of the code that implements the service. In this case, you should omit the --skeletonDeploy flag and allow Axis to generate the implementation template class. You can then edit this file to insert the code to implement the service. In the harder case, you already have some code that implements the service. If by some chance your service code already implements the SEI, then you can slip your class into the deployment descriptors and bypass using any Axis-generated provider-side stubs. You'll still need to generate them using the --server-side flag to have WSDL2Java generate the deployment descriptors for you. If your service code doesn't implement the SEI and you're lazy, you can have WSDL2Java generate the skeleton and template implementation classes for you. You can then throw away the template implementation class and use the skeleton's forwarding code to get a head start on calling your existing service code. (This is an application of the Adapter design pattern.) You can also do this with the template implementation class, because you can edit the method bodies to forward on to your existing service code.

For each <service> element in the WSDL file, WSDL2Java generates a service interface that extends the JAX-RPC Service interface and adds methods for getting an implementation of the service. This file is named with the name attribute of the <service> element and the word *Service*. WSDL2Java also generates an implementation of the Service, which is named with the name of the <service> element and the word *ServiceLocator*.

WSDL2Java generates a pair of deployment and undeployment descriptor files. There's a WSDD <service> entry for each <service> element in the WSDL file. These descriptors are ready to be used with the AdminClient program.

You should be asking yourself which Java package or packages these generated classes will end up in. The package for the generated classes depends on which namespace the associated WSDL elements appeared in. If the namespace URI associated with a WSDL element is of the form http://host.domain/path1/path2/path3, then WSDL2Java converts it into a Java package of the form domain.host.path1.path2.path3. So, if the portType BookHandler is in the target namespace with URI http://BookService.ch9.apachexml.sauria.com, WSDL2Java will generate a Java Interface in com.sauria.apachexml.ch9.BookService.BookHandler.java. Similarly, the book schema defines its elements to be in the targetNamespace http://sauria.com/schemas/apache-xml-book/book, and book is one of the top-level elements. WSDL2Java will generate a new class called _book in the package com.sauria.schemas.apache-xml-book.book.

Let's look at the command-line arguments for the WSDL2Java program and then run through a complete example to see what files are generated and where. The full syntax of the WSDL2Java command is

```
java org.apache.axis.wsdl.WSDL2Java [options] <WSDL URI>
```

The options are as follows:

- **--verbose**—Print informational messages as the file is processed.
- **--noImports**—Only generate code for the WSDL document at the URI; don't process any <wsdl:import> elements.
- **--timeout** <*seconds*>—Set the timeout for the requestor-side stubs in seconds. By default this value is 45 seconds. You can disable the timeout by setting this value to -1.
- **--Debug**—Print debugging information.
- **--noWrapped**—Don't perform wrapped document literal processing. Wrapped services are a .NET Web service compatibility mode. When you're processing a WSDL document, WSDL2Java generates a wrapped-style service if:
    - The input message has a single part.
    - The part is an element.
    - The element has the same name as the operation.
    - The element's complex type definition has no attributes.
- **--server-side**—Generate the provider-side files for the service. The --skeletonDeploy flag controls whether a skeleton class is generated. An implementation template class as well as the pair of deployment descriptors (deploy.wsdd, undeploy.wsdd) is always generated.
- **--skeletonDeploy**—If true (it's false by default), generate a skeleton class for use by the provider and modify the deployment descriptors to make Axis call the skeleton class to perform the service (instead of the implementation template class). If you set this flag true, --server-side is automatically set true, so you don't need to set --server-side if you set --skeletonDeploy.

- **--NStoPkg** ***<namespace-uri>=<package-name>***—This option lets you override WSDL2Java's rules for generating package names from namespace URIs. To do this, you provide a mapping from a namespace URI to a Java package name.
- **--fileNStoPkg**—If you want to override a number of namespace-to-package mappings, you'll probably want to put them in a file. If you use --fileNStoPkg, you can supply the name of a Java properties file that contains the mappings. Each line in the property file is a mapping of the form *<namespace-uri>=<package-name>* (note that you'll have to escape any colons in the namespace URI by prefixing them with \; for example, http://www.sauria.com becomes http\://www.sauria.com). If you use both --fileNStoPkg and --NStoPkg to declare a namespace-to-package mapping, the mapping specified by --NStoPkg takes precedence.
- **--package** ***<package-name>***—Force WSDL2Java to put all generated classes in the same package. The danger with this approach is that you could have two types with the same name in different namespaces. By putting them in a single package (WSDL2Java would put them in different packages by default), you're asking for trouble. You can't use the --NStoPkg option and the-package option at the same time.
- **--output** ***<directory>***—Specify the root directory to be used for output. Any directories needed for packages are created under this directory.
- **--deployScope** ***<scope name>***—Axis runs as a servlet, and you can ask for per-scope handling of a particular Web service. The --deployScope flag adds a scope parameter to the deploy.wsdd file. The valid values for the scope name are the three scopes available to servlets: "request", "session", and "application" ("request" is the default).
- **--testCase**—Generate a template for a provider-side JUnit test case.
- **--all**—Generate code for all the elements in a WSDL document. Normally WSDL2Java only generates code for the elements that are referenced in the document. To determine whether an element is referenced, you must see if it's reachable from some root element in the document. You'd think this should be the <service> element, but the document you're processing may not have a <service> element. So, WSDL2Java uses the *highest* element that appears in the file. <service> is higher than <binding>, <binding> is higher than <portType>, and <portType> is higher than <types>. This order is easy to see because if you start with a <service> and trace all the way through the WSDL grammar to get to <types>, you encounter <service>, <binding>, <portType>, and <types> in that order.
- **--TypeMappingVersion** ***<version>***—Specify which version of type mapping to use (SOAP 1.1 or SOAP 1.2). The default is to use the JAX-RPC compliant SOAP 1.2 mapping. You supply the version number, 1.1 or 1.2, as the option value.
- **--factory** ***<classname>***—Use the specified classname to extend the behavior of the WSDL emitter. This allows you to get custom generation behavior. The class you supply must extend JavaWriterFactory.
- **--helperGen**—Generate separate helper classes for any classes generated in a <types> section.
- **--user** ***<username>***—Supply a username for accessing the WSDL file.
- **--password** ***<password>***—Supply a password for accessing the WSDL file.

An Example

We'll show you an example that builds on the document-literal WSDL file from earlier in the chapter. You'll add a second operation to the <portType>. We'll also show you how to modularize the WSDL file. You can certainly keep all the WSDL elements in a single file, but doing so means you may have to copy and paste sections of the file if you need to reuse them in other places. Let's break the single WSDL file into four files (the *DL* prefix on these files stands for *document-literal*):

- **book.xsd**—This file will contain any XML schema types you use in the Web service. It's easy to see that you might have a set of common XML schemas you're using for various purposes throughout your organization. Having a single authoritative copy can prevent copy-and-paste errors. This schema is the same one you've been using throughout the book. This file is imported into other WSDL files using the <wsdl:import> element.
- **DLBook.wsdl**—This file will contain the <message> and <portType> elements. This is the description of the interface to the service. It doesn't get into how the service is bound to a transport protocol or serialization format. It's the most abstract description of the service. This file will import book.xsd, because the message parts will be defined using types and elements from book.xsd. When you split up a WSDL file this way, each file containing WSDL elements must be wrapped in a <wsdl:definitions> element.
- **DLBookBinding.wsdl**—We've taken the <binding> element and placed it its own file. At the moment the best-defined binding for WSDL is the SOAP/HTTP binding, but the WSDL spec defines several others, and you can expect to see even more (such as SOAP over BEEP or SOAP over JMS). By factoring the <binding> into its own file, you make it easier to add a new binding. The binding file needs to import the interface file.
- **DLBookService.wsdl**—This leaves the <service> element to be in a file by itself. This is the implementation file, and it allows you to define groups of services and ports in multiple files and publish them as appropriate.

The first listing contains the book.xsd file. This file should be familiar enough that it doesn't require any additional explanation:

```
<xsd:schema
 targetNamespace=
    "http://sauria.com/schemas/apache-xml-book/book"
 xmlns:book="http://sauria.com/schemas/apache-xml-book/book"
 xmlns:xsd="http://www.w3.org/2001/XMLSchema"
 elementFormDefault="qualified">
 <xsd:element name="address" type="xsd:string"/>
 <xsd:element name="author" type="xsd:string"/>
 <xsd:element name="book">
  <xsd:complexType>
   <xsd:sequence>
    <xsd:element ref="book:title"/>
    <xsd:element ref="book:author"/>
    <xsd:element ref="book:isbn"/>
    <xsd:element ref="book:month"/>
    <xsd:element ref="book:year"/>
    <xsd:element ref="book:publisher"/>
    <xsd:element ref="book:address"/>
   </xsd:sequence>
```

```
      <xsd:attribute name="version" type="xsd:string"
                     use="required"/>
     </xsd:complexType>
    </xsd:element>
    <xsd:element name="isbn" type="xsd:string"/>
    <xsd:element name="month" type="xsd:string"/>
    <xsd:element name="publisher" type="xsd:string"/>
    <xsd:element name="title" type="xsd:string"/>
    <xsd:element name="year" type="xsd:short"/>
   </xsd:schema>
```

The WSDL Interface File

The interface file DLBook.wsdl is shown next. In lines 11-13 you import the types from the schema file. You need to specify which namespace the types are imported into and the location of the file to import:

```
 1: <?xml version="1.0" encoding="UTF-8"?>
 2: <wsdl:definitions
 3:  targetNamespace=
 4:    "http://DLBookService.ch9.apachexml.sauria.com"
 5:  xmlns="http://schemas.xmlsoap.org/wsdl/"
 6:  xmlns:impl="http://DLBookService.ch9.apachexml.sauria.com"
 7:  xmlns:wsdl="http://schemas.xmlsoap.org/wsdl/"
 8:  xmlns:xsd="http://www.w3.org/2001/XMLSchema"
 9:  xmlns:book="http://sauria.com/schemas/apache-xml-book/book" >
10:
11:  <wsdl:import
12:     namespace="http://sauria.com/schemas/apache-xml-book/book"
13:     location="book.xsd"/>
14:
15:  <wsdl:message name="createBookResponse">
16:   <wsdl:part name="createBookReturn" type="xsd:boolean"/>
17:  </wsdl:message>
18:
19:  <wsdl:message name="createBookRequest">
20:   <wsdl:part name="book" element="book:book"/>
21:  </wsdl:message>
22:
23:  <wsdl:message name="getBookRequest">
24:   <wsdl:part name="isbn" element="book:isbn"/>
25:  </wsdl:message>
26:
27:  <wsdl:message name="getBookResponse">
28:   <wsdl:part name="getBookReturn" element="book:book"/>
29:  </wsdl:message>
30:
31:  <wsdl:portType name="DLBookHandler">
32:   <wsdl:operation name="createBook" parameterOrder="book">
33:    <wsdl:input message="impl:createBookRequest"
34:                name="createBookRequest"/>
35:    <wsdl:output message="impl:createBookResponse"
36:                 name="createBookResponse"/>
37:   </wsdl:operation>
38:
```

```
  <wsdl:operation name="getBook" paramterOrder="isbn">
   <wsdl:input message="impl:getBookRequest"
               name="getBookRequest"/>
   <wsdl:output message="impl:getBookResponse"
                name="getBookResponse"/>
  </wsdl:operation>
 </wsdl:portType>
</wsdl:definitions>
```

The WSDL Binding File

You add a getBook operation that retrieves a book based on its ISBN number. Here's the binding file, DLBookBinding.wsdl:

```
<?xml version="1.0" encoding="UTF-8"?>
<wsdl:definitions
 targetNamespace=
    "http://DLBookService.ch9.apachexml.sauria.com"
 xmlns="http://schemas.xmlsoap.org/wsdl/"
 xmlns:impl="http://DLBookService.ch9.apachexml.sauria.com"
 xmlns:wsdl="http://schemas.xmlsoap.org/wsdl/"
 xmlns:wsdlsoap="http://schemas.xmlsoap.org/wsdl/soap/">

 <wsdl:import
    namespace="http://DLBookService.ch9.apachexml.sauria.com"
    location="DLBook.wsdl"/>
```

The import statement controls which namespace elements go in. It's possible for the portTypes and the bindings to be in different namespaces. If you're using an industry-specified WSDL interface, then the <portType> is likely to be in a namespace controlled by an industry consortium or some similar group. When you're getting ready to deploy your implementation of the service, you'll probably put your bindings in a namespace related to your company:

```

 <wsdl:binding name="DLBookServiceSoapBinding"
               type="impl:DLBookHandler">
  <wsdlsoap:binding style="document"
            transport="http://schemas.xmlsoap.org/soap/http"/>

  <wsdl:operation name="createBook">
   <wsdlsoap:operation soapAction=""/>

   <wsdl:input name="createBookRequest">
    <wsdlsoap:body
     namespace="http://DLBookService.ch9.apachexml.sauria.com"
     use="literal"/>
   </wsdl:input>

   <wsdl:output name="createBookResponse">
    <wsdlsoap:body
     namespace="http://DLBookService.ch9.apachexml.sauria.com"
     use="literal"/>
   </wsdl:output>
```

```
  </wsdl:operation>

  <wsdl:operation name="getBook">
   <wsdlsoap:operation soapAction=""/>

   <wsdl:input name="getBookRequest">
    <wsdlsoap:body
     namespace="http://DLBookService.ch9.apachexml.sauria.com"
     use="literal"/>
   </wsdl:input>

   <wsdl:output name="getBookResponse">
    <wsdlsoap:body
     namespace="http://DLBookService.ch9.apachexml.sauria.com"
     use="literal"/>
   </wsdl:output>
  </wsdl:operation>

 </wsdl:binding>
</wsdl:definitions>
```

The WSDL Implementation File

Now let's look at the implementation file, DLBookService.wsdl:

```
<?xml version="1.0" encoding="UTF-8"?>
<wsdl:definitions
 targetNamespace=
   "http://DLBookService.ch9.apachexml.sauria.com"
 xmlns="http://schemas.xmlsoap.org/wsdl/"
 xmlns:impl="http://DLBookService.ch9.apachexml.sauria.com"
 xmlns:wsdl="http://schemas.xmlsoap.org/wsdl/"
 xmlns:wsdlsoap="http://schemas.xmlsoap.org/wsdl/soap/">

 <wsdl:import
    namespace="http://DLBookService.ch9.apachexml.sauria.com"
    location="DLBookBinding.wsdl"/>

 <wsdl:service name="DLBookHandlerService">
  <wsdl:port binding="impl:DLBookServiceSoapBinding"
             name="DLBookService">
   <wsdlsoap:address
    location="http://localhost:8080/apache-xml-book-web-axis/
services/DLBookService"/>
  </wsdl:port>
 </wsdl:service>
</wsdl:definitions>
```

By creating different versions of DLBookService.wsdl, you can generate different deployable configurations of ports. This approach will be important as applications make increasing use of Web services.

Running WSDL2 Java

Let's feed DLBookService.wsdl to WSDL2Java and look at the results. You want WSDL2Java to generate metadata helper classes, deployment skeletons, and a JUnit test case, and you want the files to be generated in the src subdirectory of the current directory. The command line looks like this:

```
java org.apache.axis.wsdl.WSDL2Java –helperGen –SkeletonDeploy=true
  --testCase --output src --verbose DLBookService.wsdl
```

When WSDL2Java finishes, the following files have been written in the src/com/sauria/apachexml/ch9/DLBookService subdirectory of the current directory:

- **deploy.wsdd**—Deployment descriptor.
- **DLBookHandler.java**—Interface corresponding to the WSDL <portType>. The JAX-RPC SEI.
- **DLBookHandlerService.java**—The requestor-side JAX-RPC Service interface.
- **DLBookHandlerServiceLocator.java**—The requestor-side JAX-RPC Service implementation.
- **DLBookHandlerServiceTestCase.java**—The JUnit test case.
- **DLBookServiceSoapBindingImpl.java**—The provider-side template implementation class.
- **DLBookServiceSoapBindingSkeleton.java**—The provider-side implementation skeleton class, which forwards methods in DLBookHandler to the same methods in DLBookServiceSoapBindingImpl.java.
- **DLBookServiceSoapBindingStub.java**—The provider-side implementation of the JAX-RPC Stub interface.
- **undeploy.wsdd**—Undeployment descriptor.

WSDL2Java also write these files in the src/com/sauria/schemas/apache_xml_book/book subdirectory of the current directory:

- **_book.java**—The generated Java Bean class corresponding to the <book:book> element
- **_book_Helper.java**—The generated helper class that knows how to serialize and deserialize a _book to XML

We want to show you briefly some of the files WSDL2Java generates. You won't need to look inside most of the files unless you're curious about the way Axis works. But this example includes four classes you might want to look at: DLBookHandler, _book, DLBookServiceSoapBindingImpl, and DLBookHandlerServiceTestCase. DLBookHandler and _book are important because they provide the API that's used by a service requestor. DLBookServiceSoapBindingImpl is important because it's the class where you need to place your service implementation code.

The DLBookHandler Interface

DLBookHandler contains two methods, createBook and getBook, which correspond to the operations defined in the WSDL file. They use _book as both a parameter and a return type. The _book class is basically a Java Bean (it implements java.io.Serializable) and provides a Java Bean property for each subelement of the <book:book> element. So, you have a private field and a pair of public getter and setter methods. Notice that the Java package com.sauria.apachexml.ch9.DLBookService has been derived from the namespace URI for the WSDL document, http://DLBookService.ch9.apachexml.sauria.com:

```
/**
 * DLBookHandler.java
 *
 * This file was auto-generated from WSDL
 * by the Apache Axis WSDL2Java emitter.
 */

package com.sauria.apachexml.ch9.DLBookService;

public interface DLBookHandler extends java.rmi.Remote {
    public boolean createBook(
        com.sauria.schemas.apache_xml_book.book._book book)
        throws java.rmi.RemoteException;

    public com.sauria.schemas.apache_xml_book.book._book
        getBook(java.lang.String isbn)
        throws java.rmi.RemoteException;
}
```

WSDL2Java also generates an equals and hashCode method for completeness. In general, you'll need to look at any Java classes that were generated for elements inside the <types> section of your WSDL document (the following listing is _book.java generated from the <types> section):

```
/**
 * _book.java
 *
 * This file was auto-generated from WSDL
 * by the Apache Axis WSDL2Java emitter.
 */

package com.sauria.schemas.apache_xml_book.book;

public class _book  implements java.io.Serializable {
    private java.lang.String title;
    private java.lang.String author;
    private java.lang.String isbn;
    private java.lang.String month;
    private short year;
    private java.lang.String publisher;
    private java.lang.String address;
    private java.lang.String version;  // attribute

    public _book() {
    }

    public java.lang.String getTitle() {
        return title;
    }

    public void setTitle(java.lang.String title) {
        this.title = title;
```

```
    }

    public java.lang.String getAuthor() {
        return author;
    }

    public void setAuthor(java.lang.String author) {
        this.author = author;
    }

    public java.lang.String getIsbn() {
        return isbn;
    }

    public void setIsbn(java.lang.String isbn) {
        this.isbn = isbn;
    }

    public java.lang.String getMonth() {
        return month;
    }

    public void setMonth(java.lang.String month) {
        this.month = month;
    }

    public short getYear() {
        return year;
    }

    public void setYear(short year) {
        this.year = year;
    }

    public java.lang.String getPublisher() {
        return publisher;
    }

    public void setPublisher(java.lang.String publisher) {
        this.publisher = publisher;
    }

    public java.lang.String getAddress() {
        return address;
    }

    public void setAddress(java.lang.String address) {
        this.address = address;
    }

    public java.lang.String getVersion() {
        return version;
    }

```

```
    public void setVersion(java.lang.String version) {
        this.version = version;
    }

    private java.lang.Object __equalsCalc = null;
    public synchronized boolean equals(java.lang.Object obj) {
        if (!(obj instanceof _book)) return false;
        _book other = (_book) obj;
        if (obj == null) return false;
        if (this == obj) return true;
        if (__equalsCalc != null) {
            return (__equalsCalc == obj);
        }
        __equalsCalc = obj;
        boolean _equals;
        _equals = true &&
            ((this.title==null && other.getTitle()==null) ||
             (this.title!=null &&
              this.title.equals(other.getTitle()))) &&
            ((this.author==null && other.getAuthor()==null) ||
             (this.author!=null &&
              this.author.equals(other.getAuthor()))) &&
            ((this.isbn==null && other.getIsbn()==null) ||
             (this.isbn!=null &&
              this.isbn.equals(other.getIsbn()))) &&
            ((this.month==null && other.getMonth()==null) ||
             (this.month!=null &&
              this.month.equals(other.getMonth()))) &&
            this.year == other.getYear() &&
           ((this.publisher==null && other.getPublisher()==null)
             || (this.publisher!=null &&
              this.publisher.equals(other.getPublisher()))) &&
            ((this.address==null && other.getAddress()==null) ||
             (this.address!=null &&
              this.address.equals(other.getAddress()))) &&
            ((this.version==null && other.getVersion()==null) ||
             (this.version!=null &&
              this.version.equals(other.getVersion())));
        __equalsCalc = null;
        return _equals;
    }

    private boolean __hashCodeCalc = false;
    public synchronized int hashCode() {
        if (__hashCodeCalc) {
            return 0;
        }
        __hashCodeCalc = true;
        int _hashCode = 1;
        if (getTitle() != null) {
            _hashCode += getTitle().hashCode();
        }
        if (getAuthor() != null) {
            _hashCode += getAuthor().hashCode();
```

```
        }
        if (getIsbn() != null) {
            _hashCode += getIsbn().hashCode();
        }
        if (getMonth() != null) {
            _hashCode += getMonth().hashCode();
        }
        _hashCode += getYear();
        if (getPublisher() != null) {
            _hashCode += getPublisher().hashCode();
        }
        if (getAddress() != null) {
            _hashCode += getAddress().hashCode();
        }
        if (getVersion() != null) {
            _hashCode += getVersion().hashCode();
        }
        __hashCodeCalc = false;
        return _hashCode;
    }

}
```

The Skeleton Service Class

The implementation template class DLBookServiceSoapBindingImpl contains the same methods that are declared by DLBook handler. The bodies of these methods are stubbed out so that they compile. You'll need to either modify this class to supply your information or edit DLBookServiceSoapBindingSkeleton to make it forward to an existing class:

```
/**
 * DLBookServiceSoapBindingImpl.java
 *
 * This file was auto-generated from WSDL
 * by the Apache Axis WSDL2Java emitter.
 */

package com.sauria.apachexml.ch9.DLBookService;

public class DLBookServiceSoapBindingImpl
   implements
   com.sauria.apachexml.ch9.DLBookService.DLBookHandler{
   public boolean createBook(
           com.sauria.schemas.apache_xml_book.book._book book)
             throws java.rmi.RemoteException {
       return false;
    }

    public com.sauria.schemas.apache_xml_book.book._book
            getBook(java.lang.String isbn)
                throws java.rmi.RemoteException {
        return null;
    }

```

```
}
```

A Filled-in Skeleton Service Class

Listing 11.23 shows DLBookServiceSoapBindingImpl after a simple object serialization implementation has been plugged in. The implementation of createBook creates a FileOutputStream that writes a file in /tmp. The name of the file is the value of the ISBN property of the book argument suffixed with *.ser*. The book data is stored by using Java object serialization to serialize the object to the file:

```
/**
 * DLBookServiceSoapBindingImpl.java
 *
 * This file was auto-generated from WSDL
 * by the Apache Axis WSDL2Java emitter.
 */

package com.sauria.apachexml.ch9.DLBookService;

import java.io.FileInputStream;
import java.io.FileNotFoundException;
import java.io.FileOutputStream;
import java.io.IOException;
import java.io.ObjectInputStream;
import java.io.ObjectOutputStream;
import java.rmi.RemoteException;

import com.sauria.schemas.apache_xml_book.book._book;

public class DLBookServiceSoapBindingImpl
    implements DLBookHandler {

    public boolean createBook(_book book)
        throws java.rmi.RemoteException {
        boolean status = false;
        String isbn = book.getIsbn();
        try {
            FileOutputStream fos =
                new FileOutputStream("/tmp/"+isbn+".ser");
            ObjectOutputStream oos = new ObjectOutputStream(fos);
            oos.writeObject(book);
            oos.close();
            status  = true;
        } catch (FileNotFoundException fnfe) {
            fnfe.printStackTrace();
        } catch (IOException ioe) {
            ioe.printStackTrace();
        }
        return status;
    }
```

The implementation of getBook takes the isbn string argument and opens a FileInputStream on a file in /tmp whose name is the isbn value suffixed with *.ser*. The serialized object in the file is deserialized and returned as the value of the getBook operation:

```
    public _book getBook(java.lang.String isbn)
        throws RemoteException {
        _book bk = null;
        try {
            FileInputStream fis =
                new FileInputStream("/tmp/"+isbn+".ser");
            ObjectInputStream ois = new ObjectInputStream(fis);
            bk = (_book) ois.readObject();
        } catch (FileNotFoundException fnfe) {
            fnfe.printStackTrace();
        } catch (IOException ioe) {
            ioe.printStackTrace();
        } catch (ClassNotFoundException cnfe) {
            cnfe.printStackTrace();
        }
        return bk;
    }

}
```

The Generated Test Case

If you're using JUnit, the automatically generated test case DLBookHandlerServiceTestCase provides the start of a requestor-side test suite. Here's a version of the test case that's been modified to perform a simple test against the DLBookService. We only added code to the generated code—we reformatted the code so it would fit onto book pages, but other than that, this is the code Axis generated:

```
/**
 * DLBookHandlerServiceTestCase.java
 *
 * This file was auto-generated from WSDL
 * by the Apache Axis WSDL2Java emitter.
 */

package com.sauria.apachexml.ch9.DLBookService;

import com.sauria.schemas.apache_xml_book.book._book;

public class DLBookHandlerServiceTestCase
    extends junit.framework.TestCase {

    public DLBookHandlerServiceTestCase(java.lang.String name) {
        super(name);
    }

    public void test1DLBookServiceCreateBook()
        throws Exception {
        DLBookServiceSoapBindingStub binding;
        try {
         binding = (DLBookServiceSoapBindingStub)
         new DLBookHandlerServiceLocator().getDLBookService();
        }
        catch (javax.xml.rpc.ServiceException jre) {
```

```
27:             if(jre.getLinkedCause()!=null)
28:                 jre.getLinkedCause().printStackTrace();
29:             throw
30:                 new junit.framework.AssertionFailedError(
31:                     "JAX-RPC ServiceException caught: " + jre);
32:         }
33:         assertNotNull("binding is null", binding);
34:
35:         // Time out after a minute
36:         binding.setTimeout(60000);
37:
38:         // Test operation
39:         boolean value = false;
```

In lines 41-49 you ad code to create a new _book instance:

```
40:
41:         _book bk = new _book();
42:         bk.setAuthor("Theodore W. Leung");
43:         bk.setTitle(
44:             "Professional XML Development with Apache Tools");
45:         bk.setIsbn("0-7645-4355-5");
46:         bk.setMonth("December");
47:         bk.setYear((short) 2003);
48:         bk.setPublisher("Wrox");
49:         bk.setAddress("Indianapolis, Indiana");
```

Change line 51 to use the new _book instance:

```
50:
51:         value = binding.createBook(bk);
```

Add the JUnit assertTrue to make this a complete JUnit test:

```
52:         // TBD--validate results
53:         assertTrue(value);
54:     }
55:
56:     public void test2DLBookServiceGetBook() throws Exception {
57:         DLBookServiceSoapBindingStub binding;
58:         try {
59:          binding = (DLBookServiceSoapBindingStub)
60:          new DLBookHandlerServiceLocator().getDLBookService();
61:         }
62:         catch (javax.xml.rpc.ServiceException jre) {
63:             if(jre.getLinkedCause()!=null)
64:                 jre.getLinkedCause().printStackTrace();
65:             throw
66:                 new junit.framework.AssertionFailedError(
67:                     "JAX-RPC ServiceException caught: " + jre);
68:         }
69:         assertNotNull("binding is null", binding);
70:
71:         // Time out after a minute
```

```
72:          binding.setTimeout(60000);
73:
74:          // Test operation
75:          _book value = null;
76:          value = binding.getBook("0-7645-4355-5");
```

For this test, supply an argument for the getBook operation in line 76 and the assertion in line 78 to make this a complete JUnit test:

```
77:          // TBD--validate results
78:          assertEquals(value.getAuthor(),"Ted Leung");
79:      }
80:
81: }
```

The Deployment Descriptor

The last set of files you should look at are the deployment descriptors. The deployment descriptor is in deploy.wsdd and looks like this:

```
 1: <!--Use this file to deploy some handlers/chains and services
 2:  -->
 3: <!--Two ways to do this:                                      -->
 4: <!--   java org.apache.axis.client.AdminClient deploy.wsdd   -->
 5: <!--      after the axis server is running                    -->
 6: <!-- or                                                       -->
 7: <!-- java org.apache.axis.utils.Admin client|server deploy.wsdd
 8: -->
 9: <!--      from the same directory that the Axis engine runs -->
10:
11: <deployment
12:  xmlns="http://xml.apache.org/axis/wsdd/"
13:  xmlns:java="http://xml.apache.org/axis/wsdd/providers/java">
14:
15: <!-- Services from DLBookHandlerService WSDL service -->
```

In line 18, the style and use attributes identify this as a document-literal Web service. You'll see some additional elements in the deployment descriptor:

```
16:
17:  <service name="DLBookService" provider="java:RPC"
18:           style="document" use="literal">
```

The wsdlTargetNamespace, wsdlServiceElement, and wsdlServicePort parameter values are all taken directly from the WSDL file:

```
19:   <parameter name="wsdlTargetNamespace"
20:    value="http://DLBookService.ch9.apachexml.sauria.com"/>
21:   <parameter name="wsdlServiceElement"
22:    value="DLBookHandlerService"/>
23:   <parameter name="wsdlServicePort"
24:    value="DLBookService"/>
```

The className parameter is the name of the Java class that's implementing the Web service. Here the value has been set to the generated class com.sauria.apachexml.ch9.DLBookService .DLBookServiceSOAPBindingSkeleton. If you want to use your implementation class directly, change the value of className to be the fully qualified name of your Java class. Be sure any necessary classes are in the classpath of the Web application that's running the Axis servlet:

```
<parameter name="className"
 value="com.sauria.apachexml.ch9.DLBookService.
DLBookServiceSoapBindingSkeleton"/>
```

The value of the wsdlPortType parameter is taken directly from the WSDL file:

```
<parameter name="wsdlPortType" value="DLBookHandler"/>
```

There is an <operation> element for each operation defined on the <portType>. The attributes on <operation> define the operation name and the type information for the return type of the operation. So, the qname for the operation is operNS:createBook, and operNS is the targetNamespace defined in the WSDL file. The return message is createBookReturn, and the type is an XML schema boolean:

```
<operation name="createBook"
 qname="operNS:createBook"
 xmlns:operNS="http://DLBookService.ch9.apachexml.sauria.com"
 returnQName="createBookReturn"
 returnType="rtns:boolean"
 xmlns:rtns="http://www.w3.org/2001/XMLSchema" >
```

There is a <parameter> child element for each parameter of the operation. The <parameter> element sets up the name and type of that parameter:

```
 <parameter qname="pns:book"
  xmlns:pns="http://sauria.com/schemas/apache-xml-book/book"
  type="tns:>book"
  xmlns:tns="http://sauria.com/schemas/apache-xml-book/book"/>
```

The allowedMethods parameter says that getBook and createBook are the only operations available to requestors of this Web service:

```
</operation>
<operation name="getBook"
 qname="operNS:getBook"
 xmlns:operNS="http://DLBookService.ch9.apachexml.sauria.com"
 returnQName="retNS:book"
 xmlns:retNS="http://sauria.com/schemas/apache-xml-book/book"
 returnType="rtns:>book"
 xmlns:rtns="http://sauria.com/schemas/apache-xml-book/book" >
 <parameter qname="pns:isbn"
  xmlns:pns="http://sauria.com/schemas/apache-xml-book/book"
  type="tns:string"
  xmlns:tns="http://www.w3.org/2001/XMLSchema"/>
</operation>
<parameter name="allowedMethods" value="getBook createBook"/>
```

The <typeMapping> element tells Axis which typeMapping classes to use. The class com.sauria .schemas.apache_xml_book.book._book is a Java Bean, and this is a document service. Axis tries to convert the XML in a document-literal message into a set of Java objects, according the XML-to-Java rules defined by JAX-RPC. Because the element <book:book> generates a Java Bean, you need to use the JAX-RPC rules for serializing and deserializing a Java Bean, which are implemented by the classes specified for the serializer and deserializer attributes. The fact that the encodingStyle attribute is empty signals that the rules for XML schema should be used rather than the rules for the SOAP encoding:

```

   <typeMapping
    xmlns:ns="http://sauria.com/schemas/apache-xml-book/book"
    qname="ns:>book"
    type="java:com.sauria.schemas.apache_xml_book.book._book"
    serializer=
       "org.apache.axis.encoding.ser.BeanSerializerFactory"
    deserializer=
       "org.apache.axis.encoding.ser.BeanDeserializerFactory"
    encodingStyle=""
    />
  </service>
</deployment>
```

The Undeployment Descriptor

The undeployment descriptor is in undeploy.wsdd and is very simple. The content of the <undeployment> element is one <service> element for each service to be undeployed. All you need is a name attribute on the <service> element to tell Axis the name of the service to undeploy:

```
<!-- Use this file to undeploy some handlers/chains and services
-->
<!-- Two ways to do this: -->
<!--    java org.apache.axis.client.AdminClient undeploy.wsdd -->
<!--       after the axis server is running -->
<!-- or -->
<!-- java org.apache.axis.utils.Admin client|server undeploy.wsdd
  -->
<!--       from the same directory that the Axis engine runs -->

<undeployment
    xmlns="http://xml.apache.org/axis/wsdd/">

  <!-- Services from DLBookHandlerService WSDL service -->

  <service name="DLBookService"/>
</undeployment>
```

Deploying the Web Service

After compiling all of the generated classes, you have a Web service you can deploy into Axis. You do so using the AdminClient program. You need to supply a value for the -l option because you've installed the AxisServlet into your own Web application instead of using the Axis-supplied Web application. The command line for deploying this service looks like this:

```
java org.apache.axis.client.AdminClient
 —lhttp://localhost:8080/apache-xml-book-axis-web/services/AxisServlet
 deploy.wsdd
```

Note that we indented the command to make it readable—the entire command should be on a single line in your command or shell window. This is the output you'll see if the deploy command is successful:

```
Processing file deploy.wsdd
<Admin>Done processing</Admin>
```

If you want to check that the service is running, you can execute a list command via AdminClient and check the output to see that the <service> entry for DLBookService is present:

```
java org.apache.axis.client.AdminClient
 —lhttp://localhost:8080/apache-xml-book-axis-web/services/AxisServlet
 list
```

You now have a running Web service, so you can run the JUnit test case or write your requestor code and start making service requests. The service will stay deployed until you undeploy it, and that includes restarts of the Web container. If you need to undeploy the service, execute this command:

```
java org.apache.axis.client.AdminClient
 —lhttp://localhost:8080/apache-xml-book-axis-web/services/AxisServlet
 undeploy.wsdd
```

Again, your output will look something like this:

```
Processing file undeploy.wsdd
<Admin>Done processing</Admin>
```

Java2WSDL

We left one scenario out of our discussion of WSDL2Java, and it's pretty important: What if you already have working code that implements functionality that you want to expose as a Web service? You may already have a WSDL service description that you need to use—perhaps a description that's being used in your industry or group of suppliers. If this is the case, your best choice is to use WSDL2Java and generate the provider-side classes, including the skeleton. Then throw away the template implementation class generated by WSDL2Java and use the forwarding code in the skeleton class to forward the service methods to your methods. You may need to do more than forwarding in order to get the skeleton class to talk to your code.

If you don't already have a WSDL description of the service, then you can use Java2WSDL to generate a WSDL file for you. Java2WSDL takes a Java interface or class and generates a WSDL description of a service whose operations correspond to the methods of the Java interface or class. Once you have the WSDL file, you can take that file and run it through WSDL2Java to generate any classes you need. You can either generate no skeletons and update the deployment descriptor to call your class directly, or you can generate skeleton classes and use them to forward to your class (you'll throw away the generated template implementation class).

The usage for Java2WSDL looks like this:

```
java org.apache.axis.wsdl.Java2WSDL [options]
  <fully qualified class name>
```

Java2WSDL needs compiled Java class file to work on, so you need to specify the full name of the class including its package. You also need to make sure this class is on your classpath before you run Java2WSDL. The command-line options for Java2WDSL are as follows:

- **--input** ***<wsdl-file>***—Take an existing WSDL file and add any WSDL elements generated to it. This won't replace an element that's already there.
- **--output** ***<wsdl-file>***—The name of the WSDL file to generate.
- **--location** ***<url>***—The URL of the location of the service. The component of the URL should be the name of the service port (name attribute of the <port> element).
- **--portTypeName** ***<name>***—The name of the <portType> element. If omitted, the name of the class is used.
- **--bindingName** ***<name>***—The name to use for the <binding> element. If omitted, the name is the value of -servicePortName with *SOAPBinding* appended.
- **--serviceElementName** ***<name>***—The name of the <service> element. If omitted, the name is be the value of -portTypeName with *Service* appended.
- **--servicePortName** ***<name>***—The name of the service port. If omitted, the name is the value of the last pathname component of location.
- **--namespace** ***<uri>***—The target namespace for the WSDL document.
- **--PkgtoNS** ***<package name>=<namespace uri>***—Indicate a mapping from a Java package to a namespace URI. This can be specified multiple times as needed.
- **--methods** ***<list of methods>***—A list of methods that will be exported. The list is either space- or comma-separated (you may need to quote the list). If omitted, all the methods in the interface or class are exported.
- **--all**—If specified, Java2WSDL looks at base classes or interfaces to determine which methods to export.
- **--outputWsdlMode** ***<mode>***—The kind of WSDL being generated. There are three possible values for <mode>:
    - **All** (the default)—Generate both interface and implementation WSDL elements.
    - **Interface**—Generate WSDL with interface elements only (excludes the <service> element).
    - **Implementation**—Generate WSDL with implementation elements only and use <wsdl:import> to import the interface WSDL (the -locationImport option is used to tell how to find the interface WSDL).

- **--locationImport** *<url>*—If you're generating an implementation-only WSDL file, the corresponding interface WSDL file is at <url>.
- **--namespaceImpl** *<uri>*—The target namespace for the implementation WSDL.
- **--OutputImpl** *<filename>*—The filename for the implementation WSDL. This causes Java2WSDL to generate both interface and implementation WSDL files. Using this option overrides the setting of —outputWSDLMode.
- **--implClass** *<class name>*—Look in the implementation class for additional information.
- **--exclude** *<list of methods>*—Don't include any methods in the list in the WSDL file. The list is space- or comma-separated.
- **--stopClasses** *<list of classes>*—Java2WSDL should stop searching base classes or interfaces when it encounters a class in the list. The list of classes is space- or comma-separated.
- **--typeMappingVersion** *<version>*—Select the type mapping registry to use. Valid values are 1.1 and 1.2. The default is the JAX-RPC compliant SOAP 1.2 (1.2).
- **--soapAction** *<value>*—Controls how the SOAPAction field is set. There are three options:
    - **OPERATION**—Set the value of soapAction to the name of the operation.
    - **DEFAULT**—Set soapAction according to the operation's metadata (usually "").
    - **NONE**—soapAction is "".
- **--style** *<style>*—Controls the style attribute of the <binding> element. There are three options:
    - **RPC**—Use RPC style.
    - **DOCUMENT**—Use document style.
    - **WRAPPED**—Use wrapped document-literal style. This forces -use to be literal.
- **--use** *<use>*—Controls the use attribute of the <wsdlsoap:body> element. There are two options:
    - **LITERAL**—Use XML schema to describe message parts.
    - **ENCODED**—Message parts are encoded using the SOAP encoding.
- **--extraClasses** *<list of classes>*—A list of classes that should be included in the <types> section of the WSDL. The list is a space- or comma-separated list of classnames.

An Example

Let's take the DLBookHandler SEI interface and the _book class generated by WSDL2Java and feed them back into Java2WSDL so you can see how Java2WSDL works in a familiar environment:

```
java2wsdl
 -lhttp://locahost:8080/apache-xml-book-web-axis/services/DLBookService
 --style document --use literal --output BookServiceIntf.wsdl
 --outputImpl BookServiceImpl.wsdl
 com.sauria.apachexml.ch9.DLBookService.DLBookHandler
```

You tell Java2WSDL the URL of the service—this should appear as the value of the location attribute on a <port> in the WSDL. You also ask Java2WSDL to generate a document-literal WSDL file and to output the interface WSDL to BookServiceIntf.wsdl and the implementation WSDL to BookServiceImpl.wsdl. You need to make sure compiled versions of com.sauria.apachexml.ch9.DLBookService.DLBoookHolder and com.sauria.schemas.apache_xml_book.book._book are available in the classpath used by Java2WSDL.

Java2WSDL modularizes WSDL files a little differently than the way we showed in the examples for WSDL2Java. Java2WSDL only separates between an interface WSDL file and an implementation WSDL file. The <types>, <message>, <portType>, and <binding> elements all go in the interface WSDL file, leaving only the <service> element to go in the implementation WSDL file. The BookServiceIntf.wsdl interface file appears in the following listing. The only real difference is in the <types> section. Java2WSDL has created the <complexType> declaration in the namespace that was implicitly specified by the package _book was in. It also created a set of element declarations in the interface WSDL namespace. There is one element name for each message part used by one of the messages. These differences propagate forward to the <part> and <operation> elements:

```
<?xml version="1.0" encoding="UTF-8"?>
<wsdl:definitions
 targetNamespace="http://DLBookService.ch9.apachexml.sauria.com"
 xmlns="http://schemas.xmlsoap.org/wsdl/"
 xmlns:apachesoap="http://xml.apache.org/xml-soap"
 xmlns:impl="http://DLBookService.ch9.apachexml.sauria.com-impl"
 xmlns:intf="http://DLBookService.ch9.apachexml.sauria.com"
 xmlns:soapenc="http://schemas.xmlsoap.org/soap/encoding/"
 xmlns:tns2="http://book.apache_xml_book.schemas.sauria.com"
 xmlns:wsdl="http://schemas.xmlsoap.org/wsdl/"
 xmlns:wsdlsoap="http://schemas.xmlsoap.org/wsdl/soap/"
 xmlns:xsd="http://www.w3.org/2001/XMLSchema">
 <wsdl:types>
  <schema
   targetNamespace=
    "http://book.apache_xml_book.schemas.sauria.com"
   xmlns="http://www.w3.org/2001/XMLSchema">
   <complexType name="_book">
    <sequence>
     <element name="address" nillable="true" type="xsd:string"/>
     <element name="author" nillable="true" type="xsd:string"/>
     <element name="isbn" nillable="true" type="xsd:string"/>
     <element name="month" nillable="true" type="xsd:string"/>
     <element name="publisher" nillable="true"
      type="xsd:string"/>
     <element name="title" nillable="true" type="xsd:string"/>
     <element name="version" nillable="true" type="xsd:string"/>
     <element name="year" type="xsd:short"/>
    </sequence>
   </complexType>
  </schema>
  <schema
   targetNamespace=
    "http://DLBookService.ch9.apachexml.sauria.com"
   xmlns="http://www.w3.org/2001/XMLSchema">
   <element name="in0" type="tns2:_book"/>
```

```
    <element name="createBookReturn" type="xsd:boolean"/>
    <element name="in0" type="xsd:string"/>
    <element name="getBookReturn" type="tns2:_book"/>
   </schema>
 </wsdl:types>

 <wsdl:message name="getBookResponse">
  <wsdl:part element="intf:getBookReturn" name="getBookReturn"/>
 </wsdl:message>

 <wsdl:message name="createBookResponse">
  <wsdl:part element="intf:createBookReturn"
             name="createBookReturn"/>
 </wsdl:message>

 <wsdl:message name="getBookRequest">
  <wsdl:part element="intf:in0" name="in0"/>
 </wsdl:message>

 <wsdl:message name="createBookRequest">
  <wsdl:part element="intf:in0" name="in0"/>
 </wsdl:message>

 <wsdl:portType name="DLBookHandler">
  <wsdl:operation name="createBook" parameterOrder="in0">
   <wsdl:input message="intf:createBookRequest"
               name="createBookRequest"/>
   <wsdl:output message="intf:createBookResponse"
                name="createBookResponse"/>
  </wsdl:operation>

  <wsdl:operation name="getBook" parameterOrder="in0">
   <wsdl:input message="intf:getBookRequest"
               name="getBookRequest"/>
   <wsdl:output message="intf:getBookResponse"
                name="getBookResponse"/>
  </wsdl:operation>
 </wsdl:portType>

 <wsdl:binding name="DLBookServiceSoapBinding"
               type="intf:DLBookHandler">
  <wsdlsoap:binding style="document"
   transport="http://schemas.xmlsoap.org/soap/http"/>

  <wsdl:operation name="createBook">
   <wsdlsoap:operation soapAction=""/>
   <wsdl:input name="createBookRequest">
    <wsdlsoap:body
     namespace="http://DLBookService.ch9.apachexml.sauria.com"
     use="literal"/>
   </wsdl:input>

   <wsdl:output name="createBookResponse">
    <wsdlsoap:body
```

```
      namespace="http://DLBookService.ch9.apachexml.sauria.com"
      use="literal"/>
    </wsdl:output>
   </wsdl:operation>

   <wsdl:operation name="getBook">
    <wsdlsoap:operation soapAction=""/>
    <wsdl:input name="getBookRequest">
     <wsdlsoap:body
      namespace="http://DLBookService.ch9.apachexml.sauria.com"
      use="literal"/>
    </wsdl:input>

    <wsdl:output name="getBookResponse">
     <wsdlsoap:body
      namespace="http://DLBookService.ch9.apachexml.sauria.com"
      use="literal"/>
    </wsdl:output>
   </wsdl:operation>
  </wsdl:binding>
</wsdl:definitions>
```

Aside from the changes in the <types> section, this WSDL file looks extremely similar to the file you'd obtain by combining the books schema, the interface WSDL, and the binding WSDL you saw in the WSDL2Java example. Because this is what you expect to see, it's a welcome sight.

The implementation WSDL file is also very similar to the implementation file from the WSDL2Java example, so you're in good shape here also:

```
<?xml version="1.0" encoding="UTF-8"?>
<wsdl:definitions
 targetNamespace=
  "http://DLBookService.ch9.apachexml.sauria.com-impl"
 xmlns="http://schemas.xmlsoap.org/wsdl/"
 xmlns:apachesoap="http://xml.apache.org/xml-soap"
 xmlns:impl="http://DLBookService.ch9.apachexml.sauria.com-impl"
 xmlns:intf="http://DLBookService.ch9.apachexml.sauria.com"
 xmlns:soapenc="http://schemas.xmlsoap.org/soap/encoding/"
 xmlns:wsdl="http://schemas.xmlsoap.org/wsdl/"
 xmlns:wsdlsoap="http://schemas.xmlsoap.org/wsdl/soap/"
 xmlns:xsd="http://www.w3.org/2001/XMLSchema">

 <wsdl:import
  namespace="http://DLBookService.ch9.apachexml.sauria.com"/>
 <wsdl:service name="DLBookHandlerService">
  <wsdl:port binding="intf:DLBookServiceSoapBinding"
             name="DLBookService">
   <wsdlsoap:address
     location="http://locahost:8080/apache-xml-book-web-axis/
services/DLBookService"/>
  </wsdl:port>
 </wsdl:service>
</wsdl:definitions>
```

Accessing the ServletContext

Your Web service may need to get access to information that's only available via the Java Web container/servlet engine. This might be information carried in the HttpServletRequest or carried via the ServletContext. Axis provides a mechanism for your Web service to access this information: the MessageContext class. Let's extend the implementation of the BookService to use information from the ServletContext to put the serialized book objects in a directory under the Web application directory:

```
/**
 * DLBookServiceSoapBindingImpl.java
 *
 * This file was auto-generated from WSDL
 * by the Apache Axis WSDL2Java emitter.
 */

package com.sauria.apachexml.ch9.DLBookService;

import java.io.FileInputStream;
import java.io.FileNotFoundException;
import java.io.FileOutputStream;
import java.io.IOException;
import java.io.ObjectInputStream;
import java.io.ObjectOutputStream;
import java.rmi.RemoteException;

import javax.servlet.ServletContext;
import javax.servlet.http.HttpServlet;

import org.apache.axis.MessageContext;
import org.apache.axis.transport.http.HTTPConstants;

import com.sauria.schemas.apache_xml_book.book._book;

public class DLBookServiceSoapBindingImpl
    implements DLBookHandler {


    private String getPath() {
        MessageContext mc = MessageContext.getCurrentContext();
        HttpServlet s = (HttpServlet)
            mc.getProperty(HTTPConstants.MC_HTTP_SERVLET);
```

Within a Web service, you get access to the MessageContext by calling the static method getCurrentContext on the org.apache.axis.MessageContext class. Once you have the current MessageContext, you can call the getProperty method with the correct constant name to get the object that has the data you need. In this case, you supply the constant HTTPConstants.MC_HTTP_SERVLET; it returns a reference to the current servlet, which you can use later. The source code for org.apache.axis.transport.http.HTTPConstants contains an exhaustive list of the constants you can use. The ones you're most likely to use are as follows:

- **MC_HTTP_SERVLET**—Get the current servlet.
- **MC_HTTP_SERVLET_REQUEST**—Get the current HTTP request.
- **MC_HTTP_SERVLET_RESPONSE**—Get the current HTTP response.

You can get to most data from one of these three roots.

The getRealPath method returns the real path of the root of the Web application. Once you have the servlet context, it's easy to get this information. You just return the results of calling getRealPath on "/":

```
        ServletContext sCtx = s.getServletContext();
        String path = sCtx.getRealPath("/");
        return path;
```

When the getPath method is defined, you use it to compute the prefix of the path for the serialized objects:

```
    }

    public boolean createBook(_book book)
        throws java.rmi.RemoteException {
        boolean status = false;
        String isbn = book.getIsbn();
        try {
            FileOutputStream fos =
                new FileOutputStream(getPath()+isbn+".ser");
            ObjectOutputStream oos = new ObjectOutputStream(fos);
            oos.writeObject(book);
            oos.close();
            status  = true;
        } catch (FileNotFoundException fnfe) {
            fnfe.printStackTrace();
        } catch (IOException ioe) {
            ioe.printStackTrace();
        }
        return status;
    }
```

Of course, you have to modify the getBook method to look in the new location as well:

```

    public _book getBook(java.lang.String isbn)
        throws RemoteException {
        _book bk = null;
        try {
            FileInputStream fis =
                new FileInputStream(getPath()+isbn+".ser");
            ObjectInputStream ois = new ObjectInputStream(fis);
            bk = (_book) ois.readObject();
        } catch (FileNotFoundException fnfe) {
            fnfe.printStackTrace();
        } catch (IOException ioe) {
            ioe.printStackTrace();
        } catch (ClassNotFoundException cnfe) {
            cnfe.printStackTrace();
        }
        return bk;
    }
}
```

The Axis MessageContext class implements the MessageContext interface, which is part of the JAX-RPC specification. You must use the Axis MessageContext class to perform the functions you've seen in this section, because these functions are extensions beyond the JAX-RPC 1.0 functionality. You'll see the JAX-RPC MessageContext interface again when we talk about handlers.

Message Service

In the section on WSDL and Java, you saw how to write RPC services and document/wrapped services. Now let's look at writing a message service. This message service will show how to deal with a document-literal style SOAP message. You'll implement the getBook operation from the document-literal book service using an Axis message-style service.

Recall that when you write a message-style service, you're just passing the SOAP messages around—the Axis engine barely gets involved. There is no automatic conversion of XML into Java types. Axis does save you from having to parse the XML and gives you a choice of four method signatures with which to implement a message service. Let's use the signature that requires you to supply a request and response SOAPEnvelope. This signature is the most flexible because it includes the SOAP headers as well as the Body.

The Service Requestor

Let's look at the service requestor first. It has to create a SOAP Envelope whose Body matches the getBook request used in the document-literal example. That message looks like this:

```
<soapenv:Envelope
 xmlns:soapenv="http://schemas.xmlsoap.org/soap/envelope/"
 <soapenv:Body>
  <isbn xmlns="http://sauria.com/schemas/apache-xml-book/book">
0-7645-4355-5</isbn>
 </soapenv:Body>
</soapenv:Envelope>
```

Here's the requestor:

```
/*
 *
 * MessageBookRequestor.java
 *
 * Example from "Professional XML Development with Apache Tools"
 *
 */
package com.sauria.apachexml.ch9.MessageBookService;

import java.rmi.RemoteException;

import javax.xml.rpc.ServiceException;
import javax.xml.soap.Name;
import javax.xml.soap.SOAPBody;
import javax.xml.soap.SOAPBodyElement;
```

```
16: import javax.xml.soap.SOAPException;
17:
18: import org.apache.axis.client.Call;
19: import org.apache.axis.client.Service;
20: import org.apache.axis.message.SOAPEnvelope;
21:
22: public class MessageBookRequestor {
23:
24:     public static void main(String[] args) {
25:         Call call = null;
26:         Service s = new Service();
27:         try {
28:             call = (Call) s.createCall();
29:         } catch (ServiceException e) {
30:             e.printStackTrace();
31:         }
```

You create a call object. This looks like a DII call, and it is, sort of. There's no way to generate a message service from WSDL, at least at the moment, so no stubs or dynamic proxies are available.

In lines 33-36, you building the endpoint address for the message-style service provider and set the call's target endpoint to that address. In line 38, you create an empty SOAPEnvelope that will serve as the argument for your service request:

```
32:
33:         String host = "http://localhost:8080";
34:         String path =
35:          "/apache-xml-book-web-axis/services/MessageBookService";
36:         call.setTargetEndpointAddress(host+path);
37:
38:         SOAPEnvelope env = new SOAPEnvelope();
```

Next you need to add the <isbn> element as the child of the SOAP body. In line 40, you get hold of the SOAP Body. You create a namespace-qualified name for isbn in the http://sauria.com/schemas/apache-xml-book/book namespace, and in line 45 you add a new element to the Body with that qualified name. All that's left is to add the value of the <isbn> element, which you do by adding a text node as a child of the isbn element. Note that the model for a SOAP message is based around the DOM but extended to cover the functionality needed by SOAP. In particular, the SOAPBody's addBodyElement adds the element to the Body but also declares the namespace prefix of the element:

```
39:         try {
40:             SOAPBody body = env.getBody();
41:             Name isbnName =
42:                env.createName("isbn","",
43:              "http://sauria.com/schemas/apache-xml-book/book");
44:             SOAPBodyElement bodyElt =
45:                 body.addBodyElement(isbnName);
46:             bodyElt.addTextNode("0-7645-4355-5");
47:         } catch (SOAPException se) {
48:             se.printStackTrace();
49:         }
```

Once you have the complete envelope for the request, you call the version of the invoke method that expects a SOAPEnvelope as its argument and returns a SOAPEnvelope as its result. The Axis engine maps it to the correct signature on the provider side:

```

        try {
            SOAPEnvelope result = call.invoke(env);
```

To keep the code simple, you just print the contents of the result envelope. You can use the SOAPEnvelope, SOAPBody, SOAPBodyElement, and other related classes to take the envelope apart and perform some processing. You'll see how the provider uses those classes to do that:

```
            System.out.println(result);
        } catch (RemoteException re) {
            re.printStackTrace();
        }
    }
}
```

The Service Provider

Now let's turn our attention to the provider side. The provider needs to take a SOAPEnvelope that contains the request, disassemble it, and take some action based on the contents. It needs to take the results and insert them into the response SOAPEnvelope:

```
/*
 *
 * MessageBookProvider.java
 *
 * Example from "Professional XML Development with Apache Tools"
 *
 */
package com.sauria.apachexml.ch9.MessageBookService;

import java.rmi.RemoteException;
import java.util.Iterator;

import javax.xml.soap.Name;
import javax.xml.soap.SOAPBody;
import javax.xml.soap.SOAPElement;
import javax.xml.soap.SOAPException;

import org.apache.axis.message.SOAPBodyElement;
import org.apache.axis.message.SOAPEnvelope;
import org.w3c.dom.Element;

import
com.sauria.apachexml.ch9.DLBookService.DLBookServiceSoapBindingImpl;
import com.sauria.schemas.apache_xml_book.book._book;

public class MessageBookProvider {
    public void getBook(SOAPEnvelope req, SOAPEnvelope res) {
```

The getBook method has one of the valid signatures for a message-style Axis service: It takes a pair of SOAPEnvelopes as arguments. The request envelope is the contents of the requestor's request. The Axis engine supplies an empty SOAPEnvelope for the response envelope.

You're only working with the SOAPBody, so you get the SOAPBody from the request Envelope:

```
28:         SOAPBody body = null;
29:         try {
30:             body = req.getBody();
31:         } catch (SOAPException se) {
32:             se.printStackTrace();
33:         }
```

You iterate over the children of the SOAP body, looking for one whose name is isbn. If you find a child element named isbn, then you have work to do:

```
34:         String isbnValue = "";
35:         for (Iterator i = body.getChildElements();
36:              i.hasNext();) {
37:             SOAPBodyElement sbe = (SOAPBodyElement) i.next();
38:             if (sbe.getName().equals("isbn")) {
39:                 Element e = null;
```

Next you get the content of the isbn element. You can ask for any SOAPBodyElement to be converted to a regular DOM element (lines 40-44). Once you have a DOM, then it's a matter of straightforward DOM calls to get the content of the element (lines 45-46):

```
40:                 try {
41:                     e = sbe.getAsDOM();
42:                 } catch (Exception e1) {
43:                     e1.printStackTrace();
44:                 }
45:                 isbnValue =
46:                     e.getFirstChild().getNodeValue();
```

Instead of reimplementing the code for getBook, you use the implementation in DLServiceSoapBindingImpl to retrieve a serialized book. Now you're ready to return the contents of that book as a SOAP message. Again, you want to mimic the message you get back from the document-literal service:

```
47:             }
48:         }
49:
50:         DLBookServiceSoapBindingImpl imp =
51:             new DLBookServiceSoapBindingImpl();
52:
53:         try {
54:             _book book = imp.getBook(isbnValue);
```

After obtaining the SOAPBody from the response envelope (line 56), you create the <books:book> element by creating a qualified name and prefix on the response envelope (lines 58-60) and then creating a SOAPBodyElement with that name:

```
55:
56:                 SOAPBody b = res.getBody();
57:
58:                 Name bkName =
59:                   res.createName("book","books",
60:                   "http://sauria.com/schemas/apache-xml-book/book");
61:                 SOAPBodyElement bk = (SOAPBodyElement)
62:                     b.addBodyElement(bkName);
```

By adding the children of the <books:book> element, you add the data obtained by the getBook call. You do this by creating a child element of the <books:book> element, remembering what that child is (line 65), and then adding a text node child containing the actual data to that new child (line 66). You then repeat this until all the fields have been added (lines 67-78):

```
63:
64:                 SOAPElement child;
65:                 child = bk.addChildElement("author","books");
66:                 child.addTextNode(book.getAuthor());
67:                 child = bk.addChildElement("title","books");
68:                 child.addTextNode(book.getTitle());
69:                 child = bk.addChildElement("isbn","books");
70:                 child.addTextNode(book.getIsbn());
71:                 child = bk.addChildElement("month","books");
72:                 child.addTextNode(book.getMonth());
73:                 child = bk.addChildElement("year","books");
74:                 child.addTextNode(Short.toString(book.getYear()));
75:                 child = bk.addChildElement("publisher","books");
76:                 child.addTextNode(book.getPublisher());
77:                 child = bk.addChildElement("address","books");
78:                 child.addTextNode(book.getAddress());
79:             } catch (RemoteException re) {
80:                 re.printStackTrace();
81:             } catch (SOAPException se) {
82:                 se.printStackTrace();
83:             }
84:     }
85: }
```

The Deployment Descriptors

The deployment descriptor for the provider is the last thing you need before you can put your new service into action. The style attribute is "message", indicating that this is an Axis message-style service:

```
<deployment
 name="test" xmlns="http://xml.apache.org/axis/wsdd/"
 xmlns:java="http://xml.apache.org/axis/wsdd/providers/java"
 xmlns:xsi="http://www.w3.org/2000/10/XMLSchema-instance">
 <service name="MessageBookService" style="message">
```

You supply the classname of the provider class as the value of the className parameter, so that Axis knows which class is providing the provider implementation:

```
  <parameter
    name="className"
    value=
"com.sauria.apachexml.ch9.MessageBookService.MessageBookProvider"
```

You export the getBook method from the service so it can be called:

```
 />
   <parameter name="allowedMethods" value="getBook" />
 </service>
</deployment>
```

For the sake of completeness, here's the undeployment descriptor:

```
<undeployment
 name="test"
 xmlns="http://xml.apache.org/axis/wsdd/">
  <service name="MessageBookService"/>
</undeployment>
```

The output of the requestor program is as follows:

```
<soapenv:Envelope
 xmlns:soapenv="http://schemas.xmlsoap.org/soap/envelope/"
 xmlns:xsd="http://www.w3.org/2001/XMLSchema"
 xmlns:xsi="http://www.w3.org/2001/XMLSchema-instance">
 <soapenv:Body>
  <books:book
   xmlns:books="http://sauria.com/schemas/apache-xml-book/book">
   <books:author
    xmlns:books=
     "http://sauria.com/schemas/apache-xml-book/book">
    Ted Leung
   </books:author>
   <books:title
    xmlns:books=
     "http://sauria.com/schemas/apache-xml-book/book">
    Professional XML Development with Apache Tools
   </books:title>
   <books:isbn
    xmlns:books=
     "http://sauria.com/schemas/apache-xml-book/book">
    0-7645-4355-5
   </books:isbn>
   <books:month
    xmlns:books=
     "http://sauria.com/schemas/apache-xml-book/book">
    October
   </books:month>
   <books:year
    xmlns:books=
     "http://sauria.com/schemas/apache-xml-book/book">
    2003
```

```
      </books:year>
      <books:publisher
       xmlns:books=
        "http://sauria.com/schemas/apache-xml-book/book">
       Wrox
      </books:publisher>
      <books:address
       xmlns:books=
        "http://sauria.com/schemas/apache-xml-book/book">
       Indianapolis, Indiana
      </books:address>
    </books:book>
  </soapenv:Body>
</soapenv:Envelope>
```

This is semantically equivalent to the response message from the document-literal example. The big difference is the declaration of the books namespace on each child of <books:book>.

Handlers

Axis provides an implementation of the JAX-RPC handler facility that allows you to insert handlers that intercept the processing of a message at well-defined points. On the requestor side, interception occurs before the message leaves the requesting host and after the response message has been received (but before it's processed). Similarly, on the provider side, interception occurs after the request message has been received from the requestor, but before it's passed to the service code; and after the response message has been generated, but before it's transmitted back to the requestor.

Let's look at implementing a simple handler that can be used on both the requestor and the provider sides. This handler logs the SOAP representation of the message using log4j. You can imagine using a handler like this when you need records of every transaction that passes through the system—in particular if you want to prove to the business partner that's providing or using the Web service that, in fact, a particular request was or wasn't made or was or wasn't processed.

The example is based on the document-literal example we've used before. Let's begin by looking at how to register a handler on the requestor side. You'll build up a pointer to the WSDL file for the document-literal service:

```
/*
 *
 * DLBookHandlerClient.java
 *
 * Example from "Professional XML Development with Apache Tools"
 *
 */
package com.sauria.apachexml.ch9.DLBookService;

import java.net.MalformedURLException;
import java.net.URL;
import java.rmi.RemoteException;
import java.util.List;

import javax.xml.namespace.QName;
```

```
16: import javax.xml.rpc.Service;
17: import javax.xml.rpc.ServiceException;
18: import javax.xml.rpc.ServiceFactory;
19: import javax.xml.rpc.handler.HandlerInfo;
20:
21: import
22: com.sauria.apachexml.ch9.DLBookService.handlers.LoggingHandler;
23: import com.sauria.schemas.apache_xml_book.book._book;
24:
25: public class DLBookHandlerClient {
26:     static String router =
27:        "http://localhost:8080/apache-xml-book-web-axis/";
28:     static String service = "DLBookService.wsdl";
```

You create a ServiceFactory instance (line 32) and use that instance to create a Service instance (line 38) using the WSDL document (line 33) and the QName of the service (lines 34-37):

```
29:
30:     public static void main(String[] args) {
31:         try {
32:             ServiceFactory sf = ServiceFactory.newInstance();
33:             URL u = new URL(router + "/" + service);
34:             QName serviceName =
35:                new QName(
36:                "http://DLBookService.ch9.apachexml.sauria.com",
37:                "DLBookHandlerService");
38:             Service s = sf.createService(u,serviceName);
```

Next you create a QName for the port (lines 40-43), which you need so you can get the handler chain for this port (lines 45-46) (and so you can create the dynamic proxy to the service later):

```
39:
40:             QName portName =
41:                new QName(
42:                "http://DLBookService.ch9.apachexml.sauria.com",
43:                "DLBookService");
44:
45:             List handlerChain =
46:             s.getHandlerRegistry().getHandlerChain(portName);
```

To register the handler in the port's handler chain, you create an instance of HandlerInfo (line 47-49) that takes the class of the handler you're registering (in this case, LoggingHandler.class), a Map containing configuration information for the handler (none in this case), and an array of QNames that specifies the headers this handler will process (again, none in this case because you process every message). Once you have the HandlerInfo, you use the regular add method on List to add the handler to the handlerChain:

```
47:             HandlerInfo hi =
48:                 new HandlerInfo(LoggingHandler.class,
49:                                 null,null);
50:             handlerChain.add(hi);
51:
52:             DLBookHandler h =
```

```
                    (DLBookHandler) s.getPort(portName,
                                             DLBookHandler.class);

                _book bk = new _book();
                bk.setAuthor("Theodore W. Leung");
                bk.setTitle(
                   "Professional XML Development with Apache Tools");
                bk.setIsbn("0-7645-4355-5");
                bk.setMonth("December");
                bk.setYear((short) 2003);
                bk.setPublisher("Wrox");
                bk.setAddress("Indianapolis, Indiana");

                boolean value = h.createBook(bk);
                System.out.println(value);
            } catch (RemoteException re) {
                re.printStackTrace();
            } catch (ServiceException se) {
                se.printStackTrace();
            } catch (MalformedURLException mue) {
                mue.printStackTrace();
            }
        }
}
```

Those are the only header-specific lines on the requestor side. Everything else is a regular dynamic proxy invocation, construction of the argument values, and so on. The handlers interact with the requestor code by causing SOAP faults if there's a problem, so this is handled using the standard mechanism for handling faults (exceptions).

Your handler class needs to implement the JAX-RPC javax.xml.rpc.handler.Handler interface. The interface has init and destroy lifecycle methods for dealing with configuration. The method getHeaders returns an array of the QNames of the headers the handler knows how to process. Most of the work is done by the handleRequest, handleResponse, and handleFault methods. These methods are called when a request, response, or fault message, respectively, passes through the handler. Each of these methods takes a JAX-RPC MessageContext as an argument, which is how the method can access the details of the message being handled. The methods return true if the message should be processed by the next handler in the handler chain, or false if no further handlers in the chain should be executed.

The handler is relatively simple. It has a dedicated log4j Logger channel:

```
/*
 *
 * LoggingHandler.java
 *
 * Example from "Professional XML Development with Apache Tools"
 *
 */
package com.sauria.apachexml.ch9.DLBookService.handlers;

import javax.xml.namespace.QName;
import javax.xml.rpc.handler.Handler;
import javax.xml.rpc.handler.HandlerInfo;
```

```
13: import javax.xml.rpc.handler.MessageContext;
14: import javax.xml.rpc.handler.soap.SOAPMessageContext;
15: import javax.xml.soap.SOAPException;
16: import javax.xml.soap.SOAPMessage;
17:
18: import org.apache.log4j.Logger;
19:
20: public class LoggingHandler implements Handler {
21:     Logger log;
22:
23:     public void destroy() {
24:     }
25:
26:     public QName[] getHeaders() {
27:         return null;
28:     }
```

The handleFault, handleRequest, and handleResponse methods log their context to the logger (line 31) and then call getEnvelope to obtain a SOAP representation of the message (line 32). The SOAP representation is also logged (line 32), and then the handler chain is signaled to continue handler processing by returning true (line 33):

```
29:
30:     public boolean handleFault(MessageContext mc) {
31:         log.error("requestor fault");
32:         log.error(getEnvelope(mc));
33:         return true;
34:     }
35:
36:     public boolean handleRequest(MessageContext mc) {
37:         log.info("requestor request");
38:         log.info(getEnvelope(mc));
39:         return true;
40:     }
41:
42:     public boolean handleResponse(MessageContext mc) {
43:         log.info("requestor response");
44:         log.info(getEnvelope(mc));
45:         return true;
46:     }
```

You use the handler's init method to set up the log4j logger:

```
47:
48:     public void init(HandlerInfo hi) {
49:         log = Logger.getLogger(this.getClass());
50:     }
```

getEnvelope downcasts the MessageContext to a SOAPMessageContext (line 53). This is necessary because only SOAPMessageContext has the method you need in order to obtain the SOAP form of the message (line 54):

```
51:
52:     private String getEnvelope(MessageContext mc) {
```

```
        SOAPMessageContext smc = (SOAPMessageContext) mc;
        SOAPMessage msg = smc.getMessage();
```

Once you have the SOAP message, you get the message as a SOAPPart, obtain the Envelope from the part, and convert the Envelope to a string that can be logged:

```
        String value = "";
        try {
            value = msg.getSOAPPart().getEnvelope().toString();
        } catch (SOAPException se) {
            se.printStackTrace();
        }
        return value;
    }
}
```

The code for the requestor side showed how to install a requestor-side handler. JAX-RPC 1.0 doesn't specify how to install handlers on the provider side. Axis uses an entry in the deployment descriptor to fulfill this function. This is the deployment descriptor generated by WSDL2Java for the document-literal example—we've added the information needed to register the handler:

```
<!--Use this file to deploy some handlers/chains and services-->
<!--Two ways to do this:                                      -->
<!--  java org.apache.axis.client.AdminClient deploy.wsdd     -->
<!--     after the axis server is running                     -->
<!-- or                                                       -->
<!-- java org.apache.axis.utils.Admin client|server deploy.wsdd
   -->
<!--     from the same directory that the Axis engine runns   -->

<deployment
 xmlns="http://xml.apache.org/axis/wsdd/"
 xmlns:java="http://xml.apache.org/axis/wsdd/providers/java">

<!-- Services from DLBookHandlerService WSDL service -->

 <service name="DLBookService" provider="java:RPC"
          style="document" use="literal">
  <parameter name="wsdlTargetNamespace"
   value="http://DLBookService.ch9.apachexml.sauria.com"/>
  <parameter name="wsdlServiceElement"
   value="DLBookHandlerService"/>
  <parameter name="wsdlServicePort"
   value="DLBookService"/>
  <parameter name="className"
   value="com.sauria.apachexml.ch9.DLBookService.
DLBookServiceSoapBindingImpl"/>
  <parameter name="wsdlPortType" value="DLBookHandler"/>
  <operation name="createBook"
   qname="operNS:createBook"
   xmlns:operNS="http://DLBookService.ch9.apachexml.sauria.com"
   returnQName="createBookReturn"
   returnType="rtns:boolean"
   xmlns:rtns="http://www.w3.org/2001/XMLSchema" >
```

```
    <parameter qname="pns:book"
     xmlns:pns="http://sauria.com/schemas/apache-xml-book/book"
     type="tns:>book"
     xmlns:tns="http://sauria.com/schemas/apache-xml-book/book"/>
   </operation>
   <operation name="getBook"
    qname="operNS:getBook"
    xmlns:operNS="http://DLBookService.ch9.apachexml.sauria.com"
    returnQName="retNS:book"
    xmlns:retNS="http://sauria.com/schemas/apache-xml-book/book"
    returnType="rtns:>book"
    xmlns:rtns="http://sauria.com/schemas/apache-xml-book/book" >
    <parameter qname="pns:isbn"
     xmlns:pns="http://sauria.com/schemas/apache-xml-book/book"
     type="tns:string"
     xmlns:tns="http://www.w3.org/2001/XMLSchema"/>
   </operation>
   <parameter name="allowedMethods" value="getBook createBook"/>

   <typeMapping
    xmlns:ns="http://sauria.com/schemas/apache-xml-book/book"
    qname="ns:>book"
    type="java:com.sauria.schemas.apache_xml_book.book._book"
    serializer=
       "org.apache.axis.encoding.ser.BeanSerializerFactory"
    deserializer=
       "org.apache.axis.encoding.ser.BeanDeserializerFactory"
    encodingStyle=""
    />
```

WSDD uses the <requestFlow> and <responseFlow> elements to add handlers to the request-handling chain and response-handling chain, respectively. The <handler> elements inside them are the same; the only difference is whether they appear as a child of <requestFlow> or <responseFlow>. Because you want to log requests (to make sure you received them) and responses (to make sure you sent them), you install the logging handler in both flows.

The type attribute specifies that you're using a JAX-RPC handler. Axis has its own notion of handlers that was developed prior to the introduction of JAX-RPC:

```
   <requestFlow>
    <handler type="java:org.apache.axis.handlers.JAXRPCHandler">
```

After that are two parameters. The scope parameter says there's one handler instance per session. The className parameter gives the name of the class that's providing the handler functionality:

```
     <parameter name="scope" value="session"/>
     <parameter name="className"
          value=
"com.sauria.apachexml.ch9.DLBookService.handlers.LoggingHandler"/>
    </handler>
   </requestFlow>
   <responseFlow>
```

```
    <handler type="java:org.apache.axis.handlers.JAXRPCHandler">
     <parameter name="scope" value="session"/>
     <parameter name="className"
          value=
"com.sauria.apachexml.ch9.DLBookService.handlers.LoggingHandler"/>
    </handler>
   </responseFlow>

 </service>
</deployment>
```

This is a relatively simple handler. As Web services deployments become more common, and people gain experience with architectures based on networks of Web services, we'll see the use of SOAP headers to carry information around those networks. That's when the use of handlers will really take off.

.jws Web Services

Axis provides a mechanism for quickly deploying simple Web services. If you take a service provider class and change the file suffix from .java to .jws, you can then put that file into an appropriately configured Web application directory (the Web application needs to have a url-mapping from .jws files to the AxisServlet). When you access the URL for that file, Axis automatically compiles the file and processes any SOAP request that accompanies the access.

Here's an example. This is the service code generated by WSDL2Java for the RPC-encoded Web service example. The only change that has been made is to comment out the package declaration in line 8. If you drop this file into a properly configured Web application directory, you'll have a running Web service, and you can use the various requestors we showed earlier to perform service requests:

```
 1: /**
 2:  * BookServiceSoapBindingImpl.java
 3:  *
 4:  * This file was auto-generated from WSDL
 5:  * by the Apache Axis WSDL2Java emitter.
 6:  */
 7:
 8: //package com.sauria.apachexml.ch9.BookService;
 9:
10: public class BookServiceSoapBindingImpl
11:     implements
12:       com.sauria.apachexml.ch9.BookService.BookHandler {
13:     public boolean createBook(java.lang.String author,
14:         java.lang.String title,
15:         java.lang.String isbn,
16:         java.lang.String month,
17:         int year,
18:         java.lang.String publisher,
19:         java.lang.String address)
20:         throws java.rmi.RemoteException {
21:         return author.equals("Ted Leung");
22:     }
23: }
```

The biggest drawback to .jws Web services is that right now the functionality only works for RPC-encoded Web services. Because the WS-I basic profile mandates document-literal Web services, the usefulness of .jws Web services has been reduced, at least until the Axis team updates them to work with document-literal style. The other drawback is that you don't have as much control as when you use deployment descriptors, which WSDL2Java can generate for you.

Tools

Let's look at a pair of tools that can make your life much easier when you're working with Axis. The first is useful for debugging Web services, and the second will keep you from going typing-crazy.

TCPMon

The first tool is called TCPMon, and it gives you a way to look at the SOAP messages that are exchanged between two hosts. The command line for TCPMon is

```
java org.apache.axis.utils.tcpmon listenPort targetHost targetPort
```

When you execute this command, TCPMon connects the *listenPort* on the current machine to the *targetPort* on the target machine. All the arguments are optional, and if you leave them out, TCPMon starts you with a GUI page where you can fill in the values interactively. Here's a screenshot of TCPMon in action:

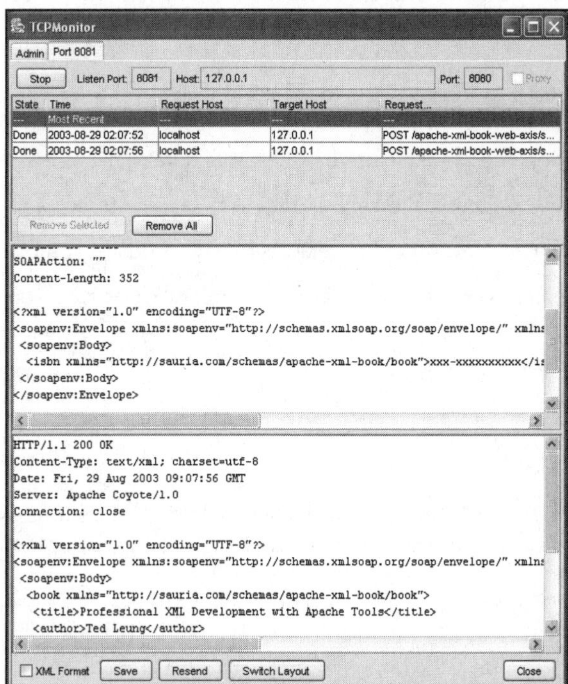

TCPMon is very useful for telling whether the SOAP that's being exchanged is the SOAP you *think* is being exchanged. It's particularly useful when the requestor and provider are using different SOAP runtimes, because it lets you see what might be causing any interoperability problems.

Ant Tasks

The other tool you'll want are the Ant tasks for Axis. They're included in the Axis distribution in the axis-ant.jar file in the lib directory. Tasks are provided for WSDL2Java, Java2WDSL and AdminClient. These tasks can save you lots of typing when you're working with Axis. Let's go through each of these tasks.

WSDL2Java

The element name for the WSDL2Java task is <axis-wsdl2java>. The attributes correspond to the command-line options, shown in parentheses, for WSDL2Java. Attributes are optional unless noted:

- **all**—Generate all elements. Defaults to false. (--all)
- **debug**—Turn on debug output. Defaults to false. (--debug)
- **deployscope**—Set the deployment scope: "Application", "Session", or "Request". (--deployScope)
- **factory**—Name of the WSDL2Java emitter factory. (--factory)
- **helpergen**—Generate helper classes. Defaults to false. (--helperGen)
- **namespacemappingfile**—Name of the namespace mapping file. (--filetoNsPkg)
- **noimports**—Don't generate code for elements in imported WSDL. Defaults to false. (--noImports)
- **output**—Name of the output directory. (--output)
- **serverside**—Generate provider-side files. Defaults to false. (--server-side)
- **skeletondeploy**—Generate skeleton files. Defaults to false. (--skeletonDeploy)
- **testcase**—Generate a JUnit test case. Defaults to false. (--testcase)
- **timeout**—Set the requestor timeout. Defaults to 45 seconds. -1 disables timeouts. (--timeout)
- **typemappingversion**—Set the type-mapping version (1.1 or 1.2). Defaults to 1.1. (--typeMappingVersion)
- **url**—URL of the WSDL file (required).
- **verbose**—Verbose output. Defaults to false. (--verbose)

Java2WSDL

The element name for the Java2WSDL task is <axis-java2wsdl>. The attributes correspond to the command-line options, show in parentheses, for Java2WSDL. Attributes are optional unless noted:

- **bindingname**—Name of <binding>. (--bindingName)
- **classname**—Name of the class for which to generate WSDL (required).
- **exclude**—Methods to exclude. (--exclude)
- **extraclasses**—List of extra classes. (--extraClasses)
- **implclass**—Implementation class. (--implClass)

- **input**—Input WSDL file. (--input)
- **location**—Location of the service. (--location)
- **locationimport**—Location of the interface WSDL. (--locationImport)
- **methods**—Methods to export. (--methods)
- **namespace**—Target namespace for the WSDL (required). (--namespace)
- **namespaceimpl**—Target namespace for the implementation WSDL. (--namespaceImpl)
- **output**—Name of the output WSDL file. (--output)
- **outputimpl**—Name of the output implementation WSDL file. (--outputImpl)
- **porttypename**—Name of the <portType>. (--portTypeName)
- **serviceelementname**—Name of the <service>. (--serviceElementName)
- **serviceportname**—Name of the <port>. (--servicePortName)
- **stopclasses**—List of classes that stop the inheritance search. (--stopClasses)
- **style**—Style of the WSDL document. Valid values are "document", "wrapped", and "rpc". (--style)
- **typemappingversion**—Type-mapping version (1.1 or 1.2). Defaults to 1.1. (--typeMappingVersion)
- **use**—Set the WSDL use option. Valid values are "encoded" and "literal". (--use)
- **useinheritedmethods**—Export inherited methods if true. Defaults to false. (--all)

AdminClient

The element name for the AdminClient task is <axis-admin>. The attributes correspond to the command-line options, shown in parentheses, for AdminClient. Attributes are optional unless noted:

- **debug**—Turn on debug output. (-d)
- **failonerror**—The Ant build should fail on an error if true. Defaults to true.
- **fileprotocol**—If the value is a filename, use a simple file protocol. (-f)
- **hostname**—The hostname to connect to. (-h)
- **newpassword**—Change the password to the value of this attribute.
- **password**—The password needed to log in. (-w)
- **port**—The port to connect on. (-p)
- **servletpath**—The path to the Axis servlet. (-s)
- **transportchain**—The transport chain to use. (-t)
- **url**—The full URL to the Axis servlet. (-l)
- **username**—The username needed to log in. (-u)
- **xmlfile**—The deployment or undeployment descriptor file (required).

Sample build.xml

The following code is a cut-down version of the Ant file used to build the document-literal example in this chapter. Create a property that points to the Axis installation:

```
<project name="axis-samples" default="wsdl">
 <property name="axis.home" value="/work/lib/axis-1_1"/>
```

Create a classpath that contains the Axis jars:

```
 <path id="axis.classpath">
  <fileset dir="${axis.home}/lib">
   <include name="**/*.jar"/>
  </fileset>
 </path>
```

Find the Axis taskdef:

```
 <taskdef resource="axis-tasks.properties"
     classpathref="axis.classpath" />
```

This target runs Java2WSDL, generating a test case and provider stubs, including skeletons. The output level is verbose, and the Java files are written directly into a directory in the Eclipse project:

```
 <target name="wsdl-dl">
  <axis-wsdl2java url="DLBookService.wsdl"
   serverside="true"
   skeletondeploy="true"
   output=
   "/work/workspace-1.4/apache-xml-book-web-axis/WEB-INF/src"
   testcase="true"
   verbose="true">
  </axis-wsdl2java>
 </target>
```

Here you set some properties to make it easier to do administration. You set properties for the port, host, and admin servlet path. You also set a partial path that helps find the generated deployment descriptors:

```
 <property name="axis.port" value="8080"/>
 <property name="axis.host" value="localhost"/>
 <property name="axis.adminService"
    value="apache-xml-book-web-axis/services/AdminService"/>
 <property name="descriptor.path"
     value="com/sauria/apachexml/ch9"/>
```

This task is used to deploy the service. The values of the attributes are supplied by the properties defined earlier:

```

<target name="deploy-dl">
 <axis-admin
  port="${axis.port}"
  hostname="${axis.host}"
  servletpath="${axis.adminService}"
  xmlfile="${descriptor.path}/DLBookService/deploy.wsdd"/>
</target>
```

This task undeploys the service:

```

<target name="undeploy-dl">
 <axis-admin
  port="${axis.port}"
  hostname="${axis.host}"
  servletpath="${axis.adminService}"
  xmlfile="${descriptor.path}/DLBookService/undeploy.wsdd"/>
</target>

</project>
```

This Ant build file makes it easy to run WSDL2Java and to deploy and undeploy your service. It can save you a lot of typing.

Practical Usage

Let's emphasize a few things we've mentioned over the course of the chapter. First, you should focus on building Web services that use the document-literal scheme. This is the scheme that's being promoted by the WS-I in its basic profile. It also has much better potential for interoperability, especially with .NET applications.

Second, you should use WSDL if at all possible. If you have existing Java code, use Java2WSDL to generate a first cut at a WSDL file. Then you can clean up the file and modularize it. You can use the modularization we showed in the WSDL2Java example, or you can use the one that Java2WSDL uses (if you use Java2WSDL, you can have Java2WSDL do it for you). Once you have a good WSDL file, you should use WSDL2Java to generate the Java classes you need. If you need to work with existing code, then have WSDL2Java generate the skeleton classes, and use the prewritten forwarding methods in the skeleton to connect the skeleton to your existing code. Don't forget to throw away the template implementation class if you use the skeleton this way.

Third, use TCPMon as a tool when you're debugging. Doing so can save you many hours of frustration and give you some insight into what your code is doing.

Fourth, ask Axis to generate a JUnit test case for you and write a decent set of tests for your application.

Fifth, make sure you use the Ant tasks to save you from repetitive typing. You can also use the JUnit task for Ant to run your generated test case.

Applications

Much like XML-RPC, the applications for Axis and Web services are broad. Anywhere you can think of invoking a method on an object is a possible candidate for a Web service. The primary areas where Web services can make a difference are as follows:

- Invoking functionality on a machine not owned by you.
- Invoking functionality on a machine that uses a different language and/or platform.

Today, most of the activity in Web services involves using Web services to integrate heterogeneous applications within the same organization. We're beginning to see some use of Web services to integrate applications across the Internet. eBay, Google, and Amazon.com have started developer programs that allow access to their applications via Web services technologies.

Perhaps your company will be the next one to expose pieces of an application to the world using Web services. Or, maybe you'll create a new application that talks to one of the big players. In either case, Axis is a capable and reliable Web services toolkit.

10

XML Security

XML is being accepted as a way of transferring information between application programs and computers. The volume of data that's being marked up in XML documents is increasing daily. Some of that data is being used to conduct everyday business. The interoperability benefits of using a format like XML are significant; the drawback is that XML makes data human-readable, even when humans shouldn't be reading that data. In this chapter, we'll look at the problem of how to protect the integrity and secrecy of data stored in XML documents.

You might wonder why this is an issue. After all, the existing techniques for protecting documents should work fine. If you want to protect a document, you run it through an encryption algorithm, and the document comes out encrypted. If you want to certify something about a document, then you sign the document with a digital signature. Declaring the integrity of a document is easy—compute a message digest, and someone else can use it to verify that the document hasn't been tampered with. To satisfy more than one of these goals at once, we know how to combine these techniques. What does XML bring to the table that requires a new solution?

The answer is that you may not want to sign or encrypt the entire document. You may only want to sign or encrypt an element or a few elements. Perhaps an XML document represents a bunch of information, but you only care about or want to be responsible for part of that information. Think of a document that represents a complex agreement among multiple parties. Each part may only want to sign the part of the document they're responsible for. Likewise, some of the terms of the agreement may be between only two parties, but the entire agreement stands or falls together. In this situation, some of these terms may be a secret between the two parties, and they would like to keep those terms secret. You can implement this requirement by allowing that section of the document to be encrypted so only the relevant parties can decrypt it. Many applications of XML involve workflows (this is true of Web services as well), which have these kinds of requirements.

Technically, the solution rests with a pair of specifications from the World Wide Web Consortium (W3C): the XML Signature Syntax and Processing Recommendation and the XML Encryption Syntax and Processing Recommendation. The XML Signature Recommendation describes how to use digital signatures and hashing/message digesting to digitally sign entire XML documents and portions of XML documents. The XML Encryption Recommendation performs a similar function for using symmetric key encryption to encrypt part or all of an XML document. The XML Signature Recommendation uses the Canonical XML and Exclusive XML Canonicalization Recommendations.

XML Security is the xml.apache.org project that's implementing these four recommendations. The project was started in September 2001 when the XML Security project at the University of Siegen in Germany donated a code base that implemented the Canonicalization and part of the XML Signature Recommendations. Since then, the project has completed implementation of the required portions of the XML Signature Recommendation and has begun implementation of the XML Encryption Recommendation. There has been some cooperation with the Apache Axis project, in particular a set of Axis handlers that can be used to digitally sign SOAP messages. These handlers use the older SOAP Signature specification, which has been superseded by the WS-Security specifications. The Web services project is interested in building a complete WS-Security implementation.

Prerequisites

To get the most out of this chapter, you need to be familiar with XML, XML namespaces, and the DOM APIs. You also need to know some of the basics of cryptography. We'll go over the concepts at a basic level so you have an idea of what's going on. If you're familiar with cryptographic concepts, then you can skip ahead to the next section.

One-Way Hashing

A *hash function* is a function that takes an array consisting of an arbitrary number of bytes as input and converts it to an output array of fixed size. The output array is usually shorter than the input array. This is a loose definition, but if you've dealt with hashing, this is exactly the way hash functions work.

A one-way hash function is a hash function that works in only one direction—it should be very difficult, if not almost impossible, to obtain the input array from the hash value. A good one-way hash function won't map two different input arrays to the same hash value. This makes one-way hash functions a good way to summarize or fingerprint some data.

In the cryptography world, the terms *one-way hash function; cryptographic checksum*, and *message digest* all mean the same thing. These functions are used to check whether data has been tampered with. You do this by taking the data and computing the hash value for it. Then you transmit the data and the hash value to someone else. The recipient takes the data, computes the hash value for it (the hash algorithm is usually public), and compares the computed hash value with the received hash value. If they're the same, the data hasn't been altered. If they're different, then the data has been altered, because no two input values yield the same hash value.

You may also see the term *message authentication code* (MAC). This is a one-way hash function that's combined with a secret key. Unless you have the secret key, the recipient can't verify the hash function. An easy way to implement a MAC is to compute a one-way hash value and then encrypt the hash value with a symmetric key encryption scheme.

Common one-way hashing algorithms are Secure Hash Algorithm 1 (SHA1) and Message-Digest 5 (MD5). SHA1 is the algorithm of choice because MD5 is based on the MD4 algorithm, which has been broken. SHA1 produces a 160-bit hash value, whereas MD5 produces a 128-bit hash value.

Symmetric Key Encryption

Symmetric key encryption is also known as *secret key encryption*. With these encryption schemes, you can exchange data securely with anyone who knows the encryption key. The details of the encryption algorithm can be well known, but as long as the key is a secret, your data will be safe. When people say *encryption*, they're usually referring to symmetric key encryption. Usually, the strength of a symmetric key algorithm depends on the size of the encryption key: The longer the key, the stronger the algorithm.

Some common symmetric key algorithms are DES, Triple DES (or 3-DES), Advanced Encryption Standard (AES), CAST, International Data Encryption Algorithm (IDEA), and Blowfish. DES is the U.S. Governments Data Encryption Standard, which until recently was the algorithm approved for all U.S. Government encryption. Triple DES is just what it sounds like: The data to be encrypted is encrypted using the DES algorithm three times. DES was replaced by the Advanced Encryption Standard (AES) in 2000. IDEA is considered a very secure symmetric key algorithm; CAST was designed in Canada and has been used in some commercial products. Blowfish was designed by Bruce Schneier of CounterPane and is in the public domain. Blowfish has been widely implemented and will appear in the Linux 2.6 series kernels.

Public Key Encryption

Public key encryption uses two keys: a private key, which is kept secret; and a public key, which is distributed to whoever wants it. In public key systems, the private key and public key are generated together. Public key encryption works like this. A person who wants to send a message to the holder of a private key takes that person's public key and uses it to encrypt a message. The only way to decrypt a message that has been encrypted with that public key is to use the corresponding private key. If everyone has a public key and a private key, then you have a system in which a person can send secret messages to any other person.

Public key encryption algorithms are much slower than symmetric key algorithms. For this reason, in practice public key methods are used to safely communicate a shared key for a symmetric encryption algorithm. Once the symmetric key has been safely transmitted, then the two parties can communicate via symmetric key encryption. Two of the most popular public key encryption algorithms are the RSA algorithm originally developed at MIT and the ElGamal algorithm.

Digital Signatures

The goals of digital signature algorithms are fairly straightforward. The recipient of digitally signed data must be sure the signature is actually the signature of the person who claims to have signed the document, and that signature should be difficult, if not impossible, to forge or reuse. It should be impossible for someone to digitally sign a document and then later claim that they didn't sign the document. Finally, a digital signature is no good unless you can be sure the data it's attached to hasn't been tampered with.

One method of implementing digital signatures is to use public key encryption. We'll explain how this works using public key encryption terminology, but you should be aware that not every public key encryption algorithm can be used this way. In some public key algorithms, you can use the private key to encrypt data, which can only be decrypted using the corresponding public key (this is in addition to the normal usage of the public and private keys). The digital signature protocol works like this. To digitally sign some data, the signer encrypts the data using their private key. Verifying the signature is simple: The recipient of the signed data uses the sender's public key to decrypt the data. This neatly satisfies all the requirements for a digital signature algorithm: Only one private key can be used to encrypt the data and have it still be decryptable with the public key. This means you know which key signed the data. (This is the best you can do. If the signer leaves their computer unprotected, then it's conceivable that someone else could use their private key to generate a signature—such attacks are beyond what digital signatures can protect against.) You can't generate the signature without having possession of the private key, making it difficult to forge the signature. Because the value of the signature depends on the data being encrypted by the private key, the signature can't be reused for other data. It's hard to claim that a document wasn't signed by a particular private key, because verification with the public key indicates which private key was used to generate the signature. Finally, modifying the encrypted data means that it can't be verified with the public key, so you'll be able to tell whether the data has been tampered with.

One important issue that arises from the use of public key encryption for digital signatures is how to obtain and trust a public key. The distribution of public keys is a big area, and we'll just point out that the ITU's X.509 standard is helping to solve this problem.

The issue of how to trust a public key takes us to the topic of certificates. A *digital certificate* is a public key that has been digitally signed by a trusted third party. This third party is often known as a Certification Authority (CA). The CAs are supposed to be well known and highly trustworthy entities. You've probably heard of Verisign, Entrust, or Thawte—names that appear when you're dealing with SSL certificates.

Remember that public key encryption is computationally expensive. One way to improve the practical efficiency of computing digital signatures is to sign a one-way hash value of the data being signed. The one-way hash is usually much smaller than the data being signed, and it's less expensive to sign the hash value than to sign the data. Using this method, verifying a signature involves the following steps: independently generate the hash value for the received data, verify the signed hash value, and test the two hash values for equality.

Two digital signature algorithms are in wide use today: the RSA public key cryptosystem and the DSA algorithm proposed by the U.S. National Institute of Standards and Technology (NIST).

Concepts

Now let's look at the concepts in the various W3C recommendations that are implemented by XML Security. We'll look at XML Canonicalization first, because both XML Signature and XML Encryption use it. Then we'll look at XML Signature and XML Encryption.

Canonicalization

When there are multiple representations for a piece of data, we often pick one representative to be the most desirable to work on. What it means to be desirable often depends on the kind of work we want to do. This selected form is sometimes known as a *canonical form*. Usually canonical forms are picked so they're simple and easy to work with. In the case of XML, the canonical form of an XML document obeys a set of rules regarding its structure but is still equivalent to the original XML document. Think about the number of ways you can have the same XML document. If you take a document and change the order in which the attributes appear, the document is essentially the same. If you take empty tags like <book/> and write them as <book><book/>, you haven't changed the meaning of the document.

One of the goals of the XML Canonicalization Recommendation is to specify a canonical form for XML documents that can be used to determine whether two documents are identical. This is important for cryptography applications because we want to encrypt the canonical form of an XML document, not the document itself—the canonical form can tell you whether a document has been modified (at least, in certain ways).

> *You'll often see the word canonicalization written as c14n—the first and last characters of the word plus 14, which stands for the 14 characters between c and n. This is a short form that's growing in usage.*

Here are the rules for an XML document that's in canonical form, according to the Canonical XML Recommendation:

- The document is encoded in UTF-8.
- Line breaks are normalized to #A in input before parsing.
- Attribute values are normalized according to the rules for validating XML processors.
- Character and parsed entities are replaced.
- CDATA sections are replaced with their character content.
- The XML declaration and DTD are removed.
- Empty elements are converted to start-end tag pairs.
- Whitespace outside the document element and within start and end tags is normalized.
- All whitespace in character content is retained (aside from characters removed during line-feed normalization).
- Attribute value delimiters are set to quotation marks.
- Special characters in attribute values and character content are replaced by character references.
- Superfluous namespace declarations are removed from each element.
- Default attributes are added to each element.
- Lexicographic order is imposed on the namespace declarations and attributes of each element.

The recommendation describes the process by which you can convert any XML document into a canonical form that obeys all of these rules. (There are actually two canonical forms: one that includes any comments from in the original document and one that doesn't.) The details of how a document is converted into canonical form aren't really important for you to understand, but the result of that process is. It means you can write a library to canonicalize XML documents.

Here's a document using the book schema:

```
 1: <?xml version="1.0" encoding="UTF-8"?>
 2: <book xmlns="http://sauria.com/schemas/apache-xml-book/book"
 3:   xmlns:xsi="http://www.w3.org/2001/XMLSchema-instance"
 4:   xsi:schemaLocation=
 5:    "http://sauria.com/schemas/apache-xml-book/book
 6:     http://www.sauria.com/schemas/apache-xml-book/book.xsd"
 7:   version="1.0">
 8:   <title>Professional XML Development with Apache Tools</title>
 9:   <author>Theodore W. Leung</author>
10:   <isbn>0-7645-4355-5</isbn>
11:   <month>December</month>
12:   <year>2003</year>
13:   <publisher>Wrox</publisher>
14:   <address>Indianapolis, Indiana</address>
15: </book>
```

This is what the document looks like after it's been converted into XML canonical form. We inserted line breaks in the book element (lines 1-6) in order to make it more readable:

```
 1: <book xmlns="http://sauria.com/schemas/apache-xml-book/book"
 2:  xmlns:xsi="http://www.w3.org/2001/XMLSchema-instance"
 3:  version="1.0"
 4:  xsi:schemaLocation=
 5:   "http://sauria.com/schemas/apache-xml-book/book
 6:       http://www.sauria.com/schemas/apache-xml-book/book.xsd">
 7:   <title>Professional XML Development with Apache Tools</title>
 8:   <author>Theodore W. Leung</author>
 9:   <isbn>0-7645-4355-5</isbn>
10:   <month>December</month>
11:   <year>2003</year>
12:   <publisher>Wrox</publisher>
13:   <address>Indianapolis, Indiana</address>
14: </book>
```

The big changes are the removal of the XML declaration from line 1 of the original and the sorting of the namespace declarations and attributes (lines 2-7 of the original and 1-6 of the canonical form).

Exclusive Canonicalization

It turns out that there's a problem with the way XML canonicalization works when it's applied to the digital signature environment or any encapsulated protocol environment. The issue arises when you want to canonicalize just a subelement of a document. In this situation, XML canonicalization may capture namespace declarations and attributes in the xml: namespace from the enclosing elements/document. These values are used when computing a digital signature for this subelement. This will be a problem if the signed subelement is extracted from the original document and/or inserted into another document. Exclusive XML Canonicalization was created to address this and other limitations. It adds two new rules to the set of rules for XML Canonicalization when canonicalizing a document subset:

- Attributes in the XML namespace, such as xml:lang or xml:space, aren't imported into the document subset.
- Namespace nodes that aren't on the InclusiveNamespacesPrefixList are expressed only in start tags where they're visible and only if they aren't declared in an enclosing element in the subset. The InclusiveNamespacesPrefixList is a parameter to the Exclusive Canonicalization algorithm, which specifies a list of namespace prefixes that should be handled according to the canonical XML rules.

With the advent of exclusive canonical XML, canonical XML is also known as *inclusive canonical XML*.

XML Signature

The XML Signature Recommendation describes an XML syntax for digital signatures. These signatures can be applied to any kind of data, not just XML. There are two kinds of signatures. In an *enveloped* (or *enveloping*) signature, the signature and the data being signed are in the same document. A *detached* signature signs data that's external to the document containing the XML signature element.

We'll explain how XML Signature works by taking you through an example. This is the book document after being signed using XML signature:

```
<book xmlns="http://sauria.com/schemas/apache-xml-book/book"
 xmlns:xsi="http://www.w3.org/2001/XMLSchema-instance"
 version="1.0"
 xsi:schemaLocation=
  "http://sauria.com/schemas/apache-xml-book/book
      http://www.sauria.com/schemas/apache-xml-book/book.xsd">
  <title>Professional XML Development with Apache Tools</title>
  <author Id="author">Theodore W. Leung</author>
  <isbn>0-7645-4355-5</isbn>
  <month>December</month>
  <year>2003</year>
  <publisher>Wrox</publisher>
  <address>Indianapolis, Indiana</address>
```

Everything up to this point is the original book document, except that the book document has been converted into inclusive canonical XML form. Everything after this is related to XML signature. In order to fit the document into the pages of this book in a readable fashion, we've done a small amount of pretty-printing, and we've truncated the base64 data that appears in the example.

The Signature Element

The <Signature> element is the element defined by XML Signature to represent a digital signature. Its namespace URI is http://www.w3.org/2000/09/xmldsig#, and in this document you use the prefix ds for the URI. A <Signature> element contains a <SignedInfo>, which is the element that's signed, along with a description of how to sign it. The <SignedInfo> element can also describe other data to be signed. Returning to the <Signature> element, after the <SignedInfo> element it contains a <SignatureValue> element whose content is the digital signature value. Optionally, it contains a <KeyInfo> element that describes how to obtain the key needed to verify the signature. It also optionally contains some number of <Object> elements that can be used to associate additional information with the signature.

The SignedInfo Element

A <SignedInfo> element contains a <CanonicalizationMethod>, a <SignatureMethod>, and one or more <Reference> methods:

```
<ds:Signature xmlns:ds="http://www.w3.org/2000/09/xmldsig#">
<ds:SignedInfo>
```

Before the <SignedInfo> element is signed, it's converted to canonical XML using the algorithm specified by the Algorithm attribute. The XML Signature spec requires support for inclusive canonical XML without comments. Canonical XML with comments is also allowed. The Algorithm attribute value is a URI, allowing URIs for other canonicalization algorithms, such as exclusive canonical XML (with and without comments) to be specified, but these aren't required in any way by the XML Signature spec:

```
<ds:CanonicalizationMethod Algorithm=
  "http://www.w3.org/TR/2001/REC-xml-c14n-20010315">
</ds:CanonicalizationMethod>
```

The <SignatureMethod> element describes the algorithm used to digitally sign the <SignedInfo> element. The Algorithm attribute is used the same way as in the <CanonicalizationMethod> element. The XML Signature specification uses algorithms that are a combination of a message digest algorithm and a digital signature algorithm. The spec requires the support of the DSA digital signature algorithm with SHA1 as the digest algorithm, which is what's used in this example. It recommends that implementations support the RSA digital signature algorithm, again with SHA1 as the digest algorithm:

```
<ds:SignatureMethod
  Algorithm="http://www.w3.org/2000/09/xmldsig#dsa-sha1">
</ds:SignatureMethod>
```

Referencing Data to Be Signed

The <SignedInfo> element can contain one or more <Reference> elements. These elements are used to specify data that should be signed. A <Reference> element contains an optional <Transforms> element, a required <DigestMethod>, and a required <DigestValue>. A <Reference> element is generated during signing of the data. In the simplest case, the data referred to by the reference is digested (using a message digest algorithm), and the digest value is stored as the content of the <DigestValue> element. If the optional <Transforms> element has been supplied, then the transforms specified are applied to the data before it's digested.

The URI attribute of the <Reference> element specifies a data object that's the target of the reference. Here you reference the <author> element whose id attribute is "#author". To specify the entire document without comments, leave the value of URI empty. To specify the entire document with comments, the value of URI should be "#xpointer(/)":

```
<ds:Reference URI="#author">
```

The <Transforms> element contains a sequence of <Transform> elements. You can think of the <Transforms> element as a pipeline of <Transform>s. The input of each <Transform> is the output of the one before it, except the first and the last. For the first <Transform>, the input is the referenced data object; for the last <Transform>, the output serves as input to the message digest algorithm. This example has two <Transform>s: the enveloped signature transform and an inclusive XML canonicalization with comments:

```
<ds:Transforms>
<ds:Transform
 Algorithm=
   "http://www.w3.org/2000/09/xmldsig#enveloped-signature">
</ds:Transform>
<ds:Transform
 Algorithm=
 "http://www.w3.org/TR/2001/REC-xml-c14n-20010315#WithComments">
</ds:Transform>
```

XML Signature specifies a set of transform algorithms:

- **A canonicalization algorithm**—Any canonicalization algorithm that can be used for <CanonicalizationMethod> can be used as a transform.
- **A base64 decoding transform**—Assumes the input is base64 and returns the decoded data as output.
- **An XPath filtering transform**—The XPath expression is evaluated, and the result is the output. XML Signature defines a new XPath function here that can be used in this transform. The here function returns a node set containing the attribute, processing instruction, or parent node of the text node containing the XPath expression. Support for the XPath filtering transform is optional.
- **The Enveloped Signature Transform**—Removes the entire <Signature> element that contains the enveloped signature transform. This means the digest won't include the <Signature> element.
- **XSLT Transform**—The output is the result of applying an XSLT stylesheet to the data object. The stylesheet is the child element of the <Transform> element. Support for the XSLT transform is optional.

In this example, the data object is the <author> element in <book> (due to the #author fragment identifier specified as the value of the <Reference> URI attribute). So, the <author> element has the enveloped signature transform applied (which does nothing, because the Signature element isn't part of the referenced data), and then it's canonicalized using inclusive XML canonicalization with comments. The last step is to use the algorithm specified by <DigestMethod> to compute a message digest value:

```
</ds:Transforms>
<ds:DigestMethod
 Algorithm="http://www.w3.org/2000/09/xmldsig#sha1">
</ds:DigestMethod>
```

The <DigestMethod> element specifies the algorithm to be used to compute the <DigestValue>. The input is the output of the last <Transform>, or the data object if no <Transforms> element is supplied. Here you use SHA1 as the digest method. The XML Signature Recommendation requires SHA1 to be available as a digest method. It also states that MD5 is *not recommended* due to recent advances in cryptanalysis.

<DigestValue>'s content is the base64-encoded SHA1 digest of the referenced data:

```
<ds:DigestValue>198q+YUGo9GC27hTpZO093eUF3Y=</ds:DigestValue>
```

The SignatureValue Element

Now we're ready to talk about the <SignatureValue>, whose content is the digital signature of the <SignedInfo> element:

```
</ds:Reference>
</ds:SignedInfo>
<ds:SignatureValue>Su0ucZAbiIs4+0HJB1BBmnBKbbJvhyQ1OISCrl/rXuzbhw
</ds:SignatureValue>
```

The value of <SignatureValue> is computed as follows:

1. For each data object being signed, apply the transforms specified in <Transforms>, compute the digest using the digest algorithm, and construct a <Reference> element with the appropriate information.
2. Create a <SignedInfo> element and the correct <SignatureMethod> and <CanonicalizationMethod> elements. Include the <Reference> elements generated in step 1.
3. Use the canonicalization method specified in <CanonicalizationMethod> to canonicalize the <SignedInfo> element.
4. Use the algorithm specified in <SignatureMethod> to compute a signature value.
5. Obtain the content of <SignatureValue> by base64-encoding the result of step 4.

There you have it. You can then combine the <SignedInfo> and <SignatureValue> elements to construct a complete <Signature> element.

The KeyInfo Element

Let's continue on and expand the example to include some of the other elements you may see in a <Signature> element. The optional <KeyInfo> element tells how to find the public key that can be used to verify the <Signature> element. A number of possible elements can appear as the children of <KeyInfo>:

- **<KeyName>**—The content of <KeyName> is a text string name for the key. You must assume that the recipient will know how to use this name to find the key.
- **<KeyValue>**—The content of the <KeyValue> element is a single public key. The specification defines two types of children (but allows for more):
    - **<DSAKeyValue>**—The parameters of a DSA public key (in subelements).
    - **<RSAKeyValue>**—The fields of an RSA public key (in subelements).
- **<RetrievalMethod>**—Retrieve the KeyInfo via a URI and optionally apply a set of <Transforms> to it. The optional Type attribute specifies the type of data being retrieved.

- ❑ **<X509Data>**—Specify that the key information is to be found via X509. This is done by using one or more of the following:
    - ❑ **<X509IssuerSerial>**—X.509 issuer distinguished name and serial number.
    - ❑ **<X509SKI>**—Base64-encoded value of an X.509 SubjectKeyIdentifier.
    - ❑ **<X509SubjectName>**—An X.509 subject distinguished name.
    - ❑ **<X509Certificate>**—Base64-encoded X509 certificate.
    - ❑ **<X509CRL>**—Base64-encoded certificate revocation list.
- ❑ **<PGPData>**—Data from a PGP public key. One of the following:
    - ❑ Base64-encoded PGP public key identifier followed by a base64 PGP Key Material Packet.
    - ❑ Base64-encoded PGP Key Material Packet.
- ❑ **<SPKIData>**—Base64-encoded SPKI canonical S-expression.
- ❑ **<MgmtData>**—Use of this method is *not recommended*.

More than one of these methods can appear as the content of <KeyInfo>:

```
<ds:KeyInfo>
<ds:X509Data>
<ds:X509Certificate>
MIIC4DCCAp4CBD9RdNcwCwYHKoZIzjgEAwUAMFYxCzAJBgNVBAYTAlVTMQ4wDAYDV
dzEQMA4GA1UEBxMHTm93aGVyZTESMBAGA1UEChMJS2V5cyBSIFVzMREwDwYDVQQDE
ZTAeFw0wMzA4MzEwNDA4NTVaFw0wMzExMjkwNDA4NTVaMFYxCzAJBgNVBAYTAlVTM
EwVOb2hvdzEQMA4GA1UEBxMHTm93aGVyZTESMBAGA1UEChMJS2V5cyBSIFVzMREwD
b2huIERvZTCCAbcwggEsBgcqhkjOOAQBMIIBHwKBgQD9f1OBHXUSKVLfSpwu7OTn9
Hj+AtlEmaUVdQCJR+1k9jVj6v8X1ujD2y5tVbNeBO4AdNG/yZmC3a51QpaSfn+gEe
t8Yb+DtX58aophUPBPuD9tPFHsMCNVQTWhaRMvZ1864rYdcq7/IiAxmd0UgBxwIVA
spK5gqLrhAvwWBz1AoGBAPfhoIXWmz3ey7yrXDa4V7l51K+7+jrqgvlXTAs9B4JnU
cQcQgYC0SRZxI+hMKBYTt88JMozIpuE8FnqLVHyNKOCjrh4rs6Z1kW6jfwv6ITVi8
8b6oUZCJqIPf4VrlnwaSi2ZegHtVJWQBTDv+z0kqA4GEAAKBgFDE4IMEhajzZWWO2
y81NHLZx9Rxda+UQnjyATvTrCg0dP9wTSMH3hlBXtVE0b8m+Hmq7CmoaPrTO4WpPZ
iQDhZMEK/a3FudKQSIlFhsaeFUGxehDHEbkhLay/hfiU7GK/IBxRLBWEwjEHZiq9O
SM44BAMFAAMvADAsAhQhD7rJv3laaI5wUTWIJEQMRNyPqAIUYPRYMOPy39mJgbG9o
</ds:X509Certificate>
</ds:X509Data>
<ds:KeyValue>
<ds:DSAKeyValue>
<ds:P>
/X9TgR11EilS30qcLuzk5/YRt1I870QAwx4/gLZRJmlFXUAiUftZPY1Y+r/F9bow9
HTRv8mZgt2uZUKWkn5/oBHsQIsJPu6nX/rfGG/g7V+fGqKYVDwT7g/bTxR7DAjVUE
K2HXKu/yIgMZndFIAcc=
</ds:P>
<ds:Q>l2BQjxUjC8yykrmCouuEC/BYHPU=</ds:Q>
<ds:G>
```

```
9+GghdabPd7LvKtcNrhXuXmUr7v6OuqC+VdMCz0HgmdRWVeOutRZT+ZxBxCBgLRJF
zwkyjMim4TwWeotUfI0o4KOuHiuzpnWRbqN/C/ohNWLx+2J6ASQ7zKTxvqhRkImog
Zl6Ae1UlZAFMO/7PSSo=
</ds:G>
<ds:Y>
UMTggwSFqPNlZY7agITcI0dqSDnLzU0ctnH1HF1r5RCePIBO9OsKDR0/3BNIwfeGU
arsKaho+tM7hak9npx7/G8AC6TmJAOFkwQr9rcW50pBIiUWGxp4VQbF6EMcRuSEtr
HFEsFYTCMQdmKr04Qlo=
</ds:Y>
</ds:DSAKeyValue>
</ds:KeyValue>
</ds:KeyInfo>
```

In the example, you have two ways to obtain the key: via the enclosed x.509 certificate or via an attached DSA public key value.

The Object Element

The <Object> element is used to attach other kinds of information to the <Signature>:

```
<ds:Object>
 <Manifest xmlns="http://www.w3.org/2000/09/xmldsig#">
 </Manifest>
```

This <Object> has been used to attach an (empty) <Manifest>. A <Manifest> can contain a sequence of <Reference> elements. These <Reference>s are checked in an application-specific manner. They aren't checked as part of the digital signature verification.

This <Object> element is used to attach a <SignatureProperties> element to the <Signature>. A <SignatureProperties> contains a sequence of <SignatureProperty> elements. The <SignatureProperty> element provides a way to provide additional information about the generation of the signature. A property has an ID that can be used to reference it. The Target attribute identifies the property via a URL, and the content of the <SignatureProperty> is the value of the property:

```
</ds:Object>
<ds:Object>
 <SignatureProperties xmlns="http://www.w3.org/2000/09/xmldsig#">
  <SignatureProperty Id="hardware"
   Target="http://www.sauria.com">smartcard</SignatureProperty>
 </SignatureProperties>
</ds:Object>
</ds:Signature>
</book>
```

Validating a Signature

To validate a <Signature>, you perform two steps: You validate each reference, and you validate the signature of the <SignedInfo> element. Here are the steps for reference validation:

1. Use the <CanonicalizationMethod> in <SignedInfo> to get the canonical form.
2. For each <Reference> in the <SignedInfo>:
    a. Retrieve the data to be digested.
    b. Perform any transforms specified in the <Transforms> element for the <Reference>.
    c. Compute the digest value using the method specified in <DigestMethod>.
    d. Compare the computed digest value with the content of <DigestValue>.

To validate the <SignedInfo> signature:

1. If the key information has been specified using <KeyInfo>, obtain the key; otherwise obtain the key some other way.
2. Use the algorithm specified in <CanonicalizationMethod> to compute the canonical form of <SignatureMethod>.
3. Use the algorithm specified in the canonical form of <SignatureMethod> to compute a signature value.
4. Compare the computed value with the content of <SignatureValue>.

This concludes our brief tour of XML Signature. We haven't covered all the details or technical points in the XML Signature Recommendation, but this should give you a good start toward understanding how to use XML Security to work with XML Signature.

XML Encryption

The XML Encryption Recommendation describes how to encrypt data and represent the result as XML. You can use XML Encryption to encrypt XML documents, XML elements, XML element content, or any other kind of data. When you encrypt data using XML Encryption, the result is an <EncryptedData> element that's included in an XML document, depending on what data you encrypted:

- If you encrypted an XML document or arbitrary data, then <EncryptedData> is the root element of a new XML document or becomes a child element of a document supplied by your application.
- If you encrypted an XML element, then the <EncryptedData> element replaces the element you encrypted.
- If you encrypted the content of an XML element, then the <EncryptedData> element replaces the element content you encrypted.

Just as we did with XML Signature, we'll explain XML Encryption by walking through an example. This example has also been slightly modified in order to fit with the formatting of the book (just like the signature example). Again, let's take the book document and encrypt the <author> element:

```
<?xml version="1.0" encoding="UTF-8"?>
<book version="1.0"
 xmlns="http://sauria.com/schemas/apache-xml-book/book"
 xmlns:xsi="http://www.w3.org/2001/XMLSchema-instance"
 xsi:schemaLocation=
```

```
"http://sauria.com/schemas/apache-xml-book/book
     http://www.sauria.com/schemas/apache-xml-book/book.xsd">
<title>Professional XML Development with Apache Tools</title>
```

According to the XML Encryption spec, when you're encrypting an XML element like <author>, the <EncryptedData> element replaces the element being encrypted. So here, where <author> used to be, you see <EncryptedData>. <EncryptedData> has its own namespace URI, http://www.w3.org/2001/04/xmlenc#, and you use the prefix xenc. An <EncryptedData> element contains an optional <EncryptionMethod> element, followed by an optional <ds:KeyInfo> (from the XML Signature Recommendation) element. After these two optional elements is a required <CipherData> element, followed by an optional <EncryptionProperties> element:

```
<xenc:EncryptedData
 Type="http://www.w3.org/2001/04/xmlenc#Element"
 xmlns:xenc="http://www.w3.org/2001/04/xmlenc#">
```

The <EncryptedData> element can have some optional attributes:

- **Type**—Type information about the unencrypted form of the content. This is specified as a URI. The spec describes two types that must be implemented. These two types are used to discriminate between an XML element that has been encrypted and XML element content that has been encrypted:
    - **Element**—http://www.w3.org/2001/04/xmlenc#Element.
    - **Element content**—http://www.w3.org/2001/04/xmlenc#Content.
- **Id**—An ID-valued attribute that can be used to refer to the element.
- **MimeType**—The MIME media type of the data that was encrypted.
- **Encoding**—The encoding used by the data.

The <EncryptionMethod> element specifies the algorithm used to encrypt the data. The content of the <EncryptionMethod> element is determined by the value of the Algorithm attribute, which is a URI that specifies the particular encryption algorithm:

```
<xenc:EncryptionMethod
 Algorithm="http://www.w3.org/2001/04/xmlenc#aes256-cbc"
 xmlns:xenc="http://www.w3.org/2001/04/xmlenc#"/>
```

Algorithms detailed by the XML Encryption specification include:

- **Triple DES**—www.w3.org/2001/04/xmlenc#tripledes-cbc. Support is required.
- **AES-128 (128 bit key)**—www.w3.org/2001/04/xmlenc#tripledes-cbc. Support is required.
- **AES-256 (256 bit key)**—www.w3.org/2001/04/xmlenc#tripledes-cbc. Support is required.
- **AES-192 (192 bit key)**—www.w3.org/2001/04/xmlenc#tripledes-cbc. Support is optional.

An optional <ds:KeyInfo> element may come after the <Encryption> method, although one isn't shown in this example. The XML Encryption spec defines two new child elements of <ds:KeyInfo>:

- **<xenc:EncryptedKey>**—Allows the message to carry an encrypted key along with it. It can have two child elements, zero or more <ReferenceList>s followed by zero or more <CarriedKeyName>s:
    - **<ReferenceList>**—A sequence of <DataReference> and <KeyReference> elements. These elements take a URI that refers to different data depending on whether the element is a <DataReference> or a <KeyReference>. A <DataReference> refers to an <EncryptedData> encrypted by the key represented by the enclosing <EncryptedKey>. A <KeyReference> refers to <EncryptedKey> elements that were encrypted using the key represented by the enclosing <EncryptedKey> element.
    - **<CarriedKeyName>**—A user-readable name for a key value that's specified using a <ds:KeyName> element in a <ds:KeyInfo> element.
- **<xenc:AgreementMethod>**—Allows you to specify a Key Agreement algorithm for deriving a secret key from certain kinds of public keys. This is a topic that's beyond the scope of this chapter. If you're interested, you should look at the XML Encryption specification.

XML Encryption also augments the behavior of the <ds:RetrievalMethod> child of <ds:KeyInfo>. If you specify http://www.w3.org/2001/04/xmlenc#EncryptedKey as the Type attribute of the <ds:RetrievalMethod>, the an <EncryptedKey> element is retrieved.

The <CipherData> element is a required element that acts as a container for the encrypted data. The data may appear as either a <CipherValue> element or as a <CipherReference> element:

```
  <xenc:CipherData
   xmlns:xenc="http://www.w3.org/2001/04/xmlenc#">
```

The content of the <CipherValue> element is the base64-encoded version of the encrypted data:

```
   <xenc:CipherValue
    xmlns:xenc="http://www.w3.org/2001/04/xmlenc#">
gfI+hyGKdUiAvgW4n/+xmjNlVoAH8ZBLtqhlmoAe/aAsS3gtc5Tm8HOZyyRaANC
   </xenc:CipherValue>
```

If the <CipherReference> element appears, it specifies a resource that can be processed to yield the encrypted data. <CipherReference> uses a URI attribute to specify the resource to process. The content of the <CipherReference> element can be a <ds:Transforms> element to indicate that Transforms are to be applied to the referenced data. Support for <ds:Transforms> is optional.

The remainder of the document is as it was before:

```
  </xenc:CipherData>
</xenc:EncryptedData>
<isbn>0-7645-4355-5</isbn>
```

```
    <month>December</month>
    <year>2003</year>
    <publisher>Wrox</publisher>
    <address>Indianapolis, Indiana</address>
</book>
```

Installing and Configuring XML Security

To work with XML Security, you need to get a current build. The XML Security builds are available at http://xml.apache.org/security/download.html. Click the link to choose a mirror site. On the page listing the mirrors, click a mirror that's close to you. Doing so will take you to a distribution director with entries for the C-library version, the Java-library version, and a PGP public key file in keys.asc. When you click the link for the Java-library, you'll be presented with a list of distributions. Both binary and source distributions are provided.

For the sake of example, let's assume you're interested in the latest development release 1.0.5D2. The binary distribution is in a file named xml-security-bin-1_0_5D2.zip. The source distribution is in a file named xml-security-src-1_0_5D2.zip. XML Security is providing distributions only in zip file format. This shouldn't be a problem, because unzipping utilities exist for Windows, UNIX, Linux, and Mac OS X. There are PGP signature files for each of the distribution files—they have the same name as the associated distribution file but end in .sig. The signature file for the xml-security-bin-1_0_5D2.zip file is in the file xml-security-bin-1_0_5D2. You should create a new directory for the xml-security distribution you're unpacking and unzip the files into it. Once you've done that, the new directory contains the following directories and files:

- **ant**—Ant taskdefs used by the XML Security build file.
- **build**—The results of running the Ant build:
    - **doc**—HTML documentation.
    - **xmlsec.jar**—XML Security library.
    - **xmlsecSamples.jar**—XML Security sample programs.
    - **xmlsecTests.jar**—XML Security test suite.
- **data**—The data files for the XML Security test suite.
- **libs**—The jar files required by XML Security. Note that you need Xalan 2.2 or later if you're going to use XPath or XSLT-related functionality.
- **src_samples**—The source code for the sample applications.
- **build.xml**—The Ant build file for XML Security.
- **Install**—Simple installation instructions.
- **Keys.asc**—The PGP keys files for the XML Security developers.
- **License.txt**—The Apache Software License.
- **README**—A brief README file.
- **README.html**—The gateway to the XML security documentation.

You also need to download the Bouncy Castle JCE Provider, and if you're using JDK 1.3, the Bouncy Castle cleanroom JCE implementation for Java 1.3. You can obtain these files from the Bouncy Castle Website at www.bouncycastle.org. For JDK 1.3, you'll want the combined JCE provider and implementation jar. This file is named jce-jdk13-nnn.jar, where nnn is the version number. For JDK 1.3, you'll want the file bcprov-jdk14-nnn.jar, again, where nnn is the version number. Your classpath must include the BouncyCastle jar as well as the xmlsec.jar from the build directory and the various jars in the lib directory.

If you're running JDK 1.4, you may need to deal with two additional items. XML Security depends on a released version of Xalan with a version number of at least 2.2. The version of Xalan that's built into JDK 1.4 is Xalan 2.2D13, which is incompatible. To solve this problem, you should take the xml-apis.jar and xalan.jar files from XML Security's lib directory and install them in the JDK using the Java Endorsed Standards Mechanism. Doing so overrides the version built into the JDK.

The other JDK 1.4 issue you may run into is related to encryption strength. By default, the JDK 1.4 ships with a restricted encryption policy file. Your application may require encryption algorithms that need cryptography with unlimited strength. You can change the JCE policy file by downloading the JCE Unlimited Strength Jurisdiction Policy Files for the JDK version you're using. You can obtain these files via http://java.sun.com/products/jce/index-14.html#UnlimitedDownload. Once you've downloaded the jar file, you can follow the instructions inside it to install the needed files. Basically, you take the contents of the jar file and copy them over the corresponding files in JAVA_HOME/jre/lib/security. You should back up the old files somewhere in case you need to use them again.

Development Techniques

Now we're ready to look at using the XML Security API to perform common XML Signature and Encryption tasks. We'll do this by working through a series of examples.

Canonicalizing and Computing the Digest

The first task you'll perform is to take an XML document, compute its canonical form, and then compute a message digest for that canonical form:

```
/*
 *
 * DigestDocument.java
 *
 * Example from "Professional XML Development with Apache Tools"
 *
 */
package com.sauria.apachexml.ch10;

import java.io.ByteArrayOutputStream;
import java.io.FileInputStream;
import java.io.FileNotFoundException;
import java.io.IOException;
import java.security.MessageDigest;
import java.security.NoSuchAlgorithmException;

```

```
17: import javax.xml.parsers.ParserConfigurationException;
18:
19: import org.apache.xml.security.c14n.CanonicalizationException;
20: import org.apache.xml.security.c14n.Canonicalizer;
21: import
22: org.apache.xml.security.c14n.InvalidCanonicalizerException;
23: import org.apache.xml.security.utils.Base64;
24: import org.xml.sax.SAXException;
25:
26: public class DigestDocument {
```

Before you can call any methods on the XML Security library you must call the static function org.apache.xml.security.Init.Init to initialize the library:

```
27:
28:     public static void main(String[] args) {
29:         org.apache.xml.security.Init.init();
```

XML Security uses a class called Canonicalizer to canonicalize data. Canonicalizer can operate on a byte array, a DOM tree, or an XPath node set (represented as a DOM NodeList). In this example you use the byte array form, so lines 31-49 open a FileInputStream on the XML document being canonicalized and copy the document into a ByteArrayOutputStream. Once the ByteArrayOutputStream is full, you convert it a byte array that can be used as input to Canonicalizer:

```
30:
31:         FileInputStream fis = null;
32:         try {
33:             fis = new FileInputStream(args[0]);
34:         } catch (FileNotFoundException fnfe) {
35:             fnfe.printStackTrace();
36:         }
37:         ByteArrayOutputStream baos =
38:                new ByteArrayOutputStream();
39:
40:         byte buffer[] = new byte[2048];
41:         int count = 0;
42:         try {
43:             while ((count = fis.read(buffer)) > 0) {
44:                 baos.write(buffer,0, count);
45:             }
46:             fis.close();
47:             baos.close();
48:         } catch (IOException ioe) {
49:             ioe.printStackTrace();
50:         }
51:
52:         byte bytes[] = baos.toByteArray();
```

First you need to set up a Canonicalizer instance. You do this via the static getInstance factory method on Canonicalizer:

```
53:
54:         Canonicalizer c14n = null;
```

```
try {
    c14n = Canonicalizer.getInstance(
        Canonicalizer.ALGO_ID_C14N_OMIT_COMMENTS);
} catch (InvalidCanonicalizerException ice) {
    ice.printStackTrace();
}
```

The argument to the factory method is a String that contains the URL of the algorithm to be used. For ease of use, Canonicalizer defines a set of String constant values for all the supported algorithms. Canonicalizer supports four algorithms: inclusive XML canonicalization with and without comments (each is a different algorithm) and exclusive XML canonicalization with and without comments:

Canonicalizing the data is a matter of calling canonicalize on the byte array containing the data:

```
byte canonicalBytes[] = null;
try {
    canonicalBytes = c14n.canonicalize(bytes);
```

The result is a byte array containing the canonical form. It's a byte array whether you canonicalize a DOM tree (the method is canonicalizeSubtree) or an XPath node set (the method is canonicalizeXPathNodeSet). The DOM and XPath node set methods also have versions that let you supply a comma-separated list of inclusiveNamespaces prefixes to be treated as the InclusiveNamespacesPrefixList used by exclusive XML canonicalization.

You print the canonical form to the console for your edification:

```
} catch (CanonicalizationException ce) {
    ce.printStackTrace();
} catch (ParserConfigurationException pce) {
    pce.printStackTrace();
} catch (IOException ioe) {
    ioe.printStackTrace();
} catch (SAXException se) {
    se.printStackTrace();
}

System.out.println(new String(canonicalBytes));
System.out.println();
```

XML Security uses the Java Cryptography Architecture's MessageDigest class to compute message digests. MessageDigest provides a static factory method for creating a MessageDigest instance. The argument is a string that's the name of a message-digesting algorithm. Valid values are "SHA-1", "SHA-256", "SHA-384", "SHA-512", "MD5", and "MD2":

```
MessageDigest md = null;
try {
    md = MessageDigest.getInstance("SHA-1");
} catch (NoSuchAlgorithmException nsa) {
    nsa.printStackTrace();
}
```

You compute the digest by passing the canonicalized byte array to the digest method of MessageDigest. This gives you a byte array with the digest value:

```
        byte digest[] = md.digest(canonicalBytes);
```

Here you print out the base64 representation of the digest value, as used in the XML Signature and XML Encryption specifications:

```

        System.out.println(Base64.encode(digest));
    }
}
```

The output of running this program on the book.xml file is as follows:

```
<book xmlns="http://sauria.com/schemas/apache-xml-book/book"
xmlns:xsi="http://www.w3.org/2001/XMLSchema-instance" version="1.0"
xsi:schemaLocation="http://sauria.com/schemas/apache-xml-book/book
http://www.sauria.com/schemas/apache-xml-book/book.xsd">
  <title>Professional XML Development with Apache Tools</title>
  <author Id="author">Theodore W. Leung</author>
  <isbn>0-7645-4355-5</isbn>
  <month>December</month>
  <year>2003</year>
  <publisher>Wrox</publisher>
  <address>Indianapolis, Indiana</address>
</book>

A29reHPotuzItyi749JCC6qBMtg=
```

Signing

The next topic is signing a document. This example serves two purposes: It introduces you to the XML Security digital signature API and also leaves you with a class you can use to sign documents in your applications:

```
/*
 *
 * DocumentSigner.java
 *
 * Example from "Professional XML Development with Apache Tools"
 *
 */
package com.sauria.apachexml.ch10;

import java.io.File;
import java.io.FileInputStream;
import java.io.FileNotFoundException;
import java.io.FileOutputStream;
import java.io.IOException;
import java.io.OutputStream;
import java.net.MalformedURLException;
```

```
import java.security.KeyStore;
import java.security.KeyStoreException;
import java.security.NoSuchAlgorithmException;
import java.security.PrivateKey;
import java.security.PublicKey;
import java.security.UnrecoverableKeyException;
import java.security.cert.CertificateException;
import java.security.cert.X509Certificate;
import java.util.ArrayList;
import java.util.Iterator;
import java.util.List;

import javax.xml.parsers.DocumentBuilder;
import javax.xml.parsers.DocumentBuilderFactory;
import javax.xml.parsers.ParserConfigurationException;

import org.apache.xml.security.exceptions.XMLSecurityException;
import org.apache.xml.security.signature.Manifest;
import org.apache.xml.security.signature.ObjectContainer;
import org.apache.xml.security.signature.SignatureProperties;
import org.apache.xml.security.signature.SignatureProperty;
import org.apache.xml.security.signature.XMLSignature;
import org.apache.xml.security.signature.XMLSignatureException;
import
    org.apache.xml.security.transforms.TransformationException;
import org.apache.xml.security.transforms.Transforms;
import org.apache.xml.security.utils.Constants;
import org.apache.xml.security.utils.SignatureElementProxy;
import org.apache.xml.security.utils.XMLUtils;
import org.w3c.dom.Document;
import org.w3c.dom.Node;
import org.xml.sax.SAXException;

public class DocumentSigner {
    protected Document document;
    protected PrivateKey privateKey;
    protected X509Certificate certificate;
    protected PublicKey publicKey;
    protected String baseURI;
    protected String signatureMethod;
    protected String digestMethod;
    protected String transformArray[] = null;
    protected List objectList = null;
```

The class has a number of protected member variables that hold data the class needs. In particular, you need a Document to place the signature in (document) and a private key to do the signing with (privateKey). You need the algorithms to be used for the <SignatureMethod> (signatureMethod) and <DigestMethod> (digestMethod) elements. If you want to use transforms, then you need to store them somehow (transformArray). Should you decide to use <KeyInfo> to specify the public key needed for verification, you may need a public key (publicKey) or a digital certificate (certificate). Any optional <Object> elements need to be stored until you're ready to do the signing.

Here you initialize the XML Security library so that you can call any methods you need:

```
60:
61:     static {
62:         org.apache.xml.security.Init.init();
63:     }
```

You define a default constructor (line 65) and a constructor that fills in the simple fields (lines 67-77). The actual work of signing a document is done by the sign method. It assumes that other methods have been called to fill in the values of any object fields that are needed:

```
64:
65:     public DocumentSigner() {}
66:
67:     public DocumentSigner(Document doc,
68:         PrivateKey privateKey, X509Certificate cert,
69:         PublicKey publicKey, String baseURI,
70:         String signatureMethod, String digestMethod) {
71:         this.document = doc;
72:         this.privateKey = privateKey;
73:         this.certificate = cert;
74:         this.publicKey = publicKey;
75:         this.baseURI = baseURI;
76:         this.signatureMethod = signatureMethod;
77:         this.digestMethod = digestMethod;
78:     }
79
```

The XMLSignature class is used to create an XMLSignature element. The <Signature> element is related to document. It needs a BaseURI that resolves any relative URIs it encounters, and it needs an algorithm to use for signing:

```
80:     public Document sign() {
81:         XMLSignature sig = null;
82:         try {
83:             sig =
84:                 new XMLSignature(document,
85:                     baseURI, signatureMethod);
86:         } catch (XMLSecurityException xse) {
87:             xse.printStackTrace();
88:         }
```

This class always creates the signature as the last child of document. So, you get the DOM DocumentElement (line 90) and append the signature (as an Element) as a child of that element (line 92):

```
89:
90:         Node root = document.getDocumentElement();
91:
92:         root.appendChild(sig.getElement());
```

Next you execute the addReferences method in DocumentSigner, whose job is to add any <References> to data that needs to be signed:

```
93:
94:         try {
95:             addReferences(sig);
96:         } catch (XMLSignatureException xse) {
97:             xse.printStackTrace();
98:         }
```

If the certificate or publicKey fields have been filled in, then you add a KeyInfo to the signature using the addKeyInfo method. If there's a certificate, you add the certificate and the public key from the certificate (lines 101-103). If there's no certificate and a public key, then you add the public key (lines 107-108):

```
99:
100:        try {
101:            if (certificate != null ) {
102:                sig.addKeyInfo(certificate);
103:                sig.addKeyInfo(certificate.getPublicKey());
104:            }
105:
106:            if (publicKey != null && certificate == null) {
107:                sig.addKeyInfo(publicKey);
108:            }
```

Next you check to see if the objectList contains any values. If it does, you iterate over those values; for each one, you create an ObjectContainer (lines 113-116) whose child is the element from the objectList (line 117). You add this new ObjectContainer to the signature object using appendObject (line 118). Note that ObjectContainers are related to the DOM document:

```
109:
110:            if (objectList != null) {
111:                for (Iterator i = objectList.iterator();
112:                    i.hasNext();) {
113:                    SignatureElementProxy sep =
114:                        (SignatureElementProxy) i.next();
115:                    ObjectContainer oc =
116:                        new ObjectContainer(document);
117:                    oc.appendChild(sep.getElement());
118:                    sig.appendObject(oc);
119:                }
120:            }
```

After all the information has been added to the signature element, you sign the <SignedInfo> by calling the sign method on XMLSignature and passing it the private key:

```
121:        } catch (XMLSecurityException xse) {
122:            xse.printStackTrace();
123:        }
124:
125:        try {
126:            sig.sign(privateKey);
```

The result of the method is the original document with a new child <Signature> element, all filled in with the data for the signature:

```
127:        } catch (XMLSignatureException xse) {
128:            xse.printStackTrace();
129:        }
130:
131:        return document;
132:    }
133:
```

Now let's look at some of the support methods you need to make this work. The addReferences method is called to add <Reference> elements to the <Signature> element represented by an XMLSignature instance (sig). Remember that each reference element specifies the URI of the data to be digested, a set of transforms to be applied, and a specification of the digest algorithm to be used for that reference. This method is protected because it shouldn't be called by any method other than the sign method. The sign method is an instance of the Template method design pattern, with addReference as one of the primitive operations. To change the set of References to add, you need to extend DocumentSigner and override addReferences with your own implementation that adds the correct references with their transformations and digest methods:

```
134:    protected void addReferences(XMLSignature sig)
135:        throws XMLSignatureException {
136:
```

You add transforms by creating an instance of Transforms (which depends on document) (line 137). You can then call the addTransform method on this instance to add as many transforms as you like. The Transforms class defines String constants whose values are the URIs for the transforms defined by the XML Signature spec. There are constants for all the transforms specified in the XML Signature spec and for the two variants of exclusive XML canonicalization. In this case, you use the enveloped signature transform (lines 140-141) to exclude the <Signature> element from the signature, and you use inclusive XML canonicalization with comments (lines 142-143):

```
137:        Transforms transforms = new Transforms(document);
138:
139:        try {
140:            transforms.addTransform(
141:                Transforms.TRANSFORM_ENVELOPED_SIGNATURE);
142:            transforms.addTransform(
143:                Transforms.TRANSFORM_C14N_WITH_COMMENTS);
144:        } catch (TransformationException te) {
145:            te.printStackTrace();
146:        }
```

The addDocument method on XMLSignature adds a referenced object to the signature. In this case, you add the URI "#xpointer(/)", which stands for the entire document including comments. So, you're signing the document that includes the <Signature> element. If you wanted to reference the entire document without comments, you'd give the empty string for the URI. You can reference elements with IDs by placing the fragment identifier in the URI, so you can reference the author element in the book file by supplying "#author" as the URI. For more complicated specifications, you should specify the entire document and then use the XPath transform:

```
147:
148:        sig.addDocument("#xpointer(/)", transforms,
149:            digestMethod);
150:    }
```

The URI is transformed using the set of transforms you added earlier, and the digest method is the value of the digestMethod field. You can have multiple calls to addDocument to add multiple URIs. Each call can have different transform and digestMethod argument values. There are multiple versions of the addDocument method.

writeSignature writes a DOM tree to an output stream in inclusive canonical form with comments. You can call this method after the signature has been produced:

```
    public void writeSignature(OutputStream outputStream) {
        XMLUtils.outputDOMc14nWithComments(document,
            outputStream);
    }
```

The addManifest method creates a new Manifest object and returns it to you. You can then call the addDocument method on Manifest to add references to the Manifest. There's only one version of the addDocument method on Manifest, and it requires you to specify a URI, a Transforms, a digestMethod URI, an ID for the <Reference>, and a type for the <Reference>, in that order:

```
    public Manifest addManifest() {
        if (objectList == null) {
            objectList = new ArrayList();
        }
        Manifest manifest = new Manifest(document);
        objectList.add(manifest);
        return manifest;
    }
```

The addSignatureProperties method lets you add a <SignatureProperties> element to the signature. It returns a SignatureProperties object. You can call the addSignatureProperty method to add a <SignatureProperty> to the <SignatureProperties> element. You have to construct a new SignatureProperty object—this is cumbersome because it needs a DOM document object as an argument to the constructor— the sole function of the getDocument method on the SignatureProperties instance to is get this object. You should also pass the target URI and ID value of the SignatureProperty to the constructor. Call the addText method on the SignatureProperty instance to add the value of the property:

```
    public SignatureProperties addSignatureProperties() {
        if (objectList == null) {
            objectList = new ArrayList();
        }
        SignatureProperties signatureProperties =
            new SignatureProperties(document);
        objectList.add(signatureProperties);
        return signatureProperties;
    }
```

This main program shows how to use the DocumentSigner. You instantiate an instance, and then you fill in all the fields that are necessary and call the sign method. This process is encapsulated in a method called testSigning, which we'll talk about next. Note that testSigning gets its two argument values from the command line:

```
175:
176:     public static void main(String[] args)  {
177:         DocumentSigner signer = new DocumentSigner();
178:         testSigning(signer, args[0], args[1]);
179:     }
```

The first thing testSigning does is parse a document that will be the host for the signature. The URI for the document comes from the argument list:

```
180:
181:     public static boolean testSigning(DocumentSigner signer,
182:         String uri, String outputFile) {
183:         Document doc = getInputDocument(uri);
```

Next, it opens a KeyStore (line 185) and gets a private key (line 188). Note that the keystore name and password, the alias for the private key, and the private key password are all hardwired to keep the example short:

```
184:
185:         KeyStore ks = getKeyStore("keystore.jks", "password");
186:
187:         PrivateKey privateKey =
188:             getPrivateKey(ks, "johndoe", "password");
```

You also attempt to get the certificate for the entity if it exists in the keystore:

```
189:
190:         X509Certificate certificate = null;
191:         try {
192:             certificate = (X509Certificate)
193:                 ks.getCertificate("johndoe");
194:         } catch (KeyStoreException kse) {
195:             kse.printStackTrace();
196:         }
```

The document with the signature in it will be written to a file. The filename is the other argument in the argument list. The base URI is set to the URI for the file containing the signature:

```
197:
198:         File signatureFile = new File(outputFile);
199:
200:         String baseURI = getBaseURI(signatureFile);
```

Next you call some setters to set the values you've computed thus far:

```
201:
202:         signer.setDocument(doc);
203:         signer.setPrivateKey(privateKey);
204:         signer.setCertificate(certificate);
205:         signer.setBaseURI(baseURI);
```

You also call some setters to set the <SignatureMethod> and <DigestMethod>. XMLSignature defines String constants for the names of the digital signature algorithms in the XML Signature Recommendation, and Constants defines constants for the digest algorithm names. Here you use DSA for signing and SHA1 for digesting references:

```
206:         signer.setSignatureMethod(
207:             XMLSignature.ALGO_ID_SIGNATURE_DSA);
208:         signer.setDigestMethod(Constants.ALGO_ID_DIGEST_SHA1);
```

In line 210 you add an empty manifest:

```
209:
210:         Manifest m = signer.addManifest();
```

Next you add a SignatureProperty. To do this, you ask the signer for a SignatureProperties by calling addSignatureProperties (lines 212-213). Next you construct a new SignatureProperty from the SignatureProperties' document, a URI, and an ID (lines 216-218). Calling addText on the SignatureProperty sets the value of the property to "smartcard".

```
211:
212:         SignatureProperties sps =
213:             signer.addSignatureProperties();
214:         SignatureProperty sp = null;
215:         try {
216:             sp = new SignatureProperty(sps.getDocument(),
217:                                        "http://www.sauria.com",
218:                                        "hardware");
219:             sp.addText("smartcard");
220:         } catch (XMLSignatureException xse) {
221:             xse.printStackTrace();
222:         }
223:         sps.addSignatureProperty(sp);
```

At last all the fields have been set up, so you're ready to call the sign method and generate a signed document:

```
224:
225:         signer.sign();
```

Finally, you write the file containing the signature to disk:

```
226:
227:         try {
228:             FileOutputStream signatureStream =
229:                 new FileOutputStream(signatureFile);
230:
231:             signer.writeSignature(signatureStream);
232:
233:             signatureStream.close();
234:         } catch (FileNotFoundException fnfe) {
235:             fnfe.printStackTrace();
236:         } catch (IOException ioe) {
```

```
237:                ioe.printStackTrace();
238:            }
239:            return true;
240:        }
241:
```

The getBaseURI method computes the URI of a File object. It assumes that this is how you'll construct the base URI. You're free to generate the base URI some other way:

```
242:        public static String getBaseURI(File signatureFile) {
243:            String BaseURI = null;
244:            try {
245:                BaseURI = signatureFile.toURL().toString();
246:            } catch (MalformedURLException mue) {
247:                mue.printStackTrace();
248:            }
249:            return BaseURI;
250:        }
```

getInputDocument hides all the boilerplate code associated with parsing a document using a JAXP DocumentBuilder. The only factor to notice is that the parser should be namespace enabled (line 256).

```
251:
252:        public static Document getInputDocument(String uri) {
253:            DocumentBuilderFactory dbf =
254:                DocumentBuilderFactory.newInstance();
255:
256:            dbf.setNamespaceAware(true);
257:
258:            Document doc = null;
259:            try {
260:                DocumentBuilder db = dbf.newDocumentBuilder();
261:                doc = db.parse(uri);
262:            } catch (ParserConfigurationException pce) {
263:                pce.printStackTrace();
264:            } catch (SAXException se) {
265:                se.printStackTrace();
266:            } catch (IOException ioe) {
267:                ioe.printStackTrace();
268:            }
269:            return doc;
270:        }
```

The getPrivateKey method takes a KeyStore, an alias for a private key, and the password for that private key, and returns a PrivateKey:

```
271:
272:        public static PrivateKey getPrivateKey(KeyStore ks,
273:            String privateKeyAlias, String privateKeyPassword) {
274:               PrivateKey privateKey = null;
275:                try {
276:                    privateKey = (PrivateKey)
277:                        ks.getKey(privateKeyAlias,
```

```
                            privateKeyPassword.toCharArray());
            } catch (KeyStoreException kse) {
                kse.printStackTrace();
            } catch (NoSuchAlgorithmException nsae) {
                nsae.printStackTrace();
            } catch (UnrecoverableKeyException uke) {
                uke.printStackTrace();
            }
        return privateKey;
    }
```

The getKeystore method takes the filename of a keystore and the password for accessing that keystore, and returns a KeyStore object that can be searched for keys and certificates:

```

    public static KeyStore getKeyStore(String filename,
        String keystorePassword) {
        KeyStore ks = null;
        try {
            ks = KeyStore.getInstance("JKS");
        } catch (KeyStoreException kse) {
            kse.printStackTrace();
        }

        FileInputStream fis = null;
        try {
            fis = new FileInputStream(filename);
        } catch (FileNotFoundException fnfe) {
            fnfe.printStackTrace();
        }

        try {
            ks.load(fis, keystorePassword.toCharArray());
        } catch (NoSuchAlgorithmException nsae) {
            nsae.printStackTrace();
        } catch (CertificateException ce) {
            ce.printStackTrace();
        } catch (IOException ioe) {
            ioe.printStackTrace();
        }
        return ks;
    }
```

The remainder of the class definition is the getters and setters for the fields in DocumentSigner:

```

    public String getBaseURI() {
        return baseURI;
    }

    public X509Certificate getCertificate() {
        return certificate;
    }

```

```
    public String getDigestMethod() {
        return digestMethod;
    }

    public PrivateKey getPrivateKey() {
        return privateKey;
    }

    public String getSignatureMethod() {
        return signatureMethod;
    }

    public String[] getTransformArray() {
        return transformArray;
    }

    public Document getDocument() {
        return document;
    }

    public void setBaseURI(String string) {
        baseURI = string;
    }

    public void setCertificate(X509Certificate certificate) {
        this.certificate = certificate;
    }

    public void setDigestMethod(String string) {
        digestMethod = string;
    }

    public void setPrivateKey(PrivateKey key) {
        privateKey = key;
    }

    public void setSignatureMethod(String string) {
        signatureMethod = string;
    }

    public void setTransformArray(String[] strings) {
        transformArray = strings;
    }

    public void setDocument(Document d) {
        document = d;
    }

    public List getObjectList() {
        return objectList;
    }

    public PublicKey getPublicKey() {
        return publicKey;
```

```
    }

    public void setObjectList(List list) {
        objectList = list;
    }

    public void setPublicKey(PublicKey key) {
        publicKey = key;
    }
}
```

Even after almost 400 lines, we haven't covered everything you can do. DocumentSigner is useful for simple to medium signing applications and can serve as a source of code to help you build your own classes for signature handling.

Verification

Signature verification is much simpler than signing. You don't need to provide a lot of additional data, and the API is pretty simple. Almost all of the information you need to verify the signature is in the document, so there's no need to create an object to store the information:

```
/*
 *
 * DocumentVerifier.java
 *
 * Example from "Profesional XML Development with Apache Tools"
 *
 */
package com.sauria.apachexml.ch10;

import java.io.File;
import java.io.IOException;
import java.net.MalformedURLException;
import java.security.PublicKey;
import java.security.cert.X509Certificate;
import java.util.ArrayList;
import java.util.List;

import javax.xml.parsers.DocumentBuilder;
import javax.xml.parsers.DocumentBuilderFactory;
import javax.xml.parsers.FactoryConfigurationError;
import javax.xml.parsers.ParserConfigurationException;
import javax.xml.transform.TransformerException;

import org.apache.xml.security.exceptions.XMLSecurityException;
import org.apache.xml.security.keys.KeyInfo;
import
org.apache.xml.security.keys.keyresolver.KeyResolverException;
import org.apache.xml.security.signature.SignedInfo;
import org.apache.xml.security.signature.XMLSignature;
import org.apache.xml.security.signature.XMLSignatureException;
import org.apache.xml.security.signature.XMLSignatureInput;
import org.apache.xml.security.utils.Constants;
```

```
33: import org.apache.xml.security.utils.XMLUtils;
34: import org.apache.xpath.XPathAPI;
35: import org.w3c.dom.Document;
36: import org.w3c.dom.Element;
37: import org.xml.sax.SAXException;
```

You initialize the XML Security library:

```
38:
39: public class DocumentVerifier {
40:     static {
41:         org.apache.xml.security.Init.init();
42:     }
```

The verifySignedDocument method does all the work. It takes a DOM tree containing a signed document and a base URI for resolving relative URI references. It returns an empty List if the signature can be verified and a List of References that could not be verified if the signature can't be verified:

```
43:
44:     public static List verifySignedDocument(Document doc,
45:         String baseURI) {
```

In lines 47-48, you set up some variables that are used to hold results:

```
46:
47:         List result = new ArrayList();
48:         boolean coarseResult = false;
```

You set up an element that declares the ds prefix for the XML Signature namespace URI:

```
49:
50:         Element namespaceContext =
51:             XMLUtils.createDSctx(doc,"ds",
52:                 Constants.SignatureSpecNS);
```

Here you take the namespace context you created earlier and pass it to the XPathAPI's selectSingleNode method. You're locating the <Signature> element within the tree:

```
53:
54:         Element signatureElement = null;
55:         try {
56:             signatureElement =
57:                 (Element) XPathAPI.selectSingleNode(
58:                     doc,
59:                     "//ds:Signature[1]",
60:                     namespaceContext);
```

Once you've located the <Signature> element, you construct an XMLSignature using it and the base URI:

```
61:         } catch (TransformerException te) {
62:             te.printStackTrace();
```

```
63:         }
64:
65:         XMLSignature signature = null;
66:         try {
67:             signature =
68:                 new XMLSignature(
69:                     signatureElement,
70:                     baseURI);
```

DocumentVerifier assumes that the <Signature> element contains a <KeyInfo> element that specifies either an X.509 certificate or a public key that can be used to verify the signature. If these conditions aren't met, DocumentVerifier can't verify the signature:

```
71:         } catch (XMLSignatureException xse) {
72:             xse.printStackTrace();
73:         } catch (MalformedURLException mue) {
74:             mue.printStackTrace();
75:         } catch (XMLSecurityException xse) {
76:             xse.printStackTrace();
77:         } catch (IOException e2) {
78:             e2.printStackTrace();
79:         }
80:
81:         KeyInfo ki = signature.getKeyInfo();
```

You test the KeyInfo object to see if it contains X.509Data. If it does, you extract the X.509 certificate:

```
82:
83:         if (ki != null) {
84:             if (!ki.containsX509Data()) {
85:                 System.out.println("No X.509 data");
86:             }
87:
88:             X509Certificate cert = null;
89:             try {
90:                 cert = ki.getX509Certificate();
91:             } catch (KeyResolverException kre) {
92:                 kre.printStackTrace();
93:             }
```

There are two versions of the checkSignatureValue method on XMLSignature: one that works on Certificates and one that works on PublicKeys. DocumentVerifier prefers to use the X.509 certificate to verify the signature (lines 96-98). If there is no certificate present, then it tries to use a public key (lines 99-112). To do this, it must extract a PublicKey from the KeyInfo instance (lines 100-106) and then use it to check the signature (lines 108-111). The return value from checkSignature is stored as coarseResult. This tells you at a coarse granularity whether the signature verified. If it didn't, then you'd like to obtain a finer-grained explanation of what went wrong:

```
94:
95:             try {
96:                 if (cert != null) {
97:                     coarseResult =
98:                         signature.checkSignatureValue(cert);
```

```
 99:                 } else {
100:                     PublicKey pk = null;
101:                     try {
102:                         pk =
103:                             signature.getKeyInfo().getPublicKey();
104:                     } catch (KeyResolverException kre) {
105:                         kre.printStackTrace();
106:                     }
107:
108:                     if (pk != null) {
109:                         coarseResult =
110:                             signature.checkSignatureValue(pk);
111:                     }
112:                 }
```

If there was no <KeyInfo>, exit early:

```
113:             } catch (XMLSignatureException xse) {
114:                 xse.printStackTrace();
115:             }
116:         } else {
117:             System.out.println("No key included");
118:             return result;
```

If the signature didn't verify, you get the SignedInfo from the Signature and pass it, along with result, to getFailedReferences, which computes the fine-grained error result:

```
119:         }
120:
121:         if (!coarseResult) {
122:             SignedInfo si = signature.getSignedInfo();
123:             try {
124:                 getFailedReferences(result, si);
```

At the end you return the result List:

```
125:             } catch (XMLSecurityException xse) {
126:                 xse.printStackTrace();
127:             }
128:         }
129:
130:         return result;
```

The getLength method on SignedInfo returns the number of References inside that SignedInfo object (line 136). You can iterate over the References, and for each one you can ask for the verification result (line 138). If that Reference failed to verify, you add the untransformed version of it to your results List (lines 139-140):

```
131:     }
132:
133:     public static void getFailedReferences(List result,
134:         SignedInfo si) throws XMLSecurityException {
135:
```

```
        int length = si.getLength();
        for (int i = 0; i < length; i++) {
          if (!si.getVerificationResult(i))
            result.add(
             si.getReferencedContentBeforeTransformsItem(i));
        }
    }
```

main passes a single argument (the URI of the document to be verified) to the verify method, which does some setup and then calls verifySignedDocument:

```

    public static void main(String[] args) {
        verify(args[0]);
    }
```

Fortunately, the amount of setup that verify has to do is pretty small—a File to read the signed file from, a base URI computed from the file, and a DOM tree obtained by parsing the file:

```

    public static boolean verify(String uri) {
        File signatureFile = new File(uri);

        String baseURI = getBaseURI(signatureFile);

        Document doc = getInputDocument(signatureFile);
```

Here's the call to verifySignedDocument:

```

        List result = verifySignedDocument(doc, baseURI);
```

This loop prints out any References that didn't verify:

```

        if (result.size() > 0) {
            for (int i = 0; i < result.size(); i++) {
                XMLSignatureInput xsi =
                    (XMLSignatureInput) result.get(i);
                System.out.println("Reference URI " +
                    xsi.getSourceURI()+" did not verify.");
            }
```

Otherwise you print a celebratory message

```
        } else {
            System.out.println("Signature verified");
```

And return a boolean:

```
        }
        return result.size() == 0;
   4 }
```

getBaseURI computes the URI from a File object:

```
    public static String getBaseURI(File signatureFile) {
        String baseURI = null;
        try {
            baseURI = signatureFile.toURL().toString();
        } catch (MalformedURLException e) {
            e.printStackTrace();
        }
        return baseURI;
    }
```

getInputDocument hides all the DocumentBuilder boilerplate. Again, the DocumentBuilder must be namespace aware:

```
    public static Document getInputDocument(File signatureFile)
        throws FactoryConfigurationError {
        Document doc;
           DocumentBuilderFactory dbf =
                DocumentBuilderFactory.newInstance();

            dbf.setNamespaceAware(true);

            doc = null;
            try {
                DocumentBuilder db = dbf.newDocumentBuilder();

                doc = db.parse(signatureFile);
            } catch (ParserConfigurationException pce) {
                pce.printStackTrace();
            } catch (SAXException se) {
                se.printStackTrace();
            } catch (IOException ioe) {
                ioe.printStackTrace();
            }

        return doc;
    }
}
```

More Signatures

Here are two examples of how you can extend the DocumentSigner class to do signature-related tasks. The first class shows how to have the data object and the signature in separate files. The second example shows how to use the XPath transform to select the data you want to sign.

Signatures in a Separate File

DetachedDocumentSigner is a subclass of DocumentSigner that allows you to place the data to be signed and the signature in separate files. The key to making this work is to reference a data object that's distinct from the document where the signature goes. In this case, you create a detached signature of the schema for the book document. No transformations are applied, and the digest method is the default (SHA1):

```
/*
 *
 * DetachedDocumentSigner.java
 *
 * Example from "Professional XML Development with Apache Tools"
 *
 */
package com.sauria.apachexml.ch10;

import org.apache.xml.security.signature.XMLSignature;
import org.apache.xml.security.signature.XMLSignatureException;
import org.w3c.dom.Document;

public class DetachedDocumentSigner extends DocumentSigner {

    protected void addReferences(XMLSignature sig,
        Document document) throws XMLSignatureException {
        sig.addDocument(
  "http://www.sauria.com/schemas/apache-xml-book/book.xsd");
```

By specifying a separate file, blank.xml, as the destination for the signature, you make DocumentSigner place the signature into this file, while the data being signed remains untouched. The file blank.xml contains a single empty <blank/> element, which the signature is attached to:

```
    }

    public static void main(String[] args) {
        DocumentSigner signer = new DetachedDocumentSigner();
        testSigning(signer, "blank.xml",
            "detached-signature.xml");
    }
}
```

XPath Transforms

XPathTransformSigner shows how to use the XPath transform to specify which portions of an XML document should be signed:

```
/*
 *
 * XPathTransformSigner.java
 *
 * Example from "Professional XML Development with Apache Tools"
 *
 */
package com.sauria.apachexml.ch10;

import org.apache.xml.security.exceptions.XMLSecurityException;
import org.apache.xml.security.signature.XMLSignature;
```

```
12: import org.apache.xml.security.signature.XMLSignatureException;
13: import
14: org.apache.xml.security.transforms.TransformationException;
15: import org.apache.xml.security.transforms.Transforms;
16: import org.apache.xml.security.transforms.params.XPathContainer;
17: import org.w3c.dom.Document;
```

The XPath transform works by using an XPathContainer object. Like all the XML signature related objects, this one depends on the document where the <Signature> element is created (line 22). The XPathContainer contains the XPath expression (line 29), and it also provides a namespace context to provide namespace URI to prefix mappings that might be needed by the XPath expression. In this case, you only need a single mapping, from http://sauria.com/schemas/apache-xml-book/book to books (lines 24-25). You can call setXPathNamespaceContext as many times as you need to. The XPath expression selects the <author> and <isbn> nodes to be signed:

```
18:
19: public class XPathTransformSigner extends DocumentSigner {
20:     protected void addReferences(XMLSignature sig,
21:         Document document)
22:         throws XMLSignatureException {
23:         XPathContainer xpc = new XPathContainer(document);
24:         try {
25:             xpc.setXPathNamespaceContext("books",
26:                 "http://sauria.com/schemas/apache-xml-book/book");
27:         } catch (XMLSecurityException xse) {
28:             xse.printStackTrace();
29:         }
30:         xpc.setXPath("//books:author|//books:isbn");
```

You're already familiar with the enveloped signature transform (lines 33-34) and the inclusive canonicalization with comments transform (lines 37-38). The new transform here is the XPath transform. The XML Security API makes this transform easy. After you've specified the correct constant for the transform, you pass in the XPathContainer's representation as an element, which is obtained by calling getElementPlusReturns (lines 35-36):

```
31:
32:         Transforms ts = new Transforms(document);
33:         try {
34:             ts.addTransform(
35:                 Transforms.TRANSFORM_ENVELOPED_SIGNATURE);
36:             ts.addTransform(Transforms.TRANSFORM_XPATH,
37:                 xpc.getElementPlusReturns());
38:             ts.addTransform(
39:                 Transforms.TRANSFORM_C14N_WITH_COMMENTS);
40:         } catch (TransformationException te) {
41:             te.printStackTrace();
42:         }
```

You want your transforms to operate on the entire document so that the XPath expressions has the right context from which to select nodes:

```
43:
44:         sig.addDocument("#xpointer(/)",ts);
```

As before, you instantiate an XPathTransformSigner (line 47) and then call testSigning with the right filename parameters (line 48):

```
45:     }
46:
47:     public static void main(String[] args) {
48:         DocumentSigner signer = new XPathTransformSigner();
49:         testSigning(signer, "book.xml", "xpath-signature.xml");
50:     }
51: }
```

Resolvers

The XML Security library allows you to plug in resolvers that handle requests for certain kinds of information. There are three kinds of resolvers:

- **ResourceResolvers** are used by a Reference object when the Reference tries to retrieve the resource to be signed.
- **StorageResolvers** are used by a KeyInfo object to retrieve certificates that are specified by the KeyInfo or its children.
- **KeyResolvers** are used by KeyInfo when processing its children. KeyResolvers use StorageResolvers to retrieve certificates.

ResourceResolvers

You're most likely to use a custom ResourceResolver in your application. To create your own ResourceResolver, extend the class org.apache.xml.security.utils.resolver.ResourceResolverSPI and provide implementations for the engineCanResolve and engineResolve methods. Once you've implemented this class, then you can call the addResourceResolver method on XMLSignature, Manifest, or SignedInfo to attach the ResourceResolver in the correct place.

Here's a simple ResourceResolver that maps references to book.xml with no base URI to a local file:

```
/*
 *
 * BookResourceResolver.java
 *
 * Example from "Professional XML Development with Apache Tools"
 *
 */
package com.sauria.apachexml.ch10;

import java.io.FileInputStream;
import java.io.FileNotFoundException;
import java.io.IOException;

import org.apache.xml.security.signature.XMLSignatureInput;
import
org.apache.xml.security.utils.resolver.ResourceResolverException;
import
org.apache.xml.security.utils.resolver.ResourceResolverSpi;
```

```
import org.w3c.dom.Attr;

public class BookResourceResolver extends ResourceResolverSpi {

    public XMLSignatureInput engineResolve(Attr uri,
        String BaseURI)
        throws ResourceResolverException {
        if (!uri.equals("book.xml") || !BaseURI.equals(""))
            throw
                new ResourceResolverException("can't handle",
                    uri, BaseURI);
        try {
            FileInputStream fis =
                new FileInputStream("book.xml");
            return new XMLSignatureInput(fis);
        } catch (FileNotFoundException fnfe) {
            fnfe.printStackTrace();
        } catch (IOException ioe) {
            ioe.printStackTrace();
        }
        return null;
    }

    public boolean engineCanResolve(Attr uri, String BaseURI) {
        if (BaseURI.equals("") && uri.equals("book.xml"))
            return true;
        return false;
    }
}
```

StorageResolvers

Implementing a StorageResolver is relatively simple. You need to extend org.apache.xml.security .key.storage.StorageResolverSpi and provide an implementation for the getIterator method. You may end up creating your own Iterator implementation. Once you've created the StorageResolver, you can call addStorageResolver on a KeyInfo object to register the resolver with the KeyInfo.

XML Security provides a few prepackaged StorageResolvers you can use in your own code. They're in the org.apache.xml.security.keys.storage.implementations package:

- **KeyStoreResolver**—retrieves certificates from an open Java KeyStore.
- **SingleCertificateResolver**— returns a certificate that was passed into its constructor.
- **CertsInFilesystemDirectoryResolver**—retrieves certificate files (that end with .crt) that are stored in a directory in the filesystem.

KeyResolvers

KeyResolvers are the type of resolver you're least likely to use. To create a KeyResolver, you need to create a new class that extends org.apache.xml.security.keys.keyresolver.KeyResolverSpi and provide implementations for the engineResolvePublicKey, engineResolveSecretKey, and engineResolveX509Certificate methods. After you do this, you need to modify the config.xml file in org.apache.xml.security.resource and add another entry to the <KeyResolver> element.

Encryption

XML Security's support for XML Encryption is still at the alpha stage and hasn't been included in a build (at least at the time of this writing—by the time you read this, there will probably be a build containing the encryption support). To work with the XML Encryption support, you need to obtain a copy of XML Security from the Apache CVS repository.

Installation

The simplest way to get a copy of the CVS for XML Security is to use a CVS snapshot. Follow these steps:

1. Go to http://cvs.apache.org/snapshots/xml-security and pick up a CVS snapshot.
2. Unpack the .tar.gz file.

You can also use CVS to get a copy of XML Security directly from the Apache public CVS repository. Follow these steps:

1. Enter this CVS command:

    ```
    cvs -d :pserver:anoncvs@cvs.apache.org:/home/cvspublic login
    ```

2. Type "anoncvs" for the password.
3. Enter this command:

    ```
    cvs –d :pserver:anoncvs@cvs.apache.org:/home/cvspublic
      checkout xml-security
    ```

You now have a copy of the XML Security CVS. To build a copy of the most recent XML Security jars, follow these steps:

1. Change to the xml-security directory.
2. Be sure you're using at least JDK 1.3.
3. Be sure you have a copy of Ant installed.
4. Type "ant jar" to create the XML Security jars.
5. The jar files will be in the build subdirectory.

An Example

This example is designed to give you a flavor of what it will be like to work with the XML Security encryption API:

```
/*
 *
 * EncryptionMain.java
 *
```

```
 5:  * Example from "Professional XML Development with Apache Tools"
 6:  *
 7:  */
 8: package com.sauria.apachexml.ch10;
 9: 
10: import java.io.ByteArrayOutputStream;
11: import java.io.File;
12: import java.io.IOException;
13: import java.security.InvalidKeyException;
14: import java.security.Key;
15: import java.security.NoSuchAlgorithmException;
16: import java.security.spec.InvalidKeySpecException;
17: 
18: import javax.crypto.KeyGenerator;
19: import javax.crypto.SecretKey;
20: import javax.crypto.SecretKeyFactory;
21: import javax.crypto.spec.DESedeKeySpec;
22: import javax.crypto.spec.SecretKeySpec;
23: import javax.xml.parsers.DocumentBuilder;
24: import javax.xml.parsers.DocumentBuilderFactory;
25: 
26: import org.apache.xml.security.encryption.XMLCipher;
27: import org.apache.xml.security.encryption.XMLEncryptionException;
28: import org.apache.xml.serialize.DOMSerializer;
29: import org.apache.xml.serialize.Method;
30: import org.apache.xml.serialize.OutputFormat;
31: import org.apache.xml.serialize.XMLSerializer;
32: import org.w3c.dom.Document;
33: import org.w3c.dom.Element;
```

Here's your static initialization for the XML Security library:

```
34: 
35: public class EncryptionMain {
36: 
37:     static {
38:         org.apache.xml.security.Init.init();
39:     }
```

In order to encrypt a document, you need a Key to use for encryption, the name of the algorithm to use, a DOM Document that serves as a context, and a DOM Element in that document that will be encrypted:

```
40: 
41:     public static Document encrypt(Key key, String cipherName,
42:         Document contextDocument, Element elementToEncrypt) {
```

The XMLCipher class is designed to work in a way familiar to someone who has used the javax.crypto .Cipher class. First you have to get an instance of a particular Cipher (algorithm) (line 45), and then you need to initialize the Cipher in encryption mode (line 46). You have to supply the encryption key to do this:

```
43:         Document result = null;
44:         try {
45:             XMLCipher cipher = XMLCipher.getInstance(cipherName);
46:             cipher.init(XMLCipher.ENCRYPT_MODE, key);
```

The XMLCipher class defines some String constants with the names of the supported encryption algorithms. The list of supported algorithms includes AES (128-, 192-, and 256-bit variants), SHA1 and SHA (256- and 512-bit variants of SHA1), and Triple DES.

Encrypting the element is simple. You call XMLCipher's doFinal method and pass it the context document and the element (from within that document) to encrypt. This operation is destructive—contextDocument is updated in place:

```
47:             result =
48:             cipher.doFinal(contextDocument,elementToEncrypt);
49:         } catch (XMLEncryptionException xee) {
50:             xee.printStackTrace();
51:         }
52:
53:         return result;
54:     }
```

As you might expect, decrypting is very similar to encrypting. You need a key for decrypting, the name of the encryption algorithm, and a DOM document that contains an <EncryptedData> element:

```
55:
56:     public static Document decrypt(Key key, String cipherName,
57:         Document documentToDecrypt) {
58:         Document result = null;
59:         Element encryptedDataElement;
60:         XMLCipher cipher;
```

You set up your XMLCipher instance with the correct algorithm (line 63), and this time you initialize it in decryption mode (line 64):

```
61:
62:         try {
63:             cipher = XMLCipher.getInstance(cipherName);
64:             cipher.init(XMLCipher.DECRYPT_MODE, key);
```

Next, you need to find an <EncryptedData> element (from the XML Encryption namespace) somewhere in the document:

```
65:
66:             encryptedDataElement = (Element)
67:                 documentToDecrypt.getElementsByTagNameNS(
68:                     "http://www.w3.org/2001/04/xmlenc#",
69:                     "EncryptedData").item(0);
```

After you find the document, you call doFinal with the document and the element containing the <EncryptedData>. Again, this is a destructive operation:

```
70:
71:             result = cipher.doFinal(documentToDecrypt,
72:                 encryptedDataElement);
73:         } catch (XMLEncryptionException xee) {
74:             xee.printStackTrace();
```

```
75:         }
76:
77:         return result;
78:     }
```

test is a simple method that calls some helper functions to assemble all the information needed by the encrypt and decrypt functions:

```
79:
80:     public static boolean test() {
```

The test method operates on the familiar book.xml file, and you need to use the namespace URI of the book schema:

```
81:         String xmlFile = "book.xml";
82:         String bookNS =
83:             "http://sauria.com/schemas/apache-xml-book/book";
```

You set up for encryption by parsing book.xml into a DOM tree (line 85) and then using the namespace-aware getElementsByTagNameNS method to locate the <author> element, which is the element you want to encrypt (lines 86-88):

```
84:
85:         Document contextDoc = loadDocument(xmlFile);
86:         Element elementToEncrypt = (Element)
87:             contextDoc.getElementsByTagNameNS(bookNS,
88:                 "author").item(0);
```

You encrypt and decrypt the document using two different algorithms. The first is Triple DES. The get3DESKey method (line 90) obtains a Triple DES secret key, given a passphrase. You set the string cipher to the constant for the Triple DES algorithm URI (line 91):

```
89:
90:         Key key = get3DESKey("3DES or DES-EDE secret key");
91:         String cipher = XMLCipher.TRIPLEDES;
```

Next you encrypt (lines 92-93) and decrypt (lines 94-95) the document:

```
92:         Document encryptedDoc = encrypt(key, cipher,
93:             contextDoc, elementToEncrypt);
94:         Document decryptedDoc =
95:              decrypt(key, cipher, encryptedDoc);
```

To check your work, you reparse the XML file to get a fresh copy of the unencrypted document (line 97), and then you compare them by converting both DOM trees to Strings and testing the String values for equality (line 98-99):

```
96:
97:         contextDoc = loadDocument(xmlFile);
98:         boolean resultDES =
99:             toString(contextDoc).equals(toString(decryptedDoc));
100:        System.out.println(resultDES);
```

The code for AES encryption is the same, except that you need to call a different helper method to get the AESKey (line 102), and you need to provide the right value for 256-bit AES (line 103):

```
101:
102:            key = getAESKey(256);
103:            cipher = XMLCipher.AES_256;
104:            elementToEncrypt = (Element)
105:                contextDoc.getElementsByTagNameNS(bookNS,
106:                    "author").item(0);
107:            encryptedDoc =
108:                encrypt(key, cipher, contextDoc, elementToEncrypt);
109:            decryptedDoc = decrypt(key, cipher, encryptedDoc);
110:
111:            contextDoc = loadDocument(xmlFile);
112:            boolean resultAES =
113:                toString(contextDoc).equals(toString(decryptedDoc));
114:            System.out.println(resultAES);
115:
116:            return resultDES && resultAES;
117:        }
```

The main function just calls test:

```
118:
119:        public static void main(String[] args) {
120:            test();
121:        }
```

The get3DESKey method takes a passphrase and uses it to create a new Triple DES key:

```
122:
123:        public static SecretKey get3DESKey(String phrase) {
```

You need to convert the passphrase to a byte array:

```
124:            byte[] passPhrase = phrase.getBytes();
```

You then obtain a DESedeKeySpec using the byte array (lines 127-128) and pass that to a SecretKeyFactory for Triple DES (under the name DESede) (lines 131). You call the SecretKeyFactory's getInstance factory method with the name of the algorithm (lines 129-130):

```
125:            SecretKey key = null;
126:            try {
127:                DESedeKeySpec keySpec =
128:                    new DESedeKeySpec(passPhrase);
129:                SecretKeyFactory keyFactory =
130:                    SecretKeyFactory.getInstance("DESede");
131:                key = keyFactory.generateSecret(keySpec);
132:            } catch (InvalidKeyException ike) {
133:                ike.printStackTrace();
134:            } catch (NoSuchAlgorithmException nsae) {
135:                nsae.printStackTrace();
136:            } catch (InvalidKeySpecException ikse) {
```

```
137:                ikse.printStackTrace();
138:            }
139:            return key;
140:        }
```

The getAESKey method shows how to generate an AES secret key. It needs to know how many bits the AES key should use. Sanity-checking the value of bits has been omitted for the sake of brevity:

```
141:
142:        public static Key getAESKey(int bits) {
```

You start by obtaining a KeyGenerator for AES:

```
143:            KeyGenerator kgen = null;
144:            try {
145:                kgen = KeyGenerator.getInstance("AES");
146:            } catch (NoSuchAlgorithmException nsae) {
147:                nsae.printStackTrace();
148:            }
```

Next you initialize the KeyGenerator with the number of bits in the key (line 149) and then generate the key (line 151):

```
149:            kgen.init(bits);
150:
151:            SecretKey skey = kgen.generateKey();
```

Because you want to return a Key object, you need to convert the SecretKey into a SecretKeySpec (line 154). To do this, you need to obtain the secret key as a byte array (line 152) and pass it to the constructor for SecretKeySpec along with the algorithm name:

```
152:            byte[] raw = skey.getEncoded();
153:
154:            SecretKeySpec skeySpec = new SecretKeySpec(raw,"AES");
155:
156:            return skeySpec;
157:        }
158:
```

The loadDocument method is a convenience method that hides the boilerplate code needed to create a namespace-aware DocumentBuilder and build a DOM tree:

```
159:
160:        public static Document loadDocument(String uri) {
161:            Document d = null;
162:            try {
163:                DocumentBuilderFactory dbf =
164:                    DocumentBuilderFactory.newInstance();
165:                dbf.setNamespaceAware(true);
166:                DocumentBuilder db = dbf.newDocumentBuilder();
167:                File f = new File(uri);
168:                d = db.parse(f);
```

```
        } catch (Exception e) {
            e.printStackTrace();
            System.exit(-1);
        }

        return (d);
    }
```

The toString method is a convenience method that uses the Xerces serializer classes to serialize a DOM tree as a String:

```

    private static String toString(Document document) {
        OutputFormat of = new OutputFormat();
        of.setIndenting(true);
        of.setMethod(Method.XML);
        ByteArrayOutputStream baos = new ByteArrayOutputStream();
        DOMSerializer serializer = new XMLSerializer(baos, of);
        try {
            serializer.serialize(document);
        } catch (IOException ioe) {
            ioe.printStackTrace();
        }
        return (baos.toString());
    }
}
```

Practical Usage

Here are some practical tips you can use for your own applications.

Try to use JDK 1.4. This version of the JDK has the Java Cryptography Extensions built in and provides much more integrated support for cryptography than earlier versions. This translates into more algorithms being available for you to use.

When you're working with XML Security, you're working with namespace-aware XML applications. Be sure you're using the namespace-aware versions of the methods from the DOM specification. You can look at the DOM Level 2 Core Recommendation to find out what these methods are.

Cryptography operations are computationally expensive. Although it may be more work for you as a developer to encrypt only portions of a document, you save a lot of CPU cycles. If you're going to be processing a lot of documents or repeatedly processing documents, this can have a major impact on the usability of your system.

If you aren't using XML Signature or XML Encryption in your applications, you should be aware of the issues that will come up when you incorporate these technologies. You'll see the greatest effect in the design of your XML vocabularies. You should think about what information will need to be signed and/or encrypted and then put that information in independent elements, so you can sign or encrypt only the data that needs to be signed or encrypted.

Applications

You can use the XML Security library to sign and encrypt XML documents for use in your own applications. You need to decide which points in your system's work flow need to add the security mechanisms allowed by XML Signature and XML Encryption. You should also be aware of interoperability issues when you exchange data with other applications.

One of the biggest applications for XML Security is implementing the functionality specified by the WS-Security specification for Web services. This important set of standards will improve the security of Web services applications. To get a preview of how this functionality might be implemented in Axis using XML Security, you can look at the security sample in the Axis distribution, which uses XML Security to implement the older SOAP-SEC extensions for digital signatures.

Index

A

abbreviated syntax (XPath expressions), 61
absolute location paths (XPath), 54
<act> element (Cocoon), 240
actions (Cocoon), 234–235
  database action, 235
  sendmail action, 235–236
  session action, 236
action sets (Cocoon), 236
active grammar catching, 25–28
add_collection command (Xindice), 300–301
add_document command (Xindice), 301
add_indexer command (Xindice), 304–305
add_multiple command (Xindice), 301
AdminClient Ant task, 451
AdminClient program, 406–407
<aggregate> element (Cocoon), 239, 241
Al-Ghosein, Mohsen, 349
<animateColor> element (SVG), 168
<animate> element (SVG), 168
<animateMotion> element (SVG), 168
<animateTransform> element (SVG), 169
Ant tasks
  Axis
    AdminClient, 451
    Java2WSDL, 450–451
    sample build.xml file, 451–452
    WSDL2Java, 450
  FOP as, 137–138
Apache SOAP. *See* SOAP
APIs (XML parsers), 6–8
  DOM, 13–15
  SAX, 8–12
applets, Xalan applet wrapper, 84–85
asynchronous clients (XML-RPC), 361–363
Atkinson, Bob, 349
augment transformer (Cocoon), 228
authentication, BASIC (XML-RPC), 365–366
AWT renderer (FOP), 143
axes (location paths), 56–57
Axis
  .jws Web services, 448–449
  Ant tasks
    AdminClient, 451
    Java2WSDL, 450–451
    sample build.xml file, 451–452
    WSDL2Java, 450
  applications of, 454
  conceptual model, 402–403
  deploying Web services, 406–407, 427–428
  deployment descriptors, 403–406
  document-style services, 408–409
  example application, 413–414
    binding file, 415–416
    deploying, 427–428
    deployment descriptor, 425–427
    DLBookHandler interface, 417–421
    generated test case, 423–425
    implementation file, 416
    interface file, 414–415
    running, 417
    skeleton service class, 421–423
    undeployment descriptor, 427

handler chains, 402
handlers, 442–448
history, 379–380
installing, 399–401
JAX-RPC, 392–393
DII (Dynamic Invocation Interface), 396–399
dynamic proxies, 394–396
stubs, 393–394
message service, 436
deployment descriptors, 440–442
service provider, 438–440
service requestor, 436–438
message-style services, 409
RPC-style services, 407–408
ServletContext access, 434–436
TCPMon tool, 449
wrapped-style services, 408–409
WSDL (Web Services Description Language), 379, 384–386
bindings, 385–386
document-literal Web service example, 389–392
document styles, 407–409
example file, 386–389
messages, 385
ports, 385
port types, 385
services, 385
WSDL2Java, 409–413

B

BASIC authentication (XML-RPC), 365–366
Batik, 145
applications for, 209–212
CachedImageHandler classes, 174–178
font converter, 207–208
image transcoding, 187
from SVG DOM trees, 189–191
from SVG files, 188–189
installing, 169–170
JSVGCanvas, 183–187
pretty-printer, 206–207
rich client user interfaces, 212
security
application security, 197
external resource access, 197–202
Squiggle browser, 205–206
style handling, 208
SVGGraphics2D class, 171–173
options, setting, 174–178
style handling, 178–183
SVG Rasterizer, 202
as Ant task, 203–204
command-line interface, 202–203
SVG (Scalable Vector Graphics)
<circle> element, 159
compatibility issues, 208
container elements, 160–161
<desc> element, 158
DTD, 158
dynamic, 164–169, 208
<g> element, 158
Hello World example, 156–157
image caching, 174–178
<image> element, 160
image storing, 174
<line> element, 158
<path> element, 162–164
<polygon> element, 159
<polyline> element, 159
<rect> element, 158–159
size attributes, 158
<text> element, 159–160
<title> element, 158
transform attribute, 161–162
SVG scripting, 191
JSVGCanvas ECMAScript API, 191–192
Jython, 192–197
text editors, 208
BinaryResource interface (XML:DB), 290
<binding> element (WSDL), 387
bindings (WSDL), 385–386
<Body> element (SOAP), 380–381
books JavaBean example, 7–8
parsing with DOM, 13–15
parsing with SAX, 8–12
Box, Don, 349
browser selector (Cocoon), 233

C

CachedImageHandler classes, 174–178
<call> element (Cocoon), 240
canonicalization, 459–461, 471–474
CInclude transformer (Cocoon), 227–228
<circle> element (SVG), 159
Cocoon, 214
actions
database action, 235
sendmail action, 235–236
session action, 236
action sets, 236
applications of, 284
configuring, 257
databases
accessing, 258–263
actions, 263–268
database application example, 269–283
documentation, 283
generators, 223
directory generator, 223
file generator, 223
image directory generator, 223
linkstatus generator, 223
notifying generator, 223–224
request generator, 224
server pages generator, 224
status generator, 224
stream generator, 224
XPath directory generator, 224
installing, 255–257
logicsheets, 246–253
forms logicsheet, 249–252
request logicsheet, 248–249
sendmail logicsheet, 252–253
matchers, 231–232
Regexp URI matcher, 232–233
wildcard header matcher, 233
wildcard URI matcher, 232
performance, 283
<pipeline> elements, 234–235
<act> element, 240
<aggregate> element, 241
<call> element, 240
<generate> element, 220, 239
<handle-errors> element, 220, 240
<match> element, 218–220, 239
<mount> element, 240–241
<parameter> element, 240
<redirect-to> element, 240
<select> element, 220, 240
<serialize> element, 220, 239
<transform> element, 220, 239
pipelines, 214
prerequisites, 213
readers, 236
database reader, 237–238
image reader, 237
JSP reader, 237
resource reader, 236–237
resources, 239
selectors, 233
browser selector, 233
host selector, 234
parameter selector, 234
request attribute selector, 234
request parameter selector, 234
serializers
HTML serializer, 229
link serializer, 231
PCL serializer, 231
PDF serializer, 231
PS serializer, 231
SVG/JPEG serializer, 230
SVG/PNG serializer, 230
SVG/TIFF serializer, 231
SVG/XML serializer, 230
text serializer, 229–230
WAP/WML serializer, 230
XHTML serializer, 229
XML serializer, 229
zip archive serializer, 231
session management, 253–254
sitemaps, 214–222
<components> element, 217
example sitemap, 215–217
<exception> element, 218
<generators> element, 217
<matchers> element, 218
<otherwise> element, 220
<pipelines> element, 217, 218–220
<selector> element, 218
<serializers> element, 218
<transformers> element, 217
<use-cookie-parameters> element, 217
<use-request-parameters> element, 217
<use-session-parameters> element, 217
<when> element, 220

transformers
augment transformer, 228
CInclude transformer, 227–228
EncodeURL transformer, 228
filter transformer, 227
fragment extractor transformer, 225
I18N transformer, 225–226
log transformer, 226
read DOM session transformer, 227
SQL transformer, 226–227
write DOM session transformer, 227
XInclude transformer, 227
XSLT transformer, 225
URIs, 241–242
views, 238–239
XSPs (eXtensible Server Pages)
elements, 245–246
overview, 242–246
<?cocoon-process?> element (Cocoon), 245
Collection interface (XML:DB), 289
CollectionManagementService interface (XML:DB), 292
collections
creating (Xindice), 307–310
deleting (Xindice), 312–314
navigating (Xindice), 310–311
<components> element (Cocoon), 217
configuration files (FOP), 127–129
configuring
Xerces, 16–17
character encoding, 19
disallow-doctype-decl feature, 19
DOM-related features, 18–19
error-reporting features, 18
input buffer size, 19
SecurityManager, 19
URI-conformant feature, 19
validation-related features, 17
container elements (SVG), 160–161
ContentHandler interface (SAX), 10
Crimson, 1
cryptographic checksum. *See* one-way hashing
CSS (cascading style sheets), 178

D

DatabaseAddAction (Cocoon), 265
DatabaseDeleteAction (Cocoon), 265
Database interface (XML:DB), 288
DatabaseManager interface (XML:DB), 288
DatabaseQueryAction (Cocoon), 265
database reader (Cocoon), 237–238
databases
adding to (Xindice), 300–302
collections (Xindice)
creating, 307–310
deleting, 312–314
navigating, 310–311
database access (Cocoon), 258
connecting, 258
errors, 261
ESQL, 258–261
example, 262–263
stored procedures, 261–262
database actions (Cocoon), 235, 263
DatabaseAddAction, 265
DatabaseDeleteAction, 265
DatabaseQueryAction, 265
DatabaseSelectAction, 265
DatabaseUpdateAction, 265
descriptor file, 264–265
example database, 266–268
database application example (Cocoon)
add-book.xsp, 278–279
add-pub.xml, 274–275
cocoon.xconf, 270
database.xml, 270
edit-book.xsp, 276–277, 280–282
form.xslt, 282–283
index.xml, 274
list-books.xsp, 279–280
list-publishers.xsp, 275–276
sample data set, 269–270
sitemap.xmap, 271–274
table definitions, 269
deleting documents from (Xindice), 303–304
exporting collections (Xindice), 306
indexing (Xindice), 304–306
persistent storage, 285
resources, creating (Xindice)
DOM-based I/O, 321–324
SAX-based I/O, 317–321
string-based I/O, 314–317

retrieval (Xindice), 302–303
XML:DB, 285–286
API, 287–293
XUpdate, 293–299
XPath-based querying, 324–327
XUpdate, 327–329
DatabaseSelectAction (Cocoon), 265
DatabaseUpdateAction (Cocoon), 265
debugging
Web services (TCPMon tool), 449
Xalan, 85–91
command-line interface, 81
EnvironmentCheck class, 85–87
logging, 88–91
SourceLocator interface, 87
TraceListeners, 85–87, 88
XML-RPC, 373
declarations, 2–3
declarative dynamic SVG, 166–169
DefaultHandler (SAX), 9–10
default namespaces, 3–4
default values, reporting, 22
deferred DOM, 20
<definitions> element (WSDL), 386
delete_collection command (Xindice), 303–304
delete_document command (Xindice), 304
delete_indexer command (Xindice), 306
deploying Web services, 427–428
deployment descriptors
Axis, 403–406
message service (Axis), 440–442
WSDL (Web Services Description Language), 425–427
<deployment> element (Axis), 403
<desc> element (SVG), 158
<DigestMethod> element (XML Signature), 463
<DigestValue> element (XML Signature), 464
digital certificates, 458
digital signatures, 457–458
placing in separate files, 490–491
signing documents, 474–485
verification, 485–490
DII (Dynamic Invocation Interface), 396–399
directory generator (Cocoon), 223
document-literal Web service (WSDL), 389–392
document scanner (Xerces), 42
document-style services (Axis), 408–409
DOM
passing DOM trees to FOP, 131–133
SVG trees, transcoding, 189–191
TrAX API, 74–77
Xerces API, 13–15
configuration features, 18–19
deferred DOM, 20
serialization, 36–37
downloading
Axis, 399–400
Batik, 169
Cocoon, 255
FOP (Formatting Object Processor), 123
Xalan, 69
Xerces, 15
Xindice, 299
XML Encryption, 495
XML-RPC, 356
XML Security, 470–471
DTDs, 5
DTD scanner (Xerces), 42
DTD validator (Xerces), 42
DTM (Document Table Model), 80–81
dynamic proxies (JAX-RPC), 394–396
dynamic SVG, 208
declarative dynamic, 166–169
imperative dynamic, 164–166

E

ECMAScript API, 191–192
elements, 3
embedding FOP in applications, 125–127
EncodeURL transformer (Cocoon), 228
endElement method (SAX), 10–11
entities, 6
handling, 29–31
references, 31–33
XNI entity manager, 43
<Envelope> element (SOAP), 380–381
EnvironmentCheck class, debugging with, 85–87
ErrorHandler interface (SAX), 12
error reporting
Xerces features, 18
XNI error reporter, 43
ESQL, 258–259
query results, 260–261
setting connections, 259
specifying SQL statements, 259–260

<esql:get-array> element (Cocoon), 260
<esql:get-ascii> element (Cocoon), 260
<esql:get-boolean> element (Cocoon), 260
<esql:get-column-label> element (Cocoon), 261
<esql:get-column-name> element (Cocoon), 261
<esql:get-columns> element (Cocoon), 261
<esql:get-column-type-name> element (Cocoon), 261
<esql:get-date> element (Cocoon), 260
<esql:get-double> element (Cocoon), 260
<esql:get-float> element (Cocoon), 260
<esql:get-int> element (Cocoon), 260
<esql:get-long> element (Cocoon), 260
<esql:get-object> element (Cocoon), 260
<esql:get-short> element (Cocoon), 260
<esql:get-string> element (Cocoon), 260
<esql:get-struct> element (Cocoon), 260
<esql:get-time> element (Cocoon), 260
<esql:get-timestamp> element (Cocoon), 260
<esql:get-xml> element (Cocoon), 260
<esql:is-null> element (Cocoon), 260
<exception> element (Cocoon), 218
exclusive canonicalization, 460–461
expanded names (nodes), 55
experimental functionality, 2
export command (Xindice), 306
expressions (XPath), 59
  abbreviated syntax, 61
  function library, 59–61
Extensible Stylesheet Language. *See* XSL
extensions
  FOP (Formatting Object Processor), 145–146
  Xalan, 97
    extension elements, 97–98
    extension functions, 98–101
    writing, 101–103
    XSLTC, 104
  XSLT, 68

F

file generator (Cocoon), 223
filters
  FOP (Formatting Object Processor), 149–150
  order of (in chains), 152
  XSLT, 146–149
filter transformer (Cocoon), 227
flows (XSL), 115–116
font converter (Batik), 207–208
font registration (FOP), 138–139
FOP (Formatting Object Processor), 113
  as Ant task, 137–138
  command-line options, 135–137
  configuration files, 127–129
  DOM trees as input, 131–133
  embedding, 125–127
  extensions, 145–146
  filters, 149–150
  font registration, 138–139
  graphics, 143. *See also* Batik
    formats, 144
    image caching, 143–144
    JAI API, 145
    Jimi library, 144
    resolution, 143
  hyphenation options, 124–125
  installing, 123–125
  output, 140
    AWT renderer, 143
    MIF renderer, 142
    PCL renderer, 142
    PDF encryption, 140–141
    PostScript renderer, 141–142
    SVG renderer, 142
    TXT renderer, 142–143
    XML renderer, 143
  performance, 146
  rendering support, 146
  sample application, 146–153
  SAX event streams, 129–131
  XSL
    document elements, 114–115
    flows, 115–116
    generating with XSLT, 117–119
    list blocks, 116–117
    new components, 114–115
    tables, 119–123
    validating, 135
  XSLT and, 133–135
formatting objects, 113
forms logicsheet (Cocoon), 249–252
fragment extractor transformer (Cocoon), 225
functions, XPath, 59–61

G

<g> element (SVG), 158
<generate> element (Cocoon), 220, 239
generators (Cocoon), 223
directory generator, 223
file generator, 223
image directory generator, 223
linkstatus generator, 223
notifying generator, 223–224
request generator, 224
server pages generator, 224
status generator, 224
stream generator, 224
XPath directory generator, 224
<generators> element (Cocoon), 217
<globalConfiguration> element (Axiz), 403
grammar catching, 23–29
active catching, 25–28
passive catching, 23–25
graphics
FOP support
Batik, 145
formats, 144
image caching, 143–144
resolution, 143
Jimi library, 144
SVG (Scalable Vector Graphics), 155–156. *See also* SVGGraphics2D class
<circle> element, 159
container elements, 160–161
<desc> element, 158
displaying documents (JSVGCanvas), 183–187
DTD, 158
dynamic, 164–169, 208, 164–169
<g> element, 158
Hello World example, 156–157
image caching, 174–178
<image> element, 160
image storing, 174
image transcoding, 187–191
<line> element, 158
<path> element, 162–164
<polygon> element, 159
<polyline> element, 159
<rect> element, 158–159
scripting, 191–197
size attributes, 158
static, 158–164
style handling, 178–183
support, 156
<text> element, 159–160
<title> element, 158
transform attribute, 161–162

H

<handle-errors> element (Cocoon), 220, 240
handler chains (Axis), 402
<handler> element (Axis), 404
handlers (Axis), 442–448
hash functions, 456
<Header> element (SOAP), 380–381
host selector (Cocoon), 234
HTMLSerializer, 34
HTML serializer (Cocoon), 229
HTTP, as RPC transport, 354–356
HXD (Hybrid XML Database), 286
Hybrid XML Database (HXD), 286
hyphenation (FOP), 124–125

I

I18N transformer (Cocoon), 225–226
image caching
Batik, 174–178
FOP (Formatting Object Processor), 143–144
image directory generator (Cocoon), 223
<image> element (SVG), 160
image reader (Cocoon), 237
image transcoding, 187
from SVG DOM trees, 189–191
from SVG files, 188–189
imperative dynamic SVG, 164–166
import command (Xindice), 302
input buffer size (Xerces), 19
installing
Axis, 399–401
Cocoon, 255–257
FOP (Formatting Object Processor), 123–125

Xalan, 69–70
Xerces, 15–16
Xindice, 299–300
XML Encryption, 495
XML-RPC, 356
XML Security, 470–471

J

Java2WSDL, 428–433, 450–451
JavaBean for books example, 7–8
active grammar catching, 25–28
parsing with DOM, 13–15
parsing with SAX, 8–12
passive grammar catching, 23–25
XSLT stylesheet, 62–66
Java dynamic proxies (with XML-RPC), 373–378
Java types, mapping to (XML-RPC), 358–359
JAX-RPC, 392–393
Axis handlers, 442–448
DII (Dynamic Invocation Interface), 396–399
dynamic proxies, 394–396
stubs, 393–394
Jimi library, 144
JSP reader (Cocoon), 237
JSVGCanvas, 183–187
ECMAScript API, 191–192
external resource access, 197–202
.jws Web services, 448–449
Jython, SVG scripting, 192–197

K

key encryption
public, 457
symmetric, 457
<KeyInfo> element (XML Signature), 464–466
KeyResolvers (XML Security), 494–495

L

<line> element (SVG), 158
link serializer (Cocoon), 231
linkstatus generator (Cocoon), 223
list blocks (XSL), 116–117
list_collections command (Xindice), 302
list_documents command (Xindice), 302–303
list_indexers command (Xindice), 306
local parts (ZNames), 3
location paths (XPath), 54–59
axes, 56–57
node tests, 57–58
predicates, 58–59
logging (Xalan), 88–91
logicsheets (Cocoon), 246–248
forms logicsheet, 249–252
request logicsheet, 248–249
sendmail logicsheet, 252–253
log transformer (Cocoon), 226
Lotus XSL. *See* Xalan

M

MAC (message authentication code), 456
ManekiNeko, 44–45
<map:act> element (Cocoon), 240
<map:aggregate> element (Cocoon), 241
<map:call> element (Cocoon), 240
<map:generate> element (Cocoon), 220, 239
<map:handle-errors> element (Cocoon), 220, 240
<map:match> element (Cocoon), 218–220, 239
<map:mount> element (Cocoon), 240–241
<map:parameter> element (Cocoon), 240
<map:redirect-to> element (Cocoon), 240
<map:select> element (Cocoon), 220, 240
<map:serialize> element (Cocoon), 239
<map:transform> element (Cocoon), 220, 239
mapping to Java types (XML-RPC), 358–359
<match> element (Cocoon), 218–220, 239
matchers (Cocoon), 231–232
Regexp URI matcher, 232–233
wildcard header matcher, 233
wildcard URI matcher, 232
<matchers> element (Cocoon), 218
message authentication code (MAC), 456

message digest. *See* one-way hashing
message service (Axis), 436
deployment descriptors, 440–442
service provider, 438–440
service requestor, 436–438
message-style services (Axis), 409
messages (WSDL), 385
<methodCall> element (XML-RPC), 351
<methodName> element (XML-RPC), 351
MIF renderer (FOP), 142
modular database actions (Cocoon), 263
DatabaseAddAction, 265
DatabaseDeleteAction, 265
DatabaseQueryAction, 265
DatabaseSelectAction, 265
DatabaseUpdateAction, 265
descriptor file, 264–265
example database, 266–268
<mount> element (Cocoon), 240–241

N

namespace binder (Xerces), 42
namespace prefixes, 3–4
namespaces, 3–4
Native XML Database (NXD), 286
NekoHTML, 44
NekoPull, 45–48
NekoXNI tools
ManekiNeko, 44–45
NekoHTML, 44
NekoPull, 45–48
nodes, expanded names, 55
node tests (location paths), 57–58
notifying generator (Cocoon), 223–224
NXD (Native XML Database), 286

O

<Object> element (XML Signature), 466
one-way hashing, 456–457
<operation> element (WSDL), 387
<otherwise> element (Cocoon), 220
output element (XSLT), 66–67
OutputFormat options, 37–38

P–Q

<parameter> element (Cocoon), 240
parameter selector (Cocoon), 234
parser APIs, 6–8
DOM, 13–15
SAX, 8–12
passive grammar catching, 23–25
<path> element (SVG), 162–164
PCL renderer (FOP), 142
PCL serializer (Cocoon), 231
PDF encryption (FOP), 140–141
PDF serializer (Cocoon), 231
<pipeline> elements (Cocoon), 217, 218–220
<act> element, 240
<aggregate> element, 241
<call> element, 240
<generate> element, 220, 239
<handle-errors> element, 220, 240
<match> element, 218–220, 239
<mount> element, 240–241
<parameter> element, 240
<redirect-to> element, 240
<select> element, 220, 240
<serialize> element, 220, 239
<transform> element, 220, 239
pipeline interfaces (Xerces), 39–41
pipelines (Cocoon), 214
PNGTranscoder, 188–189
<polygon> element (SVG), 159
<polyline> element (SVG), 159
Portable Document Format (PDF) encryption (FOP), 140–141
<port> element (WSDL), 388–389
ports (WSDL), 385
<portType> element (WSDL), 387
port types (SWDL), 385
Post Schema Validation Infoset (PSVI), 22
PostScript renderer (FOP), 141–142
predicates (location paths), 58–59

pretty-printer (Batik), 206–207
Project X, 1
PS serializer (Cocoon), 231
PSVI (Post Schema Validation Infoset), 22
public key encryption, 457
publishing XML documents. *See* Cocoon

QNames, 3

R

read DOM session transformer (Cocoon), 227
readers (Cocoon), 236
  database reader, 237–238
  image reader, 237
  JSP reader, 237
  resource reader, 236–237
<rect> element (SVG), 158–159
<redirect-to> element (Cocoon), 240
<Reference> element (XML Signature), 462
referencing entities, 31–33
Regexp URI matcher (Cocoon), 232–233
registering fonts (FOP), 138–139
relative location paths (XPath), 54
Relax-NG, 5
remote procedure calls. *See* RPCs
reporting default values, 22
request attribute selector (Cocoon), 234
<requestFlow> element (Axis), 404
request generator (Cocoon), 224
request logicsheet (Cocoon), 248–249
request parameter selector (Cocoon), 234
reset method (FOP), 146
Resource interface (XML:DB), 289–290
ResourceIterator interface (XML:DB), 291
resource reader (Cocoon), 236–237
ResourceResolvers (XML Security), 493–494
resources (Cocoon), 239
resources, creating (Xindice)
  DOM-based I/O, 321–324
  SAX-based I/O, 317–321
  string-based I/O, 314–317
ResourceSet interface (XML:DB), 290–291
<responseFlow> element (Axis), 405–406
retrieve_document command (Xindice), 303
rich client user interfaces (SVG), 212
RPCs (remote procedure calls)
  JAX-RPC, 392–393
    DII (Dynamic Invocation Interface), 396–399
    dynamic proxies, 394–396
    stubs, 393–394
  SOAP
    faults, 383–384
    requests, 381–382
    responses, 382–383
  XML-RPC
    applications of, 373
    asynchronous clients, 361–363
    BASIC authentication, 365–366
    call side flow, 350–351
    controlling server processing, 363–365
    debugging, 373
    in existing servers, 366–368
    history, 349
    HTTP as transport, 354–356
    installing, 356
    Java dynamic proxies and, 373–378
    mapping to Java types, 358–359
    prerequisites, 350
    procedure call documents, 351–352
    response documents, 352–354
    simple client example, 357–358
    simple server example, 359–361
    SSL and, 368–372
    type matching, 373
RPC-style services (Axis), 407–408

S

SAX
  feeding event streams to FOP, 129–131
  TrAX API, 72–74
  Xerces API, 8–12
    ContentHandler interface, 10
    DefaultHandler, 9–10
    endElement method, 10–11
    ErrorHandler interface, 12
    serialization, 35–36
    startElement method, 10–11
  Xindice example application, 341–346

Scalable Vector Graphics. *See* SVG
schemaLocation, overriding, 22–23
schema validation
  Xerces configuration, 20–23
  XNI schema validator, 42
secret key encryption, 457
Secure Sockets Layer (SSL), 368–372
security
  BASIC authentication (XML-RPC), 365–366
  Batik
    application security, 197
    external resource access, 197–202
  digital certificates, 458
  digital signatures, 457–458
  one-way hashing, 456–457
  public key encryption, 457
  SSL (Secure Sockets Layer), 368–372
  symmetric key encryption, 457
  XML Canonicalization, 459–461, 471–474
  XML Encryption, 456, 467–470, 495
    example application, 495–501
    installing, 495
  XML Security, 456
    applications of, 502
    installing, 470–471
    resolvers, 493–495
    signatures in separate files, 490–491
    signature verification, 485–490
    signing documents, 474–485
    XPathTransformSigner, 491–493
  XML Signature, 455–456, 461
    <DigestMethod> element, 463
    <DigestValue> element, 464
    <KeyInfo> element, 464–466
    <Object> element, 466
    <Reference> element, 462
    <Signature> element, 461
    <SignatureValue> element, 464
    <SignedInfo> element, 462
    <Transform> element, 462–463
    validating signatures, 466–467
SecurityManager, configuring (Xerces), 19
<select> element (Cocoon), 220, 240
<selector> element (Cocoon), 218
selectors (Cocoon), 233
  browser selector, 233
  host selector, 234
  parameter selector, 234
  request attribute selector, 234
  request parameter selector, 234
sendmail action (Cocoon), 235–236
<sendmail:attachment> element (Cocoon), 253
<sendmail:bcc> element (Cocoon), 252
<sendmail:body> element (Cocoon), 252
<sendmail:cc> element (Cocoon), 252
<sendmail:charset> element (Cocoon), 252
<sendmail:from> element (Cocoon), 252
sendmail logicsheet (Cocoon), 252–253
<sendmail:on-error> element (Cocoon), 253
<sendmail:on-success> element (Cocoon), 253
<sendmail:smtphost> element (Cocoon), 252
<sendmail:subject> element (Cocoon), 252
<sendmail:to> element (Cocoon), 252
separation of concerns, 213
serialization, 34–38
<serialize> element (Cocoon), 239
serializers (Cocoon)
  HTML serializer, 229
  link serializer, 231
  PCL serializer, 231
  PDF serializer, 231
  PS serializer, 231
  SVG/JPEG serializer, 230
  SVG/PNG serializer, 230
  SVG/TIFF serializer, 231
  SVG/XML serializer, 230
  text serializer, 229–230
  WAP/WML serializer, 230
  XHTML serializer, 229
  XML serializer, 229
  zip archive serializer, 231
<serializers> element (Cocoon), 218
server pages generator (Cocoon), 224
<service> element (Axis), 405
Service interface (XML:DB), 291
services (WSDL), 385. *See also* Web services
  document-style, 408–409
  message-style, 409
  RPC-style, 407–408
  wrapped-style, 408–409
ServletContext, accessing, 434–436
session action (Cocoon), 236, 254
session manangement (Cocoon), 253–254
setStyleHandler method (Batik), 178
setStyle method (Batik), 178
shutdown command (Xindice), 307
<Signature> element (XML Signature), 461
signatures
  placing in separate files, 490–491
  signing documents, 474–485
  verification, 485–490

<SignatureValue> element (XML Signature), 464
<SignedInfo> element (XML Signature), 462
sitemaps (Cocoon), 214–222
<components> element, 217
database application example, 271–274
example sitemap, 215–217
<exception> element, 218
<generators> element, 217
<matchers> element, 218
<otherwise> element, 220
<pipeline> elements
<generate> element, 220
<handle-errors> element, 220
<match> element, 218–220
<select> element, 220
<serialize> element, 220
<transform> element, 220
<pipelines> element, 217, 218–220
<selector> element, 218
<serializers> element, 218
<transformers> element, 217
<use-cookie-parameters> element, 217
<use-request-parameters> element, 217
<use-session-parameters> element, 217
<when> element, 220
Smart Transformer Switch (XSLTC), 96
SMIL (Synchronized Multimedia Integration Language), 168–169
SML11Serializer, 34
SOAP, 380–381. *See also* Axis
<Body> element, 380–381
<Envelope> element, 380–381
<Header> element, 380–381
RPC faults, 383–384
RPC requests, 381–382
RPC responses, 382–383
SourceLocator interface, debugging with, 87
SQL transformer (Cocoon), 226–227
Squiggle (SVG browser), 205–206
SSL (Secure Sockets Layer), 368–372
startElement method (SAX), 10–11
static SVG
<circle> element, 159
container elements, 160–161
<desc> element, 158
<g> element, 158
Hello World example, 156–157
<image> element, 160
<line> element, 158
<path> element, 162–164
<polygon> element, 159
<polyline> element, 159
<rect> element, 158–159
size attributes, 158
<text> element, 159–160
<title> element, 158
transform attribute, 161–162
status generator (Cocoon), 224
StorageResolvers (XML Security), 494
stream generator (Cocoon), 224
stubs (JAX-RPC), 393–394
StyleHandler interface (Batik), 178
stylesheets, 62
SVG Browser (Squiggle), 205–206
SVG font converter, 207–208
SVGGraphics2D class (Batik), 171–173
options, setting, 174–178
style handling, 178–183
SVG/JPEG serializer (Cocoon), 230
SVG/PNG serializer (Cocoon), 230
SVG pretty-printer, 206–207
SVG Rasterizer, 202
as Ant task, 203–204
command-line interface, 202–203
SVG renderer (FOP), 142
SVG (Scalable Vector Graphics), 155–156. *See also* Batik
applications for, 209–212
compatibility issues, 208
displaying documents (JSVGCanvas), 183–187
DTD, 158
dynamic, 208
declarative dynamic, 166–169
imperative dynamic, 164–166
image caching, 174–178
image storing, 174
image transcoding, 187
from SVG DOM trees, 189–191
from SVG files, 188–189
rich client user interfaces, 212
scripting, 191
JSVGCanvas ECMAScript API, 191–192
Jython, 192–197
static
<circle> element, 159
container elements, 160–161
<desc> element, 158
<g> element, 158
Hello World example, 156–157
<image> element, 160

<line> element, 158
<path> element, 162–164
<polygon> element, 159
<polyline> element, 159
<rect> element, 158–159
size attributes, 158
<text> element, 159–160
<title> element, 158
transform attribute, 161–162
style handling, 178–183, 208
support, 156
SVG/TIFF serializer (Cocoon), 231
SVG/XML serializer (Cocoon), 230
symbol table (Xerces), 43
symmetric key encryption, 457
Synchronized Multimedia Integration Language (SMIL), 168–169

T

tables (XSL), 119–123
Tauber, James, 113
TCPMon tool, 449
templates (XSLT), 62–66
TextSerializer, 34
<text> element (SVG), 159–160
text serializer (Cocoon), 229–230
<title> element (SVG), 158
TraceListener, debugging with, 85–87, 88
TransactionService interface (XML:DB), 292–293
transform attribute (SVG), 161–162
<transform> element (Cocoon), 220, 239
<Transform> element (XML Signature), 462–463
TransformerFactory (XSLTC), 95
transformers
Cocoon
augment transformer, 228
CInclude transformer, 227–228
EncodeURL transformer, 228
filter transformer, 227
fragment extractor transformer, 225
I18N transformer, 225–226
log transformer, 226
read DOM session transformer, 227
SQL transformer, 226–227
write DOM session transformer, 227
XInclude transformer, 227
XSLT transformer, 225
TrAX, 70–71
<transformers> element (Cocoon), 217
translets, 53
TrAX API, 70–71
calling XSLTC from, 92–94
DOM version, 74–77
mixing SAX and DOM, 77–80
SAX version, 72–74
troubleshooting, Xerces, 49–50
TXT renderer (FOP), 142–143

U

undeployment descriptor (WSDL), 427
<undeployment> element (Axis), 406
URI-conformant feature (Xerces), 19
URIs, Cocoon, 241–242
<use-cookie-parameters> element (Cocoon), 217
<use-request-parameters> element (Cocoon), 217
<use-session-parameters> element (Cocoon), 217

V

validation
Xerces features, 17
XML Signature, 466–467
XSL, 135
validity, 4–6
views (Cocoon), 238–239

W

WAP/WML serializer (Cocoon), 230
Web services, 379
applications of, 454

debugging, 449
deploying, 406–407, 427–428
JAX-RPC, 392–393
DII (Dynamic Invocation Interface), 396–399
dynamic proxies, 394–396
stubs, 393–394
.jws, 448–449
ServletContext access, 434–436
SOAP, 380–381
<Body> element, 380–381
<Envelope> element, 380–381
<Header> element, 380–381
RPC faults, 383–384
RPC requests, 381–382
RPC responses, 382–383
WSDL (Web Services Description Language), 379, 384–386
bindings, 385–386
document-literal Web service example, 389–392
example file, 386–389
messages, 385
ports, 385
port types, 385
services, 385
Web Services Description Language. *See* WSDL
well-formedness (XML documents), 3–4
<when> element (Cocoon), 220
wildcard header matcher (Cocoon), 233
wildcard URI matcher (Cocoon), 232
Winer, Dave, 349
wrapped-style services (Axis), 408–409
write DOM session transformer (Cocoon), 227
WSDL2Java, 409–413
Ant task, 450
example application, 413–414
binding file, 415–416
deploying, 427–428
deployment descriptor, 425–427
DLBookHandler interface, 417–421
generated test case, 423–425
implementation file, 416
interface file, 414–415
running, 417
skeleton service class, 421–423
undeployment descriptor, 427
running, 417
<wsdlsoap:binding> element (WSDL), 387–388
<wsdlsoap:body> element (WSDL), 388–389
<wsdlsoap:operation> element (WSDL), 388
WSDL (Web Services Description Language), 379, 384–386
bindings, 385–386
document-literal Web service example, 389–392
document styles, 407–409
example application, 413–414
binding file, 415–416
deploying, 427–428
deployment descriptor, 425–427
DLBookHandler interface, 417–421
generated test case, 423–425
implementation file, 416
interface file, 414–415
running, 417
skeleton service class, 421–423
undeployment descriptor, 427
example file, 386–389
Java2WSDL, 428–433
messages, 385
ports, 385
port types, 385
services, 385
WSDL2Java, 409–413

X–Z

Xalan
applet wrapper, 84–85
command-line interface, 81
debugging, 85–91
EnvironmentCheck class, 85–87
logging, 88–91
SourceLocator interface, 87
TraceListeners, 85–87, 88
DTM (Document Table Model), 80–81
extensions, 97
extension elements, 97–98
extension functions, 98–101
writing, 101–103
XSLTC, 104
installing, 69–70
sample application, 104–111
TrAX API, 70–71
DOM version, 74–77
mixing SAX and DOM, 77–80

SAX version, 72–74
XPath, 53–54
expressions, 59–61
location paths, 54–59
XPath API, 81–84
XSLT, 62
extensions, 68
output, 66–67
result trees, 67–68
stylesheets, 62
templates, 62–66
XSLTC, 91
calling from TrAX, 92–94
command-line tools, 96
configuring, 91–92
Smart Transformer Switch, 96
TransformerFactory attributes, 95

XEDB (XML Enabled Database), 286

Xerces
applications for, 50–51
configuration, 16–17
validation-related features, 17
configuring
character encoding, 19
disallow-doctype-decl feature, 19
DOM-related features, 18–19
error-reporting features, 18
grammar catching, 23–23
input buffer size, 19
SecurityManager, 19
URI-conformant feature, 19
default values, reporting, 22
deferred DOM, 20
entity handling, 29–31
entity references, 31–33
experimental functionality, 2
grammar catching, 23–29
active catching, 25–28
passive catching, 23–25
history, 1
installing, 15–16
OutputFormat options, 37–38
parser instances, reducing, 48–49
PSVI (Post Schema Validation Infoset), 22
sample programs, 43–44
schema validation, 20–23
serialization, 34–38
standards supported, 1–2
thread safety, 48
troubleshooting, 49–50
XNI (Xerces Native Interface), 38
document scanner, 42
DTD scanner, 42
DTD validator, 42
entity manager, 43
error reporter, 43
namespace binder, 42
NekoXNI tools, 44–48
pipeline interfaces, 39–41
schema validator, 42
symbol table, 43

Xerces Native Interface. *See* XNI

XHTMLSerializer, 34

XHTML serializer (Cocoon), 229

XInclude transformer (Cocoon), 227

Xindice
command-line tools
add commands, 300–302
delete commands, 303–304
exporting, 306
indexing commands, 304–306
retrieval commands, 302–303
runtime environment, 299
shutting down server, 307
example application
deployment descriptors, 337–338
SAX-based version, 341–346
XMLServlet, 330–334
XPathResultHandler, 346–347
XSLTServletFilter, 334–337
XSLT stylesheets, 338–341
installing, 299–300
performance, 329
requirements, 329
XML:DB API
creating collections, 307–310
deleting collections, 312–314
navigating collections, 310–311
resources, creating, 314–324
XPath-based querying, 324–327
XUpdate, 327–329

XML
declarations, 2–3
DTDs, 5
elements, 3
entities, 6
namespace prefixes, 3
namespaces, 3–4
Relax-NG, 5
schema language, 5

validity, 4–6
well-formedness, 3–4
XML4J parser. *See* Xerces
XML Canonicalization, 459–461, 471–474
XML:DB, 285–286. *See also* Xindice
API
BinaryResource interface, 290
Collection interface, 289
CollectionManagementService interface, 292
Database interface, 288
DatabaseManager interface, 288
Resource interface, 289–290
ResourceIterator interface, 291
ResourceSet interface, 290–291
Service interface, 291
TransactionService interface, 292–293
XMLResource interface, 290
XPathQueryService interface, 291–292
XUpdateQueryService interface, 292
update operations, 295–299
XUpdate, 293–294
elements, 294–295
XML Enabled Database (XEDB), 286
XML Encryption, 456, 467–470, 495
example application, 495–501
installing, 495
XML parsing, 1. *See also* Xerces
APIs, 6–8
DOM, 13–15
SAX, 8–12
XML renderer (FOP), 143
XMLResource interface (XML:DB), 290
XML-RPC
applications of, 373
asynchronous clients, 361–363
BASIC authentication, 365–366
call side flow, 350–351
controlling server processing, 363–365
debugging, 373
in existing servers, 366–368
history, 349
HTTP as transport, 354–356
installing, 356
Java dynamic proxies and, 373–378
mapping to Java types, 358–359
prerequisites, 350
procedure call documents, 351–352
response documents, 352–354
simple client example, 357–358
simple server example, 359–361
SSL and, 368–372
type matching, 373
XML Schema, 5
XML Security, 456
applications of, 502
installing, 470–471
resolvers, 493–495
signatures in separate files, 490–491
signature verification, 485–490
signing documents, 474–485
XPathTransformSigner, 491–493
XMLSerializer, 34
XML serializer (Cocoon), 229
XML Signature, 455–456, 461
<DigestMethod> element, 463
<DigestValue> element, 464
<KeyInfo> element, 464–466
<Object> element, 466
<Reference> element, 462
<Signature> element, 461
<SignatureValue> element, 464
<SignedInfo> element, 462
<Transform> element, 462–463
validating signatures, 466–467
<?xml-stylesheet?> element (Cocoon), 245
XNI (Xerces Native Interface), 38
components
document scanner, 42
DTD scanner, 42
DTD validator, 42
entity manager, 43
error reporter, 43
namespace binder, 42
schema validator, 42
symbol table, 43
NekoXNI tools
ManekiNeko, 44–45
NekoHTML, 44
NekoPull, 45–48
pipeline interfaces, 39–41
XPath, 53–54
expressions, 59
abbreviated syntax, 61
function library, 59–61
location paths, 54–59
axes, 56–57
node tests, 57–58
predicates, 58–59
querying NXDs, 324–327
Xalan XPath API, 81–84
Xindice example application, 346–347
xpath command (Xindice), 303

XPath directory generator (Cocoon), 224
XPathEvaluator, 83
XPathNSResolver, 83–84
XPathQueryService interface (XML:DB), 291–292
XPathResult, 83–84
XPathTransformSigner, 491–493
XSL (Extensible Stylesheet Language), 113
documents
elements of, 114–115
root elements, 115
flows, 115–116
generating with XSLT, 117–119
list blocks, 116–117
new components, 114–115
tables, 119–123
<xsl:attribute> element, 68
<xsl:comment> element, 68
<xsl:copy> element, 68
<xsl:element> element, 67
<xsl:processing-instruction> element, 68
XSLT, 62
extensions, 68
filters, 146–149
generating XSL with, 117–119
output, 66–67
performance, 104
result trees, 67–68
stylesheets, 62
templates, 62–66
Xindice example application
XSLTServletFilter, 334–337
XSLT stylesheets, 338–341
XSLTC, 91
calling from TrAX, 92–94
command-line tools, 96
configuring, 91–92
extensions, 104
FOP and, 133–135
Smart Transformer Switch, 96
TransformerFactory attributes, 95
<xsl:text> element, 68
XSLT transformer (Cocoon), 225
XSL, validating, 135
<xsl:value-of> element, 68
XSPs (eXtensible Server Pages)
elements
<?cocoon-process?> element, 245
<?xml-stylesheet?> element, 245
<xsp:attribute> element, 245
<xsp:comment> element, 246
<xsp:content> element, 246
<xsp:expr> element, 245
<xsp:include> element, 245
<xsp:logic> element, 245
<xsp:page> element, 245
<xsp:pi> element, 246
<xsp:structure> element, 245
logicsheets, 246–248
forms logicsheet, 249–252
request logicsheet, 248–249
sendmail logicsheet, 252–253
overview, 242–246
sessions, 253–254
<xsp:attribute> element (Cocoon), 245
<xsp:comment> element (Cocoon), 246
<xsp:content> element (Cocoon), 246
<xsp:expr> element (Cocoon), 245
<xsp-formval:is-??> elements (Cocoon), 251–252
<xsp:include> element (Cocoon), 245
<xsp:logic> element (Cocoon), 245
<xsp:page> element (Cocoon), 245
<xsp:pi> element (Cocoon), 246
<xsp-request:get-attribute> element (Cocoon), 249
<xsp:-request:get-header> element (Cocoon), 249
<xsp-request:get-locale> element (Cocoon), 249
<xsp-request:get-parameter> element (Cocoon), 249
<xsp-request:remove-attribute> element (Cocoon), 249
<xsp-request:set-attribute> element (Cocoon), 249
<xsp-session:encode-url> element (Cocoon), 254
<xsp-session:get-attribute> element (Cocoon), 253
<xsp-session:get-attribute-names> element (Cocoon), 253
<xsp-session:get-creation-time> element (Cocoon), 254
<xsp-session:get-id> element (Cocoon), 254
<xsp-session:get-last-accessed-time> element (Cocoon), 254
<xsp-session:get-max-inactive-interval> element (Cocoon), 254
<xsp-session:invalidate> element (Cocoon), 254
<xsp-session:is-new> element (Cocoon), 254
<xsp-session:remove-attribute> element (Cocoon), 254
<xsp-session:set-attribute> element (Cocoon), 253
<xsp-session:set-max-inactive-interval> element (Cocoon), 254
<xsp:structure> element (Cocoon), 245
XUpdate, 293–294
elements, 294–295
update operations, 295–299
updating NXDs, 327–329
XUpdateQueryService interface (XML:DB), 292

zip archive serializer (Cocoon), 231